SCIENCE AS PRACTICE AND CULTURE

SCIENCE AS PRACTICE AND CULTURE

EDITED BY ANDREW PICKERING

THE UNIVERSITY OF CHICAGO PRESS
Chicago and London

The University of Chicago Press, Chicago 60637
The University of Chicago Press, Ltd., London
© 1992 by The University of Chicago
All rights reserved. Published 1992
Printed in the United States of America

00 99 98 97 96 95 94   5 4 3 2

ISBN (cloth): 0-226-66800-2
ISBN (paper): 0-226-66801-0

Library of Congress Cataloging-in-Publication Data
Science as practice and culture / edited by Andrew Pickering.
        p.   cm.
    Includes bibliographical references and index.
    1. Science—Social aspects. 2. Knowledge, Theory of.
I. Pickering, Andrew.
    Q175.5.S3495   1992
    303.48′3—dc20   91-28829

⊗ The paper used in this publication meets
the minimum requirements of the American
National Standard for Information Sciences—
Permanence of Paper for Printed Library
Materials, ANSI Z39.48-1984.

CONTENTS

PREFACE

A book like this has more origins than authors. For me it grew out of the experience of teaching advanced undergraduate-graduate seminars on the sociology of scientific knowledge. During the second half of the 1980s, it dawned on me that while a growing number of studies were commonly discussed under this rubric, there were important and fascinating differences between them. Especially my own interests moved further away from traditional studies that could properly be labeled as studies of scientific knowledge and toward a newer genre that took scientific practice as its organizing theme. And this created a problem for teaching. Which texts should I choose to represent the differing approaches to science-as-practice pursued by the leading authors? And how could I bring the tension between studies of science-as-knowledge and science-as-practice into focus when, as it happened, the two schools chose to concentrate upon what they held in common, at least in print?

The solution I came up with was to invite the authors that I was already discussing in class to contribute to a volume of original essays, with the suggestion that they write either to exemplify their own understandings of scientific practice or, by confronting other authors or positions, to bring out what is at stake in a focus on knowledge or practice. Not all were in a position or wanted to comply, of course; conversely, new contributors joined in, and taxing choices had to be made as the project took shape. But at any rate, the stars seem to have been in an appropriate alignment, and the present volume is the result. Part 1 maps out a range of key positions in the analysis of practice, and part 2 lays out key debates across its edges, especially, though not exclusively, with studies of science-as-knowledge.

For the depth, coherence, balance, and range which I judge this book to possess, I offer my profound thanks to all of the contributors. Mike Lynch, Harry Collins, and Steven Yearley deserve particular thanks for opening up new debates which will, I suspect, be of central concern in science studies for some time to come. I might add that seeing one of these debates into print has called forth diplomatic skills that have not hitherto been a feature of my own practice: perhaps one day I will use them again. For their advice and support and their encouragement in seeing the project through its darker hours, I thank Mary Wallace and especially Susan Abrams of the University of Chicago Press. I thank the History and Philosophy of Science Program of the National Science Foundation for a grant (DIR-8912095) which supported in part my editorial work and substantive contributions to the volume. And finally, I thank Thomas for keeping me awake while all this was going on.

Andrew Pickering

1

From Science as Knowledge to Science as Practice

Andrew Pickering

The early 1970s saw the emergence of a new approach to think-ing about science. The sociology of scientific knowledge—SSK for short—differentiated itself from contemporary positions in the phi-losophy and sociology of science in two ways. First, as its name proclaimed, SSK insisted that science was interestingly and consti-tutively social all the way into its technical core: scientific knowl-edge itself had to be understood as a social product. Second, SSK was determinedly empirical and naturalistic. Just how scientific knowl-edge was social was to be explored through studies of real science, past and present. The apriorism of normative philosophical stereo-types was to be set aside. During the 1970s, the conceptual and geo-graphical map of SSK remained simple and readily surveyed. Its twin centers were Edinburgh and Bath. In Edinburgh the writings of Barry Barnes (1974, 1977, 1982), David Bloor (1976, 1983), and Steven Shapin (1979, 1982; Barnes and Shapin 1979) laid out the macroso-cial approach to SSK, seeking to trace causal connections between classical sociological variables, typically the "interests" of relevant groups, and the content of the knowledge sustained by those groups. In Bath, Harry Collins pioneered a more microsocial approach (sum-marized in Collins 1985). His studies of scientific controversies aimed to display the production of consensual knowledge as the out-come of contingent "negotiations" between scientific actors. Of course there was considerable commerce between Bath and Edin-burgh—the controversy study became a favored empirical genre north of the border, and Collins tended to defer to Edinburgh as far as macrosocial effects were concerned—and as the field grew, other centers of SSK emerged, most notably the group around Michael Mulkay in York. Nevertheless, the map remained simple to read.

This situation started to change in the late 1970s. New ap-proaches appeared in England and abroad whose concerns clearly overlapped with SSK, but whose precise relation to SSK remained problematic. One key landmark was the appearance in 1979 of the first book-length ethnographic study of *Laboratory Life*, by Bruno

Latour and Steve Woolgar. The inspiration and fieldwork for this study came from the French author, who had no evident prior affiliation to SSK. The next laboratory-life book was *The Manufacture of Knowledge* (1981), produced by another continental independent, Karin Knorr Cetina. At the same time, in the United States, Harold Garfinkel, Michael Lynch, and Eric Livingston began to bring their distinctively ethnomethodological perspective to bear upon what goes on in the laboratory (and in mathematics) (Lynch, Livingston, and Garfinkel 1983, Lynch 1985, Livingston 1986); philosophers of science—Ian Hacking (1983), Nancy Cartwright (1983), Arthur Fine (1986)—began to develop a new empirically informed approach within their discipline that seemed to intersect in interesting ways with SSK; the Tremont group were developing their pragmatist and symbolic interactionist perspective on science studies (Fujimura, Star, and Gerson 1987); and an anthropologist, Sharon Traweek (1988), was studying the particle physicists at the Stanford Linear Accelerator Center. Back in England, the discourse analysis program of Mulkay and Nigel Gilbert (Gilbert and Mulkay 1984) led, in the texts of Mulkay (1985), Woolgar (1988), and Malcolm Ashmore (1989), into "reflexivity" and "new literary forms"—genres that turned the techniques of SSK back on itself. On the continent again, Bruno Latour (1987, 1988) went his own way, articulating an "actor network" approach to science studies in collaboration with Michel Callon, thus founding the "Paris School." And so on.

By the late 1980s, then, a variety of SSK-like approaches to understanding science were on the table, united by a shared refusal of philosophical apriorism coupled with a sensitivity to the social dimensions of science, but differing at the same time along many axes. And in one sense this collection of essays continues the 1980s tradition of periodic surveys that aim to provide an overview of where and what the action is (Knorr Cetina and Mulkay 1983; Law 1986). But the time is past when one could entertain the idea of a comprehensive survey of SSK and its younger relatives, and this book aims instead to foreground what I take to be the key advance made by science studies in the 1980s. This is the move toward studying scientific practice, what scientists actually do, and the associated move toward studying scientific culture, meaning the field of resources that practice operates in and on.[1] Now I must explain what I think is at stake.

1. Since terms like 'practice" and "culture" enjoy a rich and varied range of associations that differ from audience to audience, some preliminary clarification may be useful here. Centrally at issue is the constructivist insight that doing science is real

Oddly enough, while science has always commanded a considerable audience, scholars have traditionally shown little direct interest in scientific practice. Their primary concern has always been with the products of science, especially with its conceptual product, knowledge. Thus, for instance, for most of the twentieth century Anglo-American philosophy of science has revolved around questions concerning scientific theory and facts and the relation between the two. This is true not only of the logical-empiricist mainstream and its contemporary variants (for a review, see Suppe 1977) but even of many of the philosophers who have opposed mainstream thought, Paul Feyerabend (1975, 1978) and Norwood Russell Hanson (1958), for example. Until very recently, only isolated instances of a sustained interest in practice were to be found within the philosophical tradition: Ludwik Fleck (1935), Michael Polanyi (1958), Thomas Kuhn (1962). This is not, of course, to say that we cannot extract some image of scientific culture and practice from analyses of science-as-knowledge if we try; and I want to indicate how this works for SSK.[2]

As its name suggests, the primary problematic of the sociology of scientific knowledge is that of science-as-knowledge, and its defin-

---

work and that real work requires resources for its accomplishment. Throughout this essay, "culture" denotes the field of resources that scientists draw upon in their work, and "practice" refers to the acts of making (and unmaking) that they perform in that field. "Practice" thus has a temporal aspect that "culture" lacks, and the two terms should not be understood as synonyms for one another: a hammer, nails, and some planks of wood are not the same as the act of building a dog kennel—though a completed dog kennel might well function as a resource for future practice (training a dog, say). I repeatedly seek to exemplify my sense of "practice" and "culture" in the remainder of this essay: see n. 2 on logical empiricism, the discussion of SSK that follows that note, my introduction to Hacking's essay, and so on. It might also be useful to emphasize that my usage of "culture" here is a deflationary one. It encompasses all of the resources, many of them humble and mundane, that scientists deploy and transform in their practice (see the discussion of the patchiness and heterogeneity of scientific culture below). It is not a way of gesturing at grand, all-encompassing worldviews, for example, or at big cultural currents that flow between science and the outside world—though neither is it a way of denying that unifying characterizations of entire cultures might also be perspicuous on occasion (see chap. 2, n. 2, for some thoughts on this point).

2. For the logical empiricist, say, scientific culture consists in a field of knowledge and knowledge claims, and scientific practice consists in the appraisal of conceptual knowledge claims against observational knowledge, an appraisal ideally governed by some logic or method. The disappointing result of carrying this exercise through for modern pragmatist philosophy is indicative of the general lack of interest in exploring practice itself (see, for example, Goodman 1978, Quine 1980, and Rorty 1979, 1982).

ing mark is its insistence that scientific knowledge is constitutively social. SSK's perspective on knowledge is, however, typically underwritten by a particular vision of scientific practice that goes broadly as follows (David Bloor [chap. 8] elaborates a little in his essay here; the best extended discussion is in Barnes 1982; see also Collins 1985). Since the central problematic of SSK is that of knowledge, the first move is to characterize the technical culture of science as a single conceptual network, along the lines suggested by the philosopher of science Mary Hesse (1980). Concepts at differing levels of abstraction within the net are said to be linked to one another by generalizations of varying degrees of certainty, and to the natural world by the piling up of instances under the headings of various observable terms. When scientific culture is specified in this way, an image of scientific practice follows: practice is the creative extension of the conceptual net to fit new circumstances. And here SSK, following Ludwig Wittgenstein (1953) and Thomas Kuhn (1962), insists on two points. First, that the extension of the net is accomplished through a process of modeling or analogy: the production of new scientific knowledge entails seeing new situations as being relevantly like old ones. And second, that modeling is an open-ended process: the extension of scientific culture, understood still as a single conceptual net, can plausibly proceed in an indefinite number of different directions; nothing within the net fixes its future development.

The openness of practice captured in this observation creates a problem for SSK, as it did for Kuhn earlier. Why doesn't scientific culture continually disintegrate as scientific actors develop it in the myriad different ways that are conceivable in principle? How is closure—the achievement of consensus on particular extensions of culture—to be understood? Here comes the move that justifies the *S* for "sociology" in SSK. SSK emphasizes the instrumental aspect of scientific knowledge and the agency of scientific actors: knowledge is for use, not simply for contemplation, and actors have their own interests that instruments can serve well or ill. Introduction of the distinctively sociological concept of interest serves to solve the problem of closure in two ways. On the one hand, actors can be seen as tentatively seeking to extend culture in ways that might serve their interests rather than in ways that might not. And on the other hand, interests serve as standards against which the products of such extensions, new conceptual nets, can be assessed. A good extension of the net is one that serves the interest of the relevant scientific community best. Here, then, is the basic SSK account of practice, and with this in hand we can return to the starting point—the problematic of science-as-knowledge—and articulate a position: scientific knowledge has to be seen, not as the transparent representation of nature, but rather as knowledge relative to a particular culture, with this relativity specified through a sociological concept of interest.[3]

Various points relevant to the present volume can now be made. Positively, we can note that the SSK account of scientific practice is a plausible one and quite sufficient to SSK's avowed purpose in isolating and expressing a particular social-relativist appreciation of scientific knowledge. It says enough about practice to make clear and credible what SSK's position on knowledge is. Negatively, taken seriously as an image of practice and culture rather than as an aid to thinking about knowledge, SSK's account is thin, idealized, and reductive. The representation of scientific culture as a single conceptual network, and of practice as an open-ended process of modeling structured by interest, does not offer much purchase upon the complexities evident in the nearest laboratory. SSK simply does not offer us the conceptual apparatus needed to catch up the richness of the doing of science, the dense work of building instruments, planning, running, and interpreting experiments, elaborating theory, negotiating with laboratory managements, journals, grant-giving agencies, and so on. To describe practice as open and interested is at best to scratch its surface. And here a difference of opinion looms—the difference of opinion, actually, that is highlighted in the arguments of part 2 below.

One response to the thinness of abstract discussions of practice in SSK is to try to enrich them through empirical study, and this has been a main line of development within SSK. Thus, for example, in empirical studies, the material dimension of scientific practice, largely absent from the SSK story as just rehearsed, has been reintroduced, and to great effect. The recent interest of historians and philosophers of science in instruments, experiment, and fact production is in part at least a consequence of such studies undertaken within SSK (Gooding, Pinch, and Schaffer 1989). It is worth noting,

---

3. This is the best-known version of the SSK account of closure, developed in Barnes (1977, 1982) and exemplified in the empirical studies of Shapin (1979, 1982) and Donald MacKenzie (1981). An alternative macrosocial approach is Bloor's (1983) "grid-group" theory that builds upon the work of Mary Douglas. Collins's studies focus on the contingencies of microsocial negotiations between the parties to controversy, but he too moves to an image of interests bearing upon a conceptual network when reviewing the general features of his approach (Collins 1985, chap. 6). These differences are not central to the remarks that follow, though they should be borne in mind.

however, that the material world as it appears within SSK tends to remain harnessed to the overall reductive picture. In Shapin's (1979) classic study of the Edinburgh phrenology dispute, for example, the open-ended development of material techniques as well as concep-tualizations is represented as structured by the interests of the com-peting groups. As an exemplary work in SSK, Shapin's story revolves around interests and their relation to knowledge, and the material dimension of science appears as yet more documentation of the SSK thesis of social relativity.

An alternative response to the thinness of SSK's abstract image of science is more to the point here. It is to question whether analytic repertoires developed in the service of a problematic of knowledge can serve as the primary basis for understandings of practice. And it is, I think, fair to say that most scholars who have taken it as their task to get to grips with scientific practice in some detail have found that they cannot. Put simply, talk of conceptual nets and interests does not seem terribly perspicuous when confronted with the intri-cacies of practice. Instead, the authors in part 1 of this volume and several in part 2 have sought to devise new conceptual frame-works, frameworks built out of concepts that speak directly to prac-tice rather than to arguments concerning science-as-knowledge.[4] Examples of such frameworks are described, argued about, and put to various uses in the essays that follow. I will talk about them fur-ther in a moment, but first a question needs to be addressed. Why bother? Given that the science-as-knowledge traditions can already offer a range of images of culture and practice adequate to their pur-poses, why plunge into the complexity of actual science and struggle to create new images? Here are some answers:

- The attempt to understand scientific practice is interesting in its own right and also bears directly upon the development of critical and policy-oriented perspectives on science, on the con-cerns of cognitive science, and so on. From the latter standpoints,

---

4. I must emphasize that empirical studies within SSK do not, of course, simply enforce the abstract SSK analysis outlined above. As empirical studies they go beyond that picture (often, it seems to me, in ways that challenge it). There is therefore much to be learned about practice from SSK studies, including, for example, Shapin's study just mentioned. What is challenged in studies of scientific practice is SSK's analytic framework, both in itself and as an organizing problematic for research. Concerning the latter, the problematic of finding social explanations for distributions of belief serves to foreground and thematize certain features of science at the expense of oth-ers. Studies of scientific practice foreground features of science that fade into the background from the viewpoint of SSK.

what scientists do is just as important as the knowledge they produce.

- All of the stock appreciations of scientific knowledge—as objective (logical empiricism), as relative to culture (Kuhn, Feyerabend), as relative to interests (SSK)—can be translated into particular understandings of scientific practice. We can move in the opposite direction too, and it is an interesting challenge to read new understandings of practice back into the problematic of knowledge. The essays that follow achieve all sorts of interesting effects by doing just this. Likewise we can read studies of practice back into social theory and historiography.

- The study of practice can have far-reaching implications for disciplinarity. To see this, we can note that the images of practice sustained within the science-as-knowledge traditions typically have the quality of distinctively disciplinary reductions. Thus positivist philosophy of science (in a broad sense) seeks to represent scientific practice as the operation of reason and in that act identifies itself as philosophy: talking about reason is a characteristic task of philosophers. Likewise SSK's causal arrow from the social to the technical locates it securely in the professional field of sociology. In contrast, there is no guarantee that in seeking to understand practice in its own right we will arrive at concepts proper to any discipline, traditionally understood. Again, several of the essays that follow suggest that the study of practice works to undermine traditional disciplinary reductions. At stake here, then, are not just technical arguments within philosophy, social theory, historiography, and so on, but challenges to the very disciplinary frameworks and boundaries within which technical argument is conducted. It is worth noting, though, that to say that traditional disciplinary conceptualizations and boundaries are put under pressure in the study of science-as-practice is not to point to an anarchic disintegration of scholarship. The reverse, if anything, is the case. The confluence of philosophers, historians, sociologists, and anthropologists exemplified in this volume points to the possibility of a new, wide-ranging, and for once genuine multidisciplinary synthesis in science studies. If philosophers, sociologists, and so on tend to lose the clarity of their disciplinary identities in this synthesis, it is no great loss.

- It is probably too mild a formulation to describe the conceptualizations challenged in studies of scientific practice as disciplinary ones. In fact they are central to modern thought in general. As many of the essays that follow seek in different ways to convey, such basic distinctions as subject:object and nature:society are

7

put into question. And this brings me to the last degree of selectivity implicit in this book: the contributions that follow are intended to foreground this point. To question such taken-for-granted distinctions is by definition a trademark of "postmodern" thought—though none of the contributors actually uses the word (see Galison 1990, Haraway 1985; Latour 1990; Rouse 1991). Here there is an opportunity for alliances and arguments that extend far beyond the field of science studies.

Positions

The essays that follow can speak for themselves. I want just to provide a brief overview of their contents, of how they fit together, and of how they bear upon the issues just raised. The volume is divided into two parts. Part 1, "Positions," contains self-contained pieces that aim to represent individual perspectives on practice. The first contributor is Ian Hacking, whose *Representing and Intervening* (1983) was a landmark in its attempt to shift the focus of the philosophy of science toward practice, to emphasize that science is doing (intervening) as well as knowing (representing). I want to discuss his essay on "The Self-Vindication of the Laboratory Sciences" (chap. 2) at some length because it isolates and clarifies some important themes that run through this volume. Hacking begins by challenging conventional reductive representations of scientific *culture*. Where the science-as-knowledge traditions routinely think of scientific culture as a single unitary entity—a conceptual network in SSK, a theory in positivist philosophy, a paradigm for Kuhn—Hacking insists on the multiplicity, patchiness, and heterogeneity of the space in which scientists work. Scientific culture is made up of all sorts of bits and pieces—material, social, conceptual—that stand in no necessary unitary relation to one another.[5] This is a recurring refrain in studies of science-as-practice, and Hacking drives it home by offering a taxonomy of disparate and distinguishable cultural elements that figure in laboratory practice. There are fifteen

5. The multiplicity of scientific culture is not, strictly speaking, news to SSK or to history, philosophy, and sociology of science more generally. Nevertheless, very little has traditionally been made of it within SSK; it is an aspect of science that tends to disappear within abstract discussions (see the previous note on "backgrounding"). Attention was first systematically drawn to the importance of thinking about the patchiness of culture for understanding scientific and technological practice in the "actor network" approach of Michel Callon and Bruno Latour (see, for example, Callon 1980, Latour 1987, and Law 1987; see also Smith 1988 for a similar perspective in literary theory).

elements on Hacking's list—broken down under three headings: "ideas," "things," and "marks"—and Hacking insists that the list is not exhaustive, even if we confine our attention to the technical culture of science as he does.

This once more invites the question, why bother? Why is Hacking investing so much energy in thinking through these distinctions? The answer is that to observe the multiplicity of culture is to open a new space for thinking about *practice.* If we go back for a moment to SSK's analysis of practice, the following chain of reasoning is clear. SSK insists on the openness of extension of a single conceptual net. Nothing in that net decides how it is to be extended into the future. Therefore something else must determine closure, and that something else, for SSK, is interest. In contrast, if we recognize the multiplicity of the technical culture of science, any number of somethings else beside interest become available to explain closure: any single cultural element may be open-endedly extended, but the task of fitting various extensions together, of bringing disparate elements into association, is not. As Hacking points out, Duhem-type problems continually arise and have to be managed in practice: particular cultural elements projected in particular ways fail to fit together as desired. Experiments, not to put too fine a point on it, go wrong all the time. To successfully engineer an association of disparate cultural elements is, then, a nontrivial achievement that can itself be taken as the explanation of a degree of closure in scientific practice, of a limit where practice can rest (temporarily, at least). And this is the image of scientific practice that Hacking offers us: the production of instruments, facts, phenomena, and interpretations in the laboratory is precisely the hard, uncertain, and creative work of bringing together the kinds of disparate cultural elements that he lists.

So what? Well, to return to the first item in my list of reasons for studying practice, one accomplishment of Hacking's essay is just that it outlines a new vision of what practice is like, a vision different not only from that supported by SSK but from all of the images that emerge from studies of science-as-knowledge. Further, Hacking's analysis takes us straight into the temporality of practice—the realm of real-time struggles to make things work—that conspicuously escapes other accounts.[6] But Hacking is not content to come

6. Again I should emphasize that the temporality of practice is not totally edited out of empirical studies in SSK: Collins's study of laser building, for example, speaks directly to this topic; but again, what one learns there about temporality is backgrounded in the general discussion that follows (Collins 1985; compare chaps. 3 and 6).

up with a new and improved understanding of practice, and he therefore makes the second move on my list, reading his analysis of practice back into the traditional problematic of knowledge. Hacking's
account of practice as the mutual adjustment of cultural elements
leads directly to his notion that stable sciences are artfully contrived
"self-vindicating" constellations of instrumental and interpretative
procedures, natural phenomena, and theoretical understandings.
And according to Hacking, there is no reason to suppose that such
cultural packages are necessarily unique. He believes that they are
not and thus arrives at a full-blooded articulation of the incommensurability of different stable sciences. He agrees with Kuhn (1962)
and Feyerabend (1975) that different stable sciences constitute different worlds, but importantly, he rejects the tendency in Kuhn and
especially in Feyerabend to reduce the difference to one of theory
(another classic disciplinary reduction). There is no causal arrow
from theory to observation in Hacking's account. In accord with the
slogan of *Representing and Intervening* that "experiment has a life
of its own," Hacking denies that theory has any special priority in
the self-vindication that concerns him. New instruments, for example, are just as likely to issue in new stable sciences as new
theory. Hacking's discussion of incommensurability thus offers a
challenge to the theory-obsessed philosophical discussions of the
topic over the past thirty years. This is a nice example of how attention to practice can rejuvenate and transform debates begun in the
philosophy of science-as-knowledge.

David Gooding's "Putting Agency back into Experiment" (chap.
3) offers detailed exemplification of the processes of mutual adjustment of cultural elements in experimental practice that Hacking
refers to. Gooding reconstructs the trajectory of Giacomo Morpurgo's recent quark-search experiments and, drawing upon his research over the past decade (Gooding 1990), Michael Faraday's route
to the prototypical electric motor. In both instances, Gooding puts
to work his new diagrammatic system for getting to grips with the
temporality of practice, foregrounding the emergence of Duhem-
type problems, or "recalcitrances" as he calls them, in material practice, and the accommodations that his subjects made to them. In
each case, the upshot of these passages of practice was the "interactive stabilization" (my phrase) of a package of cultural elements of
just the form that Hacking describes. Gooding's cases, though, serve
to emphasize that beyond instruments, facts, phenomena, and theories, the embodied skill of the experimenter is one of the elements
entering into the process of mutual adjustment and stabilization.

Like Hacking, Gooding too seeks to run his analysis of practice back into the philosophy of science-as-knowledge. But while Hacking takes the "macro" route, addressing the incommensurability of whole sciences, Gooding is more "micro." He criticizes the traditional philosophical way of thinking about experiment as theory testing, which "makes empirical access inherently mysterious . . . a mystery usually thought to be penetrable only by a robust sort of realism." The problem with this way of thinking is that it begins once facts about the material world have already been split off from interpretations and conceptualizations. Gooding's reconstructions of practice begin before this splitting has taken place and show, as he says, "that natural phenomena are bounded by human activity." There is no mystery of empirical access, to put it another way—facts and conceptualizations (and many other elements of scientific culture) are built together along the lines Gooding and Hacking lay out—and no special scientific realism is needed to explain it. Once more, then, the examination of scientific practice promises to undermine entrenched positions—here realist and antirealist alike—in the philosophy of science-as-knowledge.

In "The Couch, the Cathedral, and the Laboratory" (chap. 4), Karin Knorr Cetina elaborates themes clearly related to those of Hacking and Gooding, via a reflection upon what can be gained by taking the laboratory rather than individual experiments as the unit of ethnographic analysis. Her answer is that there is a rich and fascinating laboratory culture that becomes evident when we make this move, and her concern in this essay is with the relation between that culture and the culture of daily life. The traditional philosophical picture is that the former depends upon the latter but is made distinctive by the addition of some special element, a special scientific rationality or method. Knorr Cetina concludes instead that scientific culture is continuous with that of daily life, in the sense that the culture of the laboratory *is* that of the everyday world, but artfully transformed and enhanced. She speaks of the laboratory as the dwelling place of "enhanced nature" and "enhanced agents." The molecular biology laboratories that she has studied, for example, process biological materials through sequences of states that have no natural counterparts. There is an evident link here to Hacking's insistence that most natural phenomena of interest to science are unique to the laboratory and to the instruments that produce them. On enhanced agents, Knorr Cetina speaks of scientists as "'methods' of going about enquiry . . . a technical device in the production of knowledge." She notes, for example, that a certain skill or tacit

11

knowledge is required to use the "gel electrophoresis" technique in molecular biology: a transformation or enhancement is thus required of the actor entering the laboratory. This observation connects back to Gooding's discussion of the stabilization of skills in scientific practice. Knorr Cetina takes this line of thought further by examining the ways in which particular reconfigurations of nature hang together with particular reconfigurations of agents in the different "forms of life" (my phrase) characteristic of such different sciences as empirical social science, molecular biology, and high-energy physics. Knorr Cetina's essay thus points to the making of social actors and relations alongside, and in mutual accommodation to, the making of the material world of facts, phenomena, and instruments.

"Constructing Quaternions" (chap. 5), by Adam Stephanides and me, continues the analysis of practice along the lines set out by Hacking and Gooding, as well as in my own earlier writing (Pickering 1989, 1990). Unlike the other contributors to this volume, though, we are not concerned here with experimental or sociotechnical practice in science. Our interest is instead in the nature of conceptual practice, an area that has so far been allowed to remain pretty much unexplored (though see Latour 1987, chap. 6, and Livingston 1986). In our analysis of the algebraic researches of the nineteenth-century mathematician Sir William Rowan Hamilton, we try to show that there is in fact no special problem in understanding conceptual practice. The idea that practice consists in the making of associations within a patchy culture comes once more to the fore, and our central concern is to understand how "resistance"—our word for Gooding's "recalcitrance"—to such associations can arise in a realm where the otherness of the material world and other people is not immediately present. To this end we decompose the process of modeling into what we describe as free and forced moves. The constitutive intertwining of these moves, we suggest, gives modeling a distinctive double character, at once embodying active choices (free moves) and a correlative surrender of agency (forced moves). This double character implies that the upshot of particular modeling sequences has genuinely to be found out in conceptual practice, and that the achievement of intended associations through such sequences is a nontrivial accomplishment. On our analysis, then, the emergence of resistance should be seen as just as endemic to conceptual practice as it is to material and sociotechnical practice. We conclude by running our analysis back into issues central to studies of science-as-knowledge. We argue that the analysis of conceptual practice cuts across traditional discussions of the objectivity, relativity, and historicity of scientific and mathematical knowledge in interesting and significant ways.

The last contribution to part 1 is Joan Fujimura's "Crafting Science: Standardized Packages, Boundary Objects, and 'Translation'" (chap. 6). Fujimura is one of the original members of the Tremont group mentioned earlier, and here she exemplifies their pragmatist and symbolic-interactionist approach to science studies. Her essay continues the analysis of heterogeneity and association in scientific culture and practice, but along lines that are complementary to those of the earlier essays. There the heterogeneity in question resides principally in the technical culture of science: theory, instruments, skills, and so on. Fujimura is more concerned with heterogeneity that is at once technical and social. Her focus is on the wide variety of "social worlds," each having its own problematic, methods, and conceptual apparatus, that came together in what she calls the "molecular biology bandwagon in cancer research." These social worlds include those of clinicians, patients, and medical and basic researchers in all sorts of subspecialties, as well as those of the National Cancer Institute, Congress, and the U.S. public at large. Fujimura is interested here not so much in what practice is like within any one of these worlds but rather in the process of establishing links between them that constituted the molecular biology bandwagon. In this respect she stresses the significance of what she calls "boundary objects" (Star and Griesemer 1989) and "standardized packages" (Fujimura 1988) thereof. These are cultural elements that in one way or another are central to the establishment of productive relations between social worlds. Her examples include the cells that circulate between the operating room and medical and basic researchers, the recombinant-DNA techniques that flow between the different laboratories that constitute the various fields of technical practice, the computerized databases that transport findings from one social world to the next (albeit at the expense of a standardized and restrictive format), and the oncogene theory that serves to organize conceptual, social, and material relations between all of the social worlds involved. Drawing upon Callon and Latour's actor-network approach, Fujimura emphasizes both that such boundary objects are actively "crafted" in a process of "mutual enrollment," and that the production of successful boundary objects reacts back upon the social worlds thus linked and upon the larger whole they make up, reconstituting the very objects of study, as well as the material, conceptual, and social practices that surround them. Again, then, Fujimura offers us an image of the interactive stabilization of a plethora of cultural elements, while enriching our understanding of that process in her focus on the new patterns of intersection and circulation that come into sight when one recognizes the social heterogeneity of practices.

Arguments

Part 2 of the collection is "Arguments" and I can introduce it by picking up the line of thought introduced earlier concerning the relation between studies of science-as-practice and SSK. The essays of part 1 map out a rich and rather coherent perspective on scientific culture and practice, and there is prima facie case for seeing them as marking a significant break from SSK within the overall science-studies tradition. They serve to foreground a new topic, practice, as worthy of study and analysis in its own right. Further, it is notable that none of the authors finds it appropriate to thematize "the social" as a central organizing and explanatory concept. The essays of part 1 seem in fact to point away from the idea that there is some special social component of science that can constitute a privileged center around which narratives of practice can be made to revolve. Instead, the image of science that emerges is one in which all of the different elements of scientific culture that one might care to distinguish—social, institutional, conceptual, material—evolve in a dialectical relation with one another. The different elements are interactively stabilized against one another, as I put it, are "coproduced" as Latour and Callon put it below, with no particular element or set of elements having any necessary priority. The essays of part 1, then, encourage us to delete both the K of SSK, since the central topic is practice not knowledge, and the first S, since there seems no warrant for assigning causal priority to the social in understanding scientific practice and culture.[7] Or, to declare an interest that must be evident already, so it seems to me.

---

7. The point here is not to deny that science is constitutively "social" in the everyday sense of the word. It is rather to question the tenability of *disciplinary reductions* of this idea in sociology (the typical reduction to "interest" in SSK, for example). Such reductions may on occasion be perspicuous and persuasive (see the case studies reviewed in Shapin 1982), but one should see such situations as contingent limit cases of the more general phenomenon: that all of the different dimensions of scientific culture are produced, change, and evolve together in scientific practice. A more general formulation of this point is to note that studies of practice tend to cut across all traditional disciplinary reductions, not just sociological ones. While such reductions rely on identifiable and enduring variables—like "interests" or "standards"—to explain the production of knowledge, it appears that those very variables

There is, though, a different way of thinking about the essays of part 1. It could be said, for example, that the analysis of closure in terms of the making of associations in a patchy and discontinuous culture is interesting, but it could also be noted that such closures are not definitive. And therefore we need to return to "the social," perhaps understood as a distribution of interests, to understand which of the many closures that might be thus achieved are in the long run communally adopted. This is one of the many ways in which analyses of science-as-practice might be subsumed within the overall SSK enterprise, rather than being seen as breaking away from it. None of the authors of part 1 speaks directly to this issue, but it is the explicit concern that runs through the first two arguments of part 2. The question there is whether studies of science as practice should be seen as a genuine and viable departure from classical SSK, and if so, whether this departure is a step forward or backward. The various answers to this question are, I think, extremely instructive in clarifying both the substance of several important positions within contemporary science studies and what follows from them as regards topics for research, forms of accounting, and in the widest sense, politics.

I do not want to preempt the debates of part 2 and I do not intend to map out all of their twists and turns. To introduce them, I will simply mention what I take to be their central themes. The first debate features Michael Lynch speaking for the ethnomethodological study of practice, and David Bloor speaking for classical SSK. Their argument hinges upon different readings of the philosophy of the later Wittgenstein which, with its emphasis on the constitutive embedding of knowledge in social practice—in "language games" and "forms of life"—has figured as a key resource in the development of science studies since the 1970s. The bone of contention is Wittgenstein's analysis of rule following. Wittgenstein asks what it is to follow a rule: how do we know that we have followed a rule correctly? He then insists, first, that nothing in the verbal formulation of a rule determines its next application, and second, that it is fruitless to invoke yet more rules to determine how to apply the rule

---

are themselves mangled in practice: they are subject to transformation in a process that cannot itself be reduced to similarly disciplinary variables (Pickering forthcoming). This observation argues not only against accounts centered in a single discipline but also against disciplinary eclecticism that conjoins, say, a philosophical view of rationality with a sociological account of interests (though since the mid-1980s much scholarly work at the intersection of history, philosophy, and sociology of science has taken just this form).

in any fresh instance: such a strategy leads only to an infinite regress of rules for following rules. The parallel between this argument concerning rule following and the one I rehearsed earlier about the openness of cultural extension is clear, and there is a case for saying that the former is just a special case of the latter. This is why the central dispute between Lynch and Bloor over the relative merits of ethnomethodology and SSK can be played out in terms of rule following: conclusions reached there can be carried over more or less directly to the analysis of scientific practice.

Although Lynch opens the debate here, it is easier to begin this overview with Bloor's reply. In "Left and Right Wittgensteinians" (chap. 8), as in his book on Wittgenstein (Bloor 1983), Bloor appropriates Wittgenstein along the lines I sketched out earlier. He argues that Wittgenstein's analysis opens a space between the formulation of a rule and the practice that properly accompanies it: the one does not determine the other. Therefore something else which is not itself a formulation of a rule must connect the two and, making a leap from Wittgensteinian philosophy to classical sociology, that something else, for Bloor, is the social, construed as interest or whatever. We should, that is, look to the social for an understanding of how rules and practices are joined together. But this is just the point that Lynch refuses to accept, and in his "Extending Wittgenstein" (chap. 7) he finds grounds for his refusal in Wittgenstein's texts. In well-known writings Wittgenstein argues that to grasp a rule—to get the hang of what it calls for—requires at the same time a grasp of the field of practical activities to which the rule speaks. The two are, as Lynch puts it, "internally related" and thus, he argues, there is "no room in the world" for something else beyond the rule and the practices to which it speaks that is necessary to relate them. There is, in particular, no room for the causal, sociologically reductive concepts like interest on which Bloor would like to ground SSK. And this, for Lynch, is the Wittgensteinian legitimation of and inspiration for an antireductive ethnomethodological approach to enquiry into scientific practice. Such an approach seeks to explore and display the "internal relation" between scientific formulations and practices. And the most that we can hope for from this exercise is a perspicuous rendering; on Lynch's reading of Wittgenstein, we cannot hope for more. Here, then, Lynch aligns himself, in the name of the later Wittgenstein, with the radically antidisciplinary position within ethnomethodology: "death to (classical) sociology" might be the slogan.

Before sketching out Bloor's reply to Lynch, it might be worth offering my own understanding of what Lynch is up to in his essay.

I may well be mistaken—what follows is not intended in any way to prejudge Lynch's own words—but it is at least one way for outsiders to ethnomethodology and Wittgensteinian philosophy to come to terms with what is being asserted. Lynch's claim, it seems to me, is a relative of the one just sketched out regarding the analyses of practice in part 1. If practice carries within itself a teleological principle of making associations between disparate cultural elements, there is no need to look outside practice thus construed for explanations of particular closures in cultural extensions (though neither, of course, is it forbidden to do so). Practice has its own integrity, and once we have grasped that integrity, we no longer feel the need for an explanatory "something else." Now for David Bloor's reply.

Lynch in effect argues that the ethnomethodological study of science-as-practice marks a distinct and important break from SSK. Bloor replies that what is good about ethnomethodology actually continues the work of SSK, enriching the associated image of practice but leaving the overall explanatory framework unchallenged, while the rest is a mistake. In general Bloor acknowledges that support for ethnomethodology's antitheoretical posture can be found in Wittgenstein's writings, but he dismisses this strand of thought as an unfortunate failing of the great philosopher. More particularly, Bloor argues that Lynch has actually smuggled "the social" into his account of practice by means of a notion of "silent agreement." Bloor understands this notion as referring to a consensus of rule followers on proper practice and sees no reason not to theorize consensus as, like interest, a causal social principle distinguishing right from wrong rule following. Lynch has the last word on this topic in "From the 'Will to Theory' to the Discursive Collage" (chap. 9), the thrust of which is that "sociology's general concepts and methodological strategies are simply overwhelmed by the heterogeneity and technical density of the language, equipment, and skills through which mathematicians, scientists, and practitioners in many other fields of activity make their affairs accountable." Here I have to leave the reader to arrive at her own appreciation of this encounter between SSK and ethnomethodology, but it is clear what is at stake. Bloor and SSK stand for the study of distributions of knowledge as a function of classically theorized social variables; Lynch and ethnomethodology for a detailed scrutiny of practices that aims to grasp them in their integrity and that challenges any disciplinary hegemony (here, of sociology) over the understanding of scientific practice and knowledge.

Similar themes and tensions are manifest in the second argument of part 2, though taking a somewhat different form. This is a complicated three-way affair in which Harry Collins and Steven Yearley speak for traditional SSK, Steve Woolgar speaks for reflexivity in science studies, and Michel Callon and Bruno Latour speak for their own actor-network approach.[8] These exchanges take for granted the fact that reflexivity and the actor-network approach are possible continuations of SSK; what is at stake is whether these continuations move in a profitable direction. Collins and Yearley argue that reflexivity and the actor network are, in different ways, steps backward from SSK; neither Woolgar nor Callon and Latour agree.

Taking a leaf from one of Wittgenstein's books, the strategy of Collins and Yearley's "Epistemological Chicken" (chap. 10) is to ask "not for the meaning, but for the use" of the various positions at issue. Thus they defend the "social realism" of SSK—its reconstrual of natural scientists' accounts of the natural world on the basis of sociological accounts of the social world—not as a privileged epistemological position but as an effective position for social action. Collins and Yearley want to challenge what they see as an unwarranted hegemony of the natural sciences in contemporary society. The social realism of SSK, Collins and Yearley believe, exposes the epistemological pretensions of accounts that grant the natural sciences some special access to their subject matters, and thus demystifies our appraisals of science. "Making science," they say, "a continuous part with the rest of our culture should make us less intimidated and more ready to appreciate its beauty and accomplishments. It should make us more ready to use it for what it is, to value its insights and wisdom within rather than without the political and cultural process." Later they mention specifically the public understanding of science and technology and science education as areas in which SSK can make an important contribution to social debate (n. 19). Here, then, something new comes to the surface, that there can be in the broadest sense a political dimension to the debate between SSK and its younger relatives. Judgments are at stake of the political effectivity of differing accounts of science as knowledge

8. I doubt whether reflexivity falls under the heading of studies of science-as-practice as exemplified in part 1. One can describe it as, say, a study of representational practices, but its characteristic feature is its self-awareness of how its own representations are built up. What is interesting in the present context, however, is the affinity between reflexivity and the actor-network approach which does focus directly upon scientific (and technological) practice—an affinity made evident in Collins and Yearley's decision to mount a critique of reflexivity and the actor network within a single essay and in the responses to the critique. I suspect that this affinity could be profitably explored further, though, as far as I am aware, no one has yet tried to do so.

and practice. And Collins and Yearley leave us in no doubt about their appreciation of the effectivity of their presumptive heirs. They see both reflexivity and the actor-network approach as regressive.

Collins and Yearley take on reflexivity first. Reflexivity can, they admit, be seen as one way of pursuing the relativist thrust of SSK itself. According to SSK, scientific knowledge has to be seen not as a transparent representation of its object but rather, in the Collinsian variant, as the upshot of particular processes of negotiation between human actors. Clearly there is no way of stopping this kind of relativism from spreading to SSK itself: knowledge in SSK has to be seen as the upshot of exactly the same kind of negotiations. But the traditional reaction to this point within SSK has been first to acknowledge its truth—it is the fourth of David Bloor's tenets of the strong program in SSK (Bloor 1976, 4)—and second to treat it as rather uninteresting. Reflexivists like Steve Woolgar, on the other hand, take the point extremely seriously and want to explore the general properties of representation, including representation within SSK. To that end they seek to explore and display actors' representational practices, including their own. This is the train of thought that has led through discourse analysis into reflexivity and "new literary forms," experimental styles of writing that seek to bring the tactics of representation to the surface by, for example, the admission of dissonant voices into the text. The idea here is that one strategy for maintaining the authority of representation is the exclusion and silencing of all but the voice of a single author; when such exclusions are relaxed, the artful construction of representation becomes apparent. All very well and good, say Collins and Yearley, but while such ways of writing may be very clever, amusing to read, fun to write, and even epistemologically radical, they in fact reduce themselves to political impotence. The serious reflexivist just leaps into the skeptical regress of deconstruction without a parachute, and is left with nothing positive or constructive to say. While SSK at least has a radical political message concerning science, technology, and society, reflexivity has no message about anything apart from itself. Its signposts lead nowhere; we should not follow them.

Collins and Yearley then turn their critical gaze upon Callon and Latour. Here they are inclined to concede that the actor-network approach has something to tell us about scientific practice in its discussion of "obligatory points of passage," of the making of "immutable mobiles," and so on, but they worry about Callon and Latour's "extended symmetry." The actor-network approach seeks to capture the nature of scientific practice in the metaphor of the making and breaking of alliances (associations, as I have been calling

19

them) between actors, human and nonhuman, while seeking to avoid imputing different properties to either category. Human and nonhuman actors are thus in effect treated as being somehow on a par with one another. Once more, Collins and Yearley are prepared to admit that this extended symmetry can be seen as a continuation of SSK. It takes further the symmetrical approach to the analysis of "true" and "false" belief already enshrined in the strong program itself. And again, they are willing to concede that in this respect the actor-network approach is epistemologically radical compared with SSK. But this time they insist that the principle of extended symmetry leads, in fact, to accounts of science that remain "prosaic" in comparison with those of SSK. SSK achieves its political effect by representing scientific knowledge as the upshot of precisely social interactions, interactions between real, human agents. This representation stands in stark contrast to traditional accounts that see scientific knowledge as largely given by the world itself, independently of the human scientists that function as nature's mouthpiece. In granting a constitutive role to nature—to scallops, say, as in Callon's classic account of aquaculture in France—the actor-network approach thus, according to Collins and Yearley, moves us back from SSK toward the prosaic accounts beloved by traditional history, philosophy, and sociology of science, not to mention the scientists themselves. The critical and demystifying thrust of SSK is lost in the actor-network approach, and this is why we should not follow the signposts of Paris.

In their different ways, Woolgar and Callon and Latour reply to Collins and Yearley along similar lines, claiming to see in SSK certain taken-for-granted conceptual dichotomies that in fact guarantee the very hegemony of the natural sciences that Collins and Yearley want to dispute. Woolgar goes first. In "Some Remarks about Positionism" (chap. 11), he associates his explorations in reflexivity with a challenge to the fundamental dichotomy of subject and object, and to the associated "ideology of representation." Woolgar argues that SSK takes one step forward in the analysis of representation by problematizing scientists' representations of the natural world, but that it takes the same step back again in offering its own quite traditional representations of how scientists produce scientific representations. SSK's social realism thus "presume[s] and reaffirm[s] the scientific idiom" instead of exploring the idiom itself. The reflexivity approach self-consciously seeks to foreground and problematize the very idiom of representation, and this, for Woolgar, is why reflexivity is an important next step in, or if necessary beyond, SSK.

Callon and Latour follow a similar strategy in "Don't Throw the Baby Out with the Bath School!" (chap. 12). The dichotomy they attack is the Kantian "Great Divide" between nature and society. They assert that traditional thought on science and society has situated itself on a spectrum with nature at one end and society at the other. In particular, scientists and their academic spokespersons in history, philosophy, and sociology have situated their accounts of science at the "nature" end of the spectrum—scientific knowledge is dictated by nature—while the radical move of SSK has been to situate itself at the other extreme: scientific knowledge is dictated by society.[9] And thus, say Callon and Latour, their extended symmetry, in admitting agency to the realm of nonhuman actors, must appear to Collins and Yearley as a step backward, meaning a step away from the society end of the spectrum and toward nature. However, Callon and Latour continue, what Collins and Yearley have failed to appreciate is that the actor-network approach rejects the very concept of the nature-society spectrum. Especially it rejects the dichotomous limit forms, such as SSK's, that seek to represent either pole as determinative. Instead Callon and Latour begin from the idea, argued in their own studies and supported in the essays of part 1, that nature and society are intimately entangled in scientific and technological practice. Practice is where nature and society and the space between them are continually made, unmade, and remade. Inasmuch, therefore, as we can confidently attribute properties to nature and society, it is as a consequence of practice; those properties cannot count as the explanation of practice. And thus, from their non-Kantian position, Callon and Latour seek to turn the tables on Collins and Yearley. If distinctions between nature and society are made in scientific practice, then Collins and Yearley's social realism indeed throws the baby out with the bathwater: a fascinating enquiry into the making of the Great Divide is ruled out of court by reaching too quickly for explanatory closure. And, of course, in appealing to the social as the explanatory principle, Collins and Yearley grant the very premise of the Great Divide between nature and society on which the authority of the natural scientist rests.

Collins and Yearley respond to Callon and Latour in "Journey into Space" (chap. 13), but it is time for me to leave the reader to think through the debate further.[10] I do, however, have one last point to

9. And of course all sorts of hybrid positions have been taken up: see n. 7.

10. While this volume was in preparation, Collins and Yearley insisted that their right to reply to the responses from Woolgar and Callon and Latour was a condition for the inclusion of "Epistemological Chicken" (chap. 10) in the collection. In the

make in this connection. In one sense, Woolgar, Callon, and Latour have answered to Collins and Yearley's demand for the use, not the meaning. Their responses both claim to carry through the disputation of the hegemony of the natural sciences to a new and deeper level than SSK. But one needs to be careful here. It seems to me that Collins and Yearley's social realism is as politically radical as can be while remaining on known and familiar terrain. But worrying about the dualisms of subject and object, nature and society goes pretty deep. The foundations of modern thought are at stake here; this is precisely the point at which science studies converges with all sorts of postmodernisms. If one follows either Woolgar or Callon and Latour, one is leaving the known and familiar for terra incognita, and it is doubtful whether sailing into the unknown can be seen as a continuous extension of any Old World enterprise. It is not easy to imagine what a politics would be like in which the boundaries between subject and object, nature and society could no longer be taken for granted (try Haraway 1985). As Woolgar says: "Go this route and *who knows* what will happen." He puts these words into the mouths of Collins and Yearley, but I suspect that they are his own, and those of Callon and Latour, when uttered in an approving, not disapproving, tone of voice.

The last argument of part 2 is constructed in the juxtaposition of essays by Steve Fuller and Sharon Traweek. Though Fuller and Traweek do not make direct contact with one another, I pair them because they criticize science studies in general and implicitly all of the essays collected here from opposite flanks. Fuller thinks that science studies is insufficiently scientific, while Traweek wants to expose a residual scientism running through the field. Fuller's program of "social epistemology" (Fuller 1988, 1989) participates in the traditional philosophical desire to tell people what to do. But it departs from the tradition in rejecting the usual appeal to a priori normative standards of reason and method. The standards we hold scientists to must be realistic ones, deriving from studies of actual practice. Unfortunately, existing studies of science-as-practice are useless for such purposes because of their commitment, as Fuller sees it, to achieving a phenomenological "actor's perspective." Normativity requires externality, and in "Social Epistemology and the Research Agenda of Science Studies" (chap. 14), Fuller argues that

---

event, they waived their right to reply here to Woolgar, but a reply in the style of "new literary forms" may be obtained by sending enough to cover copying, postage, and packing ($5 or equivalent) to Professor Collins.

the required degree of detachment is to be achieved by studying scientific practice (more) scientifically—in studies of, for example, the psychology of scientific reasoning or the influence of communication patterns on scientific productivity. In this way his social epistemology seeks to develop normative standards against which particular practices can be assessed. Fuller's aim is, then, to make a direct connection between his kind of studies of science-as-practice and science policy by looking at the doing of science in the same way as Frederick Taylor looked at shoveling coal. He looks forward to a genuine science of science that can serve as the instrument for the scientific management of scientists.

Traweek is traveling in the opposite direction from Fuller as fast as she can. Like Woolgar, she wants to explore alternatives to scientific writing (in the broadest sense) as a way of getting beyond its taken-for-granted conceptualizations and dichotomies, not to produce more of it. And speaking from within a section of her discipline, anthropology, that has been interrogating the ideology of representation for quite a while, her "Border Crossings" (chap. 15) challenges the conventions of representation in ways that new literary forms in science studies have yet to explore. Despite speaking with a single voice, for example, she positions herself as author securely within the frame of her essay, thus cutting across any taken-for-granted subject-object distinction. And she rejects the format of conventional narrative in favor of "reverberating strings of ironic stories" circling around her ethnographic researches into high-energy physics in Japan and the United States.

Traweek remarks that we need more self-awareness of the relation between how and what we write, and the essays collected here—including this one—are probably manifestations of the kind of rhetorical naïveté that she wants to get away from. I am not going to display it further by attempting the kind of summary of her essay that I offered for the others. I risk saying that "Border Crossings" made me think about scientific culture and practice, about power and marginality, gender, and narration in science and in science studies, and about ethnography and Sharon Traweek, in ways that seem unlikely to surface within more conventional genres.

REFERENCES

Ashmore, M. 1989. *The Reflexive Thesis: Wrighting Sociology of Knowledge.* Chicago and London: University of Chicago Press.

Barnes, B. 1974. *Scientific Knowledge and Sociological Theory.* London and Boston: Routledge and Kegan Paul.

———. 1977. *Interests and the Growth of Knowledge.* London and Boston: Routledge and Kegan Paul.

———. 1982. *T.S. Kuhn and Social Science.* London: Macmillan.

Barnes, B., and S. Shapin, eds. 1979. *Natural Order: Historical Studies of Scientific Culture.* Beverly Hills: Sage.

Bijker, W. E., T. P. Hughes, and T. J. Pinch, eds. 1987. *The Social Construction of Technological Systems: New Directions in the Sociology and History of Technology.* Cambridge: MIT Press.

Bloor, D. 1976. *Knowledge and Social Imagery.* London and Boston: Routledge and Kegan Paul.

———. 1983. *Wittgenstein: A Social Theory of Knowledge.* London: Macmillan.

Callon, M. 1980. The State and Technological Innovation: A Case Study of the Electrical Vehicle in France. *Research Policy* 9:358–76.

Cartwright, N. 1983. *How the Laws of Physics Lie.* Oxford: Oxford University Press.

Collins, H. M. 1985. *Changing Order: Replication and Induction in Scientific Practice.* Beverly Hills: Sage.

Feyerabend, P. K. 1975. *Against Method.* London: New Left Books.

———. 1978. *Science in a Free Society.* London: New Left Books.

Fine, A. 1986. *The Shaky Game: Einstein, Realism, and the Quantum Theory.* Chicago: University of Chicago Press.

Fleck. L. 1935. *Entstehung und Entwicklung einer Wissenschaftlichen Tatsache: Einführung in die Lehre vom Denkstil und Denkkollektiv.* Basel: Benno Schwabe. Reprinted in English translation with a foreword by T. S. Kuhn and a preface by T. J. Trenn as *Genesis and Development of a Scientific Fact.* Chicago: University of Chicago Press, 1979.

Fujimura, J. H. 1988. The Molecular Biological Bandwagon in Cancer Research: Where Social Worlds Meet. *Social Problems* 35:261–83.

Fujimura, J. H., S. L. Star, and E. Gerson. 1987. Méthodes de Recherche en Sociologie des Sciences: Travail, Pragmatisme et Interactionnisme Symbolique. *Cahiers de Recherche Sociologique* 5:65–85.

Fuller, S. 1988. *Social Epistemology.* Bloomington: Indiana University Press.

———. 1989. *Philosophy of Science and Its Discontents.* Boulder, Colo.: Westview Press.

Galison, P. 1990. Aufbau/Bauhaus: Logical Positivism and Architectural Modernism. *Critical Enquiry* 16:709–52.

Gilbert, G. N., and M. Mulkay. 1984. *Opening Pandora's Box: A Sociological Analysis of Scientists' Discourse.* Cambridge: Cambridge University Press.

Gooding. D. 1990. *Experiment and the Making of Meaning.* Dordrecht, Boston, and London: Kluwer Academic.

Gooding, D., T. J. Pinch, and S. Schaffer, eds. 1989. *The Uses of Experiment: Studies in the Natural Sciences.* Cambridge: Cambridge University Press.

Goodman, N. 1978. *Ways of Worldmaking.* Indianapolis: Hackett.

Hacking, I. 1983. *Representing and Intervening.* Cambridge: Cambridge University Press.

Hanson, N. R. 1958. *Patterns of Discovery: An Inquiry into the Conceptual Foundations of Knowledge.* Cambridge: Cambridge University Press.

Haraway, D. 1985. A Manifesto for Cyborgs: Science, Technology, and Socialist Feminism in the 1980s. *Socialist Review* 80:65–107.

Hesse, M. B. 1980. *Revolutions and Reconstructions in the Philosophy of Science.* Brighton: Harvester Press.

Knorr Cetina, K. 1981. *The Manufacture of Knowledge: An Essay on the Constructivist and Contextual Nature of Science.* Oxford and New York: Pergamon.

Knorr Cetina, K., and M. Mulkay, eds. 1983. *Science Observed: Perspectives on the Social Study of Science.* Beverly Hills: Sage.

Kuhn, T. S. 1962. *The Structure of Scientific Revolutions.* Chicago: University of Chicago Press. 2d ed. 1970, with a new postscript.

Latour, B. 1987. *Science in Action.* Cambridge: Harvard University Press.

———. 1988. *The Pasteurization of France.* Cambridge: Harvard University Press.

———. 1990. Postmodern? No Simply Amodern. Steps Towards an Anthropology of Science: An Essay Review. *Studies in History and Philosophy of Science* 21:145–71.

Latour, B. and S. Woolgar. 1979. *Laboratory Life: The Social Construction of Scientific Facts.* Beverly Hills: Sage. 2d ed. Princeton: Princeton University Press, 1986.

Law, J. 1987. Technology and Heterogeneous Engineering: The Case of Portuguese Expansion. In Bijker, Hughes, and Pinch 1987, 111–34.

Law, J. ed. 1986. *Power, Action, and Belief: A New Sociology of Knowledge?* Sociological Review Monograph 32. London: Routledge and Kegan Paul.

Livingston, E. 1986. *The Ethnomethodological Foundations of Mathematics.* Boston: Routledge and Kegan Paul.

Lynch. M. 1985. *Art and Artifact in Laboratory Science: A Study of Shop Work and Shop Talk in a Research Laboratory.* London: Routledge and Kegan Paul.

Lynch, M., E. Livingston, and H. Garfinkel. 1983. Temporal Order in Laboratory Work. In Knorr Cetina and Mulkay 1983, 205–38.

MacKenzie, D. A. 1981. *Statistics in Britain, 1865–1930: The Social Construction of Scientific Knowledge.* Edinburgh: Edinburgh University Press.

Mulkay, M. 1985. *The Word and the World: Explorations in the Form of Sociological Analysis.* London: George Allen and Unwin.

Pickering, A. 1989. Living in the Material World: On Realism and Experimental Practice. In Gooding, Pinch, and Schaffer 1989, 275–97.

———. 1990. Knowledge, Practice, and Mere Construction. *Social Studies of Science* 20:682–729.

Pickering, A. Forthcoming. Objectivity and the Mangle of Practice. A.

Megill, ed., *Deconstructing and Reconstructing Objectivity.* Special Issue of *Annals of Scholarship.*

Polanyi, M. 1958. *Personal Knowledge: Towards a Post-Critical Philosophy.* Chicago: University of Chicago Press.

Quine, W. V. O. 1980. *From a Logical Point of View: Nine Logico-Philosophical Essays.* 2d ed. revised. Cambridge: Harvard University Press.

Rorty, R. 1979 *Philosophy and the Mirror of Nature.* Princeton: Princeton University Press.

——. 1982. *Consequences of Pragmatism (Essays: 1972–1980).* Minneapolis: University of Minnesota Press.

Rouse, J. 1991. The Politics of Post-Modern Philosophy of Science. *Philosophy of Science* 58.

Shapin, S. 1979. The Politics of Observation: Cerebral Anatomy and Social Interests in the Edinburgh Phrenology Disputes. In Wallis 1979, 139–78.

——. 1982. History of Science and Its Sociological Reconstructions. *History of Science* 20:157–211.

Smith, B. H. 1988. *Contingencies of Value.* Cambridge: Harvard University Press.

Star, S. L, and J. R. Griesemer. 1989. Institutional Ecology, "Translations," and Boundary Objects: Amateurs and Professionals in Berkeley's Museum of Vertebrate Zoology. *Social Studies of Science* 19:387–420.

Suppe, F., ed. 1977. *The Structure of Scientific Theories.* 2d ed. Urbana: University of Illinois Press.

Traweek. S. 1988. *Beamtimes and Lifetimes: The World of High Energy Physicists.* Cambridge: Harvard University Press.

Wallis, R., ed. 1979. *On the Margins of Science: The Social Construction of Rejected Knowledge.* Sociological Review Monograph 27 (University of Keele).

Wittgenstein, L. 1953. *Philosophical Investigations.* New York: Macmillan.

Woolgar, S., ed. 1988. *Knowledge and Reflexivity: New Frontiers in the Sociology of Knowledge.* Beverly Hills: Sage.

PART 1 POSITIONS

2

The Self-Vindication of the Laboratory Sciences

Ian Hacking

1 Theses

The unity of science was once a battle cry, but today it is the fashion to emphasize the disunities among the sciences. I am right up there on the bandwagon (Hacking 1991). Some suggest that there is nothing in general to be said about science unless it be the message of Latour (1987) that everything in the world and our knowledge of it is to be understood on the model of politics, or maybe, *is* politics. I am partial to Wittgenstein's word "motley"—as in "the motley of mathematics" (Wittgenstein 1956, 88). We all want to give an account of the motley of the sciences. But here I shall try to say something quite general about established laboratory sciences. In philosophy we must strive for both the particular and the general.

What follows is metaphysics and epistemology, a contribution to our radically changing vision of truth, being, logic, reason, meaning, knowledge and reality. Such a contribution from a disunifier such as me is necessarily more local than traditional metaphysics. I address just one pervasive aspect of the laboratory sciences. Despite our recent enthusiasm for refutation and revolution, these sciences lead to an extraordinary amount of rather permanent knowledge, devices, and practice. It has been too little noted of late how much of a science, once in place, stays with us, modified but not refuted, reworked but persistent, seldom acknowledged but taken for granted. In days gone by an easy explanation of the growth of knowledge satisfied almost everyone: science discovers the truth, and once you find out the truth, then, in a liberal society, it sticks. As Ernest Nagel put it in *The Structure of Science* (1961), more powerful theories subsume their predecessors as special cases. Today, after *Kuhn's Structure of Scientific Revolutions* (1962), we are more circumspect. It has become surprising that so much empirical knowledge has accumulated since the seventeenth century.

My explanation of this stability is that when the laboratory sciences are practicable at all, they tend to produce a sort of self-vindicating structure that keeps them stable. This is not to suggest that they are mental or social constructs. I am not about to argue for idealism but rather for down-to-earth materialism. Mine is a thesis about the relationships between thoughts, acts, and manufactures. It can be thought of as an extension of Duhem's doctrine that a theory inconsistent with an observation can always be saved by modifying an auxiliary hypothesis, typically a hypothesis about the working of an instrument such as the telescope. His was a thesis about thoughts; like most philosophers of theory he did not reflect on how we change not only our ideas but also the world. His doctrine, especially for those who read Quine, is taken to imply the underdetermination of scientific knowledge. When properly extended, it has quite the opposite effect, of helping us to understand how the world and our knowledge of it are so remarkably determinate.

Duhem said that theory and auxiliary hypothesis can be adjusted to each other; he left out the whole teeming world of making instruments, remaking them, making them work, and rethinking how they work. It is my thesis that as a laboratory science matures, it develops a body of types of theory and types of apparatus and types of analysis that are mutually adjusted to each other. They become what Heisenberg (e.g., 1948) notoriously said Newtonian mechanics was, "a closed system" that is essentially irrefutable. They are self-vindicating in the sense that any test of theory is against apparatus that has evolved in conjunction with it—and in conjunction with modes of data analysis. Conversely, the criteria for the working of the apparatus and for the correctness of analyses is precisely the fit with theory.

The theories of the laboratory sciences are not directly compared to "the world"; they persist because they are true to phenomena produced or even created by apparatus in the laboratory and are measured by instruments that we have engineered. This "true to" is not a matter of direct comparison between theory and phenomenon but relies on further theories, namely, theories about how the apparatus works and on a number of quite different kinds of techniques for processing the data that we generate. High-level theories are not "true" at all. This is not some deep insight into truth but a mundane fact familiar since the work of Norman Campbell (1920, 122–58), who noted that fundamental laws of nature do not directly "hook on to" the discernible world at all. What meshes (Kuhn's word) is at most a network of theories, models, approximations, together with understandings of the workings of our instruments and apparatus.

My thesis is materialist, both in its attention to the material side of what we do in science and in its opposition to the intellectualism of Duhem. The thesis has almost nothing to do with recent manifestations of scientific realism or antirealism, being compatible with almost all the significant assertions made by either party. There is only one way in which my thesis is contrary to a bundle of metaphysical doctrines loosely labeled "realist." Realists commonly suppose that the ultimate aim or ideal of science is "the one true theory about the universe." I have never believed that even makes sense. The present picture suggests that there are many different ways in which a laboratory science could have stabilized. The resultant stable theories would not be parts of the one great truth, not even if they were prompted by something like the same initial concerns, needs, or curiosity. Such imaginary stable sciences would not even be comparable, because they would be true to different and quite literally incommensurable classes of phenomena and instrumentation. I say incommensurable in the straightforward sense that there would be no body of instruments to make common measurements, because the instruments are peculiar to each stable science. It is just this literal incommensurability which also enables us to understand how a "closed system" can remain in use and also be superseded, perhaps in a revolutionary way, by a theory with a new range of phenomena.

The crude idea of my thesis, although at odds with most traditional metaphysics and epistemology, is hardly novel. Our preserved theories and the world fit together so snugly less because we have found out how the world is than because we have tailored each to the other. One can think of my detailed account below as a gloss on Heisenberg's "closed systems." Once we recovered from the impact of *The Structure of Scientific Revolutions*, the question of the stability of science was immediately raised. For example, the "finalization" of science has become a lively topic for people who have learned most from Habermas (Böhme et al. 1983). There are more striking agreements with contributors to the present volume. My emphases, and in the end my philosophy, differ from Pickering's, but for present purposes my materialism lives happily as a mere part of what he calls his "pragmatic realism," in which "facts, phenomena, material procedures, interpretations, theories, social relations etc. are, in Latour's words (borrowed from Marx) 'co-produced'" (Pickering 1990, 708). The list in this quotation begins with "forms of life," which I do not omit by inadvertence; on the other hand, the taxonomy of elements of laboratory experiment, given later in this paper, expands his "etc." in ways of which he can only approve.

Another author in this volume, David Gooding (chap. 3), has another "etc." list: he speaks of an "experimental sequence" which appears as the "production of models, phenomena, bits of apparatus, and representations of these things." He points the way in which "the representations and the phenomena gradually *converge* (his emphasis) to a point where the resemblance between what can be observed and what is sought is [as Faraday put it] 'very satisfactory.' " We agree that the interplay of items in such a list brings about the stability of laboratory science. I think of the matériel of an experiment as more central to its stabilization than do writers in the tradition of social studies of science. By the matériel I mean the apparatus, the instruments, the substances or objects investigated. The matériel is flanked on the one side by ideas (theories, questions, hypotheses, intellectual models of apparatus) and on the other by marks and manipulations of marks (inscriptions, data, calculations, data reduction, interpretation). Thus where my colleagues in this book are content with lists and etc.'s, I venture a doubtless imperfect organization or "taxonomy" of elements of laboratory experiment. The agency that Gooding puts back into experiment is just that work that is done by people, which brings the elements in my "taxonomy" into consilience and thereby creates a world of things, ideas, and data that is stable.

2 Contents

First, in (3) I say what I mean by a laboratory science. In (4) I suggest one source in the history of twentieth-century science for the present conviction of philosophers (but not of scientists) that science is rather unstable. Then I argue for the contrary point of view. In (5) I point to some reasons we might think that science is stable, reasons that seem to me superficial or misleading, and which are not my concern.

In (6)–(9) I give my taxonomy of elements of experiment which, I claim, are mutually adjusted to produce the self-vindicating character of laboratory science. I am at pains to list these because it is so easy to slip back into the old ways and suppose there are just a few kinds of things, theory, data, or whatever. My taxonomy is among other things a demonstration of the "motley of experimental science," which at the same time strives for some breadth of vision and does not merely meander from fascinating case to fascinating case. And then in (10) I mention some items, assuredly relevant to laboratory science, which are omitted from my taxonomy because they are not items that experiments literally use. (For example, Millikan did not "use" an atomistic weltanschauung when he measured the charge on the electron, although without a certain vision of how the world is, his research would have proceeded quite differently, and as we know from his rival Ehrenhaft, might have come to contrary conclusions.)

The remainder of the paper develops the theses of (1) in such a way that it is possible to jump there immediately, skipping the taxonomy in (4)–(9) and referring back to it only when need arises. In (11) I discuss my extension of Duhem's thesis. In (12) I discuss what happens to a laboratory science as it matures and stabilizes. In (13) I examine the relationship between self-vindication and our expectations that good theories should be true. The thesis of self-vindication seems to make the sciences all too internal to the laboratory; how then are they applied outside? In (14) I sketch two answers, one for a practical worry of this sort and one for a metaphysical one. Finally, in (15) I remark that the stability of the laboratory sciences has nothing to do with the problem of induction. But an experimentally oriented philosophy does paint that problem in slightly different but no less skeptical colors than Hume, Russell, or the logical empiricists would. The worry is that nothing would work any more.

3 Laboratory Science

I do not want to invite arguments about what a laboratory is, or whether such and such is a laboratory science. The laboratory is a cultural institution with a history (or rather histories) that I shall not discuss in this abstract presentation. "Laboratory" is a far more restricted idea than "experiment"; many experimental sciences are not what I call laboratory sciences. I have in mind laboratories that have "come of age" (chap. 4). Laboratory sciences are surely connected by a family of resemblances and by a central core of examples from which they more or less differ. "Laboratory science" is a radial category in the sense of Lakoff (1986); what he would call the "prototype" laboratory sciences are those whose claims to truth answer primarily to work done in the laboratory. They study phenomena that seldom or never occur in a pure state before people have brought them under surveillance. Exaggerating a little, I say that the phenomena under study are created in the laboratory. The laboratory sciences use apparatus in isolation to interfere with the course of that aspect of nature that is under study, the end in view being an increase in knowledge, understanding, and control of a general or generalizable sort. Botany is thus not what I call a laboratory science, but plant physiology is. Paleontology is not a laboratory science, even though carbon dating has usually been done in a laboratory, where one also uses Italian iridium to test hypotheses about the extinction of dinosaurs. Likewise, although there is plenty of experimentation in sociology, psychology, and economics, not much of it is what I call laboratory science, not even when there is a university building called the psychology laboratory. There is too little of that "apparatus used in isolation to interfere." In saying this I neither praise nor condemn, nor do I argue that only laboratory sciences are stable—Linnaean botany may hold the palm for stability, if not for growth. Boundaries matter little; I wish only to say from the start that the sciences that are chiefly observational, classificatory, or historical are not the subject of the following discussion.

According to my definition, astronomy, astrophysics, and cosmology cannot be laboratory sciences, for they cannot in general interfere with the nature that they study. They cannot create astrophysical phenomena. But I have found that a number of people with entirely different agendas protest that astronomy and astrophysics are or have become laboratory sciences. So let me to some extent agree. Cosmology does include much laboratory work, such as investigations of gravity or an alleged fifth force (we make a laboratory in Greenland, dropping objects through a hole bored in a kilometer of ice, enriched by myriad detectors). High energy physics projects that are intended to simulate some of the birth pangs of the universe bring some cosmology down to earth, trapping it in a very big Swiss or Texan laboratory. I thus agree with G. Munevar, who insisted on this point in discussion.

Nor is the use of laboratories for astronomy novel. Old and new instruments used in astronomy and astrophysics, from spectrometers to space-launched gyroscopes to neutrino detectors, include laboratory apparatus; indeed laboratories are now put in space. Simon Schaffer (forthcoming) implies in a recent paper that in the nineteenth century there was enough experimentation in astrospectroscopy to think of it as a laboratory science. Much of what I say below about stability applies to the very work of Huggins and Maxwell that Schaffer describes, so there may be little at issue here.

Knorr Cetina might push me one step further. She notes that imaging is being radically changed, so that data are now stored digitally. The stored data become the object of investigation rather than anything that is directly observed. "Once the transition is complete," she writes, "astronomy will have been transformed from an observational field science to an image-processing laboratory science" (chap. 4). I am more cautious about this than about most other statements in her paper, partly because it has been a long time since

astronomy was an "observational field science." The caricature of
the astronomer as the one who peers through the telescope is as
absurd as the cartoon of the scientist in the white lab coat. The
painting by Vermeer called *The Astronomer,* dated 1658, portrays a
somewhat androgynous figure in an attractive closet, protractors in
hand, with what I think is a chart partially unrolled on a table (Stä-
delsches Kunstinstitut, Frankfurt am Main).

Although image-processing laboratory science is indeed a part of
astronomical and cosmological research, there remains much more
to astronomy and astrophysics than that. Image processing creates
many phenomena of its own. It also provides transportable data that
can be analyzed by anyone. Nevertheless, in my realist mode I
would not say that it creates any astronomical phenomena in the
same sense in which experimenters created the phenomenon of lasing. And I don't think it is true to say with Knorr Cetina that "the
objects of investigation become 'detached' from their natural environment." The digitized data are no more and no less detached than
the material confronting Vermeer's astronomer. (He is *working* his
data, just like the lab that buys data from Mount Palomar.) Mean-
while the objects of investigation, Saturn, superconducting cosmic
strings, or the strangely oscillating Beta-lactantae don't become detached, even if we study them by images that are detached and reconstituted electronically. I am too much of a literalist to say that
"the processes of interest to astronomers become miniaturized," or
that "planetary and stellar time scales are surrendered to social order time scales." (Once again, how is it different with Vermeer's astronomer?) But even if I did assent to Knorr Cetina's sentences, we
would still discern a sense in which astronomy and astrophysics are
not laboratory sciences in the sense explained above. And it is the
stability of laboratory sciences, in my sense given there, that is my
topic, and my account does bear on those parts of astronomy increasingly incorporated into the laboratory.

There are yet other definitions of the laboratory, hardly recognized as such by laboratory scientists, but which cannot escape the
keen eye of the ethnographer. Thus Latour (1987, chap. 6) characterizes the laboratory as a center of calculation. This vision is to be
expected from an author who regards the production and manipulation of inscriptions as the central scientific activity.[1] The laboratory

---

1. Collins and Yearley (chap. 13) also draw attention to Latour's fascination with
inscriptions. Latour is a bracing reminder of that glorious Parisian world of long ago,
the late sixties, when inscriptions were the reality and text was substance. In my
opinion Collins and Yearley misunderstood this. They are so locked in to their Anglo-

arm of science will be that which calculates. The paleontologists and the astrophysicists have, then, their laboratories for sure. Vermeer on this view painted his calculating astronomer not in a closet but in the laboratory. Latour writes in a letter of 21 February 1990, referring to Latour (1990), that explorers too are creatures of the lab. Moreover, my list of laboratory sciences "could nicely be expanded to collections and museums and archives."

That vision of science, verging on what I have labeled lingualism or linguistic idealism (Hacking 1975, 174, 182), is not mine. Mine is thoroughly materialist and interventionist, and my laboratory is a space for interfering under controllable and isolable conditions with matter and energy, often done in museums—my office is a hundred meters from a great museum whose basement is full of what I call laboratories—but seldom in archives. But let me make peace: one-third of my taxonomy—section (9)—is about marks and the manipulation of marks, so I claim to honor Latour's insight without losing my materialist focus.

Latour has encouraged a new problematic. We must not lose sight of an old one, the relation between theory and experiment. The laboratory sciences are of necessity theoretical. Another third of my taxonomy—section (7)—is about several distinct kinds of theory. *By a laboratory science I don't just mean that part of a science that is conducted in a laboratory; I include all the theoretical superstructure and intellectual achievements that in the end answer to what happens in the laboratory.* I hope my taxonomy will serve those who realize that there are quite different types of theory.

Latour has another criticism of my approach. He writes in the same letter that "curiously your materialist outlook—with which I agree—does not include 'new phenomena' as the main production of the laboratory. I am in this sense more realist than you." Oddly, my very first essay on experiment was called "Speculation, Calcu-

---

phone theory of language that they cannot conceive of inscriptions as being other than "representational." They even cite Travis as showing that certain mass spectrometer inscriptions "were not universally accepted as representing reality," as if that were germane. Parisian inscriptions don't represent anything (let alone reality). They are autonomous objects, material beings that work without signifying. I doubt that actant theory particularly derives from inscriptionalism in the way that Collins and Yearley suggest. Unlike those two authors, I have no objection to Latour's theory of actants. I object only to something quite different, namely, the metonymic definition of the laboratory in terms of merely one of its activities, namely, inscribing. Maybe I go further than Latour, for I might take inscriptions to be among the actants, right up there with fishers and molluscs, working and worked on, everywhere people go since the moment that our species came into being as *Homo depictor*.

lation, and the Creation of Phenomena," published in German in Duerr 1981, 2, and rewritten for Hacking 1983 (chaps. 10, 12, and esp. 13, "The Creation of Phenomena"). Latour continues, "You do not leave room for the creation of new entities in the lab through the lab (what I call a new object, that is, a list of actions in trials that will later coalesce in a thing and will later be thrown 'out there' as the ultimate cause of our certainty 'about it')." One difference between my 1981 self and Latour is that I did not think of electrons being created, but did think of the photoelectric effect being created, in a pure state. I asserted that the most cautious metaphysical realist should admit that nowhere on earth did the pure photoelectric effect exist on earth until we made it. Nowhere in the universe, so far as we know, did anything lase anywhere in the universe before 1945 (maybe there were a few masers around in outer space). But now there are tens of thousands of lasers within a few miles of me as I write. Lasing is a phenomenon created in the lab. This is not a constructionalist theme, and so Latour and I go different ways with it. I do not know that new phenomena are the "main production" of the laboratory, as Latour says, but they are one of its most important products. I am glad that Latour's criticism has enabled me to reiterate one of my favorite themes, the creation of phenomena, previously left out of this essay. And I also can avoid the misunderstanding of Latour when he writes of the items in my taxonomy below that they are "a fixed list of elements shaping phenomena." Nothing was further from my mind than the idea that experiments merely shape phenomena that already exist in the world ready to be shaped.

Finally I should make two disclaimers about stable laboratory science. First, I am not in general discussing research at the frontiers of inquiry. That can be as unstable as you please, even when it is what Kuhn called normal science. As a matter of fact such research is usually highly regimented. Results are more often expected than surprising. We well understand why: it is not that sort of short-term stability that is puzzling. I am concerned with the cumulative establishment of scientific knowledge. That has been proceeding apace since the scientific revolution. Secondly, I regard stability not as a virtue but as a fact. If values are to be mentioned, stability upon which one cannot build is a vice. The noblest stability, perhaps, is that of a science that has been surpassed by deeper enquiries and new types of instrumentation and yet which remains humbly in place as a loyal and reliable servant for our interventions in, our interactions with, and our predictions of the course of events: one thinks of geometrical optics or Galilean mechanics. I shall repeat this, because I am regularly misunderstood: *This paper does not praise stability. It does not imply that stability is a good thing. It does not admire stability. It observes it and tries to explain it.*

4 Origins of the Instability Myth

Talk of stability flies in the face of recent wisdom about revolutions, but an emphasis on the fallibility of science is in part the consequence of unusual circumstances in physics early in the twentieth century. The shake-up that resulted at a certain historical moment was splendid. The comfortable belief that science is cumulative had been held for all too long. Mistakes, so ran the official story, are often made. Gigantic muddles long persist. But in due course and after hard work some truths will out, become established, and serve as steps upon which to advance into the unknown. This complacency fell apart under the criticisms first of Popper and then of Kuhn. They were wonderfully liberating. They turned that dutiful inductive discipline, philosophy of science, weary with years, into something sparkling, even if sometimes tinctured with fantasy. I am here using the names "Popper" and "Kuhn" to denote not only individuals but also successive generations. Now why did stability suddenly become unstuck? Popper, like so many of his peers, was deeply moved by Einstein's successive revolutions in space-time, special and then general relativity. They were matched by the old and new quantum mechanics of 1900 and 1926–27. Stirring times, but also anomalous ones. They stand out because so many of the eternal verities, in the form of a priori knowledge about space, time, continuity, causation, and determinism, were abandoned. Refutation and revolution were in vogue where stability and subsumption had been the norm.

To a quite extraordinary degree these transitions, especially Einstein's, were thought out and made convincing almost entirely independently of any experimental work. Pure thought, it seemed, could anticipate nature and then hire experimenters to check out which conjectures were sound. Although relativity was often presented in its day as a refutation of Kant's transcendental aesthetic, while quantum mechanics wrecked the transcendental analytic, this was an utterly Kantian moment in the philosophy of science. Any sense of the subtle interplay between theory and experiment— or between theoretician and experimenter—was lost. The conception of physical science as unstable, as a matter of refutation and revolution, went hand in hand with a total lack of interest in the role of experimental science. So it is not surprising that today we should start to think about stability again; for the present decade has seen the revival, among historians, philosophers, and sociologists of science, of serious thinking about the laboratory.

Why do I speak so confidently of stability? For a number of reasons. One is quite familiar to students of the physical sciences, whose practitioners in moments of philosophizing speak of theories being valid in their domain. Thus Heisenberg wrote (1948, 332) that "some theories seem to be susceptible of no improvement . . . they signify a *closed system* of knowledge. I believe that Newtonian mechanics cannot be improved at all . . . with that degree of accuracy with which the phenomena can be described by the Newtonian concepts, the Newtonian laws are also valid" (for convenient references to the development of Heisenberg's idea, see Chevalley 1988). I would amend this slightly, for the phenomena are not described directly and without intermediary by Newtonian concepts. It is rather certain measurements of the phenomena, generated by a certain class of what might be called Newtonian instruments, that mesh with Newtonian concepts. The accuracy of the mechanics and the accuracy of the instruments are correlative, and that is one of the explanations of the stability of laboratory science.

Before even entering the research laboratory, the student, like it or not, finds that many mature sciences are pedagogically stable. We learn geometrical optics when young, the wave theory as teenagers, Maxwell's equations on entering college, some theory of the photon in senior classes, and quantum field theory in graduate school. Each of these stages is taught as if it were true, although of course many byways, such as Newton's corpuscular light rays, are omitted. Science teachers have to bear the brunt of a familiar criticism. They teach science as if it were dead. In a way that is right. Much science *is* dead. That does not excuse bad teaching; there is probably a greater proportion of lively classes in classical Greek than in thermodynamics. Unlike the conjugations, which are the luxury of a few, the Carnot cycle must be taught.

There are perennial debates on American college campuses: should every student have some acquaintance with the great books of the West? The issues are ideological and hinge on a conception of the nature of culture and civilization. There is nothing comparably ideological about learning how to use Planck's constant or the mechanical equivalent of heat. No physicist would dream of compelling students to read Planck or Dirac, let alone Boltzmann or Joule. But the students have to master the dead and digested science associated with those names, not because of their cultural or even pedagogical value, but because that is part of the stable knowledge with which many of the students will change bits of the world, and on which a few of the research oriented among them will build new knowledge.

Our editor remarks that according to Feyerabend (1978) this is a bad way of teaching. There is a lot of bad teaching, but I doubt that it is wrong to teach stable science. The error is reverence for what is established, and a dulling of the critical spirit, but that is an entirely distinct point. The only science education on near-Feyerabendian lines with which I am acquainted is offered at the Ontario Science Centre in Toronto. Twenty-five high school seniors are told to find things out and are given remarkable experimental material—the castoffs from what five years earlier was frontline research—and quite strong theoretical resources. They spend a semester doing two of physics, chemistry, or biology, and to satisfy an English requirement, learn science writing. The morale is extraordinary; the quality of learning superb. The depression that results when the students proceed to a university classroom amounts to trauma and Feyerabendian disillusion with science. Nevertheless one of the things that the students are constantly forced to do is to acquire on their own the chunks of stable theoretical knowledge and experimental technique demanded by their own learning and research. The students don't revere it. They believe it when they need it and doubt it when it does not work. And that is the way in which old stable science is an essential part of science education.

Let it be granted that there is some stability. Is that not the road to boredom and stultification? It is tempting to suppose that although the making and solidifying of an established science might have been intensely creative, once the work is in place it is to be used only for pedestrian purposes. The action lies elsewhere, in the creating of new science. We use geometrical optics all the time, but it is hardly a topic for live research, or so it may be said. We may rely on Newtonian mechanics for launching the Hubble space telescope, but the mechanics is not itself a topic for investigation. Yet of course there are Newtonian problems that remain deeply challenging, the many-body problem being the classic example. Ergodic theorems, in which one shows how stochastic processes can arise from within a deterministic world, lead on to chaos theory, a domain that blends mathematics, experiment, and concept formation in ways that may in retrospect come to seem quite novel. Even at the level of plain laboratory science, established knowledge—which we had thought superseded except in application—can be combined with new facilities for instrumentation to yield profound innovations. S. S. Schweber (1989) has a telling example. In 1981, workers at the University of Washington devised the Penning trap, which contains a single electron in a definite space. Everything they did was planned according to, and can be explained by, the prerelativistic (pre-Dirac) theory of the electron, which might have seemed to be a dead closed system of interest only to the so-called philosophers of quantum mechanics, who write as if quantum field theory does not exist. But not only was prerelativistic theory used by the Washington workers: it is also not clear that their work could have been conceived or made sense of otherwise. For their purposes, the crude old account of the electron is better than any other. One reason that a stable laboratory science may come to life is that advances in technique or technology developed for other purposes can sometimes be applied only in its old mature intellectual and experimental framework.

5 Seeming Stability

There are a number of reasons to expect established science to feel or look stable, which are independent of the more radical metaphysical theses advanced in this paper. I shall mention three. The first is our habit of splendid anachronism. We cheerfully speak of Maxwell's equations or the Zeeman effect, but what we understand by these things is very different from what was meant by those whom we honor. In the case of experimental techniques, a great many of them fade away, and only the most gifted experimenter can duplicate what the textbooks casually say was done. New instruments make obsolete the skills needed to build old instruments; replication requires perverse antiquarianism.

Thus old science is not preserved, the cynic will say: what is stable is that various events have been turned into facts that are no longer of immediate interest. We do other things and accept on faith most knowledge derived in the past. It can be well argued that the Zeeman effect and the anomalous Zeeman effect are not now what they were when they were discovered, and it is the practice of teaching and naming that makes things seem so constant.

Second, a secure sense of stability arises from the fact that scientific practice is like a rope with many strands. One strand may be cut, but others survive intact: the rope, it seems to the unreflective, holds unchanged. Peter Galison (1987, chap. 5) observes that in any laboratory science several traditions are at work at any one time. There are, for example, theoretical, experimental, and instrumental traditions. There may be a break in a theoretical tradition which has little effect on the instruments that are used or the ways they are used. The strong sense of continuity during such a theoretical mutation results from the fact that instrumental and experimental practices may continue largely unaffected by changes in theory. Even when the explanations for the practices change, so that people understand what they are doing differently, very much the same skills and material apparatus may be used as before (e.g., Heinz Post's example of seeing anthracene ring molecules: Hacking 1983, 199ff.). Likewise an ongoing theoretical tradition can make us experience continuity in a time of radical instrumental innovation.

A third and much more common source of felt stability is our practice of turning various elements of science into what Latour (1987, 2) calls "black boxes." These include not only off-the-shelf apparatus but also all sorts of systems for operating on symbols, for example, statistical techniques for assessing probable error. Material black boxes include standard pieces of apparatus bought from an instrument company, borrowed from the lab next door, rented from the Bureau of Standards, or abandoned by a military research facility when it has moved on to fancier gadgets. The laboratory worker seldom has much idea how the box works and cannot fix it when it is broken. Yet it encodes in material form a great deal of preestablished knowledge which is implicit in the outcome of an experiment. Indeed theoretical assumptions may be *"built into the apparatus itself"* (Galison 1987, 251; emphasis his)—and that is true not only of Galison's high energy physics but of some of the most simple and direct observational devices (Hacking 1989, 268).

If we had to build every piece of equipment from scratch, not only would laboratory science be vastly more labor-intensive but it would also be a great deal less stable. Devices that worked last year for one purpose would—as anyone who has spent some time in a laboratory will know—not work this year for the next project. We are tempted to say that it is the commercial or semicommercial instrument makers and salespeople that have long kept science on an even keel. We do not just buy an instrument and switch it on. As long as there have been instruments there have been facilitators who show how an instrument or class of instruments can be put to all sorts of new purposes. Historians have hardly begun to tell us about the great instrument makers of London or Berlin in the eighteenth century, let alone those of Lisbon in the fifteenth. I doubt that they were so different, except in point of specializations, from what we find running through the *Proceedings* of an electron-microscopy conference that is being held as I write. We find sessions for the fairly new scanning tunneling (electron) microscope (STM), with talks on how to apply it to Planar membranes, Doped polypyrole on ITO glass, vapor-deposited and electrodeposited metal films, etc.

The speakers are from Shell Development, Westinghouse Research and Development, Fuji, the Advanced Research Laboratory of Hitachi, Philips Analytical Electron Optics Laboratory, as well as academic institutions in Basel, Ithaca, Freiburg, and Moscow (Bailey, 1989). At such a conference we can get a bird's-eye glance at how a type of device barely out of the research stage becomes a black box that the next generation will use as a stable laboratory tool. The consumer won't have much idea how the tool works: unlike transmission electron microscopes, whose theory is in some weak sense understood by those who use it, the new microscopes are built according to principles of quantum tunneling that sorely vex even the most diligent student of macromolecules or metallurgy. And we do not yet know quite what the black box may do: a Berkeley undergraduate playing with an STM after hours found he could image DNA molecules, contrary to anyone's expectations based on extant theory of the apparatus.

6 Items Used in the Laboratory

Thanks to the many recent studies by philosophers, historians, ethnographers, and sociologists of experimental science, we have much richer sources of information about the laboratory than were available a decade ago. This welter of colorful examples makes it hard to produce any tidy formal characterization of experiment. Hence our powers of generalization are limited. I shall try to return some degree of abstraction to the philosophy of science by listing some familiar elements in laboratory experimentation. We must guard against too strict a set of distinctions. Descriptions of experimental procedures have long been regimented to make them look as if experiments have much in common. The format for writing up a laboratory report is inculcated in school and preserved, modified, or reinforced—in ways that vary from discipline to discipline—in preprints and journals. The modest uniformity is largely an artifact of how our scientific culture wants to conceive itself and has much to do with our construction of what we call objectivity. Admitting as I do that there is less in common among experiments than we imagine, I shall nevertheless list some elements that are often discernible. Their prominence and even their presence varies from case to case and from science to science.

The items are not of the same kind. When I develop the theme of the self-vindication of laboratory science, I shall hop from category to category, and so in the following section I present a taxonomic scheme of reference. My list of elements could be thought of as dividing into three groups: ideas, things, and marks. These three monosyllabic labels should be inoffensive. There is nothing invidious in calling various kinds of questions and theories "ideas." They are among the intellectual components of an experiment. The material substance that we investigate or with which we investigate is not always best called a "thing"; instruments are things; are Norway rats or polarized electrons or bacteriophages things? But "things" serves; it is the briefest contrast with "idea." I speak of the outcomes of an experiment as marks, and subsequent manipulation of marks to produce more marks. This is reminiscent of Latour's insistence that a laboratory instrument is simply an "inscription-device" and that the immediate product of a laboratory is an inscription (1987, 68). For me, "mark" is not only the shorter word but also more suitably ambiguous, allowing it to cover a number of my items. According to my dictionary, marks are "visible impressions," "signs or symbols that distinguish something," "written or printed signs or symbols," "indications of some quality," and also "goals."

We shall never confuse theory with apparatus (an idea with a thing), and seldom shall we find it difficult to distinguish an instrument from the data that it generates or the statistical analysis that we make of them (although marks are things, we won't here confuse a thing with marks or the manipulation of marks). But within my three subgroups of ideas, things, and marks, some of the elements run into each other, and we may disagree about how to file items within my list. That is of no moment here, for stability arises from the interplay of these elements, and an account of it does not require a rigid taxonomy.

7 Ideas

1. *Questions.* There is a question or questions about some subject matter. The question answered at the end of the experiment may be different from the one with which the investigators began. Questions range from those rare ones emphasized by philosophers: "which of these competing theories is true or false?" to the commonplace, "what is the value of this quantity?" or "does treating X with Y make a difference, and if so what good differences and what bad ones?" When a question is about a theory, I shall speak of the *theory in question.* Crucial experiments have two theories in question.

2. *Background knowledge.* In what is so often called theory we should distinguish at least three distinct kinds of knowledge about the subject matter of the experiment. The divisions (2, 3, and 4) that I propose are sharp in some disciplines and vague or almost nonex-

istent in others. First is the background knowledge and expectations that are not systematized and which play little part in writing up an experiment, in part because they are taken for granted. These are surely inescapable. Science without background beliefs makes no sense.

3. *Systematic theory:* theory of a general and typically high level sort about the subject matter, which by itself may have no experimental consequences.

4. *Topical hypotheses,* as I shall call them, are part of what in physics is commonly named phenomenology. Because that term has another meaning in philosophy, and because it can also be used for (5), we want another name. We are concerned with what connects systematic theory to phenomena. Logical empiricism, with its strong emphasis on language, spoke of bridge principles (Hempel 1966, 72–5). The name is attractive, although "principles" suggests something that cannot readily be revised, whereas we are concerned with what is revised all the time in laboratory work. Indeed the core bridge principle idea was revealingly expressed by a writer not in the classic mold of logical empiricism, namely, N. R. Campbell (1920, 122–58), who spoke of a "dictionary" to connect purely theoretical concepts with observational terms. The connections I have in mind are too revisable for me to speak of principles or a dictionary. I call them topical hypotheses. *Hypothesis* is here used in the old-fashioned sense of something more readily revised than theory. It is overly propositional. I intend to cover whole sets of approximating and modeling procedures in the sense of Cartwright (1983), and more generally the activity that Kuhn (1962, 24–33) called the "articulation" of theory in order to create a potential mesh with experience. It is a virtue of recent philosophy of science that it has increasingly come to acknowledge that most of the intellectual work of the theoretical sciences is conducted at this level rather than in the rarefied gas of systematic theory. My word *topical* is meant to connote both the usual senses of "current affairs" or "local," and also to recall the medical sense of a topical ointment as one applied to the surface of the skin, i.e., not deep.

5. *Modeling of the apparatus.* There are theories, or at least background lore, about the instruments and equipment listed below as (6–8). To avoid ambiguity I shall speak of the (theoretical) modeling of the apparatus, an account of how it works and what, in theory, it is like. We are concerned with phenomenological theory that enables us to design instruments and to calculate how they behave. Seldom is the modeling of a piece of apparatus or an instrument the same as the theory in question (1) or the systematic theory (3).

Sometimes it may just be vague background knowledge (2). It may overlap with the topical hypotheses (4). The apparatus of Atwood's machine (1784) for determining local gravitational acceleration is a turning fork with a brush on one prong that is dropped so that the brush sweeps out a curve on the detector, a plate of glass with white-wash on it. The theory (and practice) of the tuning fork is plainly part of the theoretical modeling of the apparatus, and it has almost nothing to do with the systematic theory of gravitational accelera-tion or Galilean mechanics. Note that in this case there is no topical hypothesis. To heighten the contrast between modeling of the ap-paratus and topical hypotheses, consider the plight of the grandest of unified theories, superstring theory. Constructed in at least nine dimensions, it has no experimental consequences at all. The task of one kind of phenomenology is to articulate the theory so that it does mesh with our three- or four-dimensional reality. That is a matter of devising topical hypotheses. A quite different task is the design of apparatus and understanding how it works, the job of theories about and modeling of the apparatus.

8 Things

6. *Target.* This together with elements (7)–(10) comprises the matériel of the experiment. These items—not all of which need to be present in an experiment—are often, in physics, described using a military analogy. First is a target, a substance or population to be studied. The *preparation* of the target—in old-fashioned micro-biology by staining, use of microtomes, etc.—is best kept separate from the modification of the target, say by injecting a prepared cell with a foreign substance. Similar distinctions can be made in ana-lytic chemistry.

7. *Source of modification.* There is usually apparatus that in some way alters or interferes with the target. In certain branches of physics, this is most commonly a source of energy. Traditional in-organic chemical analysis modifies a target by adding measured amounts of various substances, and by distillation, precipitation, centrifuging, etc. In the case of Atwood's machine we have neither target nor source of modification; it is a detector pure and simple. There is nothing ultimate about my classification: a classic descrip-tion of apparatus due to James Clerk Maxwell, best adapted to phys-ics, would divide this item into a source of energy and devices for transport of energy, the latter divided into eight functions (Galison 1987, 24). Note that although most energy sources are controlled by us, one of the most powerful, with one of the most distinguished

track records, comes from on high: the cosmic rays. And the next major neutrino project, called DUMAND, will use neutrinos as a source of energy vastly greater than any hitherto used in high energy physics.

8. *Detectors* determine or measure the result of the interference or modification of the target. I also count as a detector a modest cosmological laboratory device such as Atwood's machine, where no target is influenced (certainly not gravity). Commonly we include both detectors and sources of modification as apparatus. In many circumstances the detectors are called instruments, but they are not the only instruments. Many of the most imaginative detectors can become what I shall call tools: Michelson's interferometer, once the subtlest detector on earth, has, for example, become a tool for eliminating some of the instrumental error that plagues astronomical imaging (Cornwell 1989).

9. *Tools.* As we contemplate proton-antiproton colliders and scanning tunneling electron microscopes, let us not forget the more humble things upon which the experimenter must rely. In the preparation of the target, I mentioned microtomes to slice organic matter thin, stains that color it, chemicals that react, taken off the shelf, or altered a little for this or that purpose. They are hardly worthy to be ranked with sources of modification or detectors, but we cannot get along without them: we also use them at least in the light of background lore (how a stain or a slicer will alter a specimen, and how it will not), and often in the light of a good deal of topical and apparatus lore. This residual category of tools overlaps with preceding ones. Is litmus paper tool or detector? In the child's chemistry set, it is a detector of acidity, but in the high school lab, it is a tool like a screwdriver. Any off the shelf device, especially one developed in a discipline unrelated to the immediate experiment, could be classified as a tool, so that we would restrict (7) and (8) to instruments that were actually made or adapted in the course of the experiment. From this perspective many data generators (10), such as machines to photograph, count, or print out events of interest, would register as tools. And what shall we say of frog's eggs? They are available from suppliers by the kilo, eggs into which a designated genetic string is injected because they reproduce it by the eggful, some minuscule fraction of it serving as a target for an experiment. Are these eggs tools? Let us say they are. What of the Norway rat, loyal servant of anatomists, physiologists, and nutritionists in the nineteenth century, and after much inbreeding and induced mutation, at the forefront of immunogenetics and recombinant experiments at this very moment? (Gill et al. 1989). Are these Norway rats tools? What

about their pituitary glands, used in endocrinology assays in ways made familiar to philosophers by Latour and Woolgar (1979)?

10. *Data generators.* Atwood's machine needs a person or robot with a ruler to measure the distances between successive passages of the brush over the center line. People or teams who count may be data generators. In more sophisticated experiments, there are micrographs, automatic printouts, and the like. There is no need to insist on a sharp distinction in all cases between detector and data-generating device. In the early days a camera taking micrographs from an electron microscope was a data generator that photographed a visible image for study, analysis, or the record. Today the camera is more often the detector; the data generator may be a scanner working from the micrograph.

9 Marks and the Manipulation of Marks

11. *Data:* what a data generator produces. By data I mean uninterpreted inscriptions, graphs recording variation over time, photographs, tables, displays. These are covered by the first sense of my portmanteau word "mark." Some will pleonastically call such marks "raw data." Others will protest that all data are of their nature interpreted: to think that there are uninterpreted data, they will urge, is to indulge in "the myth of the given." I agree that in the laboratory nothing is just given. Measurements are taken, not given. Data are made, but as a good first approximation, the making and taking come before interpreting. It is true that we reject or discard putative data because they do not fit an interpretation, but that does not prove that all data are interpreted. For the fact that we discard what does not fit does not distinguish data from the other elements (1)–(14): in the process of adjustment we can sacrifice anything from a microtome to a cyclotron, not to mention the familiar Duhemian choice among the hypotheses in the spectrum (1)–(5) for the ones to be revised in the light of recalcitrant experimental results.

12. *Data assessment* is one of at least three distinct types of *data processing.* It may include a calculation of the probable error or more statistically sophisticated versions of this. Such procedures are supposed to be theory neutral, but in complex weighing of evidence they are sensibly applied only by people who understand a good many details of the experiment—a point always emphasized by the greatest of statistical innovators, R. A. Fisher, although too often ignored by those who use his techniques. Slang talk of statistical cookbooks—recipes for making computations of confidence intervals or whatever—has more wisdom in it than is commonly sus-

pected. Good cooks must know their foodstuffs, their fire, their pots; that is true by analogy of the person who tends the apparatus, but it is equally true that good statisticians have to know their experiment. Data assessment also includes a nonstatistical aspect, the estimation of systematic error, which requires explicit knowledge of the theory of the apparatus—and which has been too little studied by philosophers of science.

13. *Data reduction:* large or vast amounts of unintelligible numerical data may be transformed by supposedly theory-neutral statistical or computational techniques into manageable quantities or displays. Fisher used the word "statistic" to mean simply a number that encapsulated a large body of data and (independently of Shannon) developed a measure of the information lost by data reduction, thus determining the most efficient (least destructive) types of reduction.

14. *Data analysis:* an increasingly common form is well described by Galison (1987) in connection with high energy experiments. The events under study in an experiment are selected, analyzed, and presented by computer. This may seem like a kind of data reduction, but the programs for analyzing the data are not supposedly theory-neutral statistical techniques. They are chosen in the light of the questions or focus of the experiment (1) and of both topical hypotheses (4) and modeling of the apparatus (5). In this case, and to a lesser extent in the case of (11) and even (12), there is now commonly an echelon of workers or devices between the data and the principal investigators; Galison argues that this is one of the ways in which experimental science has recently been transformed. There are many other new kinds of data processing, such as the enhancement of images in both astronomy and microscopy. And (11)–(14) may get rolled into one for less than $2,000. "With the new $1,995 EC910 Densitometer, you can scan, integrate, and display electrophoresis results in your lab PC. Immediately! No cutting, no hand measuring. Programs accept *intact* gel slabs, columns, cellulose acetate, chromotography strips and other support media" (Software extra, $995; from a typical 1989 ad on a back cover of *Science*).

15. *Interpretation* of the data demands theory at least at the level of background knowledge (2), and often at every other level, including systematic theory (3), topical theory (4), and apparatus modeling (5). Pulsars provide an easy example of data interpretation requiring theory: once a theory of pulsars was in place, it was possible to go back over the data of radio astronomers and find ample evidence of pulsars that could not have been interpreted as such until there was theory. The possibility of such interpretation also mandated new

data reduction (12) and analysis (13), and the systematic error part of the data assessment (11) had to be reassessed. More about interpretation below.

10 Qualifications

It is tempting to follow Galison (1988, 525) and take (2)–(5) as the "establishment of knowledge prior to experimentation." That suggests something put in place before the experiment and enduring throughout it. My picture of experimentation is, in contrast, one of potential modification of any of the elements (1)–(15), including the prior "knowledge." Many things are "established" before the experiment—not just knowledge but also tools and techniques of statistical analysis. But none of these is established in the sense of being immutable. As promised, far from rejecting Popperian orthodoxy, we build upon it, increasing our vision of things than can be "refuted."

Second, I have omitted from my list something that is rather rigid during the time span of even the most extended experiment—what we indicate with words like weltanschauung or Holton's (1978, 1987) "themata" and "thematic presuppositions," or even A. C. Crombie's "styles of scientific reasoning" (Hacking 1982, 1992). We have expectations about what the world is like and practices of reasoning about it. These govern our theories and our interpretation of data alike. Quite aside from our Humean habits, we think of Kelvin's dictum so characteristic of positive science at the end of the nineteenth century: we do not understand a thing until we can measure it. That smacks more of metaphysics than methodology—the world comes as measurable. We think of Galileo's doctrine that the author of nature wrote the book of the universe in the language of mathematics. We think of the twinned aspects of post-Baconian science to which Merchant (1980) and Keller (1986) have drawn attention: (a) the expectation that we find out about the world by interfering with it, ideally in military fashion with targets; (b) the expectation that nature "herself" works that way, with forces and triggering mechanisms and the like, and in general a master-slave mode of interaction among her parts. These conceptions, be they mathematical or magisterial, are visions of what the world is like.

I have omitted such things from (1)–(15) because experimenters do not literally use them. Some philosophers would say that experiments presuppose large-scale entities such as themata or styles or paradigms. Many a cynic would say that there are no such things. In the present essay I need not engage in that debate, because whatever the status of such entities—be they analytical concepts or mind-framing schemata or sheer fiction—experimenters do not change their ideal conceptions of the universe in the course of, or at any rate because of, experimental work. Such notions are not molded to fit into (1)–(15): they stand above them. It is true that systematic theory (2), black-box tools (9), and procedures of data assessment (12) or reduction (13) are seldom much affected by experimental work, but they can be, and they certainly are explicitly used in ways in which weltanschauungs or *Denkstile* aren't.[2]

Finally, I have said nothing about the most important ingredient of an experiment, namely, the experimenters, their negotiations, their communications, their milieu, the very building in which they work or the institution that foots the bills. I have said nothing of authors, authority, and audience. In short, nothing of what Latour indicates by his titles *Science in Action* and *Laboratory Life*. This is once again because I am concerned with elements that are used in the experiment. But that is weak, because experimenters use money, influence, charisma, and so forth. We can nevertheless to some extent hold on to the difference between what the experimenters use in the experiment and what is used in order to do the experiment or in order to further its results (Latour would protest that stable science arises only when the world of the laboratory is embedded in a far-larger social network). Those tired words "internal" and "external" seem useful here; I have been offering a taxonomy of elements internal to an experiment.

Despite my restriction to the internal, my concern with stability

---

2. Andrew Pickering noted at this point that "the recent move to microanalyses of practice seems to have left these big, underlying, unifying aspects of culture hanging (if they exist)," and rightly urged more discussion (letter of 28 November 1989). I agree; a talk given on 6 October began, "A philosophical task in our times is to connect (*a*) social and micro-social studies of knowledge, (*b*) metaphysics, and what we might call (*c*) the Braudelian aspects of knowledge" (Hacking 1992a). By (*c*) I meant "relatively permanent, growing, self-modulating, self-revising features of what we call science," exemplified by entities mentioned in the paragraph above. My own view is that there is no one story to tell about all the disparate Braudelian entities, but I have attempted to give an account of (*a*)–(*c*) for my notion of styles of reasoning. These are not matters for the present paper. But I show how the theory of self-vindication advanced here would be located within my theory of the self-authentication of styles of reasoning. Laboratory science forms one of my six designated styles of reasoning, but vindication is distinct from authentication. I use "self-authentication" to mean the way in which a style of reasoning generates the truth conditions for the very propositions which are reasoned to using that style, suggesting a curious type of circularity. Thus self-authentication is a logical concept. Self-vindication is a material concept, pertaining to the way in which ideas, things, and marks are mutually adjusted.

accords quite well, if in a conservative and conservationist fashion, with studies of the social construction of scientific facts. Unlike pedestrian antirealists of an instrumentalist or empiricist or positivist sort, constructionalists hold that facts and phenomena are made, not observed, and that criteria for truth are produced, not preordained. They hold that scientific facts are real enough once the making has been done, but that scientific reality is not "retroactive." My investigation of stability is precisely an investigation of that kind of product from a different vantage point. I am moved to the investigation by a curiosity about the death that follows laboratory life, about the cumulative inaction that follows science in action.

11 Extending Duhem's Thesis

Duhem (1906) observed that if an experiment or observation was persistently inconsistent with theory, one could modify theory in two ways: either revise the systematic theory (3) or revise the auxiliary hypotheses (in which we include both topical hypotheses [4] and modeling of the apparatus [5]). His classic example was astronomy, not a laboratory science, but the message was clear. Should a theory about the heavens be inconsistent with data, he said, we may revise astronomy, or modify either the theory of the transmission of light in space or the theory of telescope (5). But that is only the beginning of the malleability of my fifteen elements. For example, we can try to modify the telescope or build a different kind of telescope. That is, try to save the systematic hypothesis by adapting the detector (8).

Several recent contributions help to enlarge the Duhemian vision. Pickering (1989) regards the topical hypotheses (4), the modeling of the apparatus (5), and the matériel as three "plastic resources." He has an elegant example, retold with a different emphasis in Pickering 1990, of getting an experiment to work. The same example is also used, with purposes not unlike mine, by Gooding (chap. 3).[3] There were two competing theories in question (1): free charges come either in units of e, the charge on the electron, or $1/3\ e$, the

3. The repetition of the example is now becoming embarrassing, and I welcome Gooding's providing two more examples that make additional points. I appropriated Pickering's example after reading an unpublished paper of his (1986), partly because I had been following the other side of the investigation, that of Fairbanks at Stanford, who established that there are free quarks (Hacking 1983, 23ff.). If the example is ever used again, Morpurgo and Fairbanks should be considered together. As it happens, many of the things Pickering said about Morpurgo are remarkably transferrable to Fairbanks's work on supercooled niobium balls.

charge on a quark (there was also the background assumption (2) that these alternatives exhaust the possibilities). The matériel was a highly modified version of Millikan's oil drop apparatus to determine the charge on the electron. This nicely divides into target, source of modification, and detector. The initial results of the experiment were consistent with there being a continuum of free charges. The investigator had to change both his source of modification (7) and his modeling of the apparatus (5). That is, he had to tinker with the equipment (it was a matter of moving condenser plates in a way counter to that predicted by the original theoretical model of the apparatus), and he had to revise the account of how the apparatus worked. The experiment ended by producing data that could be consistently interpreted by only one of the two competing systematic theories: no free quarks were there to be observed.

Pickering emphasizes apparatus, modeling, and topical hypotheses. Ackermann (1985) draws our attention to other groupings of my elements, well summed up in his title, *Data, Instruments, and Theory*. He is concerned with a dialectical relationship between data (11), interpretation (15), and systematic theory (2). Despite his title he has, like Duhem and unlike Pickering, a passive attitude to instruments, for he thinks of them pretty much as black boxes, as established devices that generate data which is literally given. He thinks of an instrument in the way in which an eighteenth-century navigator would regard a chronometer, or a cell biologist would think of a nuclear magnetic resonance spectrometer—as off-the-shelf reliable technology. According to Ackermann, the primary task of the scientist is to interpret data in the light of theory and to revise theory in the light of interpretation. Thus his story is like most traditional philosophy of science, except that his data are my (11). They are not theory laden but are material artifacts, photographs, or inscriptions, the productions of instruments—marks, in short.

The data themselves are something given by instruments, or by a set of instruments of a certain kind, which Ackermann calls an instrumentarium, and each instrumentarium has its own data domain. The instrumentarium of classical mechanics, he says, is different from that of quantum mechanics, and the old mechanics interprets data delivered by one kind of instrument, while the newer mechanics interprets data produced by another kind. Ackermann proposes that a laboratory science becomes stable when there is a class of instruments that yield data of a certain kind such that there is a body of theory that can interpret the data uniformly and consistently. A theory, as I understand him, is then true to the data generated by a certain class of instruments, and different theories can be true to different classes of data delivered by different instrumentaria. This suggests a new and fundamental type of incommensurability. It used to be said that Newtonian and relativistic theory were in-commensurable because the statements of one could not be expressed in the other—meanings changed. Instead I suggest that one is true to one body of measurements given by one class of instruments, while the other is true to another. I have already remarked that Ackermann's discussion of instruments is far too respectful and that his conception of disjoint instrumentaria is farfetched. The texture of instrumentation and its evolution is vastly more subtle than he makes it to be. Nevertheless his simplistic picture has the germ of an important truth.

Duhem, Pickering, and Ackermann point to interplay among several subsets of the elements (1)–(15). Pickering attends to the modeling of the apparatus and the working of the instruments: we acknowledge data as data only after we have gotten handmade apparatus to work in ways that we understand. Duhem emphasized the intellectual elements (1)–(5). Ackermann, observing that data can be understood in many ways or not at all, put the emphasis on a dialectic involving theories and interpretation, regarding instruments and the data that they produced as fixed points. We should learn from all these authors. Let us extend Duhem's thesis to the entire set of elements (1)–(15). Since these are different in kind, they are plastic resources in different ways. We can (1) change questions; more commonly we modify them in midexperiment. Data (11) can be abandoned or selected without fraud; we consider data secure when we can interpret them in the light of, among other things, systematic theory (3). But it is not just Ackermann's interpretation of data by theory that is in play. Data processing is embarrassingly plastic. That has long been familiar to students of statistical inference in the case of data assessment and reduction, (12) and (13). Because statistics is a metascience, statistical methodologies are seldom called into question inside a laboratory, but a consultant may well advise that they be. Data analysis is plastic in itself; in addition any change in topical hypotheses (4) or modeling of the apparatus (5) will lead to the introduction of new programs of data analysis.

We create apparatus that generates data that confirm theories; we judge apparatus by its ability to produce data that fit. There is little new in this seeming circularity except taking the material world into account. The most succinct statement of the idea, for purely intellectual operations, is Nelson Goodman's summary (1983, 64) of how we "justify" both deduction and induction: "A rule is amended if it yields an inference we are unwilling to accept; an inference is rejected if it violates a rule that we are unwilling to amend." There is also more than a whiff of Hanson's (1965) maxim that all observation is theory loaded, and of the corresponding positivist doctrine that all theory is observation loaded. The truth is that there is a play between theory and observation, but that is a miserly quarter-truth. There is a play between many things: data, theory, experiment, phenomenology, equipment, data processing.

12 Maturing Science

Adjustment does not imply stability. All that is said in the preceding section is consistent with the "underdetermination of theory by data"—the usual lesson drawn from Duhem's reflections. Yet the common experience of the laboratory sciences is that there are all too few degrees of freedom. All of those items like (1)–(15) and more can be modified, but when each one is adjusted with the others so that our data, our machines, and our thoughts cohere, interfering with any one throws all the others out of whack. It is extraordinarily difficult to make one coherent account, and it is perhaps beyond our powers to make several. The philosophical task is less to understand an indeterminacy that we can imagine but almost never experience than to explain the sheer determinateness of mature laboratory science. On the one hand it is utterly contingent that our intellectual structure (1)–(5) is what it is, but given that it is the way it is, only rarely can it be changed, although it can be superseded.

How, then, does a laboratory science mature? Here is a very liberal adaptation of Ackermann's idea. A collection of kinds of instruments evolves—an instrumentarium—hand in hand with theories that interpret the data that they produce. As a matter of brute contingent fact, instrumentaria and systematic theories mature, and data uninterpretable by theories are not generated. There is no drive for revision of the theory because it has acquired a stable data domain. What we later see as limitations of a theory are not data for the theory.

For example, geometrical optics takes no cognizance of the fact that all shadows have blurred edges. The fine structure of shadows requires an instrumentarium quite different from that of lenses and mirrors, together with a new systematic theory and topical hypotheses. Geometrical optics is true only to the phenomena of rectilinear propagation of light. Better: it is true of certain models of rectilinear propagation. It is the optics and the models and approximations that comprise the topical hypotheses (4) that are jointly true to the phenomena. No matter how it is supplemented, geometrical optics is not true to the phenomenon of blurred edges of shadows—a phenomenon that, unlike most, is there for the noticing. Theories and phenomenology true to the phenomena of shadows became established because they were true to the phenomena elicited by a new family of instruments that began to be developed in the nineteenth century. There is no requirement that theories that address one kind of data should address another.

Stable laboratory science arises when theories and laboratory equipment evolve in such a way that they match each other and are mutually self-vindicating. Such symbiosis is a contingent fact about people, our scientific organizations, and nature. In referring to nature I do not imply that nature causes or contributes to such symbiosis in some active way. I do not invoke nature as an explanation of the possibility of science, in the way in which those fantasists called scientific realists sometimes invoke nature or underlying reality to explain the "success" of science. I mean only that we might have lived in an environment where laboratory science was impracticable. Also, as I note in my final section on induction, we may live today in an environment in which all our apparatus ceases to work tomorrow.

Symbiosis and stability are one contingency; there is another more interesting one. Laboratory science might have been the sort of enterprise that either stagnates or else is revisable only by abandoning all that has gone before. The contingency that prevents stagnation without nullifying an existing order of theory and instrumentation is this: new types of data can be produced, thought of as resulting from instruments that probe more finely into microstructure, and which cannot be accommodated at the level of accuracy of which established theory is capable. A new theory with new types of precision is needed (recall Heisenberg on closed systems, mentioned above). Space is created for a mutual maturing of new theory and experiment without dislodging an established mature theory, which remains true of the data available in its domain.

Kuhn (1961) noticed almost all of this with characteristic precision. Fetishistic measurement sometimes hints at anomaly that can only be tackled by devising new categories of instruments that generate new data that can be interpreted only by a new sort of theory: not puzzle solving but revolution. This is the overriding theme of his study of black-body radiation (Kuhn 1978). He omitted only the fact that the old theory and its instruments remain pretty much in place, in their data domain. Hence new and old theory are incommensurable in an entirely straightforward sense. They have no common measure because the instruments providing the measurements for the one are inapt for the other. This is a scientific fact that has nothing to do with "meaning change" and other semantic notions that have been associated with incommensurability.[4]

This iconoclastic (but practical) vision makes good sense of the disunity of science. We staunchly believe that science must in the end be unified, because it tries to tell the truth about the world, and there is surely only one world. (What a strange statement, as if we had tried counting worlds.) The sciences are disunified for all sorts of reasons as cataloged in Hacking (1990). One of these is the sheer proliferation of specializations so well recounted by Suppes (1984, chap. 5). But it is also disunified in a way that has not hitherto been much discussed. It is disunified in part because phenomena are produced by fundamentally different techniques, and different theories answer to different phenomena that are only loosely connected. Theories mature in conjuncture with a class of phenomena, and in the end our theory and our ways of producing, investigating, and measuring phenomena mutually define each other.

13 Truth

Could two theories with no common measure, in the above literal sense, both be true? Is not at most one theory true, the old mature one or an aspiring new one that takes account of a new data domain? Only if we suppose that there is in the end only one true ultimate theory that corresponds to the world. Some philosophers who are halfway along this road find solace in saying that different theories are true of different aspects of reality, but what work is "reality" doing here? We need say no more than this: the several systematic and topical theories that we retain, at different levels of application, are true to different phenomena and different data domains. Theories are not checked by comparison with a passive world with which we hope they correspond. We do not formulate conjectures and then just look to see if they are true. We invent devices that produce data and isolate or create phenomena, and a network of different levels of

4. A great many distinct ideas can be associated with the "no common measure" theme. I distinguished three of them in Hacking 1983, 67–74. In unpublished work, Kuhn expresses a preference for the more ordinary word "untranslatable," to be explained less by a theory of meaning than by a theory of natural kinds and a lexicon of natural-kind terms. I try to develop consequences of this idea in Hacking 1992b. The literal version of "no common measure" above—called a "new kind of incommensurability" above—is one aspect of what Pickering (1984, 407–11) calls "global incommensurability," which he illustrates with the contrast between the "new" and the "old" high energy physics of the 1970s and early 1980s.

theory is true to these phenomena. Conversely we may in the end count them as phenomena only when the data can be interpreted by theory. Thus there evolves a curious tailor-made fit between our ideas, our apparatus, and our observations. A coherence theory of truth? No, a coherence theory of thought, action, materials, and marks.

We don't want here a theory of truth at all. Not that I'm against truth, or the word "true" in its place. One of the uses of the word, as has often been remarked, is to enable us to agree with, approve of, or commit ourselves to a batch of assertions that we don't want to bother asserting—out of a desire for brevity or a quest for style, or because we lack the time to talk at length, or because we don't know in detail what the assertions actually assert. We dearly need this use of the word "true" in science, since few can remember what any theory, systematic or topical, is in all its complexities. Hence we refer to theories by their names and say that what we name is true. It is no metaphysics that makes the word "true" so handy, but wit, whose soul is brevity.

We modify, I have said, any or all of my fifteen elements in order to bring them into some kind of consilience. When we have done so we have not read the truth of the world. There usually were not some preexisting phenomena that experiment reported. It made them. There was not some previously organized correspondence between theory and reality that was confirmed. Our theories are at best true to the phenomena that were elicited by instrumentation in order to get a good mesh with theory. The process of modifying the workings of instruments—both materially (we fix them up) and intellectually (we redescribe what they do)—furnishes the glue that keeps our intellectual and material world together. It is what stabilizes science.

14 Application

When defining the laboratory sciences, I said that the end in view was an increase in knowledge, understanding, and control of a general or generalizable sort. If mature laboratory sciences are self-vindicating, answering to phenomena purified or created in the laboratory, how then are they generalizable? For nothing is more notable than our success, from time to time, in transferring stable laboratory science to practical affairs. The aim of most "mission-oriented" science (to use the jargon of a decade ago) in industrial, medical, military, and ecological spheres is precisely to increase our knowledge and our skills to solve a practical problem that existed before and remains outside the laboratory.

I don't think that there is a problem here. Sometimes techniques and devices developed in the laboratory move into our larger environment and indeed help us in some already-chosen mission. Sometimes they don't. When prototypes have been made industrial (be they machines or medicines), they will work reliably in controlled conditions. They may or may not be useful in the more luxuriant foliage of everyday life. In fact, few things that work in the laboratory work very well in a thoroughly unmodified world—in a world which has not been bent toward the laboratory. That of course is a contingent matter; it could have been different. But whatever was the case, success or failure in a mission does not vindicate or refute a theory which is true to phenomena generated in the laboratory. Vindication and refutation occur only on that site; value in a mission is something else. All the jokes about military gadgetry hinge on this banal fact. If people opposed to conventional medicine had a sense of humor, and if the rest of us didn't feel that jokes about disease were sick, then they could make exactly the same jokes about medical research that we peaceniks make about weapons research. The military like to advertise their gadgets as working with surgical precision. When was the last time they were in a surgery?

I must, however, acknowledge a metaphysical worry in the offing. I invite it even with my halfhearted use of the phrase "true to." Suppose I am right, that the mature laboratory sciences are true to phenomena created in the laboratory, thanks to mutual adjustment and ensuing self-vindication. If so, the applicability of laboratory science is no mere contingency but something of a miracle. There are two distinct responses to this, depending on what kind of miracle the protester has in mind. I think a metaphysical miracle is intended, but first a more modest one.

Taking as an example Pasteur's success with anthrax, a perfect instance of rapid movement of knowledge and technique from laboratory to the field, Latour writes that "if instead of gaping at this miracle we look at how a network is extended, sure enough we find a fascinating negotiation between Pasteur and the farmers' representatives on how to *transform the farm into a laboratory*" (Latour 1987, 249; emphasis his). That indicates a special case of an enormously important observation. We remake little bits of our environment so that they reproduce phenomena first generated in a pure state in the laboratory. The reproduction is seldom perfect. We need more than the (4) topical hypotheses and the (5) modeling of the laboratory apparatus; we need more thinking of the same kind as (4) and (5). But the application of laboratory science to a part of the world remade into a quasi-laboratory is not problematic, not miraculous, but rather a matter of hard work.

Latour's response nevertheless leads to the metaphysical miracle. For it invites the observation that anthrax has been eliminated from many regions. Smallpox no longer exists on the face of the earth, and the potential for making a person sick of smallpox now exists, we believe, only in a small number of securely locked refrigerators in a few national laboratories. Isn't that because we have found out something about our environment outside the laboratory and then applied our hard-won knowledge? And does that not mean that there are (and were) certain truths about anthrax, in addition to Pasteur's speculations being true to phenomena generated in the laboratory?

The source of this worry is the metaphysical mistake of thinking that truth or the world explains anything. "If the treatment works, then the world or the truth about the world makes it work, and that is what we found out in the laboratory and then applied to the world." Not so. I said that mature laboratory sciences are true to the phenomena of the laboratory. In so saying I was describing, not explaining anything. A science is true to the phenomena when it fits the analyzed data generated by instruments and apparatus, when modeled by topical hypotheses. Every one of those fifteen items of mine that is germane to a test has to be brought in for the vindication of the science, and when the science is mature, they are in such mutual adjustment that there is what I call self-vindication. Indeed, what we want to be the case in mission-oriented research is that the reproducible apparatus (or chemical or whatever) also has happy effects in the untamed world. But it is not the truth of anything that causes or explains the happy effects.

15 Induction

The doctrine of mature self-vindicating laboratory sciences has no more to do with the problem of induction than does Popper's methodology of conjectures and refutations or Kuhn's analysis of scientific revolutions. That is as it should be. The problem of induction was posed in connection with bread, postmen, and billiards. It has nothing special to do with science, although it has everything to do with civilization, for the question was posed for the wares of cooks and craftsmen (bread and billiard balls) and for institutionalized people (postmen). The problem of induction must nevertheless take its own form within my conception of science, just as it must, or should, within every other.

The problem of induction must not be confused with our manifest fallibility. Quite aside from questions about the projection of the past onto the future, there is no guaranteed irrefragable eternal self-vindication of a laboratory science. Sometimes a theory may be true to a body of phenomena and have a closed data domain in the way that I have suggested and yet fail to survive. The transformation of the particle theory of light into the undulatory theory is of just this sort. In the beginning it was not a new kind of instrument that did in the old ideas: the phenomena that made the wave theory compelling were elicited by what one might call Newtonian instrumentation (much of it worked by the adamant corpuscularian David Brewster) even before Fresnel had provided the mathematics of the wave theory that was fully able to interpret the data. A longish period of stability within a data domain does not promise that things have come to an end.

A more interesting case is the caloric theory of sound. Laplace calculated the velocity of sound assuming a substance he called caloric, and it fit the experimental determinations of the day. Yet it looks as if they are out by 30 percent. The velocity of sound is indeed nontrivial (there are at least three distinguishable "velocities of sound"), but even so we can't understand what Laplacean experimenters were doing. We abandon their phenomena as gladly as we forget caloric. So much is familiar conjecture and refutation. It may invite cynicism about stability but not philosophical skepticism, to which I now turn.

I should like to reverse the emphasis of philosophical skepticism. In our time it has chiefly focused on propositions; those true of the past might not hold true of the future. Our expectations and beliefs might not rightly project onto the future. The philosopher of experiment must descend from semantics and think about things and actions instead of ideas and expectations.

A laboratory science could become genuinely unstable. Our technologies might cease to work. Phenomena might no longer oblige. What would change, in my skeptical fantasy, is that our apparatus would no longer be able to elicit phenomena. Nothing that I have said about stability should prevent that form of wonder we call the problem of induction. The question, "why expect the future to be like the past?" takes on a new form for the laboratory and for the phenomena that it produces. "Why should types of devices that we have made, and have made to behave in certain ways in the past, continue to do so in the future?"[5]

REFERENCES

Ackermann, Robert. 1985. *Data, Instruments, and Theory: A Dialectical Approach to Understanding Science.* Princeton: Princeton University Press.

Bailey, G. W., ed. 1989. *Proceedings: Forty-Seventh Annual Meeting, Electron Microscopy Society of America* (in San Antonio, 6–11 August 1989). San Francisco: San Francisco Press.

Böhme, G., et al. 1983. *Finalization in Science.* Dordrecht: Reidel.

Campbell, Norman R. 1920. *Physics, the Elements.* Reference is to the reprint, *Foundations of Science: The Philosophy of Theory and Experiment.* New York: Dover, 1957.

Cartwright, Nancy. 1983. *How the Laws of Physics Lie.* Oxford: Clarendon Press.

Chevalley, Catherine. 1988. Physical Reality and Closed Theories in Werner Heisenberg's Early Papers. In D. Batens and J. P. van Bendegem, eds., *Theory and Experiment: Recent Insights and New Perspectives on their Relation,* Dordrecht: Reidel, 159–76.

Cornwell T. J. 1989. The applications of closure phase to astronomical imaging. *Science* 245: 263–69.

Duerr, P. 1981. *Versuchungen.* Stuttgart: Suhrkampf.

Duhem, Pierre. [1906] 1954. *The Aim and Structure of Physical Theory.* Princeton: Princeton University Press.

Feyerabend, Paul. 1978. *Science in a Free Society.* London: NLB.

Franklin, Allen. 1987. *The Neglect of Experiment.* Cambridge: Cambridge University Press.

Galison, Peter. 1987. *How Experiments End.* Chicago, University of Chicago Press.

———. 1988. Philosophy in the laboratory. *The Journal of Philosophy* 85: 525–27.

Gill, Thomas J. III, et al. 1989. The Rat As Experimental Animal. *Science* 245: 269–76.

Goodman, Nelson. [1954] 1983. *Fact, Fiction and Forecast.* Cambridge: Harvard University Press.

Hacking, Ian. 1975. *Why Does Language Matter to Philosophy?* Cambridge: Cambridge University Press.

5. A first version of this paper was given at the American Philosophical Association meeting, 28 December 1988, and a summary of that talk was printed in *The Journal of Philosophy* 85 (1988) 507–14. I thank my commentator on that occasion, Peter Galison, for useful advice. I had a good deal of help from the philosophy of science group at the University of Toronto in the fall of 1989, and wish especially to thank Randall Keen and Margaret Morrison. Our editor, Andrew Pickering, has been splendidly attentive.

———. 1982. Language, Truth, and Reason. In S. Lukes and M. Hollis, eds., *Rationality and Relativism,* Oxford: Blackwell.

———. 1983. *Representing and Intervening.* Cambridge: Cambridge University Press.

———. 1989. The Life of Instruments. *Studies in the History and Philosophy of Science* 20:265–70.

———. 1991. The Disunified Sciences. In R. J. Elvee, ed., *The End of Science?*

———. 1992a. Statistical Language, Statistical Truth, and Statistical Reason. In Ernan McMullen, ed., *Social Dimensions of Science,* Notre Dame, Ind.: Notre Dame University Press.

———. 1992b. Working in a New World: The Taxonomic Solution. (To appear in a volume in honor of T. S. Kuhn, edited by Paul Horwich.)

Hanson, Norwood Russell. 1965. *Patterns of Discovery.* Cambridge: Cambridge University Press.

Heisenberg, Werner. 1948. Der Begriff "Abgeschlossene Theorie" in der modernen Naturwissenschaft. *Dialectica* 2:331–36.

Hempel, C. G. 1966. *The Philosophy of Natural Science,* Englewood Cliffs, N.J.: Prentice-Hall.

Holton, Gerald. 1978. Themata in Scientific Thought. In *The Scientific Imagination.* Cambridge: Cambridge University Press, 3–24.

———. 1981. Thematic Presuppositions and the Direction of Science Advance. In A. F. Heath., ed., *Scientific Explanation.* Oxford: Oxford University Press, 1–27.

Keller, Evelyn Fox. 1986. *Gender and Science.* New Haven: Yale University Press.

Kuhn, T. S. [1961] 1977. The Function of Measurement in Modern Physical Science. *The Essential Tension.* Chicago: University of Chicago Press, 178–224.

———. 1962. *The Structure of Scientific Revolutions.* Chicago: University of Chicago Press.

———. 1978. *Black-Body Theory and the Quantum Discontinuity. 1894–1912.* Chicago: University of Chicago Press.

Lakoff, George. 1986. *Women, Fire, and Dangerous Things: What Categories Teach About the Human Mind.* Chicago: University of Chicago Press.

Latour, Bruno. 1987. *Science in Action.* Cambridge: Harvard University Press.

———. 1990. The Force and the Reason of Experiment. In Homer Le Grand, ed., *Experimental Enquiries.* Dordrecht: Reidel, 49–80.

Latour, Bruno, and Steve Woolgar. 1979. *Laboratory Life.* Beverly Hills: Sage.

Merchant, Carolyn. 1980. *The Death of Nature.* San Francisco: Harper and Row.

Nagel, Ernest. 1961. *The Structure of Science: Problems in the Logic of Scientific Explanation.* New York: Harcourt, Brace and World.

Pickering, Andrew. 1984. *Constructing Quarks*. Edinburgh: Edinburgh University Press.

———. 1989. Living in the Material World: On Realism and Experimental Practice. In D. Gooding et al., eds., *The Uses of Experiment: Studies of Experimentation in the Natural Sciences*. Cambridge: Cambridge University Press, 275–97.

———. 1990. Knowledge, Practice, and Mere Construction. *Social Studies of Science* 20:652–729.

Schaffer, S. Forthcoming. Experimenting with Objectives: Herschel and Huggins. (To appear in a volume edited by J. Z. Buchwald.)

Schweber, S. S. 1989. Molecular Beam Experiments, the Lamb Shift, and the Relation between Experiments and Theory. *American Journal of Physics* 57:299–307.

Suppes, Patrick. 1984. *Probabilistic Metaphysics*. Oxford: Blackwell.

Wittgenstein, L. 1956. *Remarks on the Foundations of Mathematics*. Oxford: Blackwell.

3

Putting Agency Back into Experiment

David Gooding

This chapter is about agency in a world of magnets, wires, vacuum chambers, ionizers, images, sketches, concepts, and beliefs. I am interested in agency that is embodied. As Dr. Johnson saw, our embodied state enables us to do far more than receive experiences and utter sentences about them; it enables us to provoke the world to impinge on our senses. Even in thought experiments, fictional embodiment enables us to explore possible worlds.[1] This should be obvious. It isn't, however, because most people encounter science through retrospective, narrative forms such as textbooks and films, in which research processes have been reconstructed into the orderly stream of narratives. Philosophers order these narratives further as logically structured verbal activity. Manipulative practices, barely glimpsed through such texts, don't appear at all in philosophical discussions of science. Since received views of knowledge restrict knowledge to what has been represented, the neglect of agency in observation and experiment seemed so natural as to be unoticed. A major survey of mainstream philosophy of science, for example, mentions experiment only twice, and neither reference has anything to do with experimentation.[2] Most Anglo-American philosophy has sought to reduce the interaction of theory and experiment to a logical relationship, that is, a relationship between propositions. This makes ex-

Parts of this chapter were read in 1988 at the Center for Advanced Studies, University of Illinois, Urbana, and to the joint 4-S/EASST meeting at Amsterdam, and in 1989 to the Fourteenth Annual Conference on Philosophy of Science at the Inter-University Centre of Postgraduate Studies, Dubrovnik, and to the British Society for the Philosophy of Science. I would like to thank participants for their comments and Andrew Pickering for many constructive criticisms and for help with Morpurgo's quark-hunting narrative. Figures 3.1–3.5, 3.7–3.10, 3.12, 3.16–3.17 are reprinted by permission of Kluwer Academic Publishers.

1. See Gooding 1990b, chapter 8.
2. The first deals with theories of data and experimental design which form the base of Patrick Suppe's hierarchy of theories; the second discusses Feyerabend's pragmatic theory of observation sentences: Suppe 1974, 106–8, 178–79.

periment into a means of generating propositions which bear some logical relationship to statements derived from theory.

But this is an untenably simple view of how theories and observations interact: it makes out that the material world constrains theory as simply as Dr. Johnson thought he could refute Berkeley. The promise of a logically proper methodology of experiment no longer justifies the naïveté of a position which denies scientists as many ways of interacting with the world as nonscientists (and many nonhumans) have and which makes empirical access inherently mysterious.[3] The mystery is supposed to be penetrable only by a robust sort of realism.[4] But it is a false mystery, perpetuated by ignoring everything that has not been elevated to the lofty heights of theoretical discourse. Its falsity emerges when we recover the complexities of practice, once advocated by Kuhn, and the importance of know-how, as advocated even earlier by Ryle.[5]

Philosophers such as Putnam and Rescher have recommended a more practice-oriented approach, but this has not affected philosophical practice, until recently.[6] After all there is a practical problem, which is particularly acute for philosophies of experiment. Much of what experimenters do involves nonverbal doing as well as saying. Such activity is often skilled and unpremeditated, especially at the frontiers where new experience is elicited, represented, and fashioned into empirical evidence. Moreover, scientists themselves write such agency out of the narratives they publish in papers and texts, along with many other things they have used or produced along the way. Where philosophers have argued that natural phenomena are bounded by theory, I shall argue that natural phenomena are bounded by human activity.[7] To assert this is to deny the hallowed independence of the world of representations from the world of embodied practices. Experiment is a situated form of learning in which the manipulation of conceptual objects is often inseparable from the manipulation of material ones, and vice versa.

3. See Giere 1988, 109–10.

4. Namely, one that explains the success of science and scientists' talk about the world in terms of correspondence to an independently existing reality: see Boyd 1973, Brown 1982, Putnam 1975, 1982, for versions of realism that postulate convergence of theories to true statements about a world independent of our interventions.

5. See Kuhn 1961, 1962; and Ryle 1949, chapter 1.

6. Putnam 1974; Rescher 1980; discussions emphasizing experimental practice include Ackermann 1985; Beller 1988; Galison 1987; Giere 1988; Gooding 1982, 1990b; Hacking 1983; Lenoir 1988; Rouse 1987.

7. The most extreme statement of the "theory-dominated" view is Popper 1959, 107; it is criticized extensively in Hacking 1983. For the reduction of experimentation to theory testing, see also van Fraassen 1980.

Agency involves the manipulation of objects of many kinds—represented, unrepresented, material, conceptual, imaginary—the sorts of thing inventoried in Ian Hacking's chapter (chap. 2). The perceived independence of experimenters' representations from the world they invoke is only apparent; that appearance is achieved through further effort.

Four properties of experimental practice

Are there ways of reaching the practical parts that more literary approaches cannot reach? I shall approach observation and experiment through the broader concept of the agency that enables what Quine called the semantic ascent.[8] I want to show how philosophy and history of science might deal with agency in observation and experiment. In the next two sections I focus on the context of experimental practice from which talk and thought about the world emerge. It is therefore necessary to represent experimentation as a process and not simply in terms of its antecedents and outcomes. I do this with diagrams I call *experimental maps.* In their fully developed form the maps visualize some of the complexities of experimentation as a learning process and should enable comparison of different processes (for example, exploratory, developmental, demonstrative, and rhetorical uses of experiment). The changing relationships between experimental practice and argumentation emerge from a comparison of maps of different accounts of an experiment. I believe that these changes will help us to understand how scientists move what they know from the local, situated uses of particular practices to the realm of general, theoretically significant argument.

I introduce the maps by representing two sorts of empirical activity: exploratory observation and hypothesis testing. Here too I argue against the assumption (embodied in the distinction between discovery and justification) that exploration and testing are essentially different. They are alike in four important respects. These are important properties of *all* experimentation (including thought experimentation, an idea I develop elsewhere). The first is the interaction of hand, eye, and mind in the fine structure of observation. I illustrate this by looking at exploratory observation by Michael Faraday, in the early stages of the study of electromagnetism. This work highlights the interaction of an observer's manipulations of objects, tentative construals of these manipulations, and interpre-

8. Quine 1960, 270–76.

tative concepts.[9] The same interaction of conceptual and material manipulations enables theory testing, exemplified by the first few months of Giacomo Morpurgo's large-scale, long-term project to test a precise theoretical prediction using a complex experimental system. Though very different from Faraday's bench-top exploration for new phenomena, Morpurgo's search for quarks also illustrates the interaction of experimental technology, instrumental practices, and theories. Both examples show how theory's incompleteness and nature's recalcitrance combine to necessitate a process of learning and refining practices that build and operate an experimental system. The familiar distinction between observation and experiment is another artifact of the disembodied, reconstructed character of retrospective accounts.

The second common feature is human agency. Here the linguistic bent of philosophy proscribes consideration of most of what science is made of: when statements about outcomes (logical consequences, observations) are all that matter, instruments become irrelevant (or are at best mere practical means to theoretical ends) and experimenters' agency does not appear at all. The maps are meant to display this ingredient in the making of empirical knowledge. To depict agency in this way does not, of course, prove any philosophical thesis: my purpose is to make an important fact about science harder to ignore.

The third feature shared by observation and testing is the occurrence of unexpected events. To appreciate this we must come to terms with how head and hand or theory and experiment interact. The accounts of experiments by Morpurgo and by Faraday display enough complexity to show that making sense of experimental phenomena is a dynamical process in which unexpected events can make formerly intelligible activity and its outcomes meaningless and perplexing. This shows that expectations (concepts, gestalts) do not always govern experience. The examples also show that observers have to work to get the experience they want, or at the very least, to construct something they can communicate. Unexpected events may indicate several things: a want of skill, a lack of theoretical explicitness about how some set of propositions practically engages the world, the recalcitrance of apparatus, the recalcitrance of other observers, or the recalcitrance of nature.

A fourth feature—or perhaps a nonfeature—is the absence of linear, logical structure. Structure emerges in the same way as the perceived independence of representations from their objects does, that

9. For construals in observation see Gooding 1986, 1990b.

is, through the construction of narratives and their subsequent re-construction for demonstrative and pedagogical purposes. I return to these processes later. When we abandon the dogma that ratiocina-tion is the only sort of activity deserving philosophical attention, then it makes sense to ask how reasoning interacts with other ac-tivities. This opens the possibility of a different picture of how what Andrew Pickering calls "out-thereness"—the perceived correspon-dence between things and events in the world and our representa-tions of them—is constructed.

Corrigibility in practice

This last feature—development of a logical structure—enables ex-periments to function in arguments. The first three features enable experimentation to make a difference to theorizing (and vice versa). How? Unexpected events show where "theory" (by which I mean a complex of theories and enabling assumptions) does not match the complexity of nature as implicated by the practices associated with a particular method of observation or experimentation. Theoreti-cians cannot work out every implication of a theory. Recalcitrance in experiment helps identify just those assumptions (or associated theories) that are actually implicated by the experimental methods adopted by a particular laboratory. Each test of what may be called the same theory in different laboratories will invoke different back-ground knowledge, enabling assumptions, local resources, and com-petences (Hacking offers a comprehensive taxonomy of things and ideas useful to experimenters in chap. 2). Experimentation is largely about identifying just the assumptions that matter in *the world as engaged* in that particular laboratory.

Observable output is not all that matters. There are many in-structive results that create competences and confidence sufficient to match theoreticians' commitment to theory. Such events pro-vide what I call *corrigibility in practice.* Like the chaotic motions Morpurgo's team observed early in their work and the unexpected side-to-side-motions Faraday recorded around the middle of a day's work with currents and magnets, these events are not reported (or are soon dropped from accounts) because they have no direct signifi-cance for the main theory or theories under test. Recalcitrances indicate a discrepancy between theory, instrumentation, practice and results. Because they shape and refine practices, they are as important to the invention of a simple device like Faraday's rotation motor as they are to building, operating, and learning how to read a complex system such as Morpurgo's quark detector. They show experimenters how to get the experimental system to engage with that bit of the world they are interested in and to create confidence in the system.

Recalcitrances shape and constrain the development of experimentation: they enable empirical constraint. Recalcitrances are different from observations, which provide corrigibility in theory. Hidden as they are in the fine structure of experiment, it is not surprising that philosophers overlook them. My examples identify a few of these practically important but theoretically insignificant events. These examples show that traditional empiricist views of science are fundamentally flawed: in seeking empirical constraints on theory exclusively in stable observation reports, empiricists have been looking for constraints that do not exist in experimental research (though they do of course appear in journal science and are common enough in textbooks). Philosophies that deal only in representations cannot hope to explain (let alone justify) scientists' confidence in the existence of experimental phenomena. As Hacking has argued, experimenter's realism is not, after all, based upon statements about facts intended to test theories.[10]

Representing Experimental Objects

To illustrate the difference between traditional views of experiment and the procedurally explicit one to be developed here, I shall intruduce a graphic representation of experiment in terms of a familiar task, the methodology of theory testing. For the time being I also adopt the bifurcation of the world into theoretical representations and representations of observations: this is a convenient but temporary fiction. Circles denote ideas or concepts (mentally represented sorts of thing) and squares denote things taken to be in the material world (bits of apparatus, observable phenomena). On the usual view, the relationship between these must be linear and logical, because the significance of experimental results (observations) is purely evidential (or *epistemic*). The familiar theory-observation relationship would look as shown in figure 3.1, which shows a hypothesis H_1 derived from theory T_1, where H_1 implies observation O_H. A real-world possibility is imagined in which O_H occurs in the material situation realized by setup A. This is realized; a result O_A is observed. Comparison of O_A with O_H shows whether the result obtained is sufficiently similar to the one predicted to support the original theory (via the hypothesis).

10. Hacking 1983, chapter 16.

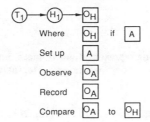

Figure 3.1   Received view of theory-observation relationship (Gooding 1990b)

Many statements in scientists' discourse are about entities that might exist in some world—say, of formally defined objects, or of theoretically imaginable objects, or of physical objects. They are based in turn on claims containing information about such worlds. I combine the squares and circles to represent the *ontological ambiguity* of the entities in play. There are mental representations of things which are taken to be in the real world, but which enter discourse only as interpreted through a complex of theories. A schematic model of an electroscope or microscope represents our understanding of an actual class of instruments, so these would appear in the map as a square (material artifact) inside a circle (concept or model of artifact): see figure 3.2*a*. A model of a hypothetical, possible but not yet constructed instrument would also be shown as a square inside a circle (fig. 3.2*a*). Uninterpreted traces on a bubble-chamber photo would appear as a square (an event in the world). However, after interpretation as the tracks of elementary particles, the square representing these traces would appear inscribed within a circle, indicating its theory ladenness. Similarly, a representation or model of a putatively real entity or mechanism (such as a bacterium or an electron) would have the same composite form until such time as it is realized (or made actual), when it could be represented simply by a square. A material realization of a model (say, an orrery or a wire-and-putty model of a crystal lattice) would be represented as in figure 3.2*b*.

Dualism

"Realizing" means observing in a manner that has come to be accepted as "direct," i.e., it is supposed to be as straightforward as Dr. Johnson's method of refuting idealism. But in practice even the most exemplary observation is not that direct. The directness of observations is a function of the concealment of their history, in which

2a   2b

Figure 3.2   Symbols denoting representations of ideas, images, mental models, etc. (a), and things such as phenomena, instruments, etc. (b) (Gooding 1990b)

people have done things in, to, and with a natural and social world.[11] The maps illustrate this by representing the changing ontology of an experiment as a changing mix of circles, squares, and composite "squurkles." They display the fact that realizing is a historical process in which the ontological status of observable things is worked out as observational techniques are developed and disseminated through the mastery and transfer of skills. As we shall see, once scientists reach consensus about the status of a phenomenon, entity, or mechanism and write this into experimental narratives, the ontological ambiguity of that phenomenon and the temporal dimension of its production are lost.

The notation can display the changing status of the objects in play. In empirical science as distinct from, say, pure mathematics, we might expect many of the "objects" of mental and material manipulations to be "composite"—either mental models of material entities (e.g., a model of an atom) or material embodiments of possibilities (iconic models and instruments, phenomena-producing setups). The maps therefore record the undecided ontological status of much of what is talked about and recorded during experiments. The ontological ambiguity of manipulated objects is important: it allows free movement between possible and actual worlds, enabling new phenomenal possibilities to be constructed. These objects are later hypostatized as necessarily having been (say) conceptual rather than material things. The ambiguous status of manipulated objects is essential to the creative development of thought experiments as well as real ones.

I am not asserting the practice ladenness of theory as a counter to the theory ladenness of observation; both theses presuppose a dualism which is suspect. Nevertheless, to start with I use the received philosophical distinction between the conceptual world of "theory" and the material world in which "observations" are made in order to show later on how the distinction between conceptual and mate-

11. Realizing is therefore a process of articulating material, verbal, and symbolic procedures and writing these into accounts of how phenomena are produced. This is quite different from Radder's notion of "material realization" (Radder 1988) which I criticize elsewhere (Gooding 1990b, chap. 7).

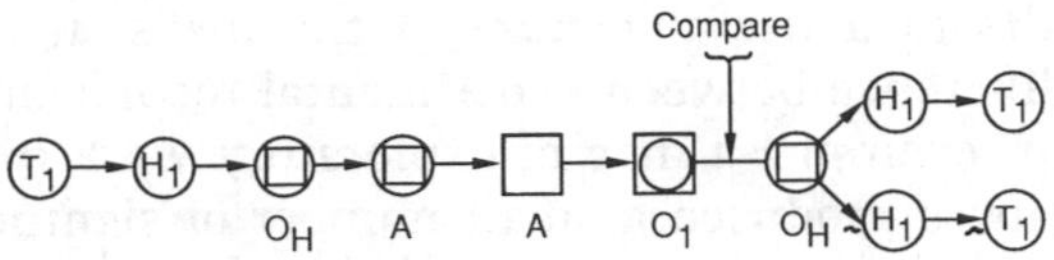

Figure 3.3   Map of simple hypothesis testing (Gooding 1990b)

rial problem spaces breaks down in unreconstructed practice. As we unravel reconstruction and move into the detail, we reach a level of analysis at which the dualistic ontology underlying the distinction between theory-concept and experiment-material world becomes untenable.

The composite symbols of figure 3.2 denote representations of actual states of affairs and realizations of prerepresented possibilities. The idealized notion of hypothesis testing might look as in figure 3.3. The sequence of theoretical and observational states is structured, as before, by a logic of testing, where both the goal and the content can be clearly specified in advance. The map of Morpurgo's work will show that actual hypotheses testing has a very different structure. Before turning to this we must represent what enables scientists to move from one state or object to the next.

Representing Agency

I shall represent agency as a connective, denoted by lines against which an appropriate verb is printed. Each square, circle, or composite "squurkle" identifies something produced or used or entertained in imagination by a scientist or group of scientists. Hacking's more comprehensive inventory of ideas, things, and marks includes only the *objects* of human agency (see chap. 2). Human agency is absent from virtually every discussion of scientific practice, including his. In the maps, each line represents an action or procedure. Combining them gives a sequence of thoughts and actions, including thoughts about objects, about actions and their outcomes, and actions leading to new thoughts or objects.

The orientation of the procedure lines is important. I use it to convey interpretative judgments about whether a particular act or procedure resulted in change, (e.g., novel experience, a sketch, artifacts, concept, or possibility). A horizontal orientation indicates a judgment that something new is introduced; vertical orientation indicates that nothing new results. Such judgments are part of any interpretative process: the notation is meant to make them explicit (and therefore challengeable), not to reify them. Further, this convention results in a useful feature of the maps: it allows us to illustrate a difference between experimental records and published narratives. For example, a map of exploratory work (where a large number of moves produced a small number of significant results) will show far more vertical and much less horizontal movement than a map of the published discovery narratives, where the ratio of horizontal to vertical is reversed.[12] This gives a graphic illustration of how narratives are simplified through reconstruction intended to juxtapose results to theoretical issues. We will see later how comparison of the map of Faraday's record of his discovery of electromagnetic rotations to a map of his instructions on how to make rotations with the device he invented illustrates the packaging of skills into instruments and their disappearance from experimental narratives.[13]

According to philosophers, the repetition of experiment has only two roles: there is replication (where one result confirms or challenges an earlier one), and there is the accumulation of evidence, or inductive support. In real science, repeating procedures is important to learning how to do an experiment. This may involve developing observational skills or revising the apparatus itself or the theory of the apparatus. The notation allows us to represent repetition to enable learning so that it looks quite different from repetition that accumulates similar results to increase inductive support.[14] A forty-five-degree orientation of a line allows us to construct loops representing trials that accumulate experimental skill or the fine-tuning of apparatus. Suppose that the previous sequence included several repetitions of observational procedures. It would appear as the loop shown in figure 3.4, in which the accumulation of skill precedes the first recorded observations. Repetition of established procedures to accumulate further instances appears as a vertical, linear sequence.

Resources

The brackets in figure 3.4 indicate that an experimenter draws on resources, say, to enable particular operations or processes. Such resources include mathematical or logical procedures (used in deriving H_1 from T_1); technological precedents for a proposed device or component of a system; a theory of the instrumentation or design work to generate a viable piece of apparatus A_1; skilled procedures and

12. See chapter 7 and the endpapers of Gooding 1990b.
13. See also Gooding 1990a.
14. For details see Gooding 1990b, chapter 6.

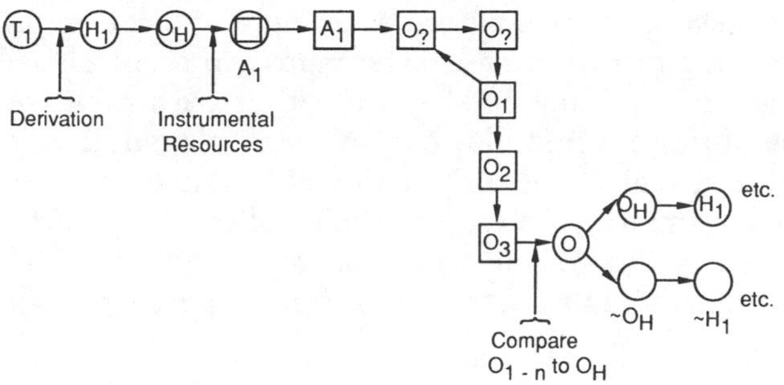

Figure 3.4 Sequence showing repetition of observational procedures and resources utilized (Gooding 1990b)

specialized techniques; computational or other representational procedures which enable (say) comparison of numerical output or observed phenomena O_{1-n} to what was predicted by H_1, and so on. Such comparisons involve similarity judgments. These are based on consensus-seeking processes which I shall not attempt to map here.[15] Selection of a particular resource often indicates that heuristic considerations are in play, but the use of maps to identify heuristic strategies also lies beyond the scope of this chapter.

Experimenter's space

Experimentation is a play of operations in a field of activity, which I call the *experimenter's space*. The place of experiment is not so much a physical location (workbench, laboratory, field station) as a set of intersecting spaces in which different skills are exercised. Of necessity, the experimental maps are printed in a two-dimensional field. But this ranges over several fields of activity: the space of concrete manipulations; mental spaces in which exploratory imaging and modeling take place; computational spaces in which analytical procedures are carried out; the social space in which observers negotiate interpretations of each other's actions; the physical space of the laboratory or field, in which observations are fashioned; and the rhetorical and literary space in which they are reported and put to work in arguments.[16] The "actual" discovery path is a chimera

15. Empiricist methodologies take these judgments pretty much for granted, as if the world caused different observers to see things the same way. For the assumptions involved, see Bloor 1983 and Gooding 1990b, chapters 1 and 3.

16. The rhetorical and literacy contexts are discussed in Shapin and Schaffer 1985 and Bazerman 1988.

which the reconstructive nature of thought and action prevents us from accessing retrospectively. The maps represent plausible pathways through experimenters' space; other pathways are possible and some of these were followed.[17] A map's plausibility depends on how well it interprets the information available to the historian, including contemporary notes, knowledge of contemporary practices, retrospective accounts, the repetition of experiments and study of surviving instrumentation to help interpret these texts, and so on.[18]

Construction as Reconstruction

So far we have a notation that represents agency and its objects. What structure do experimental processes have? The formalistic bent of philosphy of science made it unnecessary to look for sources of the logical structure that scientific narratives have. For rationalists this structure evinced a transcendent homology between the structure of thought and that of reality. For the more empirically minded, good scientific reasoning seemed to reduce to logical argument, because after all, scientists' own accounts highlight logical norms embedded in the methodological canons of their discipline. There was little here to challenge the presumption that all reasoning must have the linear form of deductive argument. But these accounts reconstruct, to ensure that the contingencies and messiness of empirical work are precisely situated (if they appear at all). Most thought is actually convoluted and reflexive; it is "reticular" (that is, folded like the outer cortex).[19] Philosophies of science ignore this, so committing what Tom Nickles labeled the "one-pass fallacy": they treat scientists' narratives as realistic accounts of a single, linear "pass" or sequence of operations.[20] This ignores the fact that such accounts involve complex reconstructions; they are not records.

Grasping the nettle of reconstruction means acknowledging that all accounts of experiments—even those made as experiments are done—involve reconstruction. Reconstruction is needed to produce an account ordered enough to enable action or to communicate what is going on. For example, in the accounts we find in notes, records, correspondence, and working drafts of papers, new images, interpre-

17. For some alternative pathways, see Gooding 1990b, chapter 6.
18. On the use of repetition to aid the interpretation of experimental texts, see Gooding 1989b, 1990b.
19. This term is due to Agnes Arber (1985).
20. See Nickles 1988, especially 34.

tations and concepts are being articulated alongside arguments.[21] This type of reconstruction is *cognitive:* it generates accounts that make experimental behavior intelligible to the actors involved. I distingish it from *demonstrative* reconstruction that generates evidential arguments from accounts of particular experiments. We can distinguish this (though not too sharply) from *methodological* reconstruction of an account. This brings the evidential argument into conformity with the methodological canons governing a particular experimental discourse.[22] Medawar's well-known complaint that the inductive style of evidential argument of published papers misrepresents the discovery process (which he took to be conjectural and fallibilistic) identifies reconstruction of this kind.[23] It is rhetorical in intent. A more extreme example of *rhetorical* reconstruction is Galileo's exaggeration of values in his account of the famous tower experiment.[24] This is not so far removed from the exemplary demonstrations found in science texts, which involve considerable streamlining of the actual research by selection of the most straightforward methods and data. Rewriting (once) actual examples has a didactic as well as a demonstrative role, so I shall call it *didactic* reconstruction. Didactic reconstruction enables the dissemination of what Kuhn called exemplars.[25] As Kuhn also pointed out, science texts and science teaching are the main source of the concept of experimentation that most nonscientists have.[26] Finally, philosophers' reconstructions remove remaining traces of the reticular structures of thought, action, and interaction to leave a smooth sheet on which methodologically acceptable or logically transparent structures can be printed. This attempt to formalize scientists' deliberations involves *normative* reconstruction.[27]

These distinctions (see table 1) are loosely drawn. I make them to highlight the cognitive, situational, procedural, conceptual, formal, and other sources of the argumentative structure that experimental narratives actually have. The invisibility and ubiquity of

21. For examples of the articulation of theoretical concepts, see Holmes 1987 on Lavoisier, and Wise 1979 on Thomson; for examples from exploratory observation, see Gooding 1986 and 1990b, chapter 2.

22. These canons are specific to different disciplines: for examples see Bazerman 1988 and case studies in Donovan et al. 1988.

23. Medawar 1963.

24. Naylor 1989, 126.

25. See Kuhn 1974.

26. Kuhn argued that this fact has helped reinforce a nonscientific approach to theory confirmation; see Kuhn 1962, 80, and 1961, 185–86.

27. Its chief proponents are those who expect to find support for philosophical theories of rationality in empirical case studies: Lakatos 1970 and Laudan 1988.

Table 1 Types of Reconstruction

	Activity	Narrative	Enables
Cognitive (real-time, nonlinear)	Constructive, creative, reasoning	Notebook, sketches, letters	Representation, communication, argument
Demonstrative (real-time, nonlinear)	Reasoning, argument	Drafts of papers and letters	Ordering, description, demonstration
Methodological (retrospective and linear)	Demonstration	Research papers, monographs	Communication, criticism, persuasion, reconstructions
Rhetorical (prospective and linear)	Demonstration	Papers, treatises	Persuasion, dissemination
Didactic (prospective and linear)	Exposition	Textbook, treatise	Dissemination of exemplars
Normative (linear)	Reconstruction	—	Logical idealization

these reconstructive processes makes it important to examine scientists' material practice as well as their verbal practice. Whereas philosophers might seek evidence of formalizable, preferably deductive strategies, I want to open the very *structure* of experimental processes to investigation. Since this structure is made rather than given, we should recover it empirically.

Comparison of maps of successive accounts of experiment shows construction and reconstruction at work. For example, narrative accounts of the same experiment show the disappearance through editing of human artifice and of the ambiguous ontological status of objects. This happens progressively, as possibilities are realized (as instruments, phenomena, etc.), as skilled procedures are embodied in instruments, and as decisions are made about the reality of a phenomenon or construct. As remarked earlier, the ontological status accorded to the entities to which language refers is conferred through reconstruction; its self-evidence is conferred through *concealment* of that reconstruction. In more familiar language, judgments about the reality of an entity or about the directness of an observation are retrospective. Their status reflects confidence based on certain representations being made and tried, on distinctions being drawn, skilled practices established, and so on.

The experimental paths mapped in this chapter involve mainly cognitive and demonstrative reconstruction. But mapping successive accounts of an experiment and comparing the maps (as I do elsewhere) also displays the ordering effects of other kinds of reconstruction. For example, it is well known that most logically crucial experiments acquire crucial status through retrospective constructions (often in textbooks) which give a false view of the actual status experiments had when proposed or when performed.[28]

Choices and Decisions

If experimental practice is less logically ordered than we thought, how does it emerge? To answer this question requires a final piece of preparatory work. Agency is always motivated, so we must represent choices or decisions that define the direction taken at any particular point. Broadly speaking the lines in figures 3.3 and 3.4 denote "actions," while the circles and squares denote things which can be communicated or manipulated (concepts, images, artifacts, etc). The term "action" connotes a rationale (usually including a verbally articulated goal). In retrospective accounts all acts appear to have had goals. For rhetorical reasons, published accounts emphasize long-term nonsituational and long-term theoretical goals rather than contextual, practical ones. I want to avoid the assumption that every act must have been premeditated, so I treat the lines as representing bits of behavior or "procedures." This is not to deny that procedures are motivated or that motivation may be quite complex.

I have distinguished choices (made with intuitive or partially articulated understanding of a situation) from decisions (made on the basis of a rationale that was invoked when the decision was made). Let choices be represented by white triangles; decisions by black ones, as in figure 3.5. This convention situates decisions as responses to outcomes. Of course there are many more levels of embeddedness than the two introduced here. Finally, because getting experiments to work involves exploring perplexing results, we need to show when a sequence fails. This failure can be conceptual (say, a derivation by argument of a model or hypothesis from theory) or practical (a setup proves impossible to construct or to operate, or fails to behave as expected, or produces unexpected output, or an observer lacks dexterity necessary for carrying out procedures). Unanticipated outcomes are indicated by terminating the action line with a T or a reversed arrowhead.

28. See Schaffer 1989, Worrall 1989.

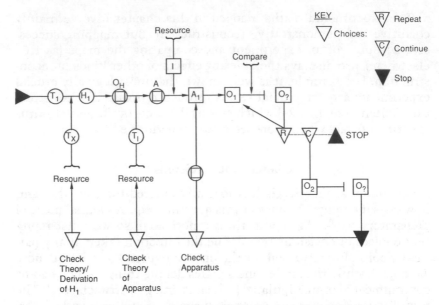

Figure 3.5   Sequence showing decisions and choices (Gooding 1990b)

When comparing a (relatively) unreconstructed laboratory record with a published narrative describing the same experiment, we would expect the effects of demonstrative and rhetorical reconstruction to appear as changes in the sequence of procedures, made in order that certain (contingent) choices could be promoted to decisions. To illustrate the method I compare a map of Faraday's notebook record of making a new phenomenon with his much briefer instructions for obtaining that same phenomenon with a newly invented demonstration device. This shows a clearer differentiation of unrepresented, material aspects of experience from represented ones. The reduction in the number of moves needed to see the phenomenon illustrates the packaging of skill.

The Dynamics of an Experimental Test: Morpurgo's Search for Quarks

During 1964 Giacomo Morpurgo began to design experimental tests of a proposal by Murray Gell-Mann and G. Zweig that nature is made up of fundamental entities called quarks. I begin with a map based on a retrospective account given by the team leader, Morpurgo, because it is much easier to *introduce* the notation for an account that has been ordered and simplified by the reconstructive processes discussed earlier. The extent of the editing will be appar-

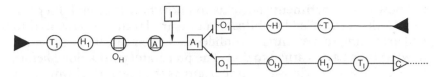

Figure 3.6   Testing the quark hypothesis: reconstructed view

ent when we come to the detail of a nonretrospective account of Faraday's electromagnetic experiments. Morpurgo and his team conducted their experiments from 1965 onward. These experiments sought to detect quantities whose theoretical significance, as well as their values, was precisely specified. On Morpurgo's interpretation of it, quarks, not electrons, might carry charges of 1/3 or 2/3 of *e* (the charge of an electron discovered by J. J. Thomson and established by Robert Millikan).

How experiments begin

For later comparison to the process-oriented map I develop below, figure 3.6 maps Morpurgo's problem situation as it would look according to the received philosophy of experiment. From a fallibilist standpoint, figure 3.6 displays all there is to know about a good experimental test. There is a precise prediction with little room for the recognition of anomalous results or ad hoc moves. Such quantitative precision is of course a good thing. It increases the likelihood of falsification by increasing the likelihood of obtaining quantities other than those specified. According to fallibilist methodology, this would show that something is wrong with the hypothesis, its derivation, or the theory. Thus, figure 3.6 maps a theoretician's rationale; it tells us why the experiments might end, not how they began.

However, precision has another side: in real science, experiment produces values other than those predicted. These are readily treated as indicating that something is amiss: the *apparatus* (or the practitioner) is not working properly. The "hardness" of published results is linked as directly to the quality of a setup and the competence of experimentalists as it is to theory. The ladder of discovery that enables ascent to formal methods of justification is indispensable for dealing with subsequent challenges to a result because—as sociological studies have shown—these are often addressed to experimental procedures and competences.[29] Thus, it is as important

29. Collins 1985; Pickering 1981, 1984; Pinch 1985.

to know how experiments begin as to know how they end. Preparatory work—dismissed by philosophers as irrelevant—is essential to understanding that scientists' confidence in their results is grounded in what they have learned to do.[30] The preparatory work done before trials could even begin was as important as the theoretical work that prompted it. This preparatory work enabled the group to refine their work before any results were injected into the realm of controversy. For example, it included reevaluating one set of results in terms of a later set, showing that the status of any particular set of observations was linked to judgments about other sets.

I shall summarize the main stages of the first year's work, leading up to their first published observation, their doubts about that result, and their subsequent confirmation of it. This is based on a narrative by team leader Morpurgo, and it draws on Pickering's analysis of these experiments.[31] He interprets Morpurgo's narrative in terms of the interaction of three sorts of activity: *material practice* (building apparatus, debugging, and learning to operate it), *instrumental modeling* (evaluating existing instruments, designing alternatives; modeling procedures), and *phenomenal modeling* (constructing models which specify what sorts of phenomena are possible, where such models support judgments about the believability of reality of experimental results). The interaction of the three activities produces a succession of problems, or "destabilizations." Stability—an unstable equilibrium between the three types of activity—is restored when solutions are found.

I argue in *Experiment and the Making of Meaning* (1990b) that this analysis could be applied as readily to theoretical practices as to experimental ones. However, to address the hypothetico-deductivist ideal that "theories are guides to action," we must foreground the *interaction* of acts in the material and theoretical domains.[32] It turns out that theories are *incomplete* guides to action. This incompleteness is a function of the complexity of experimentation. It helps to define the empirical role of experimentation as something more subtle and active than performing the logical equivalent of kicking at stones.

Following Pickering's analysis of Morpurgo's early tests into periods of stability punctuated by destabilizing events (of which more later), I divide the first few months' work into eight stages, each

30. See Franklin 1986 on "epistemological strategies" and Hacking 1983 and chapter 2 of this volume on "self-vindication."
31. Pickering 1989 and "Making sense of science," (1987).
32. See Putnam 1974.

ending in a stabilization (shown as S_{1-n}, etc.) This gives the following sequence:

Stage 1. A goal is defined in terms of a culturally situated problem, namely, the desirability of testing the hypothesis that hadrons are made up of two or three quarks. Testing this possibility would involve realizing effects in the laboratory which can be interpreted as instances of one of the phenomenal models at issue (indicated as M_{1-n}, where the value of the subscript denotes the version in play). The team's search for means begins with a search from available precedents—actual apparatus and associated techniques. They propose a possible setup, a version of the oil-drop method Millikan had used to establish the unitary charge of the electron. (In Millikan's famous experiments, minute oil droplets expressed from an atomizer "captured" electric charges. Though the droplets entered the chamber carrying charges due to friction, the size of new charges captured by a droplet could be calculated from changes in its behavior. Some droplets drifted downward into an electrostatic field between two horizontal plates. The field could be manipulated while a given droplet was observed. Changes in its rate of ascent (against gravity) indicated the capture of some quantity of charge, which could be calculated, since the field strength and the mass of the droplet were known.) Morpurgo's team supposed that fractional charges might attach to oil drops, just as unitary charges attached to the drops in Millikan's experiments. I denote a theoretical or schematic model of a possible instrument as I_n, where the value of the subscript denotes the version in play. When realized as a piece of hardware, it will be denoted by A_n, (apparatus). Again, the subscript denotes the version in use. I_1 denotes a modeled setup of which many examples (that is, A_1's) already exist.

This investigation is in what Pickering calls "conceptual space." At this point there is a temporary convergence of theory (which generates a model M_1 of the effect sought), theory of the instrumentation (which generates model I_1), and available apparatus (with its associated methods), A_1. Further investigation of the practicability of A_1 persuaded Morpurgo that it would not be feasible to use the Millikan type of apparatus. This decision "destabilizes" the model which embodied the team's understanding of possible instruments. The Millikan method is revised (by scaling up, through the application of classical electrostatics) to give another model of a possible apparatus (A_2). The basic theory of this instrument has not changed (see below), so I denote this model as I_1' (rather than I_2). The proposed change of scale enables another stabilization, still in conceptual space.

Stage 2. The possible apparatus A_2 is evaluated theoretically (i.e., as the model I_1') and is rejected as impracticable because the voltage needed for electrostatic suspension of samples of matter larger than oil drops would be too high. For the moment, there is no workable realization of conditions required to test the prediction. An alternative method of suspension (a dielectric liquid, CCl_4) is considered. They decide to build a device using a liquid suspending grains of graphite instead of oil drops. This restores stability and enables the action to move into the material world of the laboratory.

This is an appropriate point to map the moves so far. They are shown in figure 3.7. The "squares" that appear are circumscribed in circles because all decisions and manipulations are still in the realm of representations. So far the team has not built, tried, or experienced anything in the world of material procedures, apparatus, or phenomena.

Stage 3. A device (A_3) is built and tried. The test particles whizz all over the place. The team regarded this as a test of the instru-

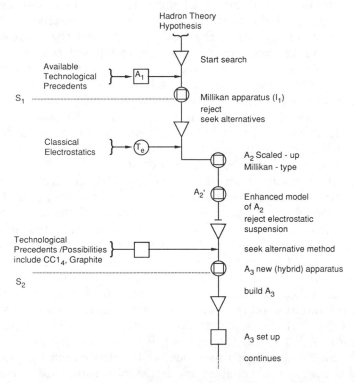

Figure 3.7   Map of the first part of Morpurgo's narrative (Gooding 1990b)

mentation, not of theory. They concluded that further experiment was not possible with this setup. This is a good example of a result that philosophers of science would regard as irrelevant because it doesn't test the theory. Yet it is an encounter with a bit of the world not anticipated by any theory, requiring a decision about what to do next. For now we note that the first bit of experimental work showed up a discrepancy between what Pickering calls material practice (which says the setup doesn't work) and the instrumental model (I_1'), the theory of which says it should work. This shifted the action back to conceptual space, where the problem was diagnosed.

Stage 4. Further theoretical work suggested that the odd behavior observed with A_3 was due to the particles exchanging too much charge with the suspending medium, and that the model of the apparatus (I_1') should be revised accordingly. This change (new model I_2) makes the theory being used to generate the predicted values of a supposedly observable quantity compatible with the models being used to construct and refine the team's understanding of their instruments and their experimental practices. This new compatibility could be maintained in practice by adopting some other method of suspending the particles to which the charges should attach. Having already rejected Millikan's electrostatic method and the dielectric liquid, the team now selected magnetic levitation. This gives I_2'. There is another search for technological precedents that could be adapted into a working device. With this stabilization (S_4) the team moved back to the material context of building and trying devices (A_4).

Stage 5. Trials with electromagnets show up a new problem: the apparatus they needed would not fit between the largest electromagnet available. They use classical field theory to redesign the magnet poles and ordered a new model to these specifications. They tried this back in the laboratory and found that it worked to a 14 mm separation of the plates that supply the electrostatic field. This is compatible with their vacuum chamber. Further work with A_5 involves frequent shifts between trying, modeling, troubleshooting.[33] These stages of the work, culminating in the decision to proceed to serious observation, are shown in figure 3.8.

33. For example, it took a long time to obtain grains carrying a low-enough charge. The solution came in the form of a familiar bit of technology (an ultraviolet lamp fitted as an ionizer). The apparatus with ionizer is A_6. At this point they also worried that a high temperature gradient across the vacuum would introduce extraneous forces on the graphite grains, but decided to continue with this system nonetheless.

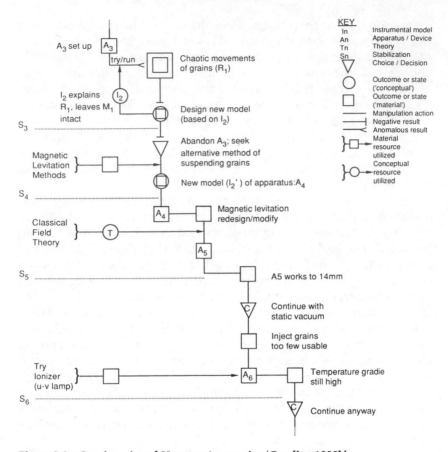

KEY
In — Instrumental model
An — Apparatus / Device
Tn — Theory
Sn — Stabilization
▽ — Choice / Decision

○ — Outcome or state ('conceptual')
□ — Outcome or state ('material')
— Manipulation action
— Negative result
< — Anomalous result
⊢□→ — Material resource utilized
⊢○→ — Conceptual resource utilized

A_3 set up A_3

try/run <

Chaotic movements of grains (R_1)

I_2 explains R_1, leaves M_1 intact I_2

Design new model (based on I_2)

S_3

Abandon A_3; seek alternative method of suspending grains

Magnetic Levitation Methods

New model (I_2') of apparatus: A_4

S_4

Classical Field Theory T

A_4 Magnetic levitation redesign/modify

A_5

S_5 A5 works to 14mm

Continue with static vacuum

Inject grains too few usable

Try Ionizer (u-v lamp) A_6 Temperature gradie still high

S_6

Continue anyway

Figure 3.8   Continuation of Morpurgo's narrative (Gooding 1990b)

Stage 6. This work makes experiment (procedures) and theory (of the instrumentation) mutually compatible. They now have an instrument that enables the observation of relatively stable grains of low charge, and now need to learn to operate it, identify grains, etc. This requires a complex of skills: once a grain has been located, a field can be applied, and the resulting displacement observed and calculated. They make their first runs, observing a displacement of a grain. This procedure is included in figure 3.9. The behavior of other grains suggested that no fractional charges were present. Note the vertical orientation of lines denoting operations with different grains. This indicates that successive observations provide the same sort of information. Here what changed was their confidence in the method and use of the apparatus. Increased confidence encouraged them to infer from the now stable result (the neutrality of the grains)

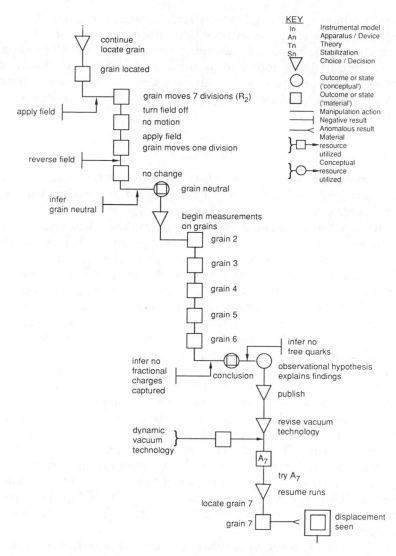

Figure 3.9 Continuation of Morpurgo's narrative (Gooding 1990b)

that there are no free quarks. They published this preliminary finding.

The system now produced results they could report, but the unstable equilibrium of theory, instrumentation, and practice was soon disturbed by the problem with the temperature gradient across the vacuum. They had earlier decided to stay with a static vacuum because they assumed that practical difficulties of maintaining a dynamic vacuum could not be overcome. However, the near impossibility of eliminating gradients (which introduced unwanted forces) obliged them to reconsider a dynamic vacuum system. When tried, this system (A₇) was found to be more practicable than they had expected. They observed further displacements of another test grain with the improved system. This event concludes the sequence shown in figure 3.9.

Anomalies

Their experimentation was now good enough to produce anomalies. These events could not readily be dismissed as artifacts because of the team's new confidence that their system worked properly. The recognition of possible anomalies shows that theoretical commitments were now balanced by a growing commitment to the instrumental practices they had worked out. The first anomalous displacement occurred when, reversing the electric field with grain 7 in place, they observed a displacement in the same direction as before. This might have indicated the presence of a quark. Morpurgo recalled that the difference in the two displacements "corresponded to one fourth (or with 'some goodwill' to one third) of the difference in displacements when the object had captured an electron."[34] Although the value obtained did not correspond to that required by theory, the possibility had to be taken seriously. The team was excited by this possibility until further observation showed that other grains displayed similar behavior. These results were consistent neither with their earlier (published) results nor, strictly, with the predicted values. These observations would not have been made had the team not allowed the enabling assumption that the observed value (1/4) is "close enough" to one of the required values (1/3 of *e*). This continuation is shown in figure 3.10. Again the delicate balance of practice, instrumentation, interpretation, and theory had been disturbed.

Stage 7. They moved back into conceptual space where they now faced a different problem: their instruments and procedures gave results that conflict with theory. As Morpurgo read it, this permits only two values (*e* or 1/3 *e*). Morpurgo's somewhat strict interpretation of theory meant that they did not consider, say, 1/4 *e* as a possible value. Instead they applied theory to reexamine the setup. This suggested that the unacceptable subelectronic results might be explained as an artifact of some aspect of the setup; their instrumen-

---

34. Pickering 1989, 287.

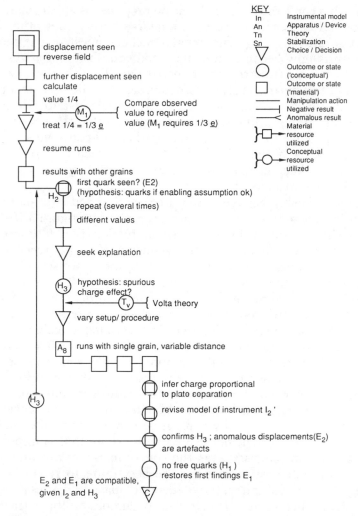

KEY

In	Instrumental model
An	Apparatus / Device
Tn	Theory
Sn	Stabilization
▽	Choice / Decision
○	Outcome or state ('conceptual')
□	Outcome or state ('material')
——	Manipulation action
⊣	Negative result
≺	Anomalous result
⊣□→	Material resource utilized
⊣○→	Conceptual resource utilized

displacement seen
reverse field

further displacement seen
calculate

value 1/4

Compare observed
value to required
value (M_1 requires 1/3 $\underline{e}$)

(M_1)

treat 1/4 = 1/3 $\underline{e}$

resume runs

results with other grains

first quark seen? (E2)
(hypothesis: quarks if enabling assumption ok)

H_2

repeat (several times)

different values

seek explanation

hypothesis: spurious
charge effect?

H_3

(T_v) — Volta theory

vary setup/ procedure

A_8 runs with single grain, variable distance

infer charge proportional
to plate separation

revise model of instrument I_2 '

(H_3)

confirms H_3 ; anomalous displacements(E_2)
are artefacts

no free quarks (H_1)
restores first findings E_1

E_2 and E_1 are compatible,
given I_2 and H_3

Figure 3.10   Final section of Morpurgo's narrative (Gooding 1990b)

tal model suggested, for example, that there could be a spurious
charge effect. This hypothesis (based on classical field theory) restored stability in the conceptual space.

Stage 8. It was practicable to test this hypothesis. If a charge effect
exists, it would be shown by increasing the separation of the plate-
lets that supply the field while a given grain is in place. A variation
of A_7 was proposed (A_8) and a new set of runs initiated. They found
that measured charge on a grain varied with the separation of the

plates. This confirmed the explanation proposed as an alternative to the possibility that there really are quarks with values other than those permitted by the phenomenal model being tested. The anomalous results now became an artifact and equilibrium was restored once more. This time the phenomenal model, the earlier observations, and the apparatus all remained intact. On the basis of a more complete understanding of the experimental system Morpurgo could reaffirm the earlier, tentative conclusion that there are no free quarks. Of course the existence of quarks is still controversial; rival experiments by William Fairbanks have produced over one dozen quark events, keeping open the possibility that Morpurgo's "anomalies" were not artifacts after all.[35]

The relationship between Morpurgo's earlier and later published results is shown by the arrow connecting them in figure 3.10. This relationship would be lost in a reconstruction that followed the logic of empirical support. As this sequence of events recedes into the past (and finds its way into textbooks), these two sets of results would come to share the same evidential status. The histories of experiments judged to have had the "right" results in the light of the closure of a controversy show that consensus alters the status of each result (usually) in relation to later ones. Such judgments enable logical cruciality to supersede consensual cruciality. The route to these and later results would therefore become even more streamlined, eventually resembling more the pathway shown in figure 3.6 than the one mapped in figures 3.7–3.10. However, reinterpretation of the first set of nonanomalous results in terms of the later set that made the two sets mutually supportive is never beyond challenge.

As I remarked earlier, figure 3.6 maps a route that is impossible for the research scientist: it is the sort of map you can draw only when both your destination and the best route to it are known. Though far from complete, the sequence of maps in figures 3.7–3.10 shows that much more was involved. What does all the extra detail of figure 3.10 tell us about how a destination is reached? It displays the frequent remodeling of the understanding of apparatus and procedures. This shows the efficacy of agency. The next example extends this analysis of agency to the fine structure of observation, showing features that the large-scale Morpurgo sequence did not. I want to bring out the interaction of ideas, objects, and manipulative skill and to recover some detail of the transition between different versions of models. This illustrates what experimentation with flexible phenomenal possibilities is like. For examples of observation in

35. See Pickering 1981.

process I move back a century and a half, to early work on electro-magnetism by Michael Faraday. This move from hypothesis testing to observation takes us from the most familiar use of experiment to the most neglected.

Making New Phenomena

There is a conventional distinction between observation (as record-ing what is presented) and experiment (as intervening in the course of nature). Observation is thought to be descriptive and passive (it involves looking, not doing). Experiment is active (it involves doing and then looking). There is also a third, exploratory, active form of observation of the sort that anatomists or field geologists engage in.[36] The conventional distinction is misleading because observation involves the same sort of agency as experiment, that is, the inven-tion and manipulation of mental and material entities. This simi-larity has escaped us because philosophical preoccupations with a world of *stable* representations (and consequent neglect of how per-ception is ordered) have made the role of agency in assimilating new information seem unimportant. Passive observation (looking at things given in experience) occurs only in finished science in which the meaning and status of experience is clear or is for the time being uncontested. Observation is passive when observers are dealing with situations in which nothing new is presented, or with highly prescribed observational possibilities (the theory-based stability of Morpurgo's model of possible phenomena is an example). By con-trast, what goes on at the observational frontier highlights the task of learning to translate novel experience into intelligible discourse about the world. This also brings out a quality that agency has: *skill*.

My example of exploratory observation is Michael Faraday's cre-ation of a new electromagnetic effect: the continuous rotation of a current-carrying wire around a magnet. This illustrates the selec-tion and development of aspects of a phenomenon. In 1820 H. C. Oersted showed that a current-carrying wire affects a magnetized needle. This had an enormous impact because it demonstrated a connection between two large but separate phenomenal domains: electricity and magnetism.[37] Within a few months of Oersted's an-nouncement in September 1820, many scientists were writing about the "ease" or "self-evidence" of seeing certain phenomena in certain ways, and about the "necessity" of inferences made about them.

36. Harré 1981, 21–23.
37. See Williams 1985; Gooding 1989a, 1990b.

Philosophers tend to conflate these two steps by reducing all of observation either to seeing what is "given" or seeing what is prescribed by preconceptions, expectations, or gestalts. Anyone who tries to make similar observations will find that the behaviors of a magnetized needle near a current are in fact unruly. In 1820 everyone involved was inexperienced—a novice—when exploring the new phenomena.

It is hard to understate the importance of this situation: it is as normal for scientists to be laymen with respect to science outside their own specialty as it is for them to be novices with respect to new phenomena, procedures, etc.[38] We should read their claims about ease and self-evidence as rhetorical emphasis in the experimental narrative. However, these phrases also show that these experimentalists had mastered observational techniques and constructed representations. These made the phenomena easy to see, thus making them self-evident to other, less-skilled observers.

It is important to see how the stability of phenomena is achieved and to recognize that—as in the Morpurgo sequence—it depends on skill. The Faraday example involves a different sort of skill. Seeing—whether in the mind's eye or in the concrete experimental situation—depends upon doing and the *cognitive reconstruction* of its outcomes. I show elsewhere, for example, how Faraday's contemporary, J. B. Biot, did what all expositors of new situations do, taking care to describe a frame of operation for lay observers who would witness the phenomena only through his account. This framework had emerged from his investigations as a way of making sense of what each new operation disclosed. His account is unintelligible unless the reader can *visualize* the setup and the framework of the experimenter's action so as to imagine the experimenter moving the wire continuously around the needle. Biot reconstructed the resulting needle movements, compressing a sequence of actions and outcomes into a single instant. Successive, discrete positions of the wire became a continuous "circular contour," not seen directly "in the world," but as traced by the experimenter's hand. The circular needle motions were a property of the experimenter's *behavior* and his ability to elicit a coherent, communicable structure out of phenomenal chaos.[39]

38. J. W. N. Watkins points out that scientists live in a world largely affected by developments they do not understand, because "the amount of science which an individual scientist is *ignorant* of is only slightly less than that of which the non scientist is ignorant" (Watkins 1964, 65).

39. See Gooding 1990b, chapter 2.

A great deal of activity lay behind Biot's apparently simple observation, as Faraday discovered when he tried to repeat these and other observations during the summer of 1821. His laboratory notes record observations which were made as part of a process of learning by doing rather than working to a preconceived plan.

Discovery: Faraday's "new magnetic motions"

In discovery, scientists cannot reason *to* an experiment as directly as their retrospective narratives usually suggest. They articulate their understanding of it, and of the bit of nature it implicates, so as to reason *about* it in images or in propositions. A great deal of invention and construction depends on the manipulation of nonverbal tokens, images, and objects. Practical manipulation is necessary to propositional representation. Afterwards phenomena are distinguished from the instruments and actions that produce them, semantic ascents are made, and the observer's agency falls out of the picture. Once that degree of abstraction has been achieved it is impossible to recover the ambiguity and openness of the early, least articulate stages of the process. Faraday's laboratory notebooks record many examples of observation in experiment in which, *during* the observation process, interpreting new phenomena is inseparable from constructing devices that produce (and re-produce) them. My second example therefore looks at the invention of instruments, as well as images and procedures.

We can follow the process of articulating concepts and instruments in the sequence of sketches from the notebook, reproduced in Martin's transcription (figure 3.11). During the summer of 1821 Faraday had made a careful study of the interaction of magnetized needles near the wire (2–5 in figure 3.11) because he was convinced that earlier investigations by Davy, Biot, and others had failed to disclose the complexity of interactions of magnets and wires. I have described the context of these experiments elsewhere; here I pick up the process at the point at which he had resolved chaotic needle motions into the circular image. The drawings represent needle motions like those Biot had produced; below them are Faraday's attempts to interpret these, and (in fig. 3.13) different configurations of a moving wire and stationary magnet, and finally the possible (prototype) rotation motor. Although his sketches identify more signposts than a retrospective account would, they convey little about the manipulations of which these words, images, instruments, or phenomena are the residue.

SEPT. 3RD, 1821.

Electromagnetic expts. with Hare's Calorimotor. To be re- ELECTRO-
membered that this is a single series? MAGNETISM.
1. Position of the expt. wire A*.
2. Positions at first ascertained were as follows

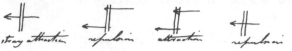

3. On examining these more minutely found that each pole had
4 positions, 2 of attraction and 2 of repulsion, thus

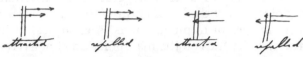

4. Or looking from above down on to sections of the wire

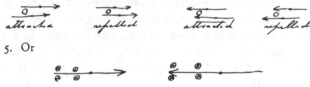

5. Or

6. These indicate motions in circles round each pole, thus

Hence the wire moves in opposite circles round each pole
and 'or the poles move in opposite circles round the wire. To
establish the motion of the wire a connecting piece was placed
upright in a cork on water; its lower end dipped into a little
basin of mercury in the water and its upper entered into a little
7. inverted silver cup containing a globule of mercury; the arrangement of battery poles always as at first. Magnets of different

FDI   4

**Figure 3.11   First part of Faraday's laboratory notes for 3 September 1821 (as
transcribed by T. Martin, 1932–36, vol. 1, 49)**

Mapping manipulations: process and know-how

The Morpurgo example illustrates the interaction of findings obtained at quite different times (shown by the feed-back arrows in fig.
3.10). Here I want to show the recursive, cyclical character of such
mundane processes as acquiring manual dexterity by sensory exploration (say, with a hand-held sensor), adjusting apparatus to give a
maximum (or a null) effect, and mental play with the configuration
of elements of a model. By the time he drew the circular images at
the bottom of figure 3.11, Faraday had passed from exploratory work

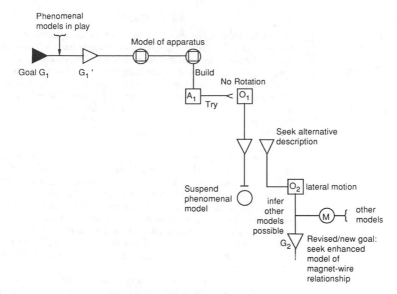

Figure 3.12 Map of the first part of Faraday's record, to paragraphs 8–9

like Biot's and was using the circle image as a heuristic for further trials (see in fig. 3.11). This suggested that he could produce motion of some other sort. He passed the wire through a cork to provide flotation on a conducting solution. These first experiments with the floating wire and magnet (in 6–9) are a typical example of the plasticity and ephemerality of new experience. The first part of the sequence is shown in 3.12, which represents Faraday's decision (6) to build a setup, experiment with it, and represent the outcomes we see recorded. The first move invents a new construction (model M_1), the second realizes that as a material model (apparatus A_1), and the third (closing the electric circuit) produces a new empirical outcome.

This result does not resemble the phenomenon sought. Its role is analogous to the "chaos" produced by Morpurgo's first working setup. The reversed head of the line denoting the first trial of the apparatus (A_1) indicates that the outcome was problematic. Instead of the axial motion implied by one of the models in play, Faraday got the wire moving from side to side as the magnet was brought up to it.[40] Paragraphs 8–9 in figure 3.13 show that Faraday bent the wire

40. Here the study of instrumentation is important: we know from the configuration of his apparatus that this outcome was not expected; had he been looking for it, he would have used a different method of maintaining electrical contact (Gooding 1989b).

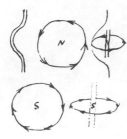

power brought perpendicularly to this wire did not make it revolve as Dr. Wollaston expected, but thrust it from side to side.
8, 9. The wire then bent into a crank form, thus, and by repeated
applications of the poles of the magnets the following motions
were ascertained, looking from above down on the circle described by the bent part of the wire, different Magnetic poles
shewn by letters, North pole in centre. The rod in the circle is
merely put there to shew the front and back part.
10. Magnetic poles on the outside of the circle the wire described*.
11. The effort of the wire is always to pass off at a right angle
from the pole, indeed to go in a circle round it; so when either
pole was brought up to the wire perpendicular to it and to the
radius of the circle it described, there was neither attraction nor
repulsion, but the moment the pole varied in the slightest manner
either in or out the wire moved one way or the other.
12. The poles of the magnet act on the bent wire in all positions
and not in the direction *only* of any axis of the magnet, so that
the current can hardly be cylindrical or arranged round the axis
of a cylinder?
13. From the motion above a single magnet pole in the centre
of one of the circles should make the wire continually turn round.
Arranged a magnet needle in a glass tube with mercury about it
and by a cork, water, etc. supported a connecting wire so that
the upper end should go into the silver cup and its mercury and
the lower move in the channel of mercury round the pole of the
needle. The battery arranged with the wire as before. In this way
got the revolution of the wire round the pole of the magnet. The
direction was as follows, looking from above down [see diagram].

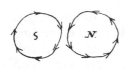

Very Satisfactory, but make more sensible apparatus.

TUESDAY, SEPT. 4.

14, 15†. Apparatus for revolution of wire and magnet. A deep
basin with bit of wax at bottom and then filled with mercury,
a Magnet stuck upright in wax so that pole just above the surface
of mercury, then piece of wire floated by cork, at lower end

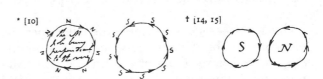

Figure 3.13 **Continuation of Faraday's laboratory notes for 3 September 1821 (from
T. Martin, 1932–36, vol. 1, 50)**

and pursued the magnetic interactions with this new version of the apparatus. His pursuit of this interaction led to a new and more general model of this relationship. It reappears as *one* of the elements that make up the successful prototype of the first rotation device. Faraday's exploratory behavior can be mapped as shown in figure 3.14, picking up from the last outcome in figure 3.12. He records (fig. 3.13, 8–9) that he bent the wire to achieve the rotation of something ("the magnetism") about an axis. This no longer coincides with the course of the wire. I surmise that he thought that the crank would enable him to analyze the unexpected "side-to-side" motions. He recorded the initial set of explorations with the magnet simply as "repeated applications of the poles," but elaborated it in terms of a geometrically modeled relationship between magnet and wire. This is expressed both visually and verbally in figure 3.13, 11–12. I have inferred this pathway, which is therefore shown in dotted lines in figure 3.14.

Cognitive skills

Faraday was getting a feel for relationships between positions and polarities of the magnets and the corresponding directions of motion of the wire. His working understanding of these relationships sug-

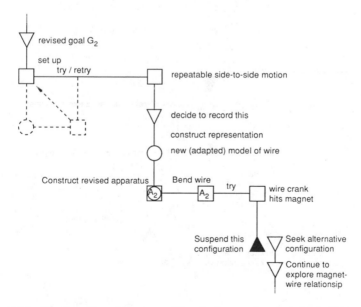

Figure 3.14 Continuation of the map of Faraday's record, to paragraph 11

gested that moving the *pole* would keep the *wire* moving. He made this change to overcome a constraint of his material setup: introducing the magnet close enough to "push" the wire also made the magnet a physical obstacle to continuous motion, were it to occur. Given his feel for the interplay of magnets and wires, this move need not have been made deliberately. Thus, in the next map (fig. 3.15) the step I have labeled "infer" tells us nothing about the modeling of the latest set of manipulations. These led to continuous motion

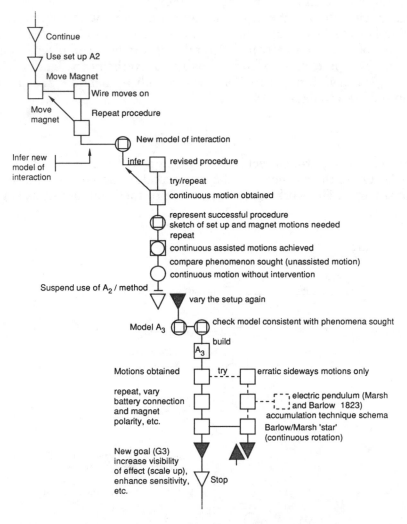

Figure 3.15   Final section of the map, from paragraph 11 onward

of the curve, recorded as the drawing to his in fig. 3.13 (10). Further analysis of inferences requires a computational representation that can deal with the recursivity of such processes.[41]

Faraday's laboratory diary shows a wide variety of mental and material procedures, indicated by verbs such as: put, arranged, bent, immersed, inverted, connected. Seemingly transparent procedures are often complex: "ascertained" in figure 3.11, 2, and "found" in 3, imply a goal reached by a whole set of operations to which Faraday alluded merely as "examining" in 3 (fig. 3.11). Any reference to a diagram implies that he observed an outcome, and this tells us that he would first invent or assemble images that could represent it, and then try to draw them. One example is particularly important. At (8–10) (fig. 3.13) Faraday had only a tentative conception of the relationship between the electromagnetic and magnetic forces. This is shown by his writing instructions to himself at the end of (9) (fig. 3.13). These ensured that he would remember how to read his own drawings. This shows how tenuous his grasp of this new phenomenon was. So far the effects were unique. They existed only in this record and depended on the skills that enabled just one individual to make them.

Read in the light of the difficulty of producing stable, visualizable phenomena (established in recent repetitions of these experiments), Faraday's instructions show that far more detailed mapping is needed for procedures denoted by verbs such as "record" and "draw." We usually take it for granted that "recording" has no effect on the articulation or conceptualization of the experience (including experimenter's behavior) of what is being recorded. This example shows an observer who was not yet able to make the distinction between the representation and its object. The activity that enables new procedures and experiences to be introduced is usually invisible: we see it here only because Faraday was still unsure about recovering his interpretations as represented in these drawings.

Pathways

Let us return to the existence and subsequent history of the little side-to-side motions. Through bits of cork, wires, and magnets Faraday was grappling with the natural world. At this point Faraday had

41. For the representation of recursivity in dynamical maps of experimental processes, see D. Gooding and T. Addis, "Towards a Dynamical, Interactive Representation of Experimental Procedures," in *Bath 3: Rediscovering Skills: Abstracts*, Science Studies Centre, University of Bath, July 1990, 61–68.

effects which he construed as "side-to-side" motions. These were actual enough, but they resembled neither the circles (of fig. 3.11, 6) nor other models of phenomenal possibilities he had in play. This encounter required that he revise his model of the possibile inter-action and alter the apparatus as a tool for the pursuit of a different phenomenon. The horizontal orientation of the procedure lines in figure 3.14 indicates that he had learned something about the con-ditions required to realize such motion. The lateral motions sug-gested new lines of investigation, involving the revision of his present understanding of the magnet-wire interactions. These ef-fects were important only for the short time that they suggested new lines of investigation. They lost significance as soon as Faraday was able to produce effects that more closely resembled aspects of one of those he sought. However, the lateral motions could be produced and demonstrated with the electric pendulum, invented by Peter Barlow and James Marsh in 1822.[42] Faraday did not pursue the lateral motions because he wanted to produce continuous rather than pe-riodic motion and (I surmise) he did not see (as Barlow soon did) how such motion could be elicited from what he had obtained.

The fact that Faraday could have pursued the lateral aspect of the wire-magnet interactions is represented by the dotted-line pathway in figure 3.15. This indicates the route to continuous motion of an-other kind, realized by Barlow's star, a device derived from the elec-tric pendulum. The existence of such alternative pathways to new phenomena shows that no necessity attaches to a particular route: hence the caveat I made earlier, that no map definitively shows the pathway actually followed. The apparent necessity or obviousness of a discovery path emerges—like the self-evidence of new phe-nomena—from cognitive and demonstrative reconstruction and the stabilization of accounts.

Faraday's manipulations were now informed by a better under-standing of the material setup in which, with sufficient manual dex-terity with the magnet, one can in fact produce jerky but continuous motion of the wire. The "repeated applications" of north and south poles are represented by a triangular circuit in figure 3.15. This tri-angle identifies a trial-and-error learning strategy embedded within a larger set of strategies represented by the whole map. According to his notes he moved (via a further query about the implications of his findings for another possibility, Wollaston's hypothesis that the wire should rotate on its axis) to the final, successful device: "From

42. See Gooding 1990b, chapter 6.

the motion above [infer that] a single magnet pole . . . should make the wire continually turn round." This articulates verbally a model of something he can test.

Testing a Construct

Practical activity is necessarily particular. How is it brought to bear on general, theoretical matters? The received view is that experiments test hypotheses by realizing conditions—specified by the theory—in which a hypothesis can be seen to be true or false.[43] However, the hypothesis-conjecture-test model lacks the resources needed to describe and interpret the close interaction of thought and action. What I've unpacked so far supports the conclusion I drew from the Morpurgo sequence—that theories are only rather loose guides to practice. For example, halfway down figure 3.15 the goal (to realize continuous motion) is unchanged, but there is a decision to obtain this motion without active intervention. This defines a new problem whose solution lies in altering the configuration of magnet and wire. On the received view it is hard to see why this problem should arise at this point, because that view never comes to grips with how intellect grapples with the material world.

Faraday's new problem involved a conflict between an *intellectual* (and long-term) objective—to produce *natural* (i.e., continuous) motions—and the physical configuration of the *apparatus*, which prevents effective expenditure of the chemical forces driving the current through the wire. So far, human action had been a necessary condition of any motions Faraday had seen. This involved the expenditure of a "force" that lay outside the scope of his investigations. Faraday had now refined the *material* situation to a point at which it was possible to recognize the larger, *intellectual* aspect of the overall problem and to deal with it *practically*, as a difficulty with the real geometry of his setup. He now changed the configuration of the wire and magnet, returning to the configuration used in the first, inconclusive, straight-wire trial of (6) (figure 3.11). The explicit inference in the first sentence of (13) (fig. 3.13) indicates the existence of a new model of the apparatus. Faraday's account finishes with description of the new setup (A_3) and the results, which he is soon able to produce anywhere.

43. In van Fraassen's formulation testing also involves "filling in the blanks" in a developing theory; i.e., experiment is the continuation of theory by other means (1980, 73ff.).

Skill, convergence and correspondence

Faraday's detailed account shows what is left out of more general, retrospective accounts such as Morpurgo's. This first working motor combined four distinct, yet closely related, elements: (1) empirical knowledge about the conditions in which the wire would move past the magnet; (2) mental models of the phenomenon produced and of the phenomenon sought; (3) a much-revised mental model of his apparatus, and (4) a requirement that phenomena be produced and exhibited independently of human action. These are ideas and images about possibilities and about objects on his laboratory bench. To realize continuous circular motion he implemented many *procedures* on or with these things. For example: *comparing* the phenomenon sought (continuous "circular motion" as goal) with the phenomena produced (which were either discontinuous or required human agency); *evaluating* particular outcomes in the light of this comparison; *manipulating* the model of his apparatus to obtain a configuration which might produce motion more consistent with the other elements. To construct a working apparatus from these four elements he drew on a fifth: *experimental skill*. Faraday's manipulations drew on knowledge of earlier outcomes (such as the null result of fig. 3.13, 11 and the sideways motions obtained in fig. 3.13, 8–9) and also his tacit, "sensorimotor" understanding of the interaction of magnet and wire. This he acquired through the "repeated applications" mapped in figure 3.16. Although skills cannot be represented directly, the nonlinear structures in the figures, such as the empirical learning "loops," together with the frequent revision of experimental apparatus, suggest the accumulation of skill.

Construals

The experimental sequence thus appears as the production of a succession of models, phenomena, bits of apparatus, and representations of these things. Such processes have another property: the representations and the phenomena gradually *converge* to a point where the resemblance between what can be observed and what is sought is "self-evident," or as Faraday himself put it at the end of his day's work, "Very Satisfactory." Space allows only four points about convergence, a notion I develop elsewhere.[44] First, we need to recall the ephemeral and plastic nature of the representations.

44. See Gooding 1990b, chapter 7.

New phenomena are not necessarily experienced and communicated by adapting ready-made modes of representation. Bringing new phenomena into the domain of discourse calls for a succession of construals, or tentative representations of *possible* outcomes. Construals are continually constructed and revised to describe and communicate *actual* outcomes. The process is actually more complex: there is a convergence of successive *material arrangements* (the apparatus) and successive *construals* (or tentative models) of manipulations of and with apparatus, and of the outcomes of these manipulations.

Second, how do we know that achieving a convergence of material and mental objects requires practical skill as well as imagination? Actual repetition of Biot's and Faraday's play with wires and magnetized needles showed that a novice observer's experience does not resemble even what the textbooks describe.[45] This shows that Kuhn's and Hanson's gestalt model of perception is overworked: sometimes observers lack the manipulative skills needed to see what they are supposed to see. Increased *convergence* of material practice to expectations therefore reflects increased observational *skill* rather than a preordained fit. Retrospectively, of course, consensus about the "out-thereness" of what is represented indicates the dissemination of skills, through training, black-boxing, or literary means. The effectiveness of what Shapin calls the literary technology of vicarious witnessing depends upon readers' willingness to believe that they too could reproduce the same processes and get the same correspondence of a concept to a percept. This is largely also why thought experiments work so well.

Third, wider acceptance reflects confidence in those to whom observation has been delegated. What is *said*, however, conceals this social process: scientists say that a phenomenon or law has been discovered, or a hypothesis tested; philosophers conclude that a better fit of theory to nature has been achieved. Expertise has an important social dimension which the diagrams do not represent. The outcomes of any observer's activity include responses elicited from other observers to construals (the tokens of shared experience). These "collaborative utterances" are as essential to the process of observation as obtaining physical responses from the natural world.[46] The "currencies" of such exhanges are the ephemeral con-

---

45. Gooding 1989b.
46. C. Goodwin discusses the inadequacy of considering speech acts independently of a complex physical and social environment, and proposes "collaborative

struals of phenomenal possibilities. These may consist of images (as in Biot's verbal picture and the sketches in Faraday's diary) or may be realized as concrete objects which function initially as mnemonics or—as we've just seen—as heuristics for further investigation, leading to instruments which reproduce aspects of phenomena as natural phenomena.

A final point concerns the relationship between observers' skill and their confidence in the veridicality of their representations. Some of these eventually become so stable that they cease to be seen as constructs that emerged from a process in which the possible and the actual converge. Instead, they are regarded as *corresponding to* (equally stable) things in the world. They cease to be seen as resulting from human agency. Lay observers who read retrospective accounts of experiments do not have to learn to observe (they are shown how). The recovery of skills helps explain the apparent mystery of the successfully referential function of much of scientists' talk; it is skilled agency that brings about the convergence of material and verbal practices. Convergence engenders belief in the correspondence of representations to things in the world.

This explanation underlines the epistemological importance of knowing how experiments begin. I have argued that the correspondence of representations to their natural objects is the result of a process of making convergences, both in experiment and in narratives that reify the distinction between words and the world while removing traces of the work that enabled the distinction to be drawn. Philosophies of scientific theory approach epistemological issues through reconstructed accounts in which convergence has proceeded past the point at which correspondence seems self-evident. The alternative developed here displays the constructed nature of representations and of the ontological status they acquire as consensus is formed about the meaning of observations; thus my emphasis on the ambiguous ontological status of the objects that agents manipulate. I represented this by superimposing circles and squares (or "mental" and "material" objects). Comparison of accounts of experiments should show the disappearance of false starts and dead ends, and the development of skills that enable success, as

---

utterances" as the verbal tokens through which local consensus is formed about what observers are seeing (in "Hunting the Snark: Perception, Technology and Interaction on a Scientific Research Vessel," presented at Bath 3: Rediscovering Skill in Science, Technology, and Medicine). Semiverbal, context-dependent tokens of communication are also important to AI: see, e.g., Bobrow and Winograd 1989.

well as the emergence of a confident differentiation of material things, events, and processes from ideas. Differentiation depends on two complementary processes: one packages skills into instruments and practices that can be disseminated as exemplars; the other assimilates empirical results into theoretical frameworks in which phenomena are either accorded real status or set aside as empirical embarrassments.

Making Skills Disappear

The ontological disambiguation through packaging of skills can be illustrated by comparing two figures. Faraday's first day's work on electromagnetic rotations is mapped out in figure 3.16. This ended with an important change of goal: he decided to scale up the effect with a more "sensible" apparatus (see fig. 3.13). He soon built other versions of the rotation motor to give rotations visibility as a phenomenon for display and to show that the interaction is symmetrical: a magnet can be made to move continuously around a fixed wire.[47] He made several copies of a small device to send to various European scientists. This packaged most of the resources and skills he had brought together on 3 September, avoiding both the pitfalls of the path he had just explored and the ambiguities of written instructions on how to build a motor from scratch. He enclosed simple instructions on how to set up the "pocket" device.[48] These are mapped in figure 3.17.

By comparison to the full map of his first day's work (fig. 3.16), this figure shows that far fewer number moves were needed to make the device produce phenomena. These are analyzed in table 2. Most are operations on an unambiguously material device: little conceptual work is needed to vary the setup to alter the phenomena produced. The ease of making and manipulating the effects makes them unambiguously natural phenomena rather than human products. Accounts in textbooks on electromagnetism that began to appear

47. See Faraday 1821, 1822a, 1822b.
48. See, for example, Faraday to G. de la Rive, 12 September 1821, in Williams et al., 1971, 122–24, and 16 November 1821, 128–29. By November the instructions read: "To make the apparatus act it is to be held upright with the iron pin downwards the north or south pole of a magnet to be placed in contact with the external end of the iron pin and then the wires of a voltaic combination connected one with the upper platinum wire the other with the lower pin or magnet. The wire within will then rotate if the apparatus is in order in which state I hope it will reach you. Good contacts are required in these experiments." (Ibid., 129.)

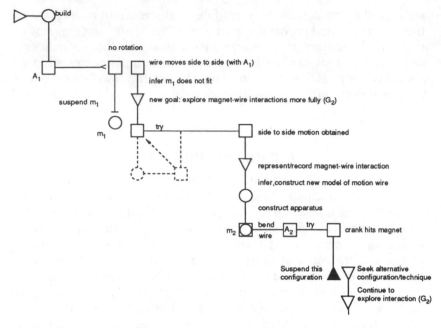

Figure 3.16 Discovery path for 3 September 1821 (Gooding 1990b) *Continued on facing page.*

during the 1820s are even briefer. Thus a new bit of the phenomenal world was worked into the experience and the language of other scientists.[49]

Putting Phenomena in Context

The experimental maps are not meant to reconstruct thought as a rational process. They show instead how intellect implicates and articulates the natural world, by situating thought in the context of empirical activity in a material and social world. The notation illustrates—in a way that a verbal narrative does not—that cognition and action are highly interactive. Every sequence is initiated by and ends with a problem and decision. More important still, every outcome is embedded in a sequence of procedures. This representation of experiment challenges the Cartesian divorce of the mental from the material, which has made the "connection" between thought,

49. These included some, such as Ampère and Biot—for whom theory and mathematical methods dictated that the rotations could not be physically significant phenomena; see Gooding 1990b, chapter 2.

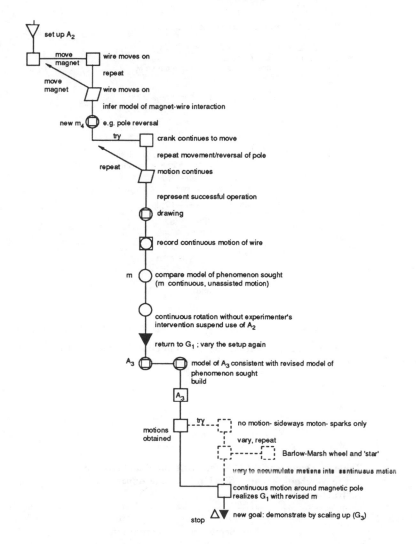

behavior, and the world so mysterious. Earlier I stressed the importance to models of discovery of the interaction of mental and material manipulations, and stressed that these are often *interdependent* (rather than distinct, interactive processes). This interdependence is represented by two properties of the procedural map: one is a property of the *whole map,* that is, its structure in two dimensions. The pattern of activity changes and we see its objects change (new models, artifacts, problems). The other property that expresses interdependence is inherent in the notation: neither the lines (representing procedures) nor the symbols (representing choices, decisions,

107

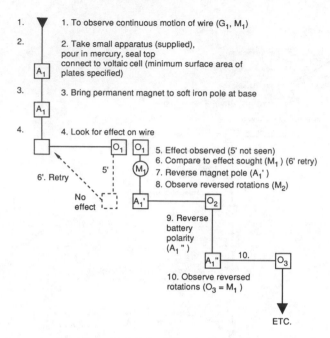

1. 1. To observe continuous motion of wire (G_1, M_1)

2. 2. Take small apparatus (supplied),
pour in mercury, seal top
connect to voltaic cell (minimum surface area of
plates specified)

A_1

3. 3. Bring permanent magnet to soft iron pole at base

A_1

4. 4. Look for effect on wire

O_1 O_1 5. Effect observed (5' not seen)
6. Compare to effect sought (M_1) (6' retry)
5' M_1 7. Reverse magnet pole (A_1')
6'. Retry 8. Observe reversed rotations (M_2)

No
effect A_1' O_2

9. Reverse
battery
polarity
(A_1'')

A_1'' 10. O_3

10. Observe reversed
rotations ($O_3 = M_1$)

ETC.

Figure 3.17   Map of Faraday's instructions for producing electromagnetic rotation with the portable apparatus (Gooding 1990b)

Table 2   Occurrence of Different Outcomes and Actions
in the Notebook Account (fig. 3.16) and the Apparatus
Instructions (fig. 3.17)

	Notebook for 3 September	Apparatus Instructions
Decision points	12	2
Outcomes		
Squares	16	10
Circles	6	1
Composite	6	0
Actions		
Vertical	25	8
Diagonal	3	(1)
Horizontal	10	3
Totals	78	24

108

events, objects, etc.) have any significance independently of the other. Thus—contrary to what many philosophers tacitly suppose—phenomena *always* appear as outcomes of human activity. No map begins or ends with a phenomenon; there are no disembodied acts and no meaningfully disembodied thoughts, decisions, or conclusions.

This shows something that received philosophies of science could not even contemplate, that natural phenomena are bounded by human activity. This consists of decisions and actions carried out with intellectual, practical, and material resources derived, to a greater or lesser extent, from work by other scientists. The maps enable us to show where such activity engages the material world that its representations purport to be about and (with further development) to show where it mainly engages other observers. The maps will also help to show how demonstrative structure and ontological distinctions are woven into the fabric of evidential arguments. In short, they display what historians and sociologists have been saying about science for some time: that all natural phenomena are bounded by human activity whose products express the culture in which it occurs.

REFERENCES

Ackermann, R. J. 1985. *Data, Instruments, and Theory: A Dialectical Approach to Understanding Science.* Princeton: Princeton University Press.

Arber, A. [1954] 1985. *The Mind and the Eye.* Cambridge: Cambridge University Press.

Bazerman, C. 1988. *Shaping Written Knowledge.* Madison: University of Wisconsin Press.

Beller, M. 1988. Experimental Accuracy, Operationalism, and the Limits of Knowledge—1925 to 1935. *Science in Context* 2: 147–62.

Bloor, D. 1983. *Wittgenstein: A Social Theory of Knowledge.* London: Macmillan.

Bobrow, D., and T. Winograd. 1989. Overview of KRL. In A. Clark, ed., *Microcognition: Philosophy, Cognitive Science, and Parallel Data Processing.* Cambridge: MIT Press.

Boyd, R. 1973. Realism, Underdetermination, and a Causal Theory of Evidence. *Nous* 7: 1–12.

Brown, J. R. 1982. The Miracle of Science. *Philosophical Quarterly* 32: 232–44.

Collins, H. M. 1985. *Changing Order: Replication and Induction in Scientific Practice.* Beverly Hills: Sage.

Donovan, A., L. Laudan, and R. Laudan, eds. 1988. *Scrutinizing Science: Empirical Studies of Scientific Change.* Boston: Kluwer Academic, 3–44.

Edge, D., ed., 1964. *Experiment: A Series of Scientific Case Histories.* London: BBC.

Faraday, M. 1821. On Some New Electromagnetical Motions, and on the Theory of Magnetism. *Quarterly Journal of Science* 12: 74–96. Reprinted in Faraday 1839–55, vol. 2.

———. 1822a. Electro-Magnetic Rotation Apparatus. *Quarterly Journal of Science* 12: 186. Reprinted in Faraday 1839–55, vol. 2.

———. 1822b. Description of an Electro-Magnetical Apparatus for the Exhibition of Rotatory Motion. *Quarterly Journal of Science* 12: 283–85. Reprinted in Faraday 1839–55, vol 2.

Franklin, A. 1986. *The Neglect of Experiment.* Cambridge: Cambridge University Press.

Galison, P. 1987. *How Experiments End.* Chicago: University of Chicago Press.

Giere, R. 1988. *Explaining Science: A Cognitive Approach.* Chicago: University of Chicago Press.

Gooding, D. 1982. Empiricism in Practice: Teleology, Economy, and Observation in Faraday's Physics. *Isis* 73: 46–67.

———. 1986. How Do Scientists Reach Agreement about Novel Observations? *Studies in History and Philosophy of Science* 17: 205–30.

———. 1989a. "Magnetic Curves" and the Magnetic Field: Experimentation and Representation in the History of a Theory. In Gooding, Pinch, and Schaffer, 1989, 183–223.

———. 1989b. History in the Laboratory: Can We Tell What Really Went On? In F. James, ed., *The Development of the Laboratory: Essays on the Place of Experiment in Industrial Civilization.* London: Macmillan. New York: American Institute of Physics, 1989, 63–82.

———. 1990a. Mapping Experiment as a Learning Process. *Science, Technology, and Human Values* 15: 165–201.

———. 1990b. *Experiment and the Making of Meaning.* Boston: Kluwer Academic.

Gooding, D., and F. A. J. L. James, eds. 1985. *Faraday Rediscovered: Essays on the Life and Work of Michael Faraday, 1791–1867.* London: Macmillan: Reprinted 1989: Macmillan and American Institute of Physics.

Gooding, D, T. J. Pinch, and S. Schaffer, eds. 1989. *The Uses of Experiment: Studies in the Natural Sciences.* Cambridge: Cambridge University Press.

Hacking, I. 1983. *Representing and Intervening: Introductory Topics in the Philosophy of Natural Science.* Cambridge: Cambridge University Press.

Harré, R. 1981. *Great Scientific Experiments.* Oxford: Phaidon.

Holmes, F. L. 1987. Scientific Writing and Scientific Discovery. *Isis* 78: 220–35.

Jardine, N. 1978. Realistic Realism and the Philosophy of Science. In C. Hookway and P. Pettit, eds., *Action and Interpretation.* Cambridge: Cambridge University Press, 107–25.

Kuhn, T. S. 1961. The Function of Measurement in Modern Physical Science. *Isis* 52: 161–90. Reprinted in Kuhn 1977.

———. 1962. A Function for Thought Experiments. In *L'aventure de la science, Mélanges Alexandre Koyré*. Paris: Hermann. Vol. 2, 307–334. Reprinted in Kuhn 1977.

———. 1974. Second Thoughts on Paradigms. In Suppe 1974, 459–82.

———. 1977. *The Essential Tension*. Chicago: University of Chicago Press.

Lakatos, I. 1970. Falsification and the Methodology of Scientific Research Programmes. In Lakatos and A. Musgrave, eds., *Criticism and the Growth of Knowledge*. Cambridge: Cambridge University Press, 91–196.

Laudan, R. 1988. Testing Theories of Scientific Change. In Donovan et al., 1988, 3–44.

Lenoir, T. 1988. Practice, Reason, Context: The Dialogue between Theory and Experiment. *Science in Context* 2: 3–22.

Martin, T. 1932–36. *Faraday's Diary: Being the Various Philosophical Notes of Experimental Investigation Made by Michael Faraday, DCL, FRS, during the Years 1820–1862*. 7 vols. and index. London: G. Bell & Sons.

Medawar, P. 1963. Is the Scientific Paper a Fraud? *The Listener*. 12 September 1963, 377–78. Reprinted in Edge, 1964.

Naylor, R. 1989. Galileo's Experimental Discourse. In Gooding, Pinch, and Schaffer 1989, 117–34.

Nickles, T. 1988. Reconstructing Science: Discovery and Experiment. In D. Batcns and J. P. van Bendegem, eds., *Theory and Experiment*. Boston: Reidel, 33–53.

Pickering, A. 1981. The Hunting of the Quark. *Isis* 72: 216–36.

———. 1984. *Constructing Quarks: A Sociological History of Particle Physics*. Chicago: University of Chicago Press.

———. 1989. Living in the Material World. In Gooding, Pinch, and Schaffer, 1989, 275–297.

Pinch, T. 1985. Theory-Testing in Science—The Case of Solar Neutrinos: Do Crucial Experiments Test Theories or Theorists? *Philosophy of the Social Sciences* 15: 167–87.

Popper, K. R. 1959. *The Logic of Scientific Discovery*. London: Hutchinson.

Putnam, H. 1974. The "Corroboration" of Theories. In P. A. Schilpp, ed., *The Philosophy of Karl Popper*. La Salle: Open Court. Vol. 1, 221–40.

———. 1975. The Meaning of Meaning. In K. Gunderson, ed., *Language, Mind, and Knowledge*. Minneapolis: University of Minnesota Press, 131–93.

———. 1982. Three Kinds of Scientific Realism. *Philosophical Quarterly* 32: 195–200.

Quine, W. V. O. 1960. *Word and Object*, Cambridge: MIT Press.

Radder, H. 1988. *The Material Realization of Science*. Assen: van Gorckum.

Rescher, N. 1980. Scientific Truth and the Arbitrament of Praxis. *Nous* 14: 59–74.

Rouse, J. 1987. *Knowledge and Power. Towards a Political Philosophy of Science.* Ithaca: Cornell University Press.

Ryle, G. 1949. *The Concept of Mind.* London: Hutchinson.

Schaffer, S. 1989. Glass Works: Newton's Prisms and the Uses of Experiment. In Gooding, Pinch, and Schaffer 1989, 67–104.

Shapin, S., and S. Schaffer. *Leviathan and the Air-pump: Hobbes, Boyle and the Experimental Life.* Princeton: Princeton University Press.

Suppe, F. 1974. The Search for Philosophic Understanding of Scientific Theories. In F. Suppe, ed., *The Structure of Scientific Theories.* Urbana: University of Illinois Press, 3–232.

van Fraassen, B. 1980. *The Scientific Image.* Oxford: Oxford University Press.

Watkins, J. W. N. 1964. Confession is Good for Ideas. In Edge 1964, 64–70.

Williams, L. P. 1985. Faraday and Ampère: A Critical Dialogue. In Gooding and James 1985, 83–104.

Williams, L. P., et al., eds. 1971. *The Selected Correspondence of Michael Faraday.* 2 vols. Cambridge: Cambridge University Press.

Wise, M. N. 1979. William Thomson's Mathematical Route to Energy Conservation: A Case Study of the Role of Mathematics in Concept Formation. *Historical Studies in the Physical Sciences* 10: 49–83.

Worrall, J. 1989. Fresnel, Poisson, and the White Spot: The Role of Successful Predictions in the Acceptance of Scientific Theories. In Gooding, Pinch, and Schaffer 1989, 135–57.

4

The Couch, the Cathedral, and the Laboratory: On the Relationship between Experiment and Laboratory in Science

Karin Knorr Cetina

Introduction

Scientific laboratories have become a popular subject in social studies of contemporary science. From a status of nearly complete neglect only one decade ago they have risen to the center of analysts' attention and have given their name to a whole approach in the new sociology of science. Part of the reason for this surely lies in the general reorientation of the field in the early seventies, as a consequence of which sociologists have begun to include in their study the technical content of science and the "hard core" of scientific activity, the process of knowledge production. But this is not the whole story. In many ways the notion of a scientific laboratory in sociology of science stands for what in history and methodology of science has long been the notion of "experiment." Why should sociologists, latecomers to the study of science, choose a focus that is so clearly different from the one that earlier fields have found useful? And is there a theoretically interesting difference between the notion of an experiment and the notion of a laboratory? Or have the different fields merely chosen different labels for what is basically an orientation to the same phenomenon, knowledge production?

I shall seek an answer to this question by drawing upon the literature on laboratories and upon my own recent research in particle physics and molecular genetics.[1] My strategy in developing an answer will be twofold. I shall first summarize the theoretical relevance of the notion of a laboratory as compared to received notions of experiment. I shall argue that far from being just the physical space in which experiments are conducted, laboratories have

A short version of this paper was presented at the annual meeting of the Society for Social Studies of Science, Irvine, California, 14–19 November 1989. The research for the paper was supported by a grant from the Deutsche Forschungsgemeinschaft and was conducted with the help of the Center for Science Studies, University of Bielefeld. I want to thank Andrew Pickering, Klaus Amann, and Stefan Hirschauer for their helpful comments on an earlier version of the paper.
   1. This work is summarized in Amann 1990 and Knorr Cetina 1992.

emerged as carrying a systematic "weight" in our understanding of science.[2] This weight can be linked to the reconfiguration of the natural and social order which in my opinion constitutes a laboratory. In the second part of the paper I shall show how the instrumental shape of laboratories differs across areas of investigation in connection with these reconfigurations, and how this is associated with the "technology" employed in experimentation. As a consequence of this situation, laboratories and experiments combine differently in different fields: for example, each may be the principal agent that defines the situation, or both may be equals in a segmentary organization.

The Theoretical Relevance of Laboratories: The Malleability of Natural Objects

Why should the study of laboratories be important to the study of science, and what do laboratories account for that is not accounted for by experiment? It seems that experiments have until recently carried much of the epistemological burden in explaining the validity of scientific results and rational belief in science. This has been largely unquestioned, and it is founded upon methodology rather than upon the history or sociology of experimentation. The advantages attributed to experiments on methodological grounds include the fact that experiments disentangle variables and test them in isolation, that they use comparison and justify results through replication, or that they exclude, through blind or double-blind designs, experimenter bias and subjective expectations. As a result, experiments were thought to be capable of establishing or disestablishing hypotheses and of deciding, as crucial experiments, between competing theories. With this methodological rationale in place, the real-time processes of experimentation in different fields and at different times remained largely unexamined.[3]

When the first laboratory studies turned to the notion of a laboratory, they opened up a new field of investigation not covered by

2. This weight has not been systematically spelled out in recent surveys of the field. For examples of such surveys, see Knorr Cetina and Mulkay 1983, Giere 1988, and Cole 1990.

3. While this has recently changed on a noticeable scale, it has changed in the wake of laboratory studies and the turn toward the cultural study of scientific work which they promoted, and in the wake of other approaches within the new sociology of science. For an example of recent studies of experimentation, see Gooding et al. 1989. For some earlier cultural studies of experimentation see Collins 1975, Pickering 1984, and Shapin and Schaffer 1985.

114

the methodology of experimentation. For them the notion of a laboratory played a role which the notion of experiment, given its methodological entrenchment, could not fulfill: it shifted the focus away from methodology and toward the study of the cultural activity of science. The focus upon laboratories has allowed us to consider experimental activity within the wider context of equipment and symbolic practices within which the conduct of science is located without reverting to the traditional concerns of the study of scientific organizations. In other words, the study of laboratories has brought to the fore the full spectrum of activities involved in the production of knowledge. It showed that scientific objects are not only "technically" manufactured in laboratories but are also inextricably symbolically or politically construed, for example, through literary techniques of persuasion such as one finds embodied in scientific papers, through the political stratagems of scientists in forming alliances and mobilizing resources, or through the selections and decision translations which "build" scientific findings from within.[4] An implication of this has been the awareness that in reaching its goals, research "intervenes" (to use Hacking's terminology)[5] not only in the natural world but also—and deeply—in the social world. Another implication is that the products of science themselves have come to be seen as cultural entities rather than as natural givens discovered by science. If the practices observed in laboratories were cultural in the sense that they could not be reduced to the application of methodological rules, the facts which were the consequence of these practices also had to be seen as shaped by culture.

Thus the laboratory has served as the place in which the separate concerns of methodology and other areas such as organizational sociology could be seen as dissolved in cultural practices which were neither methodological nor social-organizational but something else that needed to be conceptualized and that encompassed an abundance of activities and aspects that social studies of science had not previously concerned themselves with. But the significance of the

---

4. The laboratory studies which have argued these points most forcefully are by Latour and Woolgar (1979), Knorr (1977); Knorr Cetina (1981), Zenzen and Restivo (1982), and Lynch (1985). For an illustration of the political nature of science see also Shapin 1979 and Wade 1981. For a more anthropological study of scientific laboratories see Traweek 1988.

5. Hacking (1983) draws a distinction between experiments which "intervene" and scientific theories which "represent." This distinction, however, does not give adequate weight to the instrumental use of theories in experimentation or to the fact that some experiments, as we shall see later, focus upon representation rather than intervention.

notion of a laboratory lies not only in the fact that it has opened up this field of investigation and offered a cultural framework for plowing this field. It lies also in the fact that the laboratory itself has become a theoretical notion in our understanding of science. According to this perspective, the laboratory is itself an important agent of scientific development. In relevant studies, the laboratory is the locus of mechanisms and processes which can be taken to account for the success of science. Characteristically, these mechanisms and processes are nonmethodological and mundane. They appear to have nothing to do with a special scientific logic of procedure, with rationality, or with what is generally meant by "validation." The hallmark of these mechanisms and processes is that they imply, to use Merleau-Ponty's terminology, a reconfiguration of the system of "self-others-things," of the "phenomenal field" in which experience is made in science.[6] As a consequence of these reconfigurations, the structure of symmetry relationships which obtains between the social order and the natural order, between actors and environments, is changed. To be sure, it is changed only temporarily and within the walls of the laboratory. But it appears to be changed in ways which yield epistemic profit for science.

What do I mean by the reconfiguration of the system of "self-others-things," and how does this reconfiguration come about? The system of self-others-things for Merleau-Ponty is not the objective world independent of human actors or the inner world of subjective impressions, but the world-experienced-by or the world-related-to agents.[7] What laboratory studies suggest is that the laboratory is a means of changing the world-related-to-agents in ways which allow scientists to capitalize on their human constraints and sociocultural restrictions. The laboratory is an enhanced environment which improves upon the natural order in relation to the social order. How does this improvement come about? Laboratory studies suggest that it rests upon the *malleability* of natural objects. Laboratories use the phenomenon that objects are not fixed entities which have to be taken as they are or left to themselves. In fact, laboratories rarely work with objects as they occur in nature. Rather they work with object images or with their visual, auditory, electrical, etc., traces, with their components, their extractions, their purified versions.

6. Merleau-Ponty's original notion in the French version of his book is "le système 'Moi-Autrui-les choses'" (1945, 69). For the English translation and the exposition of this concept see Merleau-Ponty (1962, chap. 5, and p. 57).

7. For example, a culture in which artificial light is available will have a means of extending the day and as a consequence will experience the world differently than a culture without artificial light.

There are at least three features of natural objects which a laboratory science does not need to accomodate: First, it does not need to put up with the object *as it is;* it can substitute all of its less literal or partial versions, as illustrated above. Second, it does not need to accommodate the natural object *where it is,* anchored in a natural environment; laboratory sciences bring objects *home* and manipulate them on their own terms in the laboratory. Third, a laboratory science does not need to accomodate an event *when it happens;* it does not need to put up with natural cycles of occurrence but can try to make them happen frequently enough for continuous study. Of course the history of science is also a history of varying opportunities and successes in accomplishing these transitions. But it should be clear that it is escaping the need to accommodate objects within the natural order which laboratory studies suggest is epistemically advantageous; it is the detachment of the objects from a natural environment and their installation in a new phenomenal field defined by social agents.

Consider an example. Astronomy by common definition used to be something like a field science. For a long time, astronomers were restricted to observation, even though since Galileo it was observation aided by a telescope. Now for more than a century astronomers have also used an imaging technology, the photographic plate, with the help of which photons of light emitted by stellar bodies can be captured and analyzed. Astronomy therefore appears to have been transformed from a science which surveys natural phenomena into a science which processes images of phenomena. Further developments of imaging technology since 1976 have resulted in a replacement of the photographic plate by CCD (charge-coupled device) chips.[8] For example, the light of Halley's comet in 1982 was collected by the gigantic two-hundred-inch mirror of the Hale telescope on Mount Palomar and was focused on CCDs. CCD chips constitute a major change in imaging technology. They have digitalized outputs and thus enable astronomers to transfer and process their data electronically. If CCDs are used with space telescopes, they not only improve astronomers' data but they render astronomy completely independent of the direct observation of its field. Once the transition is complete, astronomy will have been transformed from an observational field science to an image-processing laboratory science.[9]

---

8. See Smith and Tatarewicz 1985 for a summary of this development.

9. I leave open the question, which cannot be answered at this point, of whether all of scientific astronomy will switch to space telescopes. It is likely that, as with

What reconfiguration of the phenomenal field of astronomy is achieved in this process of transformation? At least the following changes are apparent:

1. Through being imaged, the objects of investigation become detached from their natural environment and are made to be continually present and available for inquiry in the laboratory; through digitalization and computer networks, the availability of the same data is extended to potentially the whole of the scientific community;

2. Through the transition to a literary technology, the processes of interest to astronomers become miniaturized;

3. Planetary and stellar time scales become social-order time scales. Astronomers all over the world who are connected to the electronic networks can now process and analyze stellar and planetary responses in parallel and continually.

The point is that with all these changes, astronomy still has not become an experimental science. The processes described all pertain to laboratories; they enable investigations to be performed in one place, without regard to natural conditions (e.g., weather, seasonal changes, regional differences in visibility, etc.), subject only to the contingencies of local situations (e.g., to the speed and the local resources that scientists can bring to bear on the work). In other words, laboratories allow for some kind of homing in of natural processes; the processes are "brought home" and made subject only to the local conditions of the social order. The power of the laboratory (but of course also its restrictions) resides precisely in its enculturation of natural objects. The laboratory subjects natural conditions to a social overhaul and derives epistemic effects from the new situation.

Playing upon the Social Order: Enhanced Agents

But laboratories not only improve upon the natural order; they also upgrade the social order in the laboratory, in a sense which has been neglected in the literature on laboratories. Received notions of science conceived of the social as extraneous and possibly averse to science. As Bloor (1976, 141) points out, social factors were brought into the picture only to explain incorrect scientific results but never to explain correct ones. The new sociology of science has eliminated this "asymmetry" in favor of models which stress the interweaving

---

older observational technologies, photographic-plate astronomy, just like observation through hand-manipulated telescopes, will become a "backyard" astronomy.

of social and scientific interests (e.g., MacKenzie 1981; Pickering 1984) and generally consider social and political strategies as part and parcel of scientists' conduct (e.g., Latour 1987). Yet studies of laboratory science have failed to specify how features of the social world, and more generally of everyday life, become played upon and turned into epistemic devices in the production of knowledge. Phrased differently, the social is not merely "also there" in science. Rather, it is capitalized upon and upgraded to become an instrument of scientific work. If we see laboratory processes as processes which align the natural order with the social order by creating reconfigured, "workable" objects in relation to agents of a given time and place, we also have to see how laboratories install "reconfigured" scientists who become workable (feasible) in relation to these objects. In the laboratory, it is not the scientist who is the counterpart of these objects. Rather it is agents enhanced in various ways so as to fit a particular emerging order of self-other-things, a particular ethnomethodology of a phenomenal field. Not only objects but also scientists are malleable with respect to a spectrum of behavioral possibilities. In the laboratory, scientists are "methods" of going about inquiry; they are part of a field's research strategy and a technical device in the production of knowledge.

How are aspects of the social order being reconfigured? Consider the scientist turned into a measurement device. By common assent, consciousness and perhaps also intentionality are defining characteristics of human beings. For example, many of the demarcationist battles waged against the programs and promises of artificial intelligence rest upon arguments from human consciousness and intentionality and draw out their manifold implications (e.g., Searle 1983). Since the computer is not a conscious, intentional actor—or so the argument goes—it will never develop the full mental capacities of human agents. Or consider one of the most basic concepts in the social sciences, the concept of action. There appears to be no definition of action which does not presuppose (conscious) intentions. In fact, meaningful intentions serve as the distinguishing characteristic which differentiates action from behavior, and which thereby delimits what is of interest to social science and what is not. Yet in molecular biology laboratories, scientists are often featured in ways which contradict these assumptions. For example, scientists figure prominently as *repositories of unconscious experience* whose responsibility it is to develop an embodied sense for resolving certain problem situations. These situations obtain when a circular relationship between procedure and outcome arises such that to optimize a methodological procedure one would have to know its out-come, but of course to get to know the outcome is the whole point of optimizing the procedure.

Let me give an example.[10] In molecular genetics, gel electropho-resis is a method for separating DNA and RNA fragments of differ-ent lengths in a gel on which an X-ray film is exposed. As a result of the procedure, one gets blackish and whitish bands which are most clearly distinguishable in the middle of the matrix which the film represents; at the bottom of the film, bands tend to be drawn apart, and on top they tend to stick together and may in fact become indis-tinguishable. Thus, to obtain a good resolution and highly analyz-able and publishable results, one should place the bands of interest in the middle of the matrix. And to achieve this, the gel run must be stopped exactly when the fragments of interest appear in the right place—which, however, is possible only if one knows the length of the expected fragments (and bands) in advance. But this, of course, is never the case, since it is precisely the goal of the gel run to deter-mine the length of the fragments one is interested in. Thus the cir-cular relationship between gel run and its outcome results from the fact that the optics of the gel can only be optimized through knowl-edge of the expected bands, while at the same time the optics is already presupposed in any attempt to determine the bands.

There are several ways in which we can deal with this situation. For example, we can break up the circle by dividing it into its com-ponents and then run several subtests simultaneously in order to place limits around what will be a likely outcome; to know the range of likely outcomes is often sufficient to adequately fine-tune a method. Thus scientists can try to identify the procedure most likely to yield optimum results by varying the crucial ingredients and running many tests in parallel before choosing a final method. Alternatively to the breakup strategy, we can choose a framing strategy to deal with the problem, for example, by turning to theory or computer simulation to discover the likely range of the results of interest. Molecular biologists mostly do not do simulations, and there are no phenomenological theories closely linked to experi-ments such that they would be helpful for molecular biologists. Hence the framing strategy is not an option. On the other hand, molecular biologists do not want to use the circle breakup strategy either. Their reluctance is based on the shared assumption that sys-

10. For a full ethnography of the molecular biology laboratory from which this and other examples in this paper are derived, see Amann 1990.

tematic breakup strategies are too time-consuming. For example, running several subtests simultaneously to determine an optimum procedure usually means not only that there are more tests to be performed but also that the number of preparatory steps needed to obtain the reaction mixes for the subtests grows by a factor x, and depending on how many steps are involved in preparing a reaction mix, the total number of tasks can be large. Molecular biologists reason that it is not only the number of tasks that grows proportionately with such a strategy. Also each step in a multiply layered procedure would be affected by the difficulty and uncertainty of having to work in the absence of appropriately delimited expectations, and thus each step would be subject to the same sources of error as the original problem. The susceptibility to error multiplies with the number of steps.

Given such reasoning, molecular biologists situate themselves somewhere between what they perceive as the methodical-systematic strategy of breaking up the circle and the framing strategy which I described above. The intermediate method which they turn to is that of the *holistic gloss:* they leave it to individual scientists to develop a sense for a reasonable strategy in response to the challenge. Scientists are expected to make a good guess about what procedure might work best and to thereby optimize procedures holistically (without attempting systematic optimization of substeps) and locally (without recourse to procedurally external sources like theory or simulation). The required sense of successful procedure draws heavily upon an individual's experience: upon the prognostic knowledge which individuals must somehow synthesize from features of their previous experience, and which remains implicit, embodied, and encapsulated within the person. It is a knowledge which draws upon scientists' *bodies* rather than their minds. Consciousness and even intentionality are left out of the picture. And there is no native theory as to what this body without mind is doing, or should be doing, when it develops sense.

My point is that we have to be prepared to encounter scientists who function as instruments or objects in the laboratory, or as illustrated elsewhere, as collective organisms, just as we have to be prepared to encounter organisms that have been transformed into images, extractions, or agents. By the time the reconfigurations of self-others-things which constitute laboratories have taken place, we are confronted with a new emerging order that is neither social nor natural, an order whose components have mixed genealogies and continue to change shape as laboratory work goes on.

Types of Reconfigurations: From Laboratory to Experiment

What I have said so far refers to laboratory processes in general. I have neglected the phenomenon whereby concrete laboratory reconfigurations are shaped in relation to the kind of work which goes on within the laboratory. This is where experiments come into the picture; through the technology they use, experiments embody and respond to reconfigurations of the natural and social order. In this section, I will draw attention to three different types of laboratories and experiment in the contemporary sciences of particle physics, molecular biology, and the social sciences. In distinguishing between these types, I shall take as my starting point the constructions placed upon natural objects in these different areas of science and their embodiment in the respective technologies of experimentation. I want to show how, in connection with these different constructions, laboratories and experiments become very different entities and enter very different kinds of relationships with each other. For one thing, laboratories and experiments can encompass more-or-less distinctive, more-or-less independent activities: they can be assembled into separate characters which confront and play upon each other, or disassembled to the degree to which they appear to be mere aspects of one another.[11] For another thing, the relationship between local scientific practice and environment also changes as laboratories and experiments are differently assembled. In other words, reconfigurations of the natural and social order can in fact *not* be entirely contained in the laboratory space. Scientific fields are composed of more than one laboratory and more than one experiment; the reconfigurations established in local units have implications for the kind of relationship which emerges between these units, and beyond.

In the following, I shall only document some of these issues in a most cursory manner. My point is to draw attention to and to illustrate some of these matters rather than to provide a full analysis of a complex issue.[12] What I want to draw attention to in this section are the diverse *meanings* of "experiment" and "laboratory" which are indicated in different reconfigurations, and which have been gen-

11. It is clear that we can have laboratories without experiments as traditionally understood, as in the science of astronomy or in the many cases of nonresearch laboratories in which specimens are merely tested. And we know that experiments may occur in nonlaboratory settings, for example, as natural experiments. But even when laboratories and experiments tend to go together, as in the examples to be discussed, there can be different matches and combinations.

12. For a detailed analysis and documentation of these issues, see Knorr Cetina 1992.

erally ignored in recent empirical studies of science.[13] I want to indicate the differential significance and the mutual relationship of laboratories and experiments in three situations, which I distinguish in terms of whether they use a technology of representation, a technology of treatments and interventions, or a technology of signification. The construction placed upon the objects of research varies accordingly; in the first case, objects in the laboratory are *representations* of real-world phenomena; in the second, they are *processed partial versions* of these phenomena; in the third, they are *signatures* of the events of interest to science. Note that the distinctions drawn are not meant to point to some essential differences between fields but rather attempt to capture how objects are primarily featured and attended to in different areas of research. To illustrate the differences, and to emphasize the continuity between mechanisms at work within science and outside of it, I shall first draw upon examples of laboratories and experimentation invoked outside natural science, those of the psychoanalyst's couch, the twelfth-and-thirteenth century cathedral, and the military war game.

Experiments (almost) without laboratory: construing objects as representations

I begin with the war game. The hallmark of a war game in the past was that it took place on a sand table, a kind of sandbox on legs in which the geographic features of a potential battle area were built out of sand and whole battles were fought between hostile toy armies. The setup and the action were similar to the actual terrain and the likely movements of soldiers. The landscape made of sand had to be modeled on the supposed spot of a real enemy engagement in all relevant respects, and the movements made by the toy armies had to correspond as closely as possible to the expected moves of real soldiers. The war game in the sandbox was an invention of the eighteenth century which was developed further by Prussian generals. Its modern equivalent is the computer simulation. This has become widely used not only in the military but in many areas of science in which real tryouts are impracticable for one reason or another. Computer simulations are also increasingly used in laboratory sciences to simulate experiments; indeed, the computer has been called a laboratory in descriptions of this development (e.g., Hut and Sussman 1987).

13. Philosophers have started to devote some attention to the issue. See, among others, Hacking 1983.

The point here is that many real-time laboratory experiments bear exactly the same kind of relationship to the reality they deal with as the war game on the sand table bears to the real engagement, or the computer simulation bears to the action that is simulated: they *represent* the action. As an example, consider most experiments in the social sciences, particularly in social psychology, in economics, in research on problem-solving, and the like. To illustrate, experimental research on jury decision making uses mock juries; in these experiments, participants (mostly college students) are asked to reach judgments on a simulated trial.[14] Research on the heuristics of problem solving sets up simulated problem situations and asks participants to search for a solution to the problem.[15] Social science experiments, as is well known, characteristically get the same criticism as computer simulations: what is usually questioned is whether generalizable results can be reached by studying mock reality behaviors when the factors distinguishing this mock reality from real-time events are not known or have not been assessed.

Aware of this criticism, researchers in these areas take great care to design experimental reality so that in all relevant respects they come close to perceived real-time processes. In other words, they exemplify and deploy a *technology of representation.* For example, they set up a system of assurances through which correct correspondence with the world is monitored, and they set up procedures designed to implement the proper performance simulation of the world. One outstanding characteristic of this system of assurances is that it is based on a theory of nonintervention. In blind and double-blind designs, researchers attempt to eradicate the very possibility that the researcher will influence the outcomes of the experiments. In fact experimental design consists in, on the one hand, implementing a world simulation and, on the other hand, implementing a thorough separation between the action of experimental subjects, which is to take its natural course, and the action, interests, and interpretations of the researchers.

Consider the laboratory in these situations. It does not as a rule involve a richly elaborated space, a place densely stacked with instruments and materials and populated by researchers. In many social sciences, the laboratory reduces to the provision of a one-way mirror in a room that includes perhaps a table and some seating

14. An example of this kind of research can be found in MacCoun 1989.
15. For a review of the literature in this area, see, for example, Kahneman, Slovic, and Tversky 1982.

facilities. In fact, experiments may be conducted in researchers' offices when a one-way mirror is not essential. But even when a separate laboratory space exists, it tends to become activated only when an experiment is conducted, which, given the short duration and special "entitivity" of such experiments, happens only rarely. The laboratory is a virtual space and in most respects coextensive with the experiment. Like a stage on which plays are performed from time to time, the laboratory is a storage room for the stage props that are needed when social life is instantiated through experiments. The objects which are featured on the stage are players of the social form. The hallmark of their reconfiguration seems to be that they are called upon to be performers of everyday life, to be competent to behave under laboratory conditions true to the practice of real-time members of daily life.

Laboratories come of age: the construal of objects as processing materials

Consider now a second example from outside the sciences. In the twelfth and thirteenth centuries, cathedrals were built in Paris, Canterbury, Saint Denis (an abbey church), and later in Chartres, Bourges and other places, that were modeled upon earlier, smaller churches. Between them they demonstrate a rapid transmission of design innovations, manifest, for example, in the spread of the flying buttress.[16] After structural analyses of these churches, Mark and Clark argue that "cathedral builders learned from experience, using the actual buildings in the way today's engineer relies on instrumental prototypes" (1984, 144). The builders seemed to have observed wind pressure damage and cracking in the mortar of older churches, flaws in the original buttressing scheme, the flow of light, and generally how a particular design held up in relation to its purpose and usage.

The point about learning from wind pressure damage to cathedral towers by changing the structure of the buildings in response to their observed deficiencies is that on the one hand a system of surveillance must have existed which permitted those participating in the observational circuit to build upon (rather than to deplore, find who was guilty of, ignore, or otherwise deal with) mistakes. Since there were at the time no design drawings which were circulated, the system of surveillance must have depended on travel between

16. For a detailed analysis of buttressing patterns and apparent spread of information between building sites, see Mark and Clark 1984.

cathedrals and on communication of orally transmitted observations. The observation circuit together with the actual buildings acted as a kind of laboratory (Mark and Clark 1984) in which builders experimented. But the second point is that experimenting in this laboratory consisted of changing architectural designs and building cathedrals accordingly. In other words, it involved *manipulation* of the object under study, a sequence of cures classified today as architectural innovations. Consider now a typical experimental setup in a molecular genetics bench laboratory which focuses on gene transcription and translation. Like the work of twelfth-century cathedral building, the work in this laboratory is not concerned with stage playing a reality from somewhere else. The most notable feature of experimentation in this laboratory is that it subjects specimens and substances to procedural manipulations. In other words, experimentation deploys and implements a technology of intervention. For example, a routine procedure in such a laboratory is DNA hybridization, in which genes are isolated and then used to identify other genes of the same kind. In this procedure, scientists chemically cut double-stranded DNA from a particular species into fragments, then separate the fragments by size, and clone them on a lawn of bacteria. Once the clones have multiplied, the plaques which form are transferred to a filter, and the DNA on the filter is chemically separated into single strands and exposed to a radioactively labeled probe which contains single-stranded DNA from the gene through which the DNA on the filter is supposed to be identified. Then the unbound probe is removed and a photographic film exposed on the dish with the plaques to determine whether the probe did in fact bind, that is, identify the probed DNA as structurally similar. Finally, dark spots on the film which indicate binding sites are aligned with the corresponding plaques to show which of the plaques on the dish contain the targeted genes.

With a view to the reconfiguration of objects, the hallmark of this experimental technology is that it treats natural objects as *processing materials,* as *transitory object states* which correspond to no more than a temporary pause in a series of transformations. Objects are decomposable entities from which effects can be extracted through appropriate treatment; they are ingredients for processing *programs* which are the real threads running through the laboratory.[17] Objects are subject to tens, and often hundreds, of separately attended to *interferences* with their "natural" makeup, and so are

17. For an elaboration of the role of treatment programs in a medical field, see Hirschauer 1991.

the natural sequences of events in which objects take part. Through these interferences, natural objects are smashed into fragments, made to evaporate into gases, dissolved in acids, reduced to extractions, mixed up with countless substances, shaken, heated and frozen, reconstituted, and rebred into workable agents. In short, they are fashioned as working materials subject to almost any imaginable intrusion and usurpation, never more than a stage in a transition from one material state to another. The transitions effected during experimentation are not intended to imitate similar transitions in nature. Rather, they are intended to generate or explore a particular effect. There is no assumption that the transitory object states obtained in the laboratory and the manipulations which generate these objects correspond to or are supposed to correspond to natural events. Consequently the conclusions derived from such experiments are not justified in terms of the equivalence of the experiments to real-world processes.[18] And the assurances installed with such experiments do not set up a separation between experimentor and experiment. They are not based on a doctrine of noninterference by the experimenter and object integrity, which sees objects of experiments as not-to-be-tampered-with performances of natural courses of events. And how could such a doctrine be warranted if the whole point of experimentation is to influence the materials of the experiment through direct or indirect manipulation by the researcher.

If we now turn to the laboratories within which the manipulation takes place, it comes as no surprise that they are not, as in the first case, storage rooms for stage props. It seems that it is precisely with the above-mentioned processing approach and object configuration that laboratories *come of age* and are established as distinctive and separate entities. What kind of entities? Take the classical case of a bench laboratory as exemplified in molecular genetics. This bench laboratory is always activated; it is an actual space in which research tasks are performed continuously and simultaneously. The laboratory has become a *workshop* and a *nursery* with which specific goals and activities are associated. In the laboratory, different plant and animal materials are maintained, bred, nourished, kept warm, observed, prepared for experimental manipulation, and generally tended and cared for. They are surrounded by equipment and apparatus and are used themselves as technical devices to producing experimental effects. The laboratory is a repository of processing

18. Though of course there are such experiments in the biological sciences, like the ones which attempt to simulate the origin of life.

materials and devices which continuously feed into experimentation. More generally, laboratories are objects of work and attention
over and above experiments. Laboratories employ caretaking person-
nel for the sole purpose of tending to the waste, the used glassware,
the test animals, the apparatus, the preparatory and maintenance
tasks of the lab. Scientists are not only researchers but spend part of
their time as caretakers of the laboratory. Certain kinds of work *on*
the laboratory becomes focused in laboratory leaders who tend to
spend much of their time representing, promoting, and recruiting for
"their" laboratory. In fact, laboratories are also social and political
structures which "belong" to leaders and provide for the career goal
of "heading one's own laboratory." Laboratories become identified
in terms of their leaders; they are the outfits installed for senior
scientists and a measure of successful scientific careers. Thus the
proliferation of laboratories as objects of work is associated with the
emergence of a two-tier system of laboratory-level and experiment-
level social organization of agents and activities. Experiments, however, tend to have little entitivity. In fact, they appear to be dissolved
into processing activities parts of which are occasionally pulled together for the purpose of publication. As laboratories gain symbolic
distinctiveness and become a focus of activities, experiments lose
some of the wholeness and unity they display in social science
fields. When the laboratory becomes a permanent facility, experiments can be conducted continuously and in parallel, and begin to
blend into each other. Thus experiments dissolve into experimental
work, which in turn is continuous with laboratory-level work.

But there is also a further aspect which is of interest in regard to
the permanent installation of laboratories as internal processing environments. This has to do with the phenomenon that laboratories
now are collective units which encapsulate within themselves a
traffic of substances, materials and equipment, and observations. In
other words, the laboratory houses within itself the circuits of observation and the traffic of experience which twelfth- and thir-
teenth-century cathedral builders brought about through travel, and
it includes an exchange of specimens, tools, and materials. Through
this traffic, researchers participate in each other's experimental procedures, and outcomes are watched, noticed, and learned from by a
number of researchers. If the existence of such a traffic can be associated with acceleration effects, such effects are now appropriated
by laboratories. Nonetheless, they are not limited to laboratories; it
appears, and this is a last point I want to consider in regard to the
present type of laboratory, neither the traffic of specimens and ma-

terials nor the system of surveillance are wholly contained in the laboratory. In fact, if the laboratory has come of age as a continuous and bounded unit that encapsulates *internal environments*, it has also become a *link between internal and external environments*, a *border* in a *wider* traffic of objects and observations. For example, experiments are not as a rule conducted completely and exclusively by the scientist in charge (with the help of technicians). Rather researchers draw upon other researchers from whom components of the work are extracted and obtained. These pieces of work may come from inside the laboratory, but they also often come from other laboratories. In contrast to work that deploys a technology of representation, the present type of work tends to produce composite and assembled outcomes. With the reconfiguration of objects as material states in successive transitions, experiments become composable in chunks, and the chunks correspond to the results of processing stages. Chunks of work are transferable like written or visual records, they travel between and within laboratories. Since the respective pieces of work are often obtained through gift exchange rather than through formal collaborations indicated by joint authorship, the degree of "assemblage" embodied in research products and the degree of traffic upon which these products are built is not apparent from publications.

The continuation of laboratory-internal processes of exchange through external processes is just one indication that the reconfiguration of objects (and agents) has implications beyond the borders of a lab. It is clear that single laboratories in benchwork sciences are situated in a landscape of other laboratories, and it appears that it is this landscape upon which they imprint their design. The laboratory in the present situation *focuses a life world* within which single laboratories are locales, but which extends much further than the boundaries of single laboratories.

Laboratories vs. experiments: when objects are signs

The phenomenon of the laboratory as a (internally elaborated) locale of a more extended life world is interesting in that it contrasts sharply with the third case to be considered, in which much of this life world appears to be drawn into experiments which are no longer merely streams of work conducted under the umbrella of a laboratory, but which "confront" and play upon the latter. This is also a situation in which objects are reconfigured neither as not-to-be-interfered-with players of natural events nor as decomposable material ingredients to processing programs, but as *signs*. The example from outside the natural sciences is psychoanalysis.[19] Freud repeatedly referred to psychoanalysis as analogous to chemistry and physics, and he likened the method of stimulating patient recollection through hypnosis with laboratory experimentation.[20] He also compared psychoanalysts to surgeons, whom he envied because they could operate on patients removed from everyday social and physical environments under clinical conditions—a situation Freud emulated by what he called the special "ceremonial" of the treatment situation (1947, vol. 11, 477ff., and vol. 8, 467). In a nutshell, this ceremonial consisted in the patient being put "to rest" on a couch while the analyst took his seat behind the facility in such a way that the patient could not see the analyst. The patient was not supposed to be influenced by the analyst's nonverbal behavior, and the analyst was supposed to remain emotionless during the encounter. This ceremonial, together with certain rules of behavior which the patient was asked to observe in everyday life during the analysis, helped patients in "disengaging" from everyday situations and in sustaining a new system of self-others relationships which the analyst set up in his office. One could say that Freud went some length to turn psychoanalysis into a laboratory science. But my point refers to the kind of activity performed in this setup rather than to the setup itself. In essence the analyst starts from a series of pathological symptoms. These s/he tries to associate with basic drives which, by means of complicated detours having to do with events in the patient's biography, are thought to motivate the symptoms. Analysis is the progress from outward signs (the patient's symptoms) to the motivating forces which are the elements of psychic activity. Unlike the previous type of science, psychoanalysis is not processing material objects but processing signs; it is *reconstructing the meaning and origin of representations*.

Now consider contemporary particle physics, a science that indubitably involves laboratories and experiments, and in fact the largest and most complex ones in all of the sciences. In the collider experiment (called UA2)[21] we observe at the European Center for

---

19. I am grateful to Stefan Hirschauer for alerting me to this example.

20. For Freud's likening psychoanalysis to chemistry, see, for example Freud's *Gesammelte Werke* (1947), vol. 10, 320; or vol. 12, 5, 184, 186. For a reference to laboratory experimentation, see vol. 10, 131.

21. "UA2" stands for underground area 2, the site of the UA2 detector along the beam pipe several miles from CERN. UA2 is the sister experiment of UA1. In both experiments were discovered the W and Z intermediate bosons which are thought to carry the weak electromagnetic force. Experiment UA2 has been studied since 1987.

Particle Physics (CERN) in Geneva, protons and antiprotons are accelerated in a p$\bar{\text{p}}$ collider and hurled against each other, thereafter decaying into secondary and tertiary particles which travel through different detector materials before they get "stuck" in the outer shell of a calorimeter. Detectors can "see" the traces left by these particles, which may consist of "holes" from electrons knocked out of orbit by incoming particles in a silicon detector, optical images (scintillation light) converted into electrical pulses in a scintillating fiber detector, etc. Detectors announce the presence of these signals to "readout chains" through which signals are amplified, multiplexed, and converted from analog into digital values, and written on tape by an on-line computer. Events and particle tracks are reconstructed off-line, through the application of data production and track reconstruction programs. These construct—and extract—those signals which count as data and are to be analyzed for their physics content. Analysis continues the process of reconstruction in that it is concerned, in the case observed, with, (statistically) differentiating "interesting" signals (e.g., candidates for top quarks) from background events and with placing confidence limits around the estimates. In reality the chain of conversions, transformations, evaluations, selections, and combinations which leads from particle "footprints" to the supposed footprint-generating "real" events, that is, to specific particles and their properties, includes many more steps and details. But it remains a process through which signs become, with a certain likelihood, attached to events (production of particles), just as in the case of psychoanalysis we saw a process through which symptoms were attached to basic motivating drives.

Thus in particle physics experiments the natural order is reconfigured as an order of signs. Signs appear incorporated in particle physics experiments in a far more extensive sense than they are in other fields. This is not to deny that all sciences involve sign processes and can potentially be analyzed from a semiotic perspective. It is rather to say that in particle physics the construction of objects as signs[22] shapes the whole technology of experimentation. To give some simple examples, molecular genetics includes incipient forms of sign processing at the stage where protodata are transformed into publishable evidence, and there are signs involved in intermediary controls, as when a test tube is checked against the light to see whether the substance it includes has reached a certain stage, e.g., has formed a "pellet" (Amann and Knorr Cetina 1988). Signs in this

22. More precisely: the construction of objects as signatures and footprints of events.

case are used as indicators of the state of a process; they are not the objects which are processed. For the most part experiments describable in terms of a technology of intervention process material substances rather than their signatures. Experiments in particle physics, on the other hand, seem to start where processes not focusing upon signs leave off. Signs occur in many varieties and extend far back in the process of experimentation; they cannot be limited to the written output or "inscriptions" (Latour and Woolgar 1979), which in other sciences are the (intermediary) *end products* of experimental processes. But the exclusive focus upon signs is but one aspect of the particle physics technology of signification. Other aspects have to do with features of the "closedness" of a universe in which knowledge derives from the (laboratory-) internal reconstruction of "external" events, with particle physics's use of language as a plastic resource and with its play upon shifts between language games as a technical instrument in reconstruction. If particle physics experiments reconstruct an external world from signs, they also constantly transcend—through their play upon language—sign-related limitations.

A proper exploration of particle physics's rather complicated technology of signification would be too technical for this paper.[23] Instead I want to turn now to the meaning of experiment in particle physics as compared to in the previously discussed sciences. Particle physics seems to upgrade features which are also present in other sciences, and to sustain them as special characteristics of its pursuits. For example, in excluding whatever material processes lead to the production of signs, particle physics experiments rely on a division of labor between laboratory and experiment which we encountered in a rudimentary version in the distinction between "work on the laboratory" and experimental work in bench laboratories. In particle physics, however, this loose division between kinds of work which nonetheless remain continuous with each other appears transformed into a new separation between laboratory and experiment, a separation through which the laboratory becomes technically, organizationally, and socially divorced from the conduct of

23. I also want to turn the reader's attention to the fact that my argument is not that this technology of signification somehow "causes" all features of laboratories or experiments which use such a technology. Laboratories and experiments embody construals of objects, and in that sense, different construals imply different laboratories. On the other hand, there is more to be considered in the makeup of a laboratory than the construal of objects, and the construal of objects needs to be considered in more detail than is feasible in this paper. A full exploration of this can be found in Knorr Cetina 1992.

experiments. Technically, laboratories build, maintain, and run accelerators and colliders, while experiments build, maintain, and run detectors. Experiments process signs. Laboratories become segregated providers of signs—they provide for the particle clashes whose debris leaves traces in detectors. Organizationally, science is conducted in experiments, while laboratories provide the (infra) structure for the conduct of science—they supply office space, computer time, living quarters, means of transportation, a local management that recruits financial resources, and above all, particle collisions. One laboratory sustains many smaller-scale fixed-target experiments but only a few big collider experiments. Most of the researchers and technicians that are part of the structure never have anything to do directly with experiments. And researchers on one experiment often know little of others, even if the two are sister experiments dedicated to the same goal. Experiments become relatively closed, total units, and laboratories become total institutions.

This is particularly interesting in view of the reconfiguration of the common, focused, interlinked life world we found to be the context of benchwork laboratories. Experiments in particle physics involve huge collaborations (the LEP experiments at CERN have up to five hundred participants) between physics institutes all over the world. Sometimes all physics institutes in a country join in one experiment. There are only a handful of large particle physics laboratories in the world at this time, and hardly more collider experiments. These experiments and laboratories deplete scientific environments; there are virtually no active particle physics institutes or working particle physicists who are not drawn into one of the experiments and who are not thereby associated with one of the major labs. The external life world which in molecular biology is shared inside each laboratory in particle physics has become an internal life world encapsulated within experiments. The scientific community has become an internal community, a sort of collaborating organism instead of the territorial structure of independent professional locales which characterizes benchwork sciences. Since collaborations tend to seed new collaborations when, after eight to sixteen years, an experiment ends, it is clear that experiments which have depleted whole scientific fields (and perhaps most of the field's manpower in single countries) also represent a tremendous political force. This leads to the curious situation in which experiments (collaborations) become counterparts of laboratories. Given their political force, experiments can, for example, play out their political strength. A collaboration may conduct an experiment at CERN and simultaneously submit a proposal for an experiment to be conducted in ten years at the SSC (superconducting supercollider) to be built in Texas, while keeping its options open for a bid at the LHC (large hadron collider) should it be built at CERN. Collaborations do not have to be loyal to laboratories (some are, if core members of a collaboration are employed by a laboratory), though of course they need laboratories, just as much as laboratories need good (technically and financially powerful) collaborations. It seems that strings of collaborations (experiments) may pass between laboratories, or fasten upon one of them, much as they please.

It is interesting to note that in addition to, or despite, their political nature, experiments (collaborations) in particle physics acquire a cultural face in the sense that they identify with and become known for a particular style of work and organization. UA2, for example, the collider experiment I study at CERN, is known and sought out for its "liberal," "informal" style of organization and its "painstaking," "trustworthy" style of work that is contemptuous of strategies of self-promotion at the cost of science. If this style cost UA2 one or another prize or first publication,[24] it does make for the image of an agreeable atmosphere to which newcomers are attracted. The style is cultivated by participants not only in terms of the selection of new participants but also in terms of characteristic behaviors displayed by leading figures in the collaboration on a day-to-day basis.

Everyday Life: Foundation or Active Agent in Science?

I have argued that the notion of a laboratory in recent sociology of science is more than a new field of exploration, a site which houses experiments, or a locale in which methodologies are put into practice. I have associated laboratories with the notion of reconfiguration, with setting up an order in laboratories that is built upon upgrading the ordinary and mundane components of social life. The configuration model claims that science derives epistemic effects from a particular reconfiguration of the natural order in relation to the social order, from, for example, reconfiguring agents and objects in ways which draw upon, yet at the same time transcend, natural courses of activities and events. From the examples it is clear how

24. This is implied by descriptions of the very different, more "ruthless" style of UA2's sister experiment UA1, which, as gossip has it, may have helped UA1 win the Nobel prize in 1984. The nobel prize went to Carlo Rubbia, leader of UA1, and Simon van der Meer, for the discovery of the W and Z intermediate bosons with the help of the UA1 detector. For a journalist's description of the style of UA1, see Taubes 1986.

this "transcendent mundanity" of science draws in features which are as diverse as those found in twelfth-and-thirteenth-century cathedral building, in the psychoanalyst's office, or in the war game played on a sand table. Reconfigurations are neither uniform nor consistent across different areas of science, and this has consequences in terms of the meaning of laboratory and experiment in different fields. It appears that in accordance with the construction of objects, some sciences endorse a correspondence model of the relationship between experimental activities and the world, others base their discovery strategy on the processibility and "trafficability" of material objects, and a third category construes its universe as a universe of signs and deploys a language-transcending[25] technology of signification. In terms of laboratory-experiment relations which respond to these constructions, some sciences display themselves as experimental sciences which manage almost without laboratories, others appear to be laboratory sciences in which experiments dissolve into streams of research tasks continuous with laboratory work, and some are sciences in which laboratories and experiments are institutionally separate units which enter into "uneasy partnerships"[26] with each other. It is clear that from a cultural perspective, the notion of "experiment" too must be reconsidered in relation to its environment and the changing meanings and alliances it embodies.

The point about juxtaposing these cases is not only that it directs attention to the enormous disparity between different empirical sciences but also that it emphasizes the necessity to understand the manifold transformations, through the order instituted in the laboratory, of the natural and social order of the wider context from which and into which laboratories are built. Edmund Husserl was among the first to criticize the sciences for their forgetfulness about the taken-for-granted modalities of experience which are the conditions of the possibility of scientific inquiry and which in his opinion are part of the makeup of our everyday life world. Through them he thought science was deeply and inextricably anchored in everyday life, despite its technical and mathematical orientation.[27] Quine made a similar argument when he pointed out that all scientific theories were ultimately rooted in "our overall home theory," by

25. I am alluding to the phenomenon that particle physics deploys different technical languages for the solution of its problems and appears to extract epistemic advantages from the transition from one language to another.

26. This expression has been used by Lazarsfeld to describe the relationship between politics and science.

27. See in particular Husserl 1976.

which he meant our everyday language (1969). Both authors accord to everyday life a role in science, but it is a *foundational* role which reduces everyday life to the common ground science shares with everything else and which construes science as a new kind of enterprise connected to everyday life through no more than a relationship of ultimate dependence. The transformations I think we need to understand between the natural and social order and the order instituted in the laboratory are not of an ultimate nature that is open only to philosophical reflection. They do not link the eidetically perceivable universe of the everyday world to some abstract concepts which are thought to lie at the core of science. These transformations are concrete and omnipresent in the conduct of science underneath the cover of technical jargon, they are entrenched in cognitive pursuits, and inscribed in methodical practices. Taken together, and through the reconfigurations they imply, they set up a contrast to the surrounding social order. Yet it is precisely through the active recruitment, the clever selection, the deployment, enhancement, and recombination of features of this order *in relation to* the natural order—and through the clever selection and enhancement of features of the natural order in relation to social practice—that this contrast is effected and that epistemic effects can be reaped for science. Everyday orders appear to be a malleable resource and an active agent in scientific development. The laboratory embodies these resources, but as we have seen, it embodies them in different ways as it reshapes itself according to different reconfigurations.

REFERENCES

Amann, K. 1990. Natürliche Expertise und künstliche Intelligenz: Eine mikrosoziologische Untersuchung von Naturwissenschaftlern. Ph.D. diss., University of Bielefeld.

Amann, K., and K. Knorr Cetina. 1988. The Fixation of (Visual) Evidence. *Human Studies* 11:133–69.

Bloor, D. 1976. *Knowledge and Social Imagery*. London: Routledge and Kegan Paul.

Cole, S. 1990. *Social Influences on the Growth of Knowledge*. Cambridge: Harvard University Press.

Collins, H. M. 1975. The Seven Sexes: A Study in the Sociology of a Phenomenon, or the Replication of Experiments in Physics. *Sociology* 9:205–24.

Freud, S. *Gesammelte Werke*. Frankfurt: Fischer.

Giere, R. 1988. *Explaining Science: A Cognitive Approach*. Chicago: University of Chicago Press.

Gooding, D., T. Pinch, and S. Schaffer, eds. 1989. *The Uses of Experiment.* Cambridge: Cambridge University Press.

Hacking, I. 1983. *Representing and Intervening.* Cambridge: Cambridge University Press.

Hirschauer, S. 1991. Die medizinische Konstruktion von Transsexualität. Ph. D. diss., University of Bielefeld.

Husserl, E. 1976. *Die Krisis der europäischen Wissenschaften und die transzendentale Phänomenologie, Husserliana Bd. VI.* 2d ed. The Hague: Nijhoff.

Hut, P., and J. Sussman. 1987. Advanced Computing for Science. *Scientific American* 257(4): 136–45.

Kahneman, D., P. Slovic, and A. Tversky. 1982. *Judgment under Uncertainty: Heuristics and Biases.* Cambridge: Cambridge University Press.

Knorr, K. D. 1977. Producing and Reproducing Knowledge: Descriptive or Constructive? Toward a Model of Research Production. *Social Science Information* 16:669–96.

Knorr Cetina, K. 1981. *The Manufacture of Knowledge: An Essay on the Constructivist and Contextual Nature of Science.* Oxford: Pergamon Press.

———— 1989. The Organization of Embeddedness: A Constructivist Approach to Micro-Macro Relations. Paper presented in the Thematic Session "From Interpretation to Structure," annual meeting of the American Sociological Association, San Francisco.

Knorr Cetina, K., and M. Mulkay, eds. 1983. *Science Observed: Perspectives on the Social Study of Science.* London: Sage.

Knorr Cetina, K. 1992. *Epistemic Cultures: How Scientists Make Sense.*

Latour, B. 1987. *Science in Action.* Stony Stratford: Open University Press.

Latour, B., and S. Woolgar. 1979. *Laboratory Life: The Social Construction of Scientific Facts.* Beverly Hills: Sage.

Lynch, M. 1985. *Art and Artifact in Laboratory Science: A Study of Shop Work and Shop Talk in a Research Laboratory.* London: Routledge and Kegan Paul.

MacCoun, R. 1989. Experimental Research on Jury Decision Making. *Science* 244:1046–49.

MacKenzie, D. 1981. *Statistics in Britain, 1865–1930.* Edinburgh: Edinburgh University Press.

Mark, R., and W. W. Clark. 1984. Gothic Structural Experimentation. *Scientific American* 251(4): 144–53.

Merleau-Ponty, M. 1945. *Phenomenologie de la perception.* Paris: Gallimard. English translation, *Phenomenology of Perception.* London: Routledge and Kegan Paul, 1962.

Pickering, A. 1984. *Constructing Quarks: A Sociological History of Particle Physics.* Chicago: University of Chicago Press.

Quine, W. V. O. 1969. *Ontological Relativity and Other Essays.* New York: Columbia University Press.

Searle, J. 1983. *Intentionality: An Essay in the Philosophy of Mind.* Cambridge: Cambridge University Press.

Shapin, S. 1979. The Politics of Observation: Cerebral Anatomy and Social Interests in the Edinburgh Phrenology Disputes. In R. Wallis, ed., *On the Margins of Science: The Social Construction of Rejected Knowledge.* Sociological Review Monograph no. 27. London: Routledge and Kegan Paul.

Shapin, S., and S. Schaffer. 1985. *Leviathan and the Air-Pump: Hobbes, Boyle, and the Experimental Life.* Princeton: Princeton University Press.

Smith, R. W., and J. N. Tatarewicz. 1985. Replacing a Technology: The Large Space Telescope and CCDs. *Proceedings of the IEEE* 73(7):1221–35.

Taubes, G. 1986. *Nobel Dreams: Power, Deceit, and the Ultimate Experiment.* New York: Random House.

Traweek, S. 1988. *Beamtimes and Lifetimes: The World of High Energy Physicists.* Cambridge: Harvard University Press.

Wade, N. 1981. *The Nobel Duel.* New York: Anchor Press.

Zenzen, M., and S. Restivo. 1982. The Mysterious Morphology of Immiscible Liquids: A Study of Scientific Practice. *Social Science Information* 21(3):447–73.

5

Constructing Quaternions:
On the Analysis of Conceptual Practice

Andrew Pickering and Adam Stephanides

Similarly, by surrounding $\sqrt{-1}$ by talk about vectors, it sounds quite natural to talk of a thing whose square is -1. That which at first seemed out of the question, if you surround it by the right kind of intermediate cases, becomes the most natural thing possible.
  Ludwig Wittgenstein, *Lectures on the Foundations of Mathematics*

How can the workings of the mind lead the mind itself into problems? ... How can the mind, by methodical research, furnish itself with difficult problems to solve?
  This happens whenever a definite method meets its own limit (and this happens, of course, to a certain extent, by chance).
  Simone Weil, *Lectures on Philosophy*

Thinking about science has traditionally meant thinking about scientific knowledge, especially about high theory in the mathematical sciences. In the last ten years or so, however, historians, philosophers, sociologists, and others have converged upon an exploration of scientific practice, and an enormous field of enquiry has thus been opened up. Perhaps in compensation for the traditional overemphasis on theory, the analysis of practice has so far focused on experimentation and on the construction of the sociotechnical networks that link the laboratory to the outside world (see the contributions to this volume). Many fascinating discoveries have been made, but the upshot has been that we still know as little as we ever did about what theoretical, conceptual practice looks like: "almost no one has had the courage to do a careful anthropological study"

Andrew Pickering's contribution to this work was supported in part by the National Science Foundation History and Philosophy of Science Program, Grant DIR-8912095, and was completed while he was a visitor at the Science Studies Unit of the University of Edinburgh, Scotland. He thanks Barry Barnes, the director of the Unit, for making its facilities available to him, Toby Morris for reviving an exploded Macintosh, Donald MacKenzie for the use of a laser printer, and David Bloor and Steven Shapin for challenging discussions. He also thanks Barbara Herrnstein Smith and Michael J. Crowe for valuable comments.

as Latour (1987, 246) puts it (but see Livingston 1986). Our intention is to begin to remedy this deficiency. Our suggestion is not that the analysis of conceptual practice calls for any special interpretive framework; we want rather to show that it is amenable to the same kind of analysis as that already developed for experimental and sociotechnical practice. Our method is to work through a case study of mathematical rather than strictly scientific practice, but as explained below, we hope that the study can serve to open up thought on conceptual practice in both mathematics and science more generally. ('Science,' below, is thus often used as an umbrella term for both disciplines.) We first review the basics of our interpretive scheme and then move to the study. We conclude with a discussion of how the analysis developed here cuts across traditional arguments concerning the objectivity, relativity, or historicity of scientific knowledge.

An idea that has proved fundamental in science studies is that practice should be seen as a process of *modeling*, of the creative extension of existing cultural elements (Barnes 1982; Bloor 1976; Hesse 1966; Knorr Cetina 1981; Kuhn 1970; Pickering 1981, 1984). And one key property of modeling that continually comes to the fore is its open-endedness, or openness for short. A given model can be extended in an indefinite number of ways; nothing within the model itself foreshadows which should be chosen. Thus part of the problem of getting to grips with practice is that of understanding closure, of understanding why some individual or group extends particular models in particular ways. The solution to this problem appears to lie in the observation that models are not extended in isolation. Modeling typically aims at producing *associations* in which a plurality of projected elements hang together in some way.[1] And the important point here is that the achievement of

---

1. The analytic terminology adopted here is taken from Pickering 1989, 1990a, b, 1991, forthcoming, but nothing hinges upon this. "Association" is perhaps the most problematic concept we use in this essay. While it is easy enough to see what it means in any specific passage of practice, we have not found any further explication of the term that runs easily across examples. In the present study, "association" amounts to a one-to-one correspondence between two mathematical systems; but in other studies quite different associations have been at stake. In Pickering 1989 the key association concerned the translatability of a material procedure through an interpretative model into one of a pair of phenomenal models; in Pickering 1990b, one important aspect of "association" concerned the harmonious functioning of various material subsystems of a scientific instrument. It may be that this last sense of "association" should be the model for thinking about the concept more generally: we can appreciate that technological artifacts are combinations of material elements that somehow hang together without being overcome by a compulsion to spell out a defi-

such associations is not guaranteed in advance—particular modeling sequences readily lead to mismatches in which intended associations are not achieved. *Resistances,* that is, arise in practice to the achievement of goals. Encounters with resistance set in train a process of *accommodation,* in which the openness of modeling is further exploited in trial-and-error revisions and substitutions of models, modeling sequences, and so on, aimed at proceeding further toward the intended association. The process of accommodation itself precipitates further resistances in and to practice, so that practice in the end appears as a goal-oriented dialectic of resistance and accommodation, with the actual achievement of association—and the production of an empirical fact, say, or of a scientific instrument—as one contingently possible end point. And the point of achievement of association is also, of course, a (possibly temporary) point of closure. It marks out the particular direction of modeling established in the dialectic of resistance and accommodation from the larger space of unsuccessful attempts.

Now the general idea that practice is a process of modeling originated in thinking about conceptual practice in science, especially about theory development. But the further elaboration of the concept of modeling, via the teleological principle of association and the dialectic of resistance and accommodation that it structures, has so far been worked out only for the cases of experimental and sociotechnical practice. And, apart from a studied lack of interest in conceptual practice, one can see why that might be. Put crudely, we expect the material world (in experimental practice) and other people (in sociotechnical practice) to resist our designs. But what might count as resistance and thus produce the characteristic dialectic in conceptual practice is less clear. How can symbols, marks on paper, thoughts, get in our way? How can the workings of the mind lead the mind itself into problems? This is the question that we want to address. We believe an answer can be found within the framework just laid out, although it requires a more careful analysis of modeling than has previously been given.

Typically, modeling is seen as a primitive notion pointing to an aspect of practice not subject to further inquiry. In contrast, in our case study we find it possible to decompose the modeling process into three simpler and better defined operations: *bridging, transcription,* and *filling.*[2] We explain the significance of these terms as

nition of "hanging together" that spans all possible artifacts. The "irreductive" thrust of this line of thought is elaborated in Latour 1988.

2. The importance of transcription (and of the related concepts of description and

we go along; for the present it is enough to note that bridging and filling can be understood as *free moves* in the modeling process, moves in which actors exercise choice and discretion, while transcription is a *forced move*, in which agency is surrendered. To appropriate the terminology of Ludwik Fleck (1979), free moves are the "active" component of scientific practice, while forced moves are "passive." Further, it is important to appreciate that these active and passive components of modeling are constitutively intertwined: the point of bridging, for example, is to create a space for transcription. This intertwining gives modeling a peculiar active-passive or free-forced character, and this is what lies behind the possibility of resistance in conceptual practice. Free moves in modeling mark tentative choices within the indefinitely open space of cultural extension, while the forced moves that intertwine with them serve to elaborate those choices in ways beyond the actor's control. The outcome of particular modeling sequences is thus at once structured by choice but not determined by it; it is something genuinely to be found in practice. This being the case, there is no reason to suppose that intended associations will be achieved through any particular modeling sequences, which is as much as to say that their expected result should be the emergence of resistance. This emergence of resistance, and the consequent dialectic of resistance and accommodation, is what we aim to exemplify and explore in the case study that follows.[3]

From Complex Numbers to Triplets

Our study is taken from the history of mathematics. We are interested in the work of the great Irish mathematician Sir William Rowan Hamilton, and in particular in a brief passage of his mathematical practice that culminated on 16 October 1843 in the construction of his new mathematical system of quaternions. Before we turn to the study, however, a few points need to be addressed. Why, for example, study mathematics in the present context? Our answer is that mathematics offers a particularly clean instance of conceptual practice, free from the material complications of experimental practice in science and from the esoteric subtleties of, say, recent

---

redescription) is stressed in Pickering 1990b, though the concepts of bridging and filling are not explicitly introduced there.

3. See also Tiles 1984 on Gaston Bachelard's concept of the "interference" of mathematical systems.

theoretical physics. Why, then, study Hamilton and his work on quaternions? First, because this work is of considerable historical interest. It marked an important turning point in the development of mathematics, involving as it did the first introduction of noncommuting quantities into the subject matter of the field, as well as the introduction of an exemplary set of new entities and operations, the quaternion system, that mutated over time into the vector analysis central to modern physics. Second, because, as it happens, Hamilton's work is relatively easy to follow: not much technical background or insight is required to follow the moves that Hamilton makes. This is unlikely to be true of, say, work of similar importance in modern mathematics. And third, and most importantly, because Hamilton himself left several accounts of the practice that led him to quaternions, especially a notebook entry written on the day of the discovery and a letter to John T. Graves dated the following day (Hamilton 1843a, b, denoted by *NBE* and *LTG* hereafter; citations to page numbers are from the reprints of these in Hamilton 1967). As Hamilton's biographer puts it: "These documents make the moment of truth on Dublin bridge [where Hamilton first conceived of the quaternion system] one of the best-documented discoveries in the history of mathematics" (Hankins 1980, 295). On this last point, some discussion is needed.

Hamilton's discovery of quaternions is not just well documented, it is also much written about. Most accounts of Hamilton's algebraic researches contain some treatment of quaternions, and at least five accounts in the secondary literature rehearse to various ends Hamilton's own accounts more or less in their entirety (Hankins 1980, 295–300; O'Neill 1986, 365–68; Pycior 1976, chap. 7; van der Waerden 1976; Whittaker 1945). We should therefore make it clear that we have no quarrel with these secondary accounts. What differentiates our account from theirs is that, as already indicated, we aim to show that Hamilton's work can be grasped within a more general understanding of practice.[4] Finally, we should acknowledge a problem facing all secondary accounts of Hamilton's work on quaternions, namely, that Hamilton's own accounts are retrospective, if only just. The dangers of relying on retrospective accounts for any attempt at real-time reconstruction of practice are well known: they can be expected to be, at best, edited, idealized, and streamlined, and

4. Our present account is part of a longer study in preparation of Hamilton's algebraic researches. Only the critical phase in the discovery of quaternions has been so substantially worked over in the secondary literature. Much remains to be said on Hamilton's earlier unsuccessful work on triplets (see below).

at worst, distorted out of recognition in the service of some enterprise quite different from the present one. However, we can think of two reasons why such worries should not weigh too heavily in this instance. First, Hamilton's accounts are plausible: though evidently streamlined, they read like accounts of practice.[5] And second, our intent is not a detailed reconstruction of Hamilton's thought processes. It is more to delineate a way of thinking about conceptual practice in general. Especially, as indicated, we want to show how it is possible for dialectics of resistance and accommodation to arise in conceptual practice.[6] As should become evident, Hamilton's retrospective accounts are adequate to that purpose.

Now for the technical background to Hamilton's work. The early nineteenth century was a time of crisis in the foundations of algebra, centering on the question of how the "absurd" quantities—negative numbers and their square roots—should be understood (Hankins 1980, 248; Pycior 1976, chap. 4). Various moves were made in the debate over the absurd quantities, only one of which bears upon our story. This was to make an association between algebra and another branch of mathematics, geometry, where the association in question consisted in establishing a one-to-one correspondence between the elements and operations of complex algebra and a particular geometrical system (Crowe 1985, 5–11). We need to go into some detail about the substance of this association, since it figured importantly in Hamilton's construction of quaternions.

The standard algebraic notation for a complex number is $x + iy$, where x and y are real numbers and $i^2 = -1$. Positive real numbers can be thought of as representing measurable quantities or magnitudes—a number of apples, the length of a rod—and the founda-

---

5. By "streamlining" we refer to the editing of accounts of practice to improve their linearity (see Nickles 1989). Thus Hamilton's account of his path to quaternions omits any details of his earlier unsuccessful attempts at constructing systems of triplets (see below), although those attempts and their outcomes undoubtedly structured his subsequent practice. We refer to those attempts as appropriate in the text and notes. Likewise, although Hamilton does mention moves that failed in the passage of practice that led to quaternions—this is why we find his account plausible—it seems reasonable to suspect that further failed moves go unmentioned. The ultimate streamlining is of course the omission of all false starts: this is how accounts of genius are produced.

6. In what follows we are exclusively concerned with Hamilton's technical, mathematical practice, but we do not dispute the importance of the considerable literature on Hamilton's metaphysics and its relation to his algebraic researches (Hankins 1980, chap. 6; Hendry 1984). Our feeling is that the intersection between Hamilton's algebra and metaphysics and the relation of both to his social position (Bloor 1981) could be analyzed along the lines suggested here. But to attempt this project here would take us too far afield.

tional problem in algebra was to think what -1 and i (and multiples thereof) might stand for. The geometrical response to this question was to think of x and y not as quantities or magnitudes, but as co-ordinates of the end point of a line segment in some "complex" plane terminating at the origin. Thus the x-axis of the plane measured the real component of a given complex number represented as such a line segment, and the y axis the imaginary part, the part multiplied by i in the algebraic expression. In this way the entities of complex algebra were set in a one-to-one correspondence with geometrical line segments. Further, it was possible to put the operations of complex algebra in a similar relation with suitably defined operations upon line segments. Addition of line segments was readily defined on this criterion. In algebraic notation, addition of two complex numbers was defined as

$$(a + ib) + (c + id) = (a + c) + i(b + d),$$

and the corresponding rule for line segments was that the x coordinate of the sum should be the sum of the x coordinates of the segments to be summed, and likewise for the y coordinate. The rule for subtraction could be obtained directly from the rule for addition—coordinates of line segments were to be subtracted instead of summed. The rules for multiplication and division in the geometrical representation were more complicated, and we need only discuss that for multiplication, since this was the operation that became central in Hamilton's development of quaternions.

The rule for algebraic multiplication of two complex numbers,

$$(a + ib)(c + id) = (ac - bd) + i(ad + bc),$$

followed from the usual rules of algebra, coupled with the peculiar definition of $i^2 = -1$. The problem was then to think what the equivalent might be in the geometrical representation. It proved to be statable as the conjunction of two rules. The product of two line segments is another line segment which (a) has a length given by the product of the lengths of the two segments to be multiplied, and which (b) makes an angle with the x axis equal to the sum of the angles made by the two segments. From this definition it is easy to check that multiplication of line segments in the geometrical representation leads to a result equivalent to the multiplication of the corresponding complex numbers in the algebraic representation.[7]

7. The easiest way to grasp these rules is as follows. In algebraic notation, any complex number $x + iy$ can be written as $re^{i\theta}$, where $x = r\cos\theta$ and $y = r\sin\theta$. But

Coupled with a suitably contrived definition of division in the geometrical representation, then, an association of one-to-one correspondence was achieved between the entities and operations of complex algebra and their geometrical representation in terms of line segments in the complex plane.

At least two important consequences for nineteenth-century mathematics flowed from this association. First, it could be said (though it could also be disputed) that the association solved the foundational problems centered on the absurd numbers. Instead of trying to understand negative and imaginary numbers as somehow measures of quantities or magnitudes of real objects, one should think of them geometrically, in terms of the orientation of line segments. A negative number, for example, should be understood as referring to a line segment lying along the negative (rather than positive) x axis, a pure imaginary number as lying along the y axis, and so on. Thus one could appeal for an understanding of the absurd numbers to an intuition of the possible differences in length and orientation of rigid bodies—sticks, say—in any given plane, and hence the foundational problem was shown to be apparent rather than real.

A more lasting significance of the association of complex algebra with a geometrical representation was that the latter, more clearly than the former, invited extension. Complex algebra was a self-contained field of mathematical practice; geometry, in contrast, was by no means confined to the plane. The invitation, then, was to extend the geometrical representation of complex number theory from a two- to a three-dimensional space, and to somehow carry along a three-place algebraic equivalent with it, thus maintaining the association already constructed in two dimensions. On the one hand, this extension could be attempted in a spirit of play, just to see what could be achieved. On the other hand, there was a promise of utility. The hope was to construct an algebraic replica of transformations of line segments in three-dimensional space and thus to develop a new and possibly useful algebraic system appropriate to calculations in three-dimensional geometry (Crowe 1985, 5–12),

---

$re^{i\theta}$ is just the location of the end of a line segment in the plane of length r at angle θ to the x axis, written in polar coordinates. The product of two arbitrary complex numbers can thus be written as $r_1 r_2 e^{i(\theta_1 + \theta_2)}$, which in the geometrical representation stands for the location of the end of a line segment having a length which is the product of the lengths of the lines to be multiplied (part a of the rule) and making an angle with the x axis equal to the sum of angles made by the lines to be multiplied (part b).

"to connect, in some new and useful (or at least interesting) way *calculation* with *geometry*, through some *extension* [of the association achieved in two dimensions], to *space of three dimensions*," as Hamilton put it (Hamilton 1967, 135).[8]

Hamilton was involved in the development of complex algebra from the late 1820s onward. He worked both on the foundational problems just discussed (developing his own approach to them via his "Science of Pure Time" and a system of "couples" rather than through geometry) and on the extension of complex numbers from two- to three-place systems, or "triplets," as he called them. His attempts to construct triplet systems in the 1830s were many and various (we hope to publish a fuller account of them in due course), but Hamilton regarded them all as failures (Hamilton 1967, 3–100, 117–42; Hankins 1980, 245–301; Pycior 1976, chaps. 3–6). Then in 1843, after a period of work on other topics, he returned to the challenge once more. Yet again he failed to achieve his goal, but this time he did not come away empty-handed. Instead of constructing a three-place or three-dimensional system, he quickly arrived at the four-place quaternion system that he regarded as his greatest mathematical achievement and to which he devoted the remainder of his life's work. This is the passage of practice that we intend to analyze.

Constructing Quaternions

On 16 October 1843, Hamilton set down in a notebook his recollection of his path to quaternions. The entry begins (*NBE*, 103):

> I, this morning, was led to what seems to me a theory of *quaternions*, which may have interesting developments. *Couples* being supposed known, and known to be representable by points in a plane, so that $\sqrt{-1}$ is perpendicular to 1, it is natural to conceive that there may be another sort of $\sqrt{-1}$, perpendicular to the plane itself. Let this new

8. The perceived need for an algebraic system that could represent elements and operations in three-dimensional space more perspicuously than existing systems is discussed in Crowe 1985, 3–12. Though Hamilton wrote of his desire to connect calculation with geometry some years after the event (the quotation is from the preface to his *Lectures on Quaternions*, published in 1853), he recalled in the same passage that he was encouraged to persevere in the face of difficulties by his friend John T. Graves, "who felt the wish, and formed the project, to surmount them in some way, as early, or perhaps earlier than myself" (Hamilton 1853, 137). Hamilton's common interest with Graves in algebra dated back to the late 1820s (Hankins 1980, chap. 17), so there is no reason to doubt that this utilitarian interest did play a role in Hamilton's practice. See also O'Neill 1986.

imaginary be j; so that $j^2 = -1$, as well as $i^2 = -1$. A point x, y, z in space may suggest the triplet $x + iy + jz$.

We can begin by immediately noting that a process of modeling was constitutive of Hamilton's practice. As is evident from these opening sentences, he did not attempt to construct a three-place mathematical system out of nothing. Instead he sought to move from the known to the unknown, to find a creative extension of the two-place systems already in existence. Of course, notions like "modeling" and "creative extension" are vague and imprecise, but in this instance at least, we can begin to clarify what is entailed. In fact, Hamilton was working in terms of two different models that we can discuss in turn.

In his reference to "points in a plane," Hamilton first invokes the geometrical representation of complex algebra, and the creative extension that he considers is to move from thinking about line segments in a plane to thinking about line segments in a three-dimensional space. In so doing, we will say that he established a bridgehead to a possible three-dimensional extension of complex algebra. As explained below, the significance of such a bridging operation is that it marks a particular destination for modeling; at the moment we want to emphasize two points about bridging that we suspect are general. First, however natural Hamilton's move from the plane to three-dimensional space might seem here, it is important to recognize that it was by no means forced upon him. In fact, in his earlier attempts at triplet systems, Hamilton had proceeded differently, often working first in terms of an algebraic model and only toward the end of his calculations attempting to find geometrical representations of his findings, representations which were quite dissimilar to that with which he begins here (Hamilton 1967, 126–32).[9] In this sense the act of fixing a bridgehead is, as we shall say, an active or free move that serves to cut down the indefinite openness of modeling. Our second point follows from this. Such free moves need to be seen as tentative and revisable trials that carry with them no guarantee of success. Just as Hamilton's earlier choices of bridgeheads had, in his own estimation, led to failure, so

9. In such attempts the intention to preserve any useful association of algebra and geometry does not seem to be present: Hamilton's principal intent was simply to model the development of a three-place algebraic system on his existing two-place system of couples. Because of the key role of association in our analysis, we should note that attention to this concept illuminates even these principally algebraic attempts. Hamilton found it necessary to transcribe parts of his development of couples piecemeal, and the goal of reassembling (associating) the disparate parts of the system that resulted again led to the emergence of resistance.

might this one. His only way of assessing this particular choice was to work with it and on it—to see what he could make of it. Similar comments apply to the second model that structured Hamilton's practice. This was the standard algebraic formulation of complex numbers, which he extended to a three-place system by moving from the $x + iy$ notation to $x + iy + jz$. This seems like another natural move to make. But again, when set against Hamilton's earlier work on triplets, it is better seen as the establishment of a bridgehead in a tentative free move.[10]

One more remark before returning to Hamilton's recollections. We noted above that complex algebra and its geometrical representation were associated with one another in a relation of one-to-one correspondence. An intent to preserve that association characterized the passage of Hamilton's practice presently under discussion. In the passage just quoted, he sets up a one-to-one correspondence between the elements defined in his two bridging moves—between the algebraic notation $x + iy + jz$ and suitably defined three-dimensional line segments. In the passage that follows, he considers the possibility of preserving the same association of mathematical operations in the two systems. This is where the analysis of modeling becomes interesting and where the possibility of resistance in conceptual practice becomes manifest. Hamilton's notebook entry continues (*NBE*, 103):

> The square of this triplet [$x + iy + jz$] is on the one hand $x^2 - y^2 - z^2 + 2ixz + 2jxy + 2ijyz$; such at least it seemed to me at first, because I assumed $ij = ji$. On the other hand, if this is to represent the third proportional to 1, 0, 0 and x, y, z, considered as *indicators of lines* (namely the lines which end in the points having these coordinates, while they begin at the origin) and if this third proportional be supposed to have its length a third proportional to 1 and $\sqrt{(x^2 + y^2 + z^2)}$, and its distance twice as far angularly removed from 1, 0, 0 as x, y, z; then its real part ought to be $x^2 - y^2 - z^2$ and its two imaginary parts ought to have for coefficients $2xy$ and $2xz$; thus the term $2ijyz$ appeared de trop, and I was led to assume at first $ij = 0$. However I saw that this difficulty would be removed by supposing that $ji = -ij$.

This passage requires some exegesis. Here Hamilton begins to think about mathematical operations on the three-place elements that his bridgeheads have defined, and in particular about the opera-

10. The foundational significance of Hamilton's couples was that the symbol i did not appear in them and was therefore absent from the attempts at triplets discussed in the previous note. A typical bridging move there was to go from couples written as (a, b) to triplets written (a, b, c).

tion of multiplication, specialized initially to that of squaring an arbitrary triplet. He works first in the purely algebraic representation, and if for clarity we write $t = x + iy + jz$, he finds:

$$t^2 = x^2 - y^2 - z^2 + 2ixy + 2jxz + 2ijyz. \tag{1}$$

This equation follows automatically from the laws of standard algebra, coupled with the usual definition that $i^2 = -1$ and the new definition $j^2 = -1$ that was part of Hamilton's algebraic bridgehead. In this instance, then, we see that the primitive notion of modeling can be partly decomposed into two more transparent operations, bridging and transcription, where the latter amounts to the copying of an operation defined in the base-model—in this instance the rules of algebraic multiplication—into the system set up by the bridgehead. And this indeed is why we use the word "bridgehead"—it defines a point to which attributes of the base model can be transferred, a destination for modeling, as we put it earlier. We can note here that just as it is appropriate to think of fixing a bridgehead as a free move, it is likewise appropriate to think of transcription as a sequence of forced moves, a sequence of moves—resulting here in equation (1)—that follow from what is already established concerning the base model. One should not, of course, think of bridging and transcription as totally independent operations: as mentioned earlier, the point of the former is to make possible the latter. This is what gives modeling its peculiar free-forced character that, as we indicated, contains within itself the seeds of genuinely emergent resistance.

We can discuss resistance shortly, but first we should note that the decomposition of modeling into bridging and transcription is only partial. Equation (1) still contains an undefined quantity—the product ij—that appears in the last term of the right-hand side. This was determined neither in Hamilton's first free move nor in the forced moves that followed. The emergence of such "gaps" is, we believe, another general feature of the modeling process. These gaps surface throughout Hamilton's work on triplets, and one of his typical responses was what we call filling: the assignment of values to undefined terms in further free moves.[11] Hamilton could here, for example, have simply assigned a value to the product ij and explored where that led him through further forced moves. In this instance, though, he proceeded differently.

The sentences that begin "On the other hand, if this is to rep-

---

11. See, for example, his development of rules for the multiplication of couples (Hamilton 1967, 80–83).

resent the third proportional," refer to the operation of squaring a triplet in the geometrical rather than the algebraic representation. Considering a triplet as a line segment in space, Hamilton was almost in a position to transcribe into his new system the rules for complex multiplication summarized earlier, but although not made explicit in the passage, one problem remained. While the first rule concerning the length of the product of lines remained unambiguous in three-dimensional space, the second, concerning the orientation of the product line, did not. Taken literally, it implied that the angle made by the square of any triplet with the x axis was twice the angle made by the triplet itself—"twice as far angularly removed from 1, 0, 0 as x, y, z"—but it in no way specified the orientation of the product line in space. Here another gap arose in moving from two to three dimensions, and in this instance, Hamilton responded with a characteristic, if tacit, filling move. He further specified the rule for multiplication of line segments in space by enforcing the new requirement that the square of a triplet remain in the plane defined by itself and the x axis (this is the only way in which we can obtain his stated result for the square of a triplet in the geometrical representation). As usual, this move seems natural enough, but the sense of naturalness is easily shaken when taken in the context of Hamilton's prior practice: one of Hamilton's earliest attempts at triplets, for example, represented them as lines in three-dimensional space, but multiplication was defined differently in that attempt.[12] Be that as it may, this particular filling move sufficed and was designed to make possible a series of forced transcriptions from the two- to the three-dimensional versions of complex algebra that enabled Hamilton to compute the square of an arbitrary triplet. He found that the "real part [of the corresponding line segment] ought to be x^2 y^2 z^2 and its two imaginary parts ought to have for coefficients $2xy$ and $2xz$." Or, returning this result to purely algebraic notation:[13]

$$t^2 = x^2 - y^2 - z^2 + 2ixy + 2jxz. \tag{2}$$

12. Hamilton (1967, 139–40) cites his notes of 1830 as containing an attempt at constructing a geometrical system of triplets by denoting the end of a line segment in spherical polar coordinates as $x = r\cos\theta$, $y = r\sin\theta\cos\phi$, $z = r\sin\theta\sin\phi$, and extending the rule of multiplication from two to three dimensions as $r'' = rr'$, $\theta'' = \theta + \theta'$, $\phi'' = \phi + \phi'$. This addition rule for the angle ϕ breaks the coplanarity requirement at issue.

13. One route to this result is to write the triplet t in spherical polar notation. According to the rule just stated, on squaring the length of the line segment goes from r to r^2, the angle θ doubles, while the angle ϕ remains the same. Using the standard relations to express $\cos2\theta$ and $\sin2\theta$ in terms of $\cos\theta$ and $\sin\theta$, we can then return to the x, y, z notation and arrive at equation (2).

Now there is a simple difference between equations (1) and (2), both of which represent the square of a triplet but calculated in different ways: the two equations are identical except that the problematic term $2ijyz$ of equation (1) is absent from equation (2). This, of course, is just the kind of thing that Hamilton was looking for to help him in defining the product ij, and we will examine the use he made of it in a moment. First, it is time to talk about resistance. The two base models that Hamilton took as his points of departure—the algebraic and geometrical representations of complex numbers—were associated in a one-to-one correspondence of elements and operations. Here, however, we see that as so far extended by Hamilton, the three-place systems had lost this association: the definition of a square in the algebraic system (equation (1)) differed from that computed via the geometrical representation (equation (2)). The association of "calculation with geometry" that Hamilton wanted to preserve had been broken; a resistance, as we call it, to the achievement of Hamilton's goal had appeared. And as we have already suggested, the precondition for the emergence of this resistance was the intertwining of free and forced moves in the modeling process. Hamilton's free moves had determined the directions that his extensions of algebra and geometry would take in the indefinitely open space of modeling, but the forced moves intertwined with them had carried those extensions along to the point at which they collided in equations (1) and (2). This, we believe, is how "the workings of the mind lead the mind itself into problems." We can now move from resistance itself to a consideration of the dialectic of resistance and accommodation in conceptual practice.

The resistance that Hamilton encountered in the disparity between equations (1) and (2) can be thought of as an instance of a generalized version of the Duhem problem (Pickering 1986; Crowe 1990; Hacking chap. 2, this volume). Something had gone wrong somewhere in the process of cultural extension—the pieces did not fit together as he desired—but Hamilton had no principled way of knowing where. What remained for him to do was to tinker with the various extensions in question—with the various free moves he had made, and thus with the sequences of forced moves that followed from them—in the hope of getting around the resistance that had arisen and achieving the desired association of algebra and geometry. He was left, as we say, to seek some accommodation to resistance. Two possible starts toward accommodation are indicated in the passage just quoted, both of which amounted to tinkering with Hamilton's algebraic bridgehead and both of which led directly to an equivalence between equations (1) and (2). The most straightforward accommodation was to set the product ij equal to zero.[14] An alternative, less restrictive but more dramatic, and eventually more far-reaching move also struck Hamilton as possible. It was to abandon the assumption of commutation between i and the new square-root of -1, j.[15] In ordinary algebra, this assumption—which is to say that $ab = ba$—was routine. Hamilton entertained the possibility, instead, that $ij = -ji$. This did not rule out the possibility that both ij and ji were zero, but even without this being the case, it did guarantee that the problematic term $2ijyz$ of equation 1 vanished and thus constituted a successful accommodation to the resistance that had emerged at this stage.[16]

Hamilton thus satisfied himself that he could maintain the association between his algebraic and geometrical three-place systems by the assumption that i and j did not commute, at least as far as the operation of squaring a triplet was concerned. His next move was to consider a less-restrictive version of the general operation of multiplication, working through, as above, the operation of multiplying two coplanar but otherwise arbitrary triplets. Again, he found that the results of the calculation were the same in the algebraic and geometrical representations as long as he assumed either $ij = 0$ or $ij = -ji$ (NBE, 103). Hamilton then moved on to consider the fully general instance of multiplication in the new formalism, the multiplication of two arbitrary triplets (NBE, 103–4). As before, he began in the algebraic representation. Continuing to assume $ij = -ji$, he wrote:

$$(a + ib + jc)(x + iy + jz) = ax - by - cz + i(ay + bx)$$
$$+ j(az + cx) + ij(bz - cy). \quad (3)$$

14. The following day Hamilton described the idea of setting $ij = 0$ as "odd and uncomfortable" (LTG, 107). He offered no reasons for this description, and it is perhaps best understood as written from the perspective of his subsequent achievement. The quaternion system preserved the geometrical rule of multiplication that the length of the product was the product of the lengths of the lines multiplied. Since in the geometrical representation both i and j have unit length, the equation $ij = 0$ violates this rule. Here we have a possible example of the retrospective reconstruction of accounts in the rationalization of free moves.

15. Pycior (1976, 147) notes that Hamilton had been experimenting with noncommuting algebras as early as August 1842, though he then tried the relations $ij = j$, $ji = i$. Hankins (1980, 292) detects a possible influence of a meeting between Hamilton and the German mathematician Gotthold Eisenstein in the summer of 1843.

16. If we multiply out the terms of equation (1), paying attention to the order of factors, the coefficient of yz in the last term on the right-hand side becomes $(ij + ji)$; Hamilton's assumption makes this coefficient vanish.

He then turned back to thinking about multiplication within the geometrical representation. Here a further problem arose. Recall that in thinking about the operation of squaring a triplet Hamilton had found it necessary to make a filling free move, assuming that the square lay in the plane of the original triplet and the x axis. This filling move was sufficient to lead him through a series of forced moves to the calculation of the product of two arbitrary but coplanar triplets. But it was insufficient to define the orientation in space of the product of two completely arbitrary triplets: in general, one could not pass a plane through any two triplets and the x axis. Once more, Hamilton could have attempted a filling move here, concocting some rule for the orientation of the product line in space, say, and continuing to apply the sum rule for the angle made by the product with the x axis. However, he followed a different strategy. Instead of attempting the transcription of the two rules that fully specified multiplication in the standard geometrical representation of complex algebra, he began to work only in terms of the first rule—that the length of the product line segment should be the product of the lengths of the line segments to be multiplied. Transcribing this rule to three dimensions, and working for convenience with squares of lengths, or "square moduli," rather than lengths themselves, from Pythagoras' theorem he could write the square modulus of the left-hand side of equation (3) as $(a^2 + b^2 + c^2)(x^2 + y^2 + z^2)$ (another forced move).[17] Now he had to compute the square of the length of the right-hand side. Here the obstacle to a straightforward application of Pythagoras' theorem was the quantity ij again appearing in the last term. If Hamilton assumed that $ij = 0$, the theorem could be straightforwardly applied, and gave a value for the square modulus of $(ax - by - cz)^2 + (ay + bx)^2 + (az + cx)^2$. The question now was whether these two expressions for the lengths of the line segments appearing on the two sides of equation (3) were equal. Hamilton multiplied them out and rearranged the expression for the square modulus of the left-hand side and found that it in fact differed from that on the right-hand side by a factor of $(bz - cy)^2$. Once again a resistance had arisen, now in thinking about the product of two arbitrary triplets in, alternatively, the algebraic and geometrical representations. Once more the two representations, extended from two- to three-place systems, led to different results. And once more Hamilton looked for some accommodation to this

17. According to Pythagoras' theorem, the square modulus of a line segment is simply the sum of the squares of the coordinates of its end points, meaning the coefficients of 1, i, and j in algebraic notation.

resistance, for some way of making the two notions of multiplication equivalent, as they were in two dimensions.

The new resistance was conditional on the assumption that $ij = 0$. The question, then, was whether some other assignment of ij might succeed in balancing the moduli of the left- and right-hand sides of equation (3).[18] And here Hamilton made a key observation. The superfluous term in the square modulus of the left-hand side of equation (3), $(bz - cy)^2$, was the square of the coefficient of ij on the right-hand side. The two computations of the square modulus could thus be made to balance by assuming not that the product of i and j vanished, but that it was some third quantity k, a *"new imaginary"* (*NBE*, 104), different again from i and j, in such a way that Pythagoras' theorem could be applied to it too.

The introduction of the new imaginary k, defined as the product of i and j, thus constituted a further accommodation by Hamilton to an emergent resistance in thinking about the product of two arbitrary triplets in terms of the algebraic and geometrical representations at once, and two aspects of this particular accommodation are worth emphasizing. First, it amounted to a drastic shift of bridgehead in both systems of representation (recall that we stressed the revisability of bridgeheads earlier). More precisely, it consisted in defining a new bridgehead leading from two-place representations of complex algebra to not three- but four-place systems—the systems that Hamilton quickly called quaternions. Thus, within the algebraic representation, the basic entities were extended from two to four, from 1, i to 1, i, j, k, while within the geometrical representation, as Hamilton wrote the next day, "there dawned on me the notion that we must admit, in some sense, a *fourth dimension* of space" (*LTG*, 108)—with the fourth dimension, of course, mapped by the new k axis. At this point, then, Hamilton could still think of a close association between his algebraic system of quaternions and a four-dimensional geometrical representation. But, and this is our second point, the association had somewhat changed its character in moving from two to four dimensions. While Hamilton had transcribed the first rule of multiplication concerning the lengths of products from two to four dimensions, he had not attempted to transcribe the second part of the rule concerning the addition of angles. To a degree, Hamilton had in fact lost contact with his original geometrical base model at this point. Or, to put the same point in a way

18. Strictly speaking, this is too deterministic a formulation. The question really was whether any amount of tinkering with bridgeheads, fillings, and so on could get past this point without calling up this or another resistance.

that is probably more perspicuous for thinking about conceptual practice in general, he had in effect *redescribed* the geometric base model in an impoverished form, taking the first part of the rule of multiplication as definitive and discarding the second, and then transcribed the base model under this redescription.[19]

Hamilton had still not completed the initial development of quaternions. The quantity k^2 remained undefined at this stage, as did the various products of i, j, and k with one another, excepting that given by his new bridgehead $ij = k$. Hamilton fixed the latter products by a combination of filling assumptions and forced moves following from relations already fixed (*LTG*, 108):

> I saw that we had probably $ik = -j$, because $ik = iij$ and $i^2 = -1$; and that in like manner we might expect to find $kj = ijj = -i$; from which I thought it likely that $ki = j$, $jk = i$, because it seemed likely that if $ji = -ij$, we should have also $kj = -jk$, $ik = -ki$. And since the order of these imaginaries is not indifferent, we cannot infer that $k^2 = ijij$ is $+1$, because $i^2 \times j^2 = -1 \times -1 = +1$. It is more likely that $k^2 = ijij = -iijj = -1$. And in fact this last assumption is necessary, if we would conform the multiplication to the law of multiplication of moduli.

Hamilton then checked to see whether the algebraic version of quaternion multiplication under the above assumptions, including $k^2 = -1$, led to results in accordance with the rule of multiplication concerning products of lengths in the geometrical representation ("the law of multiplication of moduli"), and found that it did. Everything in his quaternion system was thus now defined in such a way that the laws of multiplication in both the algebraic and geometrical ran without resistance into one another: through the move to four-place systems, Hamilton had finally found a successful accommodation to the resistances that had stood in the way of his three-place extensions. The outcome of this dialectic was the general rule for quaternion multiplication (*LTG*, 108):[20]

19. Similarly, in his earlier attempts to construct an algebraic system of triplets modeled on his system of couples, in the face of resistances Hamilton abandoned the principle of unique division (Hamilton 1967, 129–31). A richer instance of redescription and transcription under redescription as a response to resistance in science is discussed in Pickering 1990b. What becomes clear here is that the choice of description for transcription is itself another free move in modeling.

20. Hamilton's notation for an arbitrary quaternion was (a, b, c, d). In the geometrical representation, the coordinates of the end point of a line segment in four-dimensional space are given here; in algebraic notation this same quaternion would be written as $a + ib + jc + kd$.

$(a, b, c, d)(a', b', c', d') = (a'', b'', c'', d'')$, where

$$a'' = aa' - bb' - cc' - dd',$$
$$b'' = ab' + ba' + cd' - dc',$$
$$c'' = ac' + ca' + db' - bd',$$
$$d'' = ad' + da' + bc' - cb'.$$

With these algebraic equations, and the geometrical representation of them, Hamilton had in a sense achieved his goal of associating calculation with geometry, and we could therefore end our analysis here. But before doing so, we want to emphasize that the qualifier "in a sense" is significant here. It marks the fact that what Hamilton had achieved was a *local* association of calculation with geometry rather than a global one. He had constructed a one-to-one correspondence between a particular algebraic system and a particular geometric representation of that system, not an all-purpose link between algebra and geometry considered as abstract, all-encompassing entities. And this remark makes clear the fact that one important aspect of Hamilton's achievement was to redefine, partially at least, the cultural space of future mathematical and scientific practice: more new associations remained to be made if quaternions were ever to be "delocalized" and linked into the overall flow of mathematical and scientific practice, requiring work that would, importantly, have been inconceivable in advance of Hamilton's construction of quaternions.

As it happens, from 1843 onward Hamilton devoted most of his productive energies to this task, and both quaternions and the principle of noncommutation they enshrined were taken up progressively by many sections of the scientific and mathematical communities (Hankins 1980, chap. 23; Crowe 1985, chaps. 4–7). We will mention some of these developments in the following section, but for now we can discuss one last aspect of Hamilton's practice that can serve to highlight the locality of the association embodied in quaternions.

Earlier we described Hamilton's organizing aim as that of connecting calculation with geometry. And as just discussed, quaternions did serve to bring algebraic calculation to *a* geometry—to the peculiar four-dimensional space mapped by 1, *i*, *j*, and *k*. Unfortunately this was not the geometry for which calculation was desired. The promise of triplet—not quaternion—systems had been that they would bring algebra to bear upon the real three-dimensional world of interest to mathematicians and physicists. In threading his way through the dialectic of resistance and accommodation, Hamilton had, in effect, left that world behind. Or to put it another way, his practice had, as so far described, served to displace resistance rather than fully to accommodate to it. Technical resistances in the development of three- and four-place mathematical systems had been transmuted into a resistance between moving from Hamilton's four-dimensional world to the three-dimensional world of interest: it was not evident how the two worlds might be related to one another. This was one of the first problems that Hamilton addressed once he had arrived at his algebraic formulation of quaternions.

In his letter to John Graves dated 17 October 1843, Hamilton outlined a new geometrical interpretation of quaternions that served to connect them back to the world of three dimensions. This new interpretation was a straightforward but consequential redescription of the earlier four-dimensional representation. Hamilton's idea was to think of an arbitrary quaternion (a, b, c, d) as the sum of two parts; a real part, a, which was a pure real number and had no geometrical representation, and an imaginary part, the triplet, $ib + jc + kd$, which was to be represented geometrically as a line segment in three-dimensional space. Having made this split, Hamilton was then in a position to spell out rules for multiplication of the latter line segments, which he summarized as follows (LTG, 110):

> Finally, we may always decompose the latter problem [the multiplication of two arbitrary triplets] into these two others; to multiply two pure imaginaries which agree in direction, and to multiply two which are at right angles with each other. In the first case, the product is a pure negative, equal to the product of the lengths or moduli with its sign changed. In the second case, the product is a pure imaginary of which the length is the product of the lengths of the factors, and which is perpendicular to both of them. The distinction between one such perpendicular and its opposite may be made by the rule of rotation [stated earlier].
>
> There seems to me to be something analogous to *polarized intensity* in the pure imaginary part; and to *unpolarized energy* (indifferent to direction) in the real part of a quaternion: and thus we have some slight glimpse of a future Calculus of Polarities. This is certainly very vague, but I hope that most of what I have said above is clear and mathematical.

These strange rules for the multiplication of three-dimensional line segments—in which the product of two lines might be, depending upon their relative orientation, a number or another line or some combination of the two—served to align quaternions with mathematical and scientific practice concerned with the three-dimensional world. Nevertheless, the association of algebra with geometry remained local. No contemporary physical theories, for example, spoke of entities obeying Hamilton's rules. It therefore still remained to find out in practice whether quaternions could be delocalized to the point at which they might become useful. With hindsight one can pick out from the rules of multiplication a foreshadowing of modern vector analysis with its "dot" and "cross" products, and in the references to "polarized intensity" and "unpolarized energy" one can find a gesture toward electromagnetic theory, where quaternions and vector analysis found their first important use. But as Hamilton wrote, unlike the mathematics of quaternions this "slight glimpse of the future" was, in 1843, "certainly very vague." It was only in the 1880s, after Hamilton's death, that Josiah Willard Gibbs and Oliver Heaviside laid out the fundamentals of vector analysis, dismembering the quaternion system into more useful parts in the process (Crowe 1985, chap. 5). This key moment in the delocalization of quaternions was also the moment of their deconstruction.

Objectivity, Relativity, and Historicity

This is as far as we can take our discussion of Hamilton's work on quaternions. In conclusion, we want first to summarize the general form of our analysis of conceptual practice and then to indicate how it relates to other perspectives on science. Our aim has been to show that a framework already developed in the analysis of experimental and sociotechnical practice can be usefully extended to conceptual practice. Especially we have been concerned with the question of how resistances can arise in practices which do not directly encounter the otherness of the material world or other people, with Simone Weil's question, "How can the workings of the mind lead the mind itself into problems?" Our answer has relied upon a decomposition of the modeling process into a combination of free and forced moves: bridging and filling, and transcription, respectively. The constitutive intertwining of free and forced moves gives modeling a double, active-passive, character, entailing a degree of surrender of agency despite the free moves—choices—that are endemic to it. The upshot of modeling sequences has therefore genuinely to be found out in practice, as has whether intended associations can be achieved through them. There is no reason to expect that particular extensions of models, out of the indefinite number of possible extensions, should issue in such associations, and failure to do so constitutes the emergence of resistance in conceptual practice (as in other forms of practice). Resistances, then, emerge "to a certain extent, by chance"—free moves in the modeling process are genuine choices—but at the same time with a certain necessity stemming from the accompanying forced moves: "this happens whenever a definite method meets its own limit."

Having thus explored the origins of resistance in conceptual practice, we have also sought to exemplify there the practical dialectic of resistance and accommodation, analyzing accommodation as a process of trial revision of prior free moves. As we have seen, such revisions can bear upon bridging and filling moves and even upon the descriptions of base models under which they are transcribed. And finally, we have tried to show that the products of conceptual practice—in this case quaternions—can be seen as the contingently successful end points of such dialectics.

So much by way of summary. To grasp the implications of our analysis, we find it useful to consider how it bears upon the traditional debate in science studies over the objectivity or relativity of scientific knowledge (we continue to use "science" as an umbrella term covering mathematics as well). This part of the discussion has to be tentative, since on the one hand, we cannot do justice here to the nuances of established positions on objectivity and relativity, and on the other, it proves necessary to move beyond the material we have analyzed, from the level of individual practice to the social. Our aim is to get beyond stereotypical understandings of science in which objectivism and relativism figure as diametrically opposed images of science and to show that if the reference of certain key terms is displaced toward practice, we can see that scientific knowledge is at once both objective and relative to culture. Further, we want to stress that our analysis of practice points at the same time beyond relativism and toward the genuine historicity of scientific knowledge. It follows from the double character of modeling that knowledge is, on our construal, objective, relative, and truly historical.

We begin with objectivity, a topic of central philosophical concern. Reference to objectivity has traditionally been intended to express a conviction that scientific knowledge enjoys an independence from its conditions of production and use. And one standard way of trying to get at that independence is by reference to the existence of objective—meaning shared and enduring—criteria or standards for the evaluation of tentative knowledge claims.[21] The connection be-

21. The philosophy of mathematics speaks, for example, of standards for evaluating proofs. An alternative way of thinking about the objectivity of knowledge is in

tween this way of thinking about objectivity and our account of Hamilton's practice seems clear enough. The one-to-one association of elements and operations that Hamilton aimed to preserve between algebra and geometry can certainly be thought of as a relatively constant standard against which he and others could assess the success or failure of his trials. But it is important to note that we have offered no definitive account of what "association" in general might mean; nor, we suspect, is such a definitive account possible.[22] This is not to suggest that talk of standards is empty but rather that instead of hovering above practice in some special realm, standards should themselves be seen as situated and subject to change in and through practice. Hamilton's quaternions, on this view, helped redefine what might count as a "good" mathematical system. However, it is relevant to note that in one respect at least, Hamilton's work redefined the criteria of good mathematics in a *discontinuous* fashion. As Hankins (1980, 301) puts it, "quaternions were the gateway to modern algebra. The Principle of the Permanence of Forms was shattered . . . and the road was open to a wide variety of algebras that did not follow the rules of ordinary arithmetic." The Principle of Permanence of Forms was the previously accepted methodological principle that the operations of algebra should be continuous with those of arithmetic, and Hamilton's introduction of noncommuting quantities both led to new and important developments in algebra and violated this requirement. Thus we seem to arrive at a radically situated view of mathematical standards: standards are themselves tied to the details of particular technical achievements. The similarity of this view with Feyerabend's (1975) position in the philosophy of science—that the scientific method can itself change discontinuously in revolutionary technical developments—is clear. And of course Feyerabend's position is usu-

---

terms of the possible correspondence between theoretical terms or mathematical structures and the worlds to which they refer (scientific realism, mathematical Platonism). Correspondence arguments typically have a retrospective character, concerning themselves with long-run stabilities of knowledge; our analysis attempts to understand practice as it happens and does not engage with such arguments at all.

22. See n. 1 above. In mathematics the applicability of the one-to-one criterion of association is evidently very limited. An initially plausible candidate for a more general criterion is that new mathematical systems should be reducible to previously established ones. But this criterion is not satisfied for the geometrical interpretation of quaternions. Here three-dimensional space is spanned by Hamilton's three imaginaries, i, j, and k, and the real numbers have no geometrical interpretation. Thus collapsing space to a plane leads not to the original complex plane spanned by 1 and i but to a plane spanned by two of the imaginaries.

ally understood as relativistic. This line of thought, then, seems to lead us away from objectivity into relativism, which is the next topic we want to discuss. But first we want to note that although the traditional notion of objectivity can be put under pressure by a consideration of the developments in algebra surrounding Hamilton's work, a somewhat displaced sense of objectivity can be rescued from our analysis.

Talk of enduring shared standards is surely intended to draw attention, quite rightly, to the fact that the production of scientific knowledge is not a matter of individual or collective whim. "Standards" can thus be thought of as a label for the otherness with which scientists struggle in their work. And we have offered here an analysis of such otherness in terms of the double active-passive character of modeling and its bearing upon the dialectic of resistance and accommodation. The thrust of our analysis is therefore to offer an alternative articulation of the objectivity of scientific knowledge, an articulation grounded in the (situated) otherness of technical practice rather than in the (unsituated) otherness of enduring standards. If we are prepared to accept this shift in the site of objectivity toward practice, it becomes possible to see scientific knowledge as being as objective as could be.

Now for relativism. Relativism is traditionally thought of as the enemy of objectivism, and the objectivity-relativity debate is traditionally staged whenever philosophy of science and the sociology of scientific knowledge (SSK) meet (for a detailed working out of some positions, see Hollis and Lukes 1982). The defence of objectivity is one possible philosophical response to SSK's claim that scientific knowledge has to be understood as knowledge relative to a particular culture. We have argued that our analysis of practice can underwrite an appreciation of the objectivity of scientific knowledge, at least in our displaced sense of the term; now we want to note that it underwrites a certain relativism too. According to one canonical formulation of SSK (chaps. 1 and 8, this volume), scientific knowledge is doubly relative to culture. On the one hand, new knowledge is made out of old knowledge and is therefore relative to culture understood as the field of resources in and from which it is made. Our analysis straightforwardly supports this idea. Modeling processes chain new knowledges back to their origins. On the other hand, SSK insists that knowledge production is further structured by the social goals and interests of the relevant community, and here we need to proceed carefully. It would not be misleading to see Hamilton's intended association between algebra and geometry as an instantiation of, say, an instrumental interest in a mathematics useful in handling scientific and technical problems arising in a three-dimensional world. But just as in the previous discussion of objectivity, the question arises as to whether this interest should be conceptualized in the abstract as an enduring attribute of the mathematical and scientific community that hovers above and directs practice. Better, it seems to us, to turn the instrumentality of SSK back on itself and to see interests themselves as structured by the cultural field of resources that provides the instruments for their formulation and possible attainment. An advantage of this formulation is that it foregrounds the fact that interests are situated and can change in practice.[23] Thus, as noted earlier, as a model for future practice Hamilton's quaternion system transfigured the cultural space in which an interest in connecting calculation with geometry could find meaning and expression. From one viewpoint, of course, these remarks deepen the relativism of SSK. Even the enduring and comforting explanatory principle of "interest" is here softened and situated. From another viewpoint, however, an interesting connection is made back to the displaced notion of objectivity just discussed. The struggles with the otherness of resistance that we take to be the hallmark of objectivity themselves structure the cultural space in which interests are constructed and pursued.[24]

So we believe that our analysis of practice makes it possible to get to grips at once with the objectivity and relativity of scientific knowledge. To conclude, we want to note one way in which the analysis points beyond both and toward a historicist understanding of science (see also Pickering 1991, forthcoming). Neither of the stereotypical positions we have been discussing is conducive to an appreciation of the truly historical conditioning of scientific and mathematical knowledge. Each in its way appeals to some regular principle which does (interests) or should (standards) transcend time in the production of knowledge. We have no wish to deny that practice has a certain enduring regularity—our discussion of modeling, association, resistance, and accommodation is intended to bring out

23. That interests are situated and subject to change is acknowledged within SSK, but the traditional point of SSK is to show how relatively enduring interests structure particular acts of knowledge production and evaluation. SSK itself thus offers no account of the genesis and development of interests in practice.

24. We should mention here the second wing of SSK that emphasizes the role of contingent negotiation in the production of knowledge (Collins 1985; see also Kuhn 1970 on revolutionary science; and Smith 1988 on "value" in literary theory). We agree with the emphasis placed there on contingency, which we associate with our notion of free moves (see below). The relation between association, forced moves, and resistance is not, however, brought out there, making it impossible to recover objectivity along the lines suggested in the text.

that regularity. But conversely, our analysis of the double character of modeling serves at the same time to foreground the role of choice, chance, and contingency in practice—in the free moves of bridging and filling, in the emergence of resistance, and in the achievement of association. These contingencies have no regular organizing principle lying behind them—they are truly historical—and they are, we believe, just as constitutive of the production of knowledge as the regular forced moves with which they intertwine. It mattered, that is, that Hamilton made the free moves that he did in trying to develop his systems of triplets. Or at least, to offer a more guarded formulation of the same point, some special argument is required to show that in general such moves do not matter. We cannot see how such an argument could be formulated within a real-time analysis of practice, and we believe, therefore, that our analysis of practice points to a genuine historicity of its products.[25] But just to recall the preceding paragraphs, what is at stake here is a culturally situated historicity. Our analysis of the intertwining of free and forced moves argues that the contingencies of practice do not sever the links between present culture and what it is to become. Nor, on our construal, does reference to contingency and situatedness deny the objectivity of scientific and mathematical knowledge.[26] Our claim

25. Two points can be clarified here. First, our argument is not that traditional objectivist and relativist positions have to deny the historicity of knowledge; it is rather that their focus upon perceived regularities leaves the contingencies of practice unspoken and unthought. Second, we should note that in discussing Hamilton's unsuccessful attempts at constructing triplet systems, historians often invoke later mathematical existence proofs that appear to be relevant. Thus, for example, Hankins (1980, 438 n. 2) reproduces the following quotation from the introduction to vol. 3 of Hamilton's collected papers (Hamilton 1967, xvi): "Thirteen years after Hamilton's death G. Frobenius proved that there exist precisely three associative division algebras over the reals, namely, the real numbers themselves, the complex numbers and the real quaternions." One is tempted to conclude from such assertions that Hamilton's search for triplets was doomed in advance (or fated to arrive at quaternions) and that the historicity of his practice and its products is therefore only apparent. Against this, we would remark that proofs like Frobenius's are the products of sequences of practices which remain to be examined. We can see no reason to expect that analysis of these sequences would not point to the historicity of the proofs themselves. Note also that these sequences were precipitated by Hamilton's practice and by subsequent work on triplets, quaternions, and other many-place systems, all of which served to mark out what an "associative division algebra over the reals" might mean. Since this concept was not available to Hamilton, he cannot have been looking for new instances of it. On the defeasibility of "proof," see Lakatos 1976 and Pinch 1977.

26. Our attempt to dissolve stereotypical oppositions between objectivity, relativity, and historicity has much in common with the projects of Lynch, Callon and Latour, Woolgar, and Traweek represented in part 2 of this volume. The suspicion of

for the analysis of practice is thus that through a displacement of the key concepts of objectivity and interest, it can offer a unitary understanding of aspects of scientific knowledge—its objectivity, relativity, and historicity—that traditional discourses elide or oppose to one another.

---

unsituated normative or explanatory concepts like criteria or interests that are held somehow to structure practice from without does likewise.

REFERENCES

Barnes, B. 1982. *T. S. Kuhn and Social Science.* London: Macmillan.

Bloor, D. 1976. *Knowledge and Social Imagery.* London and Boston: Routledge and Kegan Paul.

——. 1981. Hamilton and Peacock on the Essence of Algebra. In H. Mehrtens, H. Bos, and I. Schneider, eds., *Social History of Nineteenth Century Mathematics.* Boston: Birkhäuser, 202–32.

Collins, H. M. 1985. *Changing Order: Replication and Induction in Scientific Practice.* Beverly Hills: Sage.

Crowe, M. J. 1985. *A History of Vector Analysis: The Evolution of the Idea of a Vectorial System.* New York: Dover.

——. 1990. Duhem and History and Philosophy of Mathematics. *Synthese* 83:431–47.

Feyerabend, P. K. 1975. *Against Method.* London: New Left Books.

Fleck, L. 1979. *Genesis and Development of a Scientific Fact.* Chicago: University of Chicago Press.

Gooding, D., T. J. Pinch, and S. Schaffer, eds. 1989. *The Uses of Experiment: Studies in the Natural Sciences.* Cambridge: Cambridge University Press.

Hamilton, W. R. 1837. Theory of Conjugate Functions, or Algebraic Couples: With a Preliminary and Elementary Essay on Algebra as the Science of Pure Time. *Transactions of the Royal Irish Academy* 17 (1837): 293–422. Reprinted in Hamilton 1967, 3–96.

——. 1843a. Quaternions. Notebook 24.5, entry for 16 October 1843. Reprinted in Hamilton 1967, 103–5.

——. 1843b. Letter to Graves on Quaternions: Or on a New System of Imaginaries in Algebra. Dated 17 October 1843. Published in *Phil. Mag.* 25:489–95. Reprinted in Hamilton 1967, 106–10.

——. 1853. Preface to *Lectures on Quaternions.* Dublin: Hodges and Smith. Reprinted in Hamilton 1967, 117–55.

——. 1967. *The Mathematical Papers of Sir William Rowan Hamilton.* Vol. 3, *Algebra.* Cambridge: Cambridge University Press.

Hankins, T. L. 1980. *Sir William Rowan Hamilton.* Baltimore: The Johns Hopkins University Press.

Hendry, J. 1984. The Evolution of William Rowan Hamilton's View of Algebra as the Science of Pure Time. *Studies in History and Philosophy of Science* 15:63–81.

Hesse, M. B. 1966. *Models and Analogies in Science.* Notre Dame: University of Notre Dame Press.

Hollis, M., and S. Lukes, eds. 1982. *Rationality and Relativism.* Cambridge: MIT Press.

Knorr Cetina, K. 1981. *The Manufacture of Knowledge: An Essay on the Constructivist and Contextual Nature of Science.* New York: Pergamon.

Kuhn, T. S. 1970. *The Structure of Scientific Revolutions,* 2d ed. Chicago: University of Chicago Press.

Lakatos, I. 1976. *Proofs and Refutations: The Logic of Mathematical Discovery.* Cambridge: Cambridge University Press.

Latour, B. 1987. *Science in Action.* Cambridge: Harvard University Press.

———. 1988. *The Pasteurization of France.* Cambridge: Harvard University Press.

Livingston, E. 1986. *The Ethnomethodological Foundations of Mathematics.* Boston: Routledge and Kegan Paul.

Nickles, T. 1989. Justification and Experiment. In Gooding, Pinch, and Schaffer, 299–333.

O'Neill, J. 1986. Formalism, Hamilton, and Complex Numbers. *Studies in History and Philosophy of Science* 17:35–72.

Pickering, A. 1981. The Role of Interests in High-Energy Physics: The Choice Between Charm and Colour. In K. D. Knorr, R. Krohn, and R. D. Whitley, eds, *The Social Process of Scientific Investigation.* Vol. 4, *Sociology of the Sciences.* Dordrecht: Reidel, 107–38.

———. 1984. *Constructing Quarks: A Sociological History of Particle Physics.* Chicago: University of Chicago Press; Edinburgh: Edinburgh University Press.

———. 1986. Positivism/Holism/Constructivism. Paper presented at the weekly colloquium of the Institute for Advanced Study, Princeton, N.J., 8 January 1987.

———. 1989. Living in the Material World: On Realism and Experimental Practice. In Gooding, Pinch, and Schaffer, 275–97.

———. 1990a. Knowledge, Practice, and Mere Construction. *Social Studies of Science* 20:682–729.

———. 1990b. Openness and Closure: On the Goals of Scientific Practice. In H. Le Grand, ed., *Experimental Inquiries: Historical, Philosophical, and Social Studies of Experimentation in Science.* Boston: Kluwer, 215–39.

———. 1991. Beyond Constraint: The Temporality of Practice and the Historicity of Knowledge. (To appear in a volume edited by J. Z. Buchwald.)

———. Forthcoming. Objectivity and the Mangle of Practice. In A. Megill, ed., *Deconstructing and Reconstructing Objectivity.* Special issue of *Annals of Scholarship.*

Pinch, T. J. 1977. What Does a Proof Do If It Does Not Prove? A Study of the Social Conditions and Metaphysical Divisions Leading to David Bohm and John von Neumann Failing to Communicate in Quantum Physics. In E. Mendelsohn, P. Weingart, and R. Whitley, eds., *The Social Production of Scientific Knowledge*. Vol 1 of *Sociology of the Sciences*. Dordrecht: Reidel, 171–215.

Pycior, H. 1976. The Role of Sir William Rowan Hamilton in the Development of Modern British Algebra. Ph.D. diss., Cornell University.

Smith, B. H. 1988. *Contingencies of Value*. Cambridge: Harvard University Press.

Tiles, M. 1984. *Bachelard: Science and Objectivity*. Cambridge: Cambridge University Press.

van der Waerden, B. L. 1976. Hamilton's Discovery of Quaternions. *Mathematics Magazine* 49:227–34.

Whittaker, E. T. 1945. The Sequence of Ideas in the Discovery of Quaternions. Royal Irish Academy, *Proceedings* 50, sec. A, no. 6, pp. 93–98.

6

Crafting Science: Standardized Packages, Boundary Objects, and "Translation"

Joan H. Fujimura

Post-Kuhnian sociology of science argues that nature is not directing the construction of scientific knowledge. Post-Mertonian sociology of science has focused on controversies in science and has taught us that consensus is a rarity rather than the norm. Instead, scientific work is heterogeneous in both method and substance. Many different kinds of worlds are involved in constructing scientific knowledge in numerous and diverse ways. The question then is, how are scientific knowledge and technology constructed without nature and consensus as frames? That is, how do these different worlds with different methodological and substantive concerns succeed in cooperating to produce new knowledge?

This paper focuses on two concepts which are useful for analyzing how collective action is managed *across* social worlds to achieve enough agreement at various times to get work done and to produce relatively (and temporarily) stable "facts."[1] These two concepts were developed from two sets of studies where multiple social worlds intersected and managed to work relatively successfully together. The important point is that both concepts attempt to keep in the foreground the heterogeneous concerns of the different worlds involved.[2]

I would like to thank Richard Burian, Adele Clarke, James Griesemer, Michael Lynch, Andrew Pickering, Leigh Star, and Anselm Strauss for their comments on an earlier version of this paper.

1. Stability as used here is constructed by social actors and is not assumed to represent reality.

2. As a caveat, I do not assume that social worlds, e.g., disciplines, are stable entities in nature or society. I agree with Keating et al. (in press), for example, that disciplinary boundaries are also constructed and therefore can be destabilized. What molecular biology is, for instance, has changed from its birth through its "molecularization" of other realms of biological research and biological institutions. The University of California, Berkeley, has recently reorganized its many biological subdisciplines into two general "divisions," "molecular and cell biology" and "integrated biology," in part because of the general molecularization of biology. Keating et al.'s

One concept is what I have called "standardized packages" (Fujimura 1986, 1988). It consists of a scientific theory and a standardized set of technologies which is adopted by many members of multiple social worlds to construct a new and at least temporally stable definition of cancer as well as a thriving line of cancer research. Another concept is Star and Griesemer's (1989) "boundary objects," examples of which facilitated the coordination of efforts of members of several different social worlds in building the Museum of Vertebrate Zoology at the University of California, Berkeley.

I begin with a brief analysis of the difference between the boundary objects concept and the network building concept of Latour (1987) and his colleagues. Although Star and Griesemer developed their concept in response to the network model, their aim is slightly different. While Latour is concerned more with fact stabilization, Star and Griesemer focus on collective work across worlds with different viewpoints and agendas. The differences in foci are important. The value of Star and Griesemer's work is precisely their *focus*, since the coordination and management of work across multiple and divergent actors, social worlds, meanings, and uses in producing science is often invisible in both scientific and social studies of science texts. However, because boundary objects are more easily reconstructed in different local situations to fit local needs, they are equally disadvantageous for establishing the kind of "stabilization" of allies behind "facts" which Latour discusses.

I argue that "standardized packages" is a concept which handles both collective work across divergent social worlds *and* fact stabilization. A package differs from boundary objects in that it is used by researchers to define a conceptual and technical work space which is less abstract, less ill-structured, less ambiguous, and less amorphous. It is a *gray box* which combines several boundary objects (in this case, genes, cancer, and cancer genes in proto-oncogene theory) with standardized methods (in this case, recombinant DNA technologies, probes, sequence information) in ways which further restrict and define each. Such codefinition and corestriction narrows the range of possible actions and practices but does not entirely define them. Thus, using a package allows for a greater degree of fact

(1991,5) view of disciplines as "dynamic, shifting stakes and not as purely static institutions" is similar to the definition of Strauss and colleagues (Bucher and Strauss 1961; Strauss 1978; Strauss et al. 1964) of social worlds as "negotiated orders." Indeed, *social worlds* is defined as "activities and processes."

stabilization than using boundary objects. Simultaneously, however, standardized packages are also similar to boundary objects in that they facilitate interactions and cooperative work between social worlds and increase their opportunities for being transferred into, and enrolling members of, other worlds. They serve as *interfaces* between multiple social worlds which facilitates the flow of resources (concepts, skills, materials, techniques, instruments) among multiple lines of work (Fujimura 1988). An interface is the means by which interaction or communication is effected at the places "where peoples meet" (Hughes 1971) or different social worlds intersect; it is a means by which multiple intersections occur. I present an example of a standardized package which facilitated the crafting of similarities or homologies between laboratories and continuities between inscriptions and laboratories. The combination of this well-crafted oncogene theory and standardized molecular genetic technologies created a formidable package for further translations to produce a new and highly privileged *genetic* representation of cancer.

Multiple Translations versus Machiavellian Actors: Collective Work versus Fact Stabilization

Laboratory studies have provided us with understandings of the bricolage, tinkering, discourse, tacit knowledge, and situated actions that build local understandings and agreements (Cambrosio and Keating 1988; Collins 1985; Knorr Cetina 1981; Latour and Woolgar 1979; Lynch 1985; Pinch 1986).[3] Although histories of science have attended to the details of cross-situational studies of the construction of knowledge, sociologies of science have only recently begun to examine the collective construction of knowledge by different laboratories and especially by members of different social worlds through negotiation, aligning, articulation, simplification, and triangulation (Callon 1986; Clarke 1990; Fujimura 1988; Latour 1987; Law 1986; Star 1989).

In this last category, Callon's (1986), Latour's (1987), and Law's (1986) joint work proposes a compelling actor-network approach where actors' "interests" are "translated" in order to enroll them.[4] However, especially Latour's presentation of this approach has been

3. While they are not laboratory studies per se, Lave 1988 and Suchman 1987 also belong to this category of studies of local practice.
4. See also Callon and Latour 1981, Callon and Law 1982.

criticized as too Machiavellian a view in which scientific entrepreneur-generals go about waging war to conquer and discipline new allies.[5] The disagreement may be based on problems with terminology, the availability of information, and Latour's story-telling perspective. For example, in *The Pasteurization of France* (1988), Latour tells the story of Pasteur's attempt to spread his theory of the microbe. While he also demonstrates that other actors enrolled Pasteur's microbe in *their* efforts, Latour's focus is primarily on translations which facilitated Pasteur's network building.[6]

In a recent paper Star and Griesemer (1989) shift the focus of Latour's model to the *multiple translations* present in scientific work. They use an "ecological" approach framed in terms of understanding science as collective action from the viewpoints of all the actors and worlds involved, and thereby avoid the preeminence of any one actor. The ecological approach is based on views which prevailed at the University of Chicago during the first half of the twentieth century and became embedded in the pragmatist perspective in philosophy and the symbolic interactionist school in sociology. It has only recently been used to study science.[7] The ecological approach focuses on the multiple translation efforts through which scientific knowledge is constructed by standing in several positions in order to present multiple perspectives. All actors are simultaneously attempting to interest others in their concerns and objectives. The final (or temporary) outcomes of these efforts are constructed through the processes of negotiation, articulation, translation, triangulation, debating, and sometimes even coercion through "administrative persuasion" by members of different social worlds as actors attempt to install their "definitions of the situation" (Thomas and Znaniecki 1918; Hughes 1971) as the different worlds intersect.

Despite their effort to demonstrate multiple translations, how-

5. This view was expressed by two of the three speakers at a special symposium on Latour's *Science in Action* held at the 1988 meeting of the Society for the Social Studies of Science in Amsterdam. See Amsterdamska 1990. See Kondo 1990 for a nice critique of Foucault's use of violent, warlike terms for deconstructing the whole subject.

6. See Callon (1986, 1987) and Latour (1988) for efforts to take the position of nonhuman actors in the network. See also chapter 10 for a critique of this effort and Callon and Latour's (chap. 12) response to the critique.

7. For more discussion and examples of the ecological or social-worlds approach to the study of science, see Clarke 1990, in press; Clarke and Fujimura, in press; Fujimura 1987, 1988; Fujimura et al. 1987; Gerson 1983; Star 1988a, 1989; and Volberg 1983.

ever, Star and Griesemer's (1989, 390) case study is still hampered by the same difficulties faced by Latour. That is, their approach is also constrained by the availability of information and its associated story-telling perspective. Their story is based primarily on archival records, papers, and letters of Joseph Grinnell and Annie Alexander, who respectively directed and organized and funded the building of the Museum of Vertebrate Zoology at the University of California, Berkeley. Whose story gets told depends on whose life is recorded in more detail. Thus, their story is framed more in terms of the organizational and management work done by the two main characters in building the museum.

Star and Griesemer's focus on the building of the museum also distinguishes their work from Latour's. While Latour focuses on Pasteur's strategies and negotiations among social worlds to stabilize his theory of the microbe into "fact," Star and Griesemer are concerned with the problem of how members of different social worlds manage to successfully cooperate, in this case, to build the museum and to construct scientific representations despite their different viewpoints and agendas. Cooperation, they argue, is necessary to create common understandings, to ensure reliability across domains, and to gather information which retains integrity across time, space, and local contingencies. But it does not presuppose consensus. The strength of Star and Griesemer's paper lies in its focus on the viewpoints and concerns of all the participants, as far as possible, involved in building the museum.

The various actors and their interests in Star and Griesemer's study included university administrators who were attempting to make the University of California, Berkeley, into a legitimate, national-class university; amateur collectors who wanted to collect and conserve California's flora and fauna; professional trappers who wanted skins and furs to earn money; farmers who served as occasional field-workers; Annie Alexander, who was interested in conservation and educational philanthropy; and Joseph Grinnell, who wanted to demonstrate his theory that changing environments are the driving forces behind natural selection, organismal adaptation, and the evolution of species.

Star and Griesemer's contribution to the problem of how members of different social worlds interact is a new concept, *boundary objects.* They argue that boundary objects facilitate the multiple transactions needed (if we assume that nature is not directing the show) to engineer agreements among multiple social worlds (Star and Griesemer 1989, 393).

Boundary objects both inhabit several intersecting worlds . . . *and* satisfy the informational requirements of each of them. Boundary objects are objects which are both plastic enough to adapt to local needs and constraints of the several parties employing them, yet robust enough to maintain a common identity across sites. They are weakly structured in common use, and become strongly structured in individual-site use. They have different meanings in different social worlds but their structure is common enough to more than one world to make them recognizable, a means of translation.

Star and Griesemer propose that boundary objects, along with standardization of methods, were the means by which Joseph Grinnell and Annie Alexander managed the tension between heterogeneity and cooperation in their efforts to build the Museum of Vertebrate Zoology. The specific boundary objects included the museum itself as a repository, ideal-type concepts like species and diagrams, coincident boundaries like the outline of the state of California, and standardized forms like the forms Grinnell developed for trappers and amateur collectors to fill out when they obtained an animal.

These boundary objects emerged through the processes of work when the work of multiple groups coincided. They were not engineered by one individual or group. Rather, Star and Griesemer's story tells us how Grinnell *managed* these objects in such a way as to create the means for accomplishing the construction of his museum and theory. Grinnell first reconstructed California as his "laboratory in the field." California, the boundary object, was of interest to several of the participating groups. He then used this laboratory to transform himself into a preserver and conserver of California to gain support in the form of work and funding from Annie Alexander and other conservationists. Using the collected specimens and standardized information, he was able to construct unique ecological theories of evolution. Grinnell thus was able to coordinate the work of several different social worlds using several boundary objects for which each group had a *different meaning and partial jurisdiction.*

Moreover, the process of management became embedded in Grinnell's *theoretical* constructions. "Grinnell's managerial decisions about the best way to translate the interests of all these disparate worlds shaped [not only] the character of the institution he built, but also the content of his scientific claims" (Star and Griesemer 1989, 392). Griesemer (1990, 1991) argues elsewhere that the museum was Grinnell's method and data base for demonstrating his theory. It was the total museum with its ecological information that he considered important for substantiating and instantiating his theory. However, Griesemer argues that Grinnell concentrated more on specifying a standardized methodology and failed to articulate his broad theoretical views with the "methodological nitty-gritty." Rather than focusing on promoting and teaching his theory, he only promoted and taught his standard methods of collecting for building his method and data representation. Grinnell concentrated his efforts on standardizing his methods in order to get the precise ecological information he needed, along with the specimens from trappers, farmers, and amateur collectors. The end result was the disappearance of his theoretical aims from contemporary biological theory even as his careful methodology lives on. It required Griesemer's careful study of the organization of the museum's layout of specimens and Grinnell's papers in the early 1980s to reconstruct and promote the theory embedded in the museum's organization.

It should be clear by now that Star and Griesemer discuss the collective work involved in the construction of museums, claims, or theories, while Latour discusses the "hardening" of claims or theories into "facts." Grinnell used and constructed boundary objects like the "species" concept and standardized methods and forms to construct his theory qua museum. His museum, in turn, also serves as a boundary object used by *downstream users* from different social worlds for divergent purposes (e.g., by different scientists with diverse theories, conservation groups, the university administration). It is in the effort to harden his theory into fact that Grinnell failed, and this is where the very ambiguity of boundary objects which support joint organization of work across social worlds leads to the transformation of the claim it supports. Since meanings are not embodied in boundary objects, divergent uses, interpretations, and reconstructions are likely. Thus, for example, Grinnell's theory was lost, while his museum and his standardized methods continue to provide materials and methods for contemporary researchers. Multiple interpretations and uses are not necessarily a bad thing, especially for peaceful coexistence and theoretical and social change; but they are problematic for theoretical entrepreneurs, unsuccessful or successful, like Grinnell and Pasteur.

I argue, then, that although boundary objects promote collective action and coherence of information from different sites because they are more easily reconstructed (re-represented) in different local situations to fit local needs, they are equally disadvantageous for establishing the kind of "stabilization" of allies behind "facts" which Latour (1987) discusses.[8] That is, while boundary objects can promote translation for the purpose of winning allies, they can also allow others to resist translation and to construct other facts. They have a wider margin of negotiation. Latour (1987, 208–9) discusses this issue in terms of the quandary of fact builders. "They have to enrol so many others so that they participate in the continuing construction of the fact . . . , but they also have to control each of these people so that they pass the claim along without transforming it either into some other claim or into someone else's claim. . . [E]ach of the potential helping hands, instead of being 'conductor' may act in multifarious ways behaving as a 'multi-conductor': They have no interest whatsoever in the claim, shunt it towards some unrelated topic, turn it into an artefact, transform it into something else, drop it altogether, attribute it to some other author, pass it along as it is, confirm it, and so on."

Latour focuses on translation efforts to stabilize facts, while Star and Griesemer's concept of elastic boundary objects promotes our understanding of translation efforts in the management of collective work across social worlds. The strength of the concept of boundary object lies in its attention to multiple and divergent actors, social worlds, meanings, and uses. Star and Griesemer argue that boundary objects are often ill-structured, that is, inconsistent, ambiguous, and even "illogical." Yet they serve to accomplish the work to be done as defined by the actors involved. Since the local viewpoints ("interests," requirements, desires, languages, methods) of different groups are usually not identical, rigid or strongly structured entities are less likely to be able to absorb divergent instances and still maintain internal coherence or robustness.

There are both difficulties and interesting new questions in Star and Griesemer's work. What is the meaning of "getting the work done"? Whose work? Which work? For example, Grinnell succeeded in getting one of his jobs done: he built a museum, still a going concern. However, the museum (a boundary object) was and is used by many actors constructing *their* theories of speciation, evolution, and other things, while Grinnell's own theory disappeared. How did Grinnell's and Alexander's museum building affect the work of

8. Star and Griesemer's discussion differs slightly from Pickering's example of constructing coherence. Pickering (1990) focuses on the practice of theory construction and experimentation in his study of coherence formation in Morpugo's research. His concept is more similar to my concept of problem path (that is, the simultaneous construction of problem and solution as an ongoing process) (Fujimura in preparation b).

farmers and trappers? How do abstract concepts like species differ from standard forms? What are the differences between standardized forms and standardized methods? Despite the difficulties, however, the concept is valuable for its emphasis on the coordination and management of work across worlds.

Standardized Packages, Collective Work Across Worlds, and Fact Stabilization

I now want to focus on a more specific concept, standardized packages, which facilitates both collective work by members of different social worlds *and* fact stabilization (Fujimura 1986, 1988). A package differs from a boundary object in that it defines a conceptual and technical work space which is less abstract, more structured, less ambiguous, and more concrete. It is a *gray box* which combines several boundary objects (gene, cancer, oncogene or cancer gene) with standardized methods (in this case, recombinant DNA technologies) in ways which further restrict and define each object. Such codefinition and corestriction narrow the range of possible actions and practices, but also do not entirely define them. These properties of a package allow for a greater degree of "fact (and skill) stabilization" and less of the undermining which concerns Latour (1987, 208; 1990). Simultaneously, however, a standardized package is also similar to a boundary object in that it facilitates interactions and cooperative work between social worlds and increases its opportunities for being transferred into, and enrolling, other worlds; it serves therefore as an *interface* between multiple social worlds.

This combination of narrowed "work space" or range of possible practices and cross-world bridge properties is what builds bandwagons. I developed the concept of standardized packages in my effort to understand why and how the molecular biological bandwagon in cancer research developed (Fujimura 1986, 1988, in preparation. a).[9] In my case the package consisted of a scientific theory and a standardized set of technologies which succeeded in enrolling many

9. A scientific bandwagon is a situation where large numbers of people, laboratories, and organizations rapidly commit their resources to one approach to a problem. Comparative studies would help to assess the significance of theory-method standardized packages in bandwagon development. They might point to other kinds of packages or interfaces—for example, problem and data representations, problem and methods, methods and data representations, and other combinations of problem, methods, data representations, and theory—as more significant in other bandwagons.

members of multiple social worlds in constructing a new and at least temporarily stable definition of cancer.

The molecular biology cancer research bandwagon represents a major reorganization of commitments in cancer research and a major change in the organization of work for scientists and organizations. My question was how members of so many different social worlds come to agree to participate in or support molecular genetic studies of cancer, and especially studies framed in terms of a single theory of cancer. The cancer research arena previously had a host of different definitions of cancer that were developed and used by multiple lines of basic research and medical practice. Why would scientists and organizations with already-existing resource investments in different lines of research reorganize their commitments to pursue a new approach to understanding cancer? Why did they choose to commit their resources to this particular new approach? How do members of different social worlds come to practice a common approach to studying cancer? I proposed that the "translation" and "*interessement*" of members of multiple social worlds was facilitated by a standardized package of theory and methods, specifically the proto-oncogene theory and recombinant DNA and other molecular genetic technologies, which could be used to *get work done* by these many worlds; for example, researchers in many different laboratories could use it to construct and solve "doable" problems. I argued that this theory and set of methods together were used to reorganize the work yet maintain stability, integrity, and continuity in several social worlds: in laboratories in many different biological subdisciplines and medical specialties, science funding agencies (National Cancer Institute, American Cancer Society), in the U.S. Congress, in cancer research institutes, in university departments and administrations, and in biological supply organizations.

Indeed, the growth of the oncogene bandwagon was due to this capacity for maintaining the integrity of the interests of the enrolled worlds while simultaneously providing them with new tools for doing their work. For scientists in other lines of research, the theory-method package provided a theory and procedures for constructing new doable problems and the introduction of new, "sexy," recombinant DNA techniques, to augment or replace their old, well-known routines. At the same time, the oncogene theory did not challenge the theories to which the researchers had made previous commitments. Indeed, the new research provided them with ways of triangulating, of providing new evidence using new methods to support their earlier ideas. For funding organizations, it provided a means of justifying past investments whose legitimacy and productivity had been questioned, a tool for organizing and marketing their new funding agenda, and new hope for solving and possibly curing the problem of this virulent dread disease to present to Congress. The National Cancer Institute (NCI), for example, used this new research to lobby Congress for increased appropriations.[10] For Congress, it provided its members with new hope to present to their constituents. For private industry, it provided a new line of products to produce and market in the then slow biotechnology business (Johnson 1984). For university administrators, it provided a means and justification for reorganizing "old-fashioned" cancer research institutes into what seemed to be more fashionable, "hot" molecular biology institutes.[11] In other words, the package gave many different worlds ways of continuing their lines of work while simultaneously introducing novelty.

For downstream users, the package constituted conventionalized ways of carrying out tasks (or standard operating procedures) which allowed people in different lines of work to adopt and incorporate them into their laboratories and ongoing enterprises more easily and quickly. That is, it facilitated the flow of resources (concepts, skills, materials, techniques, instruments) among multiple lines of work. People in one line of research could rapidly and relatively easily adopt resources from another line of research and come to practice work in common. As such, it also served as an interface among different social worlds. An *interface* is the means by which interaction or communication is effected at the places "where peoples meet" or different social worlds intersect. It is the mechanism by which multiple intersections occur.

My argument was that the proto-oncogene theory was constructed as an abstract notion, a hypothesis, using a new unit of analysis to study and conceptualize cancer. This abstraction was general and specific enough to allow researchers in many extant lines of research to interpret the theory to fit their separate concerns all under the rubric of oncogene research. Further, the theory relied on recombinant DNA and other molecular biology technologies which by the early 1980s were standardized and conventionalized enough to be

10. Interview with Vincent de Vita, former director of NCI.

11. Interviews with respondents at the University of California, Berkeley, the University of California, San Francisco, and with a former member of the Memorial Sloan-Kettering Institute in New York. See also Boffey 1987 and Moss 1989 on Sloan-Kettering's more general shift in research from immunological to molecular biology approaches to understanding cancer.

portable from molecular biology laboratories to other biological laboratories.[12] This combination of the abstract, general oncogene theory and the specific, standardized technologies converted the novel idea into a routine. That is, the combination allowed other researchers with ongoing enterprises to *locally concretize the abstraction in different practices* to construct new problems; and the routinization allowed the new idea to move to new sites and be inserted into existing routines with manageable reorganization.

Note that I do not regard the theory-method package as constituting a necessary connection. The coupling of the oncogene theory and recombinant DNA with other molecular biology technologies is constructed and not born in nature. The theory might in the future continue to exist as an entity separate from these techniques or coupled to another set of techniques. For example, the provirus theory, which many tumor virologists consider the precursor to the present proto-oncogene theory, was coupled with traditional virological techniques (e.g., Duesberg 1983, 1985). Similarly, the technologies are coupled with quite different theories in other lines of biological research. I will discuss this issue further in the conclusion.

In the next section I discuss the construction of the oncogene theory and its advantages for enrolling others in many different lines of research with a single definition or representation of cancer as one entity. This construction and its success at enrolling others are

12. While they were new and "hot," recombinant DNA and other molecular genetic technologies for manipulating DNA in eukaryotic organisms (including humans) were also, by 1980, standardized and therefore highly transportable. That is, despite popular views of its state-of-the-art status, the protocols or requisite tasks and procedures were conventionalized and routinized in cookbook recipes and in ready-made materials and instruments. Standardized procedures reduce the amount of tacit knowledge, discretionary decision making, or trial-and-error procedures needed to solve problems. That is, what is done to what material for what reason or purpose and with what outcome are all built into the black box of transportable technologies. By the early 1980s, molecular biologists had transformed state-of-the-art tools into routine tools and made it possible for researchers in other biological specialties to be able to move these tools into their labs and for new researchers to relatively easily gain access to the tools. However, as I argue elsewhere (Fujimura 1986, 1987), articulation is never entirely eliminated even for black boxes. If we look more closely at recombinant DNA techniques, as Jordan and Lynch have done, we see that tacit knowledge has not disappeared from DNA manipulations. Even relatively mundane techniques like plasmid preps (a basic prep technique in recombinant DNA technologies) involve much tacit or local knowledge, uncertainty, and dispute. Nevertheless, novices can pick up basic plasmid prep techniques on their own from manuals and short visits with experts and without lengthy apprenticeships in other laboratories. The difference is one of degree.

based on the use of component parts which can be called boundary objects. Concepts such as "gene," "cancer," and "cancer genes" incorporated in the oncogene theory allowed members of many social worlds to adopt and adapt it while simultaneously maintaining the integrity of their local projects. However, unlike boundary objects, I argue that the package fundamentally changed local practices in enrolled scientific laboratories in ways which extend and solidify ("harden") molecular genetic representations of cancer.

Crafting the Oncogene Theory

In this section, I will focus more on how and why the oncogene theory was so successful at translating the interests of so many actors. I do not assume that the theory so closely mapped nature, so closely mapped the way that genes actually cause cancer in nature, that researchers, funding agency administrators, Congresspeople, and private entrepreneurs were convinced of its validity. Instead the plausibility and success of the oncogene theory are due to a great deal of work and the use of several key concepts and techniques which can reconcile multiple conflicting viewpoints which, in turn, allow many different groups or social worlds to cooperate in using the theory and techniques.

Scientific knowledge about cancer is constructed at the intersection of many different social worlds. There is no one world which owns the problem or the solutions. The problem of cancer is distributed among different worlds, each with its own agenda, concerns, responsibilities, and ways of working.

Clinicians frame their problems in terms of individual cases, individual patients, and standard operating procedures: how do we best treat the person given present knowledge? Medical researchers (in the fields of radiology, epidemiology, oncology, endocrinology, neurology, and pathology) work with both patients and theoretical abstractions which they construct using many cases distributed through time and space. How many patients respond to this treatment in which way? What can we say about initiation and progression of the disease when examining a number of patients over time? Basic researchers (in the fields of genetics, virology, cell biology, organismal biology, molecular biology, immunology, and neuroscience) work with theoretical abstractions and material models. How can we duplicate the cancer process in mice or cultured cells in order to use it as a tool for studying the disease? What are the origins of cancer? Among medical and basic researchers, the questions can be broken down further. What is the role of the endocrine system in causing, promoting, or retarding the initiation or growth of the disease? What is the role of chemicals, of radiation, of viruses? What are the molecular mechanisms for the initiation and progression of the disease at the levels of gene and cell? Epidemiologists track the diseases as they appear in their different manifestations (breast, liver, colon, lung, brain, cervix, prostate) across families, racial and ethnic groups, countries, parts of countries, etc. On the other end of the scale, pathologists examine cells in culture taken from tumor tissues.[13]

The point here is that participants in many different worlds work with cancer. While pathologists and physicians often interact, participants in different cancer research worlds tend to go on with their research with only cursory acknowledgment of events and research outside their narrow lines of research. There has been a proliferation of theories, methods of study, and treatments for the diseases, yielding successful treatments for a few of the leukemias, but so far no genuinely successful treatment or cure for solid tumors. Just looking at the library shelves of books, at the scores of journals and articles on cancer, can be daunting. While we have long assumed that there is some central "thing" linking these multiple representations (definitions, theories, methods, treatments), numerous attempts to "find" this elusive common denominator have failed (Shimkin 1977). Nevertheless, every so often there is a call for integration of the various lines of work. Usually these calls are ignored, not out of malice, but because of momentum and existing commitments to projects and because of difficulties in integrating the different approaches. These different worlds are working with different units of analysis, different representations of data, different scales of time and space, and different audiences.

Occasionally, however, a line of research, an approach, or a theory gains immense fame across the different worlds. Oncogene research is one such example. How does one theory gain so many adherents? I suggest several answers elsewhere (Fujimura 1986, 1988). Here I want to focus on the role of boundary objects and standardized tools in facilitating the translation of "oncogenes" from world to world to produce a robust theory.

13. Many other participants—patients, health activists groups, hospices, hospitals, alternative cancer treatment research, health insurance companies, etc.—are not on this list. I have not forgotten them but have limited my discussion here for lack of time and space.

Using boundary objects to re-represent cancer and maintain plurality

Because of the multiple ownership of, and collective work on, the problem of cancer, members of different social worlds have to successfully cooperate to construct scientific representations despite having different viewpoints on cancer. Yet as Star (1988b,9) argues, compromise between multiple and sometimes conflicting understandings and ways of dealing with phenomena while maintaining the integrity of each viewpoint is difficult to achieve. Compromise usually tends to work against pluralism, where each viewpoint maintains its own integrity. How can two entities (or objects or nodes) with two different irreconcilable epistemologies cooperate?

There are several complex answers to the question of how cooperation is accomplished.[14] I will present just two scenarios as my partial answers. The first is a brief example of a relationship between three groups of cancer researchers which allowed two of them to keep their work going through negotiation, nagging, and mutual support, or what they call "politics." This example is about hands-on work, about how researchers manage to gain the materials they need to do their research. The second scenario portrays a set of negotiations around more abstract entities. I will demonstrate that in the crafting of the oncogene theory, researchers translate the concerns of other lines of work. Boundary objects are critical elements in both of the scenarios.

Scene 1: From operating room waste to research material to research funding

In the first example, cells and cancer are concepts with different meanings in different situations. "Norma Oakdale," a cell biologist, studies the complexity of normal epithelial cells as they become or do not become cancerous.[15] One of her primary goals is to improve early detection and successful treatment of human breast cancer. Oakdale's work is based on the assumption that each individual organism's cancer is different than any other. By growing cells of each patient's tumor in culture, she can then test different treatments (e.g., various chemotherapies, prepared antibodies, hormones, etc.) in vitro and then determine the best treatment for each patient and

14. See Fujimura (1988, in prep. a) for a longer answer.
15. "Norma Oakdale" is a pseudonym, since the researcher chose to remain anonymous. Quotation marks will not be used around her pseudonym hereafter.

tumor before administering it in vivo. Oakdale and her colleagues built an institute to conduct this research and test these ideas. They located it next to a hospital in Oakland, California, where surgery on both normal and cancerous breast tissue was performed.[16] She chose a hospital which was located near a residential community in order to make it easier for the institute to obtain breast fluid secretions from women on a regular, routine basis.[17] Here I want to point to the appearance of breast tissue cells and cancer in several different worlds intersecting with the institute's work.

Human epithelial cells (cells which form the membranous lining tissues of the organism) are very difficult to grow in culture. "I grow [normal breast cells] in tissue culture in the lab. I get a very small sample from you, for example, and I put it in the laboratory, and I amplify it to a very large number. And I can then do biochemistry on them. Now that took me thirty years. I said it in one sentence, but it took me thirty years to learn how to grow those cells in culture." The few researchers who are successful at doing this all know of each other. They constitute a very small club. In part to provide a resource for her research and in part to support the institute, Oakdale grows normal and cancerous epithelial cells in culture. These cells are needed by other biological researchers for experimental purposes and were supported for a long time by National Institute of Health (NIH) grants in part because they were also necessary for experiments carried out in much more visible research.

In the late 1970s, across San Francisco Bay in a microbiological laboratory at the University of California, San Francisco, Medical Center, J. Michael Bishop and Harold T. Varmus were doing research which they decided required human epithelial cells grown in culture.[18] Instead of taking the time to grow the cells themselves, they chose to "buy" them from Oakdale's laboratory. Bishop and Varmus's laboratory did not have the time and patience, but it did have the influence to support the work done elsewhere.

It's a lot of politics, just simple politics and people interaction [to get funded by NIH]. Now, see, I've been funded to do something very fundamental and basic, and perhaps not very exciting, because Bishop and Varmus like to call me up on the phone and say, "I need cells of such-

16. Surgeons refer to normal tissue removal as reduction mammoplasty.
17. Epithelial cells are also available through lactation (breast milk) and nipple aspirations, i.e., from breast fluid secreted by normal, nonlactating women.
18. Bishop and Varmus were awarded the Nobel Prize in Physiology or Medicine in 1989 for their research on oncogenes.

and-such. Where can I get them?" Or, "Do you have them?" Or, "Will you make them for me?" And they like to have a resource like that. So my kind of work is in their interest to see that it's done. So they'll support it. [A]t some time, they need to take DNA from human cells. We've already done it on a small scale with them.

To Oakdale and her colleagues, both cancerous and normal breast tissue cells are the objects of study. Cancer cells are "cancer" in their work. I do not suggest that these researchers *believe* that cancer cells are equivalent to cancer in the organism. I do suggest that their representations of "cancer" are constructed from their work on cancer cells and not on cancer as experienced by organisms. To Bishop and Varmus, human cells are primarily sources of the valuable DNA (normal and transforming) with which they work and are sometimes used as testing grounds for the transformative (cancer-causing) properties of their DNA. Since human epithelial cells are so difficult to grow, Oakdale's cells have been transformed into sources of funds through Bishop and Varmus.

Growing human epithelial cells also requires interactions with doctors in order to obtain the human source tissues. Getting the "fresh" human tissue needed to grow epithelial cells is a difficult task for a number of reasons. Human tissue means different things to physicians and pathologists. Normal breast tissue is material to be routinely discarded in a bucket of formalin, which kills the cells. It is waste. Breast tissue diagnosed as cancerous is viewed as material for further analysis by pathologists, and otherwise as waste and as the disease cut away from the patient. Tissue is also sometimes regarded as a legal threat in the hands of others. For all these reasons, surgeons, operating room staffs, and pathologists need to be persuaded to provide the tissue.

For example, besides having "ego" difficulties, physicians and pathologists fear that researchers will find something they have missed and will subject them to malpractice suits.

> The major one is that the clinicians won't cooperate. . . Ego, primarily. [The pathologists] take a little piece [of tissue], and then they throw the rest away. When a breast is taken off, for example, a pathologist will take samples from various places—little tiny samples— and then he throws the rest away. Even though I'm sitting here dying to have it. And other research scientists as well. And if you went to the woman who gave up her breast, and you asked her for it, she'd say, "Gee, I don't need it anymore! If you can use it and if it can be of some use to the world, have it with my blessing!" I've never had a patient turn me down. But I've had doctor after doctor after doctor. They're

afraid. They're afraid I will find something that they missed. And they'll be sued. It's money. Basically money. And ego. They do not want you to suggest in any way that they missed something.

In order to overcome the legal concerns, Oakdale argued that her research on the cells could lead to better treatments and early detection of cancer, which would increase the cancer survival rate. Yet even if malpractice threats are defused, retraining surgeons and operating room staff out of old habits is another problem to be overcome. "Operating rooms and teams in operating rooms develop habits. Over the last thirty years, what they've always done with tissue is take it out, throw it in a bucket of formalin, a fixative. And once they've done that, it's finished as far as research is concerned. So that the difference in getting an operating room team to have an empty bucket or a bucket full of formalin is retraining, and that's hard to do . . . Formalin . . . inactivates—it denatures the protein. So that's a real hard problem—retraining."

Finally, while this might seem to Oakdale to be a bad habit, to physicians and surgeons it seems to be a good habit. They are not researchers. To them residual tissue is all so much waste. Retraining them to take the researcher's point of view is something that Oakdale and her colleagues, despite great effort, have not yet managed on a permanent basis. It still remains a daily task.

> Clinicians do not understand research, and how repetitive it is. So they'll say, "Well, I gave you one of those tumors two years ago, what did you do with that?" They don't understand that you need to look at them over and over and over again. So they [give it to me] once, they think that's all they need to do. So you have to tell them every single day. I get the OR [operating room] report here, I look at it, I know what [surgeries] they're doing in their operating room, and I have to call them. Every single time. I've been doing that for eight years. And if I miss one, if I'm busy and I miss one, and they dump it down the drain, they say, "Oh I didn't realize you were still collecting tumors!" . . . It's frustrating, I'll tell you.
>
> I have to have a staff that does nothing but collect specimens. Reminds people, goes and gets them, processes them. I have a liquid nitrogen bank. I can freeze and store and reconstitute cells in liquid nitrogen. So I have a liquid nitrogen bank here that is a unique resource in all the world.

Thus, tissue usually thrown into buckets of formalin becomes material for research in Oakdale's institute and in Bishop and Varmus's experimental research on oncogenes. At the same time, through Bishop and Varmus's support, tissues also turn into money, research funds for Oakdale's institute. These transformations (or translations) require careful, patient, and time-consuming management on the part of Oakdale and her colleagues.

To summarize, "cells" and "cancer" are sometimes different things to doctors, operating-room staff, patients, breast cancer cell biologists, and oncogene researchers. Yet they are similar enough to allow Oakdale and her colleagues to translate others' concerns in order to satisfy their research requirements. In order for Oakdale to do her research, she needed to coordinate her efforts with the work styles and interests of these different groups. Since she did not have the power to demand obedience, she had to persuade, cajole, badger, educate, and reciprocate with others to get them to act in her interest to preserve and give her living breast tissue cells. We see then that surgeons, patients, oncologists and operating-room staff in hospitals, and women in a community were indirect and invisible participants in the construction of the oncogene theory through work like Oakdale's and the supply of research materials.[19]

Scene 2: Crafting the oncogene theory using boundary objects

For the second scenario, I present the broader-scale crafting of the oncogene theory with an emphasis on the use of boundary objects in the processes of translation, triangulation, and re-representation. The point I want to make here is that the oncogene theory uses a package of boundary objects and standardized tools which make it possible for different worlds to cooperate in constructing a robust theory. Boundary objects in this case include *concepts* like genes, cancer, cancer genes, viral genes, cells, tumors, development, and evolution, which are quite plastic terms and often have different meanings for the various groups. The theory also relies on *data bases* of sequences which are standardized tools. Data bases allow different lines of research to share information on gene and protein sequences. These *sequences* allow different lines of research on evolution, cancer, and normal growth and development to interact in ways that had not been previously possible.

Oncogene theorists, including the aforementioned J. Michael Bishop and Harold T. Varmus, working in the late 1970s in a micro-

19. Since the time of the original interview, the National Cancer Institute has made some effort to assist accrual of specimens through legislation to protect human subjects in experimental research and through establishing regional collection networks. However, recent legal suits for property rights over commercial products constructed from tissue taken from patients have further complicated the acquisition of research materials.

biology laboratory at the University of California, San Francisco, Medical Center, drew on boundary objects and standardized tools to construct a theory which mapped onto the intellectual problems of many different scientific social worlds. For some translations (of carcinogenesis, etc.), they recrafted existing lines of research using a new unit of analysis. For other translations (of developmental biology—normal growth and development), they constructed equivalences between previously unequivalent units of analysis. For yet other translations (such as of viral oncology), they constructed continuities through time and space while introducing novelty into the scheme.

By using the concepts of genes, cancer, cancer genes, viral genes, cells, tumors, development, and evolution and standardized tools, especially data bases of sequence information, oncogene theorists succeeded in constructing working relationships with biologists in evolutionary biology and population genetics, medical genetics, tumor virology, molecular biology, cell biology, developmental biology, and carcinogenesis. The concepts were used quite loosely to allow for both variability among worlds and specificity within work sites, while the tools were used very specifically. It is this combination that allowed researchers in several fields of biology to draw on each other's work to support and extend their own lines of research and to harden their theory into fact. I will sketch a few of these interactions, which in turn show how important this combination of ambiguous concepts and specific, standardized tools were to the development of a stable oncogene theory and to the development of the bandwagon in oncogene research.

Between tumor virology and evolutionary biology: Proto-oncogenes

During the 1960s and early 1970s, tumor virologists extended their research on viral oncogenes to develop the concept of normal cellular genes as causes of human cancers by borrowing and using the concept of gene conservation from evolutionary biology. Tumor virologists reported that they had found specific "cancer" genes in the viruses which transformed cultured cells and caused tumors in laboratory animals. This experimental work was done using traditional virology and molecular biology methods to investigate RNA tumor viruses.[20] As more researchers joined in this line of research and

20. RNA tumor viruses are retroviruses which have genes constituted of RNA sequences rather than DNA. They replicate by producing a strand of DNA sequences

explored other viruses, they reported discoveries of more viral oncogenes. These viral oncogenes, however, caused cancer only in vitro
and in laboratory animals. No naturally occurring tumors in animal
and human populations were credited to viral oncogenes.[21]

In 1976 J. Michael Bishop, Harold T. Varmus, and their colleagues
at the University of California, San Francisco, announced that they
had found a normal cellular gene sequence in various normal cells
of several avian species which was very similar in structure to the
chicken viral oncogene, called src (Stehelin et al. 1976). Two years
later, after constructing a probe for their viral oncogene, they reported
that they had also discovered DNA sequences related to the src viral
oncogene in the DNA of normal cells in many different vertebrate
species from fish to primates, including humans (Spector et al.
1978).[22] Bishop and Varmus and their collaborators suggested that
the viral gene causing cancer in animals was transduced from normal cellular genes by the virus; that is, the virus took part of the
cellular gene and made it part of its own genetic structure. Based on
their research and that of others, Bishop and Varmus speculated that
some qualitative alteration (through point mutation, amplification,
chromosomal translocation) of this normal cellular gene may play
an important role as a cause of human cancer.[23] Before this theory,
human cancer research and viral oncogene research had been en-

---

through the activities of an enzyme called reverse transcriptase. See Studer and Chubin 1980 and Watson, et al. 1987.

21. However, researchers did report suspected links between some human cancers
and retroviruses. See especially Gallo 1986.

22. Molecular biologists claim that since a gene is constructed of a specific sequence of nucleotide bases along a continuous strand of DNA, simply locating a
particular gene of interest is akin to searching for the proverbial needle in a haystack.
The human genome, divided into twenty-three paired DNA molecules, for example,
is very long and complex. It contains three billion nucleotide base pairs (constituting
perhaps fifty to one hundred thousand genes). The genome of a frog is even longer.
Even the viral genome is long; for example, the DNA of the SV40 monkey tumor
virus consists of 5,243 nucleotide base pairs. Molecular biologists argue that constructing DNA probes is one way of locating homologous genes. A probe is a syntheti-
cally constructed strand of DNA, called an oligonucleotide. In 1978 probes were still
relatively difficult to construct. In 1990 most probes were constructed by automated
DNA synthesizers. The procedure is routine. See below for more discussion of probes.

23. The proto-oncogene theory in 1990 included the concept of antioncogenes (or
tumor suppressor genes) introduced by Robert Weinberg (see below). Inactivation of
these antioncogenes is another proposed mechanism by which normal genes can become cancer-causing genes. In addition, by 1990 a total of nearly thirty possible proto-
oncogenes had been reported in the literature. I discuss the early origins of the theory

tirely orthogonal to each other, despite decades of efforts to link viruses to human cancer.[24]

These speculations were based in part on an earlier theory, the oncogene hypothesis of Huebner and Todaro (1969) and on accumulated research reports about the structures and mechanisms of viral oncogenesis. The difference between the earlier theory and the Bishop and Varmus theory was Bishop's and Varmus's conjecture that the gene was originally part of the cell's normal genome rather than a viral gene implanted by viruses sometime in the organism's evolutionary history.

Bishop and Varmus's proposal that the gene which caused normal cells to become cancer cells was part of the cell's normal genetic endowment was based on arguments about "evolutionary logic." Since the gene was found in fish, which are evolutionarily quite ancient, the gene must have been conserved through half a billion years of evolution. Their critics simultaneously based their criticisms on the theory's "evolutionary illogic." Why would a cancer gene be conserved through evolution? At the time, the announcement of normal cellular genes homologous to a viral oncogene in humans was greeted with some skepticism.

> The first couple of years [after the discovery] were difficult. [Our findings that viral oncogenes had homologous sequences in normal cellular genes] were extended with some difficulty to a second and third gene . . ., and then it was rapidly extended to all the rest [of the twenty known viral oncogenes]. We had to overcome a bias in the field. Our findings were first. . . Well, they were rationalized. It was hard for us to come to grips with the idea that a gene carried by a chicken virus that caused cancer was also in human beings. It didn't make sense. *Why would we have cancer genes as part of our evolutionary dowry?* (Interview 7:7)

On the other hand, Bishop argues that their proposal was also "evolutionarily logical."

> Our first evidence that human beings had this gene, although it evolutionarily looked just fine, there are a lot of biologists who don't really accept the evolutionary logic . . . So until the gene was isolated from humans and shown to be the same as what we'd started with,

---

in this paper. See Fujimura (in preparation a) for a discussion of oncogene theory and research as it was in 1990.

24. See Fujimura 1988, in preparation a; Studer and Chubin 1980.

there was still some doubt. At the outset, there was a lot of skepticism as to whether we had really found the same gene in human beings. That's an anthropomorphism that amused me. Everyone was perfectly happy that the gene was in chickens or even mice, but it wasn't supposed to be in humans. I don't know why. But there was a lot of resistance to that. (Interview 7 : 8–9).

"Evolutionary logic" is used here to argue for and against their findings. The conservation of cancer genes fails as evolutionary logic to support their theory, while the location of gene sequences similar to the viral oncogene in many different species points to the evolutionary success of the gene sequence. The way out of this paradox was normal growth and development.

Before discussing developmental biology, I want to point out that Bishop and Varmus are here attempting to construct a *two-way relationship* with evolutionary biology. They are not simply drawing on evolutionary arguments. They are also attempting to inject their theories, inscriptions, and materials into the wealth of research, debates, and controversy in evolutionary biology.[25]

Transduction by retroviruses is the only tangible means by which vertebrate genes have been mobilized and transferred from one animal to another without the intervention of an experimentalist. How does this transduction occur? What might its details tell us of the mechanisms of recombination in vertebrate organisms? What does it reflect of the potential plasticity of the eukaryotic genome? Can it transpose genetic loci other than cellular oncogenes? *Has it figured in the course of evolution?* How large is its role in natural as opposed to experimental carcinogenesis? These are ambitious questions, yet the means to answer most of them appear to be at hand. (Bishop 1983, 347–48; emphasis added)[26]

Links to developmental biology

Normal growth and development are research problems which form the basis of developmental biology. This has been, and remains,

25. Evolutionary biology, and especially evolutionary genetics, is so embroiled in debates that oncogene researchers may succeed in this effort to propose a role for oncogenes in evolutionary biology. The units-of-selection debates so closely studied by philosophers of science are just one indication of the lack of consensus about the unit, levels, and processes by which selection and evolution occur. See, for example, Lloyd 1988 and Brandon 1990 for an overview and analysis of the units-of-selection debates.

26. Other suggestions of oncogenes as a source of genetic variation and as an indication of the course of evolution were made by Temin (1971, 1980) and by Walter Gilbert's research group (Schwartz et al. 1983), respectively.

an established and popular field of biological research. At the time of Bishop and Varmus's initial announcements, they proposed that their "normal" proto-oncogene had something to do with cell division. Later, as researchers in molecular biology and biochemistry of normal growth and development began proposing the existence of growth factor genes based on research on growth factor protein, Bishop and Varmus began to tie their work on oncogenes both theoretically and concretely to concurrent studies on growth factor proteins. For example, Michael Waterfield (Waterfield et al. 1983) of the Imperial Cancer Research Fund in London reported that a partial sequence of platelet-derived growth factor (PDGF) was nearly identical to that deduced for the protein product of the *sis* oncogene of simian sarcoma virus. In 1984, Waterfield's laboratory reported that they had found that the epidermal growth factor (EFG) receptor protein was identical to an oncogene's (*erbB*) protein product studied by the Varmus and Bishop group.

This link between normal growth factors and proto-oncogenes provided an evolutionarily acceptable (logical) explanation for finding that potentially cancer-causing genes were conserved through time.

> The logic of evolution would not permit the survival of solely noxious genes. Powerful selective forces must have been at work to assure the conservation of proto-oncogenes throughout the diversification of metazoan phyla. Yet we know nothing of why these genes have been conserved, only that they are expressed in a variety of tissues and at various points during growth and development, that they are likely to represent a diverse set of biochemical functions, and that they may have all originated from one or a very few founder genes. Perhaps the proteins these genes encode are components of an interdigitating network that *controls the growth of individual cells during the course of differentiation*. We are badly in need of genetic tools to approach these issues, *tools that may be forthcoming from the discovery of proto-oncogenes* in Drosophila and nematodes. (Bishop 1983, 347–48; emphasis added)
>
> And it took us a while to convince people that [these genes] might have a different purpose in the normal body. And then finally that perhaps they had a different purpose in the normal body, but if something went wrong with them, they would become cancer genes as they were in the virus. (Interview 7:8)

Bishop expanded the number of research problems in his laboratory from one viral oncogene to studies of several viral oncogenes and their related proto-oncogenes, and included questions regarding the normal functions of the proto-oncogenes in developmental biology.

> My laboratory doesn't much resemble what it was ten years ago. . . [How has it changed and why?] The work's evolved in response to progress in the field. You get one problem solved, and you move on to something new that presents itself. A number of people in my laboratory are explicitly interested in normal growth and development. They're here because we believe that the cellular genes we study are probably involved in normal growth and development. And I wasn't studying cellular genes involved in normal growth and development fifteen years ago. . . There is a conceptual and probably mechanistic connection between cancer and development. But I'm not a developmental biologist, and I haven't read seriously in the field. There are people in my laboratory who will probably become developmental biologists as they fashion their own careers. (Interview 7:19)

The links between viral and cellular oncogenes and developmental biology were concretized in links between his laboratory and a Drosophila genetics laboratory through a shared student.

> I have a major collaboration with another member of the biochemistry faculty here, a Drosophila geneticist, because we use genetic analysis in Drosophila to try to see what the genes we study do in development. And I'm not a geneticist, and he's not a student of oncogenes, so that's a necessary collaboration. We have joint students between us, several now. (Interview 7:20–21)

By now, retroviruses and viral oncogenes are linked to the course of evolution, Drosophila genetics, and normal growth and development in developmental biology through proto-oncogenes. Here again proto-oncogenes are the boundary object which facilitates the translation of one group's interests into the interests of other groups and link laboratories in different lines of research into a single network.

Mutual translation: molecular biological oncogenes and tumor virological oncogenes

I discussed how tumor virologists used oncogenes to translate their own interests into the interests of others. Here I present an example of mutual translation between viral oncogene researchers and a group of molecular biologists attempting to link their work to viral oncogenes.

In 1978, soon after the Bishop and Varmus announcements, a

few molecular biology laboratories began to study cancer using recombinant DNA technologies, especially gene transfer techniques, and soon reported that they had found cancer genes similar to Bishop and Varmus's proto-oncogenes.[27] In one experiment researchers in Weinberg's laboratory at the Whitehead Institute at the Massachusetts Institute of Technology first exposed "normal" mouse cells to DNA from mouse cells that had been transformed by chemical carcinogens.[28] The outcome, as reported by the researchers, was the transformation of the "normal" cells into cancer cells. They (Weinberg 1983, 127A) concluded from the experimental outcomes that "the information for being a tumor cell [was] transferred from one [mammalian] cell to another by DNA molecules." These and other research groups attempted other more sophisticated experiments where they used human tumor DNA to transform normal cells in culture. Using recombinant DNA technologies to devise a new molecular cloning approach, these researchers reported that they had finally isolated an oncogene which was the transforming factor, independent of any epigenetic (or environmental) factors. More significantly, this single gene was mutated at a single point. Weinberg claimed that a single point mutation had caused the normal gene to become a cancer-causing gene.[29]

> The successful isolation of transforming DNA in three laboratories by three different methods directly associated transforming activity with discrete segments of DNA. No longer was it necessary to speak vaguely of "transforming principles." Each process of molecular cloning had yielded a single DNA segment carrying a single gene with a definable structure. These cloned genes had potent biological activity. . . The transforming activity previously attributed to the tumor-cell DNA as a whole could now be assigned to a single gene. It was an oncogene: a cancer gene (Weinberg 1983, 130).

27. See Parada et al. 1982; Tabin et al. 1982; Land et al. 1983; and Goldfarb et al. 1982. See Angier 1988 for an account of research in Weinberg's and Wigler's laboratories.

28. These "normal" cells, called NIH 3T3 cells, are somewhat ambiguous cells. They are not entirely normal, since they have been passaged so many times in the laboratory. That is, the original cells taken from normal mouse tissue in the early 1960s have by now adapted to the artificial conditions of cell cultures (plates of agar filled with nutrients to feed them and antibiotics to prevent them from being infected with bacteria) and are no longer entirely normal. They are referred to as "immortalized cells."

29. Weinberg's claims have since been toned down. Current views are that at least two events, and perhaps up to eight events, are necessary to transform "truly normal" cells into cancer cells. See Fujimura (in preparation a) for more details.

Weinberg (1982, 136) argued that his transfected oncogenes were of a class with the oncogenes reported by tumor virologists Bishop and Varmus.

> A second question concerns the relation of these oncogenes to those which have been appropriated from the cellular genome by retroviruses and used to form chimeric viral-host genomes. The most well known of these genes is the avian sarcoma virus *src* gene, the paradigm of a class of more than a dozen separate cellular sequences. Do these two classes of oncogenes, those from spontaneous tumors and those affiliated with retroviruses, overlap with one another or do they represent mutually exclusive sets?
>
> Although the answer to this is not yet at hand, it will be forthcoming, since many of the sequence probes required to address this question are already in hand.

Weinberg (1982, 135) argued that while "the study of the molecular biology of cancer has until recently been the domain of tumor virologists," it now was also the domain of molecular biologists. In 1983, he and his associates (Land et al. 1983, 391) claimed to have confirmed this equivalence between these sets of oncogenes.

> Two independent lines of work, each pursuing cellular oncogenes, have converged over the last several years. Initially, the two research areas confronted problems that were ostensibly unconnected. The first focused on the mechanisms by which a variety of animal retroviruses were able to transform infected cells and induce tumors in their own host species. The other, using procedures of gene transfer, investigated the molecular mechanisms responsible for tumors of nonviral origin, such as those human tumors traceable to chemical causes. *We now realize that common molecular determinants may be responsible for tumors of both classes.* These determinants, the cellular oncogenes, constitute a functionally heterogeneous group of genes, members of which may cooperate with one another in order to achieve the transformation of cells. (emphasis added)

Bishop (1982, 92) supported Weinberg's arguments.

> Weinberg and Cooper have evidently found a way of transferring active cancer genes from one cell to another. They have evidence that different cancer genes are active in different types of tumors, and so it seems likely that their approach should appreciably expand the repertory of cancer genes available for study. None of the cancer genes uncovered to date by Weinberg and Cooper is identical with any known oncogene. Yet is is clearly possible that there is only one large family of cellular oncogenes. If that is so, the study of retroviruses and

the procedures developed by Weinberg and Cooper should eventually begin to draw common samples from that single pool.

To summarize, a few molecular biologists constructed an equivalence between their cancer genes and the proto-oncogenes of tumor virologists. They argued that their cancer genes were in the same class of cancer genes reported by tumor virologists. This representation expanded the category of proto-oncogenes to include genes which had been transformed by chemicals reported to be carcinogens in volumes of previous studies on cells, on whole organisms, and especially on humans. The work in Weinberg's laboratory links carcinogenesis studies, human cancer, and oncogenes. This simultaneously provided a new link between Bishop and Varmus's oncogene and carcinogenesis studies. As sets of researchers embraced one another's work, the concept of a normal gene causing cancer becomes more stable.

Re-representing cancer

By 1983 the new unified proto-oncogene theory of cancer had been adopted into and used as the basis of research of investigation in programs in several new and established lines of biological and biomedical research. The oncogene theorists constructed cancer genes which they claimed mapped onto the intellectual problems of many different scientific social worlds. They claimed that their cancer genes accounted for findings in many other lines of cancer research and represented a unified pathway to cancer in humans and other higher organisms. If one looks closely at these alliances, however, one sees that the mapping is quite *heterogeneous*. Links were constructed between evolution, developmental biology, and molecular biology as well as between established lines of biomedical research on cancer. These various links were patched together to present a coherent re-representation of cancer in molecular genetic terms.

For example, Weinberg (1983, 134) speculated broadly that the proto-oncogene theory accounted for findings in many lines of cancer research. "What is most heartening is that the confluence of evidence from a number of lines of research is beginning to make sense of a disease that only five years ago seemed incomprehensible. The recent findings at the level of the gene are consistent with earlier insights into carcinogenesis based on epidemiological data and on laboratory studies of transformation."

Bishop (1982, 91) similarly linked Bishop and Varmus's work to cancer research in medical genetics and epidemiology. "Medical geneticists may have detected the effects of cancer genes years ago, when they first identified families whose members inherit a predisposition to some particular form of cancer. Now, it appears, tumor virologists may have come on cancer genes directly in the form of cellular oncogenes."

In a volume entitled *RNA Tumor Viruses, Oncogenes, Human Cancer, and AIDS: On the Frontiers of Understanding*, editors, Furmanski, Hager, and Rich (1985, xx), also called for further links to be made between oncogene research on causation and *clinical problems* in cancer research: "We must turn these same tools of molecular biology and tumor virology, so valuable in dissecting and analyzing the causes of cancer, to the task of understanding other equally critical aspects of the cancer problem: progression, heterogeneity, and the metastatic process. These are absolutely crucial to our solving the clinical difficulties of cancer: detection, diagnosis, and effective treatment."

Cancer genes, however, do not in and of themselves mechanistically connect together the multiple viewpoints (approaches, theories, methods) mentioned above. Rather the oncogene theory is a *new* representation of cancer, this time in terms of normal cellular genes, the proto-oncogenes. The multitude of representations of chemical carcinogenesis, radiation carcinogenesis, tumor progression, metastasis, and so forth are *re-represented* using *a new unit of analysis. They are locally re-represented in laboratories, research protocols, and transforming cells in culture, and formally re-represented in a new theory.* While this new theory provides a *metaphoric* tying together of the "nodes of the system," the work is done by many heterogeneous actors. Some of these re-representations were facilitated by standardized tools such as probes and sequence data bases, which eventually became part of the standardized package of proto-oncogene theory and molecular genetic technologies.

Using Standardized Tools to Maintain Continuity by Standardizing the World inside and outside the Laboratory

Oncogene researchers went beyond speculation by reconstructing their laboratory work to pursue some of the proposed problems, as the above example of Bishop's laboratory's work on normal growth and development shows. At the same time, researchers in other lines of research took the opportunity to reconstruct work in their laboratories to pursue some of the proposed problems. This reconstruction introduced novelty into their laboratory's work while simultaneously maintaining continuity with previous and other on-going research. That is, Bishop's student was still working with oncogenes, but now in the context of a different problem: normal growth and development.

In another example, a senior biophysicist whose laboratory stud-ied the effects of radiation on carcinogenesis (on transforming cells in culture) similarly expanded his laboratory's research by incorpo-rating oncogene research to explore new levels of analysis. After much excitement about the oncogene theories of carcinogenesis, he sent his student to train in recombinant DNA techniques in a nearby laboratory in order to study two problems: first, whether ra-diation played a role in the mutating or transposing one or several proto-oncogenes and, second, whether radiation damage to cells made it easier for the viral oncogene to become integrated into the normal cellular genome. In this example, radiation stayed constant, while the experimental process and problem context changed from manipulating cells to manipulating genes.

Reconstructing laboratories can, however, lead to deconstructing theory. In order to shape these subsequent reconstructions and re-representations, oncogene theorists attempted to standardize the world. Standardizing the world outside one's laboratory is one way to maintain continuity in scientific constructions. The oncogene re-searchers' *tools for standardizing the world* include probes, data bases, and sequences.

Probes are constructed strands of DNA, called oligonucleotides, which researchers use to locate homologous gene sequences in larger strands of DNA.[30] In their efforts to allay the skepticism met by their new theory and to win converts to it, Bishop and Varmus distributed their probes for proto-oncogenes to other laboratories and to suppliers, thus specifically facilitating replication of their re-sults as well as further oncogene research in other laboratories by providing standardized tools: "We've had so many requests for our probes for [two cellular oncogenes] that we had one technician working full-time on making and sending them out. So we finally turned over the stocks to the American Type Culture Collection" (Interview 19:3). Any researcher can call or write the ATCC to order the probes at the cost of maintenance and shipping. These probes are more than physical materials. They are constructed categories which embody the specific work organizations of the laboratories in

30. See n. 22 for more details on probes.

which they had been constructed. Exporting probes is one attempt to standardize the world outside. With Bishop and Varmus's probe, researchers are more likely to find what Bishop and Varmus found than if they constructed probes of their own.

Data bases allow different lines of research to share information on gene and protein sequences. These *sequences* allow different lines of research on evolution, cancer, and normal growth and development to interact in ways that had not been previously possible.

Data bases are the computerized version of *publications* of sequence information. Before more efficient retrieval software was constructed for accessing the computerized data bases, scientific journals and books published sequence information related to particular topics. For example, some scientists served as "curators" for book "repositories" by pulling together and publishing in one document all of the published sequences on a specific research topic to aid search-and-retrieval procedures. Computerized data bases and new search-and-retrieval software increase the speed of work.[31] For example, by searching through the data base, Michael Waterfield, a technical expert on peptide mapping and amino acid sequencing, constructed ties between the epidermal growth factor (EFG) receptor protein and the *erbB* viral oncogene's protein product and between platelet-derived growth factor (PDGF) and the protein product of the *sis* oncogene of simian sarcoma virus. These earlier publications and the new computerized data bases are repositories of information which is coded in standardized forms in order that it can be used by many different scientific worlds.

Centralized, systematic data bases hold DNA, RNA, and protein amino acid sequence information—organized and annotated (for example, by selected host organisms and by taxonomies of organisms)—on many organisms, including humans. The major data bases are located at the Los Alamos National Laboratory in the United States and at the European Molecular Biology Laboratory (EMBL) in Heidelberg, Germany. The American data base, called Genetic Sequence Data Bank or GenBank, is funded by several NIH agencies (including the National Cancer Institute), the National Science Foundation, the Department of Energy, and the Department of Defense. GenBank and EMBL share the job of collecting sequence

---

31. Walter Gilbert, a molecular biologist at Harvard University, argues that these data bases and software also change the quality of work. Indeed, he argues that they are creating a paradigm shift in biology from an experimentally based discipline to a theoretically based discipline.

information and then pool their information. By 1987 GenBank contained 13 million base pairs of total DNA sequence information and 1.9 million base pairs of human DNA sequence information, and it has since rapidly expanded. Information in both data bases is organized in standardized, computer-readable form (Office of Technology Assessment Report 1988). "Access to the data is through distribution of magnetic tapes and floppy disks, direct computer-to-computer and computer-to-terminal transfer over telephone lines, and computational resources ... which provide access to both sequence-data and sequence-analysis programs for the nation's academic molecular biologists" (Friedland and Kedes 1985, 1172).[32]

The sequence data bases allow scientists a faster and more efficient method for accessing information needed for experiments or for interpreting experiments. Some of the kinds of analyses scientists can perform using the data base system include translation and location of potential protein coding regions; inter- and intrasequence homology searches; inter- and intrasequence dyad symmetry searches; analysis of codon frequency, base composition, and dinucleotide frequency; location of AT- or GC-rich regions; and mapping of restriction enzyme sites.[33] That is, for example, researchers put their DNA, RNA, or amino acid sequence information into the computer in order to seek homologies—other DNA, RNA, or amino acid sequences which are homologous to theirs. Homologies are similar sequences which are hypothesized to have a common ancestor at some point in their evolutionary history (see Fujimura 1991b for a discussion of homologies).

An oncogene researcher describes the speed and efficiency with which two previously unrelated areas of research (arteriosclerosis and growth factors) were "found to be related" through the use of computers and the sequence data bases.[34] (Note that the epidermal growth factor (EGF) receptor protein had earlier been reported to be identical to the *erbB* oncogene's protein product.)

32. For literature on sequence data bases, see Friedland and Kedes 1985, and Smith 1986.

33. See Friedland and Kedes 1985, 1172–73, for concise descriptions of these functions.

34. By streamlining the procedures and knowledge requirements for identifying sequence homologies, the computerized sequence data bases allow scientists to pass some of their tasks on to other lab members. In an academic oncogene laboratory, the director had hired an undergraduate student to handle much of the computerized data base work. The student did not have to know about the relevant journals, authors, and articles in the research topic area in order to search for sequence homologies using the computer.

In fact, nobody has to read any more. . . [A]t least nobody has to read [pages of sequence data in search of specific information], because the computer's changed the face of that aspect of science. . . . [T]he way this is usually done is to take your sequence and plug it into the computer and ask the computer to search a gene bank, a sequence bank, for relationships. So just yesterday, for example, a fellow visiting here . . . described some experiments . . . in which he was looking at the receptor for low-density lipoproteins. This is a receptor which is required to clear the blood of cholesterol. People who lack this receptor develop arteriosclerosis and myocardial infarctions at an early age. [The visitor] and his colleague . . . some years ago defined the receptor. They recently purified and cloned and sequenced the gene, that is, sequenced a copy of the messenger RNA of the gene. When they plugged their sequence into the computer, they got back information that the receptor was very similar to a protein that serves as a precursor for the growth factor we've been talking about, EGF [epidermal growth factor]. So there we're dealing not with identity but with similarity. We have the information that two genes that seem ostensibly unrelated are, in fact, closely related members of a gene family. (Interview 12:10–11)

In order for the data bases to be constructed and to be useful, information is standardized. The sequence data bases contain information in terms of the biochemical sequences of DNA, RNA, and amino acids. The sequences are used to represent genes and proteins in terms of a linear description of deoxyribonucleic acids (DNA), ribonucleic acid molecules (RNA), and amino acid molecules of proteins. If we just limit our concerns to the terms of these realist representations, the complex properties of each molecule, of each set of molecules that constitute genes and proteins, and of gene and protein interactions with other parts of its environments (cellular, organismal, extraorganismal) are eliminated from this data base.[35]

The sequence information for different types of phenomena is expressed in the same chemical language. This language standardizes the form of the representations of the phenomena. This standardization or common language is what allows for collaborative work across both laboratories and worlds.[36] It is also what allows for claims of triangulation of different lines of research on a particular phenomenon. Homologies, for instance, are coincident representations. This coincidence, however, is based on *interdependence* rather than independence. Phenomena are first represented using

35. See Fujimura 1991b for more on the constructed complexities and simplicities of DNA and proteins.
36. This is similar to the processes of naming (nomenclature) and classifying medical diseases, biological flora and fauna, and races.

one language standard, and then similarities within the language system are constructed or found.

Sequence information, then, is just one kind of re-representation of earlier theories of the gene and proteins which in turn are kinds of representations. For instance, Burian and Fogle (1990) argue that there is a qualitative difference between the traditional definition of gene, even as late as 1965, and what molecular genetics now considers to be a gene (cf. Kitcher 1982). I argue that gene and protein sequence information are markers for complex phenomena and that the homologous relationships constructed through comparing sequence information on line may be more a construction of coincident markers than of homologous phenomena. The robustness of the oncogene theory, then, is based on coincident representations or markers which in turn are based on a standardized language or form of representation.

Thus, concepts, probes, and data bases of sequences are the result of *"homologies" between laboratories as well as between representations of phenomena.* These collective constructions are then used to reconstruct laboratory work organizations as well as experimentally produced representations. Both kinds of homologies are part of creating and maintaining continuities across lines of research and through time.

Continuity and the National Cancer Institute

NCI administrators joined in the effort to promote the oncogene theory for several reasons.[37] Their sponsors were Congress and the public it represented, including other scientists. The oncogene theory provided them with both the justification for past research investments in the Virus Cancer Program (VCP) and with a product to present to Congress.

In the 1960s the National Cancer Institute focused on the role of viruses in cancer etiology through a special, well-funded Virus Cancer Program. Many virologists and molecular biologists were funded through NCI through this program, both before and after the National Cancer Act of 1971, to study what are now called DNA tumor viruses and retroviruses (or RNA tumor viruses).[38] Both the act and

37. This paper discusses one reason for NCI's promotion of oncogene research. See Fujimura 1988 for further reasons.

38. I present more detailed versions of this history below. See also Chubin and Studer 1978; DeVita 1984; Rettig 1977; Strickland 1972; and Studer and Chubin 1980.

its viral research component were controversial and much-maligned efforts. Controversy raged over both the contractual basis for dispensing research funds and the huge sums of money concentrated on the virus cancer program, that is, on what was considered by many at that time to be a high-risk bet that viruses caused human cancer.

After twenty years of research, no viruses had been linked to human cancer, and the program had been thoroughly maligned by its critics. As the following statements demonstrate, the proposed role of proto-oncogenes in causing human cancer was in the early 1980s used to justify past investments in viral oncology.

> The study of viruses far removed from human concerns has brought to light powerful tools for the study of human disease. Tumor virology has survived its failure to find abundant viral agents of human cancer. The issue now is not whether viruses cause human tumors (as perhaps they may, on occasion) but rather how much can be learned from tumor virology about the mechanisms by which human tumors arise. (J. Michael Bishop [1982,92], tumor virologist)

> Given the still prevalent unfair public misconception that the NCI Tumor Virus Program was a failure, and the new strong possibility (fact?) that most if not all of viral oncogenes have their human counterparts, the time is more than ripe for NCI to point out how well the public purse has, in fact, been used. (James D. Watson, molecular biologist)[39]

> We have often been asked if the NCP [National Cancer Program] has been a success. While I acknowledge a bias, my answer is an unqualified "yes." The success of the Virus Cancer Program which prompted this essay is a good example. Since its inception, this Program has cost almost $1 billion. If asked what I would pay now for the information generated by that Program, I would say that the extraordinarily powerful new knowledge available to us as a result of this investment would make the entire budget allocated to the NCP since the passage of the Cancer Act worthwhile. There may well be practical applications of this work in the prevention, diagnosis, and treatment of cancer that constitute a significant paradigm change. The work in viral oncology has indeed yielded a trust fund of information, the dividend

---

39. This statement was quoted by DeVita in his 1984 essay. Watson, as Nobel laureate (1956), has used his influence to push for the institutional growth of molecular biology. More recently he has been a prime mover and shaker behind the Human Genome Initiative, the three-billion-dollar effort to map and later sequence the entire human genome.

of which defies the imagination. (Vincent T. DeVita, Jr. [1984, 5], former director, National Cancer Institute)

Both oncogene researchers and cancer research administrators argued then, that the "new" oncogene research would be based on the "extraordinarily powerful new knowledge" produced by past investments. The viral cancer genes constructed from the investments of the NCI in the Viral Cancer Program during the 1960s and 1970s have in the 1980s become human cancer genes through the oncogene theory and recombinant DNA technologies. Viral cancer genes with no previous connection to human cancer have now become human cancer genes. In their view, the NCI's and James Watson's earlier choices and predictions have been proven fruitful and justified, while Bishop's theory gains credibility from De Vita's and Watson's translations. Here, then, is mutual translation for mutual benefit.[40]

Discussion and Conclusion

In a recent interview, an oncogene researcher balked at my use of the term "oncogene theory." He argued that oncogenes are a fact, not a theory. I have used the concepts of standardized packages, boundary objects, and translation to show how different social worlds interacted through time and space to collectively craft this fact. Each world is changed in some manner, yet each also maintains its uniqueness and integrity in the construction and adoption of the standardized package of proto-oncogene theory and recombinant DNA technologies. The package provided both dynamic opportunities for divergent meanings and uses as well as stability. Using recombinant DNA technologies and selected boundary objects, Bishop and Varmus constructed multiple translations between oncogene research, on the one hand, and evolutionary biology, developmental biology, cell biology, carcinogenesis research, and more, on the other hand. They are not simply drawing on arguments from these lines of research. They are also installing their theories, inscriptions and materials into these ongoing lines of research. A combination of ambiguous concepts and standardized tools are used to construct homologies between laboratories as well as between representations of phenomena.[41] These collective constructions packaged together are

40. More recently, Watson and Walter Gilbert have used the oncogene research findings as justification for the development of the Human Genome Initiative.

41. However, there are still many unanswered questions. For example, how do abstract concepts like cancer genes differ from standard forms like the precise lan-

used to reconstruct laboratory work organizations as well as experimentally produced representations. Both kinds of homologies are part of creating and maintaining continuities within and across lines of research and across time and space. Hybrid lines of research are also constructed through this process of intersection. For example, Bishop's student who worked on the problem of oncogene activities in development is a hybrid product of two formerly separate lines of research. However, the original lines of research also continue.

The package of concepts and standardized tools is useful for understanding both the stability and the dynamism of the oncogene theory. Less structured concepts, such as cancer, cells, genes, and cancer genes, and standardized tools, such as probes, the language of sequence information, and sequence data bases, were used to craft the oncogene theory. These objects provide a way of talking about a theory which appears to be both simple and complex, both static and dynamic. Together they help to explain how the theory can be continuous across time and space through different social worlds.

The newly crafted oncogene theory was then used in conjunction with newly standardized recombinant DNA and other molecular genetic technologies as a package to enroll other researchers, biological supply companies, the National Cancer Institute, the American Cancer Society, members of Congress, and the Nobel Prize Committee.

My point is that packages of ambiguous concepts and standardized tools, of theory and methods, are powerful tools for insuring fact stabilization. Whether concepts or standardized tools alone can achieve fact stabilization is an empirical question. The two examples discussed in this paper suggest otherwise.

In contrast to Grinnell's focus on standard methods of collecting and on building the museum and his relative neglect of his ecological theory of evolution, oncogene theorists immediately began to promote and teach their theory to new audiences. They also used

---

guage of sequence information? What are the differences between standardized forms and standardized methods? In this case, the more precise but static sequence language is the form, and less precise but active recombinant DNA and other molecular genetic technologies are the methods. See Fujimura 1991b. While standardized forms are static, they still act by constraining other actions. Census forms, for example, force people to fit themselves into one of several racial or ethnic categories. The only choice left for bicultural people has been the residual category of "other." Efforts are now being made to add more fluid categories, but bureaucrats are finding that a difficult task precisely because of the static property of forms. Thus, this boundary object both enables some action and disables others.

molecular genetic technologies to instantiate and substantiate their theory. The combination is what I called the standardized package. This combined theory-methods package, the triangulation of efforts by several lines of research, and a great deal of work constitute the new vision of cancer which has become part of the canon.

I do not regard the theory-methods package as constituting a necessary connection. The coupling of the oncogene theory and recombinant DNA and other molecular biology technologies is constructed, and not born in nature. The theory may in the future continue to exist as an entity separate from these techniques or coupled to another set of techniques. Similarly, the technologies are coupled with quite different theories in other lines of biological research.

I am interested in standardized packages and other such crafted tools because I would argue that they can be used by scientists to define their areas of expertise and power. It is through the use of standardized packages that scientists constrain work practices and define, describe, and contain representations of nature and reality. The same tool that constrains representations of nature can simultaneously be a flexible dynamic construction with different faces in other research and clinical and applied worlds. A standardized package is used as a dynamic interface to translate interests between social worlds. This is true for the social as well as the natural sciences. Examining the construction, maintenance, and augmentation of these packages will help us to understand not only how we came to have the representations we now hold sacred but also that there are other possible representations, other ways of knowing and practicing.

REFERENCES

Amsterdamska, O. 1990. Surely You are Joking, Monsieur Latour! *Science, Technology, and Human Values* 14:495–504.

Angier, N. 1988. *Natural Obsessions: The Search for the Oncogene.* Boston: Houghton Mifflin.

Becker, H. S. 1982. *Art Worlds.* Berkeley: University of California Press.

Bijker, W. E., T. P. Hughes and T. J. Pinch, eds. 1987. *The Social Construction of Technological Systems: New Directions in the Sociology and History of Technology.* Cambridge: MIT Press.

Bishop, J. M. 1982. Oncogenes. *Scientific American* 246:80–92.

———. 1983. Cellular Oncogenes and Retroviruses. *Annual Review of Biochemistry* 52:301–54.

Boffey, P. M. 1987. Dr. Marks' Crusade: Shaking Up Sloan-Kettering for a New Assault on Cancer. *The New York Times Magazine* (April 26) 25–31, 60–67.

Brandon, K. N. 1990. *Adaptation and Environment*. Princeton: Princeton University Press.

Bucher, R., and A. L. Strauss. 1961. Professions in Process. *American Journal of Sociology* 66:325–34.

Burian, R. M. N.d. The Current Revolution in Molecular Genetics. Virginia Polytechnic Institute.

Callon, M. 1986. Some Elements of a Sociology of Translation: Domestication of the Scallops and the Fishermen of St. Brieuc Bay. In J. Law, *Power, Action, and Belief*. Sociological Review Monograph. Boston: Routledge and Kegan Paul.

———. 1987. Society in the Making: The Study of Technology as a Tool for Sociological Analysis. In Bijker et al. 1987.

Callon M., and B. Latour. 1981. Unscrewing the Big Leviathan: How Actors Macrostructure Reality and How Sociologists Help Them. In K. Knorr Cetina and A. Cicourel, eds., *Advances in Social Theory and Methodology: Toward an Integration of Micro- and Macro-Sociologies*. London: Routledge and Kegan Paul.

Callon, M., and J. Law. 1982. On Interests and Their Transformation: Enrolment and counter-enrolment. *Social Studies of Science* 12:615–25.

Cambrosio, A., and P. Keating. 1988. Going Monoclonal: Art, Science, and Magic in the Day-to-Day Use of Hybridoma Technology. *Social Problems* 35:244–60.

Chubin, D. E., and K. E. Studer. 1978. The Politics of Cancer. *Theory and Society* 6:55–74.

Clarke, A. 1990. A Social Worlds Research Adventure: The Case of Reproductive Science. In S. Cozzens and T. Gieryn, *Theories of Science in Society*. Bloomington: Indiana University Press.

———. In press. Social Worlds Theory as Organization Theory. In D. Maines, *Social Organization and Social Process: Festschrift in Honor of Anselm L. Strauss*. Hawthorne, N.Y.: Aldine de Gruyter.

Clarke, A., and J. H. Fujimura, eds. In press. *The Right Tools for the Job: At Work in Twentieth Century Life Sciences*. Princeton: Princeton University Press.

Collins, H. M. 1985. *Changing Order: Replication and Induction in Scientific Practice*. Beverly Hills: Sage.

DeVita, V. T. 1984. The Governance of Science at the National Cancer Institute: A Perspective on Misperceptions. In *Management Operations of the National Cancer Institute That Influence the Governance of Science*. National Cancer Institute Monograph 64. Bethesda, Md.: U.S. Department of Health and Human Services, NIH Publication no. 84-2651.

Duesberg, P. H. 1983. Retroviral Transforming Genes in Normal Cells? *Nature* 304:219–25.

------. 1985. Activated Proto-onc Genes: Sufficient or Necessary for cancer? *Science* 228:669–77.

Duesberg, P. M., R.-P. Zhou, and D. Goodrich. 1989. Cancer Genes by Illegitimate Recombination. In *Viral Oncogenesis and Cell Differentiation: The Contributions of Charlotte Friend.* Annals of the New York Academy of Science 567.

Fogle, T. 1990. ˋAre Genes Units of Inheritance? *Biology and Philosophy* 5:349–71.

Friedland, P., and L. H. Kedes. 1984. Gene Machines: Fast Growth, Limited Market. *High Technology* 4:60.

------. 1985. Discovering the Secrets of DNA. *Communications of the ACM* 28:1164–86.

Fujimura, J. H. 1986. Bandwagons in Science: Doable Problems and Transportable Packages as Factors in the Development of the Molecular Genetic Bandwagon in Cancer Research. Ph.D. diss., University of California, Berkeley.

------. 1987. Constructing Doable Problems in Cancer Research: Articulating Alignment. *Social Studies of Science* 17:257–93.

------. 1988. The Molecular Biological Bandwagon in Cancer Research: Where Social Worlds Meet. *Social Problems* 35:261–83.

------. 1991a. On Methods, Ontologies, and Representation in the Sociology of Science: Where Do We Stand? In D. Maines, *Social Organization and Social Process: Festschrift in Honor of Anselm L. Strauss.* Hawthorne, NY: Aldine de Gruyter.

------. 1991b. Constructing Knowledge across Social Worlds: The Case of DNA Sequence in Molecular Biology. Paper presented to the American Association for the Advancement of Science (AAAS), Washington, D.C., Feb. 1991.

------. In preparation a. *Crafting Science and Building Bandwagons: The Case of Oncogene Research.*

------. In preparation b. Problem Paths: A Tool for Dynamic Analysis of Situated Scientific Problem Construction. Submitted to *Social Studies of Science.*

Fujimura, J. H., S. L. Star, and E. M. Gerson. 1987. Methodes de recherche en sociologie des sciences: Travail, pragmatisme et interactionnisme symbolique. (Research methods in the sociology of science and technology: Work, pragmatism, and symbolic interactionism). *Cahiers de Recherche Sociologique* 5:65–85.

Furmanski, P., J. C. Hager, and M. A. Rich, eds. 1985. *RNA Tumor Viruses, Oncogenes, Human Cancer, and Aids: On the Frontiers of Understanding.* Proceedings of the International Conference on RNA Tumor Viruses in Human Cancer, Denver, Colorado, June 10–14, 1984. Boston: Martinus Nijhoff.

Gallo, R. C. 1986. The First Human Retrovirus. *Scientific American* 255: 88–98.

Gerson, E. 1983. Scientific Work and Social Worlds. *Knowledge* 4:357–77.

Goldfarb, M., et al. 1982. Isolation and Preliminary Characterization of a Human Transforming Gene from T24 Bladder Carcinoma Cells. *Nature* 296:404–9.

Griesemer, J. R. 1990. Modeling in the Museum: On the Role of Remnant Models in the Work of Joseph Grinnell. *Biology and Philosophy* 5:3–36.

———. To appear. The Role of Instruments in the Generative Analysis of Science.

Huebner, R. J., and G. J. Todaro. 1969. Oncogenes of RNA Tumor Viruses as Determinants of Cancer. *Proc. Nat. Acad. Sci.* 64:1087–94.

Hughes, E. C. 1971. *The Sociological Eye.* Chicago: Aldine de Gruyter.

Johnson, R. S. 1984. Oncor, Oncogene Diagnostics Venture, is "Encore" for BRL Cofounder Turner. *Genetic Engineering News* 4 (4).

Jordan, K., and M. Lynch. To appear. The Sociology of a Genetic Engineering Technique: Ritual and Rationality in the Performance of the Plasmid Prep.

Keating, Peter, Alberto Cambrosio, and Michael MacKenzie. To appear. The Tools of the Discipline: Standards, Models and Measures in the Affinity-Avidity Controversy in Immunology.

Kitcher, Philip. 1982. Genes. *British Journal of Philosophy of Science* 33:337–59.

Knorr Cetina, K. 1981. *The Manufacture of Knowledge.* Oxford: Pergamon Press.

Kondo, D. K. 1990. *Crafting Selves: Power, Gender, and Discourses of Identity in a Japanese Workplace.* Chicago: University of Chicago Press.

Land, H., L. F. Parada, and R. A. Weinberg. 1983. Cellular Oncogenes and Multistep Carcinogenesis. *Science* 222:771–78.

Lappe, M. 1984. *Broken Code: The Exploitation of DNA.* San Francisco: Sierra Club Books.

Latour, B. 1987. *Science in Action: How to Follow Scientists and Engineers through Society.* (Cambridge, MA.: Harvard University Press.)

———. 1988. *The Pasteurization of France.* Cambridge: Harvard University Press.

———. 1990. Are We Talking about Skills or about the Redistribution of Skills? Paper presented at the conference on Rediscovering Skill in Science, Technology, and Medicine, Bath, England.

Latour, B., and S. Woolgar. 1979. *Laboratory Life: The Social Construction of Scientific Facts.* Beverly Hills: Sage. Reprint. Princeton: Princeton University Press, 1986.

Lave, J. 1988. *Cognition in Practice: Mind, Mathematics and Culture in Everyday Life.* Cambridge: Cambridge University Press.

Law, J. 1986. On the Methods of Long-Distance Control: Vessels, Navigation, and the Portuguese Route to India. In Law 1986.

Law, J., ed. 1986. *Power, Action, and Belief: A New Sociology of Knowledge?* Sociological Review Monograph 32. London: Routledge and Kegan Paul.

Lloyd, E. A. 1988. *The Structure and Confirmation of Evolutionary Theory.* Westport: Greenwood Press.

Lynch, M. 1985. *Art and Artifact in Laboratory Science: A Study of Shop Work and Shop Talk in a Research Laboratory.* London: Routledge and Kegan Paul.

Moss, R. W. 1989. *The Cancer Industry: Unraveling the Politics.* New York: Paragon House.

Office of Technology Assessment. 1988. *Mapping Our Genes. Federal Genome Projects: How Vast. How Fast.* Contractor Reports, vol. 1. Washington, D.C.

Parada, L. F., et al. 1982. Human EJ Bladder Carcinoma Oncogene is Homologue of Harvey Sarcoma Virus *ras* Gene. *Nature* 297:474–79.

Pickering, A. 1990. Knowledge, Practice and Mere Construction. *Social Studies of Science* 20:682–729.

Pinch, T. 1986. *Confronting Nature: The Sociology of Solar-Neutrino Detection.* Dordrecht: Reidel.

Rettig, R. A. 1977. *Cancer Crusade: The Story of the National Cancer Act of 1971.* Princeton: Princeton University Press.

Schwartz, D. E., R. Tizard, and W. Gilbert. 1983. Nucleotide Sequence of Rous Sarcoma Virus. *Cell* 32:853–69.

Shibutani, T. 1955. Reference Groups as Perspectives. *American Journal of Sociology* 60:562–69.

———. 1962. Reference Groups and Social Control. In A. Rose, ed., *Human Behavior and Social Processes.* Boston: Houghton Mifflin.

Shimkin, M. B. 1977. *Contrary to Nature: Being an Illustrated Commentary on Some Persons and Events of History of Importance in the Development of Knowledge Concerning Cancer.* Washington, D.C.: Department of Health, Education, and Welfare.

Smith, L. M. 1986. The Synthesis and Sequence Analysis of DNA. *Science* 232:G63.

Spector, D. H., H. E. Varmus, and J. M. Bishop. 1978. Nucleotide Sequences Related to the Transforming Gene of Avian Sarcoma Virus are Present in the DNA of Uninfected Vertebrates. *Proceedings of the National Academy of Sciences* 75:5023–27.

Star, S. L. 1983. Simplification in Scientific Work: An Example from Neuroscience Research. *Social Studies of Science* 13:205–28.

———. 1985. Scientific Work and Uncertainty. *Social Studies of Science* 15:391–427.

———. 1986. Triangulating Clinical and Basic Research: British Localizationists, 1870–1906. *History of Science* 24:29–48.

———. 1988a. Introduction: The Sociology of Science and Technology. *Social Problems* 35:197–205.

———. 1988b. The Structure of Ill-Structured Solutions: Boundary Objects and Heterogeneous Distributed Problem Solving. In Mike Huhns and Les Gasser, eds., *Readings in Distributed Artificial Intelligence.* Menlo Park, Calif.: Morgan Kaufman.

————. 1989. *Regions of the Mind: Brain Research and the Quest for Scientific Certainty.* Stanford: Stanford University Press.

Star, S. L., and J. R. Griesemer. 1989. Institutional Ecology, "Translations," and Boundary Objects: Amateurs and Professionals in Berkeley's Museum of Vertebrate Zoology, 1907–39. *Social Studies of Science* 19: 387–420.

Stehelin, D., et al. 1976. DNA Related to the Transforming Gene(s) of Avian Sarcoma Viruses is Present in Normal Avian DNA. *Nature* 260:170–73.

Strauss, A. L. 1978. *Negotiations: Varieties, Contexts, Processes, and Social Order.* San Francisco: Jossey-Bass.

————. 1982. Social Worlds and Legitimation Processes. *Studies in Symbolic Interaction* 4:171–90.

————. 1984. Social Worlds and Their Segmentation Processes. *Studies in Symbolic Interaction* 5:123–79.

————. 1987. *Qualitative Analysis for Social Scientists.* Cambridge: Cambridge University Press.

Strauss, A. L., and J. Corbin. 1990. *The Basics of Qualitative Research.* Newbury Park, Calif.: Sage.

Strauss, A. L., et al. 1964. *Psychiatric Ideologies and Institutions.* New York: Free Press of Glencoe.

Strickland, S. P. 1972. *Politics, Science, and Dread Disease: A Short History of United States Medical Research Policy.* Cambridge: Harvard University Press.

Studer, K. E., and D. E. Chubin. 1980. *The Cancer Mission: Social Contexts of Biomedical Research.* London: Sage.

Suchman, L. 1987. *Plans and Situated Actions: The Problem of Human-Machine Communication.* Cambridge: Cambridge University Press.

Tabin, C. J., et al. 1982. Mechanism of Activation of a Human Oncogene. *Nature* 300:143–49.

Temin, H. M. 1971. The Protovirus Hypothesis: Speculations on the Significance of RNA Directed DNA Synthesis for Normal Development and for Carcinogenesis. *J. Nat. Canc. Inst.* 46:3–7.

————. 1980. Origin of Retroviruses of Cellular Genetic Moveable Elements. *Cell* 21:599–600.

Thomas, W. I., and F. Znaniecki. 1918. *The Polish Peasant in Poland and America.* New York: Alfred A. Knopf.

Varmus, H. T., and A. J. Levine, eds. 1983. *Readings in Tumor Virology.* Cold Spring Harbor, N.Y.: Cold Spring Harbor Laboratory.

Volberg, R. A. 1983. Constraints and Commitments in the Development of American Botany, 1880–1920. Ph.D. diss., Department of Sociology, University of California, San Francisco.

Waterfield, M. D., et al. 1983. Platelet-derived Growth Factor is Structurally Related to the Putative Transforming Protein p28*sis* of Simian Sarcoma Virus. *Nature* 304:35–39.

Watson, J. D. 1987. *Molecular Biology of the Gene.* Vol. 2. Menlo Park, Calif.: W. A. Benjamin.

Watson, J. D., N. H. Hopkins, J. W. Roberts, J. A. Steitz, and A. M. Weiner. 1987. *Molecular Biology of the Gene.* 4th ed. Reading, Mass.: Benjamin Cummings.

Weinberg, R. A. 1982. Review: Oncogenes of Human Tumor Cells. In S. Prentis, ed., *Trends in Biochemical Sciences.* Vol. 7. Amsterdam: Elsevier Biomedical.

———. 1983. A Molecular Basis of Cancer. *Scientific American* 249: 126–43.

Woolgar, S. 1988. *Knowledge and Reflexivity: New Frontiers in the Sociology of Knowledge.* London: Sage.

PART 2   ARGUMENTS

Extending Wittgenstein:
The Pivotal Move from Epistemology
to the Sociology of Science

Michael Lynch

The sociology of knowledge's empirical approach to the traditional topics of epistemology has been emboldened and radicalized in recent decades.[1] At least two distinct programs in "epistemic sociology" (Coulter 1989) are currently established in social studies of science. The more familiar of these, the sociology of scientific knowledge (SSK) is an outgrowth of Bloor's (1976,1) proposal to investigate and explain the "very content and nature of scientific knowledge."[2] A second approach, ethnomethodological studies of

David Bogen and Jeff Coulter read and commented upon an earlier draft of this paper, and I'm very grateful for their help. I would also like to thank David Bloor, Harry Collins, and Steve Woolgar for their civilized and helpful replies to my sometimes tendentious arguments in this paper.

1. Epistemology is often identified with foundationalism—the philosophical attempt to ground the truth of scientific knowledge. The sociological approaches discussed here address epistemology's topics (observation, experimentation, represen tation, etc.) while maintaining one or another agnostic posture toward the validity of scientific knowledge. While such an approach is antithetical to foundationalist epistemology (and to the entrenched view of knowledge as correct belief), it is consistent with constructivist, phenomenological, and some variants of analytic and ordinary language philosophy. Hacking's paper (chap. 2) is an example of the kind of small *e* epistemology that is compatible with an interest in scientists' local practices. Sociological approaches can thus be viewed as epistemological or antiepistemological depending upon what sort of philosophical commitments are subsumed under "epistemology."

2. "Social studies of scientific knowledge" (SSK) is a shorthand way of referring to various lines of relativist, constructivist, and discourse analysis research. The most coherent and widely recognized group of studies in SSK emerged in Britain in the 1970s and is sometimes called the "strong program" in the sociology of knowledge (Barnes 1974, 1977; Bloor 1973, 1976; Collins 1975; Edge and Mulkay 1976; MacKenzie 1978; Shapin 1979; Mulkay 1979). Although by no means marching in lockstep on the issues, these studies embraced a constructivist (or in some instances, a relativist) reading of Wittgenstein (1958, 1956), as well as Hesse (1974) and Kuhn (1962), and used this as leverage against the established sociology of science implemented by Merton and his colleagues.

The past decade has seen a proliferation of schools and programs in SSK on a broad international base, and in some cases a more particularized attack on epistemology's work in the sciences and mathematics (ESW), is an extension of Garfinkel's (1967) studies of ordinary practical actions and practical reasoning.[3] Both programs investigate such epistemic matters as visual and textual representation, experimental practice, instrumentally mediated observation, argumentative reasoning, and mathematical structures. Although SSK and ethnomethodology can be traced

---

topics. Recent works have taken up such classic epistemological themes as representation (Shapin 1984; Woolgar 1988a, 1988b), the "theory-ladenness" of observation (Pinch 1986); experimental replication (Collins 1985); consensus formation (Amann and Knorr Cetina 1988); the internal-external distinction (Pickering 1988), and reflexivity (Woolgar 1988c). Latour (1987, 1988) and his colleagues (Callon 1986; Law and Callon 1988) advance what they call "actor-network theory." This framework for analyzing scientists' and engineers' world-building activities treats "social" relations between scientists, interest groups, and organizations on the same (literary) plane as the "technical" relations between scientists, equipment, and "natural" phenomena (e.g., microbes, sea scallops, ocean currents, wind, etc. Scientists and engineers succeed in creating resilient constellations of power/knowledge when they manage to enroll and enlist "heterogeneous allies" by using a variety of rhetorical and Machiavellian tactics to stabilize these networks. Another group develops themes from American pragmatism and symbolic interactionist sociology to study scientists' and engineers' activities (Star 1983; Gerson and Star 1987; Fujimura 1987). Their work links up with Latour's and his colleagues' semiotic approach, and with a related language-based emphasis in work by Cambrosio and Keating (1988).

These social constructivist programs have branched out in other directions as well: in studies of technological innovation (MacKenzie and Wajcman 1985; Law 1986; Bijker et al. 1987) and health economics (Ashmore et al. 1989), and have even been merged with the Mertonian tradition in Gieryn's work (1983; Gieryn and Figert 1990).

3. By ethnomethodological studies of work in the sciences (ESW) I refer to studies conducted since the early 1970s by Garfinkel and some of his colleagues and students (cf. Garfinkel et al. 1981; Morrison 1981; Lynch et al. 1983; Garfinkel et al. 1989; Lynch 1985a; Livingston 1986). Sharrock, Coulter, Anderson, and Hughes have also produced a body of ethnomethodological studies on science and other professions (Sharrock and Anderson 1984; Anderson et al. 1988). Their work is particularly salient to the discussion in this paper, since their explications of Wittgenstein and critiques of the strong program have largely beaten the path I'll be taking here. Suchman's (1987) studies on situated technology use are also highly relevant to the treatment in this paper.

The academic territory is complex and overlapping and is not easily divided into discrete camps. For instance, Mulkay, Woolgar, Knorr Cetina, Yearley, Collins, and Pinch all make use of ethnomethodological themes and research strategies, though their work is solidly rooted in SSK. A reciprocal regard for SSK is found in some of my work (Lynch 1985b; Lynch and Woolgar 1988), though it is notably absent in that of some of my colleagues in ESW. It also should be mentioned that SSK and ESW by no means exhaust the lines of what Donald Campbell (1979) calls "epistemologically relevant" research in sociology of science. I focus on them in part because of their common affinity to Wittgenstein's later writings, and because I find it challenging to try to clarify the relation between the programs.

through separate lines of theoretical ancestry, as Barnes (1977,24) notes, "there are interesting parallels between them, which derive from their reliance on the late work of Ludwig Wittgenstein."

Neither SSK nor ESW aim to deliver a "faithful" reading of Wittgenstein, since their main concern is to use the Wittgensteinian corpus, along with any other suggestive materials, to inspire and guide one or another program of "empirical" research.[4] Despite their common debt to Wittgenstein, SSK and ESW develop sharply different readings of his later writings.[5] In this paper I will argue that some of the key differences between the ESW and SSK research programs can be illuminated by reference to a familiar debate in philosophy over Wittgenstein's discussion of actions in accord with rules. One side of the debate, "rule skepticism," takes Wittgenstein to be arguing that the relation between rules and conduct is indeterminate, and that social conventions and learned dispositions account for orderly actions. The contrary "antiskepticist" position holds that Wittgenstein treats rules inseparably from practical conduct, so that there is no basis for explaining the relation between rules and conduct by invoking extrinsic factors. Although this debate may seem to be an arcane preoccupation within a tight circle of philosophers, I will argue that the divergent positions implicate entirely different views of what is empirical and how to study it in social studies of science. The crux of my argument will be that SSK offers a skepticist extension of Wittgenstein, and that its attempt to explain science sociologically creates a crisis for the "science" that would do the explaining. Ethnomethodology, contrary to what is often said about its program, offers a nonskepticist, but not a realist or rationalist, extension of Wittgenstein.

The problem for social studies of science is that Wittgenstein's writings not only suggest one or another path out of philosophy and into sociology, they also, as Winch (1958) argues, deeply problema-

---

4. Garfinkel explicitly renounces any attempt to tag ethnomethodology to philosophical predecessors, although he has suggested a practice of "ethnomethodologically misreading" the philosophers. His preference is to "misread" Husserl, Merleau-Ponty, and Heidegger, and unlike Sharrock, Anderson, and Coulter, he has been less explicit about possible resonances with Wittgenstein. The point of the present essay is not to show that ethnomethodology is best regarded as an offshoot of Wittgenstein's philosophy but to bring out some strong arguments from Wittgensteinian philosophy in support of research policies in ethnomethodology. To do this is not to imply that those research policies developed in an effort to follow Wittgenstein.

5. A strong inkling of the differences can be gained by reading Bloor's (1987) review of Livingston's (1986) study of mathematicians' work; or on the other hand by reading ethnomethodologists' critical reviews of the strong program (Sharrock and Anderson 1984; Anderson et al. 1988; Coulter 1989,30ff.).

tize the possibility of an explanatory sociology. I will argue that this presents a far greater problem for the SSK skepticist interpretation of Wittgenstein than for the ESW nonskepticist reading.

The Pivotal Importance of Wittgenstein

Wittgenstein's later writings are by no means the only significant source of philosophy for SSK and ESW. Existential phenomenology, pragmatism, poststructuralist literary theories, and semiotics have also been deemed important for one or another line of study. Nevertheless, Wittgenstein is widely regarded as the *pivotal* figure for a "sociological turn" in epistemology. Bloor's *Wittgenstein: A Social Theory of Knowledge* (1983) is the most extensive treatment in social studies of science, though Collins (1985), Sharrock and Anderson (1984), Woolgar (1988a), Coulter (1989), Phillips (1977), Pinch (1986), Livingston (1987), Lynch (1985a), and many others have explicitly discussed Wittgenstein's relevance for the social studies of science and mathematics. Wittgenstein's influence is also filtered through many of the "Kuhnian" themes, such as "seeing-as" and "paradigms as exemplars," so often discussed in sociology of science. An indication of Wittgenstein's importance is the fact that the concepts of "forms of life," "language games," and "family-resemblances" are often used without attribution in the social studies of science literature.

Bloor's (1983,184) central proposal is that Wittgenstein's philosophy should be interpreted as a "social theory of knowledge." For Bloor, Wittgenstein's pivotal move was to reconceptualize the central topics of epistemology as empirical problems for social science research. Although Wittgenstein made no mention of Durkheim's sociology and explicitly distinguished his approach from behaviorism (Wittgenstein 1958, §307–8; Luckhardt 1983; Hunter 1985; 129ff.), Bloor argues that in certain respects Wittgenstein's treatment is compatible with these programs in empirical social science. Indeed, when faced with glaring discrepancies between Wittgenstein's and Durkheim's writings, Bloor resolves these by repudiating some of Wittgenstein's central proposals.[6]

6. Bloor accounts for how Wittgenstein seemed so little inclined to embrace behaviorism or Durkheimian sociology (or any other empirical social science of his day) by suggesting that Wittgenstein's antiscientific predilections (perhaps reflecting Spenglerian influences) blinded him to the natural affinities between his account of language and research in the behavioral sciences.

Bloor makes it clear that he aims to supplement Wittgenstein with an empirical program, and that he is willing to read Wittgenstein creatively to suit this purpose. I have no objection to this, since as Hacking (1984) points out, there is no reason why fidelity to a particular philosophical tradition should sidetrack an attempt to do original sociological research. In any event, it would be dubious to suppose that Wittgenstein's or any other figure's "thought" is subject to a single "correct" representation (Rorty 1979). A creative misreading may serve better to carry forward the conversation on the questions Wittgenstein raises. Unfortunately, Bloor (1983,5) goes well beyond this, since he also claims that sociological research is *necessary* in order to replace Wittgenstein's "fictitious natural history with a real natural history, and an imaginary ethnography with a real ethnography." These realist proposals treat Wittgenstein's writings as speculations in need of empirical grounding or correction,[7] and they are entirely out of line with Wittgenstein's repudiation of theory and empiricism in favor of grammatical investigations. Wittgenstein's writings no doubt serve to inspire Bloor, even if they do not authorize his project, but the more serious issue is that they undermine many of Bloor's programmatic claims.

Before going further with a critique of Bloor's views on Wittgenstein, let me turn to the basic tenets of Bloor's "strong programme" in the sociology of knowledge. It is here that his philosophical commitments have had their most tangible influence. Bloor (1976,4–5) proposes four main principles to guide the "strong programme":[8]

1. It would be causal, that is, concerned with the conditions which bring about belief or states of knowledge. Naturally there will be other types of causes apart from social ones which will cooperate in bringing about belief.

---

7. As Sharrock and Anderson (1984) argue, Bloor's proposals for an empirical science take the immediate form of a philosophical treatise. Although Bloor cites and summarizes numerous historical studies and suggests what an empirical treatment might consist of, his own writings are programmatic. Livingston (1979,15–16) makes a similar point about Bloor's writings. "What Bloor seems to mean by claiming that the sociological investigation of 'scientific knowledge' should follow the canons of scientific procedure is that one should adopt a way of speaking that conforms to current, popular, philosophical theories." It is therefore appropriate to examine Bloor's arguments with reference to philosophical scholarship rather than simply view them as a substantive social theory to be evaluated on empirical grounds.

8. For the moment I will leave aside the question of whether these principles do in fact guide the various historical case studies affiliated to the strong program. Laudan (1981) argues that in several respects the relationship between the principles and the research is very doubtful.

2. It would be impartial with respect to truth and falsity, rationality or irrationality, success or failure. Both sides of these dichotomies will require explanation.
3. It would be symmetrical in its style of explanation. The same types of cause would explain, say, true and false beliefs.
4. It would be reflexive. In principle its patterns of explanation would have to be applicable to sociology itself. Like the requirement of symmetry, this is a response to the need to seek general explanations. It is an obvious requirement of principle, because otherwise sociology would be a standing refutation of its own theories.

These proposals have influenced a large body of research in the social history of science, and have also provided a target for numerous criticisms.[9] Bloor's causalist assumptions are not widely accepted in SSK,[10] but his recommendations about impartiality and symmetry (proposals 2 and 3) are advocated in all the major lines of constructionist and discourse-analytic inquiry. Even many of those who do not agree with Bloor's empiricist assumptions and social interest explanations share his skeptical posture toward scientists' and mathematicians' truth claims. In calling this a "skeptical" posture, I do not mean that Bloor advocates disbelief in scientists' theories and mathematicians' proofs. "Symmetry" and "impartiality" only require that all theories, proofs, or facts be treated as "beliefs" to be explained by social causes. Bloor's skepticist approach is primarily methodological, as it aims to neutralize the explanatory power of "internalist' accounts in order to gain purchase for one or another social or conventionalist explanation of science and mathematics. Although it has certainly proved to pay as a sociological research strategy, the skepticist posture invites some formidable philosophical arguments.

Wittgenstein and Rule Skepticism: The Externalist Reading

In his essay *Wittgenstein on Rules and Private Language* (1982), Saul Kripke reviews Wittgenstein's discussion of rule following. He reads Wittgenstein to be advancing a novel solution to a classic skeptical problem on how rules determine actions. In Kripke's view, Wittgenstein initially accepts the skepticist thesis that actions are

9. These critiques include Laudan 1981; Turner 1981; Woolgar 1981; Anderson et al. 1988; and Coulter 1989. The collection edited by Hollis and Lukes (1982) includes several papers arguing the pros and cons of the approach. Barnes 1974, 1977, 1982; and Shapin 1982 also elaborate some of the central proposals of the strong program.

10. Programmatic statements and debates on these issues are presented in the collection edited by Knorr Cetina and Mulkay (1983).

underdetermined by rules but then gives a social constructivist solution to the problem of how orderly conduct is possible. Kripke is not the only philosopher to attribute skepticist and conventionalist views to Wittgenstein (cf., Dummett 1968; and more ambiguously, Cavell 1976), but his essay provoked especially heated criticism in Wittgensteinian circles (Baker and Hacker 1984, 1985; Hanfling 1985; Shanker 1987). Wittgenstein discusses rules in several other manuscripts and collections of notes,[11] but the dispute between Kripke and his critics mainly concerns §§143–242 of the *Philosophical Investigations* (PI), where Wittgenstein discusses his famous number-series example (parts of this argument are also reproduced in Wittgenstein's *Remarks on the Foundations of Mathematics*, 1956, part 1).

As is typical of Wittgenstein's later writings, numerous threads of argument weave through the text, along with a series of partly overlapping or analogous examples. Questions are posed and seemingly left hanging, and it is sometimes difficult to keep track of when Wittgenstein is asserting his own views and when he is speaking in the voice of one of his interlocutors. In spite of, or perhaps *because of*, its difficulty, the argument has been reconstructed in numerous secondary and tertiary sources, and a fairly standard version of it runs as follows: Wittgenstein (*PI*,§143) devises a "language game" in which a teacher gives a pupil an order to write down a series of cardinal numbers according to a certain formation rule. This language game and its imaginary pitfalls has become a paradigm for rules in arithmetic, as well as in other rule-ordered activities, like the game of chess. In the main section of his argument, Wittgenstein (*PI*,§185ff.) asks us to assume that the student has mastered the series of natural numbers, and that we have given him exercises and tests for the series "$n + 2$" for numbers less than one thousand.

> Now we get the pupil to continue a series (say $+2$) beyond 1,000—and he writes 1,000, 1,004, 1,008, 1,012.
> We say to him: "Look what you've done!"—He doesn't understand.
> We say: "You were meant to add *two*: look how you began the series!"
> He answers: "Yes, isn't it right? I thought that was how I was *meant* to do it."

For the skepticist reading, what the pupil's "mistake" brings into relief is that his present action is logically consistent with an imagi-

---

11. See especially *Remarks on the Foundation of Mathematics* (1956), *Zettel* (1967), and also the collection of lecture notes on mathematics edited by Diamond (1976). Malcolm (1989) discusses material from an unpublished manuscript (Wittgenstein MS 165 *c.*, 1941–44).

nable series, "add 2 up to 1,000, 4 up to 2,000, 6 up to 3,000." Since the pupil had not been given examples past 1,000, his understanding of the rule is consistent with experience. With enough imagination, numerous permutations can be generated. Collins (1985,13), for instance, says about the rule: "add a 2 and then another 2 and then another and so forth . . . doesn't fully specify what we are to do . . . because that instruction can be followed by writing '82, 822, 8222, 82222,' or '28, 282, 2282, 22822' or '8²', etc. Each of these amounts to 'adding a 2' in some sense." Since we can think of an indefinite variety of understandings of the formula $n + 2$ based on the finite series of examples the pupil previously calculated, it seems we have arrived at a radically relativistic position: "This was our paradox: no course of action could be determined by a rule, because every course of action can be made out to accord with the rule. The answer was: if everything can be made out to accord with the rule, then it can also be made to conflict with it. And so there would be neither accord nor conflict here" (Wittgenstein *PI*,§201).

But as Wittgenstein then goes on to say, this paradox is based on the assumption that our grasp of the rule is based on an "interpretation"; that is, a private judgment about the rule's meaning in isolation from any regular practices in a community. Instead, he adds, the regularities in our common behavior provide the context in which the rule is expressed and understood. *Imaginable* variations in counting rarely, if ever, intrude upon our practice. Nor do violent disputes break out among mathematicians over the rules of their practice (*PI*,§212). They simply follow the rule "as a matter of course" (§238).

But the question now is, why? Or rather the question is, how do we manage so unproblematically to extend a rule to cover cases we haven't previously applied it to? The answer seems to appeal to sociology. Wittgenstein (*PI*,§§206ff.) likens following a rule to obeying an order, and he notes that the concepts of rule, order, and regularity can only have a place in a nexus of common behavior. How is such orderly action established? Through example, guidance, expressions of agreement, drill, and even intimidation: "When someone whom I am afraid of orders me to continue the series, I act quickly, with perfect certainty, and the lack of reasons does not trouble me" (*PI*,§212).

Since we do indeed act in accord with the rules for calculating, the reason for this is not intrinsic to *formal* mathematics, but to our "form of life" (*PI*,§241). What limits our practice, and eventually the pupil's if he learns it, is not the rule alone but the social conventions for following it in a certain way. If it makes sense to say that logic "compels" us, this is only so in the way that we are "compelled to accept certain behaviour as right and certain behaviour as wrong. It will be because we take a form of life for granted" (Bloor 1976,125).

Orderly calculation thus depends upon the social conventions we learn through drill; conventions which are inculcated and reinforced by normative practices in the social world around us (Bloor 1983, 121). Or, if we read "the common behavior of mankind" or "form of life" to apply more broadly than to the norms in a particular social group, we can invoke our common biological and psychological capacities. Given that mathematics (in this case, elementary arithmetic) is among our most rigorously rule-governed activities, then it appears that Wittgenstein is making a powerful argument for turning to sociology and other empirical sciences to explain order in mathematics.[12] What holds for rules can also be said to hold for theories in the natural sciences: they are underdetermined by facts, since no theory can be supported unequivocally by a finite collection of experimental results. Therefore if consensus is reached on a theory, it is not explained by facts alone but by the social conventions and common institutions shared by the members of a scientific community. These aspects of communal life greatly restrict the field of possible theoretical accounts to one or a very few socially recognized and approved versions. Collective habit, and at more heated times vigorous persuasion and even coercion, limits the range of sensible theoretical alternatives.

The appeal to social studies of science should seem obvious at this point. The skepticist reading of Wittgenstein seems to place the contents of mathematics and natural science at the disposal of the sociologist, since the most elementary procedures of arithmetic and the theoretical laws of physics can now be seen to express "the common behavior of mankind," and not the transcendent laws of reason or the intrinsic relations in a Platonic realm of pure mathematical forms. The externalism implied by this argument does not necessitate that the behavior of scientists or mathematicians should be explained in reference to norms or ideological forces arising from the "outside" society. Although the door has now been opened for such explanations, the argument also permits relatively small and closed disciplinary communities ("core sets" in Collins' [1975] termi-

---

12. In his 1983 book, Bloor seems more open than he was in his 1973 paper to the possibility that experimental psychology and biology can join sociology in bringing Wittgenstein's philosophy to empirical fruition. Collins (1985,15) invokes Wittgenstein's "private language" argument to bar psychology (and presumably biology) from such investigations. For a discussion of an "organic account"—but not strictly a biological one—of Wittgenstein's references to "form of life," see Hunter 1971.

nology) to be held responsible for their members' conventional practices. Controversies within scientific fields take on special significance in SSK, since they exhibit fissures within the relevant epistemic communities on fundamental matters of theory, fact, or procedure. An established procedure in SSK is to use historical study (supplemented with interviews whenever possible) to demonstrate the social process through which "closure" is reached in particular controversies. According to such studies, interpretive possibilities that remained open while the controversy raged are closed down when a successful theory gathers force in the community. After the fact, the victorious theory may seem to have vanquished its rivals by superior performance in experimental tests, but proponents of SSK argue that most of the time no such direct confrontation takes place. Theoretical possibilities that were never definitively tested or falsified are simply shut away in a black box,[13] and from then on the successful theory is treated as a correct theory whose major justification is its correspondence to "reality" and/or its congruence with "reason."[14] The difference, then, between normal and revolutionary science becomes a matter of whether some of the open possibilities for developing science or mathematics are explicitly disputed or remain submerged within the taken-for-granted habitus of "ready made science" (Latour 1987).[15]

The Wittgensteinian Critique of Skepticism

Although it may be compatible with Bloor's and other sociologists' explanatory programs, Kripke's skepticist thesis about the

13. A similar argument about technological innovation is made by Pinch and Bijker (1984), who argue that during the early phases in the social history of invention, evidences of multiple pathways abound. Eventually these alternatives are closed down, and one or a very few models of, e.g., the bicycle, refrigerator, or personal computer prevail. Pinch and Bijker emphasize the role of interest groups in this process, and they contrast their social constructivist view to a technological rationalism that supposes the convergence on a particular model to reflect laws of efficiency. For a case study critiquing this and related arguments see Jordan and Lynch 1992.

14. Bachelard (1984) notes that although rationalists and realists sit on opposite sides of an epistemic fence, their arguments play a similar justificatory role in discussions of science. Both sides subscribe to the same duality: on one side nature, on the other rational procedures for correctly discerning nature's secrets. There are of course significant differences between philosophies that put primary emphasis on one or the other; and within realism there are numerous positions, some of which strong program enthusiasts have themselves assumed.

15. There is of course much more to SSK than a working out of a particular programmatic argument. To take issue with the readings of Bloor, Collins, and others of Wittgenstein does, I think, call attention to a key set of problems, but it does not negate the many provocative discussions and interesting case studies in SSK.

rule-following example has been charged with being a fundamentally mistaken reading of Wittgenstein. Stuart Shanker (1987,14), for instance, argues that Kripke misunderstands the key passage quoted above from §201 of the *Philosophical Investigations:* "Far from operating as a skeptic, one of Wittgenstein's earliest and most enduring objectives was . . . to undermine the sceptic's position by demonstrating its unintelligibility. 'For doubt can exist only where a question exists, a question only where an answer exists, and an answer only where something *can be said.'*"

Shanker (1987,14) argues that Kripke fails to take into account that the passage "is the culmination of a sustained *reductio ad absurdum.*" The crux of Shanker's argument is that Kripke interprets Wittgenstein within the familiar terms of the realist-antirealist debate in epistemology.[16] According to Shanker (4), Wittgenstein lends support to neither camp in this debate, and considerable misunderstanding results from any attempt to enlist his arguments on either side: "But if the premise is wrong—if Wittgenstein belongs to neither school of thought, for the very reason that he had embarked on a course which would undermine the very foundation of the Realist/ Anti-realist distinction—the 'sceptical' interpretation of *Remarks on the Foundations of Mathematics* is itself undermined at a stroke."

As Shanker reconstructs it, the point of Wittgenstein's number-series argument is to demonstrate the absurdity of a "quasi-causal" picture of rule following, wherein a rule is treated as "an abstract object which engages with a mental mechanism." Wittgenstein replaces this deterministic picture with one that emphasizes the practical basis of rule following. The "impression" that the rule guides our behavior reflects *"our inexorability in applying it"* (Shanker 1987,17–18).

Thus far the argument is fairly consistent with the lesson Collins, Bloor and other proponents of SSK derive from the example. However, the positions soon diverge. The skeptic follows Wittgenstein's *reductio ad absurdum* to the point where abandonment of the quasi-causal picture is warranted but then concludes that rules provide an insufficient account of actions. Taken into the realm of sociology of knowledge, this conclusion motivates a search for alter-

16. Wittgenstein's writings are scandalously obscure, and vast amounts of academic writing have been devoted to clarifying them. Often as a prelude to mounting a criticism, many clarifications begin by affiliating Wittgenstein's positions to one side or another in familiar debates about realism-antirealism, positivism-idealism, objectivism-constructivism, and structural determinacy-methodological individualism. This has been a familiar fate for phenomenological and ethnomethodological writings as well.

native explanations on how orderly action is possible. Social conventions and interests fill the space vacated by rational compulsion.

The critical move in the skepticist strategy is to *isolate the formulation of the rule from the practice it formulates* (its extension). Once the rule statement is isolated from the practices that extend it to new cases, the relation between the two becomes problematic: no single rule is determined by the previous practices held to be in accord with it; and no amount of elaboration of the rule can foreclose misinterpretations consistent with the literal form of its statement. Such indeterminacy is then remedied by a skepticist solution, in which extrinsic sources of influence are used to explain the relation between rules and their interpretations. These extrinsic sources include social conventions, communal consensus, psychological dispositions, and socialization—a coordination of habits of thinking and action which limits the alternative interpretational possibilities. A battery of questions can then be raised for further research: How are such conventions established and sustained? How is consensus reached in the face of uncertainty and controversy? What are the relative contributions from our biological makeup, cognitive structure, and social affiliations?

Contrary to the skepticist solution, Shanker (1987,25) argues, "The purpose of the *reductio* is certainly not to question the intelligibility or certainty of the practice of rule-following." The path out of the skeptical paradox is not through an antirealist epistemological position but through an examination of "grammar." The "foundations crisis" in epistemology (the realist-antirealist debate) arose from questions that can have no answer, and Wittgenstein offered a way to "dissolve" such questions. The point of the demonstration therefore was not to undermine objectivity, but to clarify "in what sense mathematical knowledge can be said to be objective" (Shanker 1987,62), which is not the same as arguing that such knowledge has an objective or transcendental foundation. For Shanker, the "internal" relation between the rule for counting by twos and the actions done in accord with it is by no means an insufficient basis for the rule's extension to new cases. Nor is there any need to search for such a basis in psychological, biological mechanisms, or extrinsic social conventions.

Baker and Hacker (1984; 1985) also contest Kripke's skepticist reading of the number-series example, in their extended exegesis of the *Philosophical Investigations*. Their particular target is what they call "the community view," the position that rule-following behavior is determined by patterns of reasoning sanctioned by community behavior. Baker and Hacker's challenge to the community view at times is overly zealous,[17] but their most telling arguments are worth repeating. In their view the problem begins with the way the skeptic initially phrases the question. They argue that the skeptic's question, "How can an object like a rule determine the infinite array of acts that accord with it?" is miscast. As Wittgenstein says in regard to a similar question (PI,§189), "'But *are* the steps then *not* determined by the algebraic formula?'—The question contains a mistake." The question presupposes the independence of the rule and its extension, as though the rule were external to the actions performed in accord with it.

The skepticist interpretation retains the quasi-causal picture of rule following, since it never abandons the search for explanatory factors beyond or beneath the rule-following practice. The Kripkean skeptic agrees that the formula $n + 2$ cannot force compliance, but he then goes on to look elsewhere for the cause (Baker and Hacker 1984,95). But if it is agreed that an "internal" relation holds between rule and extension—that it makes no sense to even speak of the rule for counting by twos aside from the organized practices that "ex-

---

17. For instance, Baker and Hacker (1984,74) say that the community thesis "seems to imply that 'human agreement decides what is true and what is false.' But this, of course, is nonsense. It is the world that determines *truth:* human agreement determines meaning." Apparently this is a paraphrase of Wittgenstein (PI,§241): "So you are saying that human agreement decides what is true and false?—It is what people *say* that is true and false; and they agree in the *language* they use. That is not agreement in opinions but in form of life." Wittgenstein makes no mention here of the world, nor does he say anything about what determines truth. Rather his passage identifies "what is true and false" with what people "say." I read this to be locating "what is true and false" (and not "truth") in the grammar of speaking. Perhaps what people say is not a matter of "agreement" in any facile sense, but there seems to be no basis for attributing it to "the world." Wittgenstein uses different terms for "agreement" in the above passage. His term for agreement in language is more akin to English "consonance" or "attunement," as it draws upon a musical metaphor suggested in the German *Übereinstimmung* (see Bogen and Lynch 1990). Much of Baker and Hacker's critique of the community view is worth taking into account, as is their further discussion of "accord with a rule" in their 1985 book. But as Malcolm (1989) incisively argues, their zealous attack on the community view sometimes strays into individualism, denying or ignoring the overwhelming emphasis on concerted human practice in Wittgenstein's writings about rules. Malcolm greatly clarifies Wittgenstein's emphasis on "quiet agreement" and "consensus in action" in the discussion of rules. This differs from agreement in opinions, but is no less social. "It seems clear to me . . . that Wittgenstein *is* saying that the concept of following a rule is 'essentially social'—in the sense that it can have its roots only in a setting where there is *a people,* with a common life and a common language" (Malcolm 1989,23). Note that this is far from an endorsement of Kripke's view or of the sort of sociological reading of Wittgenstein Bloor gives. Hunter (1973; 1985) and Cavell (1979) also elaborate views on rules and skepticism that are not quite so hostile to all "social" readings of Wittgenstein, but their views are not very compatible with the SSK approach.

tend" it to new cases—then the epistemological mystery dissolves. "'*How* does the rule determine this as its application?' makes no more sense than: 'How does this side of the coin determine the other side as its obverse?'" (Baker and Hacker 1984,96)

This analogy may seem puzzling given the fact that formulations of rules are commonly set down on paper and posted on walls, and they are often recited separately from any acts that do or do not follow them. To clarify this further, consider the following passage from an unpublished manuscript by Wittgenstein (MS 165, ca. 1941–44,78; quoted in Malcolm 1989,8):

> A rule can lead me to an action only in the same sense as can any direction in words, for example, an order. And if people did not agree in their actions according to rules, and could not come to terms with one another, that would be as if they could not come together about the sense of orders or descriptions. It would be a "confusion of tongues," and one could say that although all of them accompanied their actions with the uttering of sounds, nevertheless there was not language.

As Malcolm (1989,9) reads this, "a rule does not determine anything *except* within a setting of quiet agreement." In the absence of such concerted action, the rule is as though "naked" and the "words that express the rule would be without weight, without life." This means more than that, for example the rules in the traffic code have little weight in Boston, since drivers routinely ignore them. It means instead that a kind of practical attunement supports a rule's intelligibility. Such attunement is produced in and as the very order of activities that is already in place when a rule is formulated, notably violated, disregarded, or evidently followed. The statement of a rule or order is a constituent part of such activities, and not a distinct causal agent impinging upon them.

When we follow a rule we do not often "interpret" it, as though its meaning were somehow fully contained in an abstract formulation. We act "blindly," and we show our understanding by *acting* accordingly and not necessarily by formulating our "interpretation." Of course it is possible to misinterpret a rule, and we do sometimes wonder what the rules are and how we can apply them in a particular situation. But such occasions do not justify a general position of rule skepticism, nor do they suggest that in the normal case we interpret rules in order to use them in our actions (Baker and Hacker 1984,93–94).

It is important to understand that the antiskepticist argument does not revert to a more familiar "internalist" or rationalist view.[18] Nor, despite Baker and Hacker's occasional realist assertions, does the argument provide a blanket endorsement of epistemological realism. Instead, it is a rejection of both variants of externalism: (1) the Platonist position that the transcendental objects of mathematics determine mathematicians' practices, and (2) the skepticist position that something else (community norms or psychological dispositions) accounts for the relation between rules and behavior.

So what do these philosophical arguments portend for SSK? The most distressing implication of the antiskepticist argument is that the "contents" Bloor's Wittgenstein delivered to sociology have now been taken back and placed firmly within mathematicians' and scientists' practices, although not in terms of an overarching rationality or reality. Following Wittgenstein's *reductio*, the rule for counting by twos stands as an adequate member's account. The student in Wittgenstein's example does not display a possible interpretation of the rule; rather, his actions do not obey the rule. For members, his actions demonstrate a failure of understanding and not the relativistic nature of the rule's sense or application. Relatedly, the rule's unproblematic extension calls for no independent justification outside the organized practices of counting. It is a rule in, of, and as counting by twos. The formulation of the rule does not cause its extension, nor does the meaning of the rule somehow cast a shadow over all the actions done in accord with it. The indefinite series of actions sustains the rule's intelligibility "blindly," without pause for interpretation, deliberation, or negotiation. Is this a social phenomenon? Definitely. Can it be explained by a body of concepts proper to a field of study called sociology? Not by what we usually think of as sociology.

18. The distinction between internal and external in Baker and Hacker's treatment should not be confused with the internalist-externalist distinction in explanations of scientific progress. There is a sense in which they affiliate to an "internalist" position. An organized practice (e.g., calculating) demonstrates its rational organization (i.e., that it is orderly, in accord with relevant rules). However, this does not mean that rationality governs the practice or that one can explain the practice by invoking a set of rules. Again, a quotation from Wittgenstein may help to clarify the sort of "internal" relation between rule and practice that is involved here: "Suppose that we make enormous multiplication—numerals with a thousand digits. Suppose that after a certain point, the results people get deviate from each other. There is no way of preventing this deviation: even when we check their results, the results still deviate. What would be the right result? Would anyone have found it? Would there be a right result?—I should say, 'This has ceased to be a calculation'" (Wittgenstein, in Diamond 1976; quoted in Malcolm 1989, 14).

The problem for sociology is that the rule for counting by twos is embedded in the practice of counting. Counting is an orderly social phenomenon, but only in a trivial sense so far as causal, explanatory, scientific sociology is concerned. Similarly for the more complex practices in mathematics. The consensual culture of mathematics is expressed and described mathematically; that is, it is available in the actions of doing intelligible mathematics. To say this does not imply that mathematicians' practices are given a complete and determinate representation by mathematical formulae but that no such representation can be constructed and none is missing. To define the contents of mathematics and science as social phenomena turns out to be a very hollow victory for sociology.

It seems we have arrived at an unhappy position for the sociology of science. The neointernalist view expressed by Shanker, Baker, and Hacker seems to provide little basis for sociology to extend Wittgenstein's project. Mathematics and science (not to speak of innumerably other theory-guided or rule-following activities) now seem to have no need for sociologists to show them what they are missing in their realist preoccupations. Latour (who is partially sympathetic with constructivist sociology of science) acknowledges this problem in a most forceful way (1988,9):

> But where can we find the concepts, the words, the tools that will make our explanation independent of the science under study? I must admit that there is no established stock of such concepts, especially not in the so-called human sciences, particularly sociology. Invented at the same period and by the same people as scientism, sociology is powerless to understand the skills from which it has so long been separated. Of the sociology of the sciences I can therefore say, "Protect me from my friends; I shall deal with my enemies," for if we set out to explain the sciences, it may well be that the *social* sciences will suffer first.

This passage succinctly identifies a dilemma for any program of "social" explanation that seeks to show that the "contents" of other disciplinary practices are determined by a distinct configuration of sociological factors. If, as Latour suggests, to explain a practice is to deploy concepts that are independent of the practice under study, SSK's explanatory concepts would have to be independent of the heterogeneous "skills" in the other disciplines explained. But since sociology's analytic language is not divorced from the vernacular terms through which scientists (and other competent language users) develop their operative relations to the world in which they act, a causal sociology of science seems to require nothing short of a complete transcendence of ordinary language.[19]

But even if the antiskepticist argument convinces us of the absurdity of regressive attempts to explain rule following, what are we to make of Wittgenstein's very clear references to training, drill, custom, common practice, and the public display of language use? Do they not constitute a "social theory of knowledge," as Bloor argues? The problem is that Bloor treats Wittgenstein's "sociological" account as licensing an extension of sociology's existing concepts and methods to cover the subject matter of logic, mathematics, and natural science. "Mathematics and logic are collections of norms. The ontological status of logic and mathematics is the same as that of an institution. They are social in nature. An immediate consequence of this idea is that the activities of calculation and inference are amenable to the same processes of investigation, and are illuminated by the same theories, as any other body of norms" (Bloor 1973,189).

What Bloor overlooks is that Wittgenstein's arguments apply no less forcefully to realist and rationalist sociology than to mathe-

---

19. Although Latour neatly identifies the problem here (also see Callon 1986), and he disavows any possibility of a causal or explanatory SSK, his solution to the problem is to turn to semiotics to borrow a stock of concepts that he holds to be analytically independent of both general (i.e., academic) sociology and the situated sociologies in the disciplines studied. He thus takes the program of "stepping back" from the field of language use to an even further extreme than do the sociologists he criticizes. In contrast, Wittgenstein attempts to make language use perspicuous, but not by distancing an "observer" from the concepts in use. Instead he draws explicit attention to the in-use (i.e., situated, occasional, indexical) properties of familiar expressions and to the "quiet agreement" that founds them. In his imaginary "anthropological" examples, Wittgenstein indicates the common ground for intelligibility provided by such primordial language games as greetings, commands and responses, giving and receiving orders, and so forth. (See Jordan and Fuller 1974 for an anthropological case study on this point.) Note that the contrast Wittgenstein draws in the following passage emphasizes the social field in which these common practices take recognizable form: "If someone came into a foreign country, whose language he did not understand, it would not in general be difficult for him to find out when an order was given. But one can also order oneself to do something. If, however, we observed a Robinson, who gave himself an order in a language unfamiliar to us, this would be much more difficult for us to recognize" (Wittgenstein MS 165,103; quoted in Malcolm 1989,24). In ethnographic studies of scientific and other specialized disciplines, familiar activities like giving orders, asking questions, giving instructions, and so forth provide an initial, though far from complete, basis for grasping the intelligibility of specialized actions. To bring more distinctive language games under examination requires an analysis situated within the settings studied. The direction of such an inquiry is more a matter of immersion than of distancing.

matical realism and logicism. Winch (1958) and Sharrock and Anderson (1985) point out that it is not so much that Wittgenstein made science and mathematics safe for sociology; he made things entirely unsafe for the analytic social sciences. This applies not only to sociology's attempts scientifically to explain science but also to its attempts to explain religious beliefs, magical rituals, and ordinary actions. If sociology is to follow Wittgenstein's lead, a radically different conception of sociology's task needs to be developed. Bloor's attempts to graft Durkheim's or Mary Douglas's schemes to Wittgenstein's arguments simply do not go far enough.

This is where ethnomethodology comes into the picture, but to make the case for it as a program for pursuing Wittgenstein's initiatives will require our clearing away certain confusions both within and about ethnomethodology.[20] Ethnomethodology has become an increasingly incoherent discipline, despite incessant efforts by reviewers and textbook writers to define its theoretical and methodological program. Although many ethnomethodologists remain committed to the more radically "reflexive" ethnomethodology exemplified in Garfinkel's (1967) central writings, an offshoot of ethnomethodology known as conversation analysis has grown increasingly compatible with the analytic social sciences. To complicate matters further, many social scientists, give a decidedly skeptical reading to ethnomethodology. Woolgar (1988a), for instance, puts some of Garfinkel's "key concepts" in the service of a skepticist treatment of science. He lists indexicality and reflexivity among the "methodological horrors" haunting all attempts at scientific representation.

The antiskepticist reading of Wittgenstein suggests a way to understand what I see as ethnomethodology's distinctive treatment of language and practical action; a treatment that avoids the twin pitfalls of sociological scientism and epistemological skepticism. To clarify this point, in the next section I shall explicate an argument by Garfinkel and Sacks about the relationship between "formula-

20. As stated in n. 4, Wittgenstein's importance is downplayed by Garfinkel and other ethnomethodologists. Schutz and phenomenology are usually given a greater role in ethnomethodology's philosophical ancestry (Heritage 1984, chap. 3). Without going into what would have to be a complicated scholarly exercise, let me simply assert that the early development of conversational analysis and Garfinkel's studies of accounting practices and everyday rule use exhibit strong Wittgensteinian overtones. I have argued elsewhere (Lynch 1988b) that Schutz's influence is undermined by much of the work on science in SSK and ethnomethodology, but the same cannot be said about Wittgenstein. But as I stated before, this does not mean that ethnomethodologists have endeavored to be faithful to the Wittgensteinian or any other philosophical tradition.

tions" and practical actions, which I believe is compatible with an antiskepticist reading of Wittgenstein. In the final sections of the paper I will discuss some of the consequences of SSK's and ESW's contrastive "empirical" commitments for analyzing mathematicians' proofs and scientists' discoveries.

Formulations and Practical Actions

In their difficult and often misunderstood paper "On formal structures of practical actions," Garfinkel and Sacks (1970) discuss ethnomethodology's interest in natural language. They mention Wittgenstein only briefly in their paper, but Sacks (1967a) gives a more elaborate discussion of Wittgenstein's relevance in a transcribed lecture that covers some of the themes discussed in the later paper.[21] In that lecture Sacks speaks of Wittgenstein's having "exploded" the problem of the referential meaning of "indicator terms" (related to what Garfinkel calls "indexical expressions"). These terms have traditionally boggled logicians, since their reference changes with each occasion of use. Prior to Wittgenstein, a common solution in the philosophy of language was to "remedy" these expressions by assigning spatiotemporal referents for each instance of their use, so that a particular use of the term "here" would be translated into a proper name for the place the speaker "intends." Such efforts at translation encounter the problem of deciding just what name should translate a particular use of an indicator term. In any particular use, does "here" refer to a geographical place, an address, a social occasion like a meeting or celebration, or all of the above? Using examples from a tape-recorded group therapy session, Sacks (1967a,8) demonstrates that indicator terms do not simply stand proxy for names, "since each formulation of 'here' may well be consequential, i.e., if 'here' is say, 'the group therapy session' there might be good reasons for wanting to say 'here,' e.g., . . . 'what are you doing here,' rather than saying 'What are you doing in group therapy.'" Sacks argues that far from being inherently ambiguous or problematic, indicator terms have "stable" uses in conversation. Speakers ordinarily use indicator terms effectively and intelligibly without having to establish (ostensively or otherwise) what they stand for.

Garfinkel and Sacks (1970) greatly expand the relevance of "in-

---

21. I take it that Sacks's lecture expresses themes arising in his collaboration with Garfinkel, and I am not suggesting that the later paper owes its main initiatives to Sacks's ideas alone.

dexicality" beyond the analysis of specific classes of words, like pronouns, deictic and anaphoric references, and indicator terms. Their
discussion develops a biting quality when they treat Durkheim's
fundamental rule of method—"The objective reality of social facts
is sociology's fundamental principle"—as an example of an "indexical expression" for members of the American Sociological Association. This expression can be used on different occasions as a
definition of professional sociologists' activities, "as their slogan,
their task, aim, achievement, brag, sales-pitch, justification, discovery, social phenomena, or research constraint" (Garfinkel and Sacks
1970,339).

The bulk of their paper focuses on a phenomenon Garfinkel and
Sacks call "formulating." Formulating includes a wide range of phenomena: naming, identifying, defining, describing, explaining, and
of course, citing a rule. Initially the paper provides a set of examples
that seem to suggest that formulations are used in "lay" and "professional" discourse as devices for clarifying the unequivocal sense
of activities.[22] Garfinkel and Sacks observe that in ordinary conver-

22. Garfinkel and Sacks (1970, 346) recommend that students of practical reasoning should remain indifferent to distinctions between "scientific" and other efforts to
formulate activities: "Persons doing ethnomethodological studies can 'care' no more
or less about professional sociological reasoning than they can 'care' about the practices of legal reasoning, conversational reasoning, divinational reasoning, and the
rest." Consequently this indifference covers any practical or academic effort to substitute "objective expressions" for "indexicals." Heritage and Watson (1980) discuss
several systematic uses of formulations in conversation. Formulations do much more
than clarify or correct prior usage. Consider, for example, the following excerpt from
an interrogation:

> MR. NIELDS: Did you suggest to the Attorney General that maybe the diversion
> memorandum and the fact that there was a diversion need not ever come
> out?
> LT. COL. NORTH: Again, I don't recall that specific conversation at all, but I'm
> not saying it didn't happen.
> MR. NIELDS: You don't deny it?
> LT. COL. NORTH: No.
> MR. NIELDS: You don't deny suggesting to the Attorney General of the United
> States that he just figure out a way of keeping this diversion document
> secret?
> LT. COL. NORTH: I don't deny that I said it. I'm not saying I remember it either.
> (Taking the Stand: The Testimony of Lieutenant Colonel Oliver L. North,
> Pocket Books, 1987, 33)

In this brief but very convoluted interchange we can see numerous interlarded "formulations" at work: formulations of prior conversations (with the attorney general),
formulations on the pragmatic implications of "not recalling" that conversation; formulations of what "I said," or might have "said," and what "I'm not saying" now;
formulations that suggest irony, etc. Without going further into this, it should be

sation, speakers use formulations reflexively to disambiguate the unfolding situation: "Was that a question?" "Are you inviting me to go along with you?" "I already answered your question"; "Would you please get to the point!" Similarly, in their professional discourses, logicians and scientists attempt to repair the indexical properties of language by substituting "objective expressions" (context-free expressions like "Water boils at one hundred degrees Celsius") for "indexical expressions" (context-bound expressions like "The water's hot enough now").[23] But far from developing an argument to the effect that formulations provide lay persons and scientists with a metalanguage through which they can "define the situation" in an unambiguous way, Garfinkel and Sacks (1970,359) go on to say (1) that the "work" of doing "accountably rational activities" can be accomplished, and recognizably so, by participants in the activity without need for formulating "this fact"; and (2) that "there is no room in the world to *definitively* propose formulations of activities, identifications, and contexts."

The first point is related to Baker and Hacker's (1985,73) discussion of formulating a rule: "Typically explanations by examples involve using a series of examples *as a formulation of the rule.* The examples, thus viewed, are no more *applications* of the rule explained than is an ostensive definition of 'red' (by pointing to a tomato) an application (predication) of 'red.' . . . The formulation of a rule must itself be *used* in a certain manner, as a canon of correct use." The series of examples acts to formulate the rule (i.e., make it evident, clear, relevant), without the rule being stated in so many words. The appropriateness, sense, intelligibility, and recognizability of the rule is displayed in and through the examples, without need for additional commentary. Garfinkel and Sacks draw a distinction between "formulating" (saying in so many words what we are

---

obvious that these formulations do not simply refer to something; they act as thrusts, parries, feints, and dodges in the interrogatory game (Bogen and Lynch 1989).

23. Genette (1980,212) also uses the above "water boils" example and contrasts it to another form of statement exemplified by "For a long time I used to go to bed early." The latter expression "can be interpreted only with respect to the person who utters it and the situation in which he utters it. *I* is identifiable only with reference to that person, and the completed past of the 'action' told is completed only in relation to the moment of utterance." But Genette goes on to say, "I am not certain that the present tense in 'Water boils at one-hundred degrees; (iterative narrative) is as atemporal as it seems." He argues that the contrast nevertheless has "operative value." As we shall see, Garfinkel and Sacks use the contrast between objective and indexical expressions as a placeholder in their argument and they do not imply an ontological distinction with it.

doing) and "doing" (what we are doing), but their point is similar: formulations have no independent jurisdiction over the activities they formulate, nor are the activities otherwise chaotic or senseless. Instead, the sense and adequacy of any formulation is inseparable from the order of activities it formulates. It does not act as a substitute, transparent description, or "metalevel" account of what otherwise occurs.

Like Wittgenstein's discussion of rules, Garfinkel and Sacks' discussion of formulating can be misunderstood to imply either of two antithetical positions: (1) a skepticist interpretation to the effect that any attempt to formulate activities is beset by the "problem" of indexicality, so that description, explanation, and the like are essentially indeterminate; and (2) a realist interpretation that recommends empirical study of formulations in order to enable social scientists to objectively understand members' activities.[24] A close reading of their argument should enable us to see that neither view is adequate.

Garfinkel and Sacks establish the second point—that there is "no room in the world" definitively to propose formulations of activity—by undermining their paper's provisional contrast between "objective" and "indexical" expressions. They argue that formulations do not "define" the sense of activities that would otherwise remain senseless.[25] Formulations themselves are used as "indexical expressions"; and in so using them, members routinely find that "doing formulating" is itself a source of "complaints, faults, troubles, and recommended remedies, *essentially*" (Garfinkel and Sacks 1970, 353). By the same token, "formulations are *not* the machinery whereby accountably sensible, clear, definite talk is done" (353–54). "Saying in so many words what we are doing" can be "recognizably incongruous, or boring, . . . [furnishing] evidence of incompetence, or devious motivation, and so forth" (354).[26] Conversationalists manage to maintain topical coherence, often without naming the

24. Garfinkel and Sacks's paper undermines the integrity of the phenomenon they initially set out to examine. "Formulating" no longer names a discrete class of linguistic objects; instead it becomes a rubric for a heterogeneous collection of actions in conversation.

25. See Filmer 1976 for an analysis of Garfinkel and Sacks's argument, particularly in reference to the way the apparent distinction between objective and indexical expressions is undermined in the course of the paper.

26. For an example of how formulating can often deepen the misery in which a speaker is enmeshed, consider the following formulation, which was made during a particularly disastrous public lecture: "I'm going to tell a joke, but it isn't very funny."

topic,[27] and as Garfinkel's breaching exercises demonstrate, attempts to "repair" the indexicality of any text or set of instructions further compound and extend the indexical properties of the text. The conclusion Garfinkel and Sacks (355) draw from this may initially seem to support a skepticist reading (emphasis and brackets in original): *"for the member it is not in the work of doing formulations for conversation that the member is doing [the fact that our conversational activities are accountably rational].* The two activities are neither identical nor interchangeable."

But carefully note the passage that follows (355; brackets in original): "In short, doing formulating for conversation itself exhibits for conversationalists an orientation to [the fact that our conversational activities are accountably rational]." This clearly differs from a constructivist argument to the effect that our activities remain indeterminate until we establish "accounts" of their meaning. But neither is this emphasis on the accountability of actions tantamount to a realist or rationalist position (355): "The question of what one who is doing formulating is doing—which is a member's question—is not solved by members by consulting what the formulation proposes, but by engaging in practices that make up the *essentially* contexted character of the action of formulating."

For the rule "add two," no formulation can provide a complete or determinate account of how the rule is to be extended to new cases (as though the rule included a representation of all of its applications). Citing the rule is an activity in its own right (an instruction, warning, correction, reminder, etc.), but the rule's formulation does not say what is to be done with it. The sense of the rule is *"essentially* contexted" by the orderly activity within which it is invoked, expressed, applied, and so forth. But this does not imply that the

27. Sacks (transcribed lecture, 9 March 1967) demonstrates that topical coherence is achieved through systematic placement of a second utterance vis-à-vis a first. The placement of an utterance answers such unasked question as Why did you say that? Why did you say that *now?* This is done "automatically," and not by any formulation: "That persons come to see your remark as fitting into the topic at hand provides for them the answer for how come you said it now. That is, it solves the possible question *automatically.* Upon hearing the statement a hearer will come to see directly, how you come to say that" (Sacks 1967b,5). Although resolved on an entirely different historical scale, Sacks's analytic approach is strikingly, if perversely, in line with Foucault's (1975,xvii) antisemiotic approach to historical discourse: "The meaning of a statement would be defined not by the treasure of intentions that it might contain, revealing and concealing it at the same time, but by the difference that articulates it upon the other real or possible statements, which are contemporary to it or to which it is opposed in the linear series of time."

activity has no rational basis, or that participants' understandings of what they are doing is necessarily incomplete or faulty.

In the concluding section of their paper, Garfinkel and Sacks (358) assert that how "members do [the fact that our activities are accountably rational] . . . is done without having to do formulations." They add further that this "work" is organizable as "a machinery, in the way it is specifically used to do [accountably rational activities]" (brackets in the original). They then spell out the critical implications of this for the social sciences (359):

> That there is no room in the world for formulations as serious solutions to the problem of social order has to do with the prevailing recommendation in the social sciences that formulations can be done for practical purposes to accomplish empirical description, to achieve the justification and test of hypotheses, and the rest. Formulations are recommended thereby as resources with which the social sciences may accomplish rigorous analyses of practical actions that are adequate for all practical purposes. . . . insofar as formulations are recommended as descriptive of "meaningful talk" something is amiss because "meaningful talk" cannot have that sense.

Insofar as the formal structures of practical actions (i.e., the "achieved fact" that activities are accountably rational) are not recovered by formulations, these structures elude constructive-analytic attempts to codify and statistically represent them. "The unavailability of formal structures is assured by the practices of constructive analysis for it *consists* of its practices" (361).

Ethnomethodology does not solve the epistemological problems arising from the effort to substitute objective for indexical expressions. By remaining indifferent to that program, ethnomethodologists aim to characterize the organized use of indexical expressions in lay and professional activities. Inevitably ethnomethodologists engage in formulating, if only to formulate the work of doing formulating. Unlike constructive analysis, ethnomethodology topicalizes the relationship between formulations and activities in other than truth-conditional terms; not as true or false statements but as pragmatic moves in a temporal order of actions. Two main questions arise from this program: (1) How do ordinary activities exhibit regularity, order, standardization, and particular cohort independence (i.e., "rationality") in advance of any formulation? (2) How, in any instance, do members use formulating as part of their activities?

From the above we can see the sharp contrast between ethnomethodology's and Bloor's "Wittgensteinian" projects. Where Bloor maintains a distinction between sociology's foundation as a science and the sociologically explained "contents" of the sciences, studied,

Garfinkel and Sacks place sociology squarely within the ordinary society ethnomethodology studies.

Developments and Applications

In the decades since the formal structures paper was written, ethnomethodology's program has diverged into two different lines of research. One line of studies, conversational analysis, investigates the sequential organization of "naturally occurring" conversations (Sacks, Schegloff, and Jefferson 1974). These studies elucidate "rational properties of indexical expressions" by describing the regular procedures for turn taking, adjacency-pair organization, referential placement and correction, topical organization, story structure, place formulation, and other phenomena. In Wittgenstein's terminology, such phenomena are included among the "language games"[28] through which order, sense, coherence, and agreement are interactionally achieved.[29]

A second line of development is Garfinkel's (1986) ethnomethodological studies of work. Garfinkel (1988) characterizes this program as an approach to the production of social order that breaks with classical conceptions of the problem of order. For Garfinkel, both the detailed methods for producing social order and the conceptual themes under which order becomes analyzable are members'

---

28. Wittgenstein's use of the term "language game" is multifaceted. Conversational analysis develops upon the sense of "language game" Wittgenstein (*PI*, §23) emphasizes when he says the term "is meant to bring into prominence the fact that the *speaking* of a language is part of an activity, or of a form of life." He then provides a list of examples, including giving and obeying orders, describing the appearance of an object, constructing an object from a description, and telling stories and jokes. Wittgenstein (*PI*, §25) characterizes some of these activities ("commanding, questioning, recounting, chatting") as "primitive forms of language," and he says that they "are as much a part of our natural history as walking, eating, drinking, playing."

29. Conversational analysis has diverged from many of Garfinkel's initiatives. The current literature in the area has increasingly dissociated itself from ethnomethodology's antipositivistic commitments. Nevertheless, particular studies can be reappropriated as precise examples for critical epistemic arguments (cf. Coulter 1989). The basic themes and procedures of conversation analysis can also be mobilized for studying the local production of scientific work (Garfinkel et al. 1981; Lynch 1985a; Amann and Knorr Cetina 1988; Woolgar 1988b) and human-machine interaction (Suchman 1987). Analyzing tape-recorded shop talk in laboratories does not require an aim to positively characterize scientific talk as a species of "speech exchange system." Recorded shop talk can be analyzed along with the graphic, photographic, and other documents produced in laboratory activities in order to deepen our access to experimental and observational praxis. Structures of "talk" per se are incidental, although indispensable, for such a study.

local achievements. There is no room in such a universe for a master theorist to narrate the thematics of an overall social structure. Instead the best that can be done is to closely study the particular *sites* of practical inquiry where participants' actions elucidate the grand themes (e.g., of rationality, agency, structure, and meaning) as part of the day's work. Of particular interest for the present discussion are ethnomethodological studies of scientists' and mathematicians' practices. In this body of research, the questions Garfinkel and Sacks raise on how formulations arise within practical activities remain much livelier than in conversational analysis.

It might initially seem that such formulations as maps, diagrams, graphs, textual figures, mathematical proofs, and photographic documents differ significantly from the formulations of activity Garfinkel and Sacks discuss. Maps, after all, represent objective terrain and territory and proofs demonstrate the logical grounds for mathematical functions. They are not in any precise sense used as formulations of "what we are doing." But to treat maps and proofs as isolated pictures or statements ignores the activities that compose and use them. To analyze a document's use does not discount its referential value, but it does demolish suppositions about the essential difference between formulations of "things" and formulations of "our activities." For example, take the following conversation recorded during a session where two laboratory assistants (J and B) review some electron microscopic data they prepared, while the lab director (H) looks on and comments (Simplified version of transcript from Lynch 1985a, 252–53):

> J: If you *look* at this stuff it—things that are degenerating are very definite, and there's no real question about it.
> B: That's the thing that really blew me *out*. Once I was looking at the three-day stuff, and the terminals were already phagocytized by the uh, by the glia.
> J: Oh yeah, there are some like that now.
> (Three seconds of silence)
> H: Yeah, I'm not worried about that. It's the false positives that worry me.
> J: Yeah, yeh.
> H: Like this.
> J: Oh yeah, well that one—I didn't mark I don't think—You know I just put a little *X* there, because that's marginal, but this one looks like it has a density right there.
> H: Yeah, and this one looks pretty good.

Roughly characterized, the fragment starts when J assesses the analytic clarity of the data he and B have just finished preparing.

B then supports J's assessment with a comparison to other data. He expresses a worry that challenges what the two assistants have just said, and J then fends off the challenge by simultaneously explicating details of the document and his method for preparing it. The fragment ends as H begins to accede to J's assessment. The interchange continues well beyond the transcribed fragment (see Lynch 1985a, 250ff. for additional details).

Without going into a detailed analysis of the fragment, let me just mention a few points relevant to the current question about formulations of things. The participants say things about the electron microscopic photographs they inspect together. These references include at least the following: [30]

1. J's initial references to "this stuff" and to "degenerating" organelles of the brain tissue presumably resulting from an experimental lesion
2. B's comparison of the present materials to "three-day stuff," where "three" formulates the number of days between the lesion and the sacrifice of the animal
3. B's reference to phagocytosis, a process through which glial cells are said to "clean up" degenerated tissue following brain injury
4. H's "worry" about "false positives," which in the present instance can be understood as visible profiles of organelles that should appear to be degenerating but look normal in the micrographs
5. J's mention of the "little X" he says he marked on the surface of the micrograph to denote a "marginal" entity
6. H's assessment that "this one" looks "pretty good"

Each of these references to things makes one point or another about the materials being inspected. Some references seem to point to visibly discriminable features of the data: instances of "degenerating" axon profiles (1), of a "marginal" case (5), and of a "this one" that looks "pretty good" (6). And these indicator terms may be accompanied by the characteristic gestures of ostension. Other references invoke temporal and conceptual horizons of the particular case at hand (e.g., B's references to other cases and phagocytosis [2,

30. My glosses on what these indexical expressions "refer to" were not generated from the transcribed text alone and rely upon my ethnography of the lab's common techniques and vernacular usage. Their intelligibility for this analysis hinges upon my (rather tenuous in this case) grasp of the disciplinary specific practices studied, above and beyond any ethnomethodological expertise I put to use in the study. To mention the tenuousness of my glossing practices is not, contrary to Latour's (1986) criticisms of my (1985a) text, a mea culpa about my ignorance as a brain scientist so much as a reminder that what I have to say about the practices is—whether adequate, inadequate, or trivial—an extension of the competency described.

3] and C's mention of a possible methodological problem [4]). Still others, for example, J's reference to "this stuff" (1), seem to point with a thick and hazy finger, which may indicate any of several things. "This stuff" could indicate the entire micrographic display, a delimited feature within the frame of the document, a series of comparable micrographs, various analytic indices and markings, or a characteristic phenomenon. But the parties do not take time out to clarify such references (except when challenged to do so), and this is not because an occult process supplies them with mental images of what the indicator terms "stand for". Moreover, each of the successive references to things is included within utterances that make a point vis-a-vis a local context of utterances and activities.

From this example we can see that references to things act simultaneously as references to (and within) activities. The participants do not act like talking machines, emitting nouns that correspond to pictorial details. Their references implicate the adequacy of J's and B's work and the success of the project (that is, the references to "definite" features of the data imply that things are going well, that a discriminable phenomenon seems to be emerging in the data). In this case the general argument that Garfinkel and Sacks made about formulations of activities is no less pertinent to formulations of things in laboratory discourse.

If we recall once again the contrasts between the skepticist and antiskepticist readings of Wittgenstein's number series argument, we can now bring into relief how ESW's program extends Wittgenstein in a very different way from SSK's. The skepticist reading treats the rule as a *representation* of an activity which fails to account uniquely for the actions done in accord with it. The skeptical solution invokes psychological dispositions and/or extrinsic social factors to explain how an agent can unproblematically extend the rule to cover new cases. The nonskepticist reading treats the rule as an expression in, of, and as the orderly activity in which it occurs. The rule formulates an orderly activity insofar as order is already produced within the activity, and the rule's use elaborates that order.

As discussed above, Garfinkel and Sacks treat indexicality as a chronic problem for logicians and social scientists in their attempts to objectively represent linguistic and social activities. This problem disappears for ethnomethodology, not because it is solved or transcended, but through a shift in the entire conception of language. As Garfinkel and Sacks elaborate in their discussion of "the rational properties of indexical expressions," such expressions are the very stuff of clear, intelligible, understandable activities. From their point of view, indexicality ceases to be a problem except under delimited circumstances. A sense of it as an ubiquitous "methodological horror" (Woolgar 1988a) only accrues when indexical expressions are treated as tokens isolated from their meanings.[31] Insofar as scientists and mathematicians use such expressions as part of a nexus of routine activities, they do not so much manage or evade indexicality by some rhetorical or interpretive strategy; the general "horror" *never arises in the first place*. This is not to say that scientists have no methodological or epistemic problems, but that such problems arise and are handled with variable success as occasional (and sometimes "demonic") contingencies in the course of disciplinary specific work.

Exemplary Debates 1: Bloor vs. Livingston on Mathematics

From Garfinkel and Sacks's argument we can take the lesson that, far from disturbing or forestalling efforts to formulate activities, "the rational properties of indexical expressions" furnish an indispensable basis for the sense, relevance, success, or failure of any formu-

---

31. The "methodological horrors" are a set of problems raised in a skeptical treatment of representation. They include the indeterminate relationships between rules and their applications, and between theories and experimental data. Woolgar (1988b, 172, 198–99 n.1) gives a methodological rationale for his general skepticism about scientists' representational practices. The policy of unrestricted skepticism licenses the sociological observer to impute methodological horrors to practices that would otherwise appear undisturbed. Part of the package Woolgar asks his readers to accept is the picture of scientists endlessly laboring to evade or circumvent the problems a skeptical philosopher could raise about their work. If this looks like a familiar move in the game of ideology critique, it is no accident. Woolgar (1988a,101) states that "science is no more than an especially visible manifestation of the ideology of representation." The latter he defines (99) as "the set of beliefs and practices stemming from the notion that objects (meanings, motives, things) underlie or pre-exist the surface signs (documents, appearances) which give rise to them." His critique is squarely aimed at scientific practice as well as a particular metaphysical view of science, and he thus may seem liable to Hacking's (1983,30) charge of conflating what specialized scientists do with what philosophers of sciences would have them do. In Woolgar's defense plenty of evidence can be mustered to show that when asked about what they are demonstrating in their studies, many scientists give realist (whether naive or otherwise) responses (cf. Gilbert and Mulkay 1984). And it would not be off base to say that scientists' writings are a particularly realistic literary genre. But while it may be appropriate to criticize the ideology, it is not at all clear whether such criticisms implicate the "vulgar competence" (Garfinkel et al. 1981,139) of scientists' routine activities. And Woolgar's statement that science is "no more than" a manifestation of an ideology is particularly off the mark, given the demonstration (even in some of his own studies) that the "ideology of representation" is a rather thin and often irrelevant account of scientists' practices.

lation. In cases where rules or related formulations are regarded as rigorous, invariant, or even transcendental descriptions of activities, the basis for their rigor is provided by the practices in which such formulations are used. The contrast between this proposal and SSK's program becomes clear when we examine issues raised in Bloor's (1987) review of Livingston's (1986) ethnomethodological study of mathematicians' work.

Livingston (1986, 1987) introduces a phenomenon he calls the "pair structure" of a mathematical proof.[32] This involves a distinction between a "proof-account" (the textual statement of a proof's "schedule") and "the lived-work of proving" (the course of activities through which a "prover" works out the proof on any particular occasion). In his demonstration of Gödel's proof and a simpler proof from Euclidean geometry, Livingston emphasizes the internal relation of proof-account to the lived-work of proving, such that neither proof-account nor its associated lived-work stand alone. For a competent mathematician, acting alone with pencil on paper or together with colleagues at the blackboard, the proof-account comes to articulate the lived-work of proving. Once worked through, it becomes a "precise description" and "transcendental account" of the work of proving.

> The puzzling and amazing thing about the pair structure of a proof is that neither proof-account nor its associated lived-work stand alone, nor are they ever available in such a dissociated state. The produced social object—the proof—and all of its observed, demonstrable properties, including its transcendental presence independent of the material particulars of its proof-account, are available in and as that pairing. A prover's work is inseparable from its material detail although, as the accomplishment of a proof, that proof is seen to be separable from it. (Livingston 1987,136–37)

The relation to the antiskepticist reading of Wittgenstein should be obvious. Livingston avoids the "question contain[ing] a mistake"

32. Livingston develops Garfinkel's theme of "*Lebenswelt* pair" (cf. Garfinkel et al. 1989,123–24). The "pair" consists in a "first segment" (e.g., the proof statement in Livingston's example) and the "'lived' work-site practices—'the work'—of proving the theorem." In this treatment I am glossing over many of the intricacies, and particularly one of the features Garfinkel et al. (1989,121ff.) and Livingston (1986) take pains to point out: that the "pair structure" is not simply another example of formulations and activities. They raise the possibility that the *Lebenswelt* pair occurs only in mathematics and other "discovering sciences of practical action." To assess this rather bold proposal would take more than I am ready to muster here. It should be clear, however, that they are not proposing to exempt mathematics and physical science from ethnomethodological study.

by insisting that the intelligibility of a proof statement does not stand isolated from the practices of proving. The lived work the proof formulates, while it is nothing other than mathematicians' work, is at the same time a social phenomenon. "One of the consequences of the discovered pair structure of proofs is that the proofs of mathematics are recovered as witnessably social objects. This is not because some type of extraneous, non-proof-specific element like a theory of 'socialization' needs to be added to a proof, but because the natural accountability of a proof is integrally tied to its production and exhibition *as* a proof" (Livingston 1987,126).

In his extensive and in some ways trenchant review of Livingston's (1986) volume, Bloor (1987) raises a set of objections that clearly expose the differences between his approach and ethnomethodology's. He enlists Wittgenstein on his side of the fray, but as I shall argue, he does so at great risk to his own position. Bloor chides Livingston for having made no mention of Wittgenstein and then lectures him about what he should have known about Wittgenstein's "social theory of knowledge." While doing so, Bloor fails to grasp how strongly Livingston's treatment accords with an antiskepticist reading of Wittgenstein. To be sure, Livingston fails to mention Wittgenstein in his (1986) volume, and in his subsequent book (1987,126ff.) he mentions Wittgenstein only in relation to a particular example. However, both texts make use of what I would argue are Wittgensteinian arguments mediated by Garfinkel's teachings. Bloor (1987,341) characterizes Livingston's position as follows:

> The amazing feat of creating universally compelling, eternal mathematical truths is managed entirely by what goes on, say, at the blackboard. If we examine the precise details we will see how transcendence is accomplished then and there. We don't need to enquire into the surroundings of the episode, or into the possibility that the feat depends on something imported into a situation from the surroundings. That would be to involve non-local features and circumstances beyond the "worksite."

Livingston can, of course, only fail by Bloor's reckoning. Bloor points out that Livingston refers to "familiar" aspects of a proof, thereby implying a wider horizon of accepted arguments and common tendencies among mathematicians. But to count this against Livingston is to miss the point of his focus on the internal relation between a proof statement and the lived work of proving. What Livingston aims to demonstrate is that the lived work of proving (the public production of mathematics at the blackboard, or with pencil and paper) generates the proof statement's precise description of that selfsame activity. In retrospect there is no better formulation than the proof statement itself, although its adequacy is established not by any referential function of the statement but through the lived activity of proving. Or if a better formulation is to be developed, it arises from the historicity of mathematicians' activities. This, of course, implicates a communal setting of "quiet agreements" and orderly practices (Malcolm 1989). But this is not enough for Bloor, since there is no sociological explanation in Livingston's demonstration. Bloor (1987,353–54) argues that the seeds of such an explanation are found in Wittgenstein's later philosophy:

> Wittgenstein, despite what is sometimes said, elaborated a *theory*. He argued that constructing mathematical proofs could be understood as a process of reasoning by analogy. It involves patterns of inference that were originally based on our experience of the world around us, and which have come to function as paradigms. They become conventionalized, and begin to take on a special aura as a result. We think that mathematics shows us the *essence* of things but, for Wittgenstein, these essences are conventions (*RFM*, I-74). We might say that in Wittgenstein, Mill's empiricism is combined with Durkheim's theory of the sacred.

In a very basic way, Bloor's Wittgensteinian critique of Livingston might as well be a critique of Wittgenstein. If Livingston fails to state a social scientific theory and fails to explain mathematical practice, so too does Wittgenstein fail as a matter of explicit policy:

> It was true to say that our considerations could not be scientific ones. . . . And we may not advance any kind of theory. There must not be anything hypothetical in our considerations. We must do away with all *explanation*, and description alone must take its place. And this description gets its light, that is to say its purpose, from the philosophical problems. These are, of course, not empirical problems; they are solved, rather, by looking into the workings of our language, and that in such a way as to make us recognize those workings: *in despite of* an urge to misunderstand them. The problems are solved, not by giving new information, but by arranging what we have always known. Philosophy is a battle against the bewitchment of our intelligence by means of language. (Wittgenstein *PI*,§109)

Far from offering a "social theory of knowledge" in line with the dream of classical sociology, Wittgenstein here disavows science, theory, and explanation. Ethnomethodology also eschews the most basic elements of scientific sociology: its explanatory aims, its disciplinary corpus, and its definition of society. In that sense, ethnomethodology "extends" Wittgenstein without having to repudiate his challenge to scientism and foundationalism.

In recommending description rather than explanation, Wittgenstein took into account that a description is not a "word-picture of the facts," and that descriptions "are instruments for particular uses" (*PI*,§291). He did not propose to deliver singularly correct descriptions of language use. Instead he advocated a kind of "reflexive" investigation, where philosophy's problems are addressed by "looking into the workings of our language." In the final section of this paper I shall return to this proposal to suggest how ethnomethodology develops a distinctive empirical approach. Before that I will review yet another debate between SSK and ESW. This debate concerns the phenomenon of scientific discovery.

Exemplary Debates 2: Collins vs. Garfinkel et al. on Discovery

Established mathematical procedures may not be the most apt exemplars of scientific practice. As Galison (1987,11) points out, "it is unfair to look to experimental arguments for ironclad implications and then, upon finding that experiments do not have logically impelled conclusions, to ascribe the experimentalists' beliefs entirely to 'interests.' But who would have thought experiments were like mathematics?" Of course advocates of the strong program are quite comfortable with treating mathematics in the same (skepticist-relativist) terms as they do experimental reasoning. The problem is that conventionalist arguments about rule following do not so readily apply to novel experimental or observational procedures. Discoveries tend to be surrounded by circumstances a great deal "noisier" than the "silent agreements" supporting established mathematical practices. Controversies surrounding discovery claims may occasionally verge upon a confusion of tongues. But when we consider a particular discovery, not as the implementation of a conventional procedure, but as an object or phenomenon—as the thing of "law" to which the discovery is referenced—we can draw a stronger analogy with mathematical practices. Realist philosophers explain observational and experimental results by citing the evident properties of the discovered object, just as Platonists explain mathematical practice in reference to ideal mathematical forms. Neither SSK or ESW accepts such "objective" determinacy, but there are significant differences between their treatments of discovery. Again, these can be considered in light of the skepticist and nonskepticist readings of Wittgenstein. In this instance I will focus on Harry Collins's criticisms of an ethnomethodological study of a discovery by Garfinkel, Lynch, and Livingston. Garfinkel et al. (1981,131–32) begin their article as follows:

247

On the evening of the discovery of the optical pulsar at Steward Observatory, January 16, 1969, by John Cocke, Michael Disney, Don Taylor and Robert McCallister, a tape recording in which they reported their series of observations was left running and before it ran out recorded the evening's "conversations" from Observation 18 through 23. This unique document . . . was made available for our examination. The tape was transcribed by us using the conventions of conversational analysis.

The article raises the question, "What does the optically discovered pulsar consist of as Cocke and Disney's night's work?"[33] The basic structure of the argument is similar to Livingston's (1986). Garfinkel et al. draw a distinction between the "Independent Galilean Pulsar" (IGP) and "the local historicity of the night's work." The IGP is the pulsar that by night's end is assigned an identity and set of astrophysical properties (e.g., *NP* 0532, with an optical period of 0.033095 sec., a primary and secondary peak of measurable intensities, etc.). Conventionally speaking, the IGP formulates the substantive discovery Cocke et al. make. In contrast to astrophysicists' usage, Garfinkel et al. speak of the IGP as a "cultural object" which

33. The "optically discovered pulsar" is Garfinkel et al.'s way of speaking of the intertwining of the astronomers' work and its astrophysical object. It contrasts to the "independent Galilean pulsar" (IGP) given standing in the astrophysicists' universe. Prior to 1969, radio astronomers had identified a class of objects they called "pulsars." These were point sources whose radio emissions pulsated at many-times-per-second frequencies. The initial discovery of the radio pulsars gave rise to considerable theoretical speculation and some very interesting stories (see Edge and Mulkay 1976; Woolgar 1976). None of the forty or so radio pulsars that had been identified by 1969 had been correlated with a visible (optical) source, and some astrophysicists calculated that the energies from pulsars would not be visible in optical wavelengths. Cocke, Disney, and Taylor, all from the University of Arizona at the time, collaborated on a project in which they used a relatively small telescope on Kitt Peak (Steward Observatory) hooked up to an electronic gadget that could be set at measured frequencies to record regular fluctuations in a light source. None of the three astronomers was very experienced in practical astronomical observation, and they later claimed that they had very little expectation of discovering anything. They guessed that the most likely sources of optical pulsars would be at the core of supernova remnants. Since one radio pulsar with an especially high frequency had been recorded near the Crab Nebula, they decided to set their telescope on a star believed to be the core of that exploding cloud of gas. After several unsuccessful runs over a few nights, on 16 January they set their telescope and electronic accumulator at the estimated frequency and then watched to see a pulse built up on their oscilloscope screen. Taylor was not on hand when the tape was recorded. McCallister, the night assistant at Steward Observatory, was present at the time, but virtually all the conversation on the tape occurs between Cocke and Disney. Garfinkel et al. collected observational logs and notes, read relevant publications on pulsars, and interviewed two of the participants (Cocke and Taylor). The study therefore was not limited to an analysis of the tape recording.

is "extracted" from a succession of observational runs with the optical and electronic equipment. They neither dispute nor adopt the claim that the IGP comes to stand as "the cause of everything that is seen and said about it" (138). For the astronomers on the tape, the IGP becomes an astronomically specific articulation of the work through which they reflexively constitute it. Garfinkel et al. do not fetishize this product of the night's work; rather they insistently point to its genealogy in and as the astronomers' praxis. Nor do they discount its status as an object. It is not a representation, and it is no less of an object than any other (cultural) object.[34]

Collins (1983,104–5) takes issue with the way Garfinkel et al. use the term "discovery." In line with Brannigan's (1981) attributional theory of discovery, Collins argues that Garfinkel et al. (GLL in his acronym) trade upon a conventional notion of discovery when they suggest that the "unique" tape documents the constituent events of a "discovery." In his view, no amount of detailed study will get a discovery out of that tape. This is because the status of the IGP as a discovery depends upon a contingent course of historical events through which Cocke et al.'s initial announcement is received, interpreted, replicated, and credited in the larger community of astronomers. For example, later in the fateful evening Cocke et al. sent out a telegram to major observatories throughout the world. The telegram announced the frequency of the pulse and the celestial coordinates of the star identified as the source. At that time, none of the few-dozen previously recorded radio pulsars had been shown to correspond to a visible star. But had another observatory sent out a similar telegram a few hours earlier, the tape of Cocke and Disney's evening's conversations would stand as a document, not of a discovery, but of a replication. Collins (1983,105) also invites us to imagine what would happen if "it later turned out that Cocke and Disney had been looking at an artifact—the result of a fault in their oscilloscope—and that this was the scientific consensus." Everything on

34. Here we can think of Wittgenstein's arguments against doubling the field of perception into objects and images of objects. It may simply confuse a description of an object to insist that the description must explicitly take account of the "fact" that the words "actually" describe a mental image or representation of the object. "The concept of representation of what is seen, like that of a copy, is very elastic, and so together with it is the concept of what is seen. The two are intimately connected. Which is not to say that they are alike" (Wittgenstein *PI*, 198). Garfinkel et al.'s (1981,142) refusal to speak of the optical pulsar as a trace on an oscillograph, a theoretical idea, a perceived figure, or an inscription divorced from any astrophysical object is not concomitant to a move into realism. It is more a matter of retaining an orientation to the "chaining" of practical action and practical reasoning "to the certain, technical, materially specific appearances of astronomy's *things.*"

the tape would stay as it was, but the retrospective sense of the event it documents would depend upon "the interaction between [Cocke and Disney] and their critics in the more extended scientific debate that followed their night's work."

Had a similar tape been left running when Pons and Fleishmann performed their infamous "cold fusion" experiments, it might also have recorded a series of excited exclamations, ad hoc proposals about what to do next in the face of one or another contingency, speculations about what it all means, projections on how to announce it, etc. But what would all this talk be a document *of*? In Pons and Fleishmann's case it remains to be seen, although it looks pretty grim for them at the moment. What Wittgenstein (*PI*,§202) says about rules seems applicable to the painful Pons and Fleishmann lesson about discoveries: "And hence also 'obeying a rule' [making a discovery] is a practice. And to *think* one is obeying a rule is not to obey a rule. Hence it is not possible to obey a rule 'privately': otherwise thinking one was obeying a rule would be the same thing as obeying it."

Collins's argument is an especially strong antidote to all cognitivist and logicist accounts of discovery, since individualistic models presuppose the status of a discovery while abstractly representing sequences of action that describe replication no less than discovery.[35] GLL's study does not advance such an individualistic model, however, since it focuses on an interactionally organized course of action. Nor does the study propose to represent a generalized discovery procedure. But Collins's point still holds that the apparent result of an isolated episode does not count as a scientific discovery until credited by members of the relevant disciplinary community. His argument seems even more pertinent to discoveries than to rules. It is consistent with the concept of "rule" to say that a person knows how to "follow a rule," but if we were to say that a person knows how to "follow a discovery" we would only be crediting his ability to replicate or understand the original act.

Collins does not denigrate GLL's study as merely an analysis of some people at work. Rather he praises it as a detailed and somewhat revealing analysis of routine scientific practices. But, he ar-

35. Slezak (1989,576) dismisses such arguments about the grammar of discovery and replication by saying that they only concern the designation, and not the substance, of a discovery. But this is no trivial matter, since it concerns what an analysis can be said to be an analysis *of* in the first place. Enthusiasts for cognitive science may have good reasons to be excited about the capabilities of computerized data reduction programs, but this gives them no basis for claiming that such programs perform discoveries when they simulate the results of historical discoveries.

gues, the "field work location" is too restrictive to have a bearing on whether or not the astronomers' "night's work" constituted a discovery. "What it is that made it that they were making a great discovery is to be found outside their night's work" (Collins 1983,105). Now this is where the issue begins to get contentious.

Recall from the above discussion of skepticism that "the critical move is to isolate the formulation of the rule from the practice it formulates." If for "rule" we substitute "discovery," and particularly "the IGP," the argument transfers nicely to the case we are now considering. It is consistent with the grammar of scientific discovery to say with hindsight that Cocke et al. made the first discovery of an optical pulsar on 16 January, 1969. This formulation presently counts as a "correct" description within astronomy; it is grammatically intelligible.[36] Astronomers commonly speak of particular objects as having been discovered by one or more individuals at a particular observatory and on a particular evening. Not all astronomical discoveries are formulated this way (cf. Hanson 1967; Woolgar 1976), but such variability does not detract from the intelligibility of this particular formulation. Philosophical realism takes liberties with the grammar of discovery by treating the Galilean object (or relatedly, the data presumably reflecting the object's properties) as an objective foundation for the activities representing it. The "conjurer's trick" is to isolate "the discovered object" from the course of action making up "the discovery" and to explain the discovery by invoking the properties of an "eternal" object.

The skeptic retains this explanatory duality but reverses the arrows: the object does not explain its representation as a discovery; rather the reverse occurs. The representation of an action as a discovery constitutes the discovered object (Woolgar 1988a,56ff.).[37] As we saw in the case of rule following, a rule becomes subject to unbounded "methodological horrors" once it is treated as a "statement" detached from the activities it formulates. As decontex-

---

36. It is possible that one or another astronomer might challenge this discovery account. For instance, an astronomer who believed that Cocke and his collaborators were unfairly credited with the discovery might disagree with the statement. But the statement is correct in the sense of being an intelligible way of formulating an astronomical discovery.

37. The policy of "inversion" is a popular one in constructivist studies. It is often linked misleadingly to the program of "deconstruction" from literary studies. As Fish (1989,211) points out, to "deconstruct" a distinction (such as, in this case, between representation and discovered object) is not a matter of inverting the conventional priority of one term over and against the other: "One deconstructs an opposition not by reversing the hierarchy of its poles but by denying to either pole the independence that makes the opposition possible in the first place."

tualized representations, discoveries also become vulnerable to an open-ended list of counterfactual conditionals (the what if? scenarios in Collins's argument). Accordingly, since the IGP does not unequivocally explain what Cocke and Disney were talking about on the tape, something else must explain how their activities came to be *represented* as making a discovery. In Collins's ungrammatical phrasing, Cocke and Disney did not make a discovery, something else "made it that they were making a great discovery."[38]

The counterfactual scenarios (and their related methodological horrors) do not come into play when we deny the skeptic's initial move of isolating the statement from the activity it formulates. Or, to be more precise, counterfactual scenarios may indeed come into play, but not as we would freely imagine them. In the antiskepticist reading of Wittgenstein, Garfinkel and Sacks's discussion of formulations, and Livingston's account of mathematical proofs, the point is driven home that no adequate use of a statement can be made in isolation from the lived order of activities it formulates. Included among these activities are the very conventional uses of the statement that establish its recognizable sense. Counterfactual scenarios do not hover idly over the night's work, as though members were haunted by the skeptic's ultimate doubts about the possibility of airtight representation. Particular doubts and methodological worries may be interjected into the course of the work, but these do not license a skeptic's global interventions.

Collins (1989,13) recognizes that the concept of discovery is relevant to the analyses of situated practices, since researchers must anticipate the potential reception of their findings when they present them to colleagues and rivals. Not only do potential discoverers recognize the possible significance and novelty of their data, they perform what Collins calls a "calculus of risk and ridicule" when formulating their findings. He argues that such anticipations of the community's reaction do not by themselves constitute discoveries, since there is no determinate relationship between the announcement of a discovery and a community's acceptance of that an-

38. The doubling of "made"/"making" here is very interesting. In the sentence prior to the one quoted, Collins (1983,105) uses a similar structure: "But to know what it is about their work that makes them scientists who *are making* a great discovery, one needs to look elsewhere." The indication of regress is dramatic here: behind the act is another act of the same category that causes its manifestation. Worse, while the application of the term "making" to Cocke and Disney's activity is unremarkable (i.e. intelligible), it is much more difficult to picture how "makes" functions in the domain of "elsewhere." It seems to me that invoking such a diffuse agency only serves to confuse otherwise intelligible usage.

nouncement. Collins is certainly correct in this, but it would be misleading to say that isolated individuals cannot make discoveries until the community renders a judgment about their claims. First, there is no clear point of separation between the activities of individuals in an observatory and the community judgments that determine whether they have made a discovery. Technical activities are not asocial acts awaiting their social determination. Secondly, the relevant community judgments are not evaluations of statements alone. In the case Garfinkel et al. analyze, the IGP is not an account of a discovery, it stands as the discovery, and no amount of consideration of the form of the discovery announcement would yield its astrophysical accountability. To see what the discovery announcement says requires some work with a telescope and observatory equipment. So rather than argue for a source of social determination outside the observatory, an appropriate policy would be to describe how the question, "Is this a discovery?" is a constituent feature of scientists' practices, whether inside the laboratory or in the discipline beyond the laboratory. In either case, the question is chained to the local historicity of the object and is not a question to be settled by the literary skills of professional social historians.[39]

The question, "Is this a discovery?" is perspicuous in the tape, as well as in GLL's analysis. (This does not mean that it ceases to be perspicuous after the tape ends.) After Disney proclaims, "We've got a bleeding *pulse here*" (Observation 18; see GLL,149), he and Cocke continue to pursue what that pulse might turn out to be. From the beginning of the tape "until the tape ends an hour later in the midst of their 23rd Run there is hardly a remark that is not either animated by or animating of the possibility of their discovery and achievement" (GLL,140). The tape records a set of actions cast into the future perfect tense. The participants clearly orient to the possibility that a discovery will have been made, and this is evident in the dialogue, where Cocke (as he said later in an interview) tended to "play the skeptic," in response to Disney's announcements. We could think of the night's work as a matter of setting up felicity conditions

---

39. Brannigan (1981) describes a number of cases where members of the relevant scientific discipline acted as practical social historians, retrospectively crediting or discrediting the "discoveries" of their predecessors. Brannigan does not delve into the practical historiographic methods, but his account suggests an interesting displacement of subject matter for history of science. If social historians were willing to own up to the consequences of such a displacement (which they seem little inclined to do), it would require that they put aside any pretentions to explain discoveries by consulting the archives. Also see Abir-Am's (forthcoming) ethnographic-historiographic study.

for the announcement of a discovery. When should they announce it? What should they include in the announcement? Who would believe it? How many more runs should they make before it will be reasonable to make an announcement? Who should they announce it to first? Clearly Cocke and Disney do not simply send out a telegram and wait for the community response, any more than saying the words "I now pronounce you man and wife" causes a marriage to happen in isolation from the appropriate arrangements (Austin 1976).

From Observation 18
Disney: This is a historic moment.
Cocke: I hope this is a historic moment. We'll know when we take another reading. That spike is right in the middle [of the screen] and that scares me.

From Observation 19
Disney: By God! We got it!
Cocke: Naow, naow.

From Observation 19
Disney: Should we go and ring Don [Taylor] up?
Cocke: Uh, let's move off that position and do somewhere else and see if we get the same thing. Arright? I hope to God this isn't some sort of artifact of the (uh) instrumentation. Maybe tonight a m-mouse got (in chewed out some of the wires). (Garfinkel et al. 1981,153)

The astronomers do not simply speculate about counterfactual possibilities. They address the possibility that "it" may turn out to be an artifact in their subsequent runs. Cocke points beyond the episode to a contingent future when he mentions the mouse in the machinery. He does not, of course, start looking for the mouse. Instead he and his colleagues monitor the instrument readings as they continue the series of runs: repeating the procedure, varying telescopic position, varying frequency settings on the electronic equipment, changing the light filters, and decreasing the aperture with a homemade diaphragm they make out of tinfoil. By the end of the sequence of runs Cocke accedes to Disney's exclamation "That's a bloody pulsar!" and he agrees that they should phone their colleague Taylor to announce their good fortune. This was far from the end of the story, and Collins is correct in his insistence that the discovery cannot be framed as a moment captured on less than an hour of tape. It would also be misleading to say that Cocke and Disney were "forced" by the data and by their methodic checks on the instrumentation to reach the only reasonable conclusion possible.

Rather the discovery was an object chained prospectively and retrospectively to the local historicity of the night's work. The work of getting it again and specifying relevant conditions for getting it supply defeasible felicity conditions for the affirmative statements Cocke and Disney make about their object. Presumably this temporal structure persisted through Cocke and Disney's subsequent discussions with Taylor, his initial skepticism about their claims and his further testing of the equipment, their announcement to other observatories, the subsequent reports of replicated sightings, and so forth. At any point the discovery could have turned out to be an artifact, and it may yet turn out to be an artifact, but such possibilities do not discount the grammatical role of the object in the local historicity of the work.

Much of the difference between Collins and Garfinkel et al. comes down to a question of whether an interjection of skeptical doubts should be a necessary part of a sociological analysis of scientific experimentation and observation. To answer yes to this is to agree to place sociology on very intimate terms with astronomy.[40] As GLL treat it, the discovery is a cultural object, not an account, and certainly not a statement separate from a course in inquiry. But

40. A parallel situation arises when philosophers treat scientists' practices as a basis for solving epistemological problems. Shapere (1982,519–20) makes much the same argument about the problems of generalized skepticism that I have made in this section. But he goes on to treat the technical practices physicists use in solar neutrino experiments as answers to general philosophical questions: "We have come to see that, and how, science builds on what it has learned, and that that process of construction consists not only in adding to our substantive knowledge, but also in increasing our ability to learn about nature, by extending our ability to observe in new ways. These conclusions constitute an important step toward seeing how it is, after all, that our knowledge rests on observation" (Shapere 1982,522). Shapere uses the pronouns "we" and "our" to affiliate what physicists do or know to his own general philosophical inquiries. His approach creates an immense burden on the philosopher, since he rests his philosophical argument on a set of technical practices in an entirely different discipline. It then becomes possible to dispute Shapere's philosophical claims by questioning his technical understanding of physics. For a relativist rebuttal to Shapere's conclusions about solar neutrino experiments, see Pinch 1986. For another case, see Galison's (1987,257–60) and Franklin's (1990,164ff.) criticisms of Pickering's (1984a, 1984b) counterfactual arguments about particle physicists' experiments on weak neutral currents. Galison is more careful than either Shapere or Franklin about treating physicists' experimental techniques as a generic ground for realist claims, but in the heat of his debate with Pickering's constructivist sociology he sometimes suggests that experimenters' judgments are "forced" by data. Pickering (1984b,97) argues in part that data exerted no "compulsive force" on particle physicists' experimental judgments, and that experimental practices and natural phenomena "stood and fell together." In this he is consistent with Wittgenstein (1969, §139–40).

how do they know it is really a discovery, and not an artifact or a replication? To treat this question seriously is to participate in the very sort of inquiry Cocke and Disney undertook. Only in GLL's case, the inquiry would have to be a vicarious one, without the benefit of an observatory. GLL make no claims about getting the discovery out of a tape recording.[41] But to say this does not imply that the discovery is explained by events outside the astronomers' practices. "Inquiries *and* objects are intertwined creatures. They are *not* philosophers' playthings" (Garfinkel et al. 1981,142). Nor are they the playthings of sociologists.

An Empirical Extension of Wittgenstein

When Wittgenstein recommended a descriptive rather than an explanatory approach to language, I take it that he advocated neither an empirical sociology of language nor an introspective form of reflection. With regard to the latter, he saw no need to develop a second-order philosophy to reflexively comprehend its unreflexive counterpart. "One might think: if philosophy speaks of the use of the word 'philosophy' there must be a second-order philosophy. But it is not so: it is, rather, like the case of orthography, which deals with the word 'orthography' among others without then being second-order" (Wittgenstein *PI*,§121).

How then are we to "look" into the workings of our language? Wittgenstein (*PI*,§122) remarks that "we do not *command a clear view* of the use of our words.—Our grammar is lacking in this sort of perspicuity." In the reflective attitude of traditional philosophy, we are easily led to ascribe essential or core meanings to such resonant terms as "know," "represent," "reason," and "true," and to develop hypostatized concepts of "knowledge," "representation," "reason," and "truth." By citing intuitive examples from ordinary usage and constructing imaginary "tribes" and language games systematically different from our customary usage, Wittgenstein is able to problematize epistemology by showing the variations, systematic ambiguities, and yet clear sensibilities in everyday usage.

As Bloor (1983) points out, Wittgenstein develops an "imaginary ethnography" and not an empirical ethnography of language. This is

41. The tape recorded electronic data from the observations as well as the voices, so it would be possible, with the right equipment, to review that data recorded that evening. Aside from the fact that a review of these data twenty years later would not count as a discovery (unless it was discovered that Cocke and Disney misread their data), the point is that such a project would be the very sort of thing Cocke and Disney were up to in the first place: getting the phenomenon out of the data.

not necessarily a failing, since Wittgenstein (*PI*,§122) devises his cases as "perspicuous representations"—examples which are arranged systematically to show "connections" in our grammar. Extending Wittgenstein's project may create a role for empirical cases, though not, as Bloor suggests, to transform a speculative method into an explanatory one. Instead, as Garfinkel (1967,38) advises, empirical investigations can be devised primarily as "aids to a sluggish imagination."

Garfinkel's well-known troublemaking exercises can be viewed as methods of perspicuous representation—interventions that disrupt ordinary scenes in order to make their practical organization visible.[42] The idea of perspicuous representation also applies to early conversation-analytic investigations. Sacks initially took up the analysis of tape-recorded conversation to supply examples of commonplace language use that tend to elude the reflective and ideal-typical modes of inquiry in ordinary language philosophy and speech-act theory.[43] In more recent work Garfinkel has suggested a set of exercises for turning the central terms in epistemology (rationality, rules, agency, etc.) into "perspicuous phenomena."[44]

The extension of Wittgenstein's later philosophy produced in ESW is therefore not a move into empirical sociology so much as an attempt to rediscover the sense of epistemology's central concepts

42. For readers unfamiliar with these interventions, they consisted in exercises where, e.g. students living at home conversed with their families while projecting the demeanor appropriate to a stranger; or where married students insistently asked their spouses to explain or give complete accounts of every utterance made in a casual conversation. Not only was ordinary interaction often found to be impossible under such circumstances, it turned out to be highly volatile and likely to erupt into accusations of betrayal, suspiciousness, and general disagreeableness.

43. Many of Sacks's early lectures were discourses touched off by one excerpt or another from his collection of transcribed conversations. In the course of one such discussion, Sacks (1967b) remarks that "what I'm trying to do here is make my transcript noticeable to me." Although Sacks also expressed scientific ambitions in his early lectures, his treatment of transcripts contrasted to his and his colleagues' later development of a rule-governed model for turn taking. In the earlier lectures, such as those reproduced in a collection of lectures from 1964–65 (Jefferson 1989), issues in logic and philosophy of language are never far from the surface. Sacks uses particular fragments of conversation to critique logical-grammatical investigations based on intuitive examples.

44. An example of this is Friedrich Schrecker's study of experimental practice (Schrecker 1980; Lynch et al. 1983), in which Schrecker (a graduate student in Garfinkel's seminars) assisted a disabled chemistry student in his laboratory work. Schrecker acted, in effect, as the student's "body" at the bench during lab exercises. The interaction between the two was videotaped. The verbal instructions from the chemistry student to Schrecker made a perspicuous issue of the work of moving and arranging equipment into a "sensible" display of the present state of the experiment.

and themes. The world "rediscover" is used here with a particular sense. Although as speakers of a natural language we already know what rules are and what it means to explain, agree, give reasons, or follow instructions, this does not mean that our understanding can be expressed in definitions, logical formulae, or even ideal-typical examples. Ethnomethodology's descriptions of the mundane and situated activities of observing, explaining, or proving enable a kind of rediscovery and respecification of how these central terms become relevant within particular context of activity. Descriptions of the situated production of observations, explanations, proofs, and so forth provide a more differentiated and subtle picture of epistemic activities than can be given by the generic definitions and familiar debates in epistemology.

The upshot is not likely to be a unitary set of rules or themes affiliated with each epistemic topic. For instance, consider the primitive epistemic operation of "counting." Treated as an ethno-methodological phenomenon, counting is by no means limited to an operation on a number series. Counting becomes perspicuous in entirely different ways depending upon the empirical setting investigated. It is an explicit procedure used by maximum security prison staff, census workers, lab technicians of all kinds, and for example Panamanian election officials.[45] In each of these settings the language games differ remarkably, though participants in each of them use the series of natural numbers in contingent ways. The work of counting in each case is socially organized, so that what is meant by "skill," "proper procedure," "error," "missing cases," "correction," and "adequate results" is not readily subsumed under what usually comes to mind when we think of arithmetic. The procedures and precautions employed by, for example, the warden's assistant to assure a correct count of prisoners several times a day is an irreducibly organizational practice. While counting prisoners incorporates mathematical relations and practices, there is little the warden's assistant can do mathematically to remedy problems having to do with missing cases, false positives, and the like.

45. Suggestions for treating counting in this way are presented in unpublished notes by Garfinkel, on "Thoughts on How Members Count Members," Department of Sociology, UCLA, 1962. The example of counting prisoners is based on informal discussions with staff at Washington State Penitentiary, Walla Walla, during meetings and on-site visits by the Whitman College Prison Research Group. Other examples of everyday arithmetic used by supermarket shoppers, dieters, and Liberian tailors are presented in Lave 1988. Lave's anthropological research draws no explicit connection to ethnomethodology or Wittgenstein but is an outstanding source of insights and examples on situated modes of measurement and calculation.

Doing counting in a practical setting like a maximum security prison may exhibit a mastery of a very concrete sort; a mastery that takes account of contingent possibilities for failure, remedy, and precaution. Such a mastery may be very different from anything Wittgenstein said or even imagined in his discussions of counting. Consequently an ethnomethodological study of such a phenomenon would extend Wittgenstein's body of work not only to cover new cases but to adapt it to the description of singular orders of embodied actions in organizational situations. Such an extension of Wittgenstein is less a substitution of a real ethnography for imaginary investigations of language use than it is a movement from an investigation of key concepts to an analysis of the integration of such concepts in mundane practical activities. Ethnomethodology is far from a complete or entirely coherent program, but it suggests how epistemology's terms can be elucidated in a distinctively empirical form of investigation.

REFERENCES

Abir-Am, Pnina. Forthcoming. Toward an Historical Ethnography of Scientific Ritual: The Fiftieth Anniversary of the First Protein X-ray Photo and the Origins of Molecular Biology. *Social Epistemology.*

Amann, Klaus, and Karin Knorr Cetina. 1988. The Fixation of (Visual) Evidence. In M. Lynch and S. Woolgar, eds., *Representation in Scientific Practice.* A special issue of *Human Studies* 11(2/3): 133–69.

Anderson, R. J., J. A. Hughes, and W. W. Sharrock. 1988. Some Initial Difficulties with the Sociology of Knowledge: A Preliminary Examination of "the Strong Programme." Departments of Sociology, Manchester Polytechnic University, Lancaster University, and University of Manchester.

Ashmore, Malcolm, Michael Mulkay, and Trevor Pinch. 1989. *Health and Efficiency: A Sociology of Health Economics.* Milton Keynes: Open University Press.

Austin, J. L. 1976. *How to Do Things with Words.* London: Oxford University Press.

Bachelard, Gaston. 1984. *The New Scientific Spirit.* Trans. Arthur Goldhammer. Boston: Beacon Press.

Baker, G. P., and P. M. S. Hacker. 1984. *Scepticism, Rules, and Language.* Oxford: Basil Blackwell.

———. 1985. *Wittgenstein, Rules, Grammar, and Necessity.* Vol. 2 of *Analytical Commentary on the Philosophical Investigations.* Oxford: Basil Blackwell.

Barnes, S. B. 1974. *Scientific Knowledge and Sociological Theory.* London: Routledge and Kegan Paul.

———. 1977. *Interests and the Growth of Knowledge.* London: Routledge and Kegan Paul.

――――. 1982. *Thomas Kuhn and Social Science.* London: Macmillan.

Bijker, Wiebe E., Thomas P. Hughes, and Trevor J. Pinch, eds. 1987. *The Social Construction of Technological Systems: New Directions in the Sociology and History of Technology.* Cambridge: MIT Press.

Bloor, David. 1973. Wittgenstein and Mannheim on the Sociology of Mathematics. *Studies in the History and Philosophy of Science* 4:173–91.

――――. 1976. *Knowledge and Social Imagery.* London: Routledge and Kegan Paul.

――――. 1983. *Wittgenstein: A Social Theory of Knowledge.* New York: Columbia University Press.

――――. 1987. The Living Foundations of Mathematics. *Social Studies of Science* 17:337–58.

Bogen, David, and Michael Lynch. 1989. Taking Account of the Hostile Native: Plausible Deniability and the Production of Conventional History in the Iran-Contra Hearings. *Social Problems* 36(3):197–224.

――――. 1990. Social Critique and the Logic of Description: A Response to McHoul. *Journal of Pragmatics* 14:131–47.

Brannigan, Augustine. 1981. *The Social Basis of Scientific Discoveries.* Cambridge: Cambridge University Press.

Callon, Michel. 1986. Some Elements of a Sociology of Translation: Domestication of the Scallops and the Fishermen of St. Brieuc Bay. Pp. 196–223 in Law 1986.

Cambrosio, Alberto, and Peter Keating. 1988. "Going Monoclonal." Art, Science, and Magic in the Day-to-Day Use of Hybridoma Technology. *Social Problems* 35:244–60.

Campbell, Donald T. 1979. A Tribal Model of the Social System Vehicle Carrying Scientific Knowledge. *Knowledge* 2:181–201.

Cavell, Stanley. 1979. *The Claim of Reason: Wittgenstein, Skepticism, Morality, and Tragedy.* Oxford: Oxford University Press.

Collins, H. M. 1974. The TEA Set: Tacit Knowledge and Scientific Networks. *Science Studies* 4:165–86.

――――. 1975. The Seven Sexes: A Study in the Sociology of a Phenomenon, or the Replication of Experiments in Physics." *Sociology* 9:205–24.

――――. 1983. An Empirical Relativist Programme in the Sociology of Scientific Knowledge. Pp. 83–113 in Knorr Cetina and Mulkay.

――――. 1985. *Changing Order; Replication and Induction in Scientific Practice.* London: Sage.

――――. 1989. The Location of Knowledge. Paper prepared for conference on The Place of Experiment, Van Leer Jerusalem Institute and Tel Aviv University, Israel.

Coulter, Jeff. 1989. *Mind in Action.* Oxford: Polity Press.

Diamond, Cora, ed. 1976. *Wittgenstein's Lectures on the Foundations of Mathematics.* Lectures notes taken by four people. Ithaca: Cornell University Press.

Dummett, Michael. 1968. Wittgenstein's Philosophy of Mathematics.

Pp. 420–47 in G. Pitcher, ed., *Wittgenstein: The Philosophical Investigations*. Notre Dame, Ind.: University of Notre Dame Press.

Edge, David, and Michael Mulkay. 1976. *Astronomy Transformed: The Emergence of Radio Astronomy in Britain*. New York: Wiley.

Filmer, Paul. 1976. Garfinkel's Gloss: A Diachronically Dialectical, Essential Reflexivity of Accounts. *Writing Sociology* 1:69–84.

Fish, Stanley. 1989. *Doing What Comes Naturally: Change, Rhetoric, and the Practice of Theory in Literary and Legal Studies*. Durham: Duke University Press.

Foucault, Michel. 1975. *The Order of Things*. New York: Vintage Books.

Franklin, Allan. 1990. *Experiment Right or Wrong*. Cambridge: Cambridge University Press.

Fujimura, Joan. 1987. Constructing "Do-able" Problems in Cancer Research: Articulating Alignment. *Social Studies of Science* 17:257–93.

Galison, Peter. 1987. *How Experiments End*. Chicago: University of Chicago Press.

Garfinkel, Harold. 1967. *Studies in Ethnomethodology*. Englewood Cliffs, N.J.: Prentice Hall.

———. 1988. Evidence for Locally Produced, Naturally Accountable Phenomena of Order, Logic, Reason, Meaning, Method, etc., in and as of the Essential Quiddity of Immortal Ordinary Society (1 of 4): An Announcement of Studies. *Sociological Theory* 6:103–6.

Garfinkel, Harold, ed. 1986. *Ethnomethodological Studies of Work*. London: Routledge and Kegan Paul.

Garfinkel, Harold, and Harvey Sacks. 1970. On Formal Structures of Practical Actions. Pp. 337–66 in J. C. McKinney and E. A. Tiryakian, eds., *Theoretical Sociology: Perspectives and Development*. New York: Appleton-Century-Crofts.

Garfinkel, Harold, Michael Lynch, and Eric Livingston. 1981. The Work of a Discovering Science Construed with Materials from the Optically Discovered Pulsar. *Philosophy of the Social Sciences* 11:131–58.

Garfinkel, Harold, Eric Livingston, Michael Lynch, Douglas MacBeth, and Albert B. Robillard. 1989. Respecifying the Natural Sciences as Discovering Sciences of Practical Action, 1 and 2; Doing So Ethnographically by Administering a Schedule of Contingencies in Discussions with Laboratory Scientists and by Hanging Around Their Laboratories. Department of Sociology, University of California, Los Angeles.

Genette, Gerard. 1989. *Narrative Discourse: An Essay in Method*. Ithaca: Cornell University Press.

Gerson, Elihu M., and Susan Leigh Star. 1987. Representation and Re-representation in Scientific Work. Tremont Research Institute, San Francisco.

Gieryn, Thomas F. 1983. Boundary-Work and the Demarcation of Science from Non-science. *American Sociological Review* 48:781–95.

Gieryn, Thomas F., and Anne E. Figert. 1990. Ingredients for a Theory of Science in Society: O-rings, Ice Water, C-clamp, Richard Feynman, and the Press. In Susan Cozzens and Thomas Gieryn, eds., *Theories of Science in Society*. Bloomington: Indiana University Press.

Gilbert, G. Nigel, and Michael Mulkay. 1984. *Opening Pandora's Box: An Analysis of Scientists' Discourse*. Cambridge: Cambridge University Press.

Hacking, Ian. 1983. *Representing and Intervening: Introductory Topics in the Philosophy of Natural Science*. Cambridge: Cambridge University Press.

————. 1984. Wittgenstein Rules. *Social Studies of Science* 14:469–76.

Hanfling, Oswald. 1985. Was Wittgenstein a Sceptic? *Philosophical Investigations* 8:1–16.

Hanson, N. R. 1967. An Anatomy of Discovery. *The Journal of Philosophy* 64(11): 321–52.

Heritage, John. 1984. *Garfinkel and Ethnomethodology*. Oxford: Polity Press.

Heritage, John C., and D. R. Watson. 1980. Aspects of the Properties of Formulations in Natural Conversations: Some Instances Analyzed. *Semiotica* 30:245–62.

Hesse, Mary. 1974. *The Structure of Scientific Inference*. London: Macmillan.

Hollis, M., and S. Lukes, eds. 1982. *Rationality and Relativism*. London: Routledge and Kegan Paul.

Hunter, J. F. M. [1968] 1971. "Forms of Life" in Wittgenstein's Philosophical Investigations. In E. D. Klemke, ed., *Essays on Wittgenstein*. Urbana: University of Illinois Press. Reprinted (with minor corrections) from *American Philosophical Quarterly* 5:233–43.

————. 1973. Logical Compulsion. Pp. 171–202 in *Essays After Wittgenstein*. Toronto: University of Toronto Press.

————. 1985. *Understanding Wittgenstein: Studies of Philosophical Investigations*. Edinburgh: Edinburgh University Press.

Jefferson, Gail, ed. 1989. *Harvey Sacks: Lectures 1964–65*. With an introduction/memoir by Emanuel A. Schegloff. A special issue of *Human Studies* 12(3/4).

Jordan, Brigitte, and Nancy Fuller. 1974. On the Non-fatal nature of Trouble: Sense-making and Trouble-managing in Lingua Franca Talk. *Semiotica* 13:1–31.

Jordan, Kathleen, and Michael Lynch. 1992. The Sociology of a Genetic Engineering Technique: Ritual and Rationality in the Performance of the Plasmid Prep. In A. Clarke and J. Fujimura, eds., *The Right Tools for the Job At Work in Twentieth Century Life Sciences*. Princeton: Princeton University Press.

Knorr Cetina, Karin, and Michael Mulkay, eds. 1983. *Science Observed: Perspectives on the Social Study of Science*. London and Beverly Hills: Sage.

Kripke, Saul. 1982. Wittgenstein on Rules and Private Language. In I. Block, ed., *Perspectives on the Philosophy of Wittgenstein.* Oxford: Basil Blackwell.

Kuhn, Thomas S. 1962. *The Structure of Scientific Revolutions.* Chicago: University of Chicago Press.

Latour, Bruno. 1986. Will the Last Person to Leave the Social Studies of Science Please Turn On the Tape Recorder? *Social Studies of Science* 16:541–48.

———. 1987. *Science in Action.* Cambridge: Harvard University Press.

———. 1988. *The Pasteurization of France.* Trans. A. Sheridan and J. Law. Cambridge: Harvard University Press.

Laudan, Larry. 1981. The Pseudo-science of Science? *Philosophy of the Social Sciences* 11:173–98.

Lave, Jean. 1988. *Cognition in Practice.* Cambridge: Cambridge University Press.

Law, John. 1986. On the Methods of Long-Distance Control: Vessels, Navigation, and the Portuguese Route to India. Pp. 231–60 in John Law, ed., *Power, Action, and Belief.* London: Routledge and Kegan Paul.

Law, John, and Michel Callon. 1988. Engineering and Sociology in a Military Aircraft Project: A Network Analysis of Technological Change. *Social Problems* 35:284–97.

Livingston, Eric. 1979. Answers to Field Examination Questions in the Field of Sociology, Philosophy, and History of Science. Department of Sociology, University of California, Los Angeles.

———. 1986. *The Ethnomethodological Foundations of Mathematics.* London: Routledge and Kegan Paul.

———. 1987. *Making Sense of Ethnomethodology.* London: Routledge and Kegan Paul.

Luckhardt, C. G. 1983. Wittgenstein and Behaviorism. *Synthese* 56:319–38.

Lynch, Michael. 1982. Technical Work and Critical Inquiry: Investigations in a Scientific Laboratory. *Social Studies of Science* 12:499–534.

———. 1985a. *Art and Artifact in Laboratory Science: A Study of Shop Work and Shop Talk in a Research Laboratory.* London: Routledge and Kegan Paul.

———. 1985b. Discipline and the Material Form of Images: An Analysis of Scientific Visibility. *Social Studies of Science* 15:37–66.

———. 1988a. The Externalized Retina: Selection and Mathematization in the Visual Documentation of Objects in the Life Sciences. *Human Studies* 11:201–34.

———. 1988b. Alfred Schutz and the Sociology of Science. Pp. 71–100 in L. Embree, ed., *Worldly Phenomenology: The Influence of Alfred Schutz on Human Science.* Washington D.C.: Center for Advanced Research in Phenomenology and University Press of America.

Lynch, Michael, Eric Livingston, and Harold Garfinkel. 1983. Temporal Order in Laboratory Work. Pp. 205–38 in Knorr Cetina and Mulkay.

Lynch, Michael, and Steve Woolgar, eds. 1988. *Representation in Scientific*

Practice. A special issue of Human Studies 11(2/3). Republished under the same title by MIT Press, 1990.

MacKenzie, Donald. 1978. Statistical Theory and Social Interests. *Social Studies of Science* 11:35–83.

MacKenzie, Donald, and Judy Wajcman, eds. 1985. *The Social Shaping of Technology.* Milton Keynes: Open University Press.

Malcolm, Norman. 1989. Wittgenstein on Language and Rules. *Philosophy* 64:5–28.

Morrison, Kenneth L. 1981. Some Properties of "Telling-Order Designs" in Didactic Inquiry. *Philosophy of the Social Sciences* 11:245–62.

Mulkay, Michael. 1979. *Science and the Sociology of Knowledge.* London: George Allen and Unwin.

Phillips, Derek L. 1977. *Wittgenstein and Scientific Knowledge: A Sociological Perspective.* London: Macmillan.

Pickering, Andrew. 1984a. *Constructing Quarks: A Sociological History of Particle Physics.* Chicago: University of Chicago Press.

———. 1984b. Against Putting the Phenomena First: The Discovery of the Weak Neutral Current. *Studies in the History and Philosophy of Science* 15:85–117.

———. 1988. Big Science as a Form of Life. In M. De Maria and M. Grilli, eds., *The Restructuring of the Physical Sciences in Europe and the United States, 1945–1960.* Singapore: World Scientific Publishing.

Pinch, Trevor J. 1986. *Confronting Nature: The Sociology of Solar Neutrino Detection.* Dordrecht: D. Reidel.

Pinch, Trevor J., and Wiebe Bijker 1984. The Social Construction of Facts and Artifacts: Or How the Sociology of Science and the Sociology of Technology Might Benefit Each Other. *Social Studies of Science* 14:399–441.

Rorty, Richard. 1979. *Philosophy and the Mirror of Nature.* Princeton: Princeton University Press.

Sacks, Harvey. 1967a. Lecture, Department of Sociology, UCLA, 16 February 1967.

———. 1967b. Lecture, Department of Sociology, UCLA, 9 March 1967.

Sacks, Harvey, Emanuel A. Schegloff, and Gail Jefferson. 1974. A Simplest Systematics for the Organization of Turn-Taking in Conversation. *Language* 50:697–735.

Schrecker, Friedrich. 1980. Doing a Chemical Experiment: The Practices of Chemistry Students in a Student Laboratory in Quantitative Analysis. Department of Sociology, University of California, Los Angeles.

Shanker, S. G. 1987. *Wittgenstein and the Turning-Point in the Philosophy of Mathematics.* Albany, N.Y.: SUNY Press.

Shapere, Dudley. 1982. The Concept of Observation in Science and Philosophy. *Philosophy of Science* 49:485–525.

Shapin, Steven. 1979. The Politics of Observation: Cerebral Anatomy and Social Interests in the Edinburgh Phrenology Disputes. Pp. 139–78 in Roy Wallis, ed., *On the Margins of Science: The Social Construction of*

Rejected Knowledge. Sociological Review Monograph no. 27. Keele University.

————. 1982. History of Science and Its Sociological Reconstructions. *History of Science* 20:157–211.

————. 1984. Pump and Circumstance: Robert Boyle's Literary Technology. *Social Studies of Science* 14:481–520.

Sharrock, W. W., and R. J. Anderson. 1984. The Wittgenstein Connection. *Human Studies* 7:375–86.

————. 1985. Magic, Witchcraft, and the Materialist Mentality. *Human Studies* 8:357–75.

Slezak, Peter. 1989. Scientific Discovery by Computer as Empirical Refutation of the Strong Programme. *Social Studies of Science* 19:563–600.

Star, Susan Leigh. 1983. Simplification in Scientific Work. *Social Studies of Science* 13:205–228.

Suchman, Lucy. 1987. *Plans and Situated Actions: The Problem of Human-Machine Communication.* Cambridge: Cambridge University Press.

Turner, Stephen P. 1981. Interpretive Charity, Durkheim, and the "Strong Programme" in the Sociology of Knowledge. *Philosophy of the Social Sciences* 11:231–44.

Winch, Peter. 1958. *The Idea of a Social Science.* London: Routledge and Kegan-Paul.

Wittgenstein, Ludwig. 1956. *Remarks on the Foundations of Mathematics.* Trans. G. E. M. Anscombe. Oxford: Basil Blackwell.

————. 1958. *Philosophical Investigations.* Trans. G. E. M. Anscombe. Oxford: Basil Blackwell.

————. 1967. *Zettel.* Ed. G. E. M. Anscombe and G. H. von Wright. Oxford: Basil Blackwell.

————. 1969. *On Certainty.* Ed. G. E. M. Anscombe and G. H. von Wright. Oxford: Basil Blackwell.

Woolgar, S. W. 1976. Writing an Intellectual History of Scientific Development: The Use of Discovery Accounts. *Social Studies of Science* 6:395–422.

Woolgar, Steve. 1981. Interests and Explanations in the Social Study of Science. *Social Studies of Science* 11:365–94.

————. 1988a. *Science: The Very Idea.* London: Tavistock.

————. 1988b. Time and Documents in Researcher Interaction: Some Ways of Making Out What Is Happening in Experimental Science. *Human Studies* 11:171–200.

Woolgar, Steve, ed. 1988c., *Knowledge and Reflexivity: New Frontiers in the Sociology of Knowledge.* London: Sage.

8

Left and Right Wittgensteinians

David Bloor

In his paper "Extending Wittgenstein" (chap. 7), Michael Lynch puts forward two main claims. The first, positive, claim is that ethnomethodology represents a fruitful extension of Wittgenstein's insights, particularly those concerning rule following. The second, a negative claim, is that by contrast, the sociology of knowledge (in some of its current formulations) is based on a misunderstanding of Wittgenstein's account of rule following.[1] Lynch's intention is not to argue about who are the true followers of Wittgenstein but to decide on the best approach to important problems about everyday, scientific, and mathematical knowledge. A correct analysis of these problems needs a correct analysis of rule following. The spirit of his remarks is to acknowledge that both ethnomethodologists and sociologists of knowledge are aware of their shared debt to Wittgenstein, and that everyone realizes that some degree of selectivity and interpretation of Wittgenstein's writing is permissible. Nevertheless there is a marked divergence of opinion over what is to be learned from Wittgenstein, and that is the point at issue.

While I agree with Lynch that (some) work in ethnomethodology and (some) work in the sociology of knowledge share common Wittgensteinian roots, I disagree with much of his account of why and where the two approaches diverge. I think he does not always correctly locate its cause, with the result that he draws a number of false contrasts. I also suspect that he engages in some special pleading on behalf of ethnomethodology, unfairly allowing its practitioners a leeway that is denied to the sociologist. It would be a pity if the two empirically oriented "heirs to the subject that used to be called 'philosophy' "[2] fell out over imaginary differences when there are real ones to discuss. I shall therefore try to highlight the points where I believe Lynch does touch upon the real differences between

1. In what follows I will leave out the qualification "in some of its current formulations." When I speak of "the sociology of knowledge" I mean the sociology of knowledge in the form that I would want to defend it.

2. Wittgenstein 1969, 28.

266

ethnomethodology and the sociology of knowledge. When these points are made explicit and their implications are drawn out, I hope it will become clear why I prefer the sociological rather than the ethnomethodological reading of Wittgenstein. Before coming to these issues, all of which deal with Lynch's second, negative claim, I will make a few remarks on his first, positive claim.

Lynch is surely right to say that ethnomethodologists have shown us one way of turning Wittgenstein's philosophy into an empirical study of language and cognition. They study examples of linguistic behavior drawn from real life, and even create experimental confrontations designed to elicit revealing data for analysis. They have carried their investigations beyond the language games of everyday life into studies of scientific discourse. Lynch is also right to surround his claim with careful qualifications. He is cautious about using the word "empirical." The aspects of Wittgenstein's work that most appeal to ethnomethodologists are his determined contextualization of every feature of our speech and thought and his opposition to the construction of explanatory theories in philosophy. The concern with empirical data is to be understood in a way that satisfies both these requirements. The empirical investigations that are to extend Wittgenstein's work are to be nonexplanatory.

Lynch also notes that ethnomethodology is not a unified enterprise. The continuity with Wittgenstein is at its strongest in what he calls "ethnomethodological studies of the work of science and mathematics." But even here the point is simply that these studies can be seen as a "program for pursuing Wittgenstein's initiatives."[3] The connection is therefore framed, at least in the first instance, rather loosely. Despite this enough has been said to create an interesting difficulty for the alleged relationship, a difficulty that Lynch does not address. It derives from what might be called Wittgenstein's refutation of ethnomethodology. I refer here to the fact that there is a prima facie contradiction between ethnomethodology and one of Wittgenstein's most profound conclusions.

To see this contradiction let us suppose that on reading Garfinkel's powerful *Studies in Ethnomethodology*[4] we extracted from it the following two doctrines:

Doctrine 1. "Indexicality" is irreparable.

Doctrine 2. The human agent is not a cultural or judgmental "dope."

I am taking it that Garfinkel's book is a paradigm of ethnomethodol-

3. Chap. 7, 230.
4. Garfinkel 1967.

ogy and that the two doctrines effectively capture some of its most characteristic ideas. The first doctrine says that the meaning of utterances, thoughts, gestures, instructions, and rules can never be separated from the detailed circumstances of their use. They always depend on their context and its contingencies. We can never reach the ideal of pure objectivity in which meanings are made totally explicit and are formulated in a wholly context-free way.[5] The second doctrine says (roughly) that human agents are active rather than passive. It is they who construct meanings. They are not determined by their circumstances, where "circumstances" include, among other things, their definition of the situation, and the norms and values of their group.[6]

In his *Philosophical Investigations*,[7] Wittgenstein developed an argument about rule following which showed that doctrine 1 is inconsistent with doctrine 2. He therefore refuted ethnomethodology (on the above definition) before it was even born. I shall give a version of the argument in general terms and then show how it connects with ethnomethodology. The question is: how do we follow a rule? For example: someone gives us a rule and we are to act in accordance with it. By "gives us a rule" I mean that someone presents us with a sign, perhaps the spoken sentences of an instruction or a written formula in mathematics. It might seem that we could find out how we follow such a rule by reflecting on what happens when we *can't* follow it, and we ask for help. Perhaps when it is explained to us how we are to follow it we will discover what happens when we can and do follow it. But a request for help will in general only result in our being given further signs. We will be told how to interpret the first sign, where "interpret" means substituting one set of signs for another.[8] In other words, all that happens is that we will be given a rule for interpreting a rule. Although such responses can sometimes be of practical help, this cannot tell us anything fundamental about rule following. The investigatory strategy is wrong because it merely sets up an infinite regress. It only postpones the problem of how a rule is related to the actions that constitute rule following. Wittgenstein's conclusion—at once simple and profound—was that there must be a way of following a rule which is not an interpretation in the sense defined. What, then, is this way of grasping a rule which is not an interpretation? It is the way we have

5. Garfinkel 1967, 24–31.
6. Garfinkel 1967, 68.
7. Wittgenstein 1967a.
8. "We ought to restrict the term 'interpretation' to the substitution of one expression of the rule for another" (Wittgenstein 1967a, § 201)

been trained to respond: it is what we do when we then proceed "as a matter of course." In the last analysis, said Wittgenstein: "When I obey a rule I do not choose. I obey the rule blindly."[9] Only by acknowledging the importance of the blind (i.e. automatic and caused) response can we avoid the regress. This is how we get from rule to rule following.

The argument can now be connected to the two central doctrines of ethnomethodology as stated above. The endless possibility of interpretation to which Wittgenstein drew attention is the same as the irreparable indexicality of rules and instructions described by Garfinkel. So Wittgenstein was certainly committed to doctrine 1. The problem comes with doctrine 2. The necessity that in the last analysis a rule must be obeyed blindly means that contrary to doctrine 2, the actor must be some form of cultural or judgmental "dope." Wittgenstein's argument is that indexicality requires that we accept some form of the cultural dope model. Without this the phenomenon of rule following would not exist. Doctrine 1 therefore implies the falsity of doctrine 2. If ethnomethodology is taken to rest on the wholesale rejection of the cultural dope model, then its central doctrines are in contradiction.

Although it would be possible to fasten on material of this kind and argue that ethnomethodology is inconsistent, rather than consistent, with Wittgenstein's argument, I shall not do so. The root of the problem may have more to do with confusion than contradiction. Thus, while doctrines 1 and 2 represent a plausible summary of Garfinkel's book, it may be that it would be unjust to lay the contradiction at his door. The crucial issue seems not to have been addressed with sufficient clarity in his book to be certain either way.[10] In any case, such difficulties are in principle resolvable by

9. Wittgenstein 1967a, § 219.

10. It is arguable that the rejection of the cultural dope model has become even more pronounced in ethnomethodology since Garfinkel's book: cf. P. Attewell 1974, 179–210. In his impressive exposition of Garfinkel, John Heritage takes the view that Garfinkel's rejection of the cultural dope model is a qualified one; see J. Heritage 1984, 118: "It should be emphasized that although Garfinkel's critical discussions of treatments of the actor as a 'judgemental dope' may imply for some a view of the actor as an almost endlessly reflexive, self-conscious and calculative Machiavel, this is neither a necessary nor an intended interpretive consequence of his position. On the contrary, Garfinkel repeatedly stresses the *routine* nature of . . . action." Unfortunately this reading is obscured by later remarks. On page 120 there is a denial that for Garfinkel, this acceptance of routinization amounts to an acceptance of the "internalisation" of rules. Furthermore it is said that such internalization could not in any case "dictate the specifics of a course of action" (120). As Heritage emphasizes, rules are never in any sense looked upon as determinants of action. These qualifica-

decision, clarification, and adjustment, e.g., by holding fast onto Wittgenstein's blind rule following and appropriately moderating the aversion to human automatism and determinism. (Lynch, for his part, clearly *does* embrace Wittgenstein's conclusion about blind rule following. He is therefore committed to accepting that in some form, the human agent is a judgmental dope.) I assume, then, that this problem can be surmounted, so I accept the claim that some suitably clarified and qualified form of ethnomethodology could indeed be seen as a torchbearer of Wittgensteinian insights.

Now for Lynch's negative thesis, in which he claims that it is the sociological account of rule following that is defective and un-Wittgensteinian. Lynch correctly locates some of the elements out of which the sociological account is constructed, e.g., training, drill, socialization, disposition, habit, consensus, interest, and convention. Nevertheless it will be useful to prepare the ground for the ethnomethodological attack by quickly reminding ourselves how these elements are connected together.

The central idea is that the sociological importance of rules lies in their being shared practices sustained by interests, for example, by general interests that all group members have in coordinating their activities, and special interests such as become invested in prior classificatory achievements and bodies of established practices, or paradigms. New members are socialized (i.e., trained) in these practices and achieve full membership through acquiring the relevant competences. Ultimately such competences may become habitual; they turn into smoothly operating and easily available dispositions that each individual can call upon at will. Here we have the origin of our sense of the rule "guiding" the rule follower, of it going its own way as a matter of course. Nevertheless it is, ultimately, the fact that these dispositions lead to agreement in practice that gives the rule follower the sense of having followed the rule rightly or correctly. Consensus and convention thus come into the story to account for the characteristic "normativity" of rules. As Lynch correctly sees, the sociological analysis weaves together biological, psychological, and sociological strands of argument. There is one further aspect of the sociological account that Lynch does not mention, but that deserves notice. It derives from Wittgenstein's

---

tions make it difficult to be sure just how routines *are* supposed to prevent the actor from being seen as an "endlessly reflexive, self-conscious and calculative Machiavel" (i.e., as an endless interpreter in Wittgenstein's sense).

"finitism" and says that each application of a rule is in principle problematic. There is no such thing as an application of a rule being solely determined by the past applications or the meanings generated by these past applications. Meanings are constructed in a step-by-step fashion. They are effects, not causes, and do not possess intrinsic agency. In principle each application of a rule is negotiable, and the negotiation (or lack of it) is intelligible in terms of the dispositions and interests of the rule followers themselves: that is where agency truly resides.

What is meant to be wrong with this? The accusation is that this story fails to do justice to the single most important feature of rules, to what Lynch (following the philosophers) calls the "internal relationship" between a rule and its applications or instances. The underlying thought is that once we have appreciated the true nature of this "internal relationship," we will have sufficiently understood the rule and the character of rule following. We need nothing over and above, or "extrinsic" to, the internal relationship to furnish an adequate account. Sociologists of knowledge, so the argument goes, fail to appreciate this, and their introduction of consensus and other sociological ideas represents an appeal to just such extrinsic factors. Thus, to quote Baker and Hacker, whom Lynch follows in this regard: "there is no possibility of building consensus ... into the explanation of what 'correct' means except at the price of abandoning the insight that a rule is internally related to acts that accord with it."[11]

In order to assess this argument I need to explain these "internal relations" and then ask whether consensus and the other social processes mentioned really do lie outside them. To say that A and B are internally related means that the definition of A involves mention of B, while the definition of B involves mention of A. In short, two things are internally related if they are interdefined and so described that you can't have one without the other. (Having a debt and having an obligation to repay it are two moral states that are internally related.) A simple mathematical example is provided by the formula for generating the sequence of odd numbers: 1, 3, 5, 7, 9, etc. This can be given by substituting $n = 0, 1, 2, 3, 4$, etc., into the formula $2n + 1$. The formula and the sequence are internally related because the sequence can be defined as the one generated by the correct use of the formula; and the meaning of the formula can be given in terms of its producing this sequence and no other. We recognize the

11. Baker and Hacker 1985, 172.

internality of the relation when we say that the formula *must* yield this sequence; so clearly internal relations are in some sense the focus of the "compulsion" of the rule.

In reply to the charge that notions of consensus, socialization, and the rest are "extrinsic" to these internal relations, I will offer two arguments. First I will show exactly how the social theory accounts for these relations, and second I will show that without such a theory the notion of the internal relation between a rule and its application is powerless to illuminate the relevant phenomena.

From the sociological standpoint socialization, consensus, and the like, far from being outside the internal relationship, are actually *constitutive of it*. To explain this I will use an example drawn from some papers by Elizabeth Anscombe.[12] Anscombe reminds us of how we come to attach meaning to the word "must" as it is used in connection with rule following. When children are taught a rule (e.g., a rule of a game, or a rule of counting), they are told that they must do such and such, and then, if necessary, they are *made* to do it. They are shown, encouraged, physically guided, and even physically forced. Then they learn to do what is demanded as a result of verbal instigation alone. This is how the various "forcing modals" (such as "must," "have to," "necessary," etc.) get their meaning. Anscombe points out that it is impossible to produce independent reasons to back up forcing modals. If we try, we find ourselves going round in circles. An example might go like this: "You *must* move this piece like this." "Why?" "Because that's how the game is played." "What's wrong with moving it like *that*?" "It's not allowed." "But why?" "It would break the rules." "Why would it?" "Because the rules forbid it." "Why?" "That's not how the game is played." In short, there are no reasons for the rules outside the game. The game itself is cited as the reason for the rules, and yet the rules are constitutive of the game. This lack of independent reason isn't the result of the triviality of games. Rather Anscombe is showing us in quite general terms just how internal relations are constructed, and how they are grounded in social institutions, e.g., the institution of the game. What she has described in the discussion of forcing modals is clearly the process of socialization. Notice that contrary to what Lynch says, this explanation does not appeal to anything *extrinsic* to the rule-following practice; it describes something that is constitutive of that practice.

Anscombe's implicitly sociological explanation of the internal re-

12. See her "On Promising and Its Justice," and "Rules, Rights, and Promises," reprinted as chapters 2 and 10 of vol. 3 of Anscombe 1981.

lation between rules and their application is not designed to replace or displace our more ordinary talk of rules. It is the usual rule story identified in a new way. It is not as if one kind of thing is being postulated in place of another, as happens when, say, a moral or magical account of thunderstorms is replaced by a meteorological story. The situation is more like that in which talk of electrical discharge takes over from talk about flashes of lightning. Such a theory does not lead us to say that lightning doesn't exist (as we might say that the thunder god doesn't exist). The theory simply says that lightning is an electrical discharge. It is lightning better understood by being placed in a broader context and having new resources brought to bear upon it. Perhaps Lynch simply has the wrong model of explanation in mind when he criticizes the sociological approach for substituting something "extrinsic" in the place of an internal relationship. Whatever the reason, he has overlooked the important case where theories explain their subject matter by spelling out contingent identities. The internal relation between rule and application just is a social relationship. What is more, it is a relation that is clearly analyzable using precisely the conceptual apparatus that ethnomethodologists affect to dismiss.[13]

Now let us see what happens if we refuse to acknowledge this contingent identity and insist on seeing social processes as extrinsic to the link between a rule and its application, i.e., if we construe "internal relation" in a narrow, nonsociological way. The result is described in one of Wittgenstein's most celebrated examples, an example which can be read as a reductio ad absurdum of the position advocated by Lynch, Baker, Hacker, Shanker, and other antisociological commentators. In *Philosophical Investigations* §185, Wittgenstein imagined what would happen if a teacher seeking to convey a rule in arithmetic were to confront a pupil who systematically misunderstood the task. All attempts at correction fail because they too are systematically misunderstood. This is an example of the possibility of an endless regress of rules for following rules. It exhibits the limits of "interpretation" and the endlessness of the task of repairing indexicality. But another aspect of the example is what it says about internal relations. It shows that the deviant applications of a rule can themselves stand in a kind of internal relation to the

13. To say, contrary to the ethnomethodologists, that one accepts the traditional concepts and categories of a scientistic, explanatory sociology obviously does not mean that it is necessary to agree with standard theoretical accounts of these concepts. To take a well-known example, much British sociology of knowledge rejects the standard "Mertonian" account of the role of "norms" in explaining, say, scientific behavior.

rule as the deviant understands it. The teacher and the pupil here fail to make the usual kind of contact because the pupil constructs his own circle of definitions and his own set of internal relations between his signs and his practices. So the phenomenon of the internal relation between a rule and its application—if conceived narrowly—doesn't serve to define the real nature of rule following as we know it as a feature of a shared practice. At most it challenges us to define the difference between the actual rules of arithmetic and their idiosyncratic alternatives. It brings home, in the way that previous discussions of interpretation did, that something more and different is needed to define the accepted institution of arithmetic. Clearly what is required in the Wittgenstein example is something that breaks the deadlock between the competing internal relations. Such a factor would be consensus, the very thing rejected by Baker and Hacker. Ultimately it is collective support for one internal relation rather than another that makes the teacher's rule correct and the other deviant and incorrect. This is not to say that the consensus is "arbitrary," although in some cases it might be. In general a rule is a technique that must fit into our lives.[14] That again means addressing something Lynch dismisses, namely, the overall thematics of social structure.

Unless we ground rule following in the kind of sociological process that Lynch eschews, we will find that the rule by no means stands "as an adequate account" of rule-following behavior. If it is retorted that the rule itself must always be understood so as to include this consensual and conventional underpinning, then how have we escaped from the traditional, explanatory apparatus of sociology? We have merely acknowledged that these explanatory concepts do not, after all, refer to what is "external" to the rule.

I now come to my charge that Lynch is setting up false contrasts and engaging in special pleading. My evidence is that when Lynch's preferred ethnomethodological approach is closely compared with the sociological approach that he rejects, the alleged differences often evaporate. Two examples should suffice. (1) It is clear that despite his polemical opposition to such concepts as "consensus," Lynch makes use of very similar ideas. He doesn't use the term "consensus" but he makes approving references to the idea of rule following presupposing a background of "quite agreement."[15] This is just the traditional concept in thin terminological disguise. Those who use such an idea, even if only implicitly, should be prepared to

14. Cf. Wittgenstein 1967a, part 1, § 116; and on consensus, part 2, § 67.
15. Chap. 7, 226.

ask and answer some of the standard questions. How is this "quiet agreement" created and sustained? How is it transmitted? What factors might cause it to break down? Won't various "quiet interests" be at work amid this quiet agreement?

(2) Consider Lynch's charge that the sociological approach to rules depends on isolating the formulation of the rule from the practice of rule following.[16] Lynch is surely missing the point. The sociologist does *not* say that in actuality any mathematical formula exists in isolation from the practices associated with its use. Rather the claim is the reverse: the two depend on one another, as can be seen by the meaninglessness of any formulation *conceived as isolated*. The claim is exactly the same one that Lynch himself makes when he says "Formulations have no independent jurisdiction over the activities they formulate."[17] It is a denial of the agency of meaning. Suppose that on reading Lynch's sentence a sociologist were to attack him by saying: "but in order to make this very claim you must first *isolate* the 'formulation' and then argue that it renders the activity *indeterminate*." I think Lynch would (rightly) say that this was a hostile and pedantic reading that went against the whole spirit of the claim. I fear his comments about isolation and indeterminacy directed against the sociological approach have something of the same quality.

The worry about false contrasts is heightened when the ethnomethodologists' own program of research is described. For example, an ethnomethodological study of rules will treat every formulation of a rule as an indexical expression: that is, one whose meaning is anchored in its context. The use of such indexical formulations is to be seen as a kind of "work"; they are part of the way we "do" our activities. Lynch describes the corresponding program of empirical research as involving questions such as: "(1) How is it that *doing* activities exhibits regularity, order, standardization, and particular cohort independence (i.e. 'rationality') in advance of any formulation? (2) How, in any instance, do members use formulating as part of their activity?"[18] This line of enquiry is said to be in "stark contrast" to the sociology of knowledge.

For my part I must report an inability to see any contrast at all on the level of the principles just quoted. Instead I see a series of points on which practitioners of the two approaches would agree. Just like the ethnomethodologist, the sociologist of knowledge wants to

16. Chap. 7, 224.
17. Chap. 7, 234.
18. Chap. 7, 236.

"demonstrate contextures of activity" in which our understanding of words like "agree," "explain" and "rule" are embedded.[19] Is not the appeal to social interests to explain the negotiated character of the application of a rule an attempt to demonstrate a "contexture" for the activity? Just like the ethnomethodologist, the sociologist of knowledge sees the invoking of rules as "pragmatic moves in a temporal order of activities."[20] The ethnomethodologist feels free to "characterize the organized use of indexical expressions."[21] But how is the sociologist's aim other than this?

Could the difference lie in what is to count as "characterizing"? Is the sociologist perhaps looking for explanatory generalizations or laws or principles concerning these organized uses that the ethnomethodologist can prove to be unavailable? Might it be that formulating rules about the formulations of rules is impossible and incoherent? If this means trying to achieve ideally objective, nonindexical formulations (about the use of indexical formulations), then it is indeed impossible. But the sociologist of knowledge, no less that the ethnomethodologist, is aware of the fact that his own cognitive processes are as indexical and context-bound as those under study. We are doomed to speak indexically about indexicality, as about everything else.

But, conversely, we *can* speak indexically about indexicality, and Lynch is happy enough to grant that freedom to the ethnomethodologist. "Inevitably," he says, "ethnomethodologists engage in formulating, if only to formulate the work of 'doing' formulating."[22] And of course formulating (i.e., invoking some formula or rule) is an activity that can work effectively in both everyday and technical, scientific contexts. Ethnomethodologists locate such forms of cognitive work in the natural sciences and mathematics, where (it must be assumed) it contributes to the characteristic forms of generality that we associate with such knowledge. All the sociologist of knowledge asks is that he be permitted to proceed in the same way. Reading Lynch, I cannot avoid the impression that everybody is to be allowed to get on with their chosen way of making sense of the world *except* the poor sociologist.

If I am right, and Lynch's objections to the sociology of knowledge trade on false contrasts and perhaps a certain partiality, is there not, surely, still a real difference of approach? I think there is. It lies in

19. Chap. 7, 256.
20. Chap. 7, 236.
21. Chap. 7, 236.
22. Chap. 7, 236.

the points that Lynch makes about *representation*. To say that a symbol "represents" means that it operates as a surrogate for some external, independent reality. Representation implies a role for two things: (1) the symbol or representation, and (2) the reality that is symbolized or represented. Here we come to the heart of the matter. Lynch accuses the sociologist of knowledge of thinking in terms of representations in cases where the picture is inappropriate. Thus he says that the sociologist of knowledge "treats the rules as a *representation* of an activity which fails to account uniquely for the actions done in accord with it" (hence the appeal to social factors to close the gap of underdetermination). By contrast, the ethnomethodologist "treats the rule as an expression *in, of,* and *as* the orderly activity in which it occurs."[23]

What is the contrast that Lynch is making here? We seem to be invited to reject the idea of our words and symbols representing an independent reality. We must replace it by the idea of symbols referring only to other symbols. Our naive picture of our (often) talking about *things* gives way to that of our talking about *talk*. The object of our talk is always more talk. For example, notice the way that the discussion of Garfinkel and Sacks on "formulating" shifts from processes such as naming and identifying (where symbols presumably represent an external reality) and homes in on self-reflexive processes within a conversation (e.g., comments such as: "Was that a question?"). These are mentions *of* the conversation that are at the same time *in* the conversation. They are moments when the talk refers to itself; it is both subject and object. So when Lynch insists that for the ethnomethodologist the rule is an expression *in, of,* and *as* the activity in which it occurs, I take him to be trying to maximize the analogy with these self-reflexive aspects of self-referring talk about talk.

This interpretation of Lynch's meaning is strengthened by a number of other points that he makes. For example, he indicates his rejection of the "polarity" or "dualism" that is implicit in the idea of representation. He quotes with approval the idea of "denying to either pole the independence that makes the opposition possible," i.e., the "opposition" between a representation and what is represented.[24] Clearly, he wants to collapse these together. Again there is the intriguing testimony provided by Lieutenant Colonel Oliver North. Lynch describes an attempt during his cross-questioning to elicit a straight answer about what North did or did not say to the

23. Chap. 7, 240.
24. Chap. 7, 249 n.37.

277

attorney general. North concludes his responses to a certain suggestion about this matter by saying that he doesn't deny saying the thing in question, but he isn't saying that he remembers saying it either. As Lynch observes: what we have here are not simple references to something but "thrusts, parries, feints, and dodges in the interrogatory game."[25] In other words, we don't get outside the talk—we just get more talk about talk.

This is at least a tempting construction to put upon the determined commitment of writers in the ethnomethodological tradition to use language in the way they do: they are making their medium consistent with their message. They turn talk back on itself because they think that this is all there is to talk about. My conjecture is that here is the real parting of the ways between ethnomethodology and the sociology of knowledge. For ethnomethodologists the expressive, internalist, nonrepresentational picture of discourse has universal application. It yields a picture applicable, they believe, to all knowledge claims, and a program of research that is equally universal: seek out and exhibit the ways in which talk is at once the subject and object of all discourse.

Obviously I must be extremely careful in imputing such a radical thesis to anyone. There are certainly problems in making such an imputation stick. Some things that Lynch says do not fit this reading at all. The question then becomes: is the reading simply wrong, or is Lynch inconsistently offering more than one thesis? I suggest that he is being equivocal and inconsistent. My reason is that the less extreme strand in his argument is indistinguishable from the sociological position that he wants to attack. Therefore if he is to have any real basis for differentiating himself from the sociological approach, he vitally needs the more radical claim used in his attack on the notion of representation, i.e., the position defined above.

The sociological position does not deny that talk *can* be about talk. Indeed it accepts that this is an important and ubiquitous feature of discourse. A good example of self-referring systems of talk was provided in the ideas of Anscombe that were cited earlier. There the point was that the "must" that attends the following of the rule of a game is the product of a self-referring set of verbal practices. There is no reality external to the practices of the game to which the rules correspond or which they represent. Here we do indeed have a case, or a family of cases, where the duality of symbol and

25. Chap. 7, 233 n.22.

thing, subject and object, is overcome. The rules represent nothing but themselves.[26]

These cases where, as Anscombe puts it, the relevant "essences" are created by being referred to do not, however, constitute the whole of our referential practices. They work especially well in the analysis of concepts like promises, rights, and obligations. What, however, is to be made of concepts where the reality that is being discussed is not some *moral* reality but a *material* reality? How does this model of language work for natural-kind terms? The line taken by sociologists of knowledge has been to say that here discourse has both representational *and* self-referential aspects. The sociological research program could be defined as the study of how these two things are always woven together. What is intriguing and sociologically important about our representational practices, as they apply to the real world about us, is that they have an ineradicable, self-referential component. That is of course the normative and conventional component; a component that is far more subtly intertwined in our thought than standard philosophical forms of "realism" acknowledge. We must simultaneously negotiate our handling of things and our handling of people. Metaphorically we function on two channels at the same time. This even applies in the case of mathematics, where certain elementary routines in the ordering and sorting of material objects become conventionalized models of formal and abstract operations—this at least is Wittgenstein's theory.

On occasion Lynch seems to endorse a very similar approach. Thus he claims that to analyze a document's use does not discount its referential functions.[27] In his analysis of the exchange between three scientific workers looking at some electron microscope photographs, he isolates certain references that are made within the talk to a reality outside the talk and notes that "each of the successive references to 'things' is included within utterances that 'make a point' vis-à-vis a local context of utterances and activities." This example is glossed by his saying that: "we can see that references to 'things' act simultaneously as references to (and within) activities."[28] I take the simultaneity here to hold between our references to external inanimate objects and our references to other people with whom we are interacting. If this is a correct reading, then we

26. An excellent account of the role of self-referring expressions, written from the standpoint of the sociology of knowledge, is Barnes 1983. I have found this paper extremely valuable in providing a framework for understanding the present discussion.

27. Chap. 7, 238.

28. Chap. 7, 240.

have here a view very close to that developed in the book on Wittgenstein that Lynch takes himself to be attacking. In that book I offered the image of the "superposition of language-games," the idea of different purposes simultaneously informing our organized talk. I am not asking Lynch to recognize his own theory in that model but merely to acknowledge that one strand of what he says is not so very different. It is because of that similarity that he needs the more radical (and questionable) thesis that I detected earlier. Without it he cannot sustain the principled opposition he believes exists between ethnomethodology and the sociology of knowledge.

In summary, Lynch is in a dilemma. He can only create a difference between ethnomethodology and the sociology of knowledge by embracing a theory of our referring activities that is implausible, restricted, and empirically inadequate, viz, that all talk is about talk. If he draws back from such a theory and says this was not his intention, then he is forced onto the other horn of the dilemma: his position is not, after all, significantly different from that of the sociology of knowledge.

I do not pretend to have answered all of the points that Lynch raises against the sociology of knowledge approach. For example, I have not even addressed the claim that a sociological approach to science would produce a "crisis" for the science doing the explaining. On that question perhaps we should be pragmatic and wait and see. In any case an a priori reply would take the discussion too far afield, and I think it better to concentrate on the more sharply focused points that have been raised about rule following. Nor have I sought to answer Lynch's claim that the social character of mathematical rule following will be trivial if measured against the aspirations of standard sociological explanation, with its use of "consensus," "interest," and such concepts. The only reply to that is to invite readers to consult examples of such work and decide for themselves.[29] Nevertheless, I hope that I have made it clear what might be at stake in the choice between the ethnomethodological approach and the sociology of knowledge.

As regards Wittgenstein, it is certainly arguable that in some respects ethnomethodologists have a better claim to be his spiritual heirs than do sociologists of knowledge. The ethnomethodologists can rightly claim to have inherited his hostility to constructive

29. See, for example, MacKenzie 1981. It would be most instructive to read MacKenzie's book in conjunction with Livingston 1986. This would give a clear sense of the different character and direction of the two styles of analysis. It might even lead to a spontaneous preference for one over the other.

theory building. I doubt if Wittgenstein was entirely consistent in adhering to this principle, but it is an undeniable part of his personal position. It is a part that I would happily discard and hand over to whoever might find it congenial. In Wittgenstein's own case this stance probably derived from his participation in the movement of antiscientific and anticausal irrationalism associated with Oswald Spengler's *Decline of the West*.[30] Fidelity to Wittgenstein in this respect seems to me to emphasize what is least fruitful and suggestive in his work. But if ethnomethodologists choose to become the heirs to the inhibitions that used to be called *Lebensphilosophie*, that is their privilege.

Let me end with a terminological suggestion. The time is clearly past when it was useful to speak of a position being simply "Wittgensteinian" or "non-Wittgensteinian." There are different and opposed readings of Wittgenstein, and different and opposed lessons drawn from his work. Such a situation is not surprising, and there are well-known precedents. Hegel's followers split into the right Hegelians and the left Hegelians: the former emphasizing the spiritualism and idealism, the latter giving his work a more historical, social, and materialist-scientific gloss. At the moment we seem to have an analogous situation with "right Wittgensteinians" and "left Wittgensteinians." The argument of this paper I would class as left Wittgensteinian, because it emphasizes the sociological reading and, as Lynch rightly says, treats Wittgenstein's ideas as embryonic social-scientific theories. By contrast, those I would class as the right Wittgensteinians, such as Baker and Hacker, Shanker, McGinn, and, I fear, Lynch, seem to me to be committed to readings that in various ways invert Wittgenstein's best insights. In the present discussion we have seen Wittgenstein's arguments about internal relations used as if they provided ammunition against sociology, when really they open the door to that science. In Hegel's case it was his left-wing followers who, notoriously, "stood him on his head"; in Wittgenstein's case it is his right-wing followers. Hegel may indeed be improved by inversion; but I submit that Wittgenstein, for all his unnecessary and self-imposed limitations, is better seen with his feet squarely on the ground.[31]

---

30. Spengler's *Der Untergang des Abendlandes* was translated as *Decline of the West* (1939). G. H. von Wright said of Wittgenstein that "he *lived* the 'Untergang des Abendlandes'"; see von Wright, "Wittgenstein in Relation to his Times," in McGuinness 1982, 116. For a brief discussion and references, see Bloor, 1983, § 8.2.

31. The dispute between the "skeptical" and "antiskeptical" readings of Wittgenstein and the associated confrontation between collectivism and individualism will be analyzed in a forthcoming book, provisionally entitled *Rules and Obligations*.

REFERENCES

Anscombe, G. E. M. 1981. *Collected Philosophical Papers.* Vol. 3. Oxford: Blackwell.

Attewell, P. 1974. Ethnomethodology since Garfinkel. *Theory and Society* 1: 179–210.

Baker, G. P., and P. M. S. Hacker. 1985. *Wittgenstein, Rules, Grammar, and Necessity.* Oxford: Blackwell.

Barnes, B. 1983. Social Life as Bootstrapped Induction. *Sociology* 17: 524–45.

Bloor, D. 1983. *Wittgenstein: A Social Theory of Knowledge.* New York: Columbia University Press.

Garfinkel, H. 1967. *Studies in Ethnomethodology.* Englewood Cliffs, N. J.: Prentice-Hall.

Heritage, J. 1984. *Garfinkel and Ethnomethodology.* Cambridge: Polity Press.

McGuinness, B., ed. 1982. *Wittgenstein and His Times.* Oxford: Blackwell.

MacKenzie, D. 1981. *Statistics in Britain: 1865–1930.* Edinburgh: Edinburgh University Press.

Livingston, E. 1986. *The Ethnomethodological Foundations of Mathematics.* London: Routledge and Kegan Paul.

Spengler, O. 1989. *The Decline of the West.* Translated by C. F. Atkinson. New York: Knopf.

Wittgenstein, L. 1967a. *Philosophical Investigations.* Oxford: Blackwell.

———. 1967b. *Remarks on the Foundations of Mathematics.* Oxford: Blackwell.

———. 1969. *The Blue and Brown Books.* Oxford: Blackwell.

9

From the "Will to Theory" to the Discursive Collage: A Reply to Bloor's "Left and Right Wittgensteinians"

Michael Lynch

David Bloor wonders why I am so preoccupied with the differences between ethnomethodology and the sociology of scientific knowledge, and I imagine many readers also wonder. The two approaches certainly have much in common. As far as most sociologists are concerned, the very fact that Bloor and I can argue about the sociological implications of Wittgenstein's philosophy testifies to our sharing an arcane interest. Bloor and I agree that Wittgenstein offers a unique and very challenging approach to the central topics in epistemology, and that his writings are no less pertinent to the social sciences than they are to philosophy. We also agree that even the most specialized practices in mathematics and natural science are investigable social phenomena. Nevertheless I think it should be clear by now that we do not agree about exactly what is "social" about science and mathematics, and consequently we differ in our recommendations on how sociologists of science and mathematics should conduct their investigations. I appreciate Bloor's point that my arguments may convey the false impression that ethnomethodology and sociology of knowledge are entirely incompatible, and I am aware that it is easy to grow impatient with mere arguments when there is empirical work to be done. Nevertheless, I think the contrasts discussed in my paper are far from trivial, and they should not be written off as scholastic quibbles of no relevance to empirical research.

In this rejoinder, I will respond to Bloor's accusations that my paper draws "false contrasts" between ethnomethodology and sociology of scientific knowledge, and that my arguments rest upon self-contradictory and implausible theories of action and meaning. But rather than simply reiterate my earlier arguments, I will use Bloor's paper as material for a textual demonstration of our differences. I will take up four of his arguments: (1) his allegation of a contradic-

David Bogen and Jeff Coulter read an earlier draft of this paper and gave me helpful comments and criticisms.

tion between two "doctrines" in ethnomethodology, (2) his causal account of rule following, (3) his discussion of consensus, and (4) his treatment of representation. By critically examining his expository practices, I hope to move our discussion away from questions of doctrine and principle and confront the very "will to theory" that sets up and animates Bloor's arguments.

· 1. The prima facie contradiction in ethnomethodology. Early in his paper, Bloor elaborates upon a "prima facie contradiction" between two central "doctrines" in Garfinkel's ethnomethodological program. Perhaps with a touch of humor, he argues that Wittgenstein's discussion of rule following "refuted ethnomethodology . . . before it was even born." Given the notorious difficulty of both Garfinkel's *Studies in Ethnomethodology* and Wittgenstein's *Philosophical Investigations*, Bloor should be congratulated for having extracted such a decisive logical relationship between arguments in the two texts. He later qualifies his initial assertion, but it is worth going over his argument. While doing so I will aim not only to defend ethnomethodology but also to exhibit how Bloor's arguments gain their "logical" force through his deft translations of some difficult passages in Garfinkel's and Wittgenstein's texts.

Although Garfinkel (1967) strenuously avoids stating transcendent theoretical principles, Bloor proposes two central "doctrines" on behalf of ethnomethodology:

> Doctrine 1: "Indexicality" is irreparable.
> Doctrine 2: The human agent is not a cultural or judgmental "dope."

The way Bloor states the first doctrine subtly "fixes" Garfinkel's (1967) discussion of indexical expressions into a general theoretical proposition. Garfinkel argues that words, expressions, utterances, rules, and other formulations obtain their sense in the circumstances of their use. The point he makes is not (or not just) that "indexicality" is *irreparable,* or that, as Bloor puts it, "we can never reach the ideal of pure objectivity in which meanings are made totally explicit and formulated in a wholly context-free way." Although such a conclusion *can* be drawn from the text, the "ideal of objectivity" simply drops from sight when Garfinkel stresses that indexical expressions are part and parcel of the way communicative actions make sense in the first place.[1] Indexical expressions enable us to speak plainly as well as elusively, to explain what we mean as well as to obscure it, and to speak "objectively" no less than to ex-

1. See chapter 7 for a discussion and examples of indexical expressions.

press a personal point of view. For the most part indexical expressions are explicit enough on their occasions of use. To attempt to "repair" indexicality is to try to fix a machinery that isn't broken. Indexical expressions do present particular problems for programs in machine translation, survey analysis, linguistics, or other academic or practical endeavors for devising formal representations of practical actions. But once we no longer assume the classic posture of an objective observer, the general problem of indexicality dissolves. Ambiguities and misunderstandings sometimes arise in ordinary communicational activities, but even when they do they are repaired through the further use of indexical expressions.

Bloor also states doctrine 2 as though it were a proposition in a general theory of social action. He writes that it "says (roughly) that human agents are active rather than passive. It is they that construct meanings." Garfinkel's (1967,68) literary figure of the "cultural dope" (along with its close relatives, the "judgmental dope" and "psychological dope") recalls the metaphor of the "puppet" (or "dummy") that Schutz (1964) used to describe the ideal-typical "actor" in sociological theories of action. The cultural dope embodies the general patterns of normative expectancies, constraints, needs, values, and decision rules specified by a theoretical schema. This dummy is docile since it contains only what the theorist puts into it, and it does not act in any here-and-now situation. The major question Garfinkel (1967,68) addresses in his discussion of the cultural dope is not whether "the human agent" is active rather than passive, but "how is an investigator *doing* it when he is making out the member of a society to be a judgmental dope?" Again, as he does when he raises the "problem" of indexicality, Garfinkel implicates the classical mode of investigation in the very way he resolves the phenomenon. Indexicality is not "irreparable" except when decontextualized meanings are demanded in an analytic program. Similarly, the "cultural dope" is not just a misleading "model of man" in contrast to another model of a more consciously acting decision-making agent. Whether designed to be passive or active, the "agent" or "actor" in a sociological theory is an abstraction. Such an abstraction can be brought to life in empirical applications of the model, but only through the complicity of the persons studied. Garfinkel mentions (70) that investigators sometimes "instruct" their subjects on how to act in order to guarantee that they will produce the kinds of actions the investigator has in mind: "But, following Wittgenstein, persons' actual usages are rational usages in *some* 'language game.' What is *their* game? As long as that question is neglected, it is inevitable that persons' usages will fall short. The more will this be so the more are subjects' interests in usages dictated by different practical considerations." Although Garfinkel gives a specific account of how the cultural dope is a product of social science methodology, he does not elaborate a contrary conception of "the human agent." Instead, his question, "What is *their* game?" puts aside the "will to theory" and invites us to consider the varieties of ordinary settings in which persons take part in concerted social activities. This question focuses on the "games" and not on any general account of the human agent. As ethnomethodological studies demonstrate, entirely different distributions of agents and agencies emerge within diverse "games,"[2] such as driving in traffic, playing music together, conducting classroom lessons, solving mathematics problems at the blackboard, and so on. In any particular instance, how agency is articulated and whether or not any coherent sense of agency is relevant may depend upon the constellations of actions, expressions, equipment, and other scenic particulars that identify and inform a language game's course of play.

Having set up the two ethnomethodological doctrines, Bloor then explains how Wittgenstein's argument about rule following reveals a contradiction between those doctrines. According to Bloor's summary of Wittgenstein's argument, the expression of a rule cannot exhaustively define or otherwise control its contextual application. Nor will another rule for "interpreting" the rule entirely bridge the "gap" between the rule statement and the actions done in accord with it, since a similar gap appears between the secondary rule and *its* application. This, says Bloor, is akin to what Garfinkel says about the irreparable indexicality of rules and instructions. But, he adds, Wittgenstein shows how the potential regress of rules and interpretations comes to an end when we simply act as a matter of course, on the basis of our training: "When I obey a rule I do not choose. I obey the rule blindly" (*PI*, §219). "Only by acknowledging the importance of this blind (i.e., automatic and caused) response can we avoid the regress. This is how we get from rule to rule following" (Bloor). Having equated "blind" obedience to a rule with "automatic and caused" behavior, Bloor then argues that "in the last analysis, a rule must be obeyed blindly means that, contrary to doctrine 2, the actor *must* be some form of cultural or judgmental 'dope.'"

As Bloor partly acknowledges, this "contradiction" is a rather fragile construct. Aside from his formulations of ethnomethodology's

2. In a later chapter, Garfinkel (1967) criticizes the game metaphor at length, but his criticism is not germane to the present argument.

doctrines, he is asking us to treat Wittgenstein's line about obeying a rule "blindly" as a substantive characterization of caused behavior. Bloor's parenthetical substitution of "automatic and caused" for "blind" may seem innocuous enough, since "blind obedience" often connotes an unthinking compliance to an order, as in military drill. However, this translation is at least doubtful, and the way it is doubtful is instructive about Bloor's methods for turning Wittgenstein into a social theorist. In the first place, it is doubtful that Wittgenstein's line is a *causal statement* about rule following. The passage Bloor quotes from *PI*,§219 comes up in the course of Wittgenstein's critique of the hypostatic idea that the rule itself "traces the lines along which it is to be followed through the whole of space." When he speaks of following a rule "blindly," Wittgenstein writes in the first person singular, explicating an intuitive sense in which "I" act without any awareness of choice, interpretation, or guidance. As he goes on to argue, an ascription of logical determination to the meaning of a rule is "really a mythological description of the use of a rule" (*PI*,§221). That is, when we follow it "blindly," the rule "whispers" nothing to us, and we can only imagine that the rule somehow hovers over or internally guides our actions of following it. Although Wittgenstein uses this example to oppose logical determinacy, it is not at all clear that he is affirming that orderly conduct is causally determined (*PI*,§220).

Secondly, to accept Wittgenstein's conclusion about blind rule following does not commit one "to accepting that, in some form, the human agent is a judgmental dope." Bloor's argument seems to assume that judgment is a matter of conscious deliberation or ratiocination about the options inherent in a situation. But as I understand the concept, someone who obeys an order instantaneously and without hesitation is not necessarily acting without judgment, and he can certainly be held responsible for his actions. Moreover, to point to the absence of an introspective justification or reason for acting does not necessarily imply that the action was caused by an unconscious disposition or internalized norm.

Before further pursuing Bloor's account of the causes of rule following, let me summarize my response to his argument on the "contradiction" within ethnomethodology. Bloor constructs something of a syllogism to the effect that (1) Garfinkel's first doctrine (indexicality is irreparable) is equivalent to Wittgenstein's argument about blind rule following; and (2) Wittgenstein's argument implies that if agents follow rules blindly, they must in some sense be judgmental dopes; so that (3) Wittgenstein's argument contradicts Garfinkel's second doctrine, and Garfinkel's two doctrines contradict each other.

I have argued that the relevant passages in Garfinkel's and Wittgenstein's texts do not so neatly fall into place as clear-cut theoretical propositions. The "prima facie contradiction" between the two "doctrines" is a textual product of the way Bloor shapes Garfinkel's arguments into theoretical "doctrines" and translates Wittgenstein's passage about "blind" rule following into a causal proposition. Bloor's "will to theory" is an important mediator for shaping up the logical "force" of the alleged contradiction.

2. The "causes" of rule following. Bloor makes an interesting comment about how a causal explanation of rule following is compatible with the concept of an "internal" relation between rules and conduct. He cites two essays by Anscombe (1981) to elaborate upon the causes of the "blind" step from a rule to the actions of following it. It is interesting that the essay Bloor discusses most specifically, on "Rights, Rules and Promises," takes up questions raised by Hume and never mentions Wittgentstein.[3] Anscombe defines a promise as "essentially a sign and the necessitation arises from the giving of the sign" (102). By extension, Bloor says that Anscombe shows "how we come to attach meaning" to particular expressions "used in connection with rule following." One of the examples Anscombe (1981,102) gives is the following:

> Consider the learner in chess or some other game. Of course: "You have to move your king, he's in check" is equivalent to "The rules of the game require that, in this position, you move your king." But a learner may not yet have this idea: *the rules of the game require . . .* Accepting it when told "You have to move your king, he's in check," is part of learning that very concept: "the rules of the game require." *Requiring* is putting some sort of necessity on you, and what can that be? All these things hang together at some early stage: learning a game, learning the very idea of such a game, acquiring the concept of "you have to" which appears in the others' speech, grasping the idea of a rule. Nor is there a distinct meaning for "being a rule of the game" (unless the general idea has been learned from other games) which can be used to *explain* the "you have to" that comes into that learning.

As I read this passage, it describes how the sense of necessity implied in the expression "you have to" is learned together with an ensemble of actions and expressions that constitute playing the game. But, I do not see how Anscombe is giving a *causal* account of the internal relation between the rule and the game. Even if the in-

---

3. Anscombe edited and translated the *Philosophical Investigations* as well as several other works of Wittgenstein, but her essays do not necessarily represent Wittgenstein's position.

junction, "You have to move your king, he's in check," instigates a behavior that was forcibly shaped during the player's training, the role of "check" in the game of chess is not *caused* by the individual's socialization. The appropriate response is a *criterion* for playing the game we call "chess." If a player ignores the injunction and fails to move out of check, the game is effectively over. And if the player shows no comprehension of what "check" means, it is doubtful whether he or she was *in* the game in the first place. Of course players must learn the game as a condition for understanding the injunction, but the sense of "you have to" in this case does not derive from an individual's being coerced or conditioned to follow the rule. It concerns how the rule is part of the way the game is played. The concept of socialization may describe how individuals are trained to master the game, but it presupposes rather than explains what counts as a mastery of the game's constituent practices.

It is also doubtful that Wittgenstein abides by the Humean problematic of how one gets from the "sign" to the "obligation" to act in a particular way. Indeed it can be argued that Wittgenstein dissolves this very way of treating expressions of rules and promises. Wittgenstein states, for instance, that "Every sign *by itself* seems dead." He then asks, "*What* gives it life?—In use it is *alive*. Is life breathed into it there—Or is the *use* its life?" (*PI*,§432). This last question suggests something that is more plain and yet more subtle than Bloor's way of considering rules. If the "use" is the "life" of an expression, it is not as though a meaning is "attached" to an otherwise lifeless sign. We first encounter the sign in use or against the backdrop of the practice in which it has a use. It is already a meaningful part of the practice, even if each individual needs to learn the rule together with the other aspects of the practice. It is misleading to ask "how we attach meaning" to the sign, since the question implies that each of us separately accomplishes what is already established by the sign's use in the language game. This way of setting up the problem is like violently wresting a cell from a living body and then inspecting the now-dead cell to see how life would have been attached to it.

If the expression of a rule is a sign, it is one whose sense arises as part of an unfolding nexus of moves and other expressions in the language game. There is no meaning waiting to be attached to it, and there is no discrete step to be taken from sign to practice. Rather the sign is already embedded *in* a practice, and meaning arises through the very placement of the sign in accordance with the grammar of the practice. Wittgenstein mentions training as a condition for learning how to obey the rule, as well as how to use the word "rule" along with an entire nexus of interwoven concepts and activities that are brought into play together (*PI*,§225). The rule is a moment in the practical assemblage, and that assemblage includes the ongoing actions and judgments of other players.

Bloor is, of course, committed to a *social theory of knowledge*, so he is unlikely to be disturbed by my saying that Wittgenstein warns us away from an individualistic account of rule following. The problem is that Bloor's dispositional explanation retains elements of the psychologism Wittgenstein effectively attacked.[4] As I understand Wittgenstein's discussion of rules, he specifically warns against such an explanation, but not because of any anticausal irrationalism. He insists that there is no better site for the explication of a rule's sense, relevance, and agreed-to use than the ensemble of expressions and techniques that make up the practice in which it is embedded. He does not offer an alternative form of causal explanation, since a practice is not a center of agency or a causal factor. Rather than trying to explain a practice in terms of underlying dispositions, abstract norms, or interests, a task for sociology would be to describe the ensemble of actions that constitute the practice. This is precisely what ethnomethodology seeks to do.

3. Consensus and quiet agreement. Bloor argues that aside from my antisociological prejudice and anticausal irrationalism (shared with Wittgenstein), my treatment of the relationship between rules and practices is not very different from the one he advocates. He declares that I make thinly disguised use of the concept of consensus when I speak of "quiet agreement." And since I use the concept, I should be held to the "standard questions" about its origins and maintenance and the role of social interests. What truly puzzles me about Bloor's argument is his assertion that I opposed the *concept* of consensus, when I thought I had disputed a particular way that concept is used in sociology of knowledge explanations. No one who reads the *Philosophical Investigations* can ignore Wittgenstein's repeated references to "agreement."[5] The interesting, and very debatable, question is just how "agreement" is part of the practices in

4. An appreciation of this can be gained by examining Henderson's (1990) argument on how traditional epistemological values are compatible with SSK's descriptions. Henderson (131) latches onto Bloor's causal reading of Wittgenstein but then turns to cognitive psychology to fill in the details. Although Henderson advocates a kind of backdoor rationalism partially at odds with the SSK's approach, his dispositionalist account of rule following is largely compatible with Bloor's, and, I would argue, it is open to similar criticisms.

5. In previous work (Lynch 1985,179ff.) I discussed the topic of agreement at length, although in a way that I now see to be inadequate.

science and mathematics. In my paper I argued that ethnomethodology and sociology of knowledge take different positions on this question, and despite what he says about my making "false contrasts," Bloor constructs an explanation of the role of consensus in arithmetic that exemplifies precisely what I argued against in my paper.[6]

In *Philosophical Investigations* §185, Wittgenstein imagined what would happen if a teacher, seeking to convey a rule in arithmetic, were to confront a pupil who systematically misunderstood the task. All attempts at correction failed because they too are systematically misunderstood. This is an example of the possibility of an endless regress of rules for following rules. It exhibits the limits of "interpretation" and the endlessness of the task of repairing indexicality. But another aspect of the example is what it says about internal relations. It shows that the deviant applications of a rule themselves stand in an internal relation to the rule as the deviant understands it. The teacher and pupil fail to make the usual kind of contact because the pupil constructs his own circle of definitions and his own set of internal relations between his signs and his practices. So the phenomenon of internal relations between a rule and its applications—if conceived narrowly—doesn't serve to define the real nature of rule following as we know it as a feature of a shared practice. At most it challenges us to define the difference between the actual rules of arithmetic and their idiosyncratic alternatives. It brings home, in the way that previous discussions of interpretation did, that something more and different is needed to define the accepted institution of arithmetic. Clearly what is required in the Wittgenstein example is something that breaks the deadlock between the competing internal relations. Such a factor would be consensus, the very thing rejected by Baker and Hacker. Ultimately it is collective support for one internal relation rather than another that makes the teacher's rule correct and the other deviant and incorrect.

Initially Bloor says that the pupil in Wittgenstein's example "systematically misunderstood the task." Shortly thereafter he characterizes this as an application of the rule as "the deviant understands it." From that point on, he places the pupil's "idiosyncratic alternative" in a symmetrical relationship with the teacher's conventional

6. Readers who are alert for signs of incommensurability should note that Bloor prefaces his recitation of Wittgenstein's example by saying that it can be read as a "reductio ad absurdum of the position advocated by Lynch, Baker, Hacker, Shanker, and other antisociological commentators." As I stated in my paper, Shanker (1987, 14) speaks of the same argument as "a sustained *reductio ad absurdum*" of rule skepticism.

treatment of the rule; both display "competing internal relations" between the rule and a practice, and *consensus* breaks the deadlock.

There is a degree of plausibility to what Bloor is saying here. Consider, for instance, the following example of a child learning to count according to instructions given by an adult.[7] The child counts on the fingers of his hand: "one, two, three, four, five." The adult asks him, "Can you count backwards?" The child turns around, and with his back facing his questioner he counts "one, two, three, four, five." Following Bloor's recommendations, we might say that this example illustrates how the injunction to "count backwards" is indexical to the practice in which it is used. The child "misunderstands" the adult's injunction, and yet his application of the word "backwards" demonstrates an understanding of sorts by linking the adult's question to others of the form, "Can you face backwards?" There is nothing intrinsic to the form of the statement that signals its "correct" application. In Bloor's terms, the child "constructs his own circle of definitions and his own set of internal relations" for applying the words "count backwards" in a technique for counting. The "deadlock" between competing internal relations is broken when the child is laughed at, corrected, and shown examples, and he eventually comes to learn what "count backwards" means as a constituent feature of a conventional practice.

The problem with this description is that if the child "systematically misunderstands" the injunction to count backwards, he has *not* demonstrated an understanding of the relevant use of the injunction. When he turns around and counts, "one, two, three, four, five," he inadvertently produces a pun on the *words* "count backwards," but what he does is not the technique we call "counting backwards." He does show a *funny* understanding of the words "count backwards" in the very way his actions display an ignorance of the techniques of counting. There is no symmetry or "deadlock" between "competing internal relations," unless we were to assume that the child's actions establish a viable alternative to the technique invoked by the adult's injunction. But if a practice or technique is not an entirely private affair, it would not make sense to say that the child is *understanding* the words "count backwards" in terms of "his own" technique (Wittgenstein *PI*,§199).

When Baker and Hacker (1985) speak of an "internal" relation between a rule and a practice in arithmetic, they describe a gram-

7. The example was furnished by Ed Parsons, who described it to me after having seen it and another similar example on a television program called "The Best Home Videos."

matical relation between the expression of a rule and the techniques of arithmetic. This has nothing to do with the "internal relations" Bloor mentions when he speaks of a pupil's "own set of internal relations between his signs and his practices" or "his own circle of definitions." Despite the clear account of internal relations he gave elsewhere, Bloor here seems to be using the word "internal" as though it referred to the pupil's private conception of the rule's meaning. But the pupil in Wittgenstein's example performs actions that demonstrate that he only *thinks* he is following the rule. By treating the internal relation between rule and practice as an individual matter, Bloor creates the need to search for "something more and different" in order to "define the accepted institution of arithmetic." The initial characterization of the action as a "misunderstanding" of the rule only makes sense from a standpoint that is already situated within (i.e., *internal* to) the "accepted institution of arithmetic," so that there is no comparable standpoint from which to characterize what the pupil is doing as a "competing understanding."

Bloor expresses approval of Kripke's (1982) interpretation of the rule-following example. Although, as I mentioned in my earlier paper, Kripke's "community" view is disputed by a number of Wittgenstein scholars, he carefully avoids treating the "deviant's" response as a "competing internal relation."[8]

> A deviant individual whose responses do not accord with those of the community in enough cases will not be judged, by the community, to be following its rules; he may even be judged to be a madman, following no coherent rule at all. When the community denies of someone that he is following certain rules, it excludes him from various transactions such as the one between the grocer and the customer. It indicates that it cannot rely on his behavior in such transactions. (Kripke 1982,93)

There is no suggestion in Wittgenstein's example that the pupil's "misunderstanding" is to be placed on equal *theoretical* footing with the "correct" way of continuing the number series. This is not because of a lack of sympathy for the pupil's "point of view," but because there is no room in the world to place a "systematic mis-

8. By quoting the following passage I do not mean to endorse the way Kripke attributes agency and judgment to "the community." In contrast, Wittgenstein's examples suggest that there is no singular agent, so that a communal judgment is no more apt than an individual interpretation for accounting for "blind" rule following. Wittgenstein does not describe the practices of arithmetic as an institution that reflects, emanates from, or is sustained by any center of judgment.

understanding" on such footing without revising the initial terms of the description. The established practices and techniques of arithmetic are inseparable from the terms under which a relevant action is characterized as an understanding, competing understanding, or misunderstanding. If the student's practice displays "misunderstanding," it does not relativize the rule. "Competing internal relations" are precluded, since the student's practice is defined negatively in reference to the established practice of counting by twos.

I am not saying that there can be no such thing as idiosyncratic options to the usual way a practice or technique is done. Competitions certainly can arise between different internal relations. Sometimes deviant usages, such as "ungrammatical" colloquial expressions, variants of a game prohibited by official rules, or unorthodox scientific theories, later gain acceptance. The point is that none of these characterizations turns on the deviant (or "eccentric," "mistaken," or "innovative") *agent's* "own set of internal relations between his signs and his practices." The agent does not *own* the internal relations that identify his or her actions as mistakes, legitimate alternatives, or idiosyncratic instances of some practice. Rather all of these characterizations presuppose that the agent's actions already take place in relation to some concerted practice.

It would be very misleading to treat the pupil in Wittgenstein's example under the analogy of a scientist whose unconventional theory is rejected during a controversy. Despite the once-common tendency to reduce the history of science to a chronology of great men's ideas, no controversy is generated by an *individual's* "own set of internal relations between his signs and his practices." A controversial theory's very standing as a theory about which there is controversy is "internally related" to the equipment, techniques, literary practices, observation language, and accepted concepts in a field. This public relationship holds even when historians, or the scientists who originally promulgated the theory, later characterize the theory as a "misunderstanding" or "mistake." Consequently not every imaginable alternative to accepted theories in a discipline counts as a controversial theory, nor can an outside analyst presume to apply a policy of symmetry to every conceivable claim about disciplinary matters of interest. There is no room in the world for such a (non)judgmental standpoint.[9]

9. In their excellent study of the controversy between Hobbes and Boyle over the air pump experiments, Shapin and Schaffer (1985,6) devise a methodological strategy for "playing the stranger." They do this to straddle the epistemic border between (1) a member taken in by shared beliefs in the experimental community studied and

Although Bloor confidently lays claim to a "sociological" reading of Wittgenstein, while relegating me to an "antisociological" position, perhaps our "competing internal relations" to sociology are not so clearly resolved. In his recitation of the number-series example, Bloor portrays "internal" relations in a radically individualistic way; as though the pupil could have had his own understanding of arithmetic, at odds with that of the teacher. "Consensus" then becomes a factor, as though independently introduced into the equation, that "breaks the deadlock" between the pupil's and the teacher's individual understandings. Bloor is correct in saying that I used the terms "quiet agreement" to speak of a kind of consensus, but it is hardly a scandal for my position to do so. "Quiet agreement" is so thoroughly and ubiquitously a part of the production of social order that it has little value as a discrete explanatory factor. In a footnote (n. 17), I referred to Wittgenstein's well-known distinction between agreement "in opinions" and agreement "in form of life." Agreement in form of life is expressed in the very coherence of our activities. It is an evident attunement (*Übereinstimmung*) of activities and their results; an orchestration of actions and expressions that enables mistakes, disruptions, and systematic misunderstandings to become noticeable and accountable. There is no time out from such agreement, even for a student who misunderstands what he is doing or an observer who characterizes what the student is doing as a misunderstanding. To explicate this consensus and to specify its role in the activity is not to isolate a causal factor. In the case of mathematics, the competent practice of mathematics builds its consensual foundations in and as instructionally reproducible mathematical structures. As Livingston (1986) demonstrates in his ethnomethodological study of mathematics, agreement among mathematicians is a social production, but it is not a factor impinging upon that practice. It is the concerted production of mathematics.

4. Representation. Bloor does allow for at least one "real" difference between our approaches, and this is the question of representation. As he defines it, the concept of representation means that a symbol stands for an external, independent reality. He says that I

---

(2) a "true" stranger who would be entirely closed out from the technical questions at issue. By assuming a position as "virtual witnesses" to the historical scenes they describe, the historians propose to delve into the "internal relations" between Boyle's and Hobbes' arguments and the life world of seventeenth-century natural philosophy, while at the same time they avoid becoming epistemically bound by that life world. For a discussion of dilemmas arising in a similar use of the "stranger" strategy that I think should also apply in this case, see Lynch 1982.

accuse "the sociologist of knowledge of thinking in terms of representations in cases where the picture is inappropriate," and he wonders whether I am suggesting that we should altogether "reject the idea of our words and symbols representing an independent reality." He reads my paper to be saying that the "naive picture" of symbols representing objects should be replaced by one where *talk* refers only to *talk*. "The object of our talk is always more talk."

Our differences on this matter are indeed "real," and as always, Bloor's admirably bold way of stating his arguments supplies ample material for elucidating our disagreements. Bloor's remarks on representation surprised me when I first read them, since I had not realized that we differed so profoundly on this matter. To me his remarks appear to be advocating a philosophical concept of meaning that Wittgenstein criticized at the very outset of the *Philosophical Investigations.* Wittgenstein attributed this picture of language to Saint Augustine, although he could just as easily have attributed it to more modern views of language and meaning in philosophy, psychology, sociology, and communication studies. In this classical philosophy of language, "the individual words in language name objects—sentences are combinations of such names.—In this picture of language we find the roots of the following idea: Every word has a meaning" (Wittgenstein *PI,*§1). Wittgenstein does not entirely reject the Augustinian picture of language; instead he says that it "has its place in a primitive idea of the way language functions" (*PI,*§2). He adds that "Augustine, we might say, does describe a system of communication; only not everything that we call language is this system" (*PI,*§3). He goes on to give a series of arguments, analogies, and examples to demonstrate how we perform an immense variety of actions in language besides referring to objects. It is not just that we refer to different domains of objects but that acts of reference are themselves set up and sustained by prereferential or nonreferential communicational actions.

Bloor's treatment of language is of course more nuanced than the Augustinian picture. He acknowledges that "discourse has both representational *and* self-referential aspects to it," and he suggests that representational practices have numerous "components." And as far as he is concerned, I am the one who holds a restricted version of language that emphasizes only the "self-referential aspects." Again, I think Bloor is talking past my position. As I diagnose the problem, he misreads my paper by placing all of its arguments and examples within a framework of referential uses of language. This is particularly clear when he says that ethnomethodology generally advocates an extreme thesis to the effect that "talk" can *refer* only to "talk."

This is far from what I take to be the upshot of ethnomethodology's investigations of language use. Like Wittgenstein, ethnomethodologists treat linguistic expressions as *actions* more various than talking *about* things, persons, moral realities, ideas, talk itself, or any combination of such referents. This is not to say that we cannot refer to objects, but that referring is part of a much larger field of activities. Consider the following response Wittgenstein (*PI*,§27) gives to an imaginary interlocutor:

> "We name things and then we can talk about them: can refer to them in talk."—As if what we did next were given with the mere act of naming As if there were only one thing called "talking about a thing." Where as in fact we do the most various things with our sentences. Think of exclamations alone, with their completely different functions.
>
> > Water!
> > Away!
> > Ow!
> > Help!
> > Fine!
> > No!
>
> Are you inclined still to call these words "names of objects?"

It can be argued that each of these expressions does include an "underlying" referent, so that "Ow!" could be said to "refer" to the speaker's painful experience and "Help!" to the speaker's need to be rescued. But such a program in psycholinguistic analysis is exactly what Wittgenstein disputed. To say "No!" in response to a request does not primarily *refer* to a thing, mental state, or linguistic object. Instead it acts to refuse the request as part of a sequence including both the request and its refusal. To study the uses of such expressions is not to study "talk *about* talk" but to elucidate the actions such expressions accomplish. But rather than reviewing how the entire argument in the *Philosophical Investigations* bears on this point, let me simply *refer* to that text, while realizing, not without some despair, that Bloor has already read it thoroughly and thoughtfully.

I could go on. And so could Bloor. We could chop Wittgenstein's *Philosophical Investigations* into its constituent paragraphs, print them on cards, and then use them to play an endless game. Bloor could start the game by throwing a paragraph card on the table, and then I could trump it with another. He could then pull another card from his hand to trump mine, and so forth. After gaining enough proficiency, we could perhaps print the appropriate paragraph numbers on the cards, and accelerate the pace of the play. Bloor could

throw card §212 and then I could follow with §224. We could perhaps settle who reads Wittgenstein right and who reads him wrong
by defining these terms as game-specific outcomes (e.g., the first
player to use all the cards in his hands is "right"), but this would not
be very convincing to those who do not play the game.

Toward the end of his paper Bloor suggests another way of laying
our cards on the table: by spreading them from "left" to "right."
He places my arguments to the "right" of his, and he makes clear
that the "right" is the wrong side of the table to be on. As he argues, the ethnomethodologists are right Wittgensteinians, in league
with the orthodox conservators of Wittgenstein's words. Worse,
they are caught up in a reactionary *Lebensphilosophie* of "anticausal and antiscientific irrationalism." The sociologists of knowledge are "left Wittgensteinians"—*righteous* advocates of a social
theory of knowledge—and they are less concerned about Wittgenstein's explicit words than inspired to nurture his "embryonic social-
scientific theories." With some qualifications, I do think that such
"right-Wittgensteinian" scholars as Baker, Hacker, and Shanker are
right about Wittgenstein. And I also think Bloor misses the point
when he writes them off as reactionary individualists. This right-
and-left arrangement is a very unstable one, since it is easily reversed. In this rejoinder I have tried to reverse the charges by saying
that Bloor retains elements of an individualistic view of rule following, and that his discussion of representation recalls the classical
view of language that Wittgenstein criticized. To get Wittgenstein
"right," I argued, is to realize that the critical implications of his
investigations strike very close to home. If Bloor takes this position
to be orthodox, I would insist that it is orthodox only in the sense
that it refuses to go along with a revisionist program of classical
social science theorizing.

In my view Bloor underestimates the extent to which Wittgenstein's writings pose a challenge for the sociology of science. This
challenge is not akin to the familiar argument that scientific and
mathematical practices are governed by a nonsocial rationality.[10]
Quite the opposite; it is that the production of social order in these
disciplines is inseparable from the dense texture of understandings
and concerted practices that make up disciplinary specific language
games. Sociology's general concepts and methodological strategies

10. This is not to say that Wittgenstein has never been cited in support of such
arguments. Slezak (1989,586), for instance, affiliates Wittgenstein to his "decisive
disproof" of the strong program based on computer models of discovery, but at the
same time he dismisses Wittgenstein's attack on mentalistic theories of action. See
Coulter 1983 for a Wittgenstein-inspired critique of cognitivism.

are simply overwhelmed by the heterogeneity and technical density of the language, equipment, and skills through which mathematicians, scientists, and practitioners in many other fields of activity make their affairs accountable. It is not that their practices are asocial, but that they are more thoroughly and locally social than sociology is prepared to handle. The radical question for a post-Wittgensteinian sociology is, Now that we can say that every detail of science is "social," what is there *left* for sociology to do?"[11]

I am tempted to conclude that Bloor's views and mine are incommensurable. It is easy to imagine that both of us are in the grip of massive, internally consistent and mutually incompatible "conceptual frameworks," so that no amount of argument or textual exegesis will persuade either of us to change our ways. However, there are plenty of reasons to put aside the seductive and much overworked concept of incommensurability. Bloor and I are not after all cognizing subjects enunciating coherent "points of view"; nor are we isolated agents describing what we see from a fixed "standpoint." Instead both of us are speaking on behalf of perspectives that are riven with internal disputes, incompletely developed, and faced with doubtful futures. Both ethnomethodology and sociology of scientific knowledge are lightly staffed and weakly policed.[12] This is their attraction as much as a source of anxiety for those of us who work in the two areas. Neither field resembles a Renaissance painting, that is, an expansive and coherent vision converging on a fixed point of view. Instead each is a discursive collage that nobody can quite piece together. From my place within the collage of ethnomethodology, I see little support for a coherent and powerful "social theory of knowledge"; instead I see much more likelihood of fragmentary borrowings and mutual critiques that crisscross the mobile divides between our studies.

REFERENCES

Anscombe, G. E. M. 1981. *The Collected Philosophical Papers of G. E. M. Anscombe.* Vol. 3, *Ethics, Religion, and Politics.* Oxford: Basil Blackwell.

Baker, G. P., and P. M. S. Hacker. 1985. *Wittgenstein, Rules, Grammar, and Necessity.* Oxford: Basil Blackwell.

Coulter, Jeff. 1983. *Rethinking Cognitive Theory.* New York: St. Martin's Press.

Garfinkel, Harold. 1967. *Studies in Ethnomethodology.* Englewood Cliffs, N.J.: Prentice-Hall.

11. I am indebted to Melvin Pollner (1989) for this pun on "left."
12. I owe the expression "weakly policed" in this context to John Urry.

Henderson, David. 1990. On the Sociology of Science and the Continuing Importance of Epistemologically Couched Accounts. *Social Studies of Science* 20:113–48.

Kripke, Saul. 1982. *Wittgenstein on Rules and Private Language.* Cambridge: Harvard University Press.

Livingston, Eric. 1986. *The Ethnomethodological Foundations of Mathematics.* London: Routledge and Kegan Paul.

Lynch, Michael. 1982. Technical Work and Critical Inquiry: Investigations in a Scientific Laboratory. *Social Studies of Science* 12:499–534.

———. 1985. *Art and Artifact in Laboratory Science.* London: Routledge and Kegan Paul.

Pollner, Melvin. 1989. Left of Ethnomethodology. Presented at eighty-fourth annual meetings of the American Sociological Association, San Francisco.

Schutz, Alfred. 1964. The Problem of Rationality in the Social World. In A. Schutz, *Collected Papers*, vol. 2. The Hague: Martinus Nijhoff.

Shanker, S. G. 1987. *Wittgenstein and the Turning-Point in the Philosophy of Mathematics.* Albany, N.Y.: SUNY Press.

Shapin, Steven, and Simon Schaffer. 1985. *Leviathan and the Air-Pump.* Princeton: Princeton University Press.

Slezak, Peter. 1989. Scientific Discovery by Computer as Empirical Refutation of the Strong Programme. *Social Studies of Science* 19:563–600.

Wittgenstein, Ludwig. 1958. *Philosophical Investigations.* G. E. M. Anscombe. Trans. Oxford: Basil Blackwell.

10

Epistemological Chicken

H. M. Collins and Steven Yearley

The game of "chicken" involves dashing across the road in front of speeding cars. The object of the game is to be the last person to cross. Only this person can avoid the charge of being cowardly. An early crosser is a "chicken" (noun), that is, a person who is "chicken" (adjective).

Alternation

In his book *Invitation to Sociology,* Peter Berger describes the process of "alternation." Sociologists, he explains, develop the ability to switch between different frames of reference. They learn how to take on the ways of being in the world that are characteristic of the groups they study. In doing this they learn that their own taken-for-granted-reality, including their most deeply held beliefs, are but one set of beliefs among many. This ability, which seems to the sociologist to be little more than applied common sense, is surprisingly narrowly distributed within society. It is a skill that good sociologists (also anthropologists and some philosophers) acquire through their training. Most academic training narrows the viewpoint and reinforces the single way of seeing that is the trademark of the discipline. Just as Christians know that Christ was the Savior and Muslims know that Muhammad was the Prophet, so economists learn that the world is a set of rationally interlocking self-interests, physicists learn that everything can be predicted mathematically so long as it can be isolated (and so long as it is not indeterministic or chaotic), biologists learn that everything can be explained by some variant of evolutionary theory, and neurochemists know that individuals are fundamentally controlled by the flow of juices in the brain.

Sociologists don't know anything in quite this way; they only know how it is to know. The sociologist is promiscuous, experiencing many loves without ever falling in love. This is neither a happy nor an endearing state. But while promiscuity is not a recipe for love, it is for education. A well-educated person is not just a faithful specialist but one who knows how to take another's point of view— even to invade another's world of knowledge.

The achievement of the sociology of scientific knowledge (SSK) can be understood as an extension of this ability to "alternate." Where, for example, sociologists must understand the culture of religious believers and of worldly atheists, SSKers must be ready to be convinced by geological uniformitarianism *and* catastrophism; now they must know that the universe is filled with gravity waves, now that it is not; in one location they grasp the reality of psychokinesis, in another they must be sure that the universe is exhausted by the four known forces. But SSK also makes us specially aware of sharp differences not only in the content but also in the quality of knowledge. What Mr. John Doe knows as he rides the Clapham omnibus he knows with much more certainty than what Professor Jonathon Doe knows as he reads the *Philosophical Investigations.* Typically, as we have remarked, the sociologist knows less than the natural scientist, while the sociologist of science knows still less. Those engaged from day to day with the problem of reflexivity would, if they could achieve their aims, know nothing at all. We might say that SSK has opened up new ways of knowing nothing.

In spite of this achievement, all of us, however sophisticated, can switch to modes of knowing that allow us to catch buses and hold mortgages. We all engage as a matter of fact in what we might call "meta-alternation." Our argument here is that social studies of science ought to erect meta-alternation as a principle, not treat it as a failing. To treat it as a failing is to invite participation in an escalation of skepticism which we liken to the game of chicken; in this case the game is epistemological chicken.

In what follows we examine two recent tendencies or schools in science studies which play the game in different ways. The most straightforward case is the escalation from relativism through discourse analysis and "new literary forms" to reflexivity. In the end, the relativist regress leads us to have nothing to say.

A more complicated case is the French school. A clear prescription that emerged from relativism was, as Bloor (1973, 1976) put it so well, *symmetry.* That is, sociologists of scientific knowledge should treat correct science and false science equally; they should analyze what are taken by most scientists to be true claims about the natural world and what are treated by most as mistaken claims in the same way. The idea was that the construction of the boundary between the true and the false would become the topic rather than the starting point as in existing sociologies of science. The French have adopted a semiotic approach which gives rise to a much more radical symmetrism. Not only is the boundary between true and false seen as a construction, but from now on, so are all dichotomies—*poulet épistémologique.*[1] The net effect of treating the whole world as a system of signs is, however, to come full circle back to the prosaic world of John Doe. As we will explain, the philosophy may be radical, but the implications are conservative. Where there are no differences except the differences between words there are no surprises left—no purchase for skeptical levers to shift the world on its axis. If anything moves it is the world as a whole. It slides unnoticed; nothing is realigned, nothing trembles, nothing falls. The two types of epistemological escalation—reflexive and semiotic—seem very different, yet in each case the result is impotence.

The Relativist Regress

Relativism, discourse analysis, reflexivity

Since the mid-1970s each new variant of SSK has tended to be a little more radical than the one before it. Each new variant has stood longer on the relativist road. Each group in turn has made the same mistake about its foundational role. In the initial flourish, some sociologists of scientific knowledge believed they were solving epistemological puzzles that had defeated philosophers. They believed that the close study of the activity of scientists showed that even in the hardest case of knowledge "truth [was] a socially organized upshot of contingent courses of linguistic, conceptual and social behaviour" (McHugh, quoted in Collins 1975, 205). But epistemological problems are not resolved by empirical discoveries.[2] Collins should have looked more carefully at the words he quoted. McHugh actually says that "truth is only *conceivable* as a socially organized upshot" (1971, 329; emphasis added). Being inconceivable, "real" truth is hardly susceptible to empirical study. The importance of the philosophical arguments about relativism in the 1970s was, in retrospect, not that they showed that relativism was true but that it was tenable and therefore could be used as a methodology for the study of science. This was in a context where many philosophers argued that relativism was untenable and therefore could lead only to flawed research. Proponents of SSK used in-principle argu-

1. In French the term *poulet* has the not-inappropriate connotation of policeman.
2. Though what counts as doing epistemology may be radically affected by the developments of new styles of research on the problem of knowledge.

ments to show the necessity of epistemological agnosticism, while their case studies revealed the appropriateness of *methodological relativism.*[3]

Within the first few nanoseconds of the relativist big bang, nearly everyone realized that the negative levers were equally applicable to the work of the sociologists and historians themselves.[4] Under appropriate scrutiny their work too looked like a "socially organized upshot," but this did not seem very interesting; the new-style analysis of science, with its implications for the relationship between science and the rest of the world of knowledge, seemed to be the exciting thing. Before long, however, Mulkay, Potter, and Yearley (1983) announced the program of "discourse analysis."

Discourse analysis refused to accept the evidence marshaled by SSK case studies as an unproblematic representation of scientists' activities. We might say that it closely examined the way SSK practitioners used their evidence and revealed the constructional work involved in making social science out of interview material.[5] Discourse analysis revealed some features of the way people organize their talk that were of interest (see Gilbert and Mulkay 1984, 90–111; Mulkay and Gilbert 1982; Yearley 1985). The exercise would have been unexceptionable but for its proponents' insistence that discourse analysis itself was epistemologically foundational. They thought that discourse analysis comprised a critique of SSK while itself being invulnerable to the same critique. In short, they believed that because SSK was vulnerable to deconstruction it was methodologically flawed, whereas discourse analysis touched bedrock.

The discourse analysts, it seemed, had failed to appreciate the universal vulnerability of knowledge making to the methods of SSK. They also failed to understand that social analysis of science does not show the science to be wrong; by the same token, discourse analysis does not show that something other than SSK is right. In all cases validity is the outcome of social negotiation; the absence of social negotiations is not a condition of validity. Articles critical

---

3. The philosophical arguments (not the case studies) which supported epistemological agnosticism were not without epistemological force, however. They are fatal for those who claim authority in virtue of the epistemological high ground. They level out the epistemological terrain just as the empirical studies level out the scientific terrain.

4. The nanosecond joke is due to Steve Shapin.

5. In fact, first-flush discourse analysis did not examine such work very closely; rather it looked at published papers and sought to mount in-principle, methodological arguments; see, for example, Gilbert and Mulkay 1980.

of discourse analysis soon appeared (Collins 1983; Shapin 1984) and discourse analysis has been largely abandoned within SSK.[6]

Discourse analysis paved the way for more radical deconstruction which goes under the title of "reflexivity."[7] Those of the reflexive persuasion have noted the omnipervasiveness of the social construction of truth—it is, as McHugh noted, a conceptual rather than an empirical point—and have set out to sidestep all truth-making conventions. "New literary forms" are an important part of this movement, since single authorship is taken to be one conventional method of constructing certainty. Reflexive texts often use "multivocality" to avoid authority. Witty authors can write as though they were more than one person so as to prevent a text from reaching a conclusion; to each argument or rhetorical gambit there is always an answer or rhetorical counterplay. Eventually the dialogue peters out without coming to any conclusion. The absence of convergent argument draws ironic attention to the devices that are normally used to make conclusions come about. Indeed, as one of the Pinches (Pinch and Pinch 1988) points out, in the hands of less subtle authors, multivocality is merely a pernicious way of imposing authority, by making it seem as though everyone has been allowed a say, while the author retains control over the voices of opponents.

Subtle reflexivists realize that their work leads nowhere. For example, Woolgar has said that getting nowhere should be seen as an accomplishment, not a failure.[8] Nevertheless, on occasion reflexivists appear to claim that their work is associated with progress within the sociology of science: thus Woolgar and Ashmore (1988, 7) state that "The exploration of reflexivity is the next natural development of the relativist-constructivist perspective in the social study of science," and they supply a diagrammatic three-stage history of the field to reinforce their case. While they satirize their own "progressivist" depiction of the field with blithe headings and captions such as "The Next Step" (1988, 7) and by the observation that these authors would not "be quite so stupid as to introduce a definitive list of aims and arguments in the volume without their being some clever reflexive point to it all" (1988, 2), this is not taken so far as to eliminate all academic defence. One argument invokes consistency: "the growing confidence with which scholars have argued

6. But is still interesting to social psychologists; witness the success of Potter and Wetherell 1987.

7. For the most recent, full-blown, witty work in the reflexivist genre, see Ashmore 1989.

8. This was his comment from the floor (as recalled by Collins) at a conference on rhetoric and the strong program in Iowa in 1987.

that *natural* scientific knowledge is a social construct, is now accompanied by growing interest in the consequences of applying this same argument to knowledge generated by the *social* sciences" (1988, 1; emphasis in original). The interest in the social conditioning of knowledge can evidently be extended to our own knowledge claims; we have no right to exclude ourselves.

Of course such equivalence was also recommended by Bloor. But among reflexivists this assertion is accompanied by a second argument: that reflexivity brings extra dividends. Unlike Bloor, who would have science studies resemble natural science, reflexivists see the study of knowledge making as "an occasion for exploring new ways of addressing longstanding questions of knowledge and epistemology" (Woolgar and Ashmore 1988, 1–2). And, lest this be taken as one of the disingenuously listed "aims and arguments," we may note that Woolgar had earlier asserted that SSK "can only be a distraction from any attempt to come to terms with the fundamentals of knowledge production" (1983, 263). More recently the same author has noted that while SSK usefully challenges defenders of "'scientific method' . . . it leaves the distinct impression that deeper, more fundamental questions remain unanswered" (1988a, 98).

As we have implied, the consistency argument is unobjectionable. Woolgar (1983, 245) nicely makes the point that SSK has equivocated about the extent to which "the social world [is] regarded as fully a substitute for the natural world in knowledge determination." Outside of scientific Marxism, no social scientist would expect sociology to tell us the proper apperception of nature. When we talk of access to knowledge of nature we must mean access through the sciences. Of course insofar as self-appointed advocates of science seek to attribute the success of science to the pursuit of some set of rules or systematic behaviors, SSK challenges these accounts. As we have just seen, even Woolgar is happy with this "use" of SSK. These are, so to speak, the powers and limits of SSK. If SSK is turned on social science in general and on itself in particular, these powers and limitations turn with it. Just as SSK has no direct, unmediated route to nature, so reflexive study can expect no immediate access to the truths of the social world. Equally, the powers remain the same: Woolgar concludes his recent book-length study, *Science: The Very Idea*, by criticizing those who seek to prescribe rules of sociological inquiry by reference to natural scientific method (1988a, 106–8). If the call for reflexivity is simply—not "merely" but "simply"—a call for consistency, then this is all we can get from it: the powers and limitations of SSK applied to our claims to knowledge of the social world. How can it do anything more fundamental?

This prospect is, as we have said, unobjectionable. But it is not consequential. Even if, in Woolgar's words, we are left with the "distinct impression that deeper, more fundamental questions remain unanswered" (1988a, 98), reflexive analysis cannot answer these questions. Reflexivists do claim consequentiality for their work; in their writings they seek to derive it from a sort of phenomenological jump into the study not of social scientific knowledge but of knowing per se. Woolgar poses this issue in terms of the "Problem" (1983, 240–2; 1988a, 31–37). For Woolgar, the Problem concerns the revocable, indefinite, and nondemonstrable link which binds the objects of knowledge to our statements about those objects. How do we know that the chromatograph represents the chemical, that the respondent's answer represents his or her attitude, that the image in the telescope represents the world imaged through it? The Problem is thus "a general and irresolvable problem" of knowing (1983, 240). What reflexivity shows is the ubiquity of this problem. It occurs in epistemological theorizing but also at the laboratory bench and in the argumentational practice of social scientists.

According to Woolgar, the Problem is perceived by members as a series of "methodological horrors." He lists strategies by which practitioners can sidestep them (1988a, 33–36). For example, the Problem may be deemed a problem only for less sophisticated sciences (psychiatry suffers, but not medicine), or it may be construed as a technical problem whose solution will come when one's own science becomes more sophisticated (psychologists will soon be able to measure attitudes better). It may be recognized only as it applies to others, or it may be relegated to the status of a "made up" or "academic" problem.

Woolgar's identification of the Problem is very persuasive. But what are we to make of it; how does it benefit us to know of it? Clearly the Problem cannot be solved. Neither can it be bypassed by adopting a phenomenological policy of introspection. In 1983 it was, however, recommended (cautiously) that we "celebrate" it (1983, 263). Why, though, should reflexive analyses which draw attention to the Problem be valued or at least prized any more highly than other well-known skeptical philosophies? While other scientists and lay inquirers proceed by merely "managing" the Problem (and we can disclose this managing work; see Woolgar's recent emphasis on ethnography [1988b]), reflexive analyses face up to it. But facing up to it can only lead nowhere. It is hard to construe this as taking us, in Woolgar's words, into the fundamentals of knowledge production. Woolgar and the other reflexivists may stand steadfast in the path of the traffic, but a heroic description of the experience is misplaced. The traffic passes and they survive unscathed—but only because they have fallen down a hole in the road.

In sum, following the lead of the relativists, each new fashion in SSK has been more epistemologically daring, the reflexivists coming closest to self-destruction. Each group has made the same mistake at first; they have become so enamored of the power of their negative levers on the existing structures as to believe they rest on bedrock. But this is not the case. Though each level can prick misplaced epistemological pretentions, they stand in the same relationship to each other as parallel cultures; no level has priority and each is a flimsy building on the plain. Accepting this we can freely use whatever epistemological "natural attitude" is appropriate for the purpose at hand; we can alternate between them as we will. That is what methodological relativism is about—the rejection of any kind of foundationalism and its replacement, not by permanent revolution but by permanent insecurity. To reverse the vertical scale of the metaphor, while SSK showed that science did not occupy the high ground of culture, the newer developments must be taken to demonstrate not the failure of SSK, but that there simply is no high ground.

In the absence of decisive epistemological arguments, how do we choose our epistemological stance? The answer is to ask not for the meaning but for the use.[9] Natural scientists, working at the bench, should be naive realists—that is what will get the work done. Sociologists, historians, scientists away from the bench, and the rest of the general public should be social realists. Social realists must experience the social world in a naive way, as the day-to-day foundation of reality (as natural scientists naively experience the natural world).[10] That is the way to understand the relationship between science and the rest of our cultural activities. Close description of

9. We mean this in the Wittgensteinian sense. We mean that the endlessly agonizing search for essential meanings is senseless, since the meaning of something equals its use in a form of life. Meaning and use are but two sides of the same coin. When we go on to analyze the French school, we will take advantage of this idea to examine the use/meaning of the semiotic approach. In other words, we will not engage in a scholarly exercise to uncover the roots of semiotic ideas; we will ask what the wholesale adoption of these ideas would mean for the practice of the sociology and history of scientific knowledge. Whatever the roots, that is the meaning of the semiotic approach for SSK.

10. For an analysis of the use of social realism and its relation to recent debates in the philosophy of social science, see Yearley 1988.

the human activity makes science look like any other kind of practical work. Detailed description dissolves epistemological mystery and wonder. This makes science one with our other cultural endeavors without making it necessary to deny that scientists have more skill, experience, and wisdom than others in the matters they deal with.

Notice that granting skill, experience, and wisdom is not quite the same as granting the *authority* that would follow from accepting natural realism as an epistemological foundation. The difference is important for several reasons. Social realism in studies of science discourages the sterile emulation of canonical models of scientific activity by social scientists and others. It discourages ordinary people from judging science against a criterion of infallibility; since science cannot deliver infallibility, to judge it thus is to risk widespread disillusion. Making science a continuous part with the rest of our culture should make us less intimidated and more ready to appreciate its beauty and accomplishments. It should make us more ready to use it for what it is, to value its insights and wisdom within rather than without the political and cultural process.

What use are the other epistemological levels that the game of chicken has opened out? First, their very existence has led to the end of epistemology. No one can take epistemological foundationalism seriously any more. The effect of meta-alternation is similar to that of cultural alternation in its broadening and liberalizing effect. More directly, discourse analysis is useful for analyzing discourse, and clearly there is a living and some joy in reflexivity (Collins 1989). The concerns of reflexivists are close to those of rhetoricians; complete skepticism regarding the very matter of argumentation is a good starting point for the analysis of the force of argument. We believe, however, that the big job of sorting out the relationship between cultural enterprises has to be done from the level of social realism. The work can be done from no other level.

The French School

One of the most attractive approaches in the study of science to have appeared in very recent years has been that of "l'école" de l'Ecole de Mines in Paris. The principal actors are Michel Callon and Bruno Latour; Latour's sparkling writings having been especially influential in the English-speaking world. Both the French and the reflexivists have been attracted by the lure of consistency. In the French case it is a matter of consistency in the treatment of all dichotomies. For example, natural "actants" and human actors must be treated symmetrically. This strategy too requires great daring, but like full-blown reflexivity it can only bring annihilation or retreat—retreat from the traffic or retreat from the world. What does the French work do for us? What is its use?[11]

In spite of early coincidences of interest, the starting point of the French approach is quite different from that of SSK. Whereas the Anglo-American tradition of epistemological thought is concerned with how we represent reality (what the relationship is between the world and our representational devices), the Continental tradition more naturally asks how anything can represent anything else. This has led some reviewers to consider the French work to be the most progressively radical approach in science studies (see, for example, de Vries 1988, 8). Whereas Bloor's tenet of symmetry seems radical within the Anglo-American tradition, the French approach extends symmetry of treatment to many more dimensions. Treating natural "actants" and human actors symmetrically comes naturally from the semiotic starting point. Crucially, however, whereas the Anglo-American approach, with its concern with our representations of the natural world, is essentially human-centered, the semiotic extension of the question about representation has no center. From this viewpoint it is just as natural to ask how natural objects represent us as to ask how we represent natural objects. A cardboard cutout of a traffic policeman is a representation of us;[12] its power, as an actant, to control us is just as suitable a case for analysis as the power with which the mapmaker "dominates the world" (Latour 1987, 224).

The effect of SSK has been to show that the apparent independent power of the natural world is granted by human beings in social negotiation. Because the special power and authority of natural scientists comes from their privileged access to an independent realm, putting humans at the center removes the special authority. In the work of the French school, symmetry between all kinds of actants once more removes humans from the pivotal role. This is the key to understanding the "uses" of the French approach. It explains why the case studies which are emerging from this approach look prosaic when viewed from SSK. While the approach seems, on the one hand, radical and shocking, on the other hand it does not provide any countercommonsensical surprises. Where it is novel vis-á-vis earlier SSK approaches it is essentially more conservative.

11. See also some recent reviews of Latour's books (Yearley 1987; Shapin 1988).
12. In Europe, cardboard policemen are sometimes used to warn of danger on the roads.

As we will see, the extension of the principle of symmetry to other dimensions makes it less easy to be symmetrical in the original Bloorian sense. Symmetry of treatment between the true and the false requires a human-centered universe.

Laboratory life

In retrospect, the divergence between the human-centered and the French approach can be traced back to *Laboratory Life* (Latour and Woolgar 1979). A central idea in this book is the "inscription device." Latour saw the biological laboratory filled with devices for making inscriptions—inscriptions that were then transformed and combined with other transcriptions and eventually published. These representations were the reality-stuff of science—gaining truth precisely as they became separate from the messy activity of the laboratory. The scientific trick was to transform the to and fro of daily life in the laboratory into a paper transcription which could move outside the laboratory, creating the reality of the phenomenon under investigation. The representation had a power that the activity in the laboratory did not have.

The idea of the force of an inscription comes from the methodology of the study. The method espoused by Latour was observation informed by the perspective of the estranged visitor. Participation, the method of *verstehende* sociology, to which the controversy studies (Collins 1981) aspired, played no part in *Laboratory Life*. Latour may have worked in the Salk Institute, but he proudly proclaimed his failure to understand what he was doing. It is this that makes inscription devices appear autonomous. That is exactly how they are meant to look to those who are less than expert. The point is that in controversial areas it is experts who are the first consumers of inscriptions, not outsiders; to experts, everything is mutable. The participant is struck by this mutability whereas the stranger sees immutable forces.

Those who took an interpretative approach to the study of scientific controversies and who tried to grasp the expert's viewpoint were, then, less enthusiastic about granting to inscriptions the degree of autonomy implied in *Laboratory Life*. For example, Travis looked at a controversy within the biological sciences—over the chemical transfer of learned behavior—and found that the inscriptions produced by mass spectrometers in biological laboratories were not universally accepted as representing reality. A mass spectrometer, like all other technologies, requires skilled interpretation. According to Travis's study, spectrometry traces that did not fit with favored hypotheses of experts outside the source laboratory were rejected by them.

The difference, then, between the approach of the controversy studies and that of *Laboratory Life* was in the extent to which the former saw the granting of authority to inscriptions and other representations as an active and revocable process—one which could be halted at any time. *Laboratory Life* stressed the "once and for all" production and release of an inscription with autonomous power.

In the early days, we could see this as a difference in emphasis rather than principle. Furthermore, in recent passages Latour talks of the amount of work that would be required to challenge inscriptions. He leaves the door open to their deconstruction at the hands of sufficiently determined humans. On such occasions he could still be interpreted as differing from SSK only in emphasis (with the inscriptions growing steadily more powerful). But there is substantial ambiguity around this point. Certainly the idea that representations have power is clearly expressed in Latour's later formulation—the "immutable mobile" (1987, 227). Here again, agency is granted to pieces of paper—the first step on the road to granting agency to things. Admittedly the stress is on the *granting* of agency—the inscriptions have to be inscribed and the immutable mobiles have to be created and to gain assent. But once the agency has been granted, the inscriptions gain a degree of autonomy. They can compel further assent. It is in this that their immutability lies.

Scallops and things

So far we have discussed the agency of things that have been created by humans—as in the Salk Institute. But French-style radical symmetry draws no boundary between objects that have been created and those that occur naturally. Here we run into some difficulty of interpretation, for if the whole subject matter is signs and representations, it is hard to know exactly how we should make the distinction between that which occurs naturally and that which is made. Does this distinction too lie only in the way things are taken to represent one another? In the face of these complex problems we must fall back once more on asking not for the *real* meaning but for the use. What does the semiotic approach do for our understanding of the world?

Callon's (1986) paper on the scallops of St. Brieuc Bay is a good starting point. Consider first Callon's remarks on the nature of the boundary between the natural and the social:

The observer must abandon all a priori distinctions between natural and social events. He must reject the hypothesis of a definite boundary which separates the two. These divisions are considered to be conflictual, for they are the result of analysis rather than its point of departure. Further, the observer must consider that the repertoire of categories which he uses, the entities which are mobilized, and the relationships between these are all topics for actors' discussions. Instead of imposing a pre-established grid of analysis upon these, the observer follows the actors in order to identify the manner in which these define and associate the different elements by which they build and explain their world, whether it be social or natural. (200–201).

The capacity of certain actors to get other actors whether they be human beings, institutions or natural entities—to comply with them depends upon a complex web of interrelations in which Society and Nature are intertwined. (201)

In both of these quotations the principles of radical symmetry are set out.[13] Callon's analysis proceeds symmetrically, using his vocabulary of problematization, *intéressement, enrollment,* and mobilization. Here is how he treats the mobilization of the scallops.

If the scallops are to be enrolled, they must first be willing to anchor themselves to the collectors. But this anchorage is not easy to achieve. In fact the three researchers will have to lead their longest and most difficult negotiations with the scallops. (211)

The researchers are ready to make any kind of concession in order to lure the larvae into their trap. What sort of substances do larvae prefer to anchor on? Another series of transactions is necessary to answer this question.

It was noted that the development of the scallops was slower with collectors made of straw, broom, or vegetable horsehair. These types of supports are too compressed and prevent water from circulating correctly through the collector. (213)

13. Just how radical the symmetry is, however, is not entirely clear. Though as we will see, the scallops of St. Brieuc Bay are to be treated as actors on a par with the fishermen, the creation of symmetry is very much in the hands of the analysts. The analysts remain in control the whole time, which makes their imposition of symmetry on the world seem something of a conceit. Would not complete symmetry require an account from the point of view of the scallops? Would it be sensible to think of the scallops enrolling the scallop researchers so as to given themselves a better home and to protect their species form the ravages of the fishermen? Does the fact that there is no *Sociological Review Monograph* series written by and for scallops make a difference to the symmetry of the story? Fortunately we do not need an answer to these questions before we continue our analysis.

These passages are written in just the same style as the passage in the next paragraph where Callon discusses what the scientists will count as signifying successful attachment of the scallops to the collectors: "At what number can it be confirmed and accepted that scallops, in general, do anchor themselves?" To answer this question the researchers had to negotiate not with the scallops but with their scientific colleagues. It turned out that they met little resistance to their preferred definition of a "significant" degree of attachment because—and here the problem is highlighted—"of the negotiations which were carried out with the scallops in order to increase the interessement and of the acts of enticement which were used to retain the larvae (horsehair rather than nylon, etc.)" (213).

We see in these passages some of the fruits of radical symmetry. While the scientists had to negotiate with their colleagues over the meaning of "successful anchorage," their success came about partly because the scallops had already agreed to anchor themselves in reasonable numbers. The scallops are full parties to the negotiations.

Callon's account shows how all the parties—fishermen, scientists, scallops—at first give their assent to the networking ambitions of the research scientists. But catastrophe strikes in later years. The fishermen suddenly dredge up all the experimental scallops and sell them. The scallops too withdraw their cooperation:

> The researchers place their nets but the collectors remain hopelessly empty. In principle the larvae anchor, in practice they refuse to enter the collectors. The difficult negotiations which were successful the first time fail in the following years. . . . The larvae detach themselves from the researchers' project and a crowd of other actors carry them away. The scallops become dissidents. The larvae which complied are betrayed by those they were thought to represent. (219–20)

The crucial final quotation is: "To establish . . . that larvae anchor, the complicity of the scallops is needed as much as that of the fishermen" (222).

Callon's account of the negotiations between the scientists and the fishermen is a fine study in the relationships between technology and society. But as a social account of the making of knowledge it is prosaic, because the story of the scallops themselves is an asymmetrical old-fashioned scientific story. A symmetrical, SSK-type account would analyze the way it came to be agreed, first, that the scallops did anchor, and second—at a later date—that they did not anchor. Into this analysis the question of whether or not the scallops complied would not enter. The informing assumption would be that whether there were more or fewer scallops anchoring early and late in the story did not affect the extent to which scallops were seen to be anchoring early and late. No SSK story could rely on the complicity of the scallops; at best it could only rely on human-centered accounts of the complicity of the scallops.

To look at the difficulty from a different angle, let us ask what traditional SSK studies would gain from radical symmetrism and the actor-network perspective. Should the Collinsian story of gravity waves (1975, 1985) be retold granting agency to the gravity waves in addition to the scientists? Callon's description of scallops as actors gains some of its rhetorical appeal from the fact that scallops are living things. One can just about imagine them deciding whether or not to anchor themselves to the horsehair collectors. Similarly, Latour is following a familiar figure of speech when he describes tides and winds as "acting" on explorers' ships (1987, 221). It is more difficult in the case of gravity waves. But given the imaginative resources, what does it add to our understanding to say that gravity waves granted their allegiance to Joseph Weber but refused to grant it to anyone else? Far from adding to our understanding it seems to us that the resulting account would look just like the account of a conventional historian of science—except that the historian wouldn't talk of allegiances with gravity waves and failures of negotiations with gravity waves, but of discoveries and failures of experimental technique. The language changes, but the story remains the same.[14]

14. Is it just the vocabulary that is radical? Let us try the old trick of rewriting some of the quotations from Callon using the conventional language of the history of science. "If the scallops are to be enrolled, they must first be willing to anchor themselves to the collectors. But this anchorage is not easy to achieve. In fact the three researchers will have to lead their longest and most difficult negotiations with the scallops (211)." History of science version: If the scallops are to be cultivated they must anchor on the collectors. But anchorage is not easy to achieve. In fact the three researchers will have a lot of trouble developing appropriate techniques.

The researchers are ready to make any kind of concession in order to lure the larvae into their trap. What sort of substances do larvae prefer to anchor on? Another series of transactions is necessary to answer the question.

It was noted that the development of the scallops was slower with collectors made of straw, broom, or vegetable horsehair. These types of supports are too compressed and prevent water from circulating correctly through the collector. (213)

History of science version: The researchers are willing to try anything. What sort of substances do larvae prefer to anchor on? Another series of experiments is necessary to answer the question. It was noted that the development of the scallops was slower with collectors made of straw, broom, or vegetable horsehair. These types of

In any case, the complicity of the scallops (or whatever), if it is to play a part in accounts of this sort, ought to be properly recorded. How is the complicity of scallops to be measured? There is only one way we know of measuring the complicity of scallops, and that is by appropriate scientific research. If we are really to enter scallop behavior into our explanatory equations, then Callon must demonstrate his scientific credentials. He must show that he has a firm grip on the nature of scallops. There is not the slightest reason for us to accept his opinions on the nature of scallops if he is any less of a scallop scientist than the researchers he describes. In fact, we readers would prefer him to be *more* of a scallop expert than the others if he is to speak authoritatively on the subject. Is he an authority on scallops? Or did he merely report the scientists' views on the matter. If the latter, then we have two possibilities. One way of using scientists' reports is in a typical SSK study, traditionally sym-

---

supports are too compressed and prevent water from circulating correctly through the collector.

> The researchers place their nets but the collectors remain hopelessly empty. In principle the larvae anchor, in practice they refuse to enter the collectors. The difficult negotiations which were successful the first time fail in the following years. . . . The larvae detach themselves from the researchers' project and a crowd of other actors carry them away. The scallops become dissidents. The larvae which complied are betrayed by those they were thought to represent. (219–20)

> To establish . . . that larvae anchor, the complicity of the scallops is needed as much as that of the fishermen. (222)

The history of science version: The researchers place their nets, but the collectors remain hopelessly empty. In theory the larvae ought to anchor, in practice they don't. The difficult experiments which were successful the first time fail in the following years. . . . The larvae fail to attach themselves and get carried away. The larvae seem to have changed their nature—the first experiment apears to have succeeded under unrepresentative experimental conditions. To establish that larvae anchor, the tests must be safeguarded against the fishermen's interference, but this is only one factor in the experiment.

The reason why this is so easy is that the relationship between the scientists and the scallops in Callon's account is just as is found in the old history of science. Agency and responsibility are divided in the same way. In SSK, by contrast, agency is much more in the domain of the humans. For example, consider this passage from Collins's story of gravity waves (1985, 91): "It is not obvious how the credibility of the high flux case fell so low. In fact, it was not the single uncriticized experiment that was decisive; scientists rarely mentioned this in discussion. Obviously the sheer weight of negative opinion was a factor, but given the tractability, as it were, of all the negative evidence, it did not *have* to add up so decisively. There was a way of assembling the evidence, noting the flaws in each grain, such that outright rejection of the high flux claim was not the necessary inference."

metrical, and not in the least radically symmetrical. But if he really means what he says about the importance of the scallops as actors, and yet he persists with scientists' secondhand reports of scallops' behavior rather than providing firsthand expertise, then he gives us a pre-SSK study open to all the problems of asymmetry. Certainly we do not have a study that can offer us any surprises about the natural world, or one that clarifies the credibility and authority of science.

Doors and grooms

The problem of radical symmetrism, as we hope to have revealed, is that it must rest on routine methods of scientific research for that part of its evidence concerned with the nonhuman actants. There is no reason to suppose that sociologists are particularly good at gathering such evidence. The problem of method is very evident in Latour's recent work. The piece we look at is entitled "Where are the Missing Masses? Sociology of a Door."[15]

Latour treats as actors (or actants—it makes no difference) a door and an automatic door closer.[16] An automatic door closer is known colloquially in French as a "groom," by analogy with the human groom who might once have been a doorman. This does lend the door closer, like the scallops, a degree of anthropomorphic appeal, but this is certainly not true of the door itself. In the paper Latour sets out to explore the potency of doors (and other technological artifacts) as actors. In this he has a very grand purpose in mind. He intends to explain social order. His explanation of social order is that the constraints that are missing within existing social and political analysis of order (the missing masses) are to be found in things. Doors, and other artifacts, act as constant constraints upon our behavior. Though they are physical mechanisms, their effect is indistinguishable from normative or moral control: a door allows us to walk through only at a certain speed and only in a certain place in the wall; a cardboard policeman enforces the traffic code in a way similar to a real policeman; a seat-belt warning signal enforces the law on seat belts; my desk computer forces me to write instructions

15. This article has a long history. A version of it was published once in a refereed journal (Latour and Johnson 1988) and another version is due to appear in an edited volume (Latour forthcoming). The version we refer to is an in-between draft presented at the conference which spawned the edited volume. It is sometimes hard to know when Latour is being completely serious, but we will assume two publications of essentially the same article in refereed outlets is as good a sign as any.

16. Schaffer 1991 refers to the giving of life to inanimate objects as "hylozoism."

to it in an exact syntactical form. The missing masses (analogous to the missing mass that is required to explain the slow rate of expansion of the universe) are to be found in the technological things that surround us. We delegate actor status to these things and along the way we delegate power to them.

Now as explained in respect to Callon's analysis of scallops, imputing agency to things requires a method of analysis of their potency. It is no good just talking about inscriptions and immutable mobiles; I won't learn from a No Smoking sign why some people obey it while many others ignore it. Furthermore, the method must be something more than social analysis; it must be more than an analysis of what we grant to things and their representations on a moment-to-moment basis. If this was all there was to it, then, first, radical symmetry would have been abandoned and we would be back with an SSK-style human-centered, social-realist universe; and second, Latour would not have discovered the missing masses. The missing masses, if they are to count as a discovery, must lie in the agency of things outside of ourselves.

Given that we want to understand the power and agency of doors and door closers, the appropriate method, we would think, would include something of mechanical engineering, something of materials science, and something of the more engineering-oriented parts of architecture. Alternatively it might consist of detailed examination of the use of doors; some videotaping of people going in and out of doors would be a good start. It is clear that the interpretative method is unusable, since doors have no social life in which we could participate. This fits well with the scientific "unity of method" first offered in *Laboratory Life*; we may open doors a hundred times a day, but we are all strangers in the world of things.

Interpretation is no good. What method is left? It ought to be science, but Latour is not an expert in any of the fields of science that would help him understand doors, nor does he have videotapes or other close records of doors in use. How then does he convince us of the potency of the agency of doors? The question is not where are the missing masses? but where is the missing method? It turns out to be the method of counterfactual hypotheses.

In order to understand the power of doors we are asked to imagine how it would be if they were not there:

> Now, draw two columns . . . in the right column, list the work
> people would have to do if they had no door; in the left column write
> down the gentle pushing (or pulling) they have to do in order to fulfil
> the same tasks. Compare the two columns: the enormous effort on
> the right is balanced by the little one on the left, and this is all

thanks to hinges. I will define this transformation of a major effort into a minor one, by the words displacement or translation or delegation or shifting; I will say that we have delegated . . . to the hinge the work of reversibly solving the hole-wall dilemma. . . . everytime you want to know what a non-human does, simply imagine what other humans or other non-humans would have to do were this character not present. (4–5)

Latour exploits the imaginative possibilities to the limit. If there were no door in a wall, anyone wanting to enter would have to demolish part of the wall and rebuild it again after passing through. On the other hand, if there were merely a hole, then cold winds would enter causing the occupants to become ill. In the case of La Villete, the draughts would get in and the historians' drafts would not get out. One may use counterfactual method as such a rich source of jests precisely because the writer is in complete control over the counterfactual scenario. That is why it is a dangerous method in history. What was the power of the exact contour of Cleopatra's nose? What was the historical contribution of Napoleon's breakfast on the morning of the Battle of Waterloo? What is the power, not of a door, but of a row of bricks in a wall; take the bricks away and wall and roof will fall down killing everyone inside. This row of bricks, it turns out, has the force and responsibility of the row of strong men which would otherwise be required to support the wall. Precisely the same number of strong men are required to replace two rows of bricks, or half a row of bricks.[17] The counterfactual method is very exciting to use because the imagination is given

17. Actually a similar analysis of doors has already been done by a British comedian. Rik Mayall once had an act on BBC television in which he played "Kevin Turvey—Investigative Reporter." Turvey, portrayed as an unprepossessing youth from Birmingham in a horrible blue parka, sat in silhouette in a black revolving chair turning dramatically to the camera as his report began. He would begin to describe his investigation of some subject of moment, but almost immediately would lose track, and his description would degenerate into a hilarious account of the inconsequentialities of moment-to-moment existence.

In one episode, "The Supernatural," Turvey reports that he is in his kitchen when he hears a ringing noise which he eventually identifies as someone at the back door:

So I got up—right? Went out into the hall. 'Cause, well, you've got to get out into the hall to get to the back door you see. The only alternative is, like, smashing down the wall next to the cooker. And I'm not gonna get involved in all that again—right?

Anyway, I got to the back door—right? Opened it up and everything. That was easy really—it's—Well, I've done it loads of times before. Just got to twist the handle a bit and open up the door. Piece of piss really. Well it's made out of wood . . . etc.

such free rein. It is like a child's toy clock face; the hands may be set anywhere, but it is not of much use for telling the time.

The absence of methodological control over fantasy allows Latour to develop his concept of "delegation" unhindered by traditional problems. Using imaginative license to the full, he is able to tell convincing stories about the way we delegate power to technological artifacts. The lack of control over method allows control to be given to things. This way he appears to resolve a major philosophical problem—the distinction between action and behavior—but *appears* is the operative word. The distinction continues to trouble those who actually try to make machines that can appropriate human responsibilities. Latour sometimes seems to realize that things don't fulfill quite the same duties as humans: "Three rows of delegated non-human actants (hinges, springs and hydraulic pistons) replace, 90% of the time, either an undisciplined bell-boy . . . or, for the general public, the programme instructions that have to do with remembering-to-close-the-door-when-it-is-cold" (11). This 90 percent is about as far as Latour can go, and even that realization does not come from the counterfactual method (which could produce any percentage figure desired). Superficial analysis gives rise to the claim that the door closer "substitutes for the actions of people, and is a delegate that permanently occupies the position of a human; . . . and it shapes human action by prescribing back what sort of people should pass through the door" (12). But the author himself notes that harder work is required to solve this kind of problem properly: "Specialists of robotics have very much abandoned the pipe-dream of total automation; they learned the hard way that many skills are better delegated to humans than to non-humans, whereas others may be moved away from incompetent humans" (25 n. 5).[18]

The phrase "the hard way" is exactly to the point. There are a number of hard ways of finding out about our relationship to ma-

18. In a later version of the paper we find a note 9 which reads: "In this type of analysis there is no effort to attribute forever certain competences to human and others to non-humans. The attention is focussed on following how *any* set of competences is *distributed* through various entities." This note describes the position much better. To reiterate, however, if we wanted to discover the distribution of competences among nonhumans, we would not normally go first to a sociologist or philosopher. One critical reader of this paper has suggested that a more sympathetic treatment of Latour would see him as trying to produce a description of the experienced materiality of things. But we simply do not experience the materiality of doors as having anything to do with saving us from the effort of knocking down walls, whether they be those of La Villette or Kevin Turvey's kitchen (see n. 17). If we need a description of the materiality of things—we thought this was what we already had within the prosaic view of science—this is not a good way of going about it.

chines and other artifacts. Scientists, technologists, philosophers, builders of intelligent machines, and social scientists all struggle in their different ways to make progress along the route. The builders of intelligent machines have one method: they try to model human beings; the scientists, technologists, and philosophers work hand in hand using another method: it is called natural science. What sociology of scientific knowledge provides is a third method, no longer subservient to accounts of the work of the scientists and technologists and the stories of philosophers but rooted in a special understanding of social life. It would be a tragedy to surrender this new way of comprehending the world to the accounts of scientists, technologists, and philosophers. It would also be a tragedy not to exploit the particular understanding of our relationship to machines that this method allows us.

Latour's treatment of the technological world fails in three ways. First, it enrolls the false ally of the counterfactual method. Second, since the counterfactual method fails, the story of the power of things can amount to no more than technologists' secondhand accounts; it is sociologically prosaic. Third, the distinction between human action and the behavior of things and its significance for the automation of human skills is, ironically, one area where sociologists of scientific knowledge have the ability to speak authoritatively as scientists. If there were any areas where we might claim to know something, this would certainly be among the foremost;[19] yet it is just here that the French school passes the responsibility by.

Consider this third failing. SSK has put us in a position to understand what knowledge is, what humans do as they make knowledge, what the difference is between the social construction of knowledge and the asocial operation of machines and other things, how the operation of machines may seem to pass for knowledge, and what the limits are on the replacement of human skills by artificial means. All these understandings have come through exploring the difference between humans and things, the difference between actions and mere behavior, and through criticizing the mistaken attempts—for example, by rationalist philosophers of science—to describe human action as formula-bound behavior.[20]

19. Other areas would include science education and the public understanding of science and of scientific authority. See for examples, Collins and Shapin 1989; Collins 1988; Wynne 1982; Yearley 1989.

20. Interestingly, the Latour-Turvey (see n. 17) style of description of everyday things can itself be used as part of a critique of the ability of machines to act as humans. It can be used as a critique of artificial intelligence. One might think of "L-T" descriptions as ironic dramatizations of the commonsense, tacit knowledge

The consequences of the semiotic method amount to a backward step, leading us to embrace once more the very priority of techno-logical, rule-bound description, adopted from scientists and technologists, that we once learned to ignore. This backward step has happened as a consequence of the misconceived extension of symmetry that takes humans out of their pivotal role. If nonhumans are actants, then we need a way of determining their power. This is the business of scientists and technologists; it takes us directly back to the scientists' conventional and prosaic accounts of the world from which we escaped in the early 1970s.

Conclusion

In this paper we have reviewed two post-relativist positions in science studies. One group has sought to penetrate to "foundational" knowledge by turning constructionist tools on constructionism; the other has aimed to generalize symmetry by treating all actants that are party to the scientific enterprise in the same manner. We have shown the shortcomings of both approaches.

Despite their considerable differences, the two positions have one important feature in common, a feature which distinguishes them from relativism or constructionism. Both supply an elaborate vocabulary for describing the means of knowledge making, but the vocabulary does not allow explanations of why certain knowledge claims are accepted and others are not. In the case of Woolgar, for example, we have seen the labels which he gives to ways of managing the Problem in everyday life, such as treating it as merely a technical difficulty (1988a, 34). The labels delineate the range of strategies which may be adopted. Equally, Callon (1986, 206) refers to the strategy which scientists may use of trying to set up an "obligatory passage point" through which the arguments of others have to pass. And when describing the work of cartographers and

---

that humans have by virtue of their culture. These cannot be expressed in programming rules, because of their potential to ramify explosively, and because it is never clear how much needs to be said explicitly. Counterfactual hypotheses have just the same elusiveness as common sense. The elusiveness of common sense was not noticed while artificial intelligence was a dream; it has been discovered by the builders of intelligent machines only with the failure of their project. Only now is it becoming clear to them that nonhuman actants have no common sense. The counterfactual method is still unfortunately bolstering the dreams of semioticians. Dreyfus (1976) first makes this point with respect to artificial intelligence. For a more recent discussion of the problem utilizing some of the insights of SSK, see Collins 1990.

classification makers, Latour (1987, 223) talks of stages in grasping the object of knowledge: making it mobile, rendering it stable, and making it combinable. Thus, a map fixes the limits of, say, an island; allows knowledge of the island to be taken away from the island's shores; and permits this knowledge to be transmitted and used in conjunction with other geographical expertise.

Both approaches allow suggestive names to be given to common rhetorical-argumentational strategies. Other people can easily recognize things to which they too can give these names. (This may be part of the current appeal of these authors' work.) But at best these names identify common moves in knowledge making. When scientists try to establish themselves or their technique as an obligatory passage point, it will benefit the analyst to be able to put a well-known name to the strategy. That, however, does not tell us why only some actors have been able to get away with enforcing their view of the world. We still must ask: why one map rather than another? What is in the relationship between the island and the map that makes it a successful map? Is there something more than the social relations of the mapmaker with clients and colleagues? If there is, what is it? If there is not, what is all the fuss about? We have been there already and tried to explain as well as describe.

This is not to say that every piece of science studies must be an explanation, but it must leave room for explanation. In their emphasis on form, the reflexivity and actor-network theory approaches both exclude explanation in the descriptive languages they provide.[21]

In sum, the game of epistemological chicken as played by relativists and their successors has been destructive. The French actor-network model is philosophically radical, but when we ask for its use, it turns out to be essentially conservative—a poverty of method making it subservient to a prosaic view of science and technology. While the reflexivist players have escaped the fate of the foolhardy by jumping into a hole in the road from which there is no escape, the adherents of the actor network turn out to have crossed the road well before the traffic was in sight, leaving only their ventriloquist's voices echoing between the curbs. Listen and understand, but do not follow too closely. Neither program is foundational. Meta-alternation, not oblivion, is where these programs should lead.

21. Furthermore, both disavow their scientific (or naturalistic) credentials (Woolgar 1988a, 98; Latour 1988, 165). Unlike naturalistic SSK, they search for an alternative route which turns out not to be explanatory—not just in fact but in orientation (see Woolgar 1988a, 108).

The true relativist's world is a world without foundations. What follows? The discovery that the foundations of physics are not as secure as was once believed makes no difference to what it means to be a good physicist—though it does mean that physics cannot claim authority over competing knowledge claims in virtue of epistemology. Now we have the same lesson writ large. The discovery that all foundations of knowledge are as fragile as those of the physicist gives us the opportunity to alternate between worlds, but it makes no difference to what it means to be a good sociologist or a good historian of scientific knowledge. Of course we cannot claim epistemological authority either, as though we ever had a chance. We can only compete on even terms for our share of the world with all the usual weapons. In the relativist's world you have to decide what you want to do; epistemology does not make the decision for you. But once you have decided what to do, all there is left is to do it.

REFERENCES

Ashmore, M., 1989. *The Reflexive Thesis: Wrighting Sociology of Scientific Knowledge.* Chicago: University of Chicago Press.

Berger, P. L. 1963. *Invitation to Sociology.* Garden City, N.Y.: Anchor Books.

Bloor, D. 1973. Wittgenstein and Mannheim on the Sociology of Mathematics. *Studies in the History and Philosophy of Science* 4:173–91.

———. 1976. *Knowledge and Social Imagery.* London: Routledge and Kegan Paul.

Callon, M. 1986. Some Elements of a Sociology of Translation: Domestication of the Scallops and the Fishermen of St. Brieuc Bay. In J. Law ed., *Power, Action, and Belief: A New Sociology of Knowledge?* London: Routledge and Kegan Paul, 196–233.

Collins, H. M. 1975. The Seven Sexes: A Study in the Sociology of a Phenomenon, or the Replication of Experiments in Physics. *Sociology* 9:205–24.

———. 1983. An Empirical Relativist Programme in the Sociology of Scientific Knowledge. In K. Knorr and M. J. Mulkay eds., *Science Observed.* Beverly Hills: Sage, pp. 85–114.

———. 1985. *Changing Order: Replication and Induction in Scientific Practice.* Beverly Hills: Sage.

———. 1988. Public Experiments and Displays of Virtuosity: The Core-Set Revisited. *Social Studies of Science* 18: 725–48.

———. 1989. Tu Quoque. Review of Malcolm Ashmore, *The Reflexive Thesis. THES.* no. 904, 2 March 1990, 20.

———. 1990. *Artificial Experts: Social Knowledge and Intelligent Machines.* Cambridge: MIT Press.

Collins, H. M., ed. 1981 *Knowledge and Controversy: Studies of Modern Natural Science.* Special Issue of *Social Studies of Science* 11 (1).

Collins, H. M., and S. Shapin. 1989. Experiment, Science Teaching, and the New History and Sociology of Science. In M. Shortland and A. Warwick, eds., *Teaching the History of Science*. Oxford: Blackwell, 67–79.

De Vries, G. 1988. Transferring Knowledge: Science and Its Practices. Review article including Latour's book. *EASST Newsletter* 7:5–12.

Dreyfus, Hubert. 1979. *What Computers Can't Do*. New York: Harper and Row.

Gilbert, G. N., and M. Mulkay. 1980. Contexts of Scientific Discourse: Social Accounting in Experimental Papers. In K. Knorr Cetina, R. Krohn, and R. Whitley, eds. *The Social Process of Scientific Investigation*. Dordrecht: Reidel, 269–94.

———. 1984. *Opening Pandora's Box: A Sociological Account of Scientists' Discourse*. Cambridge: Cambridge University Press.

Latour, B. 1987. *Science in Action*. Milton Keynes: Open University Press.

———. 1988. The Politics of Explanation: An Alternative. In S. W. Woolgar, ed., *Knowledge and Reflexivity: New Frontiers in the Sociology of Knowledge*. Beverly Hills: Sage, 155–76.

———. Forthcoming. Where Are the Missing Masses? Sociology of a Few Mundane Artifacts. In W. Bijker and J. Law, eds., *Constructing Networks and Systems*. Cambridge: MIT Press.

Latour, B., and J. Johnson. 1988. Mixing Humans with Non-Humans: Sociology of a Door-Opener. *Social Problems* 35:298–310.

Latour, B., and S. Woolgar. 1979. *Laboratory Life: The Social Construction of Scientific Facts*. Beverly Hills: Sage.

McHugh, P. 1971. On the Failure of Positivism. In J. D. Douglas, ed., *Understanding Everyday Life*. London: Routledge and Kegan Paul, 320–35.

Mulkay, M., and G. N. Gilbert. 1982. Joking Apart: Some Recommendations concerning the Analysis of Scientific Culture. *Social Studies of Science* 12:585–615.

Mulkay, M., J. Potter, and S. Yearley. 1983. Why an Analysis of Scientific Discourse Is Needed. In K. D. Knorr Cetina and M. Mulkay, eds., *Science Observed: Perspectives on the Social Study of Science*. London: Sage, 171–203.

Pinch, T., and T. Pinch. 1988. Reservations about Reflexivity and New Literary Forms, or Why Let the Devil Have All the Good Tunes? In S. W. Woolgar, ed., *Knowledge and Reflexivity: New Frontiers in the Sociology of Knowledge*. London: Sage, 178–97.

Potter, J., and M. Wetherell. 1987. *Discourse and Social Psychology: Beyond Attitudes and Behaviour*. London: Sage.

Schaffer, S. 1991. The Eighteenth Brumaire of Bruno Latour. *Studies in the History and Philosophy of Science* 22(1):174–92.

Shapin, S. 1984. Talking History: Reflections on Discourse Analysis. *Isis* 75:276, 125–28.

———. 1988. Following Scientists Around. Review of Latour 1987. *Social Studies of Science* 18:533–50.

Travis, G. D. L. 1981. Replicating Replication? Aspects of the Social Construction of Learning in Planarian Worms. In Collins 1981, 11–32.

Woolgar, S. W. 1983. Irony in the Social Study of Science. In K. D. Knorr and M. Mulkay, eds., *Science Observed.* Beverly Hills: Sage, 239–66.

———. 1988a. *Science: The Very Idea.* Chichester: Ellis Horwood and London: Tavistock.

———. 1988b. Reflexivity is the Ethnographer of the Text. In S. W. Woolgar, ed., *Knowledge and Reflexivity: New Frontiers in the Sociology of Knowledge.* Beverly Hills: Sage, 14–34.

Woolgar, S. W. and M. Ashmore. 1988. The Next Step: An Introduction to the Reflexive Project. In S. W. Woolgar, ed., *Knowledge and Reflexivity: New Frontiers in the Sociology of Knowledge.* Beverly Hills: Sage, 1–11.

Wynne, B. 1982. *Rationality or Ritual? The Windscale Inquiry and Nuclear Decisions In Britain.* Chalfont St. Giles, Bucks.: British Soc. Hist. Sci. Monograph.

Yearley, S. 1985. Representing Geology: Davy's Presentation of Science at the Royal Institution. In T. Shinn and R. Whitley, eds., *Expository Science: Forms and Functions of Popularisation.* Dordrecht: Reidel, pp. 79–101.

———. 1987. The Two Faces of Science. Review of Latour 1987. *Nature* 326 (6115): 23–29 April, 754.

———. 1988. Settling Accounts: Accounts, Action, and Sociological Explanation. *British Journal of Sociology* 39:578–99.

———. 1989. Bog Standards: Science and Conservation at a Public Inquiry. *Social Studies of Science* 19:421–38.

11

Some Remarks about Positionism: A Reply to Collins and Yearley

Steve Woolgar

> While reflection on a problem by no means always produces a solution, reflexivity is the key to the development of both theory and methodology in social sciences.
>
> Hammersley and Atkinson 1983

> When adherents to a scientific movement flaunt their unconcern with "global inconsistency" or reflexivity, just as when they flaunt illiteracy, illogic and fanaticism, they often inadvertently reveal what it is they have to hide, and why they should not be taken seriously.
>
> Turner 1990

There is no question that the sociology of scientific knowledge (SSK) has been an important and successful perspective within the social studies of science (broadly defined to include history, philosophy, and sociology of science, as well as less visible interest from economics, psychology, and political science). It is clear, for example,

Since this is the third version of this reply, acknowledgements are due to a number of people for assisting the transition between versions. Harry Collins kindly organized an informal meeting at University of Bath on 10 February 1990. He allowed me to tape-record the helpful comments of the participants (Wiebe Bijker, Harry Collins, Dave Gooding, Bruno Latour, Dave Travis, Gerard de Vries, and Steve Yearley) but prevented me from using them in this reply. Malcolm Ashmore and Jonathan Potter persuaded me that my first (conventional) form of reply might be misunderstood as lacking consciousness of its own lack of reflexivity. Consequently in a second version I tried to situate the reply within a conversation about the limitations of conventional formats for displaying "positions" and defending them consistently (cf. Woolgar 1989b). I am grateful to Keith Grint, Leslie Libetta, Janet Low, and Andrew Pickering for suggesting that my attempt to "bolt on" disruptive voices might prove confusing to the reader. My second effort failed, it seems, because I tried to deploy reflexivity as a formulaic adjunct to a main argument. This third, current version has no voices and *appears* remarkably like the first version. One difference, of course, is the inclusion in this account of the history of its writing. Since this history (and its account) makes the almost identical third version much more reflexive than the first, I have further support for the point that formulaic mimicry (of the kind exemplified by Harry Collins in his reply: "All Together Now"—see chap. 1, n. 10) is no guarantee of good reflexive practice.

327

that many of the contributors to this volume have been affected to some degree by the "relativist" dictates associated with the work of Harry Collins. SSK has been especially important in revitalizing the epistemic dimensions of social studies of science and in engaging certain philosophical preconceptions about the nature of science.

The piece by Collins and Yearley (chap. 10)—henceforth Candy[1]—is couched as a response to what they term "postrelativist" arguments in social studies of science: principally the two positions they call "reflexivity" and "the French school." Their piece makes clear, I believe, that despite its past success, there is now a question mark over the future value of the Bath variant of SSK[2] for the overall well-being of social studies of science. Candy adopt a narrowly negative stance toward postrelativist arguments. This stance is much to be regretted, since our clear priority is to find ways of incorporating Bath-SSK within currently evolving research perspectives. Our common aim should be to find ways of retaining Bath-SSK as part of these new developments, to persuade it out of its tendency to constitute itself as a separate orthodoxy, and to make sure its proponents don't get left behind. Accordingly, the main thrust of this reply will be to diagnose the condition of insularity and offer a prognosis. The recommendation is that Bath-SSK needs to broaden its intellectual horizons so as to realize its potential to inform key ideas in social theory and to see the significance of social studies of science for wider issues in intellectual scholarship.

On one point Candy are right. The argument between them and reflexivity *is* about a failure of nerve. For Candy, postrelativist arguments constitute needless danger, a kind of reckless flirtation with unknown forces which, they suggest, can only be counterproductive. But for many of the rest of us, postrelativist arguments are a necessary and inevitable part of the overall dynamic of social studies of science. Indeed it is not hard to see that the strength and excitement of social studies of science over the years has been precisely its willingness to explore perspectives and arguments which initially seemed counterintuitive. One need only think of the initial reaction to suggestions that the content of scientific knowledge could be understood as a social product to appreciate the magnitude of the shifts which can and should be made. In this context, Candy

1. The term Candy emerged at a meeting of the Discourse Analysis workshop (Department of Social Sciences, Loughborough University, 31 April-May 1990), which the author was unable to attend.

2. The Bath variant of SSK is referred to as Bath-SSK throughout, an admittedly cumbersome way of signaling differences between the particular arguments of Candy and of others within SSK.

display a disappointing conservatism, a failure of nerve which betrays the central vitality of social studies of science. We clearly need to understand what prompted this stasis.

The central significance of social studies of science is that it addresses fundamental questions about the nature of knowing, and it works through these questions in relation to empirical examples; the power of demonstration by example is one of the secrets of SSK's success. From the outset, researchers in social studies of science recognized the special strategic value of their topic: science is not only a powerful knowledge-generating institution, a highly valued and well-supported social system; but also a highly revered belief system, encompassing especially prized methods for the generation of knowledge. Consequently although the social study of science is about a particular social institution, it is also about the practices and methods of knowing and representing which permeate every aspect of our everyday lives. To the extent that we are representing, adducing, summarizing, portraying, deducing, using evidence, interpreting, in everything we do, our practice embodies deep preconceptions about what it is to be scientific, to reason adequately, to know, and so on. Hence, science—the culture and practice of those called scientists—is only the tip of the iceberg of a much more general phenomenon: representation. This is hardly surprising, since science is both derived from and influences the practices of ordinary everyday life.

Discussions in and about science thus provide the official party line—so to speak—on the much more pervasive phenomenon of representation. Of course natural scientific practice is a strategic site to begin to confront our own entrenchment in the ideology of representation. But the big mistake made by Bath-SSK is then to presume that our own analysts' practice and culture are essentially different and distinct from the characteristics we identify in the practice and culture of science. Unfortunately, despite myriad contributions by a variety of scholars in different disciplines (for example, Foucault 1972, 1977; Lawson 1985; Lyotard 1984; Evans 1989), despite highly articulate statements about the ways our own practices presume and reaffirm the scientific idiom (Clifford and Marcus 1986; Marcus and Fischer 1986; Tyler 1987), this presumption persists. Science is treated as an object out there, and SSK practice is presumed to take place on a different level. Lyotard (1984) has shown how the end of the modern era is marked by the collapse of the metanarrative as a legitimizing or unifying force. But Candy still yearn for a metanarrative.

This partly explains the otherwise remarkable phenomenon that as soon as practitioners start talking programmatics (that is, as soon as they start talking about how the research ought to be done, rather than just doing it), they often forget the most cherished tenets of their own practice. Participants in social studies of science (this author included) are probably among the worst offenders. As soon as the discussion moves to a consideration of "the state of the field," its "prospects for future development," "possible new directions," an assessment of "what has been achieved," and so on, all commitment to relativism is dropped. What this phenomenon underscores is that the commitment to relativism in Bath-SSK has thus far been little more than narrowly instrumental, as Candy would readily concede, I think. When speaking in programmatic mode, participants resort to a rather familiar, conventional, traditional vocabulary of argument. Thus participants invoke all the standard notions of positions—perspectives, tools, rationales for approaches. These include, notably, justifications for an approach in terms of what seems interesting, or assessments of a perspective in terms of "where it gets you." This is remarkable because it is just these kinds of justification with which the sociologist of scientific knowledge is expected to take issue when they are voiced by natural scientists. When scientists account for theory choice or a change of career direction by saying "it was interesting," or "it wasn't getting us anywhere," sociologists are expected to prick up their analytical ears. Such accounts are analytically insufficient (cf. Yearley 1990). Yet in the current debate such assessments are allowed to pass without comment. Here then is further evidence of the weasel status of self-proclaimed commitment to relativism. For Bath-SSK, relativism is not a concept inviting intellectual inquiry; instead it is conceived of as a tool for pursuing what turn out to be rather parochial ends. (This is what makes it amusing that Candy should describe reflexivity as "*post*relativist." When did we finally get to relativism? Did I miss something?)

Very early in their piece, Candy display some stunning insensitivities to the nature of the enterprise in which they are engaged. First we are told that the cosmic status of SSK derives from the fact that its practitioners do not know in the same way that other disciplines know. Candy contrast the knowing of Christians, Muslims, physicists, and biologists with the knowing of a sociologist. Sociologists are said to be the only beings capable of seeing things from more than one point of view—little consideration here of anthropology, literary theory, and so on. Here, right at the start of the argument, we get a good sense of the disciplinary myopia which pervades Candy. For Candy's own versions of what it is to know in another

330

discipline are advanced as entirely unproblematic. They simply know the positions of others; they advance versions of how Christians, Muslims, and physicists know, apparently oblivious to the fact that these versions are (occasioned) products of their own efforts at knowing. Candy partition the world into groups and then assign differential positions (capabilities and actions) to these groups. As the ethnomethodologists have reminded us, this presumption of structured reality is a travesty of a key sociological phenomenon: how are structurings of this kind managed and achieved, for what purposes, by whom, and so on? Treating them as a frame for analysis is a sorry violation of topic in favor of resource; but the error is redoubled when the focus is knowing. What next? Will scientists turn out to have different genes from sociologists? Actually yes, we see that Candy's argument depends on something very close to this position.

A related insensitivity follows from this glib characterization of the world in terms of different ways of knowing. Given that there are different epistemological natural attitudes, Candy say we are free to use whatever version is appropriate for the purpose at hand. But once we recognize the constitutive function of language, the strength of the argument that we are immersed in our language games, this idea of freedom of choice is laughable. The notion that we should then decide (how) to choose an epistemological stance is ludicrous. Do Candy suppose we are so free of the constraints of conventions of language? Precisely what counts as having an epistemological stance here?

This curious aspect of their argument runs directly counter to one of the more important insights of SSK. Characterizations of philosophical position have been shown to be the post hoc and disengaged portrayal of conventional practice; they are attempts to justify practices which are conventionally embedded. Emphatically, such positions do not exist prior to practice, nor do they determine that practice. To put it most starkly, people (sociologists, scientists, and others) act; philosophers (and sociologists with certain philosophical pretensions) then deploy a repertoire of "isms" to characterize and justify these actions. The apposite Wittgensteinian slogan is that logic compels only by the sanctions of our fellow men.

Candy's cavalier use of epistemological characterizations denies this important finding. In virtue of their adoption of a philosopher's stereotype, Candy take it as obvious that scientists are (naive) "realists." But laboratory studies and discourse analysis suggest that this convenient stereotype doesn't hold up. In order to be successful, scientists must be adept at a whole range of practices. To use epistemological parlance, scientists can demonstrably be seen to act variously and interchangeably as realists, rationalists, relativists, pragmatists, deconstructionists, and the rest (Latour and Woolgar 1986; Lynch 1985; Knorr Cetina 1981). I'm sorry to disappoint both philosophers and sociologists who like to deal in unproblematic stereotypes: scientists are not just realists. OK, so the rhetoric of realism seems to be more commonly used in, say, grant applications, honorific addresses, reports to research councils, and so on (Bazerman 1988; Gilbert and Mulkay 1984; Myers 1990; Potter and Wetherell 1987, chap. 3). But the use of the realist repertoire on these specific occasions hardly makes scientists holders of the realist position when engaged in scientific practice.

For Candy it is not just that scientists *are* naive realists; they *should* hold this position. This, Candy tell us, is the only way to get things done. Here then is a clear display of irresponsibility in the face of the major questions about the relation between practice, culture, and epistemology. For Candy there is simply no question to be asked at this level. For them, apparently, realism is foundational to achievement; any other position is not.

To observe, by contrast, that realism is a discursive repertoire, not a position per se, and not a position to be unproblematically equated with scientists' work, is to pull the rug from under Bath-SSK. For Bath-SSK depends on an antithesis to natural realism in favor of social realism. Although Candy indicate that SSK is not about the resolution of epistemological problems, we see that their position depends upon the binary partition of the world in epistemological terms: villains and heroes; natural and social realists. To repeat, this particular line of attack has been very useful. The problem comes when its practitioners take this dualism as the only valuable ordering principle in social studies of science.

Reflexivity

For reasons consistent with their positionism, it is important for Candy to deploy a restricted and monistic version of reflexivity. Yet the available literature makes clear that a wide variety of kinds of reflexivity are possible. A discussion of the divergences within the reflexive position can be found both in the introduction to a recent collection (Woolgar 1988) and between the various versions discussed by different contributors. Ashmore (1989) has written an entire encyclopedia of reflexivity which details the variations. But Candy reduce these to a single tendency.

Rather than reiterate these divergences here, I shall briefly recover two key features which Candy miss. First, reflexivity aims to capitalize upon the strains and tensions associated with all research practice which can be construed as part of its own phenomenon. One route to developing this is to observe that research practice tends to abide by a series of representational conventions which delimit the manner and substance of research. To say that this engenders tensions, most vivid in cases where the research in question gestures toward relativism, is emphatically not to deny the achievements and aspirations of the research practitioners. It is not to say that the research is wrong, any more than sociologists of scientific knowledge would wish to say that the achievements of their scientist subjects is wrong. This is precisely the kind of (mis)reading which leads to the construal of reflexivity as a problem. But the more interesting writing in the area displays no wish to champion this singular response to reflexivity. Instead the idea is to take such tensions as a starting point for exploration of the questions and issues that arise. For example, what are the limits of the conventions of representation? What forms of expression engage "epistemic" matters while resisting the constraints of the conventional research format? Since such conventions tend to encourage the suppression of paradox, what forms of treatment allow us to keep paradox alive on its own terms? And why does this paragraph end with four questions?

So we see that reflexivity capitalizes on strains and tensions in the sense of using them to direct our attention to, say, the particular form of subject-object relationship which our research conventions reify and reaffirm. A second, broader, and more important sense of reflexivity is the recognition that the particular research practices, schools, perspectives, and so on through which we reckon to find out about research are themselves temporary social phenomena. This means of course that no current perspective is immortal and that current orthodoxy can furnish the grounds for its own criticism in successor perspectives. In social studies of science, for example, criticism of preceding perspectives is commonly used as the basis for moving to a new stance. The social study of science thus contains within itself the capacity for redefining the major issues and methodological questions in virtue of attention to the nature of its practice. There is, in other words, a critical dynamic—we can call this the "dynamic of iterative reconceptualization"—(Woolgar 1991) whereby practitioners from time to time recognize the defects of their position as an occasion for revisiting its basic assumptions. Once we understand the value of reflexivity in terms of the dynamic of iterative reconceptualization—in short, as an attitude for enhancing our ability to pose fresh questions about epistemic matters—we recognize that the social study of science has the capacity to revisit taken-for-granted assumptions which underpin particular phases or research perspectives.

This latter sense of reflexivity enables us to place the squabbles and arguments between sociologists of science within a wider context. For example, it becomes clear that the concept of symmetry distinguishes different phases in the history of social studies of science. Mertonian approaches to science effectively proposed a symmetry between science and other social institutions—science was to be understood as a social institution just like any other. Accordingly, social scientists drew upon existing (mainly functionalist) methods and tools to reveal the nature of social relationships between scientists. Merton thus problematized the assumption that science could not be conceived as a social institution on an analytic par with others. Bloor's (1976) articulation of symmetry as a methodological principle extended symmetry to the content of scientific knowledge itself. In particular, new sets of methods and tools were to be used without regard for the truth status of the scientific knowledge in question. SSK thus problematized the assumption that only false scientific knowledge was amenable to the sociological gaze.

Reflexivity asks us to problematize the assumption that the analyst (author, self) stands in a disengaged relationship to the world (subjects, objects, scientists, things). It asks us to push symmetry one stage further, to explore the consequences of challenging the assumption that the analyst enjoys a privileged position vis-à-vis the subjects and objects which come under the authorial gaze. It does so, needless to say, in recognition that its own privilege is temporary.

This brief review enables us to see that Candy's critique of reflexivity is seriously misconceived. In particular it is easy to show how some of their specific comments either just miss the point or have been given a misleading emphasis. The fact that reflexivity can be recognized within nanoseconds is entirely irrelevant to the business of working out the significance and ramifications of the reflexive move. The evidence suggests it will take some people much longer than others to remove their current blinkers. The fact that discourse analysis was presented by one little band of writers as a critique of SSK does not entail the claim that it is invulnerable to the same critique. In fact, that claim is entirely inconsequential for its practice. To say that discourse analysis has "been largely abandoned within SSK" is especially curious given the number of books appearing in the last few years (for example, Bazerman 1988; Gilbert and Mulkay 1984; Mulkay 1985; Myers 1990) and the lively debates that have been published (for example, Halfpenny 1988, 1989; Fahnestock, 1989; Fuhrman and Oehler, 1986, 1987; Mulkay et al. 1983; Potter 1987; Potter and McKinlay 1989; Waddell 1989). And even this is to ignore the extensive literature which is relevant to SSK through its treatment of representational issues in academic discourse outside of the natural sciences (for example, McCloskey 1985; Nelson et al. 1987; Potter and Wetherell 1987; Simons 1988). To the extent that Bath-SSK tries to ignore discourse analysis, this is much more of a comment on the parochialism of Bath-SSK than on discourse analysis. Discourse analysis did not "pave the way" for reflexivity (Potter 1988). Reflexivity does not "set out to sidestep all truth-making conventions." Nor does it seek "immediate access to the truths of the social world." Reflexivity does not believe it rests on bedrock. It does not aspire to epistemological foundationalism. And so on and so on.

Why should Candy make these alarming misreadings? The depressing answer is that such misreadings make most sense from within an especially blinkered outlook. They exactly reflect the disciplinary myopia with which Candy saddle themselves. Before proceeding with the diagnosis, we need to relate Candy's morbid fear of reflexivity to their morbid fear of foreigners.

Reflexivity and the French School

What Candy refer to as the "French school" proposes a radical symmetry with regard to agency. In line with the general thrust of reflexivity just articulated, authors like Callon and Latour wish to disprivilege a prevailing asymmetry: in their case the focus is the relationship between humans and nonhumans. Their (especially Callon's) writing grants a voice to nonhumans as well as to humans. In the variant of reflexivity known as "new literary forms," a predominant focus is the granting of voices to those humans subdued by the conventions of the text: the author's alter ego, her second thoughts, the remarks of the subject, and so on. The French school represents a semiotically informed variant of the general reflexive dynamic: a reconceptualization of the key problems and issues takes place when a key set of identities and attributes are reconfigured within the analytical frame.

Candy's complaint about reflexivity in general is that it does not get you anywhere, it poses questions which cannot be answered, and it undermines the cause of social realism. Candy's complaint about the French school is that its moves do not get you anywhere, that its followers pose questions bereft of established methodological procedure, and that they unwittingly concede too much to natural realism. It is important to be clear that these complaints acquire substance in terms of a very specific theoretical agenda. For Candy the core philosophical tradition which informs SSK stems from contention over the relationship between the natural and social sciences. Using a sociologized reading of Wittgenstein, Candy champion a Winchean vision of social science, in a kind of holy war against the position of positivist sociology. Special and different methods pertain in the study of the social world, so the argument goes, because the subjects of the social world are fundamentally different in kind from the objects of the natural world. Candy's struggle is with the ghost of Durkheim, which ironically enough hardly troubles the French school at all.

Reflexivity asks that we problematize this core assumption. It asks what happens when we take issue with the notion that entities in the social and natural world are fundamentally different. In ethnographic spirit, we thus try to make strange the central presuppositions of research: why is the moral order of representation fashioned in this particular way, and what are the consequences of its distribution of attributes and responsibilities (Woolgar 1985, 1989a)? Note here that "ethnographic" denotes a commitment to making uncertain, rather than just a formula for rendering exotic (Latour and Woolgar 1986). Typically the conventions of representation are challenged as a means of revealing the author's part in the reaffirmation of assumptions about the social-natural divide. The French school similarly challenges this divide by assigning capacities for action, thought, and intention to nonhuman elements.

Although Callon and Latour will more than likely defend themselves with vigor on this point, it is worth noting how much Candy's refusal to understand is a measure of their entrenchment within the ideology of representation. Because of their commitment to a conventional moral order of representation, they interpret the attribution of human capacities to nonhumans as mere metaphor. Candy thus hear Callon's description of scallops as involving a "figure of speech" and the deployment of "imaginative resources." For them it is just a matter of dressing up the account differently: "The language changes but the story remains the same." So much for sociology's commitment to the constitutive character of language. Here we see clearly that for Candy, there is one preferred story behind all. For them different ways of conveying this (actual) story become distractions, fancy talk, unnecessary and sometimes dangerous embellishments. This view is evident in their remark that "it is sometimes hard to know when Latour is being entirely serious" (n. 15). The supposition is that Callon (and Latour) must be joking or talking metaphorically; he cannot mean that the scallops actually comply. What is vividly clear is how these kinds of asymmetric assessments depend on profound commitments to the "actual character" of the nature-social divide.

Xenophobia and Deontological Purity

Here, then, we have a serious case of disciplinary myopia. At every turn Candy ask, what is reflexivity for, of what use is it, where does it get us? But these otherwise reasonable questions are framed entirely within the specific concerns of a well-established but increasingly narrow research agenda. So Candy inspect the arguments of reflexivity for their value in the way we might assess a new spade for its ability to dig the ground. In other words, reflexivity is only judged as a tool, for its instrumental value, in contributing to a predefined task. Of course Candy are right that reflexivity, when viewed in this way, may not help them in their task. After all, the whole point of reflexivity is that it urges reassessment of the value of the task. It asks that we reconsider whether digging the ground is the only task to which we should be devoting our attention; that we explore possible reorientations of our theoretical and methodological commitments. For Candy knowing is a bit like digging. The ground is already prepared; it's just a question of what can be turned up.

Candy's resistance to theoretical reassessment, their subscription to the role of spade-wielding journeyman rather than theoretical critic, is characteristic of what has been recognized as the Anglo-American/Continental divide. This has been noted by Barry Barnes in his discussion of the professionalization of science:

> It is interesting to note . . . that . . . the English term "sociologist of scientific knowledge" ["scientist"] is narrower in its meaning and implications than its analogues in European languages, reflecting perhaps, a peculiarly restricted and hard-boiled conception of sociological [scientific] knowledge and sociological [scientific] activity established in the English speaking world. As compared with Continental societies, we place the sociologist [scientist] further from wisdom, learn-

ing and insight, and closer to mere technique; and we make a much stronger distinction than they do between "sociologists" ["scientists"] and "intellectuals." (Barnes 1985, 9)

The substitution of "sociologist of scientific knowledge" where Barnes uses "scientist" suggests a parallel argument about deeply embedded differences in conceptions of professional sociology across the Anglo-American/Continental divide. One unfortunate consequence is that from the point of view of the purveyors of sociological technique, those concerned with "wisdom, learning, and insight" appear as outsiders and foreigners. They appear as strangers who proceed unfettered by discipline and by a "peculiarly restricted and hard-boiled conception of sociological knowledge and sociological activity established in the English speaking world."

Barnes's observation is useful because it alludes to the considerable discussion about the extent to which continental perspectives can ever be translated into Anglo-American frameworks and vice versa (see, for example, Fuller 1983; Latour 1984; White 1978; Woolgar 1986). In this context we can now see that, above all, Candy's deontological tract is a contamination story. It is a moral tale about the dangers of embracing foreign ways, an appeal for purity in the face of recently emergent impurities. Go this route and *who knows* what will happen?

Conclusion

Rather than reassert in detail the actual features of reflexivity in the way this kind of forum encourages its writers to advance definitive depictions of positions, I have chosen instead to account for Candy's negativism. I believe this is the best way of reinforcing the point that reflexivity is not a school with its own formula but rather a means of signaling opportunities for theoretical sensitizing. We have seen that Candy espouse a disappointingly parochial programme of research for social studies of science. They do so, it seems, for a complex of reasons: fear of foreigners and contamination which is bound up with a commitment to rigidly defined boundaries; love of dualisms and inflexible categorical distinctions; pure (as opposed to dangerous) use of method and technique at the expense of imagination and intellect; and possibly—this is sheer conjecture—some resentment that the accolade of "most radical" has now passed to others. This is what leads them to use inappropriately instrumental criteria in their assessment of reflexivity and the French school. But parochialism is the last thing we need at the present juncture in social studies of science. To be Anglo-American about knowledge at this point in our history is an abrogation of intellectual responsibility.

The disappointment is that as Bath-SSK settles into middle age, it espouses a predictable and safe formula. The irritation is that it also has the effrontery to castigate others for deviation from The Formula, and that it proffers advice which is condescending and avuncular. But the rest of us must insist that life goes on beyond Bath. Let us all agree that Bath-SSK has been extraordinarily useful. In certain contexts it will undoubtedly continue to be useful. But at the same time, some of us might want to relax the constraints of the one true program and abandon the wearying furrow of safe formulas. Preferably without getting our wrists slapped. Of course some people will not be persuaded: some people just need a formula.

I have stressed the dysfunctions of exacerbating differences between Bath-SSK and other more recent variants of social studies of science: it is just this "positionism" (factionalism) which needs to be resisted if we are to ensure that Bath-SSK remains part of the new developments. However, if we agree that the grounds for deciding between Bath-SSK and postrelativist positions cannot be based on truth, how should we adjudge their respective merits? Reflexivity and actor-network theory offer ways of further challenging the preconceptions and assumptions of (what are now) current orthodoxies. Those who attach paramount importance to the security of method will choose one way: they will say that when imagination is given free rein, the excitement masks a poverty of method. Those attracted by the intellectual challenge will note with regret that their potential allies' obsession with method bespeaks a poverty of imagination and excitement.

Like much advice of this kind, the injunction to others to be less dangerous is best understood as an attempt to establish our own purity. When uncles say that pop music isn't what it used to be, or that they discovered sex almost twenty years ago, or that running in front of fast cars might be dangerous, they conveniently forget (or rewrite) their own history. Although we can perhaps forgive real-life uncles more easily than our intellectual ones, our reply must be similar. We have to reassert the integrity of recurrent challenges to the established order and, by showing how they can join in, make our uncles feel young again.

REFERENCES

Ashmore, Malcolm. 1989. *The Reflexive Thesis: Wrighting Sociology of Scientific Knowledge.* Chicago: University of Chicago Press.

Barnes, Barry. 1985. *About Science.* Oxford: Blackwell.

Bazerman, Charles. 1988. *Shaping Written Knowledge: The Genre and Activity of the Experimental Article in Science.* Madison: University of Wisconsin Press.

Bloor, D. 1976. *Knowledge and Social Imagery.* London: Routledge and Kegan Paul.

Clifford, James, and George E. Marcus, eds. 1986. *Writing Culture: The Poetics and Politics of Ethnography.* Berkeley: University of California Press.

Collins, H. M. 1985. *Changing Order: Replication and Induction in Scientific Practice.* London: Sage.

Evans, Malcolm. 1989. *Signifying Nothing: Truth's True Contents in Shakespeare's Text.* 2d ed. London: Harvester/Wheatsheaf.

Fahnestock, J. 1989. Arguing in Different Forums: The Bering Crossover Controversy. *Science, Technology, and Human Values* 14:26–42.

Foucault, M. 1972. *The Archaeology of Knowledge.* London: Tavistock.

———. 1977. What is an Author? In D. F. Bouchard, ed., *Michel Foucault: Language, Counter Memory, Practice: Selected Essays and Interviews.* Ithaca: Cornell University Press.

Fuhrman, E. R., and K. Oehler. 1986. Discourse Analysis and Reflexivity. *Social Studies of Science* 16:293–307.

———. 1987. Reflexivity Redux: Reply to Potter. *Social Studies of Science* 17:177–81.

Fuller, Steve. 1983. A French Science (with English Subtitles). *Philosophy and Literature* 7:3–14.

Gilbert, G. N., and M. Mulkay. 1984. *Opening Pandora's Box: A Sociological Analysis of Scientists' Discourse.* Cambridge: Cambridge University Press.

Halfpenny, P. 1988. Talking of Talking, Writing of Writing: Some Reflections on Gilbert and Mulkay's Discourse Analysis. *Social Studies of Science* 18:169–82.

———. 1989. Reply to Potter and McKinlay. *Social Studies of Science* 19:145–52.

Hammersley, M., and P. Atkinson. 1983. *Ethnography: Principles in Practice.* London: Tavistock.

Knorr Cetina, K. D., 1981. *The Manufacture of Knowledge.* Oxford: Pergamon.

Knorr Cetina, K. D., and M. Mulkay, eds. 1983. *Science Observed: Perspectives on the Social Study of Science.* London: Sage.

Latour, B. 1984. Where Did You Put the Black Box Opener? *EASST Newsletter* 3:17–24.

Latour, B., and S. Woolgar. 1986. *Laboratory Life: The Construction of Scientific Facts.* 2d ed. Princeton: Princeton University Press.

Lawson, H. 1985. *Reflexivity: The Post-Modern Predicament.* London: Hutchinson.

Lynch, M. 1985. *Art and Artifact in Laboratory Science: A Study of Shop*

Work and Shop Talk in a Research Laboratory. London: Routledge and Kegan Paul.

Lynch, M., and S. Woolgar, eds. 1990. *Representation in Scientific Practice.* Cambridge: MIT Press.

Lyotard, Jean-Francois. [1979] 1984. *The Post-Modern Condition: A Report on Knowledge.* Manchester: University of Manchester Press.

Marcus, G. E., and M. M. Fischer. 1986. *Anthropology as Cultural Critique: An Experimental Moment in the Human Sciences.* Chicago: University of Chicago Press.

McCloskey, Donald N. 1985. *The Rhetoric of Economics.* Madison: University of Wisconsin Press.

Mulkay, Michael. 1985. *The Word and the World Explorations in the Form of Sociological Analysis.* London: George Allen and Unwin.

Mulkay, M., J. Potter, and S. Yearley. 1983. Why an Analysis of Scientific Discourse is Needed. 171–203 in Knorr Cetina and Mulkay 1983.

Myers, Greg. 1990. *Writing Biology: Texts in the Social Construction of Scientific Knowledge.* Madison: University of Wisconsin Press.

Nelson, J. S., A. MeGill, and D. N. McCloskey, eds. 1987. *The Rhetoric of the Human Sciences: Language and Argument in Scholarship and Public Affairs.* Madison: University of Wisconsin Press.

Potter, J. 1987. Discourse Analysis and the Turn of the Reflexive Screw: A Response to Fuhrman and Oehler. *Social Studies of Science* 17:171–77.

———. 1988. What Is Reflexive about Discourse Analysis? The Case of Reading Readings. 37–54 in Woolgar 1988.

Potter, J., and A. McKinlay. 1989. Discourse—Philosophy—Reflexivity: Comment on Halfpenny. *Social Studies of Science* 19:137–45.

Potter, J., and M. Wetherell. 1987. *Discourse and Social Psychology: Beyond Attitudes and Behaviour.* London: Sage.

Simons, H. W., ed. 1988. *The Rhetorical Turn: Invention and Persuasion in the Conduct of Inquiry.* Chicago: University of Chicago Press.

Turkle, S. 1988. Artificial Intelligence and Psychoanalysis: A New Alliance 241–68 in S. R. Graubard, ed. *The Artificial Intelligence Debate: False Starts, Real Foundations.* Cambridge: MIT Press.

Turner, S. 1990. Social Constructionism and Social Theory. Department of Philosophy, University of South Florida.

Tyler, S. 1987. *The Unspeakable: Discourse, Dialogue, and Rhetoric in the Postmodern World.* Madison: University of Wisconsin Press.

Waddell, C. 1989. Reasonableness versus Rationality in the Construction and Justification of Science Policy Decisions: The Case of the Cambridge Experimentation Review Board. *Science, Technology, and Human Values* 14:7–25.

White, Hayden. 1978. Foucault Decoded: Notes from underground. 230–60 in *Tropics of Discourse: Essays in Cultural Criticism.* Baltimore: Johns Hopkins University Press.

Woolgar, Steve. 1985. Why Not a Sociology of Machines? The Case of Sociology and Artificial Intelligence. *Sociology* 19:557–72.

———. 1986. On the Alleged Distinction between Discourse and Praxis. *Social Studies of Science* 16:309–17.

———. 1989a. Representation, Cognition, Self: What Hope for the Integration of the Sociology and Psychology of Science? 201–24 in S. Fuller, M. de Mey, and S. Woolgar, eds. *The Cognitive Turn: Sociological and Psychological Perspectives on Science.* Dordrecht: Kluwer.

———. 1989b. A Coffeehouse Conversation on the Possibility of Mechanising Discovery and its Sociological Analysis. *Social Studies of Science* 19:658–86.

———. 1991. The Turn to Technology in Social Studies of Science. *Science, Technology, and Human Values.* 16:20–50.

Woolgar, Steve, ed. 1988. *Knowledge and Reflexivity.* London: Sage.

Woolgar, Steve, and Malcolm Ashmore. 1988. The Next Step: An Introduction to the Reflexive Project. 1–13 in Woolgar 1988.

Yearley, Steve. 1990. The Dictates of Method and Policy: Interpretational Structures in the Representation of Scientific Work. 337–55 in Lynch and Woolgar 1990.

12

Don't Throw the Baby Out with the Bath School!
A Reply to Collins and Yearley

Michel Callon and Bruno Latour

> Mademoiselle de l'Espinasse: "Voilà ma toile; et le point originaire
> de tous ces fils c'est mon araignée"
> Bordeu: "A merveille"
> Mademoiselle de l'Espinasse: "Où sont les fils? Où est placée
> l'araignée?"
>
> Diderot, *Le Rêve de d'Alembert*

Harry Collins and Steve Yearley (from now on C&Y) are satisfied with the state of social studies of science. Most of the problems have been solved, important discoveries have been made, sociology is firm enough on its feet to study the natural sciences. Thus, according to them, there is no fundamental reason to switch to other frames of reference—and there is still less reason to let "bloody foreigners" dabble in a field where the British have been firmly in command for so many years. Wherever we go, C&Y have already been there, have given satisfactory explanations, have developed an adequate methodology, and have solved the empirical problems. Even if they recognize that there might be some residual difficulties—the problems of reflexivity, that of symmetry, the potential conflict between relativism and social realism—their solution is to shun these intellectual traps by a process of alternation, another name for blithe ignorance, and an appeal to common sense and professional

Harry Collins and Steve Yearley had the generosity to host a one-day informal seminar to play chicken "live." Steve Woolgar and Bruno Latour were the contestants and Gerard de Vries and Wiebe Bijker the referees. Members of the Bath School, David Gooding and David Travis, abstained in a gentlemanly way from pushing the contestants under the traffic. The final dinner was in a Lebanese restaurant, but we decided not to take this as an omen of future civil strife. We benefited enormously from this one-day discussion but restrict ourselves in this paper to the published materials. Many useful comments by Gerard de Vries, Steven Shapin, and Mike Lynch could not be used, since we had agreed not to alter our respective papers so much as to make them movable targets. On the whole we felt it was a welcome and clarifying debate. We thank Gabrielle Hecht and Michael Bravo for their comments and corrections.

loyalty. Sociology is good enough to do the job, and if it is not, then let them be like their brave ancestors and say, "right or wrong, my discipline." The overall tone of C&Y implies that if all those bizarre ideas were left to thrive, sociologists of science might have to retool some of their concepts, start reading new people, maybe even philosophers of the pre-Wittgenstein era, or worse, economists of technical change, political philosophers, semioticians, and while we are at it, why not novelists or technologists or metaphysicians? No, whatever other schools have to offer, none of them is better than the good old sociology we have at hand, and instead of helping the French to overcome their deficiencies, it is better to throw them out with the bathwater.

We disagree with this assessment of the field. We are dissatisfied with the state of the art, which is now in danger of dismantlement after fifteen years of rapid advance (see Latour, in press, a, for a diagnostic). We think it is about time to change the bath water, but contrary to our colleagues, we do not want to throw the baby out with it, and especially not the Bath school. We learned a great deal from Collins's work—the study of active controversies, the meticulous application of symmetry in the treatment of parasciences, the emphasis put on local skills, the careful study of replication, the dismantlement of epistemologists' hegemony, the stress on networks and entrenchment mechanisms, and above all, his crisp and witty style of reasoning. However, we do not believe that the microsociology of the Bath school has put an end to the history of the field. We are also dissatisfied with our own network theory, but contrary to C&Y, we do not see this as a reason to put our head in the sand and pretend that sociology of science is "business as usual." Our deficiencies spur us to go on looking for alternatives, original methods, and yes, a still more radical definition of the field. The domain is young. The topics of science and society have barely been touched.

For their sometimes condescending but on the whole earnest critique of the "Paris school," C&Y have chosen two papers which are explicitly "ontological manifestos" out of a production of six books, five edited volumes and about sixty articles. Fair enough. In our reply we will stick to those two papers and will abstain from using other materials, although we will cite many others for the benefit of readers interested in following through. If we agree to restrict the dispute to those two papers, then in return C&Y have to acknowledge that we wrote them in a peculiar style. We recognize that the empirical basis of those two papers and their methods are rather idiosyncratic, but their goal is to transform the definition of entities as it is accepted in the field of social studies of science by doing two ontological experiments, one on nature, the other on technology. Each of them is followed by scores of methodological and empirical papers that C&Y have the right to ignore, although the accusation of a poverty of methods, of lack of rigor, and of a failure to provide explanations would have been more compelling had a slightly larger corpus been chosen.

The major criticism made by our colleagues is that even if our position is philosophically radical and justified, its practical effect on the use of empirical material is prosaic, reactionary, and dangerously confusing. The justification for this judgment is that in spite of what we claim, we are accused of going back to the realist position to explain scientific facts and to technical determinism to account for artifacts. Since in Paris and Bath we all agree that the touchstone of any position is its empirical fruitfulness, we concede that if indeed the empirical evidence is proven messy, we waive forever the right to appeal either to the quality of our philosophy or to the purity of our intentions.

In intellectual controversies one good way to assess the quality of claims is to see which side understands not only its own position but also that of the other side (another, lighter, touchstone is checking to see which side reads the other's production completely). We feel that the exasperation of C&Y is not only respectable but understandable and important for the future of the field, and that we are able to explain both why they are wrong and why they can't help misinterpreting us in the very way they do. The yardstick they are using to qualify any given piece of work as "advanced," "radical," or "reactionary" is the following (see fig. 12.1). There is one line going from the nature pole to the social pole, and it is along this line that schools of thought may be logged. If you grant a lot of activity to nature in the settlement of controversies, then you are a reactionary, that is, a realist; if, on the contrary, you grant a lot of activity to society in settling controversies, then you are a constructivist or a radical, with various nuances which may only be logged along this line. Although the philosophical foundation of this yardstick is crucial, we will not go into that, since the debate only hinges on the empirical use of this philosophy; but see Latour 1990, in press, a.

The claim of C&Y is that social studies of science (or SSK, as they choose to call it) is engaged in a fight, a tug-of-war between two extreme positions, one which they label "natural realism" which starts with the existence of objects to explain why we humans agree about them; and the other, which they label "social realism," which starts, on the contrary, from the firm foundation of society in order to account for why we collectively settle on matters of fact. The

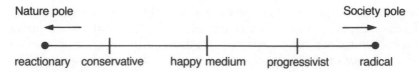

Figure 12.1 Positions in science studies debates are aligned along one line only, going from Nature to Society and using terms which are politically laden.

alternation they advocate is that we should switch from natural realism when we are scientists to social realism when we play the role of sociologists explaining science. This point is very important, because it is this alternation that C&Y call "symmetry." In this tug-of-war, any sociologist who stops being a social realist would be a traitor, since he or she would abandon the fight or, worse still, help out the other side. We in Paris are viewed as such traitors, because we give back to nature the role of settling controversies. The reflexivist is seen as less of a pest, since she places herself behind all the teams to plague them; but she is traitor nonetheless because she especially delights in bugging the "social" team with her endless bites and kicks (fig. 12.2). (But she is good enough to fend for herself [Ashmore 1989], and we will not plead on her behalf in this paper).

The reason why we may use the word "treason" is that C&Y's paper is a moral and deontological paper. The field of science studies has been engaged in a moral struggle to strip science of its extravagant claim to authority. Any move that waffles on this issue appears unethical, since it could also help scientists and engineers to reclaim this special authority which science studies has had so much trouble undermining. This is a serious claim and we cannot take it

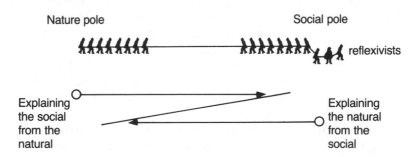

Figure 12.2 The tug-of-war between realists, on the left, and constructivists, on the right; reflexivists are those who hamstring the players of the Social team. More seriously, the sources of the explanation may come from two contradictory repertoires.

lightly. Here are the two more damning accusations of high treason, the first for science:

> Far from adding to our understanding it seems to us that the resulting account [of Collins's gravity waves phrased in Callon's ways] would look just like the account of a conventional historian of science— except that the historian wouldn't talk of allegiances with gravity waves and failures of negotiations with gravity waves, but of discoveries and failures of experimental technique. The language changes but the story remains the same.

and the second for technology:

> The consequences of the semiotic method [of Latour] amount to a backward step, leading us to embrace once more the very priority of technological, rule-bound description, adopted from scientists and technologists, that we once learned to ignore.

This is not a misreading of our position. Neither is it an anti-French prejudice, or a peculiar blindness to others' ideas, or even tunnel vision: it is a necessity of C&Y's cold war waged against realists. Our position is for them unjustifiable since it helps the traditional and conventional technologists and scientists to win the day over SSK's discoveries. The whole accusation now hinges on two questions the jury is asked to settle: did Callon and Latour commit the crime of granting to nature and to artifacts the same ontological status that realists and technical determinists are used to granting them? If so, did they commit this crime in intention or in effect, or both? The second possibility is more damning than the first and the only one that really counts for our discussion.

We have to confess that in C&Y's frame of reference—and for that matter in the whole Anglo-American tradition of science studies— the answer has to be "yes." We are guilty on both counts, and we understand why our position is bound to be read this way by social realists.

Why is this reading by C&Y so inevitable? Because they cannot imagine any other yardstick for evaluating empirical studies than the one defined above, and they cannot entertain even for a moment another ontological status for society and for things. All the shifts in vocabulary like "actant" instead of "actor," "actor network" instead of "social relations," "translation" instead of "interaction," "negotiation" instead of "discovery," "immutable mobiles" and "inscriptions" instead of "proof" and "data," "delegation" instead of "social roles," are derided because they are hybrid terms that blur the distinction between the really social and human-centered terms and the really natural and object-centered repertoires. But who provided them with this real distribution between the social and the natural worlds? The scientists whose hegemony in defining the world C&Y so bravely fight. Obsessed by the war they wage against "natural realists," they are unable to see that this battle is lost as soon as we accept the definition of society handed to them under the name of "social realism." This is now what we have to demonstrate and we will show that if there are to be traitors in this world (which might not be necessary) they might be the ones sticking to social realism, not us.

Let us first examine the yardstick we use to decide who is reactionary and who is not, and then examine what difference it makes empirically. We have never been interested in playing the tug-of-war that amuses the Anglo-American tradition so much, and C&Y are right in saying that we are born traitors, so to speak, from the early days of *Laboratory Life* and of the electric-vehicle saga (Latour and Woolgar [1979] 1986; Callon 1980a, b; Callon 1981; Callon and Latour 1981). There are many reasons for this—one of them being that realism as a philosophical tradition has never been important on the Continent (see Bowker and Latour 1987 for other factors). But the main reason is that since, like C&Y, we wish to attack scientists' hegemony on the definition of nature, we have never wished to accept the essential source of their power: that is the very distribution between what is natural and what is social and the fixed allocation of ontological status that goes with it. We have never been interested in giving a social explanation of anything, but we want to explain society, of which the things, facts and artifacts, are major components. If our explanations are prosaic in the eyes of C&Y, it is OK with us, since we have always wanted to render our texts unsuitable for the social explanation genre. Our general symmetry principle is thus not to alternate between natural realism and social realism but to obtain nature and society as twin results of another activity, one that is more interesting for us. We call it network building, or collective things, or quasi-objects, or trials of force (Callon 1980b, 1987; Callon, Law, and Rip 1986; Latour 1987, 1988, 1990, in press, a; Law 1987); and others call it skill, forms of life, material practice (Lynch 1985; Shapin and Schaffer, 1985).

To position such a symmetry, we have to make a ninety-degree turn from the SSK yardstick and define a second dimension (see fig. 12.3). This vertical dimension has its origin, 0, right at the center of the other dimension. All the studies which are at the top of the stabilization gradient are the ones which make an a priori distinction between nature and society, that is, the ones that lack symmetry (in our sense) or that muddle the issue or try to hedge out of it. All the studies that are down the stabilization gradient do not make any assumption about the social or natural origin of entities. Such is our touchstone, the one that allows us to read most of SSK as "reactionary," because they start from a closed definition of the social and then use this repertoire as an explanation of nature—most of the time to no avail. For us they are exactly as reactionary as one who would start from an a priori unconstructed definition of nature in order to explain the settlement of controversies. On the contrary, we take as progressive any study that simultaneously shows the coproduction of society and nature. The phenomenon we wish to describe cannot be framed from the two extremes on the SSK yardstick—nature out there and society up there—since on the contrary, "natures" and "societies" are secreted as by-products of this circulation of quasi-objects (Shapin and Schaffer 1985; Callon 1981, 1987; Latour 1987, 1990).

We understand from reading this diagram (fig. 12.3)—admittedly crude, but in these matters the basic frameworks are always crude—why it is that a point A on the zigzag line which we try to study, once projected in A' on the SSK yardstick is inevitably read as "reactionary," that is, as granting agency back to nature as defined by scientists. Conversely, we understand why point B, once projected

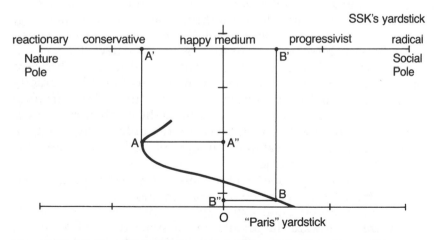

Figure 12.3 The one-dimensional yardstick of figure 1 is allowed to position any entity along the object-subject line (their longitude). The two-dimensional yardstick allows us to position objects and subjects according to their degree of stabilization as well (their latitude), and thus to offer for each entity two coordinates. Of each entity we would not only ask if it is natural or social (projected in A' and B' on the SSK yardstick) but also if it is unstable or stable (projected in A" and B" on the "Paris" yardstick).

in B', is read, this time by realists, as a blatant proof of social constructivism, that is, of society defined by social scientists. The perfect symmetry in the misreading of our work by "natural realists" and by "social realists" alike is a nice confirmation that we are in a different, although for them unthinkable, position. After scores of criticisms coming from the left side of the diagram, we welcome C&Y's critique coming from the right side, because the two together triangulate our stand with great accuracy.

Here are the four main points of contention that make this stand unthinkable for the two squabbling schools:

1. With the horizontal yardstick, there are two and only two known and fixed repertoires of agencies which are stocked at the two extremities—brute material objects, on the one hand, and intentional social human subjects, on the other. Every other entity—gravitational waves, scallops, inscriptions, or door closers, to name a few—will be read as a *combination* or mixture of these two pure repertoires. On the contrary once the two axes are drawn together, there is an indefinite gradient of agencies which are not combinations of any pure forms—although the purification work may be also documented (Latour 1988, especially part 2). We do not have to start from a fixed repertoire of agencies but from the very act of distributing or dispatching agencies.

2. The horizontal yardstick is either human-centered or nature-centered with alternation between them. The vertical axis, however, is centered on the very activity of shifting out agencies—which is, by the way, the semiotic definition of an actant devoid of its logo- and anthropocentric connotations. The very distinction between "action" and "behavior" that seems so obvious to C&Y is exactly the sort of divide that no student of science is allowed to start from (chap. 4); the only possible starting point is the attribution of intention or the withdrawal thereof, two activities different in the effects they produce, but identical in the amount of work they require. It is as difficult to turn an object into "mere matter" as it is to grant intentionality to the action of a human—on this point again, Shapin and Schaffer (1985) have made the essential moves.

3. Along the horizontal axis, explanations flow from either or both extremes toward the middle. In the other frame of reference, explanations start from the vertical axis. This is because in the first frame, nature and society are the *causes* that are used to explain the delicate content of scientific activity. It is the opposite in our frame, since the activity of scientists and engineers and of all their human and nonhuman allies is the cause, of which various states of nature and societies are the consequences. It is highly probable that we will

never again get the extremes of the nature and society poles. Scientists and engineers never use them as complacently as C&Y imagine, and this is because they are much more original, daring and progressive social philosophers and social theorists than more social scientists are. Recapturing the scientists' and engineers' social innovations—for instance those of Pasteur (Latour 1988) or French electrochemists (Callon 1987)—is what we believe we should be credited for.

4. The definition of observables is entirely different in the two frames. In the first one, social scientists were allowed to use an unobservable state of society and a definition of social relations to account for scientific work—or to alternate by using an equally unobservable state of nature. In the other frame the only observables are the traces left by objects, arguments, skills, and tokens circulating through the collective. We never see either social relations or things. We may only document the circulation of network-tracing tokens, statements, and skills. This is so important that one of us made it the first principle of science studies (Latour 1987, chap. 1). Although we have not yet fully articulated this argument, it is the basis of our empirical methods.

Since the goals and methods are so far apart, is it a mere accident that our work has been likened to those of social relativists?

There would be no reason to even discuss our position and yardstick with "social" students of science if we were interested in incommensurable objects. However, our claim is that it is utterly impossible to achieve the social students' very goals—disputing scientists' hegemony, explaining the closure of controversies, applying Bloor's principle of symmetry, calculating the entrenchment mechanisms of cognitive networks—without shifting from the horizontal axis to the vertical one, that is, without *completing* their symmetry principle with ours. We did not come to this position for the fun of it or to play the deadly game of chicken, as we have been accused of doing, but because the field is cornered in a dead end from which we want to escape (Latour, in press, a). This debate occurs in social studies of science and technology and only there, since this is about the only place in social science where the number of border cases between "nature" and "society" is so great that it breaks the divide apart. Classical social theory, or philosophy of science, never faced this problem, since they ignored either the things or the society. C&Y claim to be able to study the fabulous proliferation of borderline cases without changing the yardstick that was invented in order to keep the pure forms as far apart as possible (Shapin and Schaffer 1985). We believe this to be philosophically ill-founded and empirically sterile. And this is why the discussion should now go from ontological framework to empirical evidence. C&Y think their empirical treatment of the controversies is sufficient and progressive, and that ours is reactionary and muddled. We believe that they will not—and have never—delivered the goods they claim to have delivered, and that our methods, although unsteady and incomplete, at least begin to approach the question we are all interested in. We claim that the former symmetry principle spoils the data obtained by all of the case studies by erecting in the middle a Berlin Wall as violent—and fortunately as fragile—as the real one.

The empirical disagreement, the only one that really matters, is visible in science, and still more in technology. C&Y have read and indeed have rewritten Callon's rendering of the network of scallops, scientists, and fishermen to prove that it is "reactionary"—in their frame of reference. What would they have done instead? (Let us remember that they call "symmetry" the alternation between the two poles of their frame of reference, and that inside ours we call it "asymmetry.")

> As a social account of the making of knowledge [Callon's scallop story] is prosaic because the story of the scallops themselves is an asymmetrical old-fashioned scientific story. A symmetrical SSK-type account would analyze the way it came to be agreed, first that the scallops did anchor, and second—at a later date—that they did not anchor. Into the analysis the question of whether or not the scallops complied would not enter. The informing assumption would be that whether there were more or fewer scallops anchoring early and late in the study did not affect the extent to which the scallops were seen to be anchoring early and late. No SSK study would rely on the complicity of the scallops; at best it could rely on human-centered accounts of the complicity of the scallops.

The whole field of social studies of science pioneered by Collins and several other social realists hinges on this: nonhumans should not enter an account of why humans come to agree what they are.

There are four empirical mistakes in this position that are increasingly serious:

First, the scientists Callon portrays are constantly trying to bring the scallops to bear on the debates among colleagues and among fishermen; they simultaneously entertain dozens of ontological positions going from "scallops are like that, it is a fact"; to "you made up the data"; through positions like "this is what you think the scallops do, not what they really do"; or "some scallops tend to support your position, others don't"; to "this is your account, not what it is." To pretend that to document the ways scientists bring in nonhumans, we sociologists should choose *one* of these positions—that scallops do not interfere at all in the debate among scientists striving to make scallops interfere in their debates—is not only counterintuitive but empirically stifling. It is indeed this absurd position that has made the whole field of SSK look ridiculous and lend itself to the "mere social" interpretation (Star 1988). The only viable position is for the analyst not to take any ontological position—especially social constructivism—and to observe how the importation of various scalloplike entities modifies the controversy. Of course C&Y cannot accept that, because their yardstick forces them either to go toward the "natural realism" that they "had learned to ignore" or to embrace "social realism." The agnostic symmetric position—in our sense—is for them unreachable. This is why they make the additional empirical mistake of believing that scientists must be "naive realists" in order to do their job. If scientists were naive realists about the facts they produce they would not produce any: they would just wait (Latour and Woolgar [1979] 1986; Latour 1987; Lynch 1985; Callon 1989; chap 2; chap 4; Pickering 1984). To portray scientists as bench realists is a revealing mistake. It could be understandable from sociologists who have never met or studied science in the making, but C&Y have, so it is not out of ignorance they make this blunder but out of the impossibility of their entertaining any status for entities other than these two: either the scallops are out there and force themselves on naive realists, or they are in there made of social relations of humans talking about them. The attribution of naive realism to scientists is the mirror image of the attribution to themselves of what we should call "naive socialism." With this divide of the data they entirely forget that scallops exist under various forms at the same time (probably none of them resembles "out-thereness") and that all the scientists are busy *not* limiting their discussion to social relations but devise hundreds of ways—yes inscriptions are one among many—to mobilize the various forms of scallops. Scientists never exist simply as people talking among people about people.

The second mistake is of a greater magnitude, since it bears on our attempt to overcome the first mistake. Since it is impossible to take only one of many ontological positions in order to account for the way scientists bring in nonhumans, we the analysts have to entertain the whole range. One way to do this is to extend our principle of symmetry to vocabulary and to decide that whatever term is used for humans, we will use it for nonhumans as well. It does not mean that we wish to extend intentionality to things, or mechanism to humans, but only that with any one attribute we should be able to depict the other. By doing this crisscrossing of the divide, we hope to overcome the difficulty of siding with one, and only one, of the camps. How do C&Y debunk this enterprise? By rewriting Callon's articles and breaking the symmetry of vocabulary Callon wants to use. In their notes, C&Y limit themselves to the "object pole" of their obsessional yardstick. They rewrite only what they see as the scallops side and triumphantly argue that, once rewritten, it makes no distinction at all between the old account of historians granting agency to things in themselves and Callon's account that crisscrosses the whole gradient of agencies by not limiting things to their "out-thereness." No wonder that if they rewrite "negotiation" as "discovery," or "actant" as "actor," it seems to make no difference. But the writing was crucial in allowing the passage of words through the Great Divide and back. Of course it is not crucial for C&Y, since they believe that they possess the right metalanguage to talk about science making—the language of things in themselves alternating with the language of humans among themselves—but it matters enormously to us since we believe the symmetric metalanguage should be invented that will avoid the absurdities due to the divide of two asymmetric vocabularies (divide which has been imposed to render the very activity of building society with facts and artifacts unthinkable). Of course our two articles would have been better if instead of using the same vocabulary for the two sides we could have used an unbiased vocabulary. But is it our fault that it does not exist? If "enroll" smacks of anthropomorphism, and "attach" of zoomorphism or of physimorphism? In the future we will forge and use this symmetric vocabulary, but in the meantime we wish to avoid the deleterious effect of alternation by borrowing what is acceptable on one side to show how it can be acclimatized on the other. Here again, actors are smarter than social scientists. The repertoires they use are hybrid and impure, whether they concern catalysts which become "poisoned," researchers who are "deprogrammed," or computers which are "bugged." One of the basic tasks for future studies of science and technology is to establish a symmetrical vocabulary. We should be credited with having tried to do so, and when no other solution was available, to have chosen a repertoire which bears no insult to nonhumans.

The third mistake is still more momentous. Our colleagues see the straw in our eye but not the beam in their own eyes. C&Y accuse us of not playing their game and of limiting the task of deciding what nature is to humans, and only to humans. This implies that they, or at least Collins (since Yearley had done discourse analysis before recanting it), are able to do this for their own case studies.

Such is the irony of their attack on our symmetry principle that Collins has never been able to live up to his own rule of the game. Gravity waves (Collins 1985) do indeed often appear in the settlement of controversies about them, but how do they appear? They leak surreptitiously through the account, as we will show in the last section. Collins alternates between an account where only humans talk among themselves about gravity waves and an account, supposedly left to the scientists, where gravity waves do most of the talking, or at least the writing. Extremely good at showing the opening of controversies, the indefinite negotiability of facts, the skill necessary to transport any matter of facts, the infinite regress of underdetermination, Collins has nothing to say about the closing of controversies, the non-negotiability of facts, and the slow routinization that redistributes skills; he simply shifts the burden to the Edinburgh school. No wonder, since he rejects all these problems as belonging to the natural realist—the other side of his alternation mechanism. Alternation is supposed to be the answer, but it is the most damning solution of all. This "Don Juanism of knowledge," as Nietzsche called it, cannot posture as a highly moral position. Don Juanism is a convenient way of avoiding the constraints of marriage and forgetting in one frame every tenet that was learned in the other; it cannot pass for a solution, not a moral one at least. We prefer not to alternate at all. Ironically, it is Collins's belief that he has achieved results different from those of the traditional historian which gives him the courage to dismiss our work, work which simply tries to achieve Collins's goal not only in intention but in effect. What is our position? We do not want to accept the respective roles granted to things and to humans. If we agree to follow the attribution of roles, the whole game opens up. In practice, no one is able, and Collins no more than any one else, to deny for good the presence of nonhumans in achieving consensus (natural realism), but neither can we make them play the part of a final arbiter who settles disputes for good (social realism). So why not modify the scenario once and for all? Nonhumans are party to all our disputes, but instead of being those closed, frozen, and estranged things-in-themselves whose part has been either exaggerated or downplayed, they are actants—open or closed, active or passive, wild or domesticated, far away or near, depending on the result of the interactions. When they enter the scene they are endowed with all the nonhuman powers that rationalists like them to have, as well as the warmth and uncertainty that social realists recognize in humans. But symmetrically, humans, instead of acting like humans-among-themselves whose part has been minimized or exaggerated, are granted all the powers of discussion, speech, and negotiation sociologists like them to have, but in addition they endorse the fate of all the non-humans for whom rationalists and technologists are so concerned. The choice is simple: either we alternate between two absurdities or we redistribute actantial roles. It is not a question of asserting that there is no perceptible difference. The point is methodological. If we wish to follow a controversy through and to account for its possible closure in ways other than having recourse to the Edinburgh sociologists, then it must be accepted that the distribution of roles and competences should be left open. Are we to speak of intentionality, of behavior, of social competences, of interest or attachment? The answers are to be found mainly in the hands of scientists and engineers. Their work is exactly that of organizing and stabilizing these attributions and the classifications they lead to. Male baboons were seized by aggressive impulses before Strum arrived on the scene (Strum 1987); afterwards they were seen as manipulating social networks. To take the scientists' place in deciding on the distribution of actants' competences instead of following them in their work of constructing these competences is a methodological mistake and worse, a serious error of political judgment. Since differences are so visible, what needs to be understood is their construction, their transformations, their remarkable variety and mobility, in order to substitute a multiplicity of little local divides for one great divide. We do not deny differences; we refuse to consider them a priori and to hierarchize them once and for all. One is not born a scallop; one becomes one. A parallel could be drawn with studies on social classes or on gender differences. Who would dare to promote the idea that there are no differences between men and women or between the working class and the upper-middle class? Should these be considered differences of kind to be expressed in different repertoires? The recognition of the historicity of differences, their irreversibility, their disintegration, and their proliferation passes by way of a bitter struggle against the assertion of one great ahistorical difference.

But the fourth mistake is the most important, since it reveals the sheep behind the wolf's clothing. Several times in the paper, C&Y reject our appeal to a variety of hybrid nonhumans because we lack the scientific credentials:

> If we are really to enter scallop behavior into our explanatory equations, then Callon must demonstrate his scientific credentials. . . . There is not the slightest reason for us to accept his opinions on the nature of scallops if he is any less of a scallop scientist than the re-

searchers he describes. In fact, we readers would prefer him to be *more* of a scallop expert than the others if he is to speak authoritatively on the subject. Is he an authority on scallops? Or did he merely report the scientists' views on the matter. . . . Certainly we do not have a study that can offer us any surprises about the natural world, or one that clarifies the credibility and authority of science. . . .

. . . This backward step [of Latour] has happened as a consequence of the misconceived extension of symmetry that takes humans out of their pivotal role. If nonhumans are actants, then we need a way of determining their power. This is the business of scientists and technologists; it takes us directly back to the . . . conventional and prosaic accounts of the world from which we escaped in the early 1970s.

Callon is accused of not being a marine biologist, and he thus should not be able to talk about scallops at all—only about humans, his only terrain as a sociologist; Latour is accused of not knowing anything about technology; he should restrict himself to humans. In addition he is accused of not using the part of privileged knowledge he might have *qua* sociologist in the field of expert systems. This accusation coming from the heads of the scientific establishment is frequent. Why is it launched by sociologists of science? If they were Mertonian it would be acceptable, since Merton's tenet is to limit ourselves to the sociology of scientists and to leave science safely in the hands of the experts. But the accusation is leveled at us by sociologists who have fought for years against this limitation of sociology to social aspects, and who claim to explain the very content of science. Not only this; they also claim that they have to fight the hegemony of scientists' definition of nature! We have reached the limit of absurdity, and C&Y should be thanked for demonstrating so frankly that their fight against the hegemony of scientists over the definition of nature may be a game just as gratuitous as chicken. They never seriously believed that it was feasible. On the contrary, they accept 98 percent of the Great Divide: to the natural scientists the things, to the sociologists the remainder, that is, the humans. Either they are so deeply scientistic in their worldview that this whole enterprise is a way of defending science against attacks on their hegemony—but then what are their grounds for attacking us for doing what is an equally "reactionary" task?— or they really believe that they threaten scientists' privilege. How can this privilege be destroyed without granting sociologists the right to question the scientists' own definition of nature? Either C&Y are sheep in wolves' clothing or they chicken out of the fight. The most extravagant claim is that scientists' accounts of their own field are prosaic and boring. Have they ever seen a scientific field, ever approached a controversy, ever measured the lack of consensus, or ever felt the agitation and ranges of alternatives of professional engineers? We lack the scientific credentials, but there is one thing we can do: preserve the minority views for the benefit of the scientists themselves and preserve for the benefit of the outside public the range of alternatives on which scientists thrive. This is a much more efficient strategy for disputing hegemony than alternating between a mere social account and the condescending view that scientific practitioners are mere scientists. The beauty of studying science in action is that there is always enough dissent to let outsiders in and to offer observers with no scientific credentials a way of capturing the chaos of science. Strangely enough, we thought (until C&Y's paper came out, that is) that we had learned this lesson from Collins.

How can there be such a deep misunderstanding? How can they dismiss our work, which tries to get at the content of science and does not accept the privilege of the scientific definition of nature? Because that would mean abandoning their privilege, and that of social scientists in general, of defining the human world, the social world. And since, with their unidimensional yardstick, there is no other solution but alternating violently between two unsatisfactory explanations, they feel trapped, and their only way out is to deny that there is any difficulty or to make sure that alternative definitions are not endorsed by new students. We are not talking of intentions here, but of use and of effects, as C&Y rightly ask us to do. In effect, they are forbidding sociologists to document the vast diversity of positions entertained by scientists, either because scientists are supposed to have special access to nature and to be naive realists, or because sociologists have no scientific credentials and should stick to the human realms; this is an extraordinary step backward—since backwardness appears to be the issue. Forbidding such documentation is a serious error concerning the nature both of society and of scientific activity.

Technology is the shibboleth that tests the quality of science studies, because every mistake made in the science studies appears more blatant when we are studying technology. Like Callon's article on scallops, Latour's piece on mundane artifacts (In press b) aims at circulating through the Great Divide and deploying the whole gradient of entities from "pure" social relations to "mere" things, without giving any privilege to the two extremes. Like the piece on scallops, it is an ontological manifesto and a point about social theory. Just as scientists and fishermen in St. Brieuc Bay orchestrate a whole series of scallop-like entities, engineers and consumers dele-

gate a whole gradient of social attributes to either humanlike entities or nonhuman entities. In the former article disputed by C&Y
the point of departure is firmly positioned on the vertical axis of our
diagram, which allows us to focus not on humans or nonhumans
but on the activity of shifting, delegating, and distributing competences. In both articles the intention was not to say that scallops
have voting power and will exercise it, or that door closers are
entitled to social benefits and burial rites, but that a common vocabulary and a common ontology should be created by crisscrossing
the divide by borrowing terms from one end to depict the other. Both
articles carefully follow the large range of expressions, metaphysics,
social theories, used by humans to account for the human-nonhuman
associations; and both show that this gamut of expressions is much
larger, more interesting, and more profound than the two vocabularies of things-in-themselves and humans-among-themselves that
sociologists and technical determinists believe are necessary. But
C&Y interpret the second article the same way as they did the first:
Latour is accused of playing into the hands of the hated—but are
they really hated?—technical determinists. He is also accused, and
rightly so, of using the counterfactual method. Thought experiment
is about the only way with which we can estrange ourselves from
total familiarity with mundane artifacts. We agree that this cannot
be the solution and that many better methods should be developed,
and indeed have (Akrich 1987; Latour, Mauguin, and Teil, in press;
Latour, in press, c), but the point of the paper is clearly how to see
and position artifacts—and this is indeed what most of the critiques
of C&Y address.

Apart from their witty critique of counterfactual methods, our
colleagues show still more clearly in their analysis of the second
article their scientistic worldview. They start with an absolute dichotomy between purposeful action and mindless material behavior. Then they state that "it is clear that the interpretative method
[used for intentional humans] is unusable, since doors have no social
life in which we could participate." The matter-of-fact tone of this
extraordinary claim could not be more clearly at odds with the social theory we have developed over the years (Callon 1980b, 1987;
Callon and Latour 1981; Strum and Latour 1987; Law 1987). There
is no thinkable social life without the participation—in all the
meanings of the word—of nonhumans, and especially machines and
artifacts. Without them we would live like baboons (Strum 1987).
Technology is not far from the social realm in the hands of the technologists: it is social relations viewed in their durability, in their
cohesion. It is utterly impossible to think for even a minute about

social relations without mediating them with hundreds of entities. Of course these nonhuman entities may be dismissed—they are indeed ignored by most social theorists, even by those like Barnes (1988), who should know more about science studies—but our point is that the activity of dismissing them, of disattributing meaning and will, is as difficult, as contentious, and as revealing as the attribution of meaning, will, and intentionality to humans. Although we can waffle on the complete unification of nature and society, which we claim is our only object of study, there is no possible hesitation when dealing with artifacts, since they are man-made. Scientists may be realists on the cold and established part of their science, but engineers are constructivists about the artifacts they construct. The weight of efficiency is much lighter than that of truth—and has a less prestigious philosophical pedigree. Hence the prolongation of the use of the unidimensional yardstick in technology is less easy to forgive than in science, where after all, we cannot ask sociologists to undo the enormous preparatory work philosophers of science have done for them.

This is not the view taken by C&Y, to say the least. They take it as their brief, and moral high ground, to differentiate clearly between what humans are able to do—purposes, intentions, common sense, negotiating the rules, infinite regress—and what the machines have always been limited to doing—lacking common sense, brutish, material, asocial, and rule-bound. This is a respectable position if we are engaged in a humanistic fight against the technologists' hypes, but is uninteresting as an empirical tool to describe the daily negotiation of engineers to redistribute these very characterizations via the artifacts. As long as social scientists safely stuck to social relations—power, institutions, classes, interactions, and so forth— they might have considered artifact making as a sort of borderline case which could be put out of the picture of society. But how can we do this with sociotechnical imbroglios where every case is a borderline case? Either C&Y want to keep their yardstick alternating from mere matter to intentional humans, in which case they should study a domain other than technology, or they are interested in accounting for this activity and should abandon the worst possible standard to size it up. If they dare to say "perish the case studies as long as the moral and humanistic yardstick that allows us to extirpate social relations from mere things is safe," they can't possibly accuse us for looking for other empirical programs.

Our empirical program does not claim either that humans and artifacts are exactly the same or that they are radically different. We leave this question entirely open. A speed bump—aptly called a sleeping policeman—is neither the same as a standing policeman, nor is it the same as a sign Slow Down, nor is it the same as the incorporated caution British drivers are supposed to learn culturally from birth. What is interesting, though, is that campus managers decided to shift the program of action "slow down cars on campus" from a culturally learned action to a mere piece of behavior—the physical shock of concrete bumps on the suspension of the cars. The program of action: "Slow down please for the sake of your fellow humans" has been translated into another one: "protect your own suspension for your own benefit." Are we not allowed to follow this translation through? Who made the move from action to behavior, from meaning to force, from culture to nature? We the analysts or they, the analyzed? Who or what is now enforcing the law, the standing or the sleeping policeman? Who are supposed to have sociality embedded in themselves, the talking humans or the silent road bumper? To claim that only the humans have meaning and intentionality and are able to renegotiate the rules indefinitely is an empty claim, since this is the very reason why the engineers, tired of the indiscipline and indefinite renegotiability of drivers, shifted their program of action to decrease this pliability. By insisting on alternation, Collins can no more explain the closure of technical controversies than the closure of scientific controversies. If engineers as well as scientists are crisscrossing the very boundaries that sociologists claim cannot be passed over, we prefer to abandon the sociologists and to follow our informants.

Exactly as for science, C&Y claim that every time you appeal to the artifacts' action you have to use the technological-determinist vocabulary. This is not only a wrong interpretation of our work, it is wrong of engineers. There is a constant thread in C&Y's papers that if you document only scientists' and engineers' accounts it will be prosaic, conventional, unsurprising, uninformative, and merely technical and rule bound. Again, this portrayal of scientific activity would not be surprising from a Habermassian philosopher or from an Ellulian technophobe, but it is very surprising from social scientists who have intimate knowledge of scientific controversies. If there is one striking element in science studies—and if there is one piece of news in what we have all written—it is the amazing diversity, the liveliness, and the heterogeneity of science and engineering (even in its most deadly tasks, as can be seen in MacKenzie 1990). It is precisely because there is no such thing as "a science" with authority and complete prosaic totalitarian dominion over nature that it is so easy for us as social scientists to tread into and to demonstrate the lack of hegemony and the rich confusion between the humans and nonhumans that make up our collective.

We do not claim that our theories are right. We are looking for collaborations with English and American scholars to make them better, and in doing so we will help to achieve their goals as well as ours. But C&Y resist this enrollment; they feel they have the right to dismiss our work because they have already provided an explanation, and that our attempts are belated and muddled. This is why they accuse us of merely rephrasing the problems through the catchall network vocabulary and of not providing an explanation of the closure of controversies. This implies that they have explained something in science studies.

The accusation of not explaining things is always tricky in social science, because it ends up in a Lebanese situation, with everyone looking at the strength of the other's explanation and destroying it. In SSK it is still more difficult, because the whole pattern of "providing an explanation through the use of causes" has been largely disputed for the natural sciences (Lynch 1985; Woolgar 1988b; Collins 1985; chap. 2; Latour 1987), which makes their reimportation into the sociology of science a rather difficult job. Moreover, explanations might not be desirable after all (Woolgar 1988a). A complete description of network dynamics might provide a better explanation, in the end, than the delusive search for causes (Latour, Mauguin, and Teil, in press). Although it would take too long to argue those points, it is possible to compare our pattern of description with Collins's, especially his most elaborate work, *Changing Order* (1985), to see if he really has the grounds to discount our offer to help him out of his quandary.

Like us, Collins is better at description than explanation, but in the end of his book he feels obliged to provide a closure mechanism, and it is not uncharitable to find out how much better he is than us. His intellectual resources come from a network theory, which is not without resemblance to ours, the only difference being that we have taken ten years to document, quantify, justify, and argue it (Callon, Law, and Rip 1986; Callon, Courtial, and Lavergne 1989; Callon, Laredo, and Rabeharisoa, in press) and that Collins uses a few pages of metaphors to get rid of the problem. After describing for a hundred pages the experimenter's regress—which is a nice exemplification of Duhem's thesis that there is no *experimentia crucis*—Collins ties Weber's decision to quit the controversy to Mary Hesse's network theory: "a kind of spider's web of concepts" (1985, 131). Hesse's networks have the interesting property of explaining the choice of a theory through the notion of "entrenchment" (Law and Lodge 1984). Collins adds to this the important metaphor of "reverberation": "The point is that the whole network is mutually supporting since everything is linked to everything else. But, by virtue of the way that everything is connected a change in one link might reverberate through the whole of the network." (1985, 131)

Although this might sound like the diagnosis of one of Molière's physicians, it is OK with us if it means that in the end the solidity of a claim will be the exact measure of the resistance to a test of strength of the whole network. Hacking (chap. 2) uses a similar argument, although he provides a much richer vocabulary than Collins to account for the reverberation and the entrenchment of a claim. Once we abandon the twin resources of nature and society, we are all, it seems, looking for the same "explanation"—the stabilization of Hesse's or some other associationist network—but we disagree on what a network is made of and how to empirically calculate or account for the test.

Here Collins makes his first crucial mistake. Instead of seeking a genuine network theory—and testing the strength of a claim by operationalizing Hesse's qualitative arguments as we have done through hundreds of pages of programming language (see especially the programs Leximappe™, Lexinet™, Candide™) he reintroduces the division between social and cognitive nets with no better metaphor than that of a coin. "And just as social relations can be described in terms of social networks, their cognitive counterparts can be described in terms of Hesse net. The Hesse net and the network of interactions in society are but two sides of the same coin. To understand each, one must understand both" (132). Although the whole task is to pay the philosophical, sociological, economic, and computer price of this fusion of the two types of network—cognitive and social—Collins hedges the issue by saying that they are both different and the same and that they furthermore reflect each other, as in the crudest Marxist reflection theory.

But the second mistake is more damning, since the three notions of entrenchment, reverberation, and wider network are now used to explain the stabilization from the outside:

> The scientists, then, are faced with a choice (albeit, a highly constrained choice); at what level of inference, or externality, do they report their results? The more inferences they make the more interesting the results are to a wider and wider audience—the more they rattle the spider's web of concepts, as it were. But, if the results are not likely to preserve everyone's "socially acceptable conceptualizations of the natural world," then the more inferences they make, the

more bits of taken-for-granted reality they are threatening, and the more trouble they are going to cause" (138).

It is amusing that C&Y deride our technical use of the notion of obligatory passage point and deem the rattling of spiders a better explanation. But it is not amusing at all to see that the good old society is imported—through the spider metaphor—to brutally close the infinite experimenter's regress: "Networks ramify continuously so that reverberations induced within science have their effects outside just as influences from outside the scientific profession feed back into science proper. Science and technology are affected in quite straightforward ways by political climate." (165)

Merton would have been much more specific, much more mediated, much less "straightforward." Are these authors the same ones who mock our translation theory, which accounts with precision for the successive shifts from one repertoire (exoteric) to the others (esoteric) (Latour 1987); the same ones who deride the "quali-quantitative" work that enables us to follow in detail how politics and science might "reverberate" in each other? Yes, and they prefer empty metaphors of spider and coin to network theory because this is the only way to save their classic view of society as what abruptly puts a stop to the indefinite negotiability of scientists—a nice case of entrenchment indeed.

As long as he is in the laboratory looking for replication procedures, Collins is like Woolgar—stressing the indefinite pliability and endless negotiability of everything—but when he wishes to finish his book and closes Weber's story, he has no other issue but to jump to an Edinburgh type of interest theory: the winner will be the one who reverberates less (or more) through the entrenched interests of the wider society. (It is because of this contradiction that Collins attacks Woolgar in the same paper where he attacks us.) Duhem or Woolgar for the inner core, Edinburgh and Marxism for the outside, and in the middle a free decision that scientists make for no reason at all, in the most complete arbitrariness. What scholars like Law, Lynch, Knorr, Hacking, Jardine, Schaffer and us have shown over and over again, that is, the slow accumulation of calibrated gestures, black boxes, and routinized skills which are more and more difficult to modify, is transformed by Collins in a sudden decision to give up in a fight where nothing had force. Instead of being slowly beaten by uppercut after uppercut, the boxer Weber is touched by feathers, none of them with any weight, and suddenly he falls knocked out, without any reason whatsoever, since he could have gone on indefinitely negotiating with his adversaries: "In retrospect, Weber would have served his case better to have maintained his refusal to use electrostatic calibration—not just because the results proved unfavorable but because the assumptions taken on board by the act of calibration and the restrictions of interpretation imposed as a result" (103).

Such sentences, which combine Whiggish history ("in retrospect"), natural realism ("results proved unfavorable"), and decisionism ("would have maintained his case better") are an indicator that Collins, because he is unable to solve the link between laboratory negotiation and the wider society, may never have described in a satisfactory way what we all credit him for, that is, controversies. And this is why he is so unable to understand us. We take up the job where he leaves off. All our work aims at defining the thread in the spider's mouth, the dozens of intermediaries that slowly make Weber unable to move, the uppercuts that one after another bring him down. Instead of the empty claim that Weber should have maintained his refusal—which is like chiding a boxer after the countdown for not having stood up—we multiply the texts, the inscriptions, the instruments, the skills, the nonhumans, none of which has a decisive weight, it is true, but all of which, mobilized together, woven together, are enough to transform the indefinite pliability of a situation into an irreversible fact. Wherever we devise a hybrid that carries *some* weight—the mass spectrometer of the TRF story, the immutable mobiles, the spokesperson, the texts—Collins misunderstands us and accuses us vehemently of bringing nature back in. No, we are explaining in detail what he is unable to explain, how and why a spider makes a web, how and why one scientist is better than another, how and why a boxer is knocked out by another one. We do not want to alternate between negotiation and entrenchment. We do not feel that Collins has yet delivered the goods he claims to have delivered which allow him to get rid of us. We still want to help him out and study with him not only what he is good at: the beginning of controversy when reversibility is large and skills uncodified, but also what he is so bad at: the gradual closing of controversy and the reshuffling of the networks. We feel that if we worked together we might begin to sketch a description of society-science.

Why can't Collins understand us? Here is the core of our ethical and political disagreement. The only way for Collins to debunk scientists' hegemony is to portray them through this alternated three-stage situation:

1. Indefinite negotiation
2. Complete social determinism (delegated to the Edinburgh sociologists)
3. Free decision.

It is only if scientists are portrayed in this way that they lose the right to a special relation with nature and thus free social scientists from the domination of the natural sciences. "Do as you like, but if you close a dispute, it is not because of nature, but by alternation between free decision and social constraints. Thus you have no upper ground to invade our social realm. Stay where you are, we will stay where we are. You do not have nature on your side, so do not criticize us." Collins's solution is a good old Kantian divide. By contrast, our paradigm is twice reactionary in the eyes of Collins: first, we believe that scientists close controversies for many other reasons than arbitrariness or social entrenchment; second, we do not believe that social scientists should be left to themselves. Since we believe that there are many other ways to dispute scientists' hegemony—the first one being to dispute the very distribution of agencies between the things-in-themselves and the humans-among-themselves—we cannot be content with this resurrection of Kant's justice of peace (see Latour, in press, a, for details).

From this disagreement, however, we do not draw the same conclusion as C&Y do. They claim that our program is entirely misguided, reactionary, if not in intent, at least in use, and that it should be not followed all the way. We believe, on the contrary, that although it is experimental, uncertain, and incomplete, it should be carried all the way, with the help of the many clever and excellent scholars inspired by the various science studies schools, and that this new move will vindicate most of Collins's discoveries and insights by freeing them from their most blatant limitations. They want to throw us out. We want to change the water, but to keep the Bath baby in, since it is also *our* baby. After all, having children, even through Don Juan's immoral alternating strategy, is more fertile than playing chicken.

REFERENCES

Akrich, Madeleine. 1987. Comment décrire les objets techniques. *Technique et Culture* 5:49–63.

Ashmore, Malcolm. 1989. *The Reflexive Thesis: Wrighting Sociology of Scientific Knowledge.* Chicago: University of Chicago Press.

Barnes, Barry. 1988. *The Nature of Power.* Cambridge: Polity Press.

Bijker, Wiebe E., Thomas Hughes, and Trevor Pinch, eds. 1987. *New Developments in the Social Studies of Technology.* Cambridge: MIT Press.

Bijker, W., and J. Law, eds. In press. *Constructing Networks and Systems.* Cambridge: MIT Press.

Bowker, Geof, and Bruno Latour. 1987. A Booming Discipline Short of Discipline. *Social Studies of Science* 17:715–48.

Callon, Michel. 1980a. Struggles and Negotiations to Decide What Is Problematic and What Is Not the Sociology of Translation. In K. Knorr, P. Krohn, and R. Whitley, 197–220.

———. 1980b. "The State and technical Innovation: A Case Study of the Electrical Vehicle in France" *Research Policy* 9:358–76.

———. 1981. Pour une sociologie des controverses techniques. *Fundamenta Scientiae* 2:381–99.

———. 1986. Some Elements of a Sociology of Translation: Domestication of the Scallops and the Fishermen of St. Brieux Bay. In Law 1986b, 196–229.

———. 1987. Society in the Making: The Study of Technology as a Tool for Sociological Analysis. In Bijker et al. In press, 83–106.

Callon, Michel, ed. 1989. *La science et ses réseaux: Genèse et circulation des faits scientifiques.* La Découverte Coll. Anthropologie de la science, Paris.

Callon, Michel, and Bruno Latour. 1981. Unscrewing the Big Leviathan: How Do Actors Macrostructure Reality. In Knorr and Cicourel 1981, 277–303.

Callon, M, John Law, and Arie Rip, eds. 1986. *Mapping the Dynamics of Science and Technology.* London: Macmillan.

Callon, Michel, Jean-Pierre Courtial, Françoise Lavergne. 1989. *Co-Word Analysis: A Tool for the Evaluation of Public Research Policy: The Case of Polymers.* Report for the NSF grant PRA no.85 12-982, Paris.

Callon, Michel, Phillippe Laredo, and Vololona Rabeharisoa. In press. The Management and Evaluation of Technology: The Case of AFME. *Research Policy.*

Collins, Harry. 1985. *Changing Order: Replication and Induction in Scientific Practice.* Los Angeles: Sage.

Knorr, Karin. 1981. *The Manufacture of Knowledge: An Essay on the Constructivist and Contextual Nature of Science.* Oxford: Pergamon.

Knorr, Karin, and Aron Cicourel eds. 1981. *Advances in Social Theory and Methodology toward an Integration of Micro and Macro Sociologies.* London: Routledge and Kegan Paul.

Knorr, Karin, Roger Krohn, and Richard Whitley, eds. 1981. *The Social Process of Scientific Investigation.* Dordrecht: Reidel.

Latour, Bruno. 1987. *Science in Action: How to Follow Scientists and Engineers through Society.* Cambridge: Harvard University Press.

———. 1988. *The Pasteurization of France.* Cambridge: Harvard University Press.

———. 1990. Postmodern? No Simply Amodern. Steps towards an Anthropology of Science: An Essay Review. *Studies in the History and Philosophy of Science* 21:145–71.

————. In press a. One More Turn after the Social Turn: Easing Science Studies into the Non-Modern World. In E. McMullin, ed. *The Social Dimensions of Science.* Notre Dame: Notre Dame University Press.

————. In press b. Where are the Missing Masses? Sociology of a Few Mundane Artefacts. In Bijker and Law,

————. In press c. *Aramis ou l'amour des Techniques.* Paris: La Découverte.

Latour, Bruno, and Jim Johnson. 1988. Mixing Humans with Non-Humans: Sociology of a Door-Opener. *Social Problems* (special issue on sociology of science, ed. Leigh Star) 35:298–310.

Latour, Bruno, Philippe Mauguin, and Geneviève Teil. In press. A Note on Socio-Technical Graphs. *Social Studies of Science.*

Latour, Bruno, and Shirley Strum. Human Social Origins: Please Tell Us Another Origin Story! *Journal of Biological and Social Structures* 9:169–87.

Latour, Bruno, and Steve Woolgar. |1979| 1986. *Laboratory Life: The Construction of Scientific Facts.* Princeton: Princeton University Press.

Law, John. 1986a. On the Methods of Long-Distance Control: Vessels, Navigation, and the Portuguese Route to India. In Law 1986b, 234–63.

————. 1987. Technology and Heterogeneous Engineering: The Case of the Portuguese Expansion. In Bijker et al. 1986, 111–34.

Law, John, ed. 1986. *Power, Action and Belief: A New Sociology of Knowledge?* Keele Sociological Review Monograph, Keele.

Law, John, and Peter Lodge. 1984. *Science for Social Scientists.* London: Macmillan.

Lynch, Michael. 1985. *Art and Artifact in Laboratory Science: A Study of Shop Work and Shop Talk in a Research Laboratory.* London: Routledge.

MacKenzie, Don. 1990. *Inventing Accuracy.* Cambridge: MIT Press.

Pickering, Andrew. 1984. *Constructing Quarks: A Sociological History of Particle Physics.* Chicago: University of Chicago Press.

Shapin, Steven, and Simon Schaffer. 1985. *Leviathon and the Air Pump.* Princeton: Princeton University Press.

Star, Leigh. 1988. Introduction: Special Issue on Sociology of Science and Technology. *Social Problems* 35:197–205.

Strum, Shirley. 1987. *Almost Human: A Journey into the World of Baboons.* New York: Random House.

Strum, Shirley, and Bruno Latour. 1987. The Meanings of Social: From Baboons to Humans. *Social Science Information* 26:783–802.

Woolgar, Steve. 1988a. *Knowledge and Reflexivity: New Frontiers in the Sociology of Knowledge.* London: Sage.

————. 1988b. *Science: The Very Idea.* London: Tavistock.

13

Journey Into Space

H. M. Collins and Steven Yearley

Michel Callon and Bruno Latour's (C&L) "Don't Throw the Baby Out with the Bath School" (Chap. 12) response to our "Epistemological Chicken" (Chap. 10) is distinguished by the number of disparate issues that it raises.[1] We need to clear away some of the prickly undergrowth in their remarks before we can approach the tall trees of their argument. The central and important points in C&L's response seem to be: their claim to have moved to an orthogonal dimension of analysis, their arguments here and elsewhere about the socially constructed nature of dichotomies—probably the key to the whole debate—and their suggestion that SSK supports the traditional view of science even while it is trying to dissolve it. The last point is paired with the claim that their approach alone can get rid of the distinction between science and other cultural activities. Another major, if less penetrating, point concerns the use of networks. C&L present their case on networks through a contrast between Collins's *Changing Order*, which, they say, uses networks in a superficial and metaphorical way, and their own "hundreds of pages of programming language."

Before we can get to these important arguments, we have to hack our way through the following bramble bushes: the paper is anti-French and antiforeign; we deal with only two, presumably unrepresentative, papers taken from a much larger corpus of work; our position is smug, resting on "blithe ignorance"; in prescribing naive realism for scientists at the bench and social realism for ourselves, we act as though we are unaware that scientists have a wide repertoire of philosophical positions. Let us take these up in turn.

1. There was a famous radio series on the BBC in the 1950s called "Journey Into Space." The first moon explorers, Lemmy, Doc, and Mitch are kidnapped by an advanced civilization and transported on a strange journey, crash-landing on an unfamiliar planet. It turns out that the planet is Earth but that they have been transported back in time many millennia. The theme is familiar; it figures also in "Beyond the Planet of the Apes" and "The Hitchhiker's Guide to the Galaxy."

Through the Brambles

The paper is not intended to be anti-French. Though it may one day be the case that an attack on Callon and Latour is an attack on France, we did not think that day had yet arrived. We apologize for our contribution to the bad impression of our references to the work of C&L as the "French school." This was a mistake; it was certainly an insult to French scholars who do not share C&L's worldview. We will henceforth refer to the "actor network school," or, to be more accurate, the "*Actant* network school."[2] We are not sufficiently self-confident to think that our own work represents Britain as a whole and therefore we will ignore the suggestion that our paper is chauvinistically British.

It is true that "Chicken" deals in detail with only two papers. In debates of this sort detailed textual analysis is necessary, and it would not be possible to deal with "six books, five edited volumes, and about sixty articles" in anything less than a Ph.D. thesis. A problem for "big physics" is that it is no longer possible to test the findings of particle accelerators without the huge resources required to build one. Let us hope we are not entering an age of "big philosophy."[3]

A still more profound problem than logistics, however, is the *interpretation* of all these writings. Over the years we have found difficulty in taking some of the more flamboyant statements of the actant network school at face value, but fearing to appear foolish, we have kept quiet. This is a dilemma familiar to readers of any sophisticated body of writings. It certainly is the duty of a critic to understand what is written, but this is not, as C&L rather surprisingly suggest, a straightforward matter. Latour's "Sociology of A Door" seemed at last to make everything clear. It is an important paper—published twice and presented frequently. It is a widely admired paper. It is a very lucid paper, or so we thought. At the same time, it seems to tell us everything we always wanted to know about actant network theory but were afraid to ask.

Callon's paper is another widely admired, widely cited, and apparently clear paper. These two together were not, then, chosen at ran-

2. We now concede that the term "actant" does make a difference. When in "Chicken" we remarked that it doesn't make any difference whether C&L use the term actor or actant, we meant that since they do not make a useful distinction in their usage, it makes no difference to them. We should not, however, allow the term "actor" to be hijacked and used in places of "actant" in the way they do. The notion of an actor is much too important, and the differences between actors and actants are vital.

3. Though "big is beautiful" is certainly congruent with actant network theory.

dom but as indicative of the meaning of the main corpus while being readily accessible and addressable in a limited space. We are surprised that C&L now want to disqualify the papers from serious consideration, saying that they are mere "ontological manifestos." We believe, on the contrary, that they are indicative in just the way we have used them. Readers are of course free to consider for themselves which parts of the larger corpus, and which of the writings which follow C&L's style, do exemplify the points we make.[4]

Are we blithely ignorant? We may be ignorant, but we are not blithely ignorant. We are, then, especially grateful for the gracious comments on the second page of C&L's response. More curious is the idea that our philosophical position—alternation—can arise only out of blithe ignorance. The notion of alternation is not a new one. The concept, as we acknowledge, is Peter Berger's, and we have never heard it talked of in this way before. It is of course a position that arises out of a sensibility of ignorance, a sensibility that we cannot know enough to found a sure and certain metaphysical system. But this again is not blithe ignorance; it is a very studied kind of ignorance which has a pedigree at least as old as philosophical skepticism.

We are of course aware of the range of philosophical positions that scientists themselves adopt when working at the bench. But if we were unaware of it, it would not make the slightest difference. This strand of C&L's argument bears on nothing of consequence. It is an idle wheel. It is as though we had remarked that good priests should believe in the deity and C&L had scoffingly inquired if we were unaware that priests had interests in material things, and what is more, if they had no such interest the church would not survive. What we are saying is that just as a religious form of life requires belief—without this it does not make sense—so a scientific form of life requires belief in natural reality. We have expressed this as a kind of low-level psychological imperative. That scientists also express themselves through their concerns with the mundane is the very empirical stuff of SSK. That an analyst can think that scien-

---

4. Tom Gieryn's (1990), satirical neo-Latourian treatment of the cold-fusion controversy seems to us to bring out the points nicely. In the last resort, according to Gieryn-Latour, what Pons and Fleischman needed to do to win the scientific debate was to make a nuclear powered flashlight, or its equivalent, rather than base their claim on recalcitrant laboratory apparatus. Gieryn wittily brings out the backward-looking, technologistic implications of the Callon and Latour approach.

Simon Schaffer (1991) has written a powerful and erudite critique of Latour's *Science in Action* and *The Pasteurization of France*, which reaches many similar conclusions to those expressed here.

tists' belief in natural reality is misplaced hardly rates as C&L's discovery. That the social analyst might also claim that his or her own form of life (as analyst) makes sense only if it includes an idea of social reality, both philosophically and motivationally, seems equally unproblematic.

C&L's lengthy and oft-repeated commentary on this point has any relevance only if all we want to do is follow scientists around. If that is the aim, then when the scientist talks realistically, we too will think realistically, and when the scientist talks less realistically, we too will do the same. If, however, we want to do more than follow—if we want to make explanatory sense of what scientists do—then we will want to think in our own way. Our way will be founded in the scientists' world, it will depend on our understanding the scientists' world, but it will not simply reproduce the scientists' world. There will be concepts belonging to us as analysts that do not simply follow the scientists. The methodological prescription that emerges from relativism is that explanations should be developed within the assumption that the real world does not affect what the scientist believes about it, however much the opposite view is an inevitable part of doing science. This means that when the scientist says "scallops" we see only scientists saying scallops. We never see scallops scalloping, nor do we see scallops controlling what scientists say about them.

To put this another way, in "Chicken" we said that C&L offer some useful descriptive language, though they cannot provide explanations. We need to make it clear that a descriptive language is not the same as a description. There are no descriptions that are not at the same time explanations. Something that looks like a neutral description is in essence explanatorily conservative. It says, "this is how things are, things are as you see them." Indeed we have argued that some people are drawn to actant network theory because it provides a radical-looking descriptive terminology which, deep down, is undemandingly explanatorily conservative. SSK, on the other hand, in common with the other critical parts of the social sciences, offers descriptions-explanations which try to show that things are not as they appear. In the case of SSK, the story is that things are not as they appear to scientists, technologists, and the consumers of their material and ideological products.

Networks Revisited: Ants and Ors

C&L are doing very complicated things with networks. First, they have new ideas about what should comprise the nodes of the networks they analyze. These are "actants" and they include humans and nonhumans indiscriminately. We argued in "Chicken" that these are not good ideas, and we will return to the same argument here in the specific context of network analysis. Second, in their practice, they commonly replace analysis of networks of actants with computerized analysis of associations between words in bodies of text. The semiotic underpinnings of their approach seem to make this a natural progression, but as we will see, it is more of a reductio. Third, they take their technical virtuosity—the hundreds of pages of programming—as being in itself a warrant for the superiority of their approach. These various claims are somewhat tangled, and there is a degree of self-reference in the way they are used. Our response reflects this to some extent.

To start on the third point, C&L attack Collins's use of networks as a metaphor, but there are good reasons for being careful when the idea of a network is turned into a quantitative research program. For example, in an early study of networks of communication among scientists (Collins 1974), two arguments about the operationalization of the network metaphor are set out. One of these arguments refers to the analytic paper by Mark Granovetter (1973). Granovetter suggests that influences can only have wide effect in networks of relations via weak links. This makes the empirical study of large networks of influence difficult, because weak links are precisely the hardest to investigate. When this problem is combined with the lack of robustness of many network measures (small measurement errors result in large differences in outcome), and the conceptual difficulties of defining the nature of relations (is a friendship relation unidirectional or bidirectional?), as well as the explosive properties of network research (e. g., the number of potential relations is proportional to the square of the number of nodes), networks look empirically unpromising, however exciting they may be as a metaphor.

Now these problems of method were evident in the early 1970s, and it may be that the measurement problems and the conceptual problems of network analysis have been overcome in C&L's work. But the existence of computer programs and a body of empirically researched networks does not prove this of itself. There are, after all, vast bodies of survey literature, but this does not prove that the conceptual problems of the social survey have been solved. Certainly what is required is more than assertion supported by technical virtuosity.[5]

5. The attack on Collins's use of the network metaphor reveals another of these difficult problems of meaning. For many years, when "actor networks" were pro-

What of the replacement of humans in networks with undifferentiated actants? "There is nothing stronger than networks." This Latourian phrase is unexceptionable only so long as the nodes are not meant to be things or words but humans. Given this, the network metaphor is useful for understanding what even SSK case studies refer to as "the existing facts" of science. These are the parts of any experiment that experimenters do not at any particular moment consider to be under threat of revision.[6] The size of this set of "facts" varies from time to time. It diminishes rapidly as experimenters enter controversial areas. It is quite useful to think of the factlike parts of the scientists' universe in network terms. One may think of a factlike thing as a dense node in a network of human agreement. (Though it is not self-conscious agreement; it is concerted action within a form of life.) If we think in these terms we may imagine labels attached to dense nodes. Here one sees "gravity" there "electron," there a vestigial node, labeled "magnetic monopole." The labels float above the network, as it were. The mistake is to let the labels slip down and take the place of the nodes in the network.

It is when the labels slip down that the trouble starts. Suddenly we cease to see the way the density of the nodes is always varying, always in need of maintenance, and always vulnerable to major shifts in alliances. It makes it seem as though a node undergoes some qualitative transformation at the point in time when the label moves down and replaces the much less well defined "area of density." It makes the difference between a vestigial node such as "magnetic monopole"—which has not been replaced by a label—and a more solid node such as "gravity," seem to be more than just closure of a debate. It invests closure with an ontological significance. After

---

claimed as a new method, we had assumed that something in addition to good old network theory was being referred to. We had assumed that the crucial feature of actor network theory was not the theory of nets and di-graphs and all that, but was the *actor* part of the term. We thought that the crucial move was the semiotic turn—the use of the notion of *actant* to encompass both human and nonhuman. We thought it was the nature of the nodes and relations that was important, not the fact that there is such a thing as graph theory and that there are computer programs for analyzing networks. We thought, quite frankly, that the mathematical, computerized, analysis of networks was something to bring in the research grants rather than a revolutionary claim. If we had realized that network theory was at the heart of the matter, we would have applauded the effort and wished it luck, but there would have been nothing especially original to think about. Networks have been used in SSK since the beginning.

6. We thank Nick Jardine for stressing this point in correspondence.

this transformation we might be led to explain the existence of a node by the existence of the label. We can, in other words, think that the strength of the nodes causes the nodes to become strong. We give far too much to the nodes; we give to the nodes what ought to be reserved for the relations between the people. We begin to speak of the nodes in the way that scientists speak of them, and we may think it possible to delegate power to the labels, forgetting that all the power lies with the people who make up the areas of density and those people's concerted actions.

C&L stress in various parts of their work that these strong nodes are in need of maintenance, and that these "black boxes" may be opened up again. But if this is true, there is no need to replace the human agreements that maintain (and have the potential not to maintain) the black boxes with labels, or with things. It is only the replacement of actors with actants that enables Latour to claim to have discovered hidden power that others had neglected: "the missing masses." It is only when the labels are allowed to have reality that they can have potency beyond that granted to them by humans. This granting of potency to labels is the great mistake in C&L's version of science studies. There is simply no need for it. Put this right and the metaphysics of *actant* network theory becomes indistinguishable from *actor* network theory—a name which is quite applicable to traditional SSK, with its networks of communication (tacit and explicit), its Hesse nets, its rattling spiderwebs, and so forth. Once we strip away the metaphysics of actants, we can more readily see C&L's significant contribution to the detailed analysis of the relations of power between actors in networks.

There is, as we have indicated, a key to all the conundrums in the actant approach. The key is an interpretation of actant network theory which also seems to solve the practical and conceptual problems of network analysis. The quasi-solution is a restriction of the area of analytic interest to the relationship between terms taken from bodies of written data. Working from the theoretical end, we see the semiotic approach making written words more and more central. Working from the application of network theory end, we see association between words being more and more tractable. As in the Sistine Chapel, the finger of God (theory) reaches out toward the finger of man (practice) and everything falls into place in a flash: the nodes are words, the relations are associations between words, and there is nothing left to worry about. The problems of weak ties, complex relations, and intangible tacit knowledge dissolve.

But this cannot be the solution. The practical problems remain because the data set is not all the words in the world—including those that are only weakly linked to one another—but a small subset abstracted by varying, dubious, and somewhat obscure means. The conceptual problems remain, because the identity of word associations, on the one hand, and forms of life, on the other, has not been established. Analysis of networks of citations and other bibliometric indicators—which in the early 1970s threatened to become *the* method in the sociology of science—can touch only the surface of the scientific community. It was argued then that the transfer of tacit knowledge was much more important than the relationship between writings. "Because cognitive influences are often intangible it is unlikely that the associations between scientists discovered through the correlation of questionnaire responses or in bibliographic interconnections will reflect them."[7] Tacit knowledge is no more present in the data bases of terms analyzed by C&L than it was in the networks of citations analyzed by Diana Crane and others. This would be true even if the data base contained all the words that were ever written or spoken, and if these words represented all the machines that had ever been invented.[8] We only have what could count as a solution to the problems of networks if SSK is unraveled right back to the 1960s. This is exactly what we claim the semiotic approach threatens to do.

Networks are fine if used metaphorically. Networks can be operationalized, though if they are networks of actors, there is substantial difficulty. The trouble begins when networks are operationalized in the wrong way, as when human actors are replaced with nonhuman actants. This can happen if the labels on dense nodes of human agreement are invested with a kind of reality, or worse, when these actants are replaced with words. We should not allow the very useful idea of networks of actors, so powerfully developed by Latour in some aspects of his writing, to be hijacked by the idea of actants. To adopt C&L's metaphor, let us not drown the baby of actor network analysis in the water of actant network theory.

7. This is the second argument set out in Collins 1974.
8. In spite of Latour's argument that machines are the method by which tacit knowledge is distributed through networks, neither machines nor writing captures anything but a small and very special subset of skills. The consequences of this type of mistake were discussed in chapter 10. They include the invention of the notion of "delegation" as an unproblematic description of the transfer of power to machines. An analysis of the narrow range of human activity that can be mimicked by machines may be found in Collins 1990. This book also contains a detailed analysis of the relationship between what we know and what we can say about it.

Self-Exemplification and the Actant Network Model

But this is silly. It does not make sense to ask if the nodes and relations are more important than the computers in C&L's "revolutionary" claim. This is to miss their self-exemplifying strategy. C&L point out that new science is made with uppercut after uppercut. And here are the knockout blows: Leximappe™ (uppercut), Lexinet™ (left jab), Candide™ (right cross). We have been struck with gloves loaded with centers of calculation and immutable mobiles—nothing as ephemeral as argument, but good solid bundles of computer printout. The computers may not be the essence of the conceptual revolution, but they are the means of engendering it.

But if it were so simple to succeed in this way, the grand social survey would long have been the only method in sociological research. We could say that the argument we are having here is a microcosm of the big methodological argument within sociology. That argument too could be said to be about the power of inscriptions. Remember those sociologists of the early 1970s who strode the campuses with their bundles of computer printout? If inscriptions were less mutable, big sociology would have wiped us all out long ago. Not only does the Leximappe argument fail to convince, it exemplifies exactly what is wrong with the model as a whole. Inscriptions made by machines are just not that powerful. They cannot win this debate, and they do not have the power to match the explanatory ambitions that C&L have for them in the wider world of science.

We accuse C&L of a poverty of method, but the answer to this accusation cannot be Leximappe™ et al. That is not what is meant by method. Method is a way of getting at the world. We have the method of participation in the world. We have a theory, good or bad, about how we may gain knowledge of the world—at least of the social world. This is a problem that must be solved prior to the use of technique. Leximappe™ et al. is technique.

Dimensions and Dichotomies

Now let us move on to the crux of the debate. C&L characterize us as living in an epistemological flatland. We argue on one dimension, whereas they have leapt right out of our universe into an orthogonal dimension. We are concerned solely with the correct way to account for the findings of natural science, whereas they are concerned with the establishment of the very categories which divide natural from social science.

This is a correct characterization of our position. We recommend that scientific life be lived on one dimension at a time. Note that this is not a failure of vision or a blinkered view of the possibilities. We are well aware of the other dimensions of our universe (as we made clear in our critique of reflexivists), and the whole idea of meta-alternation is a recommendation for going from one dimension to another from time to time. We say, choose the dimension upon which you want to work according to the goals you have in mind. We are ready to relinquish foundational ambitions for this much more modest prescription. (None of this excludes an examination of the initial work of demarcating science and nonscience. We too think of Shapin and Schaffer as on our side of the debate.) The question is, how can it be that our studied position is made out to arise from smugness and a blindness to the attractions of the starry conceptual universe? The answer is, philosophical sleight of hand.

This is how it works. The first move has been described by ethnomethodologists; they call it turning resources into topics. Turning resources into topics is what got SSK off the ground. The philosopher's distinction between true and false was turned into the sociologist's topic. Scientists' distinctions, such as that between the replicated and the nonreplicated, or between the calibrated and the noncalibrated, were used as topics in more detailed sociological analyses. Now C&L ask us to turn into topics the distinction between human and nonhuman, and all the features of the world of sociology which we have been taking for granted. But why should we do this, where should we stop, and what good is it?

One available answer to the *why?* questions is philosophical radicalism. Because the possibility of moving to another level of analysis exists, it should be explored. And once you have made this move, you can look back critically at last year's analyst, since the resources used unreflectively by him or her can be seen as just as much an artifact as those resources he or she *did* turn into topics. To keep abreast of this year's analyst—to be consistent in the way that consistency is now perceived—that old resource should be turned into a new topic. This is the way of philosophical progress, gathering more and more into the analyst's domain.

On the face of it, this is an attractive idea. The earlier analysts look inconsistent, or soft-hearted, or old-fashioned, while a whole new dimension is opened up. Indeed, the force of this kind of move is seen very clearly in Woolgar's response (chap. 11). But as we argued in our treatment of reflexivists, there is no limit to the application of this procedure. Accordingly, just as C&L can thematize our resource (the distinction between the social world and the natural world), so too their resource (the distinction between the line from the natural to the social, on the one hand, and their orthogonal, Archimedean position on the other) can come to be seen as a topic. Let us see how this might happen.

First a reminder of how a new dimension is created according to C&L: "Our general symmetry principle is . . . not to alternate between natural realism and social realism but to obtain nature and society as twin results of another activity, one that is more interesting for us. We call it either network building, or collective things . . ." (chap. 12). What might the truly progressive thinker add? Something like this: "Our hypersymmetry principle is not to alternate between '(natural and social) realism' and 'networkism' but to obtain both reality and networks as twin results of another activity, more interesting for us, that we call hyperactivity." We can also follow Latour in developing a rule of method related to hypersymmetry: We see a Janus figure. The face of the old man looks backward and speaks: "Actant networks are the causes that allow facts and stable societies to be—there is nothing stronger than networks." The young man, perhaps entering the portals of the Salk Institute, speaks: "Actant network theory" will be the consequence of settling the controversy over the mode of existence of facts and stable societies (if I get my way)." To follow Latour's lead we would say that the same arguments that have been made about nature and society have to be made *symmetrically* about networks. Our *fifth rule of method* thus reads exactly like the third and fourth—the words "actant networks" replacing the words "society and nature." "Since the settlement of a controversy over the nature of facts and stable societies is the cause of the success of Actant Network Theory, we cannot use Actant Network Theory to explain how and why the controversy has been settled." (after Latour 1987, 143–44).

What is there to stop this philosophically progressive regress? Latour is certainly aware of the problem; he writes (1988): "there is another direction which allows us to maintain the necessary reflexivity without whirling helplessly in our efforts to outdo and outwit each other in proving that the other is a naive believer. I call this other tack infra-reflexivity because instead of writing about how (not) to write, it just writes." (p. 170). This solution seems unsatisfying. "Just writing" seems to provide no warrant for either starting or stopping the philosophical progress-regress of jumps to other dimensions. If the leap to the new dimension and the nonleap to yet further dimensions are to be justified, they must be justified by something more. Both *"just* writing" and *"just* following actors around" do not so much justify C&L's program as *just*-ify it.

We and the reflexivists and C&L all appreciate the potential endlessness of the progressive regress. We are content to recognize the problem and deal with it pragmatically. The reflexivists want to celebrate it—but to no practical end. Ironically, of the three parties, only C&L believe their scheme is universally stable. They set aside the difficulty with the charming naiveté of their *just*-ifications. This is the sleight of hand. The first jump to a new dimension is warranted with the rhetoric of philosophical progress, but no good reason is given for stopping there.

Empiricism Regained

Now let us find out what *just*-ification means in practice. Let us take the advice of Callon and Latour and simply follow these two technologists around as they achieve the success of actant network theory. We will in this case follow them through the arguments in their response to us (chap 12). On our quest we will travel with them to new dimensions.

The journey begins. Now something fascinating happens. It turns out that the route is too complicated to represent even with the graphics capability of an Apple Macintosh. As we follow them outward on their voyage of philosophical discovery we enter a kind of hyperspace. The universe spins nauseatingly, but the duration of the discomfort is mercifully brief. We open our eyes, blinking and squinting, but everything looks familiar, although strangely quaint and dated. Have we traveled back in time, or is it that we now inhabit a twin universe? Our companions beckon to us. They are going to give us a guided tour of their new territory. They point to things that look like part of a world left behind but talk as though they were revealing something new and exciting:

> The definition of observables is entirely different in the two frames. In the first one, social scientists were allowed to use an unobservable (sic) state of society and a definition of social relations to account for scientific work—or to alternate by using an equally unobservable (sic) state of nature. In the other frame [this frame] the only observables are the traces left by objects, arguments, skills, and tokens circulating through the collective. We never see either social relations or things. We may only document the circulation of network-tracing tokens,

statements, and skills. This is so important that one of us made it the first principle of science studies (Latour 1987, chap. 1). Although we have not yet fully articulated this argument, it is the basis of our empirical methods. (Chap. 12)

No wonder we feel so strange. The talk is of novel frames, but the vocabulary comes from long ago. They talk freely of that which cannot be observed and that which can. They state that in spite of the staggering journey through the factless nebula—not to mention the age-old stellar clouds of hermeneutics—traces of networks are there to be seen by those with an unclouded gaze. So confident are our guides that they have conquered the problems of observation and interpretation that they are ready to criticize those whom their new acuity leads them to perceive as less fortunate colleagues. We, for example, offer only groundless claims about nonobservable states of society.

Suddenly we notice a towering structure of strong iron girders (a radio transmission tower?) built on a palace of dazzling marble. In neon lights the girders are picked out with the word "Leximappe tm." The palace is identified with an inscription of gold. It reads: Empiricism.

Enough of the fable. We have no objection to C&L's claims that they can trace tokens through networks. No doubt these tokens are as observable or as unobservable as anything else. We do object, however, to empiricism masquerading as metaphysical chic. If they want to see inscriptions traveling through networks, so be it, but they are surely too sophisticated as philosophers to deny us access to states of society because they are "unobservable." We have our methods; they include participation in forms of life. To deny this on grounds of unobservability would be to resurrect the scientific sociology of the early sixties.

In this context, let us remind ourselves once more of the problem of skills, touched on above. C&L talk of "network-tracing tokens, statements, and skills"; they say "the only observables are the traces left by objects, arguments, skills, and tokens circulating through the collective." But where are the skills and what traces do they leave? The very problem for this kind of research, first put forward in the early seventies, is the intangibility of skills and cultures—the lack of tokens to represent them. Hence it is doubly ironic for C&L to rest their claims on a distinction between what is observable and what is not. We feel that in these passages they have suddenly remembered the problem of skills and have smuggled them in as though they could be treated like the other actants in their scheme.

But it does not work unless machines and inscriptions are treated as skill's embodiments—as though this were not the problem.[9]

Relativism Revisited

What, then, is *our* world like. C&L have characterized it correctly with their one-dimensional diagram. It is not that we are ignorant of the existence of multidimensional universes but that we don't think they take you anywhere useful. In the case of the reflexivists, who embark on a heady trip through as many dimensions as they can, they take you to a place of silence. In the case of C&L their universe bends back upon itself to a point around 1950 or 1960. Our world is populated, we admit, by philosophically insecure objects, such as states of society and participant's comprehension (Collins 1984). But all worlds are built on shifting sands. We provide a prescription: stand on social things—be social realists—in order to explain natural things. The world is an agonistic field (to borrow a phrase from Latour); others will be standing on natural things to explain social things. That is all there is to it. There is nowhere else to go that is significantly more interesting; at least not now or in the foreseeable future. We see the attractiveness of the idea of a comprehensive theory, but in its absence, life, although imperfect, is interesting. The battle between those of us standing on the social things and those standing on the natural things is fascinating and rewarding. The world has changed and is changing further.

The practical difference between C&L's world and our own can be seen in another way. In Latour's *Science in Action* he shows us the point beyond which the visitor to the science laboratory can no longer doubt the existence of a fact because too many forces are arrayed against him or her. The impossibility of doubt—the Cartesian point—is what repopulates C&L's world with the familiar firm objects of science undermined by SSK. That is the difference. SSK is continually stressing that familiar objects can be doubted. We think that the case studies of SSK actually show how readily great solid areas of the scientific world are doubted as soon as trouble begins to show itself. We believe in scientific revolutions. In this sense SSK is like the philosophy of the underdog so familiar from romantic portrayals of science.

SSK, then, is parasitical upon even more elements of the conven-

9. This problem emerged clearly during a discussion at Stanford University with Tim Lenoir and Mike Dettelbach. Machines cannot be used as skill tokens outside of a very simple minded notion of delegation. We criticize this notion in Chapter 10, and the problem is explained at length in Collins 1990.

tional image of science than C&L point out. It wants to use science to weaken natural science in its relationship to social science. In using science in this way, it does strengthen the whole idea of science just as C&L say. But this is not a careless error. SSK does not want to destroy the idea of science. We like science. We want to do science. We are positivists in the wider sense, favoring science as a route to knowledge. But we want all cultural endeavors to be seen as equal in their scientific potential. We don't want to make the search for gravity waves any different. What we do want to make different—as explained in the last chapter of *Changing Order*—is what happens when natural science comes into contact with other parts of the world.

These contacts include encounters with other institutions which deal in knowledge and expertise, such as legal reasoning (Smith and Wynne 1988; Wynne 1982; Yearley 1989b) and the educational system (Collins and Shapin 1989). There are also numerous occasions when science plays a contributory role in other practical projects, including attempts to assist the underdeveloped world through transfers of Western technologies (Yearley 1988), concerns over matters of public safety (Irwin 1987), or the growing clamor over green issues (Yearley 1989a, 1991). Science may even come into contact with religious expertise in novel ways, as with the recent "scientific" dating of the Turin shroud (Laverdiere 1989).

It is the potential to open up these issues which we fear has been lost during C&L's journey into space. The objects that cannot be doubted in C&L's world are of course the familiar everyday objects of science. That which cannot be doubted is the scientist's world. As Latour says in *Science in Action*, in following scientists around, he will be as relativist as the young man but as realist as the old one. It is the realism of the old one that SSK resists. It is the realism of the stranger in the Salk Institute, making his reappearance as the overawed naïf in *Science in Action*, that we want to combat. We are with the experts, trying to participate in their world so as to open it up to the rest of us, making us strong, not overawed. We want to be awed just to the extent that we admire the expertise of those whom we consult, but not overawed by the glitter and authority of banners (labels) under which they parade the agreements they have reached with their fellows.

Conclusion: A New Literary Form?

Since we have the last word in this exchange, and now that we have moved into the last paragraphs, it behooves us to try to take stock in something less than the usual partisan manner. Science studies, especially its European variants, is characterized by healthy arguments, and some that are not so healthy. This debate seems to have been a healthy one. We, at least, have learned from it, not only more about actant network theory but also more about our own position. In the following summary, we will reanalyze what we see as C&L's weaknesses, but also try to admit our own. We will also show where the two approaches seem to coincide in spite of our quarrel. Let us start with the question of whose account of the world is the more prosaic.

We say C&L produce prosaic accounts of science.[10] They say it is we who want to leave science to the scientists. But both sides are right in their way. Our ambitions are minimal compared to those of C&L. We have no great system, not even an incomplete one such as theirs. What we fear is that C&L's ambitions, brave though they are, wouldn't make any difference even if they could be fulfilled.[11] It is as though they were working for the widespread acceptance of something like solipsism. This indeed would involve a huge change in our conception of what exists, but it would affect little else. Our more modest goal is to leave most things as they are while significantly leveling the terrain. We want all cultural enterprises to be seen as having roughly the same epistemological warrant. This we think will have an effect. All manner of medium-sized things are changing and will change. We have listed some of them. On the one hand, then, there is a grand, although incomplete, system which involves following scientists and technologists around, but which we claim is essentially conservative. On the other hand, there is a less ambitious way of going about the study of science and technology, but one which is harder to do because of its countercommonsensical claims (it produces descriptions which fit far less readily with the accounts of the world of the majority of scientists and ideologists of science). We think our approach has the potential to change the relations between cultural enterprises and to give more power to those outside science.

10. "Prosaic" does not necessarily mean "boring" in its common sense. Clearly there are many areas of natural science that are not in the least boring. Prosaic means lacking the countercommonsensical surprise of the accounts of science produced by SSK. It is only in this sense that C&L's accounts of science are dull. No one could accuse their writings of being dull. We use the term "sparkling" to describe their writings.

11. With "six books, five edited volumes, and about sixty articles" already in existence, one wonders if C&L's system ever will be completed and just what would be needed to express it if it were. It is hard to think of any earlier philosophical revolution for which such a volume of writings was merely a beginning.

There are all manner of ironies in this division, some of which have been brought out clearly in the debate. For example, while C&L seemed determined to do away with the very notion of science, they fall back upon old-fashioned empiricism in their arguments. Our position, on the other hand, does not involve the dissolution of the ideals of science, yet we are happy with "unobservable states of society" as evidence.

A still more succulent irony is that while we refuse to accept scientists' accounts of the natural world in our analyses, we are ready to recognize specialist expertise within the world of science, just as much as in any other cultural enterprise.[12] What follows is that if natural things are to be given a role in analysts' explanations, if the culture of science is to enter the analysis of science, as C&L prefer, then it is scientists who must be given the principle word in these areas. We don't face that dilemma because there is no natural science, there are only accounts of natural science, in our analyses. C&L criticize us for our lack of ambition on this score, reserving for themselves the same rights as scientists to comment on the natural objects that appear in their stories. Whatever we think of the courage of this ambition, we believe that C&L's interventions on these matters must be subservient to scientists' skills. C&L, we think, will always be the puppets while the scientists remain the puppet masters. We have tried to show how this works out in detail. We think we have shown that either their grand ambitions will be subverted in their practice, or their claims to speak on behalf of things will be superficial.[13]

Another pair of matched problems concerns the status of the dichotomy between the natural and the social. Here matters become complex, with both sides alternately adopting more or less identical

12. And we are ready to recognize this expertise when it comes to prescriptions in, say, the world of policy. We believe that though our model cuts away the notion of scientific authority, the notion of expertise means that public debates involving scientific and technological decisions must involve scientists and technologists as representatives of interests, and that they have a special (though not decisive) position in such debates in relation to those less experienced in dealing with the natural world. To reiterate Collins's *Changing Order*, scientists and technologists stand roughly in the same position with regard to the natural world as travel agents stand with regard to summer holidays or property surveyors stand with regard to the value of a house. Their advice is the best available, but it does not constitute the final word.

13. Yet another irony is that the only people working in the sociology of scientific knowledge who could reasonably claim to have participated as full-blown scientific experts in an area which they were simultaneously analyzing were not Bruno Latour and Michel Callon, but Trevor Pinch and Harry Collins. For an account of their participation in the "spoon-bending" controversy, see Collins and Pinch 1982.

positions. Thus, C&L insist that the only thing that can be observed is the activities of scientists and other actants, and that there is nothing more in the world than these. In this sense, it is they rather than us who inhabit a conceptual flatland; our world is inhabited by distinct categories: people and things. And yet even as they insist on the flatness of their observational terrain, their claim to have discovered the "missing masses" in the power of "things" rests on an ontological division between the natural and the social. If the difference between the natural and the social were not of this kind, then no discovery would have been made; there would be no independent natural agents to exert the newly discovered forces. Thus they introduce this dichotomy into the very center of their argument while at the same time insisting that the dichotomy is false.

We suffer from an almost identical weakness. We insist that C&L mistakenly reify accounts and that we must work on the assumption that there is only one kind of thing—power granted by human agency. And yet our attack on the notion of "delegation" rests on the impossibility of having machines mimic human action. Thus, part of our position is based on an argument about what machines can and cannot do, and this implies that there must be more to the power and lack of power of machines than that which is granted by humans.[14] Both C&L and we, then, claim that as far as things and humans are concerned, there is (or at least we should act as if there is) only one substance from which both are made, and yet both of us rest our arguments on a more substantial distinction.

In the paragraphs preceding the last one, we set up a dichotomy between analyst and scientist outside the social analysis of science. The problem discussed in the past paragraph could be said to rest on a breakdown of this dichotomy. In the case of the study of any technology which has to do with *knowledge,* we are analysts; knowledge, after all, is the subject of our analyses; and we are scientists: knowledge is what we *know* about.[15] We complain about C&L abandoning their responsibility to act as knowledge scientists with their introduction of the simpleminded notion of delegation. But in accepting this responsibility *we* tolerate a breakdown of the very dichotomy between analyst and scientist which underlies our analyst's stance; we want to be both analysts and knowledge scientists (Collins 1990). Oddly enough, in these circumstances our treatment of

14. Steve Woolgar (1985) has been most unambiguous in putting the case that the power of machines is that which is granted by humans. It would be interesting to know his position on the question of the "missing masses."

15. Trevor Pinch and Wiebe Bijker (1987) stress this point in their work on technology.

the natural world—in the sense that we start to engage directly with scientists' accounts of the world—becomes not dissimilar to C&L's.

Although it has been surprisingly little remarked, Collins's position has shown this tension from the outset. Collins's argument, developed in his 1974 and 1975 papers and represented in his 1985 book, rests on scientists' inability to determine whether an experimental skill has been transmitted except by observation of the results of an experiment. In the case of uncontroversial science, such as the TEA laser, the claim is that there is a clear criterion for determining when skill has been acquired and when it has not: for example, the ability to burn holes in concrete. This is both a scientist's and an analyst's criterion. While circumstances can be envisaged in which the concrete-burning test could become discredited, the laser, as treated by Collins, is in what he would call a "postclosure" state (this is what Latour came to refer to as being "black-boxed"). The nexus of agreements that underlie TEA-laser performance is so strong that failure to make a laser work is treated by actors and analyst alike as representing a shortage of skill. In these instances, then, Collins's position does not differ in its practical implications from C&L's.

In more recent analyses (Collins, DeVries and Bijker 1990), there are likewise no significant ontological differences between our treatment of established skills and C&L's position. (Though our point, once more, is to talk about which human abilities can and cannot be mimicked rather than to establish more general—and, as we would have said in the more aggressive parts of this paper, "vacuous"—terms such as "delegation.") Thus, to work out what a bicycle does in relation to human skills, one must start by noting that the very idea of bike riding does not make sense without the idea of a bike. Bikes, perforce, must be treated in a commonsense way. The prescription remains, of course, to alternate back to methodological relativism for other types of analysis.

To return to our main theme, we think it is wrong to hide the problems exhibited by both approaches beneath the pretence that everything can be solved by a semiotic turn—the language of actants. The bulk of our effort has been to show why this is a false direction, a matter of cosmetics at best. We prefer to accept the problems and live within an imperfect world. Compartmentalization, with its associated alternation, seems to us to be an inevitable feature of intellectual life. All grand systems break down, but we have learned to live with this in the neo-Wittgensteinian world. Those with an overwhelming desire for consistent systems may nevertheless prefer the C&L route even though we do not believe they have found the state of intellectual grace that deep down we all yearn for.[16] We fear that if you want to change the relationship between science and technology and other cultural endeavors, and if you want to understand what can and cannot be delegated to machines, you will find it best to do analysis in a more piecemeal way, the crucial watchword being to ask for the use, not for the meaning. Whichever route is preferred, if there is anyone out there still listening, we hope the debate has clarified as many issues for you as it has for us.

16. We borrow the felicitous phrase "state of intellectual grace" from the flyer for a forthcoming book by Mike Mulkay.

REFERENCES

Bijker, W., H. M. Collins, and G. DeVries. The Grammar of Skills: Training Skills in Medical School? Paper presented at the conference on The Rediscovery of Skill at the University of Bath.

Collins, H. M. 1974. The TEA Set: Tacit Knowledge and Scientific Networks. *Science Studies* 4:165–86

———. 1975. The Seven Sexes: A Study in the Sociology of a Phenomenon, or the Replication of Experiments in Physics. *Sociology* 9:205–24

———. 1984. Concepts and Methods of Participatory Fieldwork. In C. Bell and H. Roberts, eds., *Social Researching.* London: Routledge and Kegan Paul. 54–69.

———. 1985. *Changing Order: Replication and Induction in Scientific Practice.* Beverly Hills: Sage.

———. 1990. *Artificial Experts: Social Knowledge and Intelligent Machines.* Cambridge: MIT Press.

Collins, H. M., G. DeVries, and W. Bijker. 1990. The Grammar of Skill. Paper presented at the conference on The Rediscovery of Skill at the University of Bath.

Collins, H. M., and T. J., Pinch, 1982. *Frames of Meaning: The Social Construction of Extraordinary Science.* London: Routledge and Kegan Paul.

Collins, H. M., and S. Shapin. 1989. Experiment, Science Teaching, and the New History and Sociology of Science. In M. Shortland and A. Warwick, eds., *Teaching the History of Science.* Oxford: Basil Blackwell.

Gieryn, T. F. 1990. The Ballad of Pons and Fleischmann: How Cold Fusion Became More Interesting, Less Real.

Granovetter, M. 1973. The Strength of Weak Ties. *American Journal of Sociology* 78: 1360–80.

Irwin, A. 1987. Technical Expertise and Risk Conflict: An Institutional Study of the British Compulsory Seat Belt Debate. *Policy Sciences* 20: 339–64.

Latour, B. 1987. *Science in Action.* Milton Keynes: Open University Press.

———. 1988. The Politics of Explanation: An Alternative. In Steve Woolgar, ed., *Knowledge and Reflexivity: New Frontiers in the Sociology of Knowledge*. London: Sage, 155–76.

Laverdiere, H., 1989. The Socio-Politic of a Relic: Carbon Dating the Turin Shroud, PhD. diss., University of Bath.

Pinch, T. J., and W. E. Bijker. 1987. The Social Construction of Facts and Artifacts: Or How the Sociology of Science and the Sociology of Technology Might Benefit Each Other. In W. Bijker, T. Hughes, and T. Pinch eds., *The Social Construction of Technological Systems*. Cambridge: MIT Press.

Schaffer, S. 1991. The Eighteenth Brumaire of Bruno Latour. *Studies in the History and Philosophy of Science* 22 (1): 174–92.

Smith, R., and B. Wynne, eds. 1988. *Expert Evidence: Interpreting Science in the Law*. London: Routledge and Kegan Paul.

Woolgar, S. 1985. Why Not a Sociology of Machines? The Case of Sociology and Artificial Intelligence. *Sociology* 19: 557–72.

Wynne, B., 1982. *Rationality and Ritual: The Windscale Inquiry and Nuclear Decisions in Britain*. Chalfont St. Giles, Bucks.: British Society for the History of Science.

Yearley, S. 1988. *Science, Technology, and Social Change*. London: Unwin Hyman.

———. 1989a. Environmentalism: Science and a Social Movement. *Social Studies of Science* 19:343–55.

———. 1989b. Bog Standards: Science and Conservation at a Public Inquiry. *Social Studies of Science* 19: 421–38.

———. 1991. *The Green Case: A Sociology of Environmental Issues, Politics, and Arguments*. London: Harper-Collins.

14

Social Epistemology and the Research Agenda of Science Studies

Steve Fuller

With the triumph of descriptive over normative approaches to the study of science, historians, philosophers, and sociologists of science are entering an "era of good feeling." It is the job of the social epistemologist to make sure that this era does not last long. I begin by observing that, protests to the contrary, a normative perspective is already embodied in the interpretive strategy most commonly used in science studies. The strategy imputes to scientists competence in whatever they are trying to do. What exactly the scientists are trying to do is still a matter of dispute among philosophers and sociologists. However, the social epistemologist challenges even this minimal notion of rationality because it prevents scientists from being accountable to a standard not of their own choosing and hence provides no opportunity for rethinking the ends of knowledge. I then trace the quietism of this position to the antiepistemological streak of recent neopragmatism, as represented by Richard Rorty and Richard Bernstein. I show how their pragmatism is very much against the spirit of the original pragmatism, which would have welcomed the sort of experimental approach to the study of science that social epistemology recommends. Some crucial differences between the interpretive strategies commonly used in science studies and those recommended by social epistemology are then highlighted. I then suggest how the idea of improving the production of knowledge may be modeled on principles for managing industrial labor. Finally, I address two general objections to this proposal: the first concerns the stifling of scientific creativity and the second concerns the scientific community's resistance to externally motivated change.

Many thanks to Andrew Pickering for incisive comments on earlier drafts of this paper, which kept pushing me to ever greater extremes. Thanks also to Anthony Hopwood and Ted Porter, who kept the howlers to the minimum needed for maintaining an interested readership.

The Anti-epistemological Streak in Science Studies

To stake out the conceptual space bounded by social epistemology (Fuller 1988), let me begin with an innocuous observation. Anyone who regards her activities as falling under the rubric of "science studies"—be she philosopher, historian, or sociologist—implicitly agrees to abide by the following rule:

> Science must be studied in its own terms, not in terms that are alien to the scientific enterprise.

This point of agreement recalls the common enemy of science studies, namely, the classical epistemologist, embodied most vividly in the person of Descartes, who insists on holding human knowledge accountable to such superhuman standards as incorrigibility, standards whose legitimacy perversely lay in their having been derived by a priori means, i.e., without first having consulted the relevant sciences. But as often happens when one defines a common foe, the practitioners of science studies have unwittingly taken on qualities that complement the foe's. In particular, they have developed a characteristic sense of what it means to study science "in its own terms."

If the classical epistemologist erred in trying to impose on science normative considerations that were external to it, practitioners of science studies tend to err in the opposite extreme by supposing that science has its own internally generated standards of performance, which in turn serve to define science as a self-regulating and, in that very general sense, a "rational" enterprise. Consequently practitioners of science studies tend to discuss norms only as they emerge from the facts of science, usually from facts that the scientists themselves would recognize as governing their performance. This is the "descriptive turn," which in recent years has engaged an unprecedented mix of historians, philosophers, and sociologists in cooperative research (e.g., Knorr Cetina 1981; Hacking 1983; Pickering 1984; Fine 1986; Galison 1987; Giere 1988; Hull 1988; as well as Gooding, chap. 3). From the social espistemologist's standpoint, however, the descriptive turn has emasculated the normative dimension of science studies and in the process has limited the field's potential for radical critique and revision of our knowledge enterprises. In this regard, what Herbert Marcuse said of the history of dialectics in *Reason and Revolution* can serve as an epigraph for the project of social epistemology:

> This book was written in the hope that it would make a small contribution to the revival . . . of a mental faculty which is in danger of

being obliterated: the power of negative thinking. As Hegel defines it: "Thinking is, indeed, essentially the negation of that which is immediately before us . . . "

> For to comprehend reality means to comprehend what things really are, and this in turn means rejecting their mere factuality . . . [The function of dialectical thought] is to break down the self-assurance and self-contentment of commonsense, to undermine the sinister confidence in the power and language of facts . . . to express and define that-which-is on its own terms is to distort and falisify reality. (Marcuse 1960, vii, x)

The social epistemologist does not deny that science studies presents a vast array of opinions as to the nature of these putative "internally generated standards" of scientific performance: Is science governed in ways that insulate it from the rest of society or is science simply one more arena in which the rules governing all of society are played out? Here, in a nutshell, we have the hotly contested issue of whether science runs on methodology or on interests. However, nobody seems to want to deny that science runs *well*, though again there are disagreements over what constitutes evidence for this putative fact: Increasing control over the environment or an increasing percentage of the gross national product or simply an increasing amount of time that science stays in business? Yet to the social epistemologist's ears, this litany of alternatives sounds like an elaborate overreaction to the impossible standards originally set by the classical epistemologist. It would seem that science studies has in effect thrown out the normative baby with the a priori bathwater.

According to the social epistemologist, the classical epistemologist was right about one thing, namely, that left to its own devices, science will not necessarily produce the sort of knowledge that we are interested in having. This lingering skepticism about the adequacy of the means to the ends of science engendered a robust normative sensibility, one that emboldened the epistemologist to propose ways of altering or supplementing the knowledge production process. Unfortunately, the classical epistemologist's apriorism led to speculative excesses, most of which entailed a wholesale replacement of our knowledge enterprises with ones fit only for superhuman pursuit. Instances of these excesses are still found in introductory philosophy courses that enjoin the inquirer to believe all, and only all, the logical consequences of her beliefs (let alone know which ones they are) and to adopt a belief only once the weight of the evidence has eliminated all of its rivals. Still the social epistemologist remains undaunted. It should be possible, so she argues, to remove the speculative excesses and keep the normative impulse intact. After all, just because scientists do not live up to a priori normative standards, it certainly does not follow that they live up to a posteriori ones implicit in what the scientists normally do. There is a third possibility: it may turn out that whatever pattern can be extracted from scientific practice is the result of the observer imaginatively compensating for, and hence "overinterpreting," the concatenation of events in the scientific workplace. Not exactly the stuff of which norms are normally made. Yet science studies goes astray precisely when it fails to take this third possibility seriously.

Science studies is generally seen, by insiders and outsiders alike, as a subversive cluster of disciplines—but subversive of *what* exactly? The most natural answer would seem to be science itself. Although there is considerable rhetoric to that effect, it does not explain the peculiar lineup of angels and demons in the science studies pantheon. In particular, consider the "angel" Michael Polanyi (1957) and the "demon" Karl Popper (1963). Polanyi is often invoked as inspiration for the ethnographies of scientists in the workplace that are most emblematic of empirical research in science studies. Polanyi stressed the local character of scientific knowledge, which is communicated from expert to novice largely by nonverbal means. Indeed, science is distinguished by the special sensitivity with which the scientist is attuned to her environment, a sensitivity that is expressed just as much in the handling of test tubes as in the interpretation of data. Polanyi located this sensitivity in the "tacit dimension," a deep but fluid epistemic medium which the competent scientist may be unable to articulate but which the participant observer can plainly see is responsible for the smooth operation of the scientific workplace. In light of this thumbnail sketch, it is difficult to see how Polanyi could be a patron saint of science subversives. If anything, his is the ultimate argument for science being understandable only by insiders. This point suggests to the social epistemologist that science studies has no hostile designs on science.

However, as we have seen, science studies has hostile designs on philosophy—as did Polanyi. Polanyi's polemical thrust in using such expressions as "personal knowledge" and "tacit dimension" was to foreclose the possibility that anyone other than scientists might know what is best for science. This is not to say that Polanyi thought that scientists could say what was best for science. On the contrary, it was here that philosophy was most pernicious in its influence—so much so that perhaps the intervention of a sympathetic participant-observer would be needed to tell the scientist's story correctly. Indeed, Polanyi was one of the first to propound the now-fashionable idea that philosophy-laden methodology courses were the source of the misdescriptions that scientists typically give of their own activities. But Polanyi always meant this as an attack on philosophy, not science. He still wanted us to presume that, for all their failures of verbal expression, whatever scientists did (qua scientists) was what was best for science.

Polanyi's position here could not be more alien to the modern philosophical attitude toward science. For Polanyi's main philosophical foes, the positivists and the Marxists, what makes science an epistemic advance on, say, religion is that science works by methods that are detachable from the particular people using them (i.e., a given scientific community), which in turn enables others to hold those people accountable for what they do. Thus, the important sense in which the methods of science are "objective" is not that they provide direct access to the truth (for they do not), but that they provide public access to the knowledge production process itself (cf. Porter 1991). Anyone who masters the method can challenge the scientist at her own game. The challenger need not have first become imbued with the ethos of "being a scientist" or have a vested interest in shoring up the scientific establishment. It should be clear, then, why the philosophical fixation on method would pose a threat to Polanyi: It paves the way for the *democratization* of scientific authority. The social epistemologist finds here a different sense in which science can be studied in "its own terms," namely, in accordance with the methods of science—regardless of whether those methods are representative of what most scientists actually do.

The trick for philosophers, of course, has been to specify these "methods of science." Most often they have fallen back on the pronouncements of great scientists, ones who have been demonstrably successful in the pursuit of knowledge. But this move has proven embarrassing because scientists' words and deeds tend to diverge so sharply. The matter is complicated because the scientists' "words" (i.e., their statements of method) often would have reached the right conclusions, and more efficiently at that, had they been put into practice. At least the perennial philosophical concern with perfecting an "inductive logic" (increasingly shared by cognitive scientists, e.g., Holland et al. 1986; cf. Fuller 1991) supposes that such is the case. The social epistemologist takes this supposition to be instructive, as it highlights the fact that there is a big difference between claiming that science works well enough to sustain itself and claiming that it works optimally toward a desired outcome. The first claim is borne out simply by science's continued existence, whereas the second is harder to establish, requiring as it does that we determine the relative efficacy of the possible means and ends of knowledge production. This is the project to which social epistemology is devoted. It involves asking questions such as these: Why do we want knowledge in the first place? What sorts of knowledge would satisfy our reasons for wanting knowledge? What are the relative costs and benefits of producing these sorts of knowledge, and how would the costs and benefits be distributed among the members of society?

The policy relevance of these questions becomes clear once we consider some concrete versions: Does training in the humanities increase the level of open-mindedness and civility of scientists? Is it sufficient for nonscientists to know how to use a piece of technology reliably without knowing the theory that underwrites its performance? These questions share certain presuppositions that radically depart from the ordinary conceptions of knowledge from which Polanyi and his allies have drawn intuitive support. In particular, the social epistemologist denies that any sense can be made of such locutions as "knowledge pursued for its own sake" or "the natural course of inquiry," which is usually said to correspond to "wherever the truth may lead." On the contrary, the "ends of science" (Redner 1987) are not given by science itself but by something else to which science is held accountable. If science has the image of autonomy, that is only because the standards of accountability remain obscure and unscrutinized, as in the belief, apparently common among policymakers, that scientific research is distinguished by its lack of diminishing returns (cf. Averch 1985, chap. 2). Considering the lack of systematic study of this topic, could such a belief be founded on anything more substantial than a few vivid anecdotes from the history of science? It would seem that these anecdotes—tales of forgotten speculations (e.g., Mendel's on genetics) that eventually yielded major practical payoffs—are being used to convert the self-perpetuating tendency of funding patterns into a natural law of scientific development. Under these circumstances, there is a pressing need to examine not merely how science works but whether science is working as well as it could, especially given the ever-changing and ever-more-important roles that science plays in society.

Still, the social epistemologist is not home free. For even granting that science rarely works as well as it should or could, it remains to be seen whether greater scrutiny of the scientific process is likely to improve the knowledge it produces. Democracy's signature political problem—how accountable ought the governors be to the governed— is no less its signature epistemological problem: how accountable the knowledge producers (i.e., the scientists) ought to be to the knowledge consumers (i.e., the public at large). As in the case of the political problem, the epistemological problem affords two polar so-lutions (cf. Held 1987). One pole, *plebiscitarianism*, argues that science should be subject to public scrutiny only to the extent that it can proceed with its largely self-determined business. This is Polanyi's view, as well as the ordinary citizen's natural attitude to-ward science: to wit, public participation in the scientific process is necessary only at the level of deciding whether a laboratory will be built in one's neighborhood, but certainly not at the level of research agenda setting. The other pole is *proletarianism*, which argues the opposite point, that science should proceed only to the extent that it can be subject to public scrutiny. While this view is clearly in line with socialist political agendas, it also captures the more abstractly expressed motivation for operationalism and verificationism in the philosophy of science. I emphasize this point because it is not by accident that Polanyi and other defenders of the so-called libertarian approach to the pursuit of knowledge (e.g., von Hayek 1952) have lumped together positivists and Marxists as a common foe. But far from casting aspersions on Marxism, I argue in the following sec-tions that this point should cause the science studies community to rethink its estimation of positivism.

Lest the reader be misled, I should make a disclaimer at this point. Although social epistemology is motivated by the "proletar-ianizing" impulse, the reader will not find in what follows a defini-tive refutation of plebiscitarianism. Rather, I aim to shift the burden of proof in the debate by calling into questions features of knowl-edge production that contribute to its appearance of autonomy, which in the science studies community is most clearly signaled by the alleged existence of an "internal history of science" (for a cri-tique: Fuller 1989, chap. 1). The mere fact that science studies has been able to make telling observations about the character of natu-ral scientific knowledge without having to resort to the natural scientists' own expertise bodes well for getting nonexperts involved in setting the scientific research agenda (Albury 1983). The next step toward proletarianism would be to use the educational system to subvert the most vivid reminder that science is a self-contained ac-tivity, to wit, the communication barrier between scientific and public discourse. On the one hand, in order to make the public "more scientific," elementary science courses could be taught more like elementary economics courses, which typically try to convey the pervasiveness of something as abstract as "the economy" by tracking the chain of effects across society caused by a remote event, such as a crop failure. The resources of actor-network theory (Callon et al. 1986) could be used to make the same pedagogical point about the diffuse, but no less real, implications of concentrating scientific research in a particular area. On the other hand, in order to make scientists "more public," their more professionally oriented courses could be presented as instruction, not on how to deal with "things" per se (e.g., theories and instruments), but on how to deal with people (e.g., colleagues, administrators, students, lay citizens) in the different communicative settings in which those things figure. In this way, we may concretely recover, in a Marxist spirit, relations among people that are obscured by their being presented exclusively as relations among things.

As the communication barrier between scientists and the public is broken down, the most radical phase of proletarianization may be set in motion: the elimination of any principled distinction between the "production" and "distribution" of knowledge, or in more down-to-earth terms, between "research" and "teaching." Without succumbing to anti-intellectualism, a democratic society must always be suspicious of conceptions of knowledge in which the most valued forms of knowledge are the least accessible, or more sociologically, the most esteemed knowledge producers are the ones whose goods are accessible only to an elite set of consumers (e.g., other professional knowledge producers and, indirectly, their patrons; cf. Collins 1979). As a positive program, the breakdown of the production-distribution distinction would mean making the persuasiveness of a knowledge claim part of what determines its truth value (cf. Forester 1985). But here the social epistemologist is envisaging the long term, which is to say, once we have seriously examined the patterns of knowledge consumption: *Who* uses *which* knowledge to *what* end—and should they? (cf. Machlup 1962; Fuller 1988, chap. 12). Needless to say, the social epistemologist has yet to persuade her peers of the urgency of this task. In the next section some of the intellectual grounds for this resistance are explored.

The Roots of Anti-epistemology in Neopragmatism

As we have just seen from the social epistemologist's diagnostic perch, science studies has gone astray by following Polanyi in mistaking passable for optimal performance in science. And if for Polanyi's purposes the mistake is convenient, for the purposes of science studies it is much less so. For example, the mistake has led to a hasty dismissal of positivists and Popperians as mere philosophical imperialists, just because they argue that the history of science has largely been one of suboptimal performances. More importantly, the confusion of standards for passable and optimal performance has discouraged policy-oriented thinking in science studies, especially in the United States, the world's leading manufacturer of knowledge products. In turn, science policy research in this country (say, in the pages of the journal *Knowledge: Its Creation, Diffusion, and Utilization*) has repaid the compliment by relying little on the science studies literature, drawing instead on paradigms in economics and management science.

An especially ironic way of looking at what has happened here is in terms of Ian Hacking's (1983) distinction between science as "representation" and as "intervention." When the positivists and the Popperians portrayed science as driven toward ever more comprehensive representations of a reality that exists prior to inquiry, they cast themselves as constructive critics who intervened to make the process run more smoothly. Science studies starts with the realization that these philosophical interventions served, not to govern scientific practice, but to govern talk about scientific practice. However, the more science studies practitioners have tried to remedy matters by highlighting the constructive and interventionist side of science (i.e., the extent to which scientists must transform the world in order to accomplish their goals), the more they themselves have retreated to a representational, "descriptivist" rhetoric by claiming merely to be accounting for science as it actually happens—*wie es eigenlich gewesen*, in Ranke's memorable phrase, or in Latour's (1987), updated version, "to follow scientists around society." Of course science studies practitioners are quick to admit that tracking scientists reveals things that no one had intended to find (e.g., dissent and indeterminacy where consensus and certainty were thought to reign), but it is only in this passive and incidental way that the science studies practitioner intervenes in the course of scientific inquiry. As I will now endeavor to show, this non-interventionism may be seen as reflecting the assimilation of certain pragmatist doctrines that, through the efforts of Richard Rorty (1979, 1982) and Richard Bernstein (1983), have become fashionable in recent American philosophy. Mercifully these doctrines have made their way into science studies largely without embroiling its practitioners in the "end of philosophy" debates that Rorty and Bernstein have themselves sparked (e.g., Pickering 1987).

In its heyday, during the first three decades of the twentieth century, pragmatism was a notoriously protean philosophical movement, from which Arthur Lovejoy (1908) was able to isolate at least thirteen distinct strains. All of these strains engaged in a common rhetorical appeal, namely, to the relevance of the experimental method as a guide both to inquiry and to life. Pragmatism shared with the nineteenth-century positivism of Auguste Comte and John Stuart Mill the conviction that science should be applied to everything, and that everything would thereby improve. However, the pragmatists broke with the positivists over the question of whether the "scientific attitude" is radically different from ordinary ways of knowing or merely a more highly developed version of those ways. Swallowing their Darwin with large doses of Lamarck, the pragmatists tended toward the more evolutionary account of science's ascendency. As a result, they were less concerned with locating the point at which nonscience turns into science (e.g., once a principle of verifiability or falsifiability is in place) than with showing that an inchoate scientific attitude already underwrites our successful encounters with the world.

Once we see the positivists as stressing the distinctiveness of science, as opposed to the pragmatists' emphasis on science's continuity with everyday life, we can begin to understand the difference in their preferred means of improving the epistemic enterprise. Whereas pragmatists regarded education as the way to raise one's nascent scientific awareness to self-consciousness, the positivists, who were not nearly so sanguine about the natural tractability of humans to the scientific attitude, favored legislation that explicitly constrained the discourse and practices of inquirers. For a heightened sense of this difference, consider the claims and constituencies to which pragmatism and positivism appealed as social movements in twentieth-century America: to wit, the pragmatist *progressive education* movement and the positivist *general semantics* movement. In particular, contrast the tone and structure of the pragmatist *How We Think* by John Dewey (1908) and the positivist *Language in Thought and Action* by S. I. Hayakawa (1949).

To anyone familiar with pragmatism as it was originally presented in the works of William James, Charles Sanders Peirce, and John Dewey, what is missing from the neopragmatism of Rorty and Bernstein is a positive attitude toward experimental intervention and even to science more generally. In fact, given their willingness to embrace hermeneutics as a means of staving off creeping positivism, the neopragmatists are perhaps fairly read as hostile to the very idea of a science of anything human—including certainly science itself. For a sense of the extent to which the neopragmatists have altered the terms in which pragmatism is discussed, consider that whereas Rorty and Bernstein frequently cite Heidegger's student of theology and aesthetics, Hans-Georg Gadamer (1975), as the patron saint of their position, James, Peirce, and Dewey would more likely have recognized a worthy disciple in Donald Campbell (1988), the evolutionary epistemologist who trained as a behavioral psychologist under E. C. Tolman and Egon Brunswik.

However, it is safe to say that being themselves scholars of pragmatism, Rorty and Bernstein have knowingly shifted the terms of the debate so as to highlight those tendencies in the original position that emerged most clearly from its opposition to positivism. In particular, because the original pragmatists seemed to regard the entire gamut of successful human practices as latently scientific, the term "scientific" came to take on purely honorific significance, a significance that could not be tied down to the determinate set of procedures that the positivists sought. Indeed, a similar fate befell even the term "experiment" in James's writings, such that accepting Pascal's wager to believe in God despite the inconclusive evidence would involve "experimenting" with one's life—the Jamesian point simply being that it is a risk worth taking (James 1897). In this respect, pragmatism inherited the panglossian prejudices of evolutionary theory, in which terms like "fitness" and "adaptiveness" typically do not denote specific optimizing strategies that can be used to predict the survival of a species in an environment; rather these terms are used in effect to congratulate individual organisms on their longevity, from which it is then inferred that they must have had "fitter" or "more adaptive" traits than the organisms that expired (cf. Ruse 1988, chap. 4). Unfortunately, the congratulations have been taken to imply that there is no room for improvement. If anything, this line of thinking has led the neopragmatists to conclude that in cases where someone is observed to have acted unscientifically, irrationally, or otherwise suboptimally, it is probably the observer who is at fault for having misinterpreted the context in which the observed party's actions would have appeared "naturally" scientific, rational, or optimal. In light of the pivotal role that interpretation plays in such accounts of rationality and scientificity, it is therefore not surprising that Rorty and Bernstein have veered away from pragmatism's original grounding in the natural sciences and toward hermeneutics. It is a course, as I shall now argue, that the social epistemologist believes that science studies is ill-advised to follow.

The Distinctiveness of Social Epistemology's Interpretive Strategy

I began this paper by showing how social epistemology reinterprets an axiom upheld by all who practice science studies. Let me now switch tactics and locate social epistemology as an explicit challenge to certain assumptions that have come to be shared by most philosophers, historians, and sociologists who have participated in the recent science studies debates. These assumptions may be subsumed under two general types, which are designated by the following theses:

1. Most of what scientists do in their natural settings makes some kind of sense.
2. The primary aim of science studies is to develop interpretive strategies that make the most sense possible out of what scientists do in their natural settings.

Social epistemology differs from other schools of science studies by denying these two seemingly innocuous claims. In its place, the social epistemologist affirms two of her own:

1. Most of what scientists do in their natural settings makes some kind of sense only if you do not look too closely and are of a rather charitable turn of mind.
2. The primary aim of science studies is to develop metainterpretive strategies that reveal the extent to which what scientists do makes sense only if the interpreter intervenes on the scientist's behalf by adopting roughly the scientist's frame of reference.

When a philosopher and a sociologist start talking about scientists at work, two stereotypes are immediately conjured up. The philosopher invariably evokes the image of the methodologically steadfast scientist, one who will break the rules of her disciplined pursuit only for the sake of some higher principle of truth seeking. By contrast, the sociologist's scientist is an agile opportunist who will switch research tactics, and perhaps even her entire agenda, as the situation requires. Much of the rancor that has accompanied the debates between philosophers and sociologists is traceable to this radical difference in the moral psychology of the scientist that the two sides presuppose (cf. Fuller 1988, chap. 10). Moreover, we do not need to pass judgment on whether scientists are more Kantian or Machiavellian to notice that the philosopher and the sociologist agree on more than they would probably care to admit. They agree that the scientist exercises enough control over herself and her environment to be properly ascribed responsibility for what she does. In short, what the scientist does in her natural habitats "makes sense" or "is rational," in some suitably broad understanding of these expressions, one which includes the idea that scientists succeed at what they are trying to do most of the time, or at least fail in ways that permit them to continue and improve upon their efforts.

Now at first glance this common notion of rationality seems

quite obvious. However, its obviousness may be traced to two quite distinct sources, one in philosophy and one in sociology. First, the source may be a deep point about the nature of scientists, people in general, or how one goes about interpreting one or the other. In other words, it may be that one cannot make sense of scientists (or people in general) without making sense of them as making sense of their situations. This is what analytic philosophers, following Quine (1960) and Davidson (1983), have dubbed the "principle of charity," which they take to be a necessary condition for the possibility of any interpretation whatsoever. Why is such a principle "necessary" for interpretation? The exact answer is not clear, though there are a couple of lines of thinking in support. On the one hand, it may be that interpretation is a practice that applies only to creatures who make sense of their situations. This is the "realist" reading of charity that has led followers of Wilhelm Dilthey (e.g., Taylor 1985) and the later Wittgenstein (e.g., Winch 1958) to draw a sharp metaphysical distinction between the study of persons and the study of things. On the other hand, it may be that interpretation is a practice that can apply to any creature, but only insofar as that creature can be seen as making sense of its situations. This is the "instrumentalist" reading of charity that has inspired Daniel Dennett (1979) and others to interpret computers as "intentional systems." But whichever view one has of charity, it is clear that for philosophers, charity begins at home. That is, I make sense of scientists by extending to them sense-making qualities that I first find in myself.

By contrast, the sociologists tend to see the arrow pointing in the opposite direction: namely, I had better make sense of scientists as making sense, or I will lose any basis for saying that I make sense. Here the deep point of common rationality is not charity, but *reflexivity*. It helps explain why even the more radical sociologists have been reluctant to criticize in any straightforward way the avowed rationality of scientists. A celebrated case in point is the controversy surrounding Harry Collins's (1985) attempted debunking of replication as a practice in which scientists engage. The controversy centered on whether Collins could debunk replication without implicating his own practice, since presumably Collins derived evidential support from his having observed "repeated cases" in which replication failed to occur. The irony of Collins's claim was heightened by the fact that his own analysis of the scientific situation suggested that there is no standard procedure for replicating an experiment. In that case, what could Collins's own claim mean? For his part, Collins drew a makeshift disciplinary boundary between the sociology of natural science (his own work) and the sociology of social science (the work of his critics) and claimed that inquirers in both fields may discover that the scientists they study do not replicate research—but these would be two independent findings. While confessing a certain sympathy with Collins's way out, I must add that it has not won wide acceptance among sociologists. Instead, scientists are only granted powers of reason that sociologists could tolerate having imputed to themselves. Thus, whatever surface incoherence may be detected between the words and deeds of a scientist is typically cast, not in terms of the scientist's incompetence in coordinating mouth and hands, but in terms of her dexterity in "breaking frame" and "shifting context," so that what made sense in one situation subsequently needs to be reinterpreted against entirely new background assumptions. When applied reflexively by the sociologists, this newfound nimbleness emerges as the "New Literary Forms," which have lately moved their more radical members to challenge the very distinction between fact and fiction (e.g., Mulkay 1985; Woolgar 1988).

In opposition to all this, to study science "in its own terms," as the social epistemologist understands it, is to hold the behavior of scientists accountable to the methods of science, which in practice means that the observer's interpretive framework is informed, not by a folk-psychological presumption of rationality, but by the (relatively low) level of rationality at which experts of all sorts have been scientifically shown to function (Arkes and Hammond 1986; on the fallibility of scientists specifically, cf. Faust 1985; Fuller 1989, chap. 2). In particular, the social epistemologist calls into question three assumptions frequently shared by sociologists and philosophers who study science and who may disagree on most other matters. I have arranged these assumptions with contraries that express the grounds of the social epistemologist's objections:

1. Scientists are more likely to be good at carrying out strategies designed to maximize their own interests than at carrying out strategies designed to produce interest-free knowledge.

1 . On the contrary, the fact that scientists are motivated by self-interest does not ensure their competence in the conduct of science. After all, as the expected utility formula makes painfully clear, there is a strong cognitive dimension to the pursuit of self-interest, namely, the calculation of probabilities for the relevant possible outcomes that would issue in states of pleasure or pain. In other words, even in order to promote their interests scientists

would need to take a disinterested look at the odds. Moreover, if anything, long-term self-interested pursuits may well turn out to be especially oblivious to failure, as interests are continually adapted to match what can be reasonably expected (Elster 1984).

2. Scientists can improve their performance by "learning from experience" in the research environment.

2'. On the contrary, a robust sense of learning from experience happens only in highly controlled settings, where the scientist's behavior is subject to immediate and specific feedback. A less-controlled environment, such as an ordinary research setting, is subject to irregular feedback, which makes the detection and correction difficult, if not impossible (Brehmer 1986).

3. If the interpreter has problems in rendering the scientist's behavior rational, but no one in the scientist's company has such problems, then the interpreter has failed to factor in the role that "context" or "background knowledge" plays in understanding as it occurs in natural settings.

3'. On the contrary, "context" and "background knowledge" are used so elastically as to elevate the communicative powers of the "tacit dimension" to a form of social telepathy. Indicative of this problem is the absence of agreed-upon rules for when context can and cannot be used to license inferences about the content of scientific communication; indeed, context is typically whatever the interpreter happens to need to presume in order to make sense of the particular scientists under scrutiny. Appeals to "background knowledge" work in much the same way, differing from "context" only in that the former expression suggests that what is missing is to be found in the scientist' heads, whereas the latter implies that it is a feature of the scientists' common environment. By trying ever so hard to render the scientists rational, interpreters obscure a psychologically more realistic possibility, namely, that what is not said may not have been thought or even noticed, thereby enabling long-term misunderstandings to persist among scientists (cf. Fuller 1988, chap. 6).

Since the above objections are largely based on experimental findings, a defender of the interpretive orthodoxy in science studies might argue that the social epistemologist has fallen back on a way of knowing that is expressly designed to abstract away from the detail of particular cases, even though it is only in the details that the implicit rationality of scientists can be observed (cf. Lynch, chap. 7). In short, the artificiality of experiments discourages any close examination of what scientists actually do. While this argument is common enough in the literature (e.g., Brown 1989), it misses the twofold epistemic character of experimentation. In the first place, experiments aim to decompose some overall effect into its working causal parts, thereby enabling the replacement of parts and the reconstitution of wholes. In the second place, the experimental method serves to counteract the interpreter's cognitive liabilities. Let us consider each of these points in turn.

As for the first point, someone interested in experimenting on the scientific enterprise—or "simulating social epistemology," as Michael Gorman (1992) has recently called it—would want to determine how a range of independent variables, such as group size, communication constraints, and background information, contribute to the dependent variables of interest, namely, the sort of scientist, scientific audience, and knowledge commodity that is produced. This strategy serves the normative project of social epistemology by allowing the experimenter to see how an array of means may be manipulated in an array of settings to bring about an array of ends. A somewhat more metaphysical way of putting the point is to say that the experimental method does not confer a privileged status on the "nonartificial" world outside the laboratory but rather treats it as only one of a range of possible worlds that can be manifested, maintained, and transformed under specific conditions (cf. Bhaskar 1979). But perhaps metaphysics is less needed here than a concrete example.

Since its inception as a discipline, psychology has undergone continual soul-searching about the validity of knowledge claims derived from laboratory experiments. Admittedly, the rise of what William James contemptuously called "brass instrument psychology" in the middle of the nineteenth century was crucial in psychology's establishing an identity separate from philosophy. But it was one thing to appeal to laboratory experiments in order to disavow armchair philosophical speculation and quite another to argue that such experiments provided the *via regia* to the mind. Consequently a vast literature—perhaps the most sophisticated in all the sciences—developed on the design and interpretation of experiments. From the social epistemologist's standpoint, this literature has been most interesting in its discussion of "external validity," that is, the generalizability of an experimental result to situations outside the laboratory. Until quite recently psychologists have tended to run together two distinct ways of understanding this concept (cf. Berkowitz and Donnerstein 1982). Those distrustful of psychology's external validity claims have asked whether the experimental situations are *representative* of the relevant "real world" situations. However, in response, defenders of the experimental method have typically addressed the *reproducibility* of the experimental result in real-world situations. In other words, whereas opponents have challenged the experimenter's ability to model the world as it exists independently of what happens in the laboratory, supporters have observed that what happens in the laboratory can be used as the basis for successful intervention in the world.

That these are two quite different ideas may be seen in the alternative ways we may interpret Gorman's experiments on "scientific reasoning," which, as is common with most research in this area, involves student subjects in the Wittgensteinian task of discovering the rule governing a number series (Gorman, Gorman, and Latta 1984). Gorman found that his subjects discovered the rule more quickly when they were taught a Popper-like falsificationist strategy. On the one hand, someone skeptical of this line of research can complain about the dissimilarities between Gorman's setup and the situations in which real scientists find themselves—in particular, the unlikelihood that they would be offered the kind of explicit instruction in problem solving that the experimenter provides. On the other hand, it may be said in Gorman's defense that he is more interested in constructing scenarios for making the world behave more like the laboratory than vice versa. And so if it is true that instructing real scientists in a falsificationist strategy would improve their problem-solving effectiveness, then regardless of the likelihood of such instruction in the normal course of things, Gorman will have made his point. So too would the social epistemologist, whose normative orientation is tied to this latter sense of external validity (cf. Fuller 1992).

We have just seen that efforts to change the scientific enterprise are served by the artifice of experiments. In turning to the second epistemic aspect of experimentation, we will find that artifice also enhances the critical powers of both experimenter and subject. Again, this is a point that has eluded both supporters and opponents of the experimental method.

Although it is nowadays fashionable to blame Francis Bacon for all the evils of modern science, he nevertheless realized that experiments compensate for the cognitive biases and limitations in normal observation—such as the ones highlighted in (1') through (3')—that typically prevent inquirers from penetrating the appearances. For example, controls are used in experiments as an antidote to Bacon's "Idol of the Theater," whereby we naturally notice cases in which X is followed by Y, but we need special guidance to notice what follows from an absence of X. It is precisely the artificiality of control conditions that enables the inquirer to monitor the contributions that her own cognitive liabilities might be making to an observation. This point is often lost on both friends and foes of experiment because they seem to operate with an interpretive double standard that reifies an imaginary distinction between experimental and ordinary situations. By dwelling on the artifice of the laboratory environment in which, say, a psychologist observes subjects solving a problem in scientific reasoning, critics seem to suggest that such a setting is among the relatively few situations in which the subject's full powers are constrained by the presence of someone else—in this case the psychologist—who dictates the subject's behavior and then speaks on her behalf (cf. Harre and Secord 1972).

However, one need only be a bit of an ethnomethodologist to realize that such a suggestion would be false, as even "normal" patterns of behavior in "natural" settings are the product of constraints on the subject's capacities. Admittedly most of these constraints have become so routinized as to appear invisible, or "second nature." And depending on the interpreter's favorite school of psychology, the constraints in question may be defined as "internalized" or "conditioned" or even "subliminally cued." The last expression conveys especially well the scaffolding of our "carpentered world" (Segall et al. 1966) that functions below the threshold of consciousness in everyday life. That ethnomethodologists have defended the strategic disruption of everyday situations reveals the extent to which experimental methods can serve to alert subjects—often to the point of unnerving them—to the artifice systematically built into what is typically taken as natural. We earlier alluded to a prime candidate for strategic disruption, namely, the "natural norm" that scientists and science policymakers presume governs the production of knowledge, unless subject to external interference. It is easy to fail to see the need for regulating science if we presume that science generally works as it ought to. But in that case, the science studies researcher can play the ethnomethodologist to the policymaker's naive subject by presenting the latter with the disparity between the avowed norms and actual practice of scientists, which will in turn force the policymaker to choose between either making the norms conform to the practice (i.e., a reassessment of the ends of science) or making the practice conform to the norms (i.e., a closer scrutiny of what scientist do).

It goes without saying that the interpreter's consciousness of artifice is also raised in the course of conducting the experiment. The care with which experimentalists operationalize the terms of their theories, establish control conditions, and the like demonstrates the exacting standards to which they hold their own interpretations of the subjects. These are not the standards by which we make sense of one another in everyday life, where, say, the exact contributions made by each of two parties toward defining a situation matters less than that they come to some agreement that enables future interaction. I will elaborate on this distinction in the next section, when contrasting the James and Peirce reading of the pragmatist's slogan.

In short, then, the social epistemologist's objections imply that the difference between, say, the psychologist's way of studying scientific reasoning in her own lab and the anthropologist's way of studying such reasoning "on site" in the scientist's laboratory is merely one of the *visibility*, not of the actual *presence* of constraints. Moreover, these constraints apply not only to the subject's range of expression, but also to the range of interpretations made of the subject. Thus, the anthropologist's tendency to overinterpret the scientist's actions as context-sensitive is no less preemptive of the scientist's epistemic authority than the psychologist's tendency to underinterpret similar actions as irrational. For in one breath the anthropologist "thick-describes" the scientist as a sophisticated reasoner who operates on many levels of thought at once; but in the next breath the anthropologist assures us that these levels are unconscious or "tacit" to the scientist to such an extent that we should not expect the scientist to be capable of articulating—or perhaps even recognizing—these modes of thought as her own (cf. Knorr Cetina 1981). However, the anthropologist presumably has such articulate access (though some have recently come to admit the errors of their preemptive ways; cf. Clifford and Marcus 1986).

One implication of this line of argument is that experimentation can serve as a corrective for the "situated holism" (cf. Pickering 1987, 1989) that tends to operate as a methodological assumption in science studies. According to this assumption, every feature that the interpreter identifies as significant in a scientific situation is taken to be of equal and mutual importance in bringing about that situation. In the case of Polanyi, but perhaps more especially of Friedrich von Hayek (1952), situated holism has underwritten an aversion to tinkering with the epistemic enterprise. However, from the experimenter's standpoint, situated holism looks like a rationalization for either a lack of will or a lack of power. It is no secret that nonscientists have a hard enough time being permitted to observe "science in action," let alone being allowed to interfere with how the science is actually done. As a result, it is all too convenient for a nonscientist to suppose, once she has been permitted access to the laboratory, that little would be gained by experimentally manipulating aspects of the situation, *especially* given the unlikelihood of her ever being in a position to do so (cf. Elster 1984, on "sour grapes"). By contrast, an experimental frame of mind would embolden the science studies researcher to tinker, as she would presume that the regularity of laboratory life is simply a product of artifice—in both expression and interpretation—whose traces have become carefully hidden. Although in what follows I will talk mostly as if science happens exclusively within the four walls of a laboratory, an argument for tinkering can be made even more strongly for the seemingly seamless objects of inquiry that are constructed in the writing and reading conventions of particular disciplines (cf. Bazerman 1988).

Pragmatism Revisited and Reclaimed

To bring the previous section into line with the first two, let me now sketch the features of pragmatism that social epistemology wishes to retain, features that the movement shares with positivism. A good way of getting a grip on these issues is by returning to Lovejoy's (1908) dissection of pragmatism. Lovejoy began to suspect that pragmatism was not all of one piece when he detected an ambiguity in the pragmatist slogan. "The validity of a belief is to be judged by the consequences of holding the belief for human action." The ambiguity lies in exactly what "the consequences of holding a belief" refers to. Consider these two possible readings, each associated with a particular pragmatist:

> *The James Reading:* The relevant consequences are the difference that my holding the belief makes to what I subsequently do, regardless of whether the belief corresponds to the way things really are. Thus, the validity of my accepting Pascal's wager is judged by whether my life is better off than it would have been had I not accepted it, not on whether God actually turns out to exist. Generally speaking, I should avoid holding beliefs that are likely to inhibit my commitment to what I want to do (cf. James 1907).

> *The Peirce Reading:* The relevant consequences are the difference that the truth of the belief makes to what I subsequently do. In that case, the validity of my accepting Pascal's wager is judged by how the actual existence or nonexistence of God would bear on my having decided to accept or reject the wager. Generally speaking, I should avoid trying to do things that will succeed *only* if certain improbable beliefs are true. (cf. Peirce 1964).

Whereas most of science studies tends toward the James reading of the pragmatist motto, social epistemology favors the Peirce reading instead. In thinking about how these two readings map on to the study of science, the reader should take the "I" to refer to the scientist pursuing her ends in, say, the laboratory workplace. The practitioner of science studies, including the social epistemologist, observes this "I" in action from some relatively detached stand-point. Whether the science studies practitioner has grounds for intervention depends on whether there is a sense in which she can exercise epistemic authority over what the scientist is doing. The Peirce reading allows her such an opportunity, while the James reading does not. Thus, several important issues turn on what would at first seem to be a mere question of emphasis.

In the pragmatist scheme of things, who is authorized to judge whether a belief that I hold is valid? Clearly on the James reading, I as the belief holder am the ultimate authority: if I find that the belief helps me achieve my goals, then it is valid. No further questions need be asked. By contrast, the Peirce reading entertains the possibility that I may not be the best judge, especially if an external observer knows more of the relevant facts that bear on the truth of my beliefs than I do. On the James reading, I am constantly reinterpreting the world (revising my beliefs, if you will) in order to bring my understanding of the world into greater accord with what I want from it. Thus, when I run across a feature of the world that resists my desires, I make the most of it, usually by reinterpreting the feature in some desirable way. In short, the Jamesian seems to apply Occam's razor to external reality, to wit, that the presence of a world independent of my mind should not be presumed beyond the occasions in which my mind faces resistance in its pursuits. This certainly captures a line of thinking presupposed in many social constructivist accounts of science, a line which Pickering (1990) has felicitously dubbed "situated resistance." However, the Peircean wonders, if my view of the world is so determined by my desires, then how do I manage to experience any resistance in the first place?

The Peircean's answer is that in fact reality exceeds my finite ability to anticipate what I will experience. Moreover, insofar as the stuff inside the mind is—as part of the natural evolutionary order—the same as the stuff outside the mind, then I am just as likely not to know my own mental reality as not to know any external reality. Consequently the Peircean can envisage that I may not be aware of all that I am doing when I reinterpret the world to my own advantage. In particular, I may unwittingly alter what I take "my advantage" to be. As the social psychologists would say, I may succumb to an *adaptive preference formation* and subconsciously adjust my aspirations so as to minimize their likelihood of being resisted by the world. In short, I am bound to do anything that will make me look good in the end, including radically alter what I take the end to be. And so, whereas on the James reading I appear as someone who perseveres in the face of resistance to achieve my ends, on the Peirce reading I turn out to be much more susceptible to manipulation by my environment, just as long as I am able to maintain a sense of purpose in whatever I happen to do.

For the social epistemologist interested in science policy, the Peirce reading has the advantage of alerting the observer to the difference between the veneer of rationality that results from engaging in a relatively frictionless, or "coherent," social practice and the deeper sense of rationality that comes from actually succeeding at what she originally set out to do. The Peirce reading gains this advantage by treating my activities as a sort of an experiment: Before I engage in my pursuits, the observer notes the constraints that I have imposed on the range of acceptable procedures and outcomes, including the order in which I prefer them, and then judges my subsequent actions against the original standard. Under those conditions, the observer may be able to surprise me with information concerning how well or poorly I perform. By contrast, the James reading would have the observer start her inquiry at the point when I feel that I have accomplished something; then she would reinterpret my actions up to that point as part of an overall strategy to bring about the accomplishment. Admittedly the observer need not accept my personalized sense of Whig history about the matter (i.e., how I rationalize my situation), but she will take my satisfaction with the accomplishment as evidence that my actions up to that point are to be interpreted as rational, albeit not necessarily in terms that I would approve. If nothing else, the James reading of me as naturally tending toward self-vindication captures very well the *phenomenology* of how I experience my pursuits. Indeed, the social epistemologist has no quarrel with the social constructivist about the James reading as a phenomenology of scientists' experience. The quarrel is over whether phenomenology alone makes for an adequate account of science.

And what should the Peircean make of the discrepancy between my experience of self-vindication and the observer's recognition of my convenient confoundings and forgettings? In the many cases in which social psychologists have tried to confront subjects with their failure to live up to self-imposed standards, the subjects have generally given ad hoc reasons for these failures, reasons that minimize the damage done to their sense of personal identity, and they sometimes even bolster it by means of clever casuistry (for a review of this literature, cf. Ross 1977). Appeals to imagined contextual nuances in the experimental situation often have this quality. Interestingly, though, the subjects rarely take these failures as grounds for giving up the standards themselves—a result that would probably be reproduced in the scientific case, if scientists were repeatedly shown (à la Collins 1985) that they deviated from a vast array of methodological canons. Other things being equal, it would seem that a standard acquires greater normative force in the minds of its upholders the more it is subject to empirical challenge. At the end of this article, I will suggest how we might rhetorically get beyond "other things being equal."

The potential for doublethink goes still further, to the very heart of science studies, once we delve into the mysteries surrounding the "open-endedness" of scientific practice (cf. Barnes 1982; Lynch, chap. 7). The concept of open-endedness is normally used to show that a scientist's practice is vindicated, though not in terms that the scientist herself would recognize as such. The argument is that since rules do not specify the conditions to which they apply, it should come as no surprise that scientists do not appear to follow methodological rules consistently. Indeed, the science studies practitioner goes on to claim that this is all to the good, since open-endedness is the primary source of innovation in science. Much less emphasized, however, is the fact that the very same open-endedness is equally responsible for the proliferation of error and misunderstanding in the scientific enterprise (Fuller 1988, chap. 5; cf. Lyotard 1983). Indeed, it may be a little too convenient to valorize open-endedness (perhaps even to the point of building it into the "meaning underdetermines use" account of rules), given the enormous practical difficulties that would be posed if scientists did try to synchronize their activities throughout the world in order to obtain some sort of methodological closure. Do we have here a case in which the observer has become so sympathetic to my existential plight that she helps me along in my rationalizations by revealing the open-ended character of my acts? Perhaps if Bloor's (1976) principle of symmetry were applied to the innovative-mistaken distinction with the vigor normally reserved for true-false and rational-irrational, open-endedness would appear less luminous.

We have already examined the methodologically pernicious consequences of this interpretive strategy. The source of the perniciousness is clear, namely, that on the James reading, the observer is co-opted into adopting my own frame of reference on what I am doing, even though she is potentially in a position to see much more. But the observer can acquire this extra insight only if she is willing to alternate between widening and narrowing her angle of vision and thereby refuse to accept the "context" and "background" in terms of which I make sense of what I do (cf. De Mey 1982, chap. 10). For example, even if it is true that methodological rules are inherently open-ended, it does not follow that the scientist's behavior cannot be predicted and explained on a regular basis by introducing categories and considerations that would not normally be part of the scientist's frame of reference. After all, who says that science takes place only in the region to which a scientist has immediate sensory access, namely, the laboratory work site? Who says that the science occurring in this region is restricted to those practices that most clearly set science apart from other social practices? Who says that an account of science must be framed around achieving or failing to achieve some result? Indeed, who says that science makes sense? The answer to all these questions is that scientists and their well-wishers say these things. And science studies practitioners, by implicitly adopting the James reading of the pragmatist's motto, accept what the scientists say here uncritically.

Toward the Scientific Management of Science

An instructive way of seeing how social epistemology reconceptualizes the relation between science studies and science is by recalling Frederick Winslow Taylor's (1911) "principles of scientific management," which is alleged to have revolutionized labor-management relations in the United States in the first decade of the twentieth century. There is a way of recounting the story of this revolution—largely Taylor's own—that portrays the manager as someone who, against the inertial tendencies of labor, serves the public interest by designing schemes for the efficient manufacture of consumer goods. Most historians now discount this story as so self-serving that it obscures the reasons for Taylorism being picked up only by a relatively small numbers of industries, even though Taylor himself was elevated to the status of a folk hero in the society at large (Clawson 1980). In effect, Taylorism marked the beginning of a change in the public image of the capitalist from rapacious egoist to corporate steward (cf. Miller and O'Leary 1987). However, for purposes of the argument, I want to bracket the ideological whitewash clearly involved here and focus on what it would mean to take Taylor at his word and apply it to the management of scientific labor. To translate from the previous discussion of pragmatism, "I" am now represented as a worker and "the observer" as management.

Both before and after the emergence of Taylorism, management exercised control over labor. But before Taylor came on the scene, labor was commonly regarded as the final authority over how the job was done. Management would of course offer incentives for the workers to produce more, but ultimately how much a given worker produced in a given day was left to her discretion. The most management could do was to fire an unproductive worker. The revolution came when management realized that it could intervene in the work process itself by training the worker to become more productive, or productive in the right ways. For even tasks that today seem so easily routinized, such as shoveling coal, had been typically cast in Taylor's day as unanalyzable "skills" best left to the expert workers, who would set their own pace and even choose, if not actually make, their own tools. Indeed, much of this craft-guild mentality still pervades labor unions. It encourages a strong sense of what is intrinsic and what is extrinsic to the work process. However, it is a sense that quickly diminishes once the work process is analyzed into discretely improvable routines.

For the social epistemologist, the important point here is that whether a particular job is regarded as an "organic skill" or a "mechanical routine" has little if anything to do with the nature of the work itself. Rather the judgment call reflects the amount of critical scrutiny to which the job has been subjected. Precisely because each worker had been given the last word on how the job would be done, Taylor was able to step back and observe the variety of activities that were passing without notice—or at least without question—for coal shoveling. There were differences in the time taken and amount shoveled, as well as differences in the level of interaction among workers in the course of shoveling. This variety suggested to Taylor, not that the coal shovelers embodied unique skills, but rather that each coal shoveler's behavior varied among a host of dimensions; this in turn enabled Taylor to suggest specific ways in which coal may be shoveled more efficiently to meet the various ends of production.

By confining their observations to the scientist's "natural habitat," science studies practitioners artificially restrict the range of consequences that they observe of the scientists' behavior. The claim that a coal shoveler is an expert in what she does remains persuasive only as long as coal shoveling is treated as a sui generis activity with no basis for comparison or examination outside the vicinity in which the shoveling normally takes place. However, once the observer expands her horizons, even if it merely involves comparing shovelers in different locations, then the coal shoveler starts to lose the patina of expertise. The same may be said of the scientist, though several conceptual obstacles must be overcome before seeing the full implications. However, all these may be traced to one source, namely, the language in which science is described and explained.

Even among the most antiscientific of the science studies practitioners, it is still difficult to account for knowledge production without falling back on the specialized discourse of the discipline under study or of science more generally, which in turn contributes to the illusion of science as a sui generis enterprise. In short, the image of science's natural autonomy is fostered by the typical inability of science studies practitioners to integrate their talk about science within the categories normally used to talk about the rest of society. As a result, it does not look as though science has any consequences beyond its natural habitat until it has been explicitly transferred to some more robustly "social" arena. Indeed, many thinkers have jumped on this purely linguistic point to conclude that science starts having value implications only after it has been put to some extrascientific use. And as long as these difficulties remain in conceptualizing the social consequences of science, the idea of improving science will remain a remote, if intelligible, prospect.

Hacking (chap. 2) and Law (1986, 1991) provide a nice contrast between two science studies practitioners who, respectively, do and do not tend to regard science as a sui generis activity. Both Hacking and Law are concerned with the "stabilization" of laboratory phenomena as a source of scientific credibility, but they have quite different senses of how much of society needs to be swept up in their analyses. Although Hacking loudly advertises that he has emptied science of such occult philosophical entities as theories and truth, he nevertheless retains the ontological shell that enabled the sui generis account to be given. Only now the shell is filled with experimental practices internal to the culture of a particular branch of physics. In so "disunifying" the sciences, Hacking has effectively cleared the conceptual space for many microinternal histories of science. This shows that the sciences can be portrayed as external to each other as well as to the rest of society. Such a conclusion runs counter to the one pursued here. By contrast, Law shows how scientists negotiate the amount of scrutiny focused on their activities by shaping the public's understanding of the ways in which it may react to whatever the scientists do. Like Taylor's coal shovelers, Law's scientists desire discretion to do as they please, but since the scientists ultimately need to have the phenomena they produce serve as a basis for extending their credibility across society, they must enroll the public and thereby expose themselves to its tests. Not surprisingly, then, Law's account of the stabilization of laboratory phenomena relies on economic discourse, which cuts across all sectors of society, instead of the more narrowly scientific discourse to which Hacking typically turns. Fujimura (chap. 6), comes closest to representing Law's position in this volume.

As the Taylor case indicates, science is not the only social practice whose self-image has resisted assimilation to a more comprehensive system of social analysis. And as the social epistemologist suggests, the antidote is to stop thinking about science as having a natural integrity that compels the observer to interpret it exclusively in its own terms. But how exactly does this antidote work as an interpretive strategy? The first move is to treat the word "science" as designating, not a simple practice clearly demarcated from other social practices, but rather a complex practice consisting of a cluster of behaviors each of which can be found clustered with other behaviors to form other social practices. In other words, properly analyzed, science would be shown to exhibit the power and motivation structure of other competitive fields, an organization of labor that is reminiscent of industries whose products require a similar level of technical sophistication, the flow of communication common to networks of the same spatiotemporal diffuseness, the codification of knowledge expected of traditions with similar interests in historical continuity and prospective retrieval—not to mention the deployment of capital normally found among businesses operating at a certain level of investment intensity. In each case the strategy would force the inquirer to move from the laboratory site of science to the other sectors of society in which these variables have been studied more fully (cf. Collins 1975, chap. 9; Whitley 1985).

Despite a superficial similarity, my reliance on appeals to "behavior" and "causes" reveals the vast difference in spirit between the proposed mode of analysis and Knorr Cetina's (chap. 4) phenomenology of laboratory life as the "reconfiguration" of everyday practices in novel settings. Her basis for claiming that aspects of laboratory life are like a war game or a psychoanalytic encounter seems to be the sheer resemblance of the practices in question, without much concern for the means by which such aspects might have originally been transported from one setting to the other and then maintained in that latter setting. In fact, it may be best to read Knorr Cetina as offering a stylistic analysis of science, in the fashion of art historians who also speak of reconfiguring the visual field (e.g., Arnheim 1954). In that case, her references to war games and psychoanalysis should be understood as heuristics for getting the reader to attend to certain subtle but salient features of the laboratory situation, which once established as noteworthy phenomena may be subject to the kind of analysis that I just sketched.

Some steps in this direction have been taken in Pickering's (1988, 1990) recent work on the transition from "small" to "big" science style high-energy physics in the United States, which involved incorporating military-industrial resources and attitudes into the research site of basic science. However, Pickering's account still exhibits the ambiguity in frame of reference that we have found problematic in much of science studies. When Pickering calls the new high-energy physics a "heterogeneous field," he adopts the standpoint of the observer, more specifically, someone who has yet to be persuaded of the mutual coherence of the various elements with which Luis Alvarez was trying to reconfigure physics. This is certainly the research perspective that the social epistemologist wishes to cultivate. But it does not sit well with Pickering's other tendency, much more common in science studies, namely, to refer to the different types of physics as "cultures" or "forms of life," which is more appropriate to the perspective of the scientist or someone who perceives the internal coherence of the scientist's activities and their distinctness from the rest of society. Indeed the plot of Pickering's account turns on the "interactive stabilization" of originally heterogeneous resources into coherent knowledge products (Pickering 1987, 1989). As the social epistemologist sees it, what is needed at this point is an account of how such coherence is maintained and reproduced in many situations over time and space. Moreover, this account should be cast as pertaining to a negative, not a positive, social fact, so as to heighten the observer's vantage point on the scientist's practice. Thus, the question should be phrased: How is the heterogeneity of resources continually masked in the conduct of science, such that scientists (and their well-wishers) are unable to see, say, science's dependence on various features of the military-industrial complex? Pickering (1988) actually sketches an answer to this question, but it would be interesting to see, once a full-blown answer is given, whether the "culture" or "form of life" surrounding high-energy physics turns out to be anything more than a marker for the scientists' false consciousness.

In eschewing such terms as "culture" and "form of life," the social epistemologist is concerned with demystifying the ontological significance that followers of Wittgenstein and Heidegger have tended to attach to when, where, and how an activity is performed. This is by no means to deny that the spatiotemporal dimensions of science are essential for understanding the possibilities for knowledge production. But to say that science is bounded in space and time does not entail that it can be bounded in only one way, to wit, the way in which it is actually bounded (cf. Giddens 1979). The social epistemologist takes the local character of knowledge production—the fact that science happens in a given set of labs and on a certain schedule—to be significant only as an epistemic marker, or symptom, alerting the observer to where and when to start examining how the knowledge production process works. But the examination may soon take the observer out of this setting, especially once she unravels the complexity of "science in action" into a concatenation of behavior patterns that are mutually reinforced in a given location, not only by the scientists themselves but also by the observer herself, insofar as she too sees these behaviors as contributing to the same overarching practice. Yet each of these behaviors can be analyzed separately and compared with its counterparts in the rest of society (cf. Fuller 1989, chap. 2).

The discussion so far has suggested that the social epistemologist would go about her research by examining the scientific workplace, or one of its artifacts, for the traces left by other social practices, all along expecting that nothing deeper holds these traces together than habituation in a common environment. However, this would be to enter the story in medias res. After all, the social epistemologist embarks on her research already equipped with certain expectations about how, when, and why science works. These are in turn informed by certain regularities allegedly drawn from the history of science. I say "allegedly" because in the few cases where attempts have been made to compile statistics on the frequency with which particular strategies have led to particular outcomes (e.g., Laudan et al. 1986), the results have gone against the conventional wisdom. As was suggested in earlier sections, this point has serious implications for policymakers who uncritically rely on anecdotes rooted in the folk history of science. This section will conclude with a procedure to instill a strategically critical attitude (cf. Fuller 1991).

One of the most severely challenged pieces of methodological advice in recent years (e.g., Collins 1985) has been "If you want to eliminate error from the body of empirical knowledge, then you should replicate experiments." In philosophical parlance, a strategy phrased in this way is called a "hypothetical imperative." It is designed both to summarize and to direct what scientists do. However, because the evidence for the efficacy of the imperative is largely anecdotal, it is not clear whether it is meant to apply to all scientists as individuals, regardless of their ambient social settings, or only to scientists who work in settings like the ones in which the imperative is alleged to have worked in the past. In short, the social epistemologist must decompose this sedimented piece of folk history into something that can be used to inform science policy. What follows is procedure by which history can be converted into experimentally testable hypotheses, which can then be used as the basis for informed intervention in the scientific workplace. For purposes of clarity, I have stuck with replication as the sample imperative:

1. Would the scientists who are counted as having eliminated error by replication accept that as a description of what they were doing? It is important to get this question settled at the outset, since it gauges the initial viability of issuing the imperative as a straight piece of advice to scientists.
   (a) If the answer is yes, then go to (2).
   (b) If the answer is no, then go to (4).
2. What sorts of social structures (both intra- and extrascientific) make it likely that individual scientists would eliminate error by replication? This question may be addressed in two stages: (a) compare the social structures of the historical cases in which the imperative was and was not efficacious; (b) conduct experiments in order to specify which features of the supportive structures were instrumental in rendering the imperative efficacious. Then go to (3).
3. Are the social structures supportive of the imperative the ones that are believed on independent grounds to promote human welfare? This question may be addressed by evaluating the character of human interaction in social structures supportive of the imperative.
   (a) If the answer to (3) is yes, then go to (5).
   (b) If the answer to (3) is no, then go to (4).
4. Since for either empirical (cf. 1b) or normative (cf. 3b) reasons the imperative does not work as advice to individual scientists, then perhaps the imperative is best seen as specifying a "function" in the strict sociological sense of a systemic benefit to the ongoing enterprise of science that emerges as the unintended consequence of scientists pursuing their respective ends. This would certainly explain why the scientists would neither see what they are doing as replication (cf. (1)) nor necessarily benefit from coming to see their activities in that way (cf. (3)). In that case you would not be interested in training each scientist to replicate experiments; rather you would encourage scientists to perform the kind of different but complementary tasks that regularly issue in replication as a collective effect. But which tasks are these, and what sorts of communication channels are needed to integrate the tasks in the appropriate way? Clearly constraints on permissible answers will be provided by the dimensions of the projects for which policy is being made. But within those constraints, more specific answers

are to be found by conducting small-group experiments on alternative schemes for dividing the cognitive labor. Once a suitable scheme is found, then go to (5).

5. The "only" questions that remain are whether and how our own society can be engineered to have the relevant supportive structures. We then move out of science policy proper and into social policy more generally.

Objections and Projections

There are two general lines of criticism to the project of social epistemology that are worth confronting at this point. The first, more venerable line is common among libertarian approaches to knowledge production and perhaps has received its most eloquent expression in Popper (1957). It turns on the argument that science is impossible to plan because science is distinguished by the production of new knowledge, which, if it is to remain genuinely new, must also be unpredictable, and hence unplannable. The argument can be framed in at least three distinct ways to show that any science policy that aims to legislate over the epistemic enterprise is ultimately self-defeating. First, if the social epistemologist issues a prediction about the course of science, then the relevant scientists can perversely decide to do the opposite. But if perversity is not an option, and the scientists' research turns out to conform to the prediction, a second version of the argument can be made whereby it would be impossible to tell whether the conformity was due to the independent truth of the prediction or merely to the scientists' having treated the prediction as a command that had better be obeyed. The latter possibility would surely spell the end of science pursuing the truth wherever it may lead. Indeed, on the third reading of the argument, what the scientists decide to do is irrelevant, since once the social epistemologist predicts the course of science, she will herself have made the predicted findings. Together the arguments pose a formidable challenge to the social epistemologist. To meet the challenge, she will need to do more than to remind her opponent of the bromide that discovery favors the prepared mind. For if Taylorism is an apt model, then the social epistemologist is courting a much more comprehensive sense of epistemic planning.

Putting aside for the moment the "self-defeating" character of the task, why is it so much more difficult to predict the course of science than, say, the course of business cycles? Several answers may be given to this infrequently raised question. One is that only relatively unsystematic efforts have so far been made to isolate and manipulate the variables that are thought to affect the growth of knowledge. The most systematic work has been in bibliometrics, and there one can already begin to get a sense of the boom-and-bust cycles of disciplinary specialties by examining co-citation patterns (De Mey 1982, chaps. 7–9). However, this research still leaves open important questions about the pattern of knowledge transference to new disciplines, the public sphere, and technology, which arguably has a more profound, albeit subtle, effect on long-term epistemic development. Much of the reluctance to study these matters is no doubt due to the "if it ain't broke, don't fix it" mentality that was earlier discussed in terms of the tendency to conflate passable and optimal scientific performance. In other words, people seem to be more satisfied with the "natural pace" of epistemic growth than with the "natural pace" of economic growth. Of course one reason for this difference in attitude is that there are many folk and scientific theories that license people to hold changes in the economy accountable for certain things that happen in their lives. But "we" (and here I mean both the government official and the ordinary person) are not similarly endowed with theories to tell us when to blame our successes and failures on the vicissitudes of knowledge production. Again, ignorance is bliss.

Another reason for the difficulty in predicting the course of science is that science is one of the most loosely structured social practices. Not only are the activities of scientists not monitored closely by either themselves or society at large (a by-product of the ascribed expertise of scientists), but also it is typically not clear what a scientist is trying to do until she has been recognized as having done it. At least if we want to maintain that science has been a largely "successful" enterprise in some sense of the term, then we had better accept the appropriateness of scientists rationally reconstructing their problem spaces. An important phenomenological consequence of science's structural looseness is to leave the observer with the impression that the products of science have an existence somewhat independent of the means by which they are produced. Often an element of surprise accompanies a scientific discovery precisely because the discovery was not uniquely determined by the procedures that the scientists took themselves to have been using. (A sustained comparison of scientific discoveries and religious miracles on this point would prove illuminating.) Of course this is just to lay down the challenge to the observer to search for some hidden procedures, the uncovering of which would reveal the discovery to have really been an elaborate construction. Thus, the failure to scrutinize scientific practice reinforces the myth of realism as well as the myth of expertise.

Once these two myths are dispelled, or at least demystified, it is then possible to see that scientific innovation may be understood in a way not altogether different from Taylor's analysis of industrial innovation, namely, in terms of the recombination of already-existent parts into a new gestalt (cf. Simon 1972; Langley et al. 1987). While much has been written about the "gestalt switch" as the model of scientific change, little has been said about the preconditions for such a switch, namely, that the parts which constitute the whole be analytically separable and usable for a variety of cognitive ends. And while the particular end that triggers a gestalt switch is surely context-dependent, the means that can be mobilized to serve that end must not be. Here one is reminded of Wolfgang Koehler's famous experiments on simian insight, in which the ape is able to reach a distant banana only by arranging several otherwise unrelated objects into a primitive prosthetic arm. If the psychology of scientific discovery is something like an internalization of this process (cf. Weisberg 1986), then it would seem that the "surprise" factor that scientific planning allegedly threatens to squash pertains not to the discovery process itself, but rather to where the discovery catches on and to what extent. In other words, psychologists may well be able to train scientists to reason as Darwin, Newton, or Einstein did, but that would not be sufficient to produce a new breed of scientific geniuses, since "genius" is a retrospective attribution that scientists receive for the impact that their research has on a variety of fields (Brannigan 1981). It follows that the relevant sense of surprise in scientific discovery probably has to do with the relatively unmonitored flow of scientific communication among fields. Yet again, ignorance mythified into a virtue.

The second line of criticism of social epistemology comes from pursuing the analogy with Taylorism too closely. Both critics and supporters of the scientific management idea quickly zeroed in on the biggest problem with Taylor's particular strategy: It presupposed instant compliance on the part of the workers, which was of course a pure fiction. Labor resistance to Taylorism was real, and violence not uncommon. At the very least, it showed that Taylor had designed a model of efficiency for a frictionless social medium, which when applied many real labor situations turned out to be more inefficient (in terms of people hurt, workdays lost, goods destroyed) than had the workers been left completely alone. Although Taylor had a ready audience among the "captains of industry" and the general public, he ultimately failed because the knowledge he produced (i.e., the principles of scientific management) was not consumable by his real target market, rank-and-file laborers.

There are many lessons for the social epistemologist to learn from this episode. After all, if the social espistemologist's attempts to reform scientific practice require a superhuman suppression of scientists' inclinations, then her proposals are likely to remain just as speculative as those of the classical epistemologist portrayed at the start of this paper. Either that, or she will be met with a "scientific revolution" along the lines that Taylor provoked in the workers. The trick seems to be to tread the fine line between adopting an uncompromisingly third-person perspective that unilaterally divests any sense of expertise from the scientists (the Taylor route) and uncritically capitulating to the first-person on-site authority of the scientists (the more typical science studies route). While I remain convinced that the third-person perspective cultivated by Peircean pragmatism and laboratory simulations of science is the best way to gain a truly critical perspective on our knowledge enterprises, a second-person perspective is needed to complete the normative transformation from mere criticism to genuine improvement. In other words, the scientists whose practices the social epistemologist criticizes have to be made not only part of the problem but part of the solution as well. In the management of industrial labor, this was accomplished by managers shifting their conception of authority from "power over" to "power with" labor in the workplace (Follett 1920). What does the social epistemologist offer by way of analogy?

What I am suggesting here is clearly a project in rhetoric that involves what may be called a "rehabilitation of the scientist's sense of agency." The task is in the spirit (though unfortunately not always the letter) of demystification in ideology critique (Fay 1987) and debriefing in experimental psychology (Harris 1988). If scientists have been so deeply misled about the nature of knowledge production and their own role in it, how can this fact be conveyed to them in a manner that is likely to make them want them to cooperate with the social epistemologist to improve the enterprise? It is important to note that this question is not asking for a sophistic quick fix, whereby the scientists are duped into cashing in one form of false consciousness for another. Admittedly such a proviso is easier said than done, but that simply poses a challenge to the social epistemologist to arrive at *principles of epistemic justice*, that is, principles by which knowledge producers come to change their practices in an epistemically and socially responsible manner. In a

Rawlsian gesture, let me close this paper with two such proposed principles that, I hope, will open discussion on this topic:

The Principle of Reusability: When trying to get someone to change her ways, avoid tactics that are nonreusable or likely to wear thin over time. (This captures the pragmatic punch of more ethereal appeals to the "universalizability" of the means of persuasion, namely, that the tactics must work not only here and now but at any place and any time; hence coercion and less-than-seamless forms of manipulation will not work in the long term.)

The Principle of Humility: The person whose ways you are trying to change may have good reasons to resist your efforts, which, if you gave her half a chance, she would tell you and perhaps even change *your* mind in the process. (This safeguards against the high-handed tendencies of demystification and debriefing, in which the zeal for remaking others in the image and likeness of one's theories can prevent the reformer from catching potential refutations of her own theory.)

REFERENCES

Albury, Randall. 1983. *The Politics of Objectivity.* Victoria: Deakin University Press.

Arkes, Hal, and Kenneth Hammond, eds. 1986. *Judgment and Decision Making.* Cambridge: Cambridge University Press.

Arnheim, Rudolf. 1954. *Art and Visual Representation.* Berkeley: University of California Press.

Averch, Harvey. 1985. *A Strategic Analysis of Science and Technology Policy.* Baltimore: Johns Hopkins University Press.

Barnes, Barry. 1982. *T. S. Kuhn and Social Science.* New York: Columbia University Press.

Bazerman, Charles. 1988. *Shaping Written Knowledge.* Madison: University of Wisconsin Press.

Berkowitz, Leonard, and Edward Donnerstein. 1982. Why External Validity Is More Than Skin Deep. *American Psychologist* 37: 245–57.

Bernstein, Richard. 1983. *Beyond Objectivism and Relativism.* Philadelphia: University of Pennsylvania Press.

Bhaskar, Roy. 1979. *A Realist Theory of Science.* Brighton: Harvester.

Bloor, David. 1976. *Knowledge and Social Imagery.* London: Routledge and Kegan Paul.

Brannigan, Augustine. 1981. *The Social Basis of Scientific Discoveries.* Cambridge: Cambridge University Press.

Brehmer, Berndt. 1986. *In One Word: Not from Experience.* In Arkes and Hammond 1986.

Brown, Harold. 1989. Towards a Cognitive Psychology of What? *Social Epistemology* 2:2.

Callon, Michel, John Law, and Arie Rip. 1986. *Mapping the Dynamics of Science and Technology*. London: Macmillan.

Campbell, Donald. 1988. *Methodology and Epistemology for the Social Sciences*. Chicago: University of Chicago Press.

Clawson, Dan. 1980. *Bureaucracy and the Labor Process*. New York: Monthly Review Press.

Clifford, James, and George Marcus, eds. 1986. *Writing Cultures: The Poetics and Politics of Ethnography*. Berkeley: University of California Press.

Collins, Harry. 1985. *Changing Order*. London: Sage.

Collins, Randall. 1975. *Conflict Sociology*. New York: Academic Press.

———. 1979. *The Credential Society*. New York: Academic Press.

Davidson, Donald. 1983. *Inquiries into Truth and Interpretation*. Oxford: Oxford University Press.

De Mey, Marc. 1982. *The Cognitive Paradigm*. Dordrecht: D. Reidel.

Dennett, Daniel. 1979. *Brainstorms*. Cambridge: MIT Press.

Dewey, John. 1908. *How We Think*. Boston: Houghton Mifflin.

Elster, Jon. 1984. *Sour Grapes*. Cambridge: Cambridge University Press.

Faust, David. 1985. *The Limits of Scientific Reasoning*. Minneapolis: University of Minnesota Press.

Fay, Brian. 1987. *Critical Social Science*. Ithaca: Cornell University Press.

Fine, Arthur. 1986. *The Shaky Game*. Chicago: University of Chicago Press.

Follett, Mary Parker. 1920. *The New State*. London: Longmans.

Forester, John, ed. 1985. *Critical Theory and Public Life*. Cambridge: MIT Press.

Fuller, Steve. 1988. *Social Epistemology*. Bloomington: Indiana University Press.

———. 1989. *Philosophy of Science and Its Discontents*. Boulder: Westview Press.

———. 1991. Is History and Philosophy of Science Withering on the Vine? *Philosophy of the Social Sciences*. 21: 149–74.

———. 1992. Epistemology Radically Naturalized: Recovering the Normative, the Experimental, and the Social. In Giere 1992.

Gadamer, Hans-Georg. 1975. *Truth and Method*. New York: Seabury Press.

Galison, Peter. 1987. *How Experiments End*. Chicago: University of Chicago Press.

Giddens, Anthony. 1979. *The Central Problems of Social Theory*. London: Macmillan.

Giere, Ronald. 1988. *Explaining Science*. Chicago: University of Chicago Press.

Giere, Ronald, ed. 1992. *Cognitive Models of Science*. Minneapolis: University of Minnesota Press.

Gorman, Michael. 1991. Simulating Social Epistemology: Experimental and Computational Approaches. In Giere 1992.

Gorman, Michael, Margaret Gorman, and R. M. Latta.1984. How Disconfirmatory, Confirmatory, and Combined Strategies Affect Group Problem-Solving. *British Journal of Psychology* 75: 65–79.

Hacking, Ian. 1983. *Representing and Intervening.* Cambridge: Cambridge University Press.

Harre, Rom, and Paul Secord. 1972. *The Explanation of Social Behavior.* Oxford: Oxford University Press.

Harris, Benjamin. 1988. A History of Debriefing in Social Psychology. In J. Morawski, ed., *The Rise of Experimentation in American Psychology.* New Haven: Yale University Press.

Hayakawa, S. I. 1949. *Language in Thought and Action.* New York: Harcourt Brace.

Held, David. 1987. *Models of Democracy.* Palo Alto: Stanford University Press.

Holland, James, Keith Holyoak, Richard Nisbett, and Paul Thagard. 1986. *Induction.* Cambridge: MIT Press.

Hull, David. 1988. *Science as a Process.* Chicago: University of Chicago Press.

James, William. 1987. *The Will to Believe and Other Essays in Popular Philosophy.* New York: G. P. Putnam's & Sons.

———. 1907. *Pragmatism: A New Name for Some Old Ways of Thinking.* New York: G. P. Putnam's & Sons.

Knorr Cetina, Karin. 1981. *The Manufacture of Knowledge.* Oxford: Pergamon.

Langley, Pat, Herbert Simon, Gary Bradshaw, and Jan Zytkow. 1987. *Scientific Discovery.* Cambridge: MIT Press.

Latour, Bruno. 1987. *Science in Action.* Milton Keynes: Open University Press.

Latour, Bruno, and Steve Woolgar. 1986. *Laboratory Life.* 2d ed. Princeton: Princeton University Press.

Laudan, Larry, et al. 1986. Testing Theories of Scientific Change. *Synthese* 69: 141–223.

Law, John. 1991. Notes on the Distribution of Privilege: Choices, Liquidity Struggles, and Boundary Objects. Keele University.

Law, John, ed., 1986. *Power, Action, and Belief.* London: Routledge and Kegan Paul.

Lovejoy, Arthur. 1908. The Thirteen Pragmatisms. *Journal of Philosophy.* 5: 5–12, 29–39.

Lyotard, Jean-François. 1983. *The Postmodern Condition.* Minneapolis: University of Minnesota Press.

Machlup, Fritz. 1962. *The Production and Distribution of Knowledge in the United States.* Princeton: Princeton University Press.

Marcuse, Herbert. 1960. *Reason and Revolution.* Boston: Beacon Press.

Miller, Peter, and Ted O'Leary. 1987. Accounting and the Construction of the Governable Person. *Accounting, Organizations, and Society* 12: 235–65.

Mulkay, Michael. 1985. *The Word and the World.* London: George Allen and Unwin.

Peirce, Charles Sanders. 1964. *The Essential Writings.* New York: Dover.

Pickering, Andrew. 1984. *Constructing Quarks.* Chicago: University of Chicago Press.

————. 1987. Making Sense of Science: Pragmatism, Realism, and Interactionism. Princeton University.

————. 1988. Big Science as a Form of Life. In M. De Maria and M. Grilli, eds., *The Restructuring of the Physical Sciences in Europe and the United States: 1945–1960.* Singapore: World Scientific Publishing.

————. 1989. Living in the Material World: On Realism and Experimental Practice. In D. Gooding et al. eds., *The Uses of Experiment.* Cambridge: Cambridge University Press.

————. 1990. Openness and Closure: On the Goals of Scientific Practice. In H. Legrand, ed., *Experimental Inquiries.* Boston: Kluwer.

Polanyi, Michael. 1957. *Personal Knowledge.* Chicago: University of Chicago Press.

Popper, Karl. 1957. *The Poverty of Historicism.* New York: Harper and Row.

————. 1963. *Conjectures and Refutations.* New York: Harper and Row.

Porter, Theodore. 1991. Objectivity and Authority: How French Engineers Reduced Public Utility to Numbers. *Poetics Today* (Winter).

Quine, W. V. O. 1960. *Word and Object.* Cambridge: MIT Press.

Redner, Harry. 1987. *The Ends of Science.* Boulder: Westview Press.

Rorty, Richard. 1979. *Philosophy and the Mirror of Nature.* Princeton: Princeton University Press.

————. 1982. *The Consequences of Pragmatism.* Minneapolis: University of Minnesota Press.

Ross, Lee. 1977. The Intuitive Psychologist and His Shortcomings. In L. Berkowitz, ed., *Advances in Experimental Social Psychology.* New York: Academic Press.

Ruse, Michael. 1988. *Philosophy of Biology Today.* Albany: SUNY Press.

Segall, Marshall, Donald Campbell, and Melville Herskovitz. 1966. *The Influence of Culture on Visual Perception.* Indianapolis: Bobbs-Merrill.

Simon, Herbert. 1972. *Models of Discovery.* Dordrecht: D. Reidel.

Taylor, Charles. 1985. *Human Agency and Language.* Cambridge University Press.

Taylor, Frederick Winslow. 1911. *The Principles of Scientific Management.* New York: Harper.

von Hayek, Friedrich. 1952. *The Counter-Revolution in Science.* Chicago: University of Chicago Press.

Weisberg, Robert. 1986. *Creativity: Genius and Other Myths.* New York: W. H. Freeman.

Whitley, Richard. 1985. *The Social and Intellectual Organization of the Sciences.* Oxford: Oxford University Press.

Winch, Peter. 1958. *The Idea of a Social Science.* London: Routledge and
Kegan Paul.
Woolgar, Steve, ed. 1988. *Knowledge and Reflexivity.* London: Sage.

15

Border Crossings:
Narrative Strategies in Science Studies and among Physicists in Tsukuba Science City, Japan

Sharon Traweek

Grand Récits and Revisionist Stories as Narrative Leviathans

Experimental high energy physicists usually give their talks at conferences with the lights off, the overhead projector on, and their backs to us, not, as ethologists might surmise, as a sign of submission, but as an authoritative gesture. They turn away from us to the illuminated facts as a priest might turn to the altar, and they speak to us in that masterful voice of authority and with that rather patronizing tone of certainty. Their transparencies are handwritten deliberately, as proof that the enlightened facts we are reading were so recently gleaned that word of their discovery was confirmed only a few minutes ago in a telephone call received from the laboratory. Physicists begin their talks with slides of the laboratory where their research was done and a few more of the research equipment—the detector—they used, while telling us quickly about its design and operation and modification. This part of their talks reminds me of the slides anthropologists use, the ones that attest to the researchers' technical and aesthetic skills, and of course they stand as evidence that the speakers really did go somewhere, that they really were there.

It is only in the introductory pictures that physicists and anthropologists intimate that they were involved in the production of the news to follow. The pictures tell an ambiguous story: they tell us that the speaker is an adventurer, a traveler, a discoverer, an eyewitness. They also tell us that their news is produced by the speaker's presence and ingenuity. The subjects in these tales of objectivity are introduced in act 1 and never reappear in their stories. But they survive: they are there, in control, telling their powerful tales in the

In the end it comes to this: although I would prefer to just give my word of honor, I know, unlike some of my senior colleagues, my name is not big enough for that. Economic metaphors for thinking and Victorian canons of Right Conduct mean that for you to believe that I did not steal other people's goods or that I have, out of ignorance, (re)invented their ideas, I must give credit where credit is due: the footnotes follow.

dark. I am going to leave the lights on and speak softly. I am going to write some stories for you, and I will be in some of them; I want you to know how I came to learn about these scientists and I want you to understand how the stories some anthropologists of science write might be different from what you expect.

Machines, like Galileo's telescope and the supercollider in Texas, provide the raw material for the stories that scientists tell about nature; scientists and machines and laboratories provide the not-so-raw material for the stories scientists and anthropologists can tell about making science. What kind of stories do the machines and scientists and anthropologists tell? Scientists are fond of grand explanatory systems, the sort of authoritative stories Lyotard has called the *grand récits*.[1] Scientists also like their machines to write in this way. It seems to me that almost all traditional historians, philosophers, and sociologists of science and technology must be very fond of this sort of story too. Although they question the traditionalists' easy assumption that nature coupled with genius authorizes science, almost all those writing the newer social studies of science and technology also account for everything and reject all other stories. To borrow (and disrupt) a notion from Hobbes by way of Michel Callon and Bruno Latóur, almost all these stories, whether about nature, scientists, or science, are narrative leviathans, producing and reproducing all-encompassing stories of cause and effect through the same rhetorical strategies.[2]

The social studies stories not only violate the union of nature and genius. Attending to human actions and actors has been classed as an analytic error; only "macroactors," "actants," or nameless "unclassified" voices can play a part. I certainly agree that we need to remember that human actions and actors are not natural kinds. I understand the "analytic payoff" for examining the discursive strategies of synecdochic macroactors or metonymic chains of conversational utterances, while ignoring the scientific and engineering communities' metaphoric hagiographies of their own personas and sagas of discovery, even if I am not fond of economic metaphors for thinking. When "payoff," "purchase," and "bottom line" are modified by the word "analytic," I begin to worry about the coin of the realm. For example, in American English the implication of the word *payoff* is that someone has been bribed to do something or to be silent. I am trying to add another voice to our repertoire of expansive and reductive interpretive strategies: an ironic reversal of scien-

1. Lyotard 1984.
2. Callon and Latour 1981.

tists' and engineers' epic tales of great men, great machines, great laboratories, and great ideas, to discuss their diverse strategies for producing epic tales about themselves, their tools, and their desires, to discuss why their epics have a second awed audience that supports their storytelling, and to explore their contempt for their audience, which most certainly includes all of us. Do I need to say that this is not the same as producing better tales of greatness than the subjects, and that it is not the same as studying their *values* along with their *facts*, and that it is not the same as having a retaliatory contempt for them?[3]

Charles Bazerman has given us a history of the rhetorical strategies in scientific and technical writing, and Evelyn Fox Keller has generated a rereading of the engendered scientific discourse of sixteenth- and seventeenth-century England and France; Sal Restivo and Michael Zenzen wrote to us about how they saw rhetorical forms being enforced in the grant proposal process; Bruno Latour and Steve Woolgar and Karin Knorr Cetina reported that they eyewitnessed and overheard many biologists deciding which forum to use to push which idea; Michael Lynch and several others have written about scientists' strategies for reading images.[4] In the midst of all this sophisticated rhetorical analysis of our subjects' discourse, at least one scientific journal, *Neurology,* is urging its writers not always to use the old scientific style: they tell neurologists to "use the active voice . . . the passive voice is boring, conveys lack of conviction, requires more words, extends reading time, and may be ambiguous." They are not entirely ideologically innovative; it is interesting that the old rhetorical style is still welcome in two areas: "The passive voice is acceptable in the Methods and Results."[5]

3. Woolgar 1981 and Woolgar 1989.
4. Charles Bazerman, *On Rhetoric in Science* (Madison: University of Wisconsin Press, 1988), and Bazerman 1989; Restivo and Zenzen 1982; Restivo and Loughlin 1987; Restivo 1980; Latour and Woolgar 1979; Knorr Cetina 1981; Lynch 1985.
5. Daroff, Rowland, Rossi, and Scism 1989. I am *indebted* (ironies intended) to Rachelle Doody, M.D., Assistant Professor in Neurology, Baylor University School of Medicine, Houston, Texas, and Ph.D. candidate in linguistic anthropology, Rice University, for showing me this "editorial message." Notice that among the authors of the article cited, the order is determined first by the presence or absence of an M.D. degree and only secondarily by alphabetical order. Each of our disciplines enforces its own customary order of power in these matters. An anthropologist friend refused to join a project organized by natural scientists when she was told that the "first author" on whatever she wrote would be the "PI" (principal investigator on the grant which funded the group's research project); in that field, as in many others, whoever "brought home the bacon" got primary scholarly credit, including Nobel prizes which might be given for the group's work. In return, the first author is expected to provide

What surprises me is that almost all the storytellers/writers about science and engineering practices have used the same rhetorical strategies in their own stories as the scientists and engineers conventionally do. All this narrative redundancy seems to me thoroughly to undermine their arguments about the construction of knowledge: they allow their accounts to be governed by the same narrative grammar as their subjects use, implying that there is the same sort of natural logic governing the production of good and true stories, whether about nature or about science and technology.

I am not completely naive. I know that in the social sciences we are usually expected to be scientists, collecting technical data by rigorous methods, making hypotheses and testing them, and communicating with colleagues in the proper forums in the proper way. I know that all this rigor and propriety and theoretical testimony ought to include as many numbers, mathematical symbols, and charts as possible; this sort of work is called quantitative, and the people who do it call everything else "qualitative," when they are being nice. In descending order of politeness, research which does not meet their own rhetorical criteria for science is called "case studies," "ethnographies," "anecdotal reports," or "journalism," none of which displays enough rigor and propriety and theoretical testimony.

Needless to say, many people whose research is derided in this way get rather defensive, particularly since the people doing the name-calling tend to control the publication, funding, and promotion processes in the social sciences. An unfortunate consequence of this defensive posture is that many writers of the nonquantitative studies try to write rigorous, "analytically tight," proper testimonials to their research in the same manner as their critics. Lest my friends in the humanities think that I am addressing my remarks only to economists, political scientists, psychologists, sociologists, linguists, and anthropologists, I will add that historians and philosophers of science and technology seem to share the same vice: naïvete about the implications of their own rhetorical strategies.

On various occasions I have been offered editorial assistance by

---

patronage: access to publication, academic positions, and eventually, funding. High energy physicists list in alphabetical order all members of the research group who have Ph.D.'s as authors on their publications. This practice shocks people in some other disciplines; they think that those physicists must be a docile, faceless lot to tolerate this lack of proper recognition. They do not realize that the high energy physics community most certainly allocates individual credit, but orally where it can be more carefully controlled, not in writing.

friends and colleagues in the social studies of science and technology and from the people I study: they tell me that I need to learn to remove the personal pronouns, eschew the active voice, employ the passive pervasively, use generics more than particulars, and "add some theory." One said, "It is only grammar and punctuation; I have to teach my students this all the time." I have been chided for using "most," "some," and "a few" instead of numbers. Others have offered to give me some "good theory" to add to my "descriptions." When I try to teach my students about rhetoric and writing, they ask incredulously, "Do you mean that you don't want us to be objective?" Instead I want to make a Swiftian modest proposal: let us attend to our narrative structures and our rhetorical strategies so that they complement rather than undermine our thoughts—except, of course, when we are deliberately writing for irony and paradox.

Since it may not be known to all the readers of this volume, I want to insert here that almost all social studies of science and technology (as distinct from more traditional history, sociology, and philosophy of science and technology) have been conducted by a fairly small number of sociologists and social historians in a limited set of countries: Belgium, Denmark, France, Netherlands, Norway, Sweden, and West Germany in Europe; Australia, Canada, England, and Scotland of the Commonwealth; and the United States. Almost all these researchers are white men under fifty. First we should remember that our field is still very young and very small, and that when social studies of science and technology are conducted by a broader range of scholars in a broader range of countries, our field will change. Second, while there has been a diffusion of our printed words, and scholars do travel, there are nevertheless sharply distinct traditions in theory, methods, and subjects of inquiry in sociology and social history (and our many other disciplines) which are related to our countries' different political economies and educational institutions. These diverse traditions strongly influence current social studies of science and technology. (Because acronyms carry connotations of bureaucracy, finance, and the military in the United States, I avoid using a label like SSST for our field, in spite of all the opportunities for written wordplay it offers.) I make no pretense that this chapter is an explication of our respective intellectual traditions, their influence on our diverse researches, and what has been systematically excluded, although I would very much appreciate such a study. I do want to note that we are misunderstanding each other's work because of our dissimilar discursive practices. I have learned, for example, that many anthropological features of my work have been read by my colleagues as sloppy sociology or history.

I am not claiming that my work has no weaknesses, but I do find it strange to be read as if I were trying to do sociology, whether English, French, or American. I also have no desire to eliminate our differences, because I believe that a diverse intellectual ecology will strengthen our inquiries. My desire in this chapter is to alert you to some of the differences in our theory, methods, and subjects of inquiry, in short, our rhetorical differences, and to note some of the consequences.

Reverberating Strings of Ironic Stories

Knowledge about rhetorical strategies and skill in deploying them are limited; most academics have learned only one and are unconscious of the assumptions of the one they know; they assume that there is only one way to think and write carefully and precisely about social and phenomenal worlds. I realize that when I use the words "story" and "narrative," when I use the active voice, when I write in this other form, many readers immediately know that this is not really an "article." You know that I have already transgressed the boundaries of academic writing decorum. You may conclude that there is no beginning, middle, or end here, no argument, no closure. Do you think you can make some sense without that "scientific" narrative structure but with my reverberating strings of ironic stories?

Alas, we cannot always rely on our readers to know that they should read us ironically if we use that distinctive hegemonic, totalizing authoritative scientific discourse so familiar to us all. We have been disciplined and so have they. For example, in spite of my own authorial intention, I have discovered that I cannot expect my readers to read my recently published ethnography ironically.[6] I had thought that the conventions of the genre of *anthropological* ethnography were sufficiently well known, at least among social scientists, that it would be obvious to all that I was challenging and sometimes inverting those conventions, including the theoretical ones, and occasionally even playing the genre (E. E. Vanna-Picture, the Banana Republic safari jacket-wearing intrepid lady traveler seeking adventure, sympathetically describing the rather bizarre habits of the rather pitiful locals in highly visual terms for the National Geographic-gazing armchair audience back home, substituting I-married-and-divorced-among-them for the

6. Traweek 1988.

434

more usual how-they-adopted-me-in-a-traditional-ceremony rapport story) for deadpan jokes. It is disappointing when most people do not get my jokes; I suppose it has been even more distressing to be asked if I knew what I was doing; the lady doth protest too much, you say.[7]

I learned that all the references to me in my text were being read by some as narcissistic allusions to my presumed peripatetic picaresque erotic escapades among physicists and their equipment: a sort of "Fanny in the Lab." I had thought that the notion of "subject positioning" was better known. Many scholars in cultural studies, anthropology, and feminist studies have argued for at least two decades that the role of the researcher in the production of knowledge has been erased in academic accounts for a specific set of reasons and by a specific set of narrative devices. They have also argued that the mythological abstract, absent, omniscient narrator must be replaced by other kinds of narrators and narratives, especially by stories about us finding sense in the mess of everyday life, about "situated knowledge."[8] In my case, that means telling stories not only about how I found sense being made in the mess of everyday laboratory life, but also how I happened to be in such places: who let me in there and why, and what was made of me being there, and what was made of my work, and what was made of me; how all this fitted into the senses the physicists and I were making; and whether our ways of making sense were dissonant. In short, it means I situate textually the production of my own knowledge as well as that of the physicists.

I also had thought that the canonical great books of E. E. Evans-Pritchard (called E-P by generations of graduate students) were better known; I had assumed the same about Rosaldo's and Geertz's contemporary critiques of E-P's ocular style as a restatement of English colonial administrators' desire for a landsat panoptic control

7. There is an extremely large literature on this topic. Dorinne Kondo (1990) has compellingly explored these issues in anthropological theory, fieldwork, and writing. I would also recommend Minh-ha 1989 and two collections of articles edited by Talal Asad (1988) and James Clifford and Vivek Dhareshwar (1989). My current favorite books on these issues in feminist theory are Gloria Anzaldua's *Borderlands/La Frontera: The New Mestiza* (1987) and Judith Butler's *Gender Trouble: Feminism and the Subversion of Identity* (1990). For suggestions on how these issues might shape science studies see Haraway 1988. That so many of my readers in science studies (see n. 8) and sciences (see n. 12) are surprised by my "self-positioning in the text" suggests that they are unfamiliar with this literature.

8. Reviews of my work by sociologists of science include Cozzens 1989; Latour 1990; and Pinch 1989.

of Africa.[9] I wrote my last ethnography as an ironic counterpart to E-P's books, my own ocular story about physicists' desire for pan-optical control of nature, an ironic conflation of Nuer cattle and experimentalists' detectors. E-P wrote that if we understood the diverse senses that the Africans made of cattle, we could understand the process by which they made sense. Godfrey Lienhardt modified E-P's tale by reminding us that the Nuer also knew the senses their neighbors the Dinka made of cattle and that the Nuer made certain that they did not make Dinkan sense. Later on, Raymond Kelly wrote that the Nuer and Dinka had made very different sense of their complex, shifting ecology and that made their relations with each other all the more troubled. Malinowski had already told us a story about what to make of Trobriand canoes; Annette Wiener reminded us that Malinowski only learned the Trobriand men's stories about canoes and what they got you. Marilyn Strathern had already begun her tale of how the activities and objects of men's and women's worlds in Oceania were situated not only in local ecologies but also in global ecologies.[10] My text wrote upon theirs, telling how different groups make themselves different with their cattle-detectors-canoes, how they make sense differently, and how they know it.

Using an Englishman's ethnographies of Africans as the referent for the structure and tone of my ethnographies also offered some other useful ironies. E-P contributed to the study of what has shockingly been called "primitive" thought, a field now at least a century old, trying, like Malinowski, to show the "rational" features of sense making in societies presumably unlike ours. I wanted to invoke for my study of physicists E-P's insights about the significant cognitive relations between people and their animate/inanimate artifacts while exposing his and our colonialist assumptions. E-P's work enhanced the capacity of the British colonial administration for surveillance and control of the Nuer; the black Nuer knew this, and they were not in a position to resist that white man's inquiries. A good deal of anthropological knowledge has been produced in such situations; in my case the Asian and Caucasian physicists I study are obviously in a position to resist the attentions of this white woman. I once had a conversation about my work with an

9. Rosaldo 1986; Geertz 1988. For the "primary source," see Evans-Pritchard 1978, 1976.

10. Kelly 1985; Lienhardt 1961; Malinowski [1922] 1961; Strathern 1972; Weiner 1976. For a brief discussion of Strathern's and Weiner's contributions in the 1970s and 1980s to the engendered study of "thinking social actors and the strategies they employ in day-to-day living," see Moore 1988, 38–41.

Australian aboriginal filmmaker, who found these layered ironies of race, gender, colonialism, and anthropological knowledge hilarious, if a bit overdue.

I thought we were all sufficiently self-conscious about how self-disciplined we were that I could even joke with my sister discipline sociology (which is a lot like British anthropology) about which of us had the legitimate reading of our shared ancestor Durkheim. Silly me: I had forgotten that anthropologists had noticed ages ago that siblings can joke about their uncles but not their (grand)fathers. In American anthropology Durkheim is a kindly gent, one whose name in our texts is just a reminder that we do not have to be either materialists or idealists. In sociology Durkheim seems to be a sterner fellow, standing for a specific, now decidedly archaic, position about ideas and action, and invoking his name (even on page 157) means that you defend that territory with him. The social construction of knowledge—and finding that ideas construct social relations—is hardly news in anthropology; it is even a truism after at least sixty years of ethnographies on the theme. If I had known mentioning Durkheim once would get me into so much trouble among people doing social studies of science, I might have skipped it.

I thought I could assume that we all knew about the differences between sociological and anthropological ethnography; I thought sociologists knew that cultural anthropologists have reasons why we almost never use the expressions "case study" and "qualitative" to describe our own work. I thought we all knew we had wildly different beliefs about culture, theory, and methods (sorry, I meant methodology). I did not know that many sociologists still think "culture" is syncronic, vestigial, and holistic (maybe Mertonian) "values," while "society" is diachronic, dynamic, vital conflict; I forgot some sociologists' and historians' rather tense and angry positions about rigor mortis (sorry, I meant rigorous methods). I forgot about many sociologists' need to count, and I forgot about historians' desire for accounts, quotations, and documents, because cultural anthropologists think that it is unethical to flash these fetishes in public. I thought you knew that most cultural anthropologists think that searches for cross-cultural universals, especially about "human nature," are so trivial, when they are not ideological, as to be unintellectual. I thought we knew more about each others' business, and I thought we were talking about words, not natural (sic) kinds.

To anthropologists, "culture" is not all about vestigial values, "society" is not all about agonistic encounters, and "self" is not about autonomy and initiative. A community is a group of people with a shared past, with ways of recognizing and displaying their differences from other groups, and expectations for a shared future. Their culture is the *ways*, the strategies they recognize and use and invent for making sense, from common sense to disputes, from teaching to learning; it is also their ways of making things and making use of them and the ways they make over their world. "Self" and "society" and "conflict" are parts of a set of stories that Americans and Europeans now tell themselves about their cultures. This anthropologist would be inclined to call those stories ethnoscience. That is, Americans and Europeans invoke the categories self, society, and conflict as natural kinds and build folk theories about the relationship of these kinds in different settings. To confine the social study of sciences and technologies to controversies and contested knowledge is an example. I continue to be interested in how high energy physicists build, and rebuild, a shared ground of common sense which is distinctive to them, as any anthropologist studying them would be.

Fieldwork and participant-observation do not have the same meanings for sociologists and anthropologists either, just as cattle do not have the same meanings for Nuer and Dinka (much less Texans). It is usually considered fickle in anthropology to study a people for less than twenty-five years or so; I have been attending to physicists for the fifteen years since I began graduate school and expect that I will continue for another twenty-five if I live that long. That means I have time to study how the physicists' shared ground shifts over time and maybe even to see some earthquakes. I have time to trace the fault lines. This also means I will be telling a longer story: my first book is only the first installment. Furthermore, like historians, we anthropologists only accrue our "cultural capital" by writing books; I do not think a cultural anthropologist who only wrote articles could get hired or promoted in an American research university.

Our first fieldwork should last a minimum of one year, preferably two; subsequent field trips can last as little as three months as long as they occur at least every three or four years. The questions and theories change, but we study the same people if they survive as a community, and maybe later on we also study some of their neighbors. When we do fieldwork we observe and listen. We participate, and we talk. If we do not participate and talk and write about what people make of us and our work, many would say it was not very good fieldwork. It is also widely accepted that we should not have been socialized in the community we study: we learn the locally valued ways of talking and thinking and acting by another route, one which is accompanied by a constant questioning about why this way rather than that one, an attitude almost never tolerated in conventional socialization. Consequently, although philosophers, historians, and sociologists of science and technology are encouraged to get advanced degrees in the sciences and engineering, an anthropologist of science or engineering would be expected to learn the community's cosmology and practices while doing fieldwork.

And then there are all those national differences within the genre, differences between the stories of British and French and German and American anthropologists. There are others of course, but as I wrote earlier, social studies of science and technology have been conducted almost entirely in Western Europe, North America, and Australia by sociologists and social historians; it is for that reason that I refer only to those four traditions. If I may be allowed to lapse, Dear Reader, into the approach of the (some would say hopelessly outdated) national-character and culture-and-personality schools (of American anthropologists of the thirties and forties), I think these different projects bear no small resemblance to the preoccupations of the cultures (do I mean societies?) in which they are produced, and I suggest that these diverse national research traditions also influence contemporary social studies of science. With tongue planted firmly in cheek I offer the following provocative stories about each tradition and leave it to you to write the palimpsest about science studies. In the United Kingdom my disciplinary colleagues call our subject "social anthropology," and they want to know all about the profane: social structure, social hierarchies, lineages, ownership, and social boundaries. They tell us how rationally actors engage in functional decision making and disputes about the aforementioned profanities.[11] In Francophonie they do the sacred: quite precise Marxist and structuralist analyses of the language of kinship, myth, and initiation. In Germania they do Linnaean exotica: classificatory schemata of odd human communities according to diverse amusing criteria (and on occasion there have been social Darwinist or Marxist rankings to add a rather dynamic, genetic twist to the story). There are a few polyglots who do a sort of Euro-anthropology, concentrating on how to transgress these tidy classifications, sacred languages, and social structures, how to violate the centers of these worlds.

In the United States these stories seem inadequate. We Ameri-

---

11. My colleagues from Chicago and its vassal schools call our work social anthropology too, and they do a British sort of research, all quite important and rigorous; this is the anthropology American sociologists have usually heard about, probably because of its proximity to the Chicago school of sociology.

cans have many capitals and no center. None of our largest cities—Chicago, Houston, Los Angeles, New York—is a node through which all peripheral news must travel, like London, Paris, Rome, or Tokyo. We are dispersed. Most of us acknowledge that we are "half-breeds" and we tell ourselves that we are all equal. Of course every one of us believes that the all the rest are a bunch of jerks, but we all know that we have to tolerate the jerks because it is the American thing to do. We believe that purebreds are neurasthenic and lack resolve; we believe that mongrels are stronger mentally and physically and are also full of spirit. Our preoccupations do not coalesce into stories about centers but into stories about odd couples, an infinite regress of sameness and strangeness: black and white, Time and Newsweek, men and women, Ford and Chevrolet, Republican and Democrat, Coke and Pepsi, East and West, Avis and Hertz, North and South. Our debatable differences are not about French logical exclusions which deny the excluded others; they are not about distinct English classes which define mixtures as monsters without honor. They are not about negation or rank, but polymorphous hyphens.

So we Americans usually try to tell anthropology stories differently. Naturally (slipped again) there are lots of anthropologies in the United States and each has its own organization, by-laws, membership, journal, favorite stories, and such, since we Americans always want a choice: there is an economic, legal, political, medical, psychological, ecological, humanistic, visual, demographic, and linguistic anthropology, and there are certainly others. Some of us call this mélange *cultural* anthropology and we tell stories about culture: what makes people think-feel-talk-mean-act in ways that everyone in their group takes to be normal (or a meaningful variant, including eccentricity) and everyone outside it takes to be utterly strange and ultimately meaningless, and how all this changes across generations and in shifting ecologies. I know that some say that American cultural anthropologists are the last dilettantes left in academia.

The particular branch of cultural anthropology onto which I have climbed is called many names by others, most of them impolite. We call ourselves by a lot of names too: interpretive anthropology will do for now. We usually align ourselves with those literary theorists, art historians, classicists, economists, philosophers, historians, legal studies researchers, and so on, who do "cultural studies": we all attend to patterned interactions, such as oral and written discourse, or any other "social text" such as a poem, an article, a scientist, a detector, or a conference, in which the form and the content reverberate to evoke significant strategic meaning to those who know the local patterns. "Discursive, strategic, evocative practices" are some of the key terms in our lexicon. For many years now these researchers have been concerned with how relations of power are enacted-performed-(re)produced through discursive practices-representations-evocations. This is the sort of anthropology of science I am practicing: there are certainly others.

Strategic Moves in the Margins of Power

The Rice University Anthropology Department faculty and graduate students and the journal *Cultural Anthropology*, currently published at Rice, are widely identified with the "interpretive" project; in addition, most of the cultural anthropologists in the department study the (re)production of privileged knowledge in postcolonial and postindustrial societies (psychiatrists, physicists, ayatollahs, artists, historical preservationists, museum curators, social policy makers, etc.). I joined this (internationally) notorious department so that I could pursue this part of my work, unfettered for the first time in my short career from the necessity that scientists and quasi-scientists (think they) understand everything I write. When I was first offered a position at MIT (where I worked before coming to Rice), I was given some advice by a mentor: among other things, I was told that my subject physicists, knowing nothing of anthropology, are very impressed by the name of MIT, and since they believe that scientists and engineers control much of the hiring and promotion throughout the institute, they would consider my work validated by their peers. The mentor added that after five years or so I could move on to a university which had a more visible anthropology department, any one of which would also be impressed because I had been validated by scientists and engineers.

Although you are perhaps reading an exception, to my knowledge no institution and no press has seen fit to hire me, promote me, or publish my work without first getting the opinion of extremely prominent physicists. I hasten to remind you, Dear Reader, that the physicists did not ask for this authority over my stories; it has been given to them by my senior colleagues in anthropology and science studies and by university presses. I often first hear about this from the physicists involved. We sometimes joke about what would happen if senior physicists asked leptons, hadrons, mesons, quarks, and strings to vote on the publications and promotions of junior physicists. Would the physicists begin to write with more irony and complexity, expecting the particles and fields, and perhaps their elders, to miss the point of some of their stories? If you think that the only response to such power over one's storytelling is self-censorship, I suggest reading Soviet literature. Irony and paradox are the rhetorical strategies heard from the margins of power. In the story I am now writing, physicists, particles, anthropologists, and fields all have the same status: words, words that are names. People called physicists and anthropologists use their name words to make sense and to make something happen in the world; some proper names get more clout than others. Do I need to tell you that the physicist name has more power than the anthropologist name, even to other anthropologists?

My favorite story by a physicist about my last book said that refreshingly it was neither awestruck nor muckraking, but that it went off onto some rather strange philosophical tangents. I care a great deal what physicists say and write about my work, and I am pleased that even ones I do not know come to my talks, telephone, or write and give me their reviews; of course for an ethnographer every discussion I have with them is more "data."[12] Most physicists do not seem to mind that I do not automatically agree with them. Sometimes we discuss how and why our different stories "don't compute." There are two exceptions: the first is about power and the second is about gender politics. Some physicists, ignoring my "philosophical tangents," sternly tell me that my stories are about "sociology" and "politics," that sociology and politics are easily separable from ideas, and that while these practices unfortunately exist in their community and unjustly limit their careers, physics and its facts would undoubtedly be more effectively pursued without them. I believe that I hear these stories only from those who are in the margins of power—students, discontented postdocs, physicists at less-than-central universities, those in less-than-central countries, and those in less-than-central positions at major laboratories. I do not think that "sociology" and "politics" are absent from those marginal places, only that the storytellers there rarely hear the powerful stories and that they do not get to tell their tales to those in power. Those in power tell another story: they like to tell me that they have "decoded" exactly who and what place and what events I have evoked in my stories. They think it is both odd and interesting that I did not name names but games, something they never do.

A few have been extremely irritated by my stories about their

12. The diverse meanings my ethnographic subjects make of my work can be gleaned in part by reading these five published reviews of my work: Metropolis and Quigg 1989, 215–216; Mulvey 1989; Perkowitz 1989; Riordan 1989; and Sutton 1989.

community's gender politics, and many others have criticized me for not having "exposed" what they see as the harsh consequences for women, gay men, and other minorities of the sort of engendered stories I have said that all young physicists need to learn to tell and emulate and believe. Those most critical of my stories about engendered physicists are scientists' wives and young women scientists. A few years ago I was part of a panel of researchers who were asked to describe our "work in progress" on gender in science and technology at one of the regular meetings of the MIT women faculty. I noticed that some of the assistant professors in science appeared to disapprove of what they were hearing. Eventually one stood up and said that the issues we wanted to investigate simply did not exist in the scientific community, that by the objective nature of the enterprise, issues of gender, which were issues of bias, simply did not exist. She also said that for us to persist in believing that they did exist was misguided at best and probably a reflection of either our personal psychologies or a condition of the humanities and social science, in which they were no inherent protections against biases. Several of her friends nodded in agreement.

Like the physicists who believed that "sociology" and "politics" could be separated from ideas, these women believed that gender ideology was easily separable from science. As I hesitated in order to formulate a direct but polite response to her amusingly *ad feminam* argument, a senior, influential, and powerful science professor intervened. She said that the junior faculty did not yet see gender as an issue in their work because they had not yet gotten to the career stage at which they would be defining fully independent research projects requiring their own command of significant resources. At that moment, she said, these women would realize that gender was an issue in science; and that because they did not as yet, she assumed that they were not now conceiving of fully independent research projects. Several senior faculty nodded. I was glad I had hesitated: the junior faculty would never have believed the same words from me. Hearing my stories in the margins of power in the high energy physics community seems to be very irritating: calling attention to the importance of power, including engendered power, in the making of knowledge calls attention to their lack of power, which they prefer to deny.

Disciplinary Profanities and Divinities

As the chapters in this volume suggest, most of us now doing social studies of science and technology are mired in our own disciplinary histories: our questions, our methods, our rhetorical strategies, and our boundary disputes with each other. I am not suggesting that we abandon our niches, only that we be more conscious of the limits of our little terrains so that we occasionally can, with the proper visas, passports, and adapter plugs, learn to cross those borders to discuss our different versions of what I still presume to be our shared concerns. Having acknowledged our profound and putatively honorable discursive differences, and in spite of all the inherent dangers attendant upon the transgressions I propose, I still suggest that we attend to our rhetoric, the rhetoric of our subjects, and the relationship between them. We will find our readers, in time, and our subjects (ironies intended).

Scientists and engineers tell stories all the time. I urge you to listen to them. Of course I know that the historians have told us to ignore scientists' and engineers' "retrospective accounts," their hagiographies, their self-interested anecdotes, their festschrift histories, their quaint hallway cabinets of curiosities, and their odd ways of speaking. I know that philosophers have told us to ignore scientists' and engineers' power relations and their gender politics and their colonialist assumptions about "the center of the action" and "nowhere," about their cores and peripheries. I know that all these practices are considered distractions by the properly disciplined researchers in science and technology studies. These practices are our subjects' ways of doing our job; we like to believe that they are amateurs and that we experts know how to do the job right, to get the story straight. I suggest that we not turn away politely—or smugly—from these practices: I urge a transgression, a rude return to the repressed, the boasts, the mere slips of the tongue, and the jabs, whether in the labs, in the conference halls, in the classrooms, or in the texts.

Perhaps this is a predictable suggestion from an anthropologist; we have a habit of taking the mundane seriously. Archeologists study trash heaps as well as burial mounds, and we cultural anthropologists certainly find ourselves attending to the profane activities of our subjects at least as much as to their sacred rituals. In fact we try to notice how they learn the difference between what is called sacred and profane and how they come to regard the difference as simultaneously obvious, important, pragmatic, and natural. If scientists believe in the difference between objectivity and subjectivity, between facts and stories, it is my job to listen to how they tell them apart, how and when they use this difference, and maybe even why. If I just accepted all this, believed it as much as they do, I would not be doing my job; I would be doing theirs, and perhaps yours.

So what is sacred to all these people and maybe to you too? Objectivity, facts, numbers, observation, and logic are on the list; did I forget our minds? Individuality, competition, tension, creativity, and knowing are good and proper too. These fancy parts are kept apart from the profane stuff they (we) are supposed to repress: subjectivity, stories, words, listening, and emotions; did I forget their (our) bodies? What else is missing? Play, harmony, repetition, and mystery cannot be on that first list. Oddly enough, whole people(s) get to be on one list or the other. In the jargon of some of the social sciences these so-called dichotomies are "overdetermined"; they explain both far too much and far too little. This overdetermined quality, coupled with the knowledge that it is nearly taboo to suggest that thinking people not honor these dichotomizing gestures, meet conventional definitions of ideology.

Scientists and most science studies people know where they belong in these dichotomies; most Japanese, women, and cultural anthropologists know our place: we belong on the second list with all the other illogical, markedly inscrutable ones. Naturally (did I really write that again?), those of us pushed off the first list do not like it. It is not just the assignment of the parts; unless we have been brainwashed, we do not believe in any of the characters. Pathetically, many of us put on the second list do enthusiastically play our parts in this story, as Fanon and Baldwin and Ellison and de Beauvoir and Spike Lee and many others remind us; pitifully, some of us you might expect to be on the second list proudly manage to "pass" as one of the unmarked firsts, muttering contempt to the seconds for not being clever enough to "pass." To eliminate *all* those parts we need to rewrite this colonialist play.

It amazes me that most of my students believe in all these differences, and that they even can map them on their own bodies: minds here, emotions there; eyes for observing, ears for hearsay. They say they can immediately distinguish between their thoughts and feelings, between objectivity and subjectivity, between facts and stories, that they have known how to do this for years. Of course most teachers know it is not always quite so easy and say it is our job to clarify, to disambiguate the ambiguous. But I do not agree; I have chosen to side with the complexities of ambiguity and with those who say that ambiguities are necessary for all communication, that without ambiguities we would have only repetition.

What have we lost if we take the ideological boundaries between objectivity and subjectivity, between facts and stories, between numbers and words, between observation and listening, between logic and emotion not as slashes, burning clear the contaminated ground

445

of ambiguity, but as dashes, linking what can never be cut asunder in humans? Have we lost the capacity to understand, to think, to make, to love, to talk? Did you say no, only the capacity to do all that well, effectively, productively, efficiently? I disagree. We will still have reasons for thinking well of someone's way of making sense of our world and we can still discuss that effectively. We would have lost, however, that arrogant, smug, commanding tone, that discourse of singular generics; we would have lost the cruel tension that always comes with the slashing language of cuts and exclusions. We would have gained the powerful capacity to name together the truths we want and our reasons for being unsure about them.

If ambiguities move from the repressed margins to center stage, what are they? In those ambiguities we find strings of associated meanings, not recursive, not redundant, but reverberating. We find local principles of association and dissociation; we find paradox and poetics; we find local strategies for making sense, making names, making stories. What happens when we pay attention to the stories scientists tell and when we pay attention to how the scientists read the stories their noisy machines tell? But I have gotten ahead, behind, I mean beside myself. At the risk of doubling the length of this chapter, let me tell you some stories about border crossings and some stories about alien times I heard from Amy in Japan. It irritates anthropologists to write or read commentaries devoid of ethnography.

Local Strategies for Making a Name

AMY is the name of both an international collaboration of scientists and their research equipment at KEK, the National Laboratory for High Energy Physics, in Tsukuba Science City, which is located about three hours by public transportation northeast of Tokyo. I studied them from April 1986 to August 1987. The American group leader chose the name for two reasons: his former next-door neighbors' daughter is named Amy and in his study of Japanese ideographic writing he learned that one possible pronunciation of the characters for beautiful pictures was "ay" and "mee." While he certainly hoped that his group would ultimately gain convincing visual representations of the top quark, he started with the girl's name, moved to a phonetic equivalent in Japanese, and then searched for ideographs with those pronunciations which had meanings he would consider appropriate. He knew that this is the way people make names for machines in physics: start with a word from the world of ordinary things or commonly known names, then capitalize the letters of that word and turn it into an acronym signifying something from the world of science, probably also signifying something from that group's own distinctive hardware and software.

The facility where the AMY group worked and where the AMY detector was situated is called TRISTAN. According to the laboratory director-general:

> Our accelerator plan at KEK was nicknamed as "TRISTAN" after the passionate story of the Wagner's opera, with the love and dreams for our science research, particularly for hunting quarks in Nippon. The first conception of this idea was about a decade ago, and now our TRISTAN came on stage. An opera is really a team work of singers, instrument players, the conductor, the stage manager and many more important people setting the drama behind the scenes. So is the construction of a large accelerator complex such as our TRISTAN. We could only make the TRISTAN's initial operation successful, with the excellent cooperative work of our colleagues.[13]

I forgot to tell you that TRISTAN stands for Transposable Ring Intersecting STorage Accelerator in Nippon and that there is no Japanese-language version of the annual report from which I took the director-general's words. The VENUS group said their name meant VErsatile Nlhep and Universities Spectrometer, making it a surprisingly double-layered acronym with Nlhep signifying the number one high energy physics laboratories in Nippon. In the hallway outside the offices of the group members there was a bulletin board with several snapshots of the VENUS detector's component parts; running along the top of the bulletin board was a neatly hand-lettered sign in English: VENUS lifts her veil. The SHIP group name is an acronym for Search for Highly Ionizing Particles; they also called themselves Nikko-maru after the name of the experimental hall where their detector is located (Nikko) and the Japanese word for ship (*maru*). Nikko is a famous mountainous landlocked resort in Japan; SHIP is a so-called passive detector, meaning that its component solid state track detectors are left in place for many months, removed, and only then analyzed.

Making names in this way shows that the groups know how to make the right sort of puns. Puns are the only form of wordplay I have ever heard among high energy physicists. What is it about puns they find so satisfying, and why are other kinds of wordplay so unrecognizable to them? When I am doing fieldwork, physicists occa-

---

13. Nishikawa 1987, i-ii. Notice that the name Tristan is not fully capitalized; in this title the name is not an acronym. The unusual grammatical constructions are in the original.

sionally ask why I have no sense of humor: they notice that my laughter at their puns is feigned. It is always a relief to return to anthropology territory and another kind of wordplay, where I am reputed to have at least the normal amount of wit. Reader, remember that puns bring together meanings which should be kept apart; they are a kind of verbal incest. The acronymic couplings physicists make are clever only to those who think that speech and writing ought to be kept apart, that appearances are false and hidden meanings are true. These puns directly contradict what all science and engineering students know should be kept apart.

Why is one message given in the authoritative texts and a contradictory one given in jest, one message given in print and another in speech? Bateson told us that such contradictory messages are double binds: if one message is obeyed, the other must be violated. He told us that such double binds can encode powerful cultural messages about how to think, feel, and act.[14] What a teacher says can be challenged, but it is almost impossible to stop laughing at a good joke. Every laugh is a warning to the students about exactly which borders are never to be crossed, a warning that seems to have been etched in the deep memory even of those who have left science and engineering for science and technology studies.

Did you notice that the ordinary meaning of their scientific names is only recognizable in speech, and that the fact that the name is also an acronym is only apparent in writing by the mark of its capitalized letters? While the scientific meaning of the name is hidden in the written acronym and usually is meaningful only to other scientists in the same speciality, the spoken name itself can be romantic and heroic, and it often has allusions to gender or even sexuality. Remember the names LASS and SPEAR and PEP at SLAC, the two-mile-long, perfectly straight linear accelerator at Stanford. What has been incestuously conflated in these puns? What is so important, so dangerous, so illicit that it can only be said in jest? Speech and writing, appearance and science are brought together, all under the name of heroic desire.

Do you remember that TRISTAN is the name of the desire for hunting quarks in Japan? It is not the name of a memory, of nostalgia, of things past. To return to the printed words authorized by the laboratory's director-general about TRISTAN:

> There is a famous story about the Wagner's idea in composing this opera which is based upon his original musical drama. He wrote in a letter to Franz Liszt, "Because I have never tasted the true bliss of love,

14. Bateson 1972 and 1958.

I shall raise a monument to that most beautiful of all dreams wherein from beginning to end this love may for once drink to its fill." It took about ten-years of Wagner's work before the "TRISTAN und ISOLDE" was first performed at Munich in 1865. . . . Now, we are very glad to publish this TRISTAN construction report on the occasion of the dedication ceremony for TRISTAN on April 7, 1987. Needless to say, our physics program is just about to begin. Taking the Wagner's opera, this corresponds to the beginning of the Act I, when Tristan and Isolde are about to depart to King Mark from a quay. We don't know at present how the highlights of the succeeding acts will develop. We will continue to make our best efforts so as to be able to taste the true bliss of our love, and leave the rest to Heaven.[15]

Why not a condescending name? Why not divine? Why not ironic? Why is the name of all this incest so unabashedly, sincerely heroic? Why do so many physicists around the world love nineteenth-century romantic European classical music, especially opera? Is it the tone of entitlement and authority in music written in the age of European colonialism? Is it only the simple, predicable narrative structure of beginnings, middles, and ends with characters and melodies that are known from the first, the mirror image of our academic articles with their authors and abstracts followed by theories, methods, and data? Is it that the drama is not the point, but only a reassuringly fixed text on which the musicians and actors and academics display their refined capacities for subtle variations within elaborate and precise constraints? Is it that all these players want to have a name above the title of their static texts?

What is in a desirable name? The only way that scientists can become immortal is to have equations or equipment named after them, like Maxwell's equations, Lorenz transformations, Feynman diagrams, and Cherenkov counters. Others use the power of discovery to name new particles in ways that invoke a group leader's name or a group's detector. Sam Ting supposedly named a particle "J" because that letter resembled the Chinese character for his name; SLAC's Group C named the same particle the Greek letter called "psi" after the shape of the particle's track in their computing imaging system. The conflated ontology of the particle-equation-equipment-image and its heroic maker is affirmed with each utterance, with each inscription. For a moment, repeated wherever there are scientists talking and writing, ephemeral scientists are revived by their immortal ideas—mental tools—machines. These are powerful, heroic, proper names; strangely, it is the progeny which legiti-

15. Nishikawa 1987. The unusual grammatical constructions, spellings, and punctuation are in the original.

mizes its progenitor, the source of the name. The metaphoric trope of romance, of heroism, is the only one suited to such authoritative names. The other possibilities—metonymy, synecdoche, and irony—would undermine that passionately, distinctively human authorship by their gestures of reduction, expansion, and reversal. Names like TARZAN (sorry, I meant TRISTAN), SPEAR, and PEP allude to a kind of human potency, SLAC to a certain kind of human anxiety about its loss; VENUS, LASS, TOPAZ, and AMY point to a certain kind of seductive, dazzling nature about to be revealed in the jungle of computer cables surrounding the eponymous detectors which in turn encompass the powerful (sometimes bent) accelerated beam of particles. Listing here the "passive" detector, the SHIP at anchor, captained by a woman mining the deep for heavy particles, seems out of place. (By the way, the Japanese word for people, actions, situations, and things out of place is *bachigai*.)

There are some names that tell another story, but they are not punning acronyms. Benki and Tokiwa are names for two magnets at the proton synchrotron (PS), the first research facility at KEK. These are the names of two characters in a famous historical play by Chikamatsu, a story about underdogs. Oho is the name of the experimental hall where the AMY group is located; these resident aliens chose the name of the nearest village rather than names of major sites in Japan like Fuji, Nikko, or even Tsukuba. Instead of identifying themselves with places all Japanese would recognize as imperial sites, they just used a local, inconsequential place-name, knowing that to other foreigners in the international scientific community all the names in the series would be inconsequential. It was a joke about the marginality of the whole place.

Local Strategic Uses of Marginality

I learned how marginal they thought it was when I began to have health problems. I gained fifty pounds in a few months and I lost some hair, so everyone could see I was ill. I got recommendations from M.D.s in the United States to doctors at the local, nationally known medical school hospital; I was diagnosed and eventually hospitalized and treated. My recovery, as predicted, has been gradual but steady. After leaving the hospital I encountered two reactions to my experience. Most of my fellow aliens at the lab thought that I had shown very bad judgment by not returning to the United States where they thought I could have gotten more expert care. I lost standing with these people. The Japanese scientists were clearly aware of those aliens' opinions and they asked me how I had made my decision to stay in Japan. I replied that I had felt I had Japanese friends who would help me if I needed help and I had confidence in my doctors and their diagnostic procedures, so I preferred to stay and continue my work. They said, "You really trusted Japanese doctors and Japanese hospitals?" Surprised, I replied, "Sure. Don't you?" "Of course, but you are the first foreigner we've seen who did," was the answer. I told them that I actually had never seriously thought about leaving, and they said they knew that. My standing with them had clearly risen.

National scientific communities are no longer in the margins when their scientists' findings are accepted as a matter of fact and without replication. A Thai mycologist told me that she must send her samples along with her classification and analysis to some major laboratory like Kew Gardens if she wants her papers to be taken seriously; fortunately, she has an extensive international network from having gone to graduate school in the United States, so she can at least get her samples and papers looked at. The American scientific community reached that point in the 1930s and 1940s, but the Japanese are still in the transition period. If I had not been ill, I am not sure if I would have heard the aliens' stories of suspicion about Japanese science and the Japanese scientists' awareness of their foreign colleagues' lack of confidence in their work. It was a charged subject: the Japanese needed the aliens in order for the laboratory to gain credibility in the international high energy physics community; the foreigners were afraid they were losing status by even being there. They joked a lot about their "high risk, high gain" situation. At a party one foreigner told me that no one who was really good would have to take the risk of being so far from the center of the action.

Strategic use of the margins by foreigners

Sometimes the foreigners made strategic use of being at the edge of their universe. For a while some physicists in the AMY group thought that they had found the top quark, a highly prized and predicted but then undetected particle. These physicists were very excited, but others in the group were exceedingly skeptical; they wanted to wait for more data before announcing anything that they might have to retract. The cautious ones pointed out that it would be too embarrassing to be wrong: they argued that AMY and KEK could not get away with "pulling a Rubbia." They meant that when Carlo Rubbia had had to acknowledge that data which had been announced (even in the *New York Times*) were premature, he, his group, and CERN already had massive power in the high energy physics community, unlike AMY, its leaders, and KEK; his error had to be accepted as just Carlo's bravado, but the AMY physicists were much less powerful and would be ridiculed. At one meeting the excited ones made a convincing argument: suppose they were right and AMY and KEK lost credit because they were timid outsiders. "Why have we taken the risk to be at KEK in the first place?"

A proposal was made and immediately accepted, to the silent but obvious chagrin of most of the Japanese physicists: announcement of the data would be made in Japanese at the upcoming Japan Physical Society (JPS) meeting in Osaka. The foreigners thought they were being very clever: they would suffer no embarrassment at retracting data in Japanese, but data presented at a JPS meeting had sufficient standing in case the group needed to claim precedent in a discovery dispute; they would make an official announcement, but it would not be "public." I wondered how the Japanese members of AMY would deal with this open declaration of the Japanese language and JPS meetings being *bachigai*, being "out of place," having some legal standing (like trees, animals, children, and research subjects) in international scientific discourse, but not much voice. Japanese could be seen, but not heard, a terrible reversal of the common practice among the colonized, including the Japanese, of being taught how to read the language of power but not to speak it.[16]

Strategic use of scientific Japanese

I went to the Osaka JPS meeting and I was *bachigai*, the only foreigner from KEK at the session when the AMY data were presented. The speaker began with a description of the AMY group as an unusually international collaboration for Japan, and emphasized his point about this *bachigai* group by telling his audience about how AMY even had an anthropologist studying the group: everyone laughed. I was always shocked when Japanese people, including scientists, upon hearing of my work, would say to me: "Oh, do you think physicists are like monkeys?" In Japan ethological studies of monkeys get a lot of public attention, unlike ethnological studies of people.[17] Monkeys get a lot of public attention in Japan because

16. On how telephones are altered in colonial settings to enforce power relations so that the most powerful can initiate as well as receive calls and speak as well as listen, while those with less power can speak and listen but not initiate, and those with little power can only wait for the phone to ring and listen, see Berger and Luckmann (1967).

17. For an anthropological study of the symbolic role of monkeys in Japanese cul-

they are said to have healing powers; people laughed because *gaijin* (familiarly, "foreigners"), usually regarded by Japanese people as not quite human and rather simian, are *bachigai* in Japan. Having established for his audience the considerable strangeness of AMY, he went on to mention that they had had interesting discussions in AMY about their first months' data, and that these data might well represent the signals of the top quark.

The polite discussion which ensued indicated to me that his audience regarded his data story as hypothetical and not to be taken literally: the reaction was no different than that given the other two KEK speakers who simply reported about how their TRISTAN detectors had come on line and had been nicely capable of producing very clean data signals in their early stages of operation. The English translation of the AMY JPS talk was rather more direct in tone; anyone could argue that it would simply be odd Japanese to be so blunt. It seemed to be that the speaker and his audience understood full well the distinctions being made. When I got back to KEK, some foreign AMY group members asked me if their data had attracted much attention; I said the response was mild, interest mixed with skepticism. They replied that since the point was just to have the data on record, the speaker had done his job well.

Strategic uses of American scientific slang

The then-current president of the JPS (not a high energy physicist) spoke with me about the use of English among Japanese scientists. He pointed out that everyone needed to learn to write scientific English and that some Japanese physics journals only published articles in English, although almost all the authors and readers were Japanese. He added that at his university there were now so many foreign graduate students, mostly from Asia, that they had opted to teach the graduate courses in engineering and science in English, not because any of the students were native speakers of English, but because it was at least the second language of nearly everyone and it would be very useful to all the students.

In this context scientific English is comparable to the French used by European diplomats and aristocrats internationally during

---

ture, see Ohnuki-Tierny 1987. For a study of Japanese primatology, see Haraway 1989. New research on the practice of primatology in Japan is being conducted now by both Pamela Asquith and Evelyn Vineberg. See Vineberg forthcoming and Pamela Asquith's brief commentary on the role of Japanese culture in the practice of Japanese primatology in Lebra 1987.

the eighteenth and nineteenth centuries, and the Vatican Latin used by the Catholic church in its secular as well as its religious business: using these languages for international science, diplomacy, and religion reinscribes the authority of the groups who use them with the most facility: Vatican officials, French diplomats, and American scientists. It is important to understand that the English of science is American, not British. More specifically I would claim that it is an American lower-middle- and working-class men's English, replete with the appropriate slang. I found it amusing to hear some Japanese (and Koreans and Chinese) from rather higher social classes using this idiosyncratic vernacular while giving talks at conferences: certain data points displayed by the overhead projectors onto large screens, for example, were continuously referred to as "these guys."

In the cafeteria and in the restaurant at KEK I would often overhear groups of Asian scientists using this American scientific English when I knew that they all were fluent in Japanese. Many Asians who would have been in school between about 1935 and 1945 would have been forced to learn Japanese. Such people are now the leaders in the Asian scientific community and they say that painful and hostile feelings can be elicited by speaking Japanese; speaking American scientific English is a convenient way to avoid these issues, and any influential Japanese scientist knows this, as did the then president of the JPS.

Even among Japanese scientists it is sometimes useful to speak this American scientific English. In Japanese one cannot speak or behave properly without signaling the gender and relative age and status of the participants in the conversation. Status among Japanese academics is determined first by the universally agreed upon rank of the university they attended as undergraduates, the year of their graduation, and the university where they are currently employed. This means that behaving decently requires that a person defer to the eldest male graduates of the University of Tokyo, etc., no matter what anyone thinks. Everyone knows this and evaluates the conversation accordingly. For those comfortable speaking American scientific English there is another option. On many occasions including while I was at the JPS meeting, I would say to my English-speaking Japanese friends that I would prefer that they speak Japanese so that I could learn their language more quickly. They would sometimes nod, smile, and continue speaking English. If I persisted, one would often pull me aside and tell me that because I was present (any *gaijin* would do), they had an excuse to use English and they could say certain things and make certain arrangements that might take a very different direction if the conversation were conducted in Japanese. I began to realize why some wheelers and dealers were inviting me along to their dinner parties.

Sociolinguists and linguistic anthropologists tell us that when all the speakers are fluent in the same languages, the strategic decisions they make together about which language to use in which situation are often determined by issues of power and status.[18] In the conversations I happened to witness, the Japanese speakers had for the time being collectively decided to alter their conventional power and status relations by speaking English. I am also suggesting that to speak about science in Japanese is to choose a certain demeanor and attitude about international science and its American scientific slang. The Osaka JPS meeting was conducted in Japanese, and the comments about the *gaijin* collaborators at KEK and the anthropologist there conveyed perfectly a certain distance between the data and the speaker, a distance not easily conveyed in the rather literal translation of his remarks.

Strategic use of the bachigai *name of Tsukuba*

There was another subtext to the AMY presentation at the JPS. The speaker who made the presentation was speaking in Osaka, a center for important physics research in Japan since the 1930s, and he was speaking about KEK in Tsukuba, near Tokyo, a focus of science funding in Japan for ten years. Tsukuba Gakuen Toshi (Tsukuba Science City) has more than fifty state-of-the-art science and engineering research laboratories, a new major university (in which students can be admitted on the basis of high grades in a particular discipline, as well as on the basis of high grades on a general exam which is customary at all the other prestigious universities in Japan), and a major teaching and research hospital. According to the stories I had heard, the Ministry of Education and the established public universities in Japan had wanted those resources to be allocated through them to existing research groups and departments; they were overridden by political forces in the Diet, the Japanese parliament, which had supposedly been lobbied by a very few high energy physicists (KEK was the first laboratory completed at Tsukuba). This irritated a lot of scientists based at the established universities, to say the least.

The laboratories, university, and hospital at Tsukuba had to be staffed by outsiders, although the core of the university faculty came

18. See, for example, Gumperz and Hymes 1972.

from Tokyo Metropolitan University. As in the United States, Europe, and many other places, powerful universities strongly influence the hiring at a group of less-prestigious schools, especially those nearby. Apparently none were able to turn any Tsukuba institutions into their vassals, supposedly because of the surprisingly vigorous application of government guidelines that the laboratories should be open to researchers from all national universities. Some told me that this was the result of very effective lobbying in the Diet by, again, a small set of high energy physicists with experience working abroad. In Japan it is the custom for all resources, including funding and even books and research journals, to go to the professor who heads a group of specialists; this so-called chair system was copied from the German university system over one hundred years ago. The universities and laboratories at Tsukuba are not organized this way. For example, there are open libraries, much like those in American universities, in which anyone, associate professors to undergraduates, can get books and journals if they so desire, independently of the quality of their relationship with the senior professor in their area of interest. Some physicists in established universities find this practice pernicious.

Japanese chairs in all fields also seem to be strongly identified with certain national political groups, with each subfield having the full complement of political opinion distributed in a predictable fashion through the diverse regional campuses of the national university system, such that, for example, all the chairs at Tokyo University are seen as having a similar political bent, Kyoto University another, Osaka and Sendai yet others, and so on. Through a rather arcane set of enforced regulations, none of the political groups has acquired that sort of control in any department or laboratory at Tsukuba, which was established about the same time as the political unrest on Japanese campuses in the early seventies. Each of the groups considers its exclusion from Tsukuba outrageous and repressive. Physicists are a part of this debate, and powerful contingents from these political groups are influential within the JPS.

The Japanese physicists who choose to work at KEK and Tsukuba know these stories well and realize that their affiliation with the laboratory and the science city and their alleged participation in the lobbying to keep KEK and Tsukuba outside the control of traditional forces in Japanese university physics and the JPS makes them suspect to many of their colleagues in the JPS. Who would take the risk of alienating so many colleagues? Some deeply admire the high energy physicist(s) who lobbied the Diet and thwarted the interests of the Ministry of Education and the universities and the JPS. Some are very loyal to Professor Nishikawa, the man most see as responsible for continuously bringing new resources to KEK. Many are returnees from rather long sojourns—up to twenty years—at foreign universities and laboratories, eager to finally have the chance to work both in Japan and on world-class equipment. People who have been abroad for more than about five years are said to no longer have a Japanese soul (*ki*) and to not be able lead other Japanese because they lack crucial skills (*hara-ge*); they and their children are generally treated with disdain, at best. The returnees say that they would only have returned to Tsukuba, where the traditional ways of Japanese universities are not so strong and where there might be a "critical mass" of returnees to challenge the discrimination.

Strategic uses of gaijin *physicists by* bachigai *physicists*

The scientists at Tsukuba know that they are all *bachigai*, a bunch of oddballs and out of place. Underscoring their isolation from the conventional sites of power, the science city is located in Ibaraki, an economically depressed region which has the reputation among sophisticated Tokyoites of being hopelessly déclassé: having Ibaraki license plates on one's car condemns the driver to all sorts of rude gestures and comments in Tokyo; I learned this because I had a beat-up car with such plates, and when driving in Tokyo, I startled many a Tokyoite when they realized the object of their derision was a *gaijin*, not the stereotypic Japanese hick they expected. The Japanese scientists at Tsukuba know what their colleagues around Japan think of them. Many of them eventually found the *gaijin* in their midst quite useful, because no matter how strange, how *bachigai* they seemed, the *gaijin* were reliably much more so, and so they by contrast seemed more normal. The Japanese physicist reporting AMY data at the Osaka JPS meeting made full use of the strangeness of AMY, KEK, and Tsukuba Gakuen Toshi in his presentation; simply by identifying with his audience in his jokes, he distanced himself from all sorts of strangeness, including the *bachigai* data that his arrogant *gaijin* colleagues had insisted be presented in Japanese. He spoke from the margins of power within the JPS because he was associated with everything *bachigai*: high energy physics, KEK, Tsukuba Gakuen Toshi, *gaijin*, Ibaraki, returnees. At the same time the *gaijin* physicists had made it plain that talking science in Japanese was an oxymoron. The Japanese physicists at KEK work at the edge of two empires, the very well established national scientific community in Japan and the immensely powerful multinational scientific enterprise based in North America and Europe. These physicists are learning that the borderland between empires can be dangerous and exciting; that being *bachigai* can be very useful. In that role they can tinker with Japan, its government, its universities, and physics. There is no word in Japanese for tinkering, for brico-lage, but all these Japanese physicists, willing to be *bachigai*, are finding new ways to do physics at the edge of old empires.

Borderlands, empires, and stories

Borderlands are where different standards clash, where one train gauge encounters another, where left- and right-driving cars meet head on, where nationalities fester and hyphenate. While I was at Tsukuba I began to think about my childhood, mostly because my informants asked me so many questions about myself (they seemed to find it fascinating that a single woman in her forties could also be a professor, especially at MIT, with a Fulbright Senior Researcher Grant). I grew up near Los Angeles at the margins of the old empires of the Atlantic, Spanish America and Anglo-America, and a conti-nental empire, the United States. I grew up at the beach, at lands' end between the ocean to the west; to the east a mass of aircraft factories, first built to fight the Japanese in the Pacific theater of World War II and then used to win the race with the Soviet Union to the moon; a refinery to the south named El Segundo (*el primero* was elsewhere, of course), fueled by tankers depositing their energy into a pipeline stretching far into the Pacific; and a sewage treatment facility to the north named Hyperion (after one of the ancient Greek titans, son of heaven and earth) which dumped waste through an-other pipeline into the same ocean. The air contracted rhythmically with the roar of jets leaving LAX, while the smell of oil and offal rose from the miles of sand dunes where we post-Pacific war chil-dren played "Japs (*sic*) and GIs," hunted with bows and arrows, and dug tunnels to China. Sometimes we watched adults make romantic films there about adventures in Arabia, before the birth of new em-pires and new Asian wars made the pulsing roar of the airplanes too frequent to make good movie sound tracks. I thought about that at Tsukuba as my friends showed me the huge new industrial plants along the Ibaraki coast, another part of the government's massive economic development plans for Ibaraki Prefecture. As we drove to the coast we passed the old airfields near Tsuchiura where the ka-mikaze pilots trained during World War II. My friends laughed when I said I felt like an Ibaraki native.

In elementary school our teachers, inspired by Dewey, taught us

California history by having us learn Native American ways, followed by the ways of all the conquistadores in chronological order: the Spanish, the Mexicans, the Russians, and the Americans. We made kachinas (although Native Americans in California never made them) and heard stories about how the Indians came from Asia, visited some of Serra's missions, and heard stories about the harsh rule of sword and cross, wove serapes and cooked tortillas and sang songs about *cinco de mayo*, played with animal pelts and heard stories about the pioneers from Irkutsk on Lake Baikal in Siberia, and built miniature log cabins and heard stories about the Donner party and the Gold Rush of '49. We were very proud of our frontier history and we thought that the edge of empire was the right place to be; when I go home I find everyone there still does. I thought about that at Tsukuba as I listened to physicists talk about the *tanshin funin*, the "married bachelors," who had apartments in Tsukuba but commuted to Tokyo and farther away every weekend because they did not want their children to go to school in Tsukuba.

At home I was taught that the docile stay put and the brave move on: I was told that our family had been pioneers for the past thousand years and that to fulfill the family heritage we too had to become pioneers, as our parents had, and our grandparents, and our great-grandparents, and back one thousand years; their stories were my childhood stories. In school we learned that for a brief historical moment our land had been an independent republic, with a bear flag: we sewed one and learned to sing "California, Here I Come, Right Back Where I Started From." The United States came to California in 1851, but we did not celebrate the anniversary. The biggest event in town each year was the fiesta: we all dressed like Californios and we carried the flag of the Republic.

I thought about that at Tsukuba as the foreign physicists became friendly with the Ibaraki people working at the lab and were learning to speak a bit of Ibaraki-ben, the local dialect. Some of the younger physicists, Japanese and American, were marrying Ibaraki women. Most of the Japanese physicists cultivated disdain for the locals which reminded me of all the faculty from east of the Rockies I have encountered at California universities, who have the same attitude toward their native California students; undergraduates, fully aware of the disdain, call them "carpetbaggers." I wondered what the Ibaraki people thought of the suddenly arrived scientists and engineers; gradually I began to hear. They seemed to like the foreigners much better.

I was astounded when I went "back east" for the first time and heard people say that they had more "history" than "out west;" it took me a while to realize that they did not regard the Native Americans, Spanish, and Mexicans as having a history in North America worthy of the name. We had different origin stories: when I would tell them that the oldest dwellings in the United States were built by the Native Americans in the twelfth century and by the Spanish in the sixteenth century, they thought I was untutored; I thought they were provincial. They grew up facing the Atlantic, in the newly powerful provincial margins of the old European empires; we grew up facing the Pacific, at the volatile edge of many old and new empires and with our backs to those "back east," which is what we called every part of America that drained into the Atlantic. They thought we were a joke from "the coast"; they called us lazy, shallow, and erotic—the usual stereotype for those expected to stay in their place. We had different stories to tell from the margins of different empires.

I thought about that at Tsukuba after taking the train from Ueno Station in Tokyo. Not only do soigné Tokyoites think Ibaraki Prefecture is déclassé, they think that Ueno Station and everywhere it goes are déclassé. Not surprisingly, American Japanologists tend to agree with their sophisticated Tokyo colleagues about many things; when I would meet them in Tokyo, or to a slightly lesser extent in Kyoto, they would offer condolences to me for "having to spend so much time at Tsukuba" where I never got a chance "to know the real Japan."

Because my old-fashioned (uninfluenced by Dewey) secondary school teachers decided I was smart, they thought I should learn Latin and mathematics and music theory; they also encouraged my weekly tutorials in theology with the local Methodist minister. I learned about the ancient Roman empire, Newton's calculus, harmonic structure, and Luther's theses; I did not realize that they were teaching me Queen Victoria's canon of singular generics, her universal standards for Beauty, Truth, Logic, Good Government, and Right Conduct. I kept forging putative messages from my mother to be excused from school so I could walk the dunes and watch the waves. A truant officer actually named Mr. Craven was there too, every day and all day, just to bring us all back to school from lands' end, the edge of his empire. I thought about that at Tsukuba when I heard that the universities were trying to prevent physics graduate students from getting degrees for research at KEK with KEK physicists. Their notion of the correct training for young minds was to read canonical great articles and replicate canonical great experiments.

I am not a member of the disciplinary border police; with my interdisciplinary (undisciplined) Ph.D., I am a resident alien among the anthropologists, beneficiary of a very recent and as yet fragile amnesty program for people without pedigrees in anthropology. I am an exemplar of a few anthropologists' enlightened intellectual politics; as a matter of survival, I would never repudiate the tolerance of my colleagues, nor would I ever want to rearm the border police. I will simply ask you to notice your own visas and passports and my green card, to notice the political etymology of your own language.

Did you know that the analytic language of social and cultural anthropology developed in decidedly imperialist sites? The social times and the cultural sites where anthropologists work have also been occupied by armies, colonial administrators, and those missionaries of Western cosmologies, the peripatetic expeditions of scientists and Christians. The voice of authority, of totalization, of hegemony in the anthropology of social and cultural relations is not an accident, just as the same voice in physics and science studies is no accident, developing at home that voice of entitlement, the voice of control, that accompanies the conquest of empires far from home. We all need new words and new stories.[19]

My string of stories has been written to you in an ironic mode, the only mode for stories from the margin, from the borderlands, from the edge of empires, including yours. I have written from there about the center of the action, its powerful names and its heroic acronyms and its incestuous puns. I have written about the suspicions in the borderlands, about the *gaijin* and the *bachigai* Japanese physicists and their strategic uses of each other and each other's languages. I have not written to you about negations and exclusions but about polymorphous hyphens, about odd couples. I have written about the tensions between two old empires—the Japanese national scientific community and the international scientific community based in North America and Europe—and about their recurring desires to capture the resources that the *gaijin* and the *bachigai* Japanese physicists have built there in the borderlands. I have not written to you in the mode of the center, the hegemonic mode of arguments and documents. I have not written a narrative leviathan. Did you really want another one?

19. On stories, narrative theory, and rhetoric, see, among a myriad of others, Barthes 1985; Caplan 1985; Chambers 1984; Chatman 1978; Lanham 1969; Minh-ha 1989; The Personal Narratives Group 1989; Polanyi 1989; Wallis 1987; White 1987; and just about anything by Kenneth Burke. I am especially indebted to Donna Haraway (1986).

REFERENCES

Anzaldua, Gloria. 1987. *Borderlands/La Frontera: The New Mestiza*. San Francisco: Spinsters/Aunt Lute.

Asad, Talal, ed. 1988. *Anthropology and the Colonial Encounter*. 4th ed. Atlantic Highlands, N.J.: Humanities Press.

Asquith, Pamela. 1987. Brief Commentary on the Role of Japanese Culture in the Practice of Japanese Primatology. In Takie Lebra, ed., *Japanese Culture and Behavior*. 2d ed. Honolulu: University of Hawaii Press.

Barthes, Roland. 1985. *The Responsibility of Forms: Critical Essays on Music, Art, and Representation*. Trans. Richard Howard. New York: Hill and Wang.

Bateson, Gregory. 1958. *Naven: A Survey of the Problems Suggested by a Composite Picture of the Culture of a New Guinea Tribe Drawn from Three Points of View*. Stanford: Stanford University Press.

———. 1972. *Steps to an Ecology of Mind*. New York: Ballantine Books.

Bazerman, Charles. 1988. *Written Knowledge: The Genre and Activity of the Experimental Article in Science*. Madison: University of Wisconsin Press.

———. 1989. Introduction to the Symposium: Rhetoricians on the Rhetoric of Science. *Science, Technology, and Human Values* 14 (1, Winter): 3–6.

Berger, Peter, and Thomas Luckmann. 1967. *The Social Construction of Reality*. London: Allen Lane.

Butler, Judith. 1990. *Gender Trouble: Feminism and the Subversion of Identity*. New York: Routledge, Chapman and Hall.

Callon, Michel, and Bruno Latour. 1981. Unscrewing the Big Leviathan: How Do Actors Macrostructure Reality and How Do Sociologists Help Them Do So. In K. Knorr and A. Cicourel, *Advances in Social Theory and Methodology*. London: Routledge and Kegan Paul.

Caplan, Jay. 1985. *Framed Narratives: Diderot's Genealogy of the Beholder*. Minneapolis: University of Minnesota Press.

Chambers, Ross. 1984. *Story and Situation: Narrative Seduction and the Power of Fiction*. Minneapolis: University of Minnesota Press.

Chatman, Seymour. 1978. *Story and Discourse: Narrative Structure in Fiction and Film*. Ithaca: Cornell University Press.

Clifford, James, and Vivek Dhareshwar, eds. 1989. *Traveling Theories, Traveling Theorists*. Volume 5 of *Inscriptions*.

Cozzens, Susan. 1989. The Culture of Objectivity. *Science*, 24 February 1989, 1085.

Daroff, Robert B., M.D., Lewis P. Rowland, M.D., Anne Rossi, and Carol K. Scism. 1989. Suggestions to Authors, *Neurology* 39: 1266–67.

Evans-Pritchard, E. E. 1976. *Witchcraft, Oracles, and Magic Among the Azande*. London: Clarendon Press.

———. 1978. *The Nuer: A Description of the Modes of Livelihood and Political Institutions of a Nilotic People*. New York: Oxford University Press.

Geertz, Clifford. 1988. Slide Show: Evans-Pritchard's African Transparencies. In *Works and Lives: The Anthropologist as Author*. Stanford: Stanford University Press.

Gumperz, John J., and Dell Hymes, eds. 1972. *Directions in Sociolinguistics: The Ethnography of Communication*. New York: Holt, Rinehart, and Winston.

Haraway, Donna. 1986. Primatology Is Politics by Other Means. In *Feminist Approaches to Science*, ed. Ruth Bleier. New York: Pergamon.

———. 1988. Situated Knowledges: The Science Question in Feminism and the Privilege of the Partial Perspective. *Feminist Studies* 14, 3: 575–600.

———. 1989. *Primate Visions: Gender, Race, and Nature in the World of Modern Science*. New York: Routledge.

Kelly, Raymond. 1985. *The Nuer Conquest: The Structure and Development of an Expansionist System*. Ann Arbor: University of Michigan Press.

Knorr, K., and A. Cicourel. 1981. *Advances in Social Theory and Methodology*. London: Routledge and Kegan Paul.

Knorr Cetina, Karin. 1981. *The Manufacture of Knowledge: An Essay on the Constructivist and Contextual Nature of Science*. Oxford and New York: Pergamon.

Knorr Cetina, Karin, and Klaus Amann. 1990. Image Dissection in Natural Scientific Inquiry. *Science, Technology, and Human Values* 15 (3): 259–83.

Kondo, Dorinne. 1990. *Crafting Selves: Power, Gender, and Discourses of Identity in a Japanese Workplace*. Chicago: University of Chicago Press.

Lanham, Richard A. 1969. *A Handlist of Rhetorical Terms: A Guide for Students of English Literature*. Berkeley: University of California Press.

Latour, Bruno. 1990. Postmodern? No, Simply Amodern. An Essay Review. *History and Philosophy of the Physical Sciences* 21: 145–71.

Latour, Bruno, and Steve Woolgar. 1979. *Laboratory Life: The Social Construction of Scientific Facts*. Beverly Hills: Sage.

Lebra, Takie, ed. 1987. *Japanese Culture and Behavior*. 2d ed. Honolulu: University of Hawaii Press.

Lienhardt, Godfrey. 1961. *Divinity and Experience: The Religion of the Dinka*. London: Oxford University Press.

Lynch, Michael. 1985. Discipline and the Material Form of Images: An Analysis of Scientific Visibility. *Social Studies of Science* 15: 37–66.

Lyotard, Jean-François. 1984. *The Postmodern Condition: A Report on Knowledge*. Minneapolis: University of Minnesota Press.

Malinowski, B. [1922] 1961. *Argonauts of the Western Pacific*. London: Routledge and Kegan Paul. Reprint, New York: E. P. Dutton.

Metropolis, Kate, and Chris Quigg. 1989. Notes from the Quantum Field. *Nature* 338, 16 March.

Minh-ha, Trinh T. 1989. *Woman, Native, Other*. Bloomington: Indiana University Press.

Moore, Henrietta. 1988. *Feminism and Anthropology*. Minneapolis: University of Minnesota Press.

Mulvey, John. 1989. Tribal Physics. *Times Literary Supplement*, December 22.

Nishikawa, Tetsuji. 1987. Preface, *Tristan Electron-Positron Colliding Beam Project*. KEK Report 86–14, by the Tristan Project Group, Ohomachi, Tsukuba-gun, Ibaraki-ken, 305, Japan. KEK, National Laboratory for High Energy Physics, March.

Ohnuki-Tierny, Emiko. 1987. *The Monkey as Mirror: Symbolic Transformations in Japanese History and Ritual*. Princeton: Princeton University Press.

Perkowitz, Sidney. 1989. Scientists Have Much to Gain by Studying Their Own Tribe. *The Scientist*. July 24, 13.

The Personal Narratives Group, ed. 1989. *Interpreting Women's Lives: Feminist Theory and Personal Narratives*. Bloomington: Indiana University Press.

Pinch, Trevor. 1989. Growing Up in SLAC. *Physics World*, August, 45.

Polanyi, Livia. 1989. *Telling the American Story: A Structural and Cultural Analysis of Conversational Storytelling*. Cambridge: MIT Press.

Restivo, Sal. 1980. Multiple Realities, Scientific Objectivity, and the Sociology of Knowledge. *Reflections* (1, Summer): 61–76.

Restivo, Sal, and Michael Zenzen. 1982. The Mysterious Morphology of Immiscible Liquids. *Social Science Information*.

Restivo, Sal, and Julia Loughlin. 1987. Critical Sociology of Science and Scientific Validity. *Knowledge: Creation, Diffusion, Utilization* 8, no. 3 (March): 486–508.

Riordan, Michael. 1989. The Tribe of Physics. *Technology Review*, February-March, 76–77.

Rosaldo, Renato. 1986. From the Door of His Tent: The Fieldworker and the Inquisitor. In *Writing Culture: The Poetics and Politics of Ethnography*, ed. James Clifford and George Marcus. Berkeley: University of California Press.

Strathern, Marilyn. 1972. *Women in Between: Female Roles in a Male World: Mount Hagen, New Guinea*. London: Seminar Press.

Sutton, Christine. 1989. Particicists under Scrutiny. *New Scientist*, 19 August, 54.

Traweek, Sharon. 1988. *Beamtimes and Lifetimes: The World of High Energy Physicists*. Cambridge: Harvard University Press.

Vineberg, Evelyn. Forthcoming. Translator's Introduction. In Takayoshi Kano, *The Last Ape: Pigmy Chimpanzee Behavior and Ecology*. Stanford: Stanford University Press.

Wallis, Brian. 1987. "Telling Stories: A Fictional Approach to Artists' Writings." In Brian Wallis, ed., *Blasted Allegories*. Cambridge: MIT Press.

Weiner, Annette. 1976. *Women of Value, Men of Renown*. Austin: University of Texas Press.

White, Hayden. 1987. *The Content of the Form: Narrative Discourse and Historical Representation*. Baltimore: Johns Hopkins University Press.

Woolgar, Steve. 1981. Discovery and Logic in a Scientific Text. In K.

Knorr and A. Cicourel, *Advances in Social Theory and Methodology.* Routledge and Kegan Paul.

———. 1989. What Is the Analysis of Scientific Rhetoric For? A Comment on the Possible Convergence between Rhetorical Analysis and Social Studies of Science. *Science, Technology, and Human Values* 14 (1, Winter): 47–49.

CONTRIBUTORS

David Bloor
Science Studies Unit
University of Edinburgh
34 Buccleugh Place
Edinburgh EH8 9JT
Scotland

Michel Callon
Centre de Sociologie de
 l'Innovation
Ecole Nationale Supérieure des
 Mines
62 Boulevard Saint-Michel
75006 Paris
France

H. M. Collins
Science Studies Centre
University of Bath
Bath BA2 7AY
England

Joan Fujimura
Department of Sociology
Harvard University
Cambridge, Massachusetts 02138

Steve Fuller
Science Studies
Virginia Polytechnic Institute and
 State University
Blacksburg, Virginia 24061

David Gooding
Science Studies Centre
University of Bath
Bath BA2 7AY
England

Ian Hacking
Institute for History and
 Philosophy of Science and
 Technology
Room 316, Victoria College
University of Toronto
Toronto, Ontario
Canada M5S 1K7

Karin Knorr Cetina
Fakultät für Soziologie
Universität Bielefeld
Postfach 8640
4800 Bielefeld 1
Germany

Bruno Latour
Centre de Sociologie de
 l'Innovation
Ecole Nationale Supérieure des
 Mines
62 Boulevard Saint-Michel
75006 Paris
France

Michael Lynch
Department of Sociology
Boston University
96-100 Cummington Street
Boston, Massachusetts 02215

Andrew Pickering
Department of Sociology
University of Illinois
326 Lincoln Hall
702 South Wright Street
Urbana, Illinois 61801

Adam Stephanides
Department of History
University of Illinois
309 Gregory Hall
810 South Wright Street
Urbana, Illinois 61801

Sharon Traweek
Department of Anthropology
Rice University
Post Office Box 1892
Houston, Texas 77251

Steve Woolgar
Department of Sociology
Brunel University
Uxbridge, Middlesex UB8 3PH
England

Steven Yearley
Department of Social Studies
The Queen's University
Belfast BT7 1NN
Northern Ireland

INDEX

A

Abir-Am, Pnina, 253n
Accommodation, 141–42, 152–60
Ackermann, Robert, 52–55
Acronyms, 433, 450
Actor-network theory (the French
  school), 2, 8n, 13, 18–22, 169–76,
  216n.2, 396, 398; contrasted with sociology of scientific knowledge, 302,
  309–24, 335–38, 343–66, 369–88;
  extended (radical, general) symmetry
  of, 19–21, 303, 310–18, 322, 353,
  379
Agency, 12, 32, 65–68, 90, 119, 267–68,
  271, 275, 284–86, 290, 293n, 294,
  312, 316n, 318, 350, 366, 386, 423;
  diagrammatic representation of, 73–
  76, 79–90, 94–108. *See also* Enhancement; Modeling
Alternation, in sociological practice:
  discussed by Callon and Latour, 343,
  351–52, 354–55, 358, 360–61, 365;
  discussed by Collins and Yearley,
  301–3, 308–9, 323–24, 371, 378,
  387
American Cancer Society, 177, 204
American Type Culture Collection, 197
AMY, 446–47, 450–58
Anderson, R. J., 216n.3, 271n.4, 217n.7,
  232
Anscombe, Elizabeth, 272, 278, 288
Artificial intelligence, 104n, 119,
  321n.20
Ashmore, Malcolm, 2, 305n.7, 332
Association, of cultural elements, 9, 12,
  15, 17, 140–42, 144–65, 313. *See
  also* Accommodation; Actor-network
  theory; Convergence; Duhem
  problem
Astronomy, as image processing, 34–35,
  117–18

B

Authority (hegemony) of science: discussed by Callon and Latour, 346,
  348, 357–58, 361–62, 365–66; discussed by Collins and Yearley, 309,
  321, 324, 383, 385n.12; discussed by
  Fuller, 394, discussed by Traweek,
  429, 434, 449–50, 454, 461

B

Bachelard, Gaston, 224n.14
Baker, G. P., 226–30, 235, 271, 273–74,
  281, 291–92, 298
Barnes, Barry, 1, 217, 279n.26, 337–38,
  360
Bazerman, Charles, 431
Berger, Peter, 311, 371
Bernstein, Richard, 390, 398–400
Bibliometrics, 421
Bijker, W., 224n.13, 386n.15
Biot, J. B., 92–95, 103–4
Bishop, J. Michael, 183–97, 202–3
Bloor, David, 1, 15–17, 118, 144n, 302,
  306, 310, 334; on Livingston, 241–
  45; discussed by Lynch, 215, 217n.5,
  218–21, 224n.15, 225, 227n, 229,
  231–33, 238, 256–57; 283–99; on
  mathematics, 271, 274–75, 279–80
Borderlands, 458, 461
Boundary objects, 13, 169, 172–76, 179,
  181, 186, 192, 203
Brannigan, Augustine, 249, 253n
Braudel, Fernand, 51n

C

Callon, Michel, 2, 8n, 14, 164n.26. *See
  also* Actor-network theory
Campbell, Donald, 216n.3, 399
Campbell, Norman, 30, 45
Cancer research, 169, 176–204
Cartwright, Nancy, 2, 45
Cathedral-building, 125–26, 135